T0392058

European Integration since the 1920s

European Integration since the 1920s

Security, Identity, and Cooperation

MARK HEWITSON

OXFORD
UNIVERSITY PRESS

Great Clarendon Street, Oxford, OX2 6DP,
United Kingdom

Oxford University Press is a department of the University of Oxford.
It furthers the University's objective of excellence in research, scholarship,
and education by publishing worldwide. Oxford is a registered trade mark of
Oxford University Press in the UK and in certain other countries

© Mark Hewitson 2024

The moral rights of the author have been asserted

All rights reserved. No part of this publication may be reproduced, stored in
a retrieval system, or transmitted, in any form or by any means, without the
prior permission in writing of Oxford University Press, or as expressly permitted
by law, by licence or under terms agreed with the appropriate reprographics
rights organization. Enquiries concerning reproduction outside the scope of the
above should be sent to the Rights Department, Oxford University Press, at the
address above

You must not circulate this work in any other form
and you must impose this same condition on any acquirer

Published in the United States of America by Oxford University Press
198 Madison Avenue, New York, NY 10016, United States of America

British Library Cataloguing in Publication Data
Data available

Library of Congress Control Number: 2024936383

ISBN 978–0–19–891594–2

DOI: 10.1093/oso/9780198915942.001.0001

Printed and bound by
CPI Group (UK) Ltd, Croydon, CR0 4YY

Links to third party websites are provided by Oxford in good faith and
for information only. Oxford disclaims any responsibility for the materials
contained in any third party website referenced in this work.

To my father and my mother.

Preface

I wrote much of this book in isolation during the long, often dark, days of Covid-19. Since reading and writing require extended periods of quiet, it might appear that the pandemic would have had little impact on research, but the ban on travel and the closure of the British Library obliged me—like many others, I suspect—to leave the project on which I was working in abeyance. This project, which I had started more than a decade earlier and for which I already had many of the sources, helped me to fill the void. In some respects, this is a Brexit book, which was stimulated by the convulsions and omissions of the years between 2016 and 2019, but which I would never have written without the convulsions of the years between 2020 and 2022. In other ways, however, the book has had a much longer period of gestation, for I have been teaching the history of European integration to historians, political scientists and others, as part of a programme in European Social and Political Studies (now EISPS), since the late 1990s. From this vantage point, the history of the EU, European history and European politics always seemed to be largely, and often perplexingly, separate spheres of scholarly activity. This book is one attempt, among several in recent years, to examine the intersection of such spheres. My debts in writing this study are distant, extending back to a conference on Europe before the European Community in 2008, which eventually became an edited volume in 2012. I am grateful to Berghahn for allowing me to use my contributions to the volume in reworked form. Subsequent conferences at UEA on Brexit and on Europe and the East, which resulted in another edited volume, were further sources of stimulation. I would like to thank Jan Vermeiren and Matthew D'Auria for organizing these events, as part of a much wider series of conferences and publications linked to the Institute for the Study of Ideas of Europe.

Although I did the research for this book before the onset of Covid (and Brexit), I wrote it, for the most part, during a series of unprecedented lockdowns, when restrictions on movement combined with the belated effects of the decision to leave the European Union to make trips to Yorkshire and to Les Landes, on which we had come to rely, extremely difficult and unpredictable. Thanks to my family, who remain citizens of the EU as well as of the UK, we were able to travel to France (and on to Italy) during the worst winter of a very depressing period of time, made worse by the blunders of a quasi-populist, post-Brexit government in the United Kingdom. Every European government struggled with the new demands imposed by the pandemic, including Emmanuel Macron's quasi-presidential administration in France. It was instructive to observe the very different ways in which governments coped with such demands. It was also a relief to change countries (even if still shackled to Zoom), in part because it was not possible to spend time over the New Year of 2020/21 at my parents' home in the UK. I regret that lost time, but I also cherish the short visits to Yorkshire which we were able to make between lockdowns and the longer summer holidays which we spent together in the Lake District, Cornwall, and the Yorkshire Dales. I am indebted to Delphine and Paul for allowing us to spend the winter of 2021 in France, and to Jacques and Pierrette for making our stay so unexpectedly rewarding. My memories of Anna and Camille, growing up in the winter sunshine, and of Cécile and her parents living a different life, at least for an interlude, remain vivid.

My father did not make it to the publication of this book, which is dedicated to him and to my mother, for all their strength and optimism over the last five years. They provided sustenance to all of us.

MH

London
May 2024

Acknowledgements

The author and publishers wish to thank the following for the use of copyright material:

Map 1.1 The British and French empires between the wars
Source: J. Jackson (ed.), *Europe, 1900–1945* (Oxford, 2002), 222–3, reproduced with the permission of Oxford University Press.

Map 1.4 Occupation zones in Germany and Austria, July 1945
Source: M. Allinson, *Germany and Austria, 1814–2000* (London, 2002), 117, reproduced with the permission of Taylor & Francis.

Map 1.5 US military presence in Germany in 1990
Source: A. A. Holmes, *Social Unrest and American Military Bases in Turkey and Germany since 1945* (Cambridge, 2014), 159, reproduced with the permission of Cambridge University Press.

Map 2.2 Democracy and dictatorship in Europe between the wars
Source: J. Jackson (ed.), *Europe, 1900–1945* (Oxford, 2002), 225, reproduced with the permission of Oxford University Press.

Map 4.2 Europe in 1919
Source: R. Gerwarth (ed.), *Twisted Paths: Europe, 1914–1945* (Oxford, 2007), 384–5, reproduced with the permission of Oxford University Press.

Map 4.3 Europe in 1949
Source: M. Fulbrook (ed.), *Europe since 1945* (Oxford, 2001), 304–5, reproduced with the permission of Oxford University Press.

Table 4.2 Ethnic geography of East Central Europe, 1991–92
Source: M. A. Vachudova, *Europe Undivided: Democracy, Leverage and Integration after Communism* (Oxford, 2005), 53, reproduced with the permission of Oxford University Press.

Contents

List of Maps and Tables	xiii
Introduction	1
European History and the History of Integration	2
Comparative Politics and International Relations	7
A Problematic History of Integration	13
1. Hard Power	29
Europe in a Bi-polar World	34
The German Question	50
The Limits of Détente in Europe	56
Germany and the West during the Cold War	61
2. Soft Power	89
European Cooperation and the Superpowers	91
Franco-German Friendship	100
A European Security Community?	107
3. European Stories	122
Is There a European Culture?	123
Intellectuals and the History of the Present	130
Geopolitics and the European Project	142
4. Identity	166
Deconstructing Europe	167
Nationalism in East and West	172
The National Question since 1945	181
Europeanism and Nationalism	190
5. Trade Blocs	214
Neo-Functionalism and Economic Growth	219
The Politics of Economic Integration	230
Commerce and the Common Market	237
Globalization and Regionalism	244
6. Living Europe	268
The European Social Model	270
Regional Inequalities and Social Convergence	289
What Is It to Be a European?	306
Public Spheres	316
7. Member States	333
The Politics of Integration	336
The Franco-German Shaping of Europe	341

xii CONTENTS

| The Economics of Integration and the Rise of Germany | 348 |
| Yugoslavia and the Triangulation of Europe | 357 |

8. Europolity	381
The Failure of Federalism	384
Supranationality and Intergovernmentalism	390
Reforming the European Union	397
A European Confederation	408

Conclusion	433
Cold War Europe	436
Intergovernmental Cooperation	440
A Confederation of Nation-States	444

| *Bibliography* | 459 |
| *Index* | 509 |

List of Maps and Tables

Maps

1.1 The British and French empires between the wars	38
1.2 NATO and the Warsaw Pact, 1949–56	41
1.3 The global Cold War	45
1.4 Occupation zones in Germany and Austria, July 1945	53
1.5 US military presence in Germany in 1990	72
2.1 The OEEC and Marshall Aid	92
2.2 Democracy and dictatorship in Europe between the wars	94
2.3 British Foreign Office map of Berlin, 1948	102
2.4 The European Community after enlargements in 1973, 1981, and 1986	111
3.1 The Nazi 'New Order' in Europe	126
3.2 Coudenhove-Kalergi's 'global power fields'	129
3.3 The Soviet Bloc	144
3.4 The European Economic Community in 1957	148
4.1 Ethnic structure of the population of Yugoslavia (1981)	175
4.2 Europe in 1919	185
4.3 Europe in 1949	186
6.1 GDP per inhabitant 2018	306
7.1 EFTA and the EEC, 1960–72	343
7.2 The Group of Seven (G7)	353
7.3 The Former Yugoslavia at war, 1993	361
8.1 The EEC enlargement of 1973	393
8.2 The enlargement of the EU in 2004	398

Tables

4.1 Yugoslav Census of 1981 and 1988	174
4.2 Ethnic geography of East Central Europe, 1991–92	178
4.3 Judgement on EU membership by country	191
4.4 National identity by country in 2004 (%)	197
4.5 Is membership in the EU a good thing, by group, 2007 (%)	200

xiv   LIST OF MAPS AND TABLES

4.6	Image, citizenship, trust in the EU, 2006–18	201
5.1	GDP and per capita GDP by region, 1950–92 in international dollars (1950 index)	224
5.2	Expenditure of average disposable income in West Germany, 1957–85	225
5.3	Total GNP and per capita GNP of the powers in 1950 (in 1964 dollars)	227
5.4	GDP per person in 1990 international dollars	228
5.5	Per capita real GDP growth 1870–1992 (annual average compound growth rates)	239
5.6	Foreign trade in France and the FRG, 1952–89 (% shares in total)	239
5.7	Average growth rates per period in the EU, US, and Japan, 1960–2000	247
5.8	Volume of exports as a percentage of gross domestic product, 1951–76	249
5.9	Intra-EU exports	252
5.10	Exports of goods and services as a share of GDP (%)	255
6.1	Attitudes to government intervention and equality: safety net vs freedom	273
6.2	Public social spending (% of GDP) and gross national income ($ per capita)	275
6.3	Industrial and service sectors in selected countries (% of workforce)	276
6.4	Patterns of social mobility in France, 1953–85	279
6.5	Socialist, Social-Democratic and Labour parties' share of the vote, 1945–60 (%)	281
6.6	Share of top ten per cent in total income in Europe and the United States, 1900–2010	292
6.7	Economic and social indicators in the EU-15 and accession states in 2004	297
6.8	GDP per capita (€) and real GDP growth rates (%), 2010–19	299
6.9	Perceptions of the economic basket of goods versus the political basket of goods in the Communist and current systems, 1993–94 ('better now' / 'worse now')	301
6.10	'How important is religion in your life?' or 'Independently of whether you go to church or not, would you say you are a religious person, not a religious person or a convinced atheist?'	310
6.11	To be European in the future, 2004	315

Introduction

There are many critics of the European Union. In the United Kingdom during the Brexit campaigns, there were countless references to a 'European superstate' and plans for a European army.[1] In Hungary, the Prime Minister, Viktor Orbán, called for a reduction of the powers of the European Parliament in order to stop the 'Sovietization' of the bloc: 'We want a democracy of democracies based on European nations.... We are nationally-based democrats against empire-builders,' he proclaimed in a speech marking the departure of the Soviet army from Hungarian territory.[2] In July 2021, Orbán was joined by the leaders of fifteen other right-wing populist parties, including the *Rassemblement National* in France, Law and Justice in Poland, the *Lega* in Italy, and the Freedom Party in Austria, who signed a declaration against the attempt by 'radical forces' to create a European federation: 'The EU is becoming more and more a tool of radical forces that would like to carry out a cultural, religious transformation and ultimately a nationless construction of Europe, aiming to create...a European superstate'.[3] In addition to reaffirming their belief that 'family is the basic unit of our nations' and that 'pro-family policy-making should be an answer' to Europe's 'serious demographic crisis' rather than 'mass immigration', the party leaders also demanded that the EU be reformed, with 'a set of inviolable competences of the European Union's member states, and an appropriate mechanism for their protection with the participation of national constitutional courts or equivalent bodies'.[4] It is easy to dismiss such populist confabulation and opportunism, but they reveal a fundamental set of misunderstandings and disagreements about what the EU is and what it should become.

This study attempts to separate the question of what the European Union is, which it treats historically, from questions about the EU's future, which dominate political debate. The 'radical forces' of Euroscepticism and federalism, or the endeavour to establish an overarching European political entity with the power to decide who has which competency, feed off each other and have little interest in separating the sober realities of the past and present from a fantastical future. The majority of academics who have investigated the matter, in spite of a marked preference for sobriety, have also shown little inclination to maintain a distinction between speculation about what is to come and analysis of what has already happened.

The field has been dominated by political scientists, many of whom 'seem to have concluded that the only way they can both explain the past and anticipate

---

European Integration since the 1920s: Security, Identity, and Cooperation. Mark Hewitson, Oxford University Press.
© Mark Hewitson 2024. DOI: 10.1093/oso/9780198915942.003.0001

2   EUROPEAN INTEGRATION SINCE THE 1920S

the future is to imitate the laboratory sciences, with their capacity to rerun experiments, vary the parameters, and thereby establish hierarchies of causation', in the deliberately provocative words of John Gaddis.[5] 'Social scientists try to reduce the number of variables with which they deal because this facilitates calculation, which in turn simplifies the task of forecasting,' the American historian continues: 'But if events have complex causes, forecasting based on simple ones isn't likely to work particularly well.'[6] Simple causation works on the assumption that 'Changes in one variable produce corresponding changes in the others: x when it encounters y always results in z', rendering the 'behaviour of the system...entirely predictable', yet what happens when 'the world is not ideal', the number of variables cannot be limited and causation is complex?[7] The consequence of the procedure, in Gaddis's opinion, is a 'methodological Catch-22', with political scientists seeking 'to build universally applicable generalizations about necessarily simple matters; but if these matters were any more complicated, their theories wouldn't be universally applicable. Hence, when social scientists are right, they too often confirm the obvious. When they don't confirm the obvious, they're too often wrong.'[8] Many exponents of international relations and political science who have studied 'Europe' do not conform to Gaddis's characterization, allowing for historical contingency and accounting for a varied reality.[9] Nonetheless, they have remained preoccupied by theory, quantification, and prediction, ignoring the complexity of historical events and the indeterminate relationship between European integration and the development of the European Union.[10] This history of European integration examines the relationship from varying points of view.

European History and the History of Integration

The term 'European integration' was coined by US planners in the late 1940s as a vaguer synonym for 'union' or 'unity'.[11] 'One of the most consistent aspects of post-war United States foreign policy has been the steadfast support of the economic and political integration...of Europe,' recalled a commission of inquiry of the European Coal and Steel Community document in 1956: 'This policy took shape soon after the war and has continued until the present day....European integration within the framework of an expanding Atlantic Community remains the cornerstone of its [the United States's] western European policy.'[12] For the diplomat George F. Kennan, writing to the US State Department on 1 April 1946, integration was essential for the defence of Europe against the USSR in an emerging global order of superpowers. 'The basic Soviet aim is to weaken the power-potential of all of Western Europe in order to increase the relative power of Russia in Western European affairs,' leaving Europe 'unintegrated' and blocking any power 'capable of pulling Western European countries together into an effective regional society', he wrote.[13] Part of the American project for European security centred on the 'German question', endeavouring—in the verdict of a State Department report in 1948—'to reinforce Western Europe through the integration with it of a democratic Germany'.[14] Another part rested on economic recovery, which meant 'nothing less than an integration of the Western European Economy', Paul Hoffman, the head of the Marshall Aid Program Administration, told the OEEC on 31 October 1949: 'the building of an expanding economy in Western Europe through economic integration, ... a single large market within which quantitative restrictions on the movement of goods, monetary barriers to the flow of payments and, eventually, all tariffs are permanently swept away' would 'make it possible for Europe to improve its competitive positions in the world'.[15] The 'vital objective' and 'final suggestion' of Hoffman, acting on behalf of the United States, had 'to do with the path by which this goal of integration may be reached', namely the 'creation of a single European market'.[16] 'I have made a number of references to the urgency of starting immediately on this program of integration,' Hoffman noted.[17] At the time, US planners used 'integration' interchangeably with 'unification' and the establishment of a 'federation' or, even, a 'United States of Europe'.[18] It was the adoption of the term by subsequent theorists of European integration which led to its wider, more popular usage. The label was also adopted by the EU itself.[19]

Some commentators, confronted in the early twenty-first century by a bewildering range of different definitions and by 'an odd disjunction between the rapidly increasingly knowledge of the EU, linked with a multitude of theories, and the sense of approaching a period of possible disintegration', wondered 'whether they were concerned in any way with the study of European integration', writes Paul Taylor.[20] Even Ernst Haas, the founder of 'neo-functionalism' and one of the first academic proponents of the concept, had come to claim by the 1970s that the 'theory of regional integration ought to be subordinated to a general theory of interdependence' and that integration theory in itself was obsolescent.[21] Political scientists, in particular, continue to use the term but they have been tempted to limit the scope of integration to politics. For Taylor, 'a kind of minimalist consensus view' of integration consisted, first, in the 'sense of a system, defined with regard to stated criteria, which was different from the current system', and 'a sense of dynamic processes in the current system with the potential for creating that different system'.[22] The system referred to is political, with every integration theorist requiring, 'in addition to expertise in one aspect of the system—institutional processes, policy networks, and so on—a knowledge of the minimum requirements of an integrated political system'.[23] Taylor, accordingly, emphasizes the political aspects of Haas's early theory of integration, as 'the voluntary creation of larger political units involving the self-conscious eschewal of force in relations between participating institutions' and as 'the process whereby political actors in several distinct national settings are persuaded to shift their

4 EUROPEAN INTEGRATION SINCE THE 1920s

loyalties, expectations and political activities towards a new centre, whose institutions possess or demand jurisdiction over pre-existing national states'.[24]

Haas, however, accorded much greater weight to economic interests, pushing him to make a distinction between 'political community' and 'political integration' ('conceived not as a condition but as a *process*').[25] Although 'economic integration unaccompanied by the growth of central institutions and policies does not necessarily lead to political community', since the 'removal of barriers to trade'—without 'centrally-made fiscal, labour, welfare and investment measures'—does not automatically create 'pressure for the reformulation of expectations', it has gone 'hand in hand with the gradual extension of the scope of central decision-making' in the European Coal and Steel Community (1951) and the European Economic Community (1957) 'to take in economic pursuits not initially "federated"', producing 'spill-over' from one economic sector to another and knock-on political effects.[26] 'The decision to proceed with integration or to oppose it' does not rest on economic success, but 'on the perception of interests and the articulation of specific values on the part of existing political actors'.[27] Nonetheless, perceived economic outputs were likely to lead to an evolution of economic and political 'interests', in turn affecting integration.[28] Given the centrality of Haas's work on integration, it has proved difficult to exclude consideration of the impact of economic—and other social and cultural—instances of convergence and cooperation on the definition of interests and the conception of political organization. At some points, we seem to be confronted, in the words of one recent study, by 'an engineering view of politics—one that emphasizes purposeful actors and their political choices'.[29] 'At other times, though, we are dealing with processes along different scales of social mediation and exchange, including deliberation and communication, social networks, commodity circulation and political bargaining.'[30]

Historians have been aware of such broader processes, rejecting—at least implicitly—Mark Gilbert's narrow political definition of integration as 'the historical process whereby European nation-states have been willing to transfer, or more usually pool, their sovereign powers into a collective enterprise'.[31] Scholars have long considered the significance of competing ideas of Europe, together with the European movements which professed to be their custodians.[32] They have also examined globalization, transnational networks of European politicians, businesses and unions, identities, and lived experience.[33] Yet the existence of such breadth appears to have had little effect on the field as a whole. With the exception of social historians such as Hartmut Kaelble, who has posited that there are growing social similarities between national societies in Europe compared to North America and Asia' but who is 'hardly interested in EU politics and policy-making', in Wolfram Kaiser's opinion, the majority of historians concentrate on the construction of supranational institutions or on the relationship between European integration and specific historical contexts—especially that of superpower bi-polarity—in post-war Europe.[34] The first phase of historical research was 'characterized by narrow chronological time-frames determined by the opening or availability of new archival materials and the dominance of diplomatic history themes', according to Katja Seidel, with a second phase entailing 'a broadening of themes, perspectives and time-spans' and investigating the 'origins of common policies, the creation of supranational institutions and the formation and greater activities of non-state actors'.[35] During a third phase, historians have purportedly adopted 'multilateral, multi-institutional and multi-level perspectives for understanding European integration history'.[36] Yet what has this research, which follows developments in political science and international relations (such as theories of policy networks and multilevel governance), contributed to the wider field? There is little sign that it has removed the deficit identified by Alan Milward in *The European Rescue of the Nation-State* (1992); namely, that historians, 'perhaps by the default of silence', have allowed theories of integration to come to rest 'on a historical foundation, deriving from conclusions about long-run historical trends', without actually testing and adding to that foundation, or associated theories, themselves.[37] The historical assumptions of political scientists are rarely challenged by historians.[38]

Milward concedes that European integration entails an unprecedented transfer of power which can only be explained historically. 'European integration, if we define it as the voluntary surrender of some elements of state sovereignty, may not be new, in principle,' he maintains in 'Allegiance: The Past and the Future' (1995): 'There are plausible examples from medieval history. But in modern history on the scale in which it has occurred since 1945 it is a new phenomenon.'[39] The creation and consolidation of supranational institutions, however, gives a misleading impression, even though they are the 'only new institutional characteristics' of integration: 'With every respect for the aspirations of those who support these institutions, they have not been the locus of power and decision-making.'[40] Instead, the locus has remained 'people and their ideas, the states themselves'.[41] For the British historian, the misreading of European history by 'federalists' rests in part on the justified but overblown conviction of diplomatic historians, placing faith in 'the rise and fall of nations', that the UK, France, and Germany all 'fell' during the course of the twentieth century and the USSR and USA 'rose': 'The European Communities are an attempt to protect Europe from the worst effects of its [Europe's] fall, on the whole a predictable foreign policy response to the relentless flow of historical change.'[42] Such scholars tended to see Europeanism as a response to these power-political 'facts', exaggerating the significance of early 'prophets' and overlooked movements: 'Those who see integration as an act of human will similarly see its intellectual pre-history in the interwar period, particularly in European federalist thinking and in the small number of marginal political figures, such as Coudenhove-Kalergi, who propagandised the idea of a European "unity".'[43]

6 EUROPEAN INTEGRATION SINCE THE 1920s

In Milward's judgement, economics has been more important than diplomatic and political will in stimulating, and placing limits on, integration, but its role has also been misinterpreted. 'For those, lastly, who see integration as a culmination of irreversible long-run economic trends the continuities are more broken,' he writes:

> The permeability of European national frontiers to the movement of goods, capital and people was on all measurements greater between 1870 and 1914 than in the interwar period and especially than in the 1930s. It is thus the interwar period with its temporary reversal of these immutable economic trends which is the historical puzzle. European integration is the predictable political response to the development of a universal international capitalist economy, a universal path of technological development, and the inevitable fact that the proportion of 'national' income earned outside the frontier will grow as a universal pattern of development requires national economies to choose between being open or being poor.[44]

This analysis, 'which underlies much of the writing about European integration', is historically misleading, in Milward's view, because it links 'the whole process of modern economic development since the eighteenth century to a gradual weakening of the nation-state' and relies 'on the observation that national economies, as they develop economically, become more interdependent, so that the nation-state consequently loses much of its capacity for independent policy formulation and for control over its own destiny'.[45] Some commentators 'argue that the same process actually renders the nation-state meaningless as an organizational entity, so that it will have to be replaced by some more effective form of political organization'.[46] Only an historical analysis of the changing relationship between member states and European institutions, which includes wider processes of economic, social and cultural convergence, divergence, integration, and disintegration, offers the prospect of answering such questions.

The problem with the historical literature on European integration is not only that it is—for the most part—narrow, failing to incorporate how citizens' and leaders' social circumstances and attitudes have altered over time, but also that it has not explained the changing relations of a multitude of national governments and non-governmental actors with each other and with European institutions.[47] Many scholars have been eager to go 'beyond the analysis of national policy towards "Europe"'.[48] Although it is widely accepted that 'the history of European integration is inextricably intertwined with many of the most important dynamics in post-World War II Europe and international relations' (the Cold War, transformation of the welfare state, the North–South conflict and globalization), historians remain 'more interested in the various external dimensions' of integration, 'not just western Europe's relationship with the

United States, but also the role of the Community in the Cold War and the impact of its policies on less developed countries', in Kaiser and Varsori's summary.[49] Arguably, this focus extends an existing preoccupation with the EU and European integration viewed from the centre, rather than explaining whether and why integration took place and why the European Union came to be as it is, from the point of view of those—including national governments and publics—who contributed or consented to them.[50] Despite the 'pooling of sovereignty and the increasing complexity of the EU, with greater powers for the European Parliament, for example', writes Michael Gehler, 'the member states were, and still are, the main actors in the EU', with their role transcending the 'heated debates in the post-war history of (western) Europe between different organizations of European cooperation and integration about intergovernmental versus supranational institutional forms or "negative" market integration versus positive integration with greater political ambitions'.[51] The challenge is to explain the evolution of member states' multilateral relations and their decisions to form supranational and intergovernmental institutions and mechanisms in an extensive and convincing fashion.[52]

Comparative Politics and International Relations

The terms of the debate about positive and negative economic integration, and about supranationalism and intergovernmentalism, have been set by political scientists.[53] The story of the principal academic disputes is well-known.[54] The early interest of international relations experts was tied either to neo-functionalism, with Ernst Haas and Leon Lindberg treating the European Community as a form of regionalism, or to the transactionalism of Karl Deutsch in *Political Community and the North Atlantic Area* (1957) and to the intergovernmentalism of Stanley Hoffmann in a series of essays in the 1960s and 1970s, both of which schools of thought comprehended the EC as a type of international organization.[55] Deutsch understood integration as the stabilization of the states' system and the attainment of a 'sense of community' within a territory and set of institutions, which could be established in a looser, 'pluralistic' form by independent states (the EC) or a tighter, 'amalgamated' form within a single, overarching political unit (the United States).[56] Hoffmann believed that integration was limited to agreed spheres of 'low politics' by nation-states which were mindful of their own interests—'constructs in which ideas and ideals, precedents and past experiences, and domestic forces and rulers all play a role'—and which were anxious to keep the principal spheres of policy-making ('high politics') for themselves.[57] 'The functional process was used in order to "make Europe"; once Europe began being made, the process collided with the question: "making Europe what for?"' wrote Hoffmann: 'The process is like a grinding action that can work only if someone

8 EUROPEAN INTEGRATION SINCE THE 1920s

keeps giving it something to grind. When the users start quarrelling and stop providing the machine stops.'[58] Much of the meat, according to liberal intergovernmentalists such as Andrew Moravcsik, is economic in nature and has been provided by member states.

Moravcsik adapts the notion of domestic preference formation and the engagement of national governments in a 'two-level game' to the circumstances of European politics, with international integration in specific areas strengthening states rather than weakening them. Thus, although the 'primary interest of governments is to maintain themselves in office', requiring 'the support of a coalition of domestic voters, parties, interest groups and bureaucracies, whose views are transmitted, directly or indirectly, through domestic institutions and practices of political representation', the same governments are 'able to take initiatives and reach bargains in Council negotiations with relatively little constraint'.[59] The European Community provides information 'that is not generally available', and national leaders are able to 'undermine potential opposition by reaching bargains in Brussels first and presenting domestic groups with an "up or down" choice'.[60] Moravcsik's theory is based on the models of international relations and political economy, with actors on the international and domestic stages rational, autonomous, self-interested, and risk-averse. It is relevant that the main powers of governments derive from states and their citizens. The American social scientist's propositions are framed against those of neo-functionalists and their successors.[61]

Exponents of comparative politics have regularly pitted their own arguments against those of Moravcsik, while also responding to the changing political agenda of Maastricht, with the newly consolidated institutions of the European Union and the promise of a Common Foreign and Security Policy and greater cooperation in the fields of justice and home affairs. The continuing attempts to reform the political structure of the EU in the decade and a half after 1992, culminating in the rejection of a European Constitution in 2005 and the signature of the Lisbon Treaty in 2007, raise questions about the nature of a so-called 'Euro-polity'. Unlike liberal intergovernmentalists, who examine the carefully calibrated deals struck by governments for clearly defined purposes, comparativists have focused on the construction of new, often supranational, institutions and the accretion of novel forms of 'governance', as 'the pattern or structure that emerges in socio-political systems as the "common" result or outcome of the interacting intervention efforts of all involved actors', where 'No single actor has all the knowledge and information required to solve complex, dynamic and diversified problems.'[62]

The main division within comparative politics has been between those—proponents of multilevel governance, policy networks, and Europeanization—stressing the uniqueness of the Euro-polity and those—advocates of a 'new institutionalism' or associated with a 'comparativist turn'—identifying common practices and mechanisms on the European level (the allocation and distribution of resources, representation and mediation of interests, and the formation of political cleavages) which can be compared to those in other polities.[63] Such comparison is not intended to deny the particularity of the European Union, which lacks a single executive—with competencies shared by the Commission and Council—and in which the European Parliament is not equivalent to a national legislature. Rather, it provides a mid-range theory, addressing Harold Lasswell's questions about 'who gets what, when, how', which permits a contextual analysis and evaluation of European institutions and praxis.[64] Consequently, institutionalists usually start by comparing, at least implicitly, European institutions with those in other systems of government, yet they go on—especially champions of historical or sociological institutionalism—to 'consider the issue of the autonomy of the EU's political institutions', shaped by evolving and distinct sets of norms and conventions.[65]

Proponents of multilevel governance and policy networks are more explicit in alluding to the unprecedented nature of the European Union's system of supranational and intergovernmental institutions, lacking historically and legally defined relationships with each other and with member states. 'The point of departure for this multi-level governance approach is the existence of overlapping competencies among multiple levels of government and the interaction of political actors across those levels,' write Gary Marks, François Nielsen, Leonard Ray, and Jane Salk: 'Member state executives, while powerful, are only one set among a variety of actors in the European polity' and states are 'not an exclusive link between domestic politics and intergovernmental bargaining'.[66] Nation-states continue to be relevant in this context but they become 'embedded in processes that are provoked and sustained by the expansion of transnational society, the pro-integrative activities of supranational institutions, and the growing density of supranational rules', in Alec Stone Sweet and Wayne Sandholtz's verdict.[67] The deliberate and unintended adoption of European norms and adaptation to directives and opportunity structures—or diverse processes of 'Europeanization'—seem to have accompanied this expansion of transnational society.[68]

Historians have found it difficult to resist the combined force of political and IR theories, yet their acquiescence—or, in Milward's opinion, 'silence'—has weakened their explanations of why the EU, the single market, member states, and the attitudes of European citizens have developed as they have. Most historical and political studies of European integration concentrate on actions rather than discourses.[69] Recently, 'social constructivists', influenced by constructivism within the discipline of international relations, have begun to investigate contemporary debates about what the EU—or, more broadly, 'Europe'—is and what it should be in order to assess how actors' judgements are formed and clouded by prior assumptions, and they have started to examine political actors' internalization of norms, which shape their identities and, as a corollary, their interests. 'By way of three moves (Austinian, Foucauldian and Derridean)', writes Thomas Diez, it is possible to argue 'that all our accounts of the world (and thus of European governance) are embedded in certain discourses; that the meaning of words is dependent on their discursive context; that this context is not rigid but in constant, if only slow, flux; and that recent transformations of the discursive context enable the construction of Europe as a "network".[70] Constructivists do not attempt to treat integration in exclusively discursive terms; rather, they seek to 'diversify' the 'traditional debate between (liberal) intergovernmentalism and supranationalism/neo-functionalism', which assume, respectively, that policies and coordination on the European level have been the result of rational or strategic actions on the part of governments and elites (liberal intergovernmentalism), compromises and bargaining within multilevel systems of governance (supranationalism), or economic and administrative interdependency and incremental institution-building (neo-functionalism).[71] As the German political scientist Thomas Christiansen puts it: 'A constructivist epistemology...must conceive of territorial units on all levels as social constructs..., view the political significance of [these] in the processes for which they provide containers, and such research must address the agency/structure problem, meaning that no level in the studied process must, *ex ante*, be assumed to be primary'.[72] It has proved difficult to put this agenda into practice, given the emphasis on predictive studies of power and rationality within political science.

Most political scientists studying the EU, it could be held, either assign primacy to agents pursuing their own interests 'rationally' or to structures and processes of action which operate functionally, escaping the control of governments.[73] Thus, for Moravcsik, ministers and other national actors try to realize their own interests—defined domestically—in a specific time and place, which have to be described in order to go on to 'test' theories concerning actions. 'The fundamental goal is not simply to provide narrative reconstructions of events that capture something of their complexity, uncertainty and subjective impact, but also to assess the importance of causal processes of international cooperation and institution-building which can be applied to a wide range of decisions in the E[uropean] C[ommunity] and in world politics more generally,' writes the political scientist in *The Choice for Europe* (1998): 'Obviously, not all relevant evidence can be reported, but I have sought to weight that which I present in order to give a representative sample of the quantitative and qualitative evidence available for and against any proposition.'[74] For neo-functionalist authors, against whose arguments Moravcsik frames his own, processes of European integration involve a multiplicity of agencies—ministries, companies, and other interest groups, together with supranational institutions like the European Commission—which forge direct links with each other and create 'spillover effects', or—in Lindberg's words—'a situation in which a given action, related to a specific goal, creates a situation in which the original goal can be assured only by taking further actions, which in turn create a further condition and a need for more action, and so forth'.[75] Correspondingly, Haas's investigation of 'why states voluntarily mingle, merge and mix with their neighbours so as to lose the factual attributes of sovereignty while acquiring new techniques for resolving conflict between themselves' involved detailed empirical study of instances and structures of decision-making within given historical conditions, as could be seen in his study of the European Coal and Steel Community, *The Uniting of Europe* (1958), which was based on extensive fieldwork and observation.[76] A similar interest in non-discursive actions and conditions can be detected in most historical works on European integration, whether 'federalist', 'national', or 'transnational'.[77] Communicative actions are comprehended and explained largely in this context.

Partly because of their background in international relations and partly because of their focus on politics, rather than economics, sociology, or culture, political scientists have tended to foreground the structures and operations of power. Theorists of multilevel governance and institutionalism have both, in different ways, shown how contemporaries assume that authority and power are diffuse. The former emphasize the complexity of decision-making within an undefined, evolving political structure such as the EU, where 'nine-tenths of the ... "policy iceberg" is below the water', involving day-to-day regulation and more or less routine decisions and actions.[78] The latter—'new institutionalists'—have revived political scientists' interest in the institutional basis of decision-making and 'path dependency' within the European Union. Referring to the seminal article of James March and Johan Olsen on 'The New Institutionalism: Organizational Factors in Political Life' (1984), scholars such as Simon Bulmer, Paul Pierson, Sandholtz and Stone Sweet depict institutions as embodiments of the bias that individual agents have incorporated into their society over time, which in turn leads to important distributional consequences: 'They [institutions] structure political actions and outcomes, rather than simply mirroring social activity and rational competition among disaggregated units.'[79] In part because they incorporate wider social norms, in part because they develop routine or 'rational' practices of their own, institutions— made up of formal rules, procedures, and operating practices structuring relationships between individual units of the polity and the economy—constitute sites where the exercise of power becomes almost automatic in certain circumstances.[80] They allow and foster the construction and interpretation of meaning, in March and Olsen's view, suggesting that they are not 'simple echoes of social forces', just as 'the polity is something different from, or more than, an arena for competition among rival interests', yet they also incorporate such 'social forces' and are subject to 'routines, rules and forms [evolving] through history-dependent processes that do not reliably and quickly reach unique equilibria'.[81] Individuals' actions under such conditions are informed and limited by their own institutional and social positions—their *relative positions* in a space of relations', in Pierre Bourdieu's phrase—and by their 'practical consciousness' and perceptions of circumstance.[82]

12 EUROPEAN INTEGRATION SINCE THE 1920s

Historians of European integration have accepted these premises, but they have also added to them by focusing on longer-term transformations of the decision-making process and the conditions, institutional structures, and discursive fields in which individuals acted.[83] Whether advocates of federalism (Walter Lipgens) or of 'rescued' nation-states and national interests (Alan Milward), they have paid more attention to the assumptions, ideas, and beliefs of policy-makers, intellectuals, journalists and members of the public.[84] Among other things, they have asked to what extent conceptions of 'Europe' changed during the twentieth century and what difference such shifts made to the project of European 'unity'. A widely shared notion of a European 'civilization' threatened by external enemies (the USSR and, even, the United States) and by self-destruction, as had been proved during the First World War, seems to have made economic cooperation between European states easier to envisage, despite national enmities.[85] The idea of European unity was inconceivable to most observers before 1914, but it was espoused by some of the most important European statesmen during the 1920s, including the French premier and Foreign Minister Aristide Briand and his German counterpart Gustav Stresemann. Historians have asked why plans for European integration failed during this period but succeeded after 1951, with the establishment of the European Coal and Steel Community. Partly, their answer has rested on the contention that competing discourses and ideologies, with ideas of Europe overlapping and conflicting with other political aspirations and threats (nationalism, the menace of dictatorship, the creation of welfare states, economic reconstruction, de-colonization, and international relations), variously overrode, negated, and facilitated integration.[86]

More importantly, scholars such as Tony Judt and Wilfried Loth have investigated the relationship between such discursive shifts and perceptions of threats, and the changing historical conditions in which decisions were made.[87] 'Whatever made possible the Western Europe we now have was almost certainly unique—and unrepeatable,' wrote Judt in *A Grand Illusion? An Essay on Europe* in 1996.[88] Guided by their disciplinary inclination to seek out single, transformative acts and by the nature of their evidence (with national archival records denied to political scientists by a 'thirty-year rule'), historians have revealed 'the hard-headed motivations that lay behind the multiple governmental decisions to take that most radical of steps and participate in supranational integration', in the words of Piers Ludlow.[89] They have done so, albeit unevenly, by balancing and evaluating the impact of individuals' singular actions—those, say, of the Belgian Minister of Foreign Affairs Paul-Henri Spaak, the President of the High Authority of the ECSC Jean Monnet and the Dutch Foreign Minister Johan Willem Beyen in re-instigating negotiations for a European common market in 1955, despite the failure of the project for a European Defence Community in 1954—against wider sets of institutional imperatives, competing discourses, historical conditions, and relations of power.

A Problematic History of Integration

Compared to the interwar era and the years before the First World War, the post-war period has witnessed a striking degree of political and economic integration—or 'the creation and maintenance of intense and diversified patterns of interaction among previously autonomous units' (William Wallace)—on the European level.[90] Integration has been accompanied by more sporadic forms of cooperation and it has been interspersed with periods of apparent disintegration or stasis. Institutional structures of intergovernmental cooperation, such as the European Council and the Committee of Permanent Representatives (COREPER), have been more important—I argue below—than supranational institutions such as the European Commission. What has occurred, and how we should explain and evaluate it, remains contested. That more intense and diversified patterns of interaction between previously autonomous—or more autonomous—economic and political units have occurred is not in dispute. This study aims to describe and explain these changes. It addresses a series of questions about European integration in a broad sense, rather than providing a narrative of events. Narrative approaches to European integration have long been dominant among historians, but they leave many questions and explanations, which they rely on but tend to conceal, unexamined.[91] The questions, here, concern the transformation of European institutions and a European 'polity' or political order, the policies of member states, the coordination of foreign and security policy during and after the Cold War, the political, social, and economic convergence and divergence of individual countries, and citizens' and leaders' identification with or indifference towards 'Europe' on cultural and historical grounds. Those favouring cooperation and integration on a European level faced challenges—and potential problems— in all of these areas.

My approach is to explore clusters of questions in each of these respects in accordance with the historical 'problem-orientation' outlined by François Furet.[92] To the French historian, writing in the tradition of the *Annales* school, there has been a necessary shift away from narrative history, since 'events', of which narratives have traditionally been composed, have proved 'unintelligible', if considered in isolation, and 'innumerable', if understood as occurrences. 'I do not see, *a priori*, what distinguishes one particular historical fact from another—for example, a birth, however anonymous, from a battle, however famous,' Furet contends.[93] Given the scope, novelty, and indeterminacy of the events involved in 'European integration', there is no alternative but to select evidence and occurrences, analysing the causal relationships between different acts (including communicative actions), in order to work out how and why it happened. Resting on the model of biography, narratives give 'an account of "what happened": to someone or something, to an individual, to a country, to an institution, to the people who lived before the moment of the narrative and to the products of

14 EUROPEAN INTEGRATION SINCE THE 1920s

their activity'.[94] They were originally a way of recording 'the recollections of individuals and communities' and keeping alive 'what they have chosen of their past, or of the past in general, without taking apart or reconstructing the objects within that past'.[95] They are made up of events, or moments, which are singular and ephemeral, 'the unique points in time in which something happens that cannot be assimilated to what has come before it or what will come after it'.[96] The history of European integration has usually been written in this spirit, examining the events leading to the establishment of European institutions—particularly supranational ones such as the Commission—and the actions of their founders.[97] Yet who were the principal actors, what was the role of European institutions in a wider political and economic order (involving national governments, various publics and media, international organizations, lobbies, and multinational corporations), and how can we select more and less important events? In what follows, I attempt to make such questions explicit, examining theoretical literature in political science, international relations, political philosophy, sociology, and law, in which the questions are posed, and tying a broad set of historical sources which discuss foreign powers, the governments of member states, businesses, politicians, journalists, and citizens (as well as Brussels 'insiders'), on whose actions integration and disintegration have depended.[98]

According to Furet, events such as the battle of Waterloo (or the end of the Second World War) and Stalin's death (or, say, Jean Monnet's appointment as the head of the *Commissariat général du Plan*) occurred only once, transforming history; they 'can never be compared, strictly speaking, to a preceding or subsequent fact'.[99] Yet such events have to 'be integrated into a pattern of other events', otherwise they remain 'meaningless': 'Thus, in narrative history, an event, even though it is by definition unique and not comparable, derives its significance from its position on the axis of the narrative, that is, on the axis of time.'[100] Given that the recollections of individuals and communities—and the very notions of 'individuality' and 'community'—are contestable (particularly in a new community-in-the-making like that of the EC), requiring 'conceptualization' which 'is never made explicit', how can such 'events' be arranged in a fashion that convinces the diverse readership of histories?[101] Moreover, how can unique events be combined with repeated ones? In an historical process—which is what 'integration' denotes—the relationship between singular and repeated events is especially problematic. In respect of the history of European integration, there is no 'community'—that is, a self-defining group—which could function as the subject of a 'story'.[102] Many historians take the EU as their subject but, since there was no EU (or, even, European Community), akin to a character in a novel, at the start of their story, they have to work backwards and revert to the question of why a particular institutional configuration came into being, and not others.[103] In other words, a forward-looking narrative has become a backward-looking explanation. This study does not attempt to present a narrative of integration. It explains why integration took place over time, answering a series of overlapping, secondary questions about identification, allegiance, convergence, the distribution of power and ordering of politics at home and abroad. Such a focus makes clear that integration has rested, not merely on the actions of a set of political and economic elites, but on the aspirations and responses of 'Europeans' or, less controversially, citizens of European states.

In Furet's opinion, the individuation and complex relations of events render them indescribable without some form of selection and conceptualization.[104] It is impossible simply to describe the series of events comprising 'European integration' or leading to the establishment of the European Union. Rather, historians choose what to examine of the past and, in the process, they raise 'certain problems relative to a certain period'.[105] They can no longer claim merely to detail past events, not even important events, whether in the history of humanity or in that of a part of humanity, the French historian continues.[106] This shift from narrative to problem-oriented history entails the 'construction' of an object of study 'by defining not only the period—the complex of events—but also the problems that are raised by that period and by those events and need to be solved', with the result that 'a good question or a well-formulated problem is becoming more important—and still less common—than the skill or patience needed to bring to light an unknown but marginal fact'.[107] The objects of enquiry and sources need to be integrated 'into a network of meanings', so that they are 'at least comparable within a given period of time'.[108]

Historians decide to examine a set of sources in their search for answers to a question. Since the questions concerning the extent, significance, and causes of European integration and disintegration are necessarily broad, involving a changing set of institutional structures, international relations, economic conditions, and cultural preconceptions, the sources to be considered are correspondingly varied, extending from opinion polls and data about markets to the testimony of ministers and politicians.[109] The interpretation of the sources goes beyond 'merely exposing the motives expressed by the historical agents themselves', involving explanatory hypotheses which were 'out of reach' of the people studied and which can be tested against available evidence and compared to those used to explain similar cases.[110] Even if the EU is sui generis, there are likely to be mechanisms, institutions, and processes of transformation which can be compared to those in other polities.[111] Explanations of historical events and processes are not 'scientific' or predictive, because 'there are some questions and concepts that do not lead to clear, unambiguous answers' and 'there are some questions that in principle lead to clear-cut answers yet cannot be solved, either because of a lack of data or because of the nature of the data', with the indicators 'ambiguous or 'impossible to subject to rigorous analytical techniques'.[112] Comparison, here, is used to distinguish and explain singularity as well as repetition: 'In problem-oriented history, interpretation is basically the analysis of the objective and subjective mechanisms by which a probable pattern of collective behaviour—the very one revealed by data analysis—is embodied in individual behaviour in a given period; interpretation also studies the transformation of these mechanisms.'[113] History is 'unscientific', with an 'indeterminate' object of study, but it requires principles for the selection of evidence and theoretical hypotheses to justify such selection.[114] Many narrative histories of integration ignore such requirements.

This understanding of history is designed to prevent what Roland Barthes, in his 'Introduction to the Structural Analysis of Narratives' (1966), called the '"telescoping" of logic and temporality', to which histories of integration have been especially prone.[115] 'Everything suggests ... that the mainspring of narrative is precisely the confusion of consecution and consequence, what comes *after* being read in narrative as what is *caused by*: in which case narrative would be a systematic application of the logical fallacy denounced by Scholasticism in the formula *post hoc, propter hoc*'.[116] Historians work backwards, faced with a state of affairs (the existence of the European Union or the fact of enlargement) which they wish to explain. 'The reason that events constitute what historians call "turning-points" is that they somehow change the structures that govern human conduct,' writes William Sewell: 'To understand and explain an event, therefore, is to specify what structural change it brings about and to determine how the structural change was effectuated.'[117] Yet to make sense of structural change, we need theories. We cannot comprehend—or describe—European integration without reference to a theoretical framework of explanation (why such states of affairs come into being). The problem bemoaned by political scientists—that we are unable to determine a clear outcome and dependent variable—is therefore to be expected, since integration is an open-ended process, the description of which hinges on a set of comparisons, generalizations, and theories. In this sense, it is similar to the challenges posed by the description and explanation of the 'industrial revolution', the evolution of a political party or the outbreak of a war.

This history of integration is part of a wider movement of historians away from narrative towards explanation.[118] Some studies examine the relationship between European integration and a specific historical context, particularly that of the Cold War, but few have analysed the cumulative political effects of longer-term developments and changing sets of conditions.[119] Kiran Patel, in particular, explores many of the same topics as this volume does—peace and security, economic prosperity, participation and technocracy, norms and values, and the polity—but he asks different questions, emphasizing economic integration, the role of elites and European law in the construction of the EU as the centrepiece of European cooperation.[120] Here, I ask why European governments cooperated with each other to form the European Communities, examining how they adapted—or sought to adapt—European institutions to match their changing conceptions of national interest and public opinion. This is not to deny that EU institutions have gained their own momentum, with EU leaders setting agendas. Nevertheless, national governments—in the Council, at intergovernmental conferences, and elsewhere—have remained critical, along with parties, interest groups, and the public in individual member states. As a consequence, I ask 'external' (but also relational) questions about the process: how has European integration fitted into and conflicted with the competing demands of domestic and international politics, viewed from vantage points in individual states? Arguably, most historians, following the lead of political scientists, continue to ask 'internal' questions about integration, starting with the process and institutions themselves.[121] Patel questions political assumptions about integration but concentrates, primarily (albeit not exclusively), on the development of European institutions.[122]

This study begins with an evaluation of the impact of the Cold War, which rapidly obscured and displaced citizens' experiences of dictatorship, occupation, genocide, and world war and replaced them with new anxieties about a nuclear holocaust (Chapter 1). The Cold War pushed the United States to coordinate the defence and foreign policies of European states, overcoming historical enmities and allowing the reintegration of (West) Germany. At the same time, it left many other questions about the intra-European relations of states unresolved. The incremental effects of economic and political cooperation gradually provided solutions to such problems, creating a 'security community' on the Continent (Chapter 2). Whether these forms of cooperation have had wider cultural consequences, or have required cultural affiliations and political allegiances, resting on a shared history or set of narratives, remains contested (Chapter 3). Although it appears unlikely that the types of identification and belonging characteristic of nation-states could be replicated on a European level, there is evidence of multiple, overlapping affiliations and loyalties (Chapter 4), reinforced by longstanding sets of economic interests (Chapter 5) and other forms of social convergence (Chapter 6).[123] The limited and conditional fashion in which convergence and identification have taken place has informed the actions and policies of member states (Chapter 7) and the nature of the European polity that they have helped to construct (Chapter 8).

There was nothing ready-made or inevitable about the institutional structure which was created after 1945. It came into being and was brought about as a consequence of deliberate decisions, negotiations and compromises, and unintended consequences of actions in rapidly changing circumstances in the wake of the Second World War and the Holocaust, amidst the mutually assured destruction of a nuclear arms race, the ideological struggle between Communist dictatorships and liberal, capitalist democracies, a growing division between the 'West' and the 'Third World' in the aftermath of independence and decolonization, and the uncertain establishment of a global system of freer trade, the reconstruction of domestic economies and the building of welfare states. The impression of stability in Western Europe during the 1950s and in Central and Eastern Europe in the 1990s is misleading, given European populations' recent experiences of the destruction of the Second World War, the threat of the Cold War and the proximity of the wars in Yugoslavia. Governments' actions and citizens' attitudes in these conditions were unpredictable. Although European politics often seemed distant and peripheral, taken care of by ministers and officials, they continued to depend on popular consent, as the increasingly fractious relationship between sections of 'public opinion' in individual member states and the leaders and institutions of the European Union has demonstrated.

The concept of integration only made sense in the late 1940s, 1950s, and 1960s when set against the realities of disintegration on European and national levels during the interwar era. After 1945, it can be contended, convergence and unification in Europe have occurred in different spheres and locations—and at varying speeds—but they have always been accompanied by the possibility of disunity, conflict, and divergence. In the United Kingdom, this prospect became a reality with the Brexit referendum on 23 June 2016. Over four years later, after the result of the vote had transformed domestic politics, the Irish journalist Fintan O'Toole reflected on the UK's departure in the *Observer* on 27 December 2020: 'So long, we'll miss you—we Europeans see how much you've helped to shape us.'[124] Despite his deliberate contrast between 'we Europeans' and 'you' Britons, the journalist sought to show the intertwining of both groups: 'Britain did much good for Europe', ensuring that the single market 'happened, when it happened', and that the EU 'responded so boldly to the fall of the Berlin Wall by bringing the Warsaw Pact states into its fold'; at the same time, 'Europe did much good for Britain', allowing it 'to transcend its imperial past and imagine a European future for itself', and helping it to settle 'by far its biggest internal problem', the conflict in Northern Ireland.[125] O'Toole's conclusion was a lament that the 'tedium, frustration and rancour of the past four years have wiped our memories of the historic and hopeful things that British membership of the EU allowed to happen'.[126] 'Anti-EU rhetoric in Britain has encouraged a notion in Europe that the EU will be better off without these surly and obstreperous malcontents,' he goes on, but John Donne, 'another great English poet', uttered persuasively: 'If a clod be washed away by the sea, Europe is the less.'[127] The British 'may have been cloddish at times' in the decades of their membership, but Europe was diminished by their being washed away: 'And Britain is the less for allowing itself to be so.'[128] In reality, the 'marks of engagement on both bodies' remained in place, 'and they are not wounds': 'They are the memories of mutual achievements, of the good that men and women did for each other.'[129] In O'Toole's opinion, 'At no time in its history has Britain shaped the continent so profoundly without war' and 'At no time in its history has it been able to behave towards its neighbours so much as an equal, so little as a victim of delusions of grandeur.'[130] It is not evident from his account whether Britons and 'Europeans' are the same, or indeed whether the Irish and Germans—as Europeans—are similar to each other, but they are closely related by history and, implicitly, culture. It is also not obvious why a majority of Britons had voted to leave the EU.

On the same day, the British journalist Tim Adams asked in the same newspaper: 'We're out of the European Union. Just how did we get here?'[131] Part of his answer was a bitter, tongue-in-cheek riposte to the wilder claims of the Leave campaign: 'For many, that moment will retain the liberating bravado of bedsit independence, an opportunity to refresh a midlife crisis Tinder profile.'[132] Adams's 'favourite answer to the question of how we got here came from that caller, named Mark, who contacted [Nigel] Farage's LBC phone-in show last year, to thank him for everything he had done for Britain':

> 'I used to be an ardent remainer,' Mark said. 'I believed in the European project and that staying in the union was the best thing for us, and then something monumental happened and I completely changed my opinion on all of it.'
>
> 'And what,' Farage asked, 'was that monumental thing that happened, Mark?'
>
> 'I was kicked in the head by a horse.'[133]

The rest of Adams's answer to the question of why Brexit had happened imagined schoolchildren's answers, 'within a decade', to what would become 'a staple question on their A-level papers': 'Those model Brexit answers will have to include the stubborn Euroscepticism that always characterised Britain's relationship with the union as it inched toward federalism, just as they would note the immediate crises of the Greek financial bailout, and the migrant chaos brought on by the collapse of Syria, and examine how they coincided with long years of stagnant wages and austerity at home.'[134] Examiners might look, too, 'for reference to the geographical inequalities of Britain—the sense that the vote against Brussels was also for many a cathartic "up yours" to London and Westminster'—and they could 'also give a tick to mention of the role played by tabloid media, owned by offshore plutocrats with a vested interest in deregulation and a reliably profitable line in raucous jingoism'.[135] Top marks might go to 'those framing these arguments with introductory paragraphs on the rise of populism fuelled by the unchecked influence of Facebook and fake news—and perhaps the unique combination of a prime minister in David Cameron who was the opposite of a man of the people, and a throwback opposition leader in Jeremy Corbyn, seeking to hide doubts not only about the EU but also NATO, by not showing up'.[136]

Yet perhaps what Bertrand Russell had called 'an escape from boredom', as an explanation for the outbreak of the First World War, was just as relevant, as 'enough people decided', 'a few days after England had been held to a tedious goalless draw in the European football championships by Slovakia', 'to disregard the

20 EUROPEAN INTEGRATION SINCE THE 1920S

evidence and vote leave because, well, something had to change'.[137] If this was the case, they had found 'their perfect leader in our current attention-deficit prime minister, who could never be arsed to do his homework as Brussels correspondent of the *Daily Telegraph*, so instead made up amusing caricatures about bendy bananas and condom regulations (as if history hadn't taught the world often enough to beware of Old Etonians with an unchecked sense of personal destiny and a mortal fear of appearing dull)'.[138] If these historical explanations are not convincing, we still have to work out why a majority in one member state voted to leave the European Union and those in other countries, admittedly in the absence of a referendum, consented to stay. A convincing answer is likely to go beyond the workings of European institutions to examine the relationship between national governments, voters, businesses, and the media over an extended period of time. History, identities, economic convergence, social contacts, international relations, and domestic politics have all been relevant, at different junctures, to the formation of the EU, redirecting our attention to citizens themselves. Who are 'Europeans' and how important has their support for 'Europe' been in the uneven history of European integration?

Notes

1. These myths continue in the right-wing press: for example, 'Brexit News: Britons FURIOUS after EU Superstate Plot Exposed', *Daily Express*, 5 August 2021; 'The EU Diplomat Row Shows Bexiteers Right—Brussels Does Aim to Become a Superstate', *Daily Telegraph*, 21 January 2021.
2. *Politico*, 20 June 2021.
3. 'Orbán, Le Pen, Salvini Join Forces to Blast EU Integration', *Politico*, 2 July 2021.
4. Ibid.
5. J. L. Gaddis, *The Landscape of History: How Historians Map the Past* (Oxford, 2002), 60.
6. Ibid., 65. I have argued against this overemphasis on the distinction between history and social science in M. Hewitson, *History and Causality* (Basingstoke, 2014), 86–179.
7. J. L. Gaddis, *The Landscape of History*, 74.
8. Ibid., 60.
9. Ibid., 71. See, for example, Andrew Moravcsik, *The Choice for Europe: Social Purpose and State Power from Messina to Maastricht* (Ithaca, NY, 1998), 78, who pays considerable attention to historical uncertainty. Even though Ernst Haas was worried about the absence of an agreeable outcome and dependent variable, he, too, incorporates elements of historical analysis in *The Uniting of Europe: Political, Social and Economic Forces, 1950–1957* (Notre Dame, IN, 1958); see also E. B. Haas, 'The Study of Regional Organization: Reflections on the Joy and Anguish of Pretheorizing', *International Organization*, 24 (1970), 610.
10. Moravcsik's claim in *The Choice for Europe*, 10, is unobjectionable 'In each case, a consistent set of competing hypotheses is derived from general theories; the decision is disaggregated to generate sufficient observations to test those hypotheses; and, wherever possible, potentially controversial attributions of motive or strategy are backed by "hard" primary sources (direct evidence of decision-making) rather than "soft" or secondary sources (public statements and journalistic or academic commentary in which authors have less incentive to report motivations accurately).' The main question, however, concerns the deriving of hypotheses from general theories, since the theories themselves tend to be ahistorical, based on 'rational action': 'My contention is that major integration decisions—and multilateral negotiations over international cooperation more generally—are better explained with more narrowly focused yet more broadly generalizable "mid-range" theories of economic interest, bargaining, and institutional choice drawn from the general literature on international cooperation' and employing a 'rationalist framework'

INTRODUCTION 21

(19). The testing of fully developed hypotheses on this basis tends to obscure other, broader questions about the historical context in which decision-makers operated. In Maurice Mandelbaum's opinion, in 'Causal Analysis in History', *Journal of the History of Ideas*, 3 (1942), 48–9, historians work within an extensive framework of theoretical assumptions about interactions in a given period and place, reaching 'hypotheses' from this starting point: 'we are inevitably committed to some method of comparisons, since every hypothesis refers to a class of events. It would therefore be well if in addition to the slow sifting of implicit hypotheses through the course of historical inquiry, attempts were occasionally instituted to formulate some of these hypotheses more explicitly, and to test them against a variety of cases to see how far their applicability extends.' Arguably, this type of hypothesis formulation is the reverse of that described by Moravcsik.

11. See M. Hewitson and M. D'Auria (eds), *Europe in Crisis: Intellectuals and the European Idea, 1917–1957* (New York, 2012), 326–7.
12. 'The Community's Relations with the Outside World', in the *Bulletin from the European Community for Coal and Steel*, quoted in I. T. Berend, *The History of European Integration: A New Perspective* (London, 2016), 17.
13. George F. Kennan memorandum, 1 April 1946, ibid., 26.
14. Ibid., 16.
15. Ibid., 31.
16. Ibid., 7–62.
17. Ibid.
18. Ibid.
19. See, for instance, the European Parliament's 'fact sheet' on 'The Historical Development of European Integration' (2018), at www.europarl.europa.eu, which treats integration as self-evident. Many academics likewise simply assume that integration has taken place: for example, Derek Beach, *The Dynamics of European Integration: Why and When EU Institutions Matter* (Basingstoke, 2005), 3, 22–4, 51.
20. P. Taylor, *The End of European Integration: Anti-Europeanism Examined* (London, 2008), 89.
21. Ibid. 90; E. B. Haas, 'Turbulent Fields and the Theory of Regional Integration', *International Organization*, 30 (1976), 199; E. B. Haas, 'The Obsolescence of Regional Integration Theory', *Working Paper, Institute of International Studies* (Princeton, NJ, 1975).
22. P. Taylor, *The End of European Integration*, 92.
23. Ibid., 93. Taylor also cites R. J. Harrison, *Europe in Question: Theories of Regional Integration* (London, 1974), 14, who holds that the 'integration process may be defined as the attainment within an area of the bonds of political community, of central institutions with binding decision-making powers and methods of control determining the allocation of values at the regional level and also of adequate consensus-formation mechanisms'.
24. P. Taylor, *The End of European Integration*, 89; E. B. Haas, 'The Study of Regional Organization: Reflections on the Joy and Anguish of Pretheorizing', *International Organization*, 24 (1970), 608; E. B. Haas, *The Uniting of Europe*, 16.
25. E. B. Haas, *The Uniting of Europe*, 4, 11.
26. Ibid., 12–13.
27. Ibid., 13.
28. Ibid., 486–527.
29. J. T. Checkel and P. J. Katzenstein (eds), *European Identity* (Cambridge, 2009), 3.
30. Ibid.
31. M. Gilbert, *European Integration*, 1–2. Gilbert also 'inserts the story of European integration into the wider history of this period', characterized by imperial decline and decolonization, the threat and fall of Communism, the ramifications of American foreign and economic policy, and the democratization of Southern and Eastern Europe, yet he makes 'no apology' for concentrating on the high politics of European integration, not least because 'a book that dealt in depth with the full administrative history of the European institutions or tried to trace the impact of European integration on the economies, political systems, and peoples of its member states would be many times longer'. For a much broader set of reflections on the concept of integration, see M. Gilbert, 'Narrating the Process: Questioning the Progressive Story of European Integration', *Journal of Common Market Studies*, 46 (2008), 641–62.
32. See especially W. Lipgens, *Europa-Föderationspläne der Widerstandsbewegungen 1940–1945* (Munich, 1968); W. Lipgens, *Die Anfänge der europäischen Einigungspolitik 1945–1950* (Stuttgart, 1977); W. Lipgens, 'European Federation in the Political Thought of Resistance Movements during World War II', *Central European* History, 1 (1968), 5–19; W. Lipgens, *A History of European Integration, 1945–1947* (Oxford, 1982); W. Lipgens and W. Loth (eds),

22   EUROPEAN INTEGRATION SINCE THE 1920S

Documents on the History of European Integration (Berlin, 1985–88), 3 vols. Also E. du Réau, *La construction européenne au XXe siècle. Fondements, enjeux, defies* (Nantes, 2007), 15–32, and E. du Réau, *L'idée d'Europe au XXe siècle. Des mythes aux réalités* (Brussels, 1996), 17–70; and J. L. Chabot, *Aux origines intellectuelles de l'Union européenne* (Grenoble, 2005); C. Bailey, *Between Yesterday and Tomorrow: German Visions of Europe, 1926–1950* (New York, 2013); V. Conze, *Das Europa der Deutschen. Ideen von Europa in Deutschland zwischen Reichstradition und Westorientierung 1920–1970* (Munich, 2005).

33. On the global role and situation of the EU, see L. Kühnhardt, *European Union—The Second Founding: The Changing Rationale of European Integration* (Baden-Baden, 2008); G. Garavini, *After Empires: European Integration, Decolonization and the Challenge from the Global South, 1957–1986* (Oxford, 2012); C. Kaddous (ed.), *The European Union in International Organizations and Global Governance* (Oxford, 2015); G. Bossuat (ed.), *L'Europe et la mondialisation* (Paris, 2006). On transnational networks, see W. Kaiser, *Christian Democracy and the Origins of European Union* (Cambridge, 2007); W. Kaiser and M. Gehler, 'Transnationalism and Early European Integration: The NEI and the Geneva Circle, 1947–1957', *Historical Journal*, 44 (2001), 773–98; W. Kaiser and B. Leucht, 'Informal Politics of Integration: Christian Democratic and Transatlantic Networks in the Creation of the ECSC Core Europe', *Journal of European Integration History*, 14 (2008), 35–50; R. Papini, *The Christian Democratic International* (Lanham, MD, 1997); G. Bossuat, 'Les euro-socialistes de la SFIO. Réseaux et influence', in G. Bossuat and G. Saunier (eds), *Inventer l'Europe. Histoire nouvelle des groupes d'influence et des acteurs de l'unite europeenne* (Brussels, 2003), 409–30; P. Claeys and N. Loeb-Mayer, 'Trans-European Party Groupings: Emergence of New and Alignment of Old Parties in the Light of the Direct Elections to the European Parliament', *Government and Opposition*, 14 (1979), 455–78; M. Dumoulin (ed.), *Réseaux économiques et construction européenne* (Brussels, 2004). On identities and lived experience, see R. Girault (ed.), *Identité et conscience européenne au XXe siècle* (Paris, 1994); R. Frank (ed.), *Les identités européennes au XXe siècle* (Paris, 2004); R. Girault and B. Franke (eds), *Europe brisée, Europe retrouvée. Nouvelles réflexions sur l'unité européenne au XXe siècle* (Paris, 1994); R. Hudemann et al. (eds), *Europa im Blick der Historiker* (Munich, 1995); E. du Réau (ed.), *Europe des elites? Europe des peoples? La construction de l'espace européenne 1945–1960* (Paris, 1998); E. Bussière (ed.), *Europa. L'idée et l'identité européennes de l'antiquité grecque au XXe siècle* (Anvers, 2001); H. Kaelble, *Europäer über Europa. Die Entstehung des europäischen Selbstverständnisses im 19. und 20. Jahrhundert* (Frankfurt, 2001); and G. Bossuat and G. Saunier (eds), *Inventer l'Europe. Histoire nouvelle des groupes d'influence et des acteurs de l'unité européenne* (Brussels, 2003).

34. W. Kaiser, 'From Isolation to Centrality: Contemporary History Meets European Studies', in W. Kaiser and A. Varsori (eds), *European Union History: Themes and Debates* (Basingstoke, 2010), 59. In the same volume, Lorenzo Mechi, 'Formation of a European Society? Exploring Social and Cultural Dimensions', ibid., 154, points out that Kaelble, in his latest works, has paid attention to the internal market programme from the 1980s onwards, referring 'to its facilitating of citizens' mobility, its contribution to democratic consolidation and other phenomena that became more evident only from the 1990s onwards'. On the history of supranational institutions, see M. Dumoulin (ed.), *The European Commission, 1958–72: History and Memories* (Luxembourg, 2007); K. Seidel, *The Process of Politics in Europe: The Rise of European Elites and Supranational Institutions* (London, 2010); P. Bajon, 'The European Commissioners and the Empty Chair Crisis of 1965–66', *Journal of European Integration History*, 15 (2009), 105–25; L. Warlouzet, 'Relancer la CEE avant la chaise vide. Néo-functionalists vs. fédéralistes au sein de la Commission européenne 1964–1965', *Journal of European Integration History*, 14 (2008), 69–86.

35. K. Seidel, 'Alan Milward in *The European Rescue of the Nation-State* (1992): From Pioneer Work to Refinement: Publication Trends', in W. Kaiser and A. Varsori (eds), *European Union History*, 38, 43.

36. Ibid., 43, alluding to N. P. Ludlow, *The European Community and the Crises of the 1960s: Negotiating the Gaullist Challenge* (London, 2006), A. Trunk, *Europa, ein Ausweg. Politische Eliten und europäische Integration in den 1950er Jahren* (Munich, 2007), and M. Gehler, W. Kaiser, and B. Leucht (eds), *Netzwerke im europäischen Mehrebenensystem. Von 1945 bis zur Gegenwart* (Vienna, 2009).

37. A. S. Milward, *The European Rescue of the Nation-State*, 2nd edn (London, 2000), 5. See, for instance, W. van Meurs, R. de Bruin, L. van de Grift, C. Hoetink, K. van Leewen, and C. Reijnen, *The Unfinished History of European Integration* (Amsterdam, 2018), whose 'seven strategic dilemmas' follow the political-science debates about federalism neo-functionalism, intergovernmentalism, liberal intergovernmentalism, multilevel governance, institutionalism, and constructivism.

38. One exception is R. S. Lieshout, M. L. L. Segers, and J. M. van der Vleuten, 'De Gaulle, Moravcsik and *The Choice for Europe*: Soft Sources, Weak Evidence', *Journal of Cold War Studies*, 6 (2004), 89–139, which presents a careful investigation of the political scientist's use of historical evidence. Moravcsik, 'De Gaulle between Grain and *Grandeur*: The Political Economy of French EC Policy, 1958–1970', *Journal of Cold War Studies*, 2.2 (2000), 3–43, and 2.3 (2000), 4–68, replied to earlier critics, both historians such as Milward and Gillingham, and political scientists such as Hoffmann and John Keeler, in A. Moravcsik, 'Beyond Grain and *Grandeur*: An Answer to Critics and an Agenda for Future Research', *Journal of Cold War Studies*, 2.3 (2000), 117–42. On the asymmetry between history and political science in this field and on the need for new historical approaches to integration, see L. Warlouzet, 'European Integration History: Beyond the Crisis', *Politique européenne*, 44 (2014), 98–122; and E. Mourlon-Druol, 'Rich, Vivid and Ignored: History in European Studies', *Politique européenne*, 50 (2015), 56–69.
39. A. S. Milward, 'Allegiance: The Past and the Future', *Journal of European Integration History*, 1 (1995), 12.
40. Ibid.
41. Ibid.
42. Ibid., 13.
43. Ibid.
44. Ibid., 13–14.
45. A. S. Milward, *The European Rescue of the Nation-State*, 2nd edn, 5.
46. Ibid.
47. The aim has long been recognized, of course: see, for example, Wolfram Kaiser, 'From State to Society? The Historiography of European Integration', in M. Cini and A. Bourne (eds), *Palgrave Advances in European Union Studies* (Basingstoke, 2006), 190–208. There are quite a few exceptions, usually in respect of specific events: Piers Ludlow, *Dealing with Britain: The Six and the First UK Application to the EEC* (Cambridge, 1997), for example, examines the UK's application from the German, French, and Dutch perspectives, as well as from the EEC's own standpoint.
48. W. Kaiser and A. Varsori (eds), *European Union History*, 2. E. Mourlon-Druol, *A Europe Made of Money: The Emergence of the European Monetary System* (Ithaca, NY, 2012), 5: 'Partly in reaction to the first writings on European integration by federalists, Alan Milward stressed the role of economic interests and national governments in his analysis of the origins and later development of the integration process. Yet some scholars felt that two types of actors were missing in his analysis: supranational institutions (the European Commission in particular) and transnational actors (non-state actors, political parties, formal and informal networks).' Wolfram Kaiser is one of those stressing transnational actors. The remaining problem concerns the significance of such actors and their role in decision-making.
49. W. Kaiser and A. Varsori (eds), *European Union History*, 2–3.
50. In the sphere of economic policy, for instance, Lucia Coppolaro, *The Making of a World Trading Power: The European Economic Community (EEC) in the GATT Kennedy Round Negotiations, 1963–67* (Farnham, 2013), 12, has noted that a focus on the European level tends to rule out a simultaneous exploration in depth of national policy-making.
51. M. Gehler, 'At the Heart of Integration: Understanding National Policy', in W. Kaiser and A. Varsori (eds), *European Union History*, 85. See also M. Gehler, *Zeitgeschichte im dynamischen Mehrebenensystem. Zwischen Regionalisierung, Nationalstaat, Europäisierung, internationaler Arena und Globalisierung* (Bochum, 2001).
52. Much of Gehler's chapter in W. Kaiser and A. Varsori (eds), *European Union History*, 85–108, outlines future research agendas and assumes that this has not yet been done.
53. Although historians have made separate contributions, the sheer volume of work produced by political scientists and their theoretical contributions have ensured that they continue to dominate the field. On the need for an exchange of ideas between political scientists and historians, see L. Warlouzet, 'The Interdisciplinary Challenge in European Integration History', *Journal of Contemporary History*, 49 (2014), 837–45 and E. Mourlon-Druol, 'Rich, Vivid and Ignored: History in European Studies', *Politique européenne*, 50 (2015), 56–69.
54. See, especially, B. Rosamond, *Theories of European Integration* (Basingstoke, 2000); A. Wiener, T. Börzel, and T. Risse (eds), *European Integration Theory*, 3rd edn (Oxford, 2018); B. F. Nelsen and A. Stubb (eds), *The European Union: Readings on the Theory and Practice of European Integration* (Oxford, 2003); M. Eilstrup-Sangiovanni (ed.), *Debates on European Integration: A Reader* (Basingstoke, 2006); R. Adler-Nissen and K. Kropp (eds), *A Sociology of Knowledge of European Integration: The Social Sciences in the Making of Europe* (London, 2016).

24   EUROPEAN INTEGRATION SINCE THE 1920s

55. E. B. Haas, *The Uniting of Europe*; E. B. Haas, *Beyond the Nation-State: Functionalism and International Organization* (Palo Alto, CA, 1964); L. N. Lindberg, *The Political Dynamics of European Economic Integration* (Palo Alto, CA, 1963); S. Hoffmann, 'International Systems and International Law', in K. Knorr and S. Verba (eds), *The International System* (Princeton, NJ, 1961), 205–39; S. Hoffmann, 'Obstinate or Obsolete? The Fate of the Nation-State and the Case of Western Europe', *Daedalus*, 95 (1966), 862–915; K. W. Deutsch, *Political Community and the North Atlantic Area* (Princeton, NJ, 1957).
56. K. W. Deutsch, *Political Community and the North Atlantic Area*, 6–7.
57. S. Hoffmann, *The European Sisyphus: Essays on Europe, 1964–1994* (Boulder, CO, 1995), 5.
58. S. Hoffmann, 'Obstinate or Obsolete? The Fate of the Nation-State and the Case of Western Europe', *Daedalus*, 95 (1966), 886.
59. A. Moravcsik, 'Preferences and Power in the European Community: A Liberal Intergovernmentalist Approach', *Journal of Common Market Studies*, 31 (1993), 483.
60. Ibid., 515.
61. See, for instance, A. Moravcsik, 'Preferences, Power and Institutions in 21st-century Europe', *Journal of Common Market Studies*, 56 (2018), 1648–74, which addresses questions raised by 'competitors' such as post-functionalism (Lisbet Hooghe and Gary Marks) and historical institutionalism (Paul Pierson). L. Hooghe and G. Marks, 'A Postfunctionalist Theory of European Integration: From Permissive Consensus to Constraining Dissensus', *British Journal of Political Science*, 39 (2009), 1–23; L. Hooghe and G. Marks, 'Grand Theories of European Integration in the 21st Century', *Journal of European Public Policy*, 26 (2019), 1113–33; P. Pierson, 'The Path to European Integration: An Historical Institutionalist Account', *Comparative Political Studies*, 29 (1996), 123–64; P. Pierson, *Politics in Time: History, Institutions and Social Analysis* (Princeton, NJ, 2004).
62. J. Kooiman (ed.), *Modern Governance: New Government-Society Interactions* (London, 1993), 4.
63. For the last point, see Simon Hix, *The Political System of the European Union* (Basingstoke, 1999).
64. B. Rosamond, *Theories of European Integration*, 107; H. D. Lasswell, *Politics: Who Gets What, When, How* (New York, 1950).
65. K. Armstrong and S. J. Bulmer, *The Governance of the Single European Market* (Manchester, 1998), 62; S. J. Bulmer, 'The Governance of the European Union: A New Institutionalist Approach', *Journal of Public Policy*, 13 (1994), 351–80.
66. G. Marks, F. Nielsen, L. Ray, and J. Salk, 'Competencies, Cracks and Conflicts: Regional Mobilization in the European Union', in G. Marks, F. W. Sharpf, P. C. Schmitter, and W. Streeck (eds), *Governance in the European Union* (London, 1996), 41.
67. A. Stone Sweet and W. Sandholtz, 'European Integration and Supranational Governance', *Journal of European Public Policy*, 4 (1997), 299–300.
68. Paolo Graziano and Maarten Vink (eds), *Europeanization: New Research Agendas* (Basingstoke, 2007), 7–8, claim that 'most of the contributions have mainly considered Europeanization as an adaptive process triggered by European regional integration', or 'the domestic adaptation to European regional integration', including 'the administrative adaptation of executive government to a "continuous system of negotiations" within the EU, the adaptation of interest groups and social movements to new institutional opportunity structures and also the normative consequences in terms of substantial political issues'.
69. Historians have long sought to make sense of texts about and discourses concerning 'Europe', of course, but they their studies of the 'idea of Europe' have rarely been linked to policies and decision-making on national and European levels. One recent exception, albeit concentrating largely on cultural policy, is Oriane Calligaro, *Negotiating Europe: EU Promotion of Europeanness since the 1950s* (Basingstoke, 2013); O. Calligaro, 'From "European Cultural Heritage" to "Cultural Diversity"? The Changing Core Values of European Cultural Policy', *Politique européenne*, 45 (2014), 60–85; O. Calligaro, 'Legitimation through Remembrance? The Changing Regimes of Historicity of European Integration', *Journal of Contemporary European Studies*, 23 (2015), 330–43; O. Calligaro and K. K. Patel, 'The True "EURESCO"? The Council of Europe, Transnational Networking and the Emergence of European Community Cultural Policies, 1970–90', *European Review of History*, 24 (2017), 399–422.
70. T. Diez, 'Speaking Europe: The Politics of Integration Discourse', in T. Christiansen et al. (eds), *The Social Construction of Europe* (London, 2001), 96. On the resistance of international historians and exponents of international relations to postmodernism, see P. Finney, 'Still "Marking Time"? Text, Discourse and Truth in International History', *Review of International Studies*, 27 (2001), 291–308.

INTRODUCTION 25

71. T. Christiansen, K. E. Jørgensen, and A. Wiener, 'Introduction', in T. Christiansen et al. (eds), *The Social Construction of Europe* (London, 2001), 11.
72. T. Christiansen, 'Reconstructing European Space: From Territorial Politics to Multilevel Governance', in K. E. Jørgensen (ed.), *Reflective Approaches to European Governance* (Basingstoke, 1997), 54.
73. See, for instance, Jeffrey Checkel's and Andrew Moravcsik's searing response to constructivists in 'A Constructivist Research Programme in EU Studies?', *European Union Politics*, 2 (2001), 219–49.
74. A. Moravcsik, *The Choice for Europe: Social Purpose and State Power from Messina to Maastricht* (Ithaca, 1998), 78.
75. L. N. Lindberg, *The Political Dynamics of European Economic Integration* (Stanford, 1963), 10.
76. E. B. Haas, 'The Study of Regional Organization: Reflections on the Joy and Anguish of Pretheorizing', *International* Organization, 24 (1970), 610; E. B. Haas, *The Uniting of Europe: Political, Social and Economic Forces, 1950–1957* (Notre Dame, Indiana, 1958).
77. For summaries of the literature from different points of view, see W. Loth, 'Explaining European Integration' and J. R. Gillingham, 'A Theoretical Vacuum: European Integration and Historical Research Today', *Journal of European Integration History* 14 (2008), 9–34; D. Dinan, 'The Historiography of European Integration', in D. Dinan (ed.), *Origins and Evolution*, 297–324; N. P. Ludlow, 'Widening, Deepening and Opening Out: Towards a Fourth Decade of European Integration History', in W. Loth (ed.), *Experiencing Europe*, 33–44. 'Federalist' approaches include W. Lipgens, *A History of European Integration, 1945–1947* (Oxford, 1982); W. Lipgens, *Die Anfänge der europäischen Einigungspolitik 1945–1950*; W. Lipgens and W. Loth (eds), *Documents on the History of European Integration* (Berlin, 1985–88), 3 vols; W. Loth, 'Identity and Statehood in the Process of European Integration', *Journal of European Integration History* 6 (2000), 19–31; W. Loth, 'Der Prozess der europäischen Integration', *Jahrbuch fur europaische Geschichte* 1 (2000), 17–30. For studies stressing national interest, see A. S. Milward, *The European Rescue of the Nation-State*; A. S. Milward, *The Reconstruction of Western Europe, 1945–51* (London, 1984); A. S. Milward and V. Sorensen (eds), *The Frontier of National Sovereignty: History and Theory, 1945–1992* (Routledge, 1993); also, B. Bruneteau, 'The Construction of Europe and the Concept of the Nation-State', *Contemporary European History* 9 (2000), 245–60. On transnationalism, see especially W. Kaiser, *Christian Democracy and the Origins of European Union* (Cambridge, 2007); W. Kaiser, 'Cooperation of European Catholic Politicians in Exile in Britain and the USA during the Second World War', *Journal of Contemporary History* 35 (2000), 439–65; W. Kaiser, 'No Second Versailles: Transnational Contacts in the People and Freedom Group and the International Christian Democratic Union, 1936–1945', in M. Gehler et al. (eds), *Christdemokratie in Europa im 20 Jahrhundert* (Vienna, 2001); W. Kaiser and M. Gehler, 'Transnationalism and Early European Integration: The NEI and the Geneva Circle,1947–1957', *Historical* Journal, 44 (2001), 773–98; W. Kaiser and B. Leucht, 'Informal Politics of Integration: Christian Democratic and Transatlantic Networks in the Creation of the ECSC Core Europe', *Journal of European Integration History* 14 (2008), 35–50.
78. J. Richardson, 'Policy-Making in the EU: Interests, Ideas and Garbage Cans of Primeval Soup', in J. Richardson (ed.), *European Union: Power and Policy-Making* (London, 1996), 5. See also B. Kohler-Koch and B. Rittberger, 'The Governance Turn in EU Studies', *Journal of Common Market Studies*, 44 (2006), 27–49.
79. G. Schneider and M. Aspinwall (eds), *The Rules of Integration: Institutionalist Approaches to the Study of Europe* (Manchester, 2001), 2; K. Armstrong and S. J. Bulmer, *The Governance of the Single European Market* (Manchester, 1998); W. Sandholtz and A. Stone Sweet (eds), *European Integration and Supranational Governance* (Oxford, 1998); P. Pierson, 'The Path to European Integration: A Historical Institutionalist Analysis', *Comparative European Politics*, 29 (1996), 123–63.
80. J. G. March and J. P. Olsen, 'The New Institutionalism: Organizational Factors in Political Life', *American Political Science Review*, 78 (1984), 734–49; P. Hall *Governing the Economy: The Politics of State Intervention in Britain and France* (Cambridge, 1986), 19; Maurice Mandelbaum, *Purpose and Necessity*, 151, provides a useful analysis: 'Every social institution involves a patterning of relationships among individuals: if their behaviour were not to a large extent regulated by commonly recognized rules, so that each person had a notion of what was to be expected with respect to the actions of others, there would be no institutions and no organized social life. Since one cannot speak of institutions without speaking of rules according to which individuals behave, it would seem that we should regard societies simply as a congeries of individuals who behave in a certain way. This, however, would be a mistake.... It is ... a mistake to think of society in terms of

26 EUROPEAN INTEGRATION SINCE THE 1920s

the actual behaviour of individuals, even though it is clear that were it not for the existence and activities of individuals, the society would not exist. That the individuals themselves are not to be considered the elements constituting a particular society becomes evident when we consider what is involved in describing a society: we proceed by describing its various institutions and their relations to one another, rather than by referring to the individuals who participate in its life.... Conversely, when we describe any individual, we do not simply describe his physical appearance, his capacities, his character and temperament, but we also refer to his status within his society.' Historians, though, do refer to individuals—and singular actions—more frequently as a consequence of their objective of explaining change.

81. J. G. March and J. P. Olsen, *Rediscovering Institutions: The Organizational Basis of Politics* (New York, 1989), 159. See also J. Bulpitt, *Territory and Power in the United Kingdom* (Colchester, 2008).

82. P. Bourdieu, 'Social Space and Field of Power' in P. Bourdieu, *Practical Reason*, 31. 'New institutionalists' differ in their understanding of such practical consciousness and perception of conditions, depending on whether they favour various forms of 'rational-choice', 'historical' and 'sociological' institutionalism.

83. K. K. Patel and W. Kaiser, 'Continuity and Change in European Cooperation during the Twentieth Century', *Contemporary European History*, 27 (2018), 165–82, and 'Multiple Connections in European Cooperation: International Organizations, Policy Ideas, Practices and Transfers, 1967–1992', *European Review of History*, 24 (2017), 337–57; K. K. Patel and J. Schot, 'Twisted Paths to European Integration: Comparing Agriculture and Transport in a Transnational Perspective', *European Review of History*, 20 (2011), 383–403; K. K. Patel, *Europäisierung wider Willen. Die Bundesrepublik Deutschland in der Agrarintegration der EWG, 1955–1973* (Munich, 2009); W. Kaiser and J. Schot, *Writing the Rules for Europe: Experts, Cartels and International Organizations* (Basingstoke, 2014).

84. W. Lipgens, *A History of European Integration, 1945–1947*; A. Milward, *The European Rescue of the Nation-State*.

85. For further references to historical work on concepts of Europe, see M. Hewitson and M. D'Auria (eds), *Europe in Crisis: Intellectuals and the European Idea, 1917–1957* (New York, 2012); J. L. Chabot, *Aux origines intellectuelles de l'Union européenne: l'idée d'Europe unie de 1919 à 1939* (Grenoble, 2005); E. du Réau, *L'idée d'Europe au XXe siècle. Des mythes aux réalités* (Brussels, 1996).

86. M. Hewitson, 'Inventing Europe and Reinventing the Nation-State in a New World Order', in M. Hewitson and M. D'Auria (eds), *Europe in Crisis*, 63–81.

87. W. Loth, *Der Weg nach Europa. Geschichte der europäischen Integration 1939–1957* (Göttingen, 1996); W. Loth (ed.), *Europe, Cold War and Co-existence* (London, 2004); W. Loth (ed.), *Crises and Compromises: The European Project, 1963–1969* (Baden-Baden, 2001); T. Judt, *Postwar: A History of Europe since 1945* (London, 2005); T. Judt, *A Grand Illusion? An Essay on Europe* (London, 1996).

88. T. Judt, *A Grand Illusion?*, 24.

89. N. P. Ludlow, 'Widening, Deepening and Opening Out: Towards a Fourth Decade of European Integration History', in W. Loth (ed.), *Experiencing Europe: 50 Years of European Construction, 1957–2007* (Baden-Baden, 2009), 34.

90. W. Wallace (ed.), *The Dynamics of Integration* (London, 1991), 9.

91. See, recently, Wilfried Loth, *Building Europe. A History of European Unification* (Berlin, 2015), which begins with an examination, in a Prologue rather than an Introduction, of 'four driving forces' of 'European unification', but then launches into a narrative of events.

92. F. Furet, 'From Narrative History to Problem-oriented History' (1975), in F. Furet, *In the Workshop of History* (Chicago, 1982), 54–67; F. Braudel cited in A. Megill, 'Recounting the Past: "Description", Explanation and Narrative in Historiography', *American Historical Review*, 94 (1989), 642.

93. F. Furet, 'From Narrative History to Problem-oriented History', in F. Furet, *In the Workshop of History* (Chicago, 1984), 60.

94. Ibid., 54.

95. Ibid., 55.

96. Ibid.

97. V. Martin de la Torre, *Europe, a Leap into the Unknown: A Journey Back in Time to Meet the Founders of the European Union* (Bern, 2014); A. P. Fimister, *Robert Schuman: Neo-Scholastic Humanism and the Reunification of Europe* (Saarbrücken, 2008); S. Schirmann (ed.), *Robert Schuman et les pères de l'Europe* (Bern, 2008); D. Brinkley, *Jean Monnet: The Path to European Unity* (Basingstoke, 1991); F. Duchêne, *Jean Monnet: The First Statesman of Interdependence* (New York, 1994).

98. The range of such sources is vast, requiring extensive reliance on the work, in these areas, of other scholars. Although using a range of primary materials, from opinion polls and newspaper reports to correspondence, diaries and memoirs, this study is exploratory rather than exhaustive.

99. F. Furet, 'From Narrative History to Problem-oriented History', in F. Furet, *In the Workshop of History*, 55.

100. Ibid.

101. Ibid., 56.

102. There have, of course, been many attempts to identify and tell stories about the acts of a supposed group of 'founders'. One of the main aims of this study, along with those of other recent and older works (from Milward onwards), is to challenge these assumptions and to shift the focus to the interactions of governments, business people, commentators, politicians, and 'public opinion', along with the leaders of European institutions.

103. See, for example, D. Unwin, *The Community of Europe: A History of European Integration since 1945* (London, 1991); D. Dinan, *Europe Recast: A History of European Union* (Basingstoke, 2004); M. Dedman, *The Origins and Development of the European Union, 1945–1995: A History of European Integration* (London, 1996); A. Blair, *The European Union since 1945* (London, 2014).

104. F. Furet, 'From Narrative History to Problem-oriented History', in F. Furet, *In the Workshop of History*, 56.

105. Ibid.

106. Ibid.

107. Ibid., 56–7.

108. Ibid., 57.

109. Such sources are evaluated in qualitative and comparative fashion, typical of historical enquiry, asking questions about the motives and intentions of actors, the circumstances in which sources were produced, and corroboration and contradiction in other sources. Opinion polls, on which studies of convergence tend to rely (including here), often rest on a set of leading questions. I have tried to select the most reliable polls, corroborating them by referring to other forms of commentary and reportage, where possible. H.-J. Trenz, 'The European Public Sphere: Contradictory Findings in a Diverse Research Field', *European Political Science*, 4 (2005), 407–20; P. Oleskog Tryggvason and J. Strömbäck, 'Fact or Fiction? Investigating the Quality of Opinion Poll Coverage and Its Antecedents', *Journalism Studies*, 19 (2018), 2148–67; C. Vögele and M. Bachl (eds), 'The Quality of Public Opinion Poll Coverage in German National Newspapers during Federal Election Campaigns', *International Journal of Public Opinion Research*, 32 (2019), 332–45; R. M. Worcester, *British Public Opinion: A Guide to the History and Methodology of Political Opinion* (Cambridge, 1991); P. J. Lavrakas and M. W. Traugott (eds), *Election Polls, the News Media and Democracy* (New York, 2000); F. Brettschneider, *Wahlumfragen. Empirische Befunde zur Darstellung in den Medien und zum Einfluss auf das Wahlverhalten in der Bundesrepublik Deutschland und den USA* (Munich, 1991).

110. F. Furet, 'From Narrative History to Problem-oriented History', in F. Furet, *In the Workshop of History*, 63.

111. S. Hix, 'The Study of the European Community: The Challenge to Comparative Politics', *West European Politics*, 17 (1994), 1–30.

112. F. Furet, 'From Narrative History to Problem-oriented History', in F. Furet, *In the Workshop of History*, 66.

113. Ibid.

114. Ibid., 67.

115. Cited in A. Megill, 'Recounting the Past: "Description", Explanation and Narrative in Historiography', *American Historical Review*, 94 (1989), 639.

116. Ibid.

117. Ibid., 642; F. Furet, 'From Narrative History to Problem-Oriented History' (1975), in F. Furet, *In the Workshop of History* (Chicago, 1982), 54–67. W. H. Sewell, Jr., *Logics of History: Social Theory and Social Transformation* (Chicago, 2005), 218.

118. See, for instance, Mark Gilbert, 'Narrating the Process: Questioning the Progressive Story of European Integration', *Journal of Common Market Studies*, 46 (2008), 641–8.

119. Laurent Warlouzet, *Europe contre Europe. Entre liberté, solidarité et puissance* (Paris, 2022), is one recent exception, which investigates the overlap and tensions between support for a free market, social solidarity, and political power.

120. K. K. Patel, *Project Europe: A History* (Cambridge, 2020).

28 EUROPEAN INTEGRATION SINCE THE 1920S

121. For recent historical approaches to European integration, see B. Leucht, K. Seidel, and L. Warlouzet (eds), *Reinventing Europe: The History of the European Union, 1945 to the Present* (London, 2023).
122. K. K. Patel, *Europäische Integration. Geschichte und Gegenwart* (Munich, 2022).
123. The emphasis in Chapter 5 is on trade and growth (and on welfare, reducing regional inequality and communication in Chapter 6), since they have been central for all governments and have been viewed as the principal drivers of integration. Monetary cooperation and economic and monetary union have been seen, except by their most devout proponents, largely as a means rather than a goal in themselves. EMU was, in part, put forward as a means of facilitating—and boosting—trade and, therefore, growth, and, in part, was a political decision, rejected by some governments and remaining an instance of 'differentiated integration': K. Dyson, 'Playing for High Stakes: The Eurozone Crisis', in D. Dinan, N. Nugent, and W. E. Paterson (eds), *The European Union in Crisis* (London, 2017), 54–76; K. Dyson, *States, Debt, and Power: 'Saints' and 'Sinners' in European History and Integration* (Oxford, 2014); K. Dyson, 'Norman's Lament: The Greek and Euro Area Crisis in Historical Perspective', *New Political Economy*, 15 (2010), 597–608; K. Dyson (ed.), *European States and the Euro: Europeanization, Variation, and Convergence* (Oxford, 2002), 278–304; J. I. Walsh, *European Monetary Integration and Domestic Politics: Britain, France and Italy* (Boulder, CO, 2000); F. Schimmelfennig and T. Winzen, *Ever Looser Union? Differentiated European Integration* (Oxford, 2020).
124. This was the title of O'Toole's article: *Observer*, 27 December 2020.
125. 'So Long, We'll Miss You', ibid.
126. Ibid.
127. Ibid.
128. Ibid.
129. Ibid.
130. Ibid.
131. T. Adams, 'We're Out of the European Union. Just How Did We Get Here?', *Observer*, 27 December 2020.
132. Ibid.
133. Ibid.
134. Ibid.
135. Ibid.
136. Ibid.
137. Ibid.
138. Ibid.

1
Hard Power

The establishment and consolidation of the European Communities were dependent on the new international order of the Cold War. Yet how far did Europeans help to create or shape that order? American policy was designed 'to do everything within our diplomatic power to foster and encourage democratic governments throughout the world', in the words of Franklin D. Roosevelt's aide, Harry Hopkins.[1] In Europe, this task was complicated by the presence of the Soviet Union 'as the sole great power on the Continent—a position unique in modern history'—in the judgement of the Joint Chiefs of Staff in June 1945, which eventually ensured not only that US forces remained in Western Europe, but also that Washington continued to regard mainland Europe as the nerve centre of the Cold War.[2] Gradually, the 'realization is spreading that the plight of Europe is grave beyond words, and that a new attitude to its problems is absolutely necessary', reported the correspondent of the *Economist* on 17 March 1945, after accompanying Clement Attlee, who was then the Deputy Prime Minister, on a tour around the liberated Continent.[3] 'The human problem the war will leave behind it has not yet been imagined, much less faced by anybody,' wrote Anne O'Hare for the *New York Times* on the 14th of the same month: 'There has never been such destruction, such disintegration of the structure of life.'[4] Prompted, in part, by this type of reportage and, in larger part, by strategic and political calculations, Roosevelt and Harry Truman committed military forces to Europe and underwrote a *pax americana*, coordinating European defence and foreign policy. European integration took place within such parameters.[5] The formulation and execution of a 'Common Foreign and Security Policy', articulated at Maastricht in 1992, were correspondingly halting and limited.

In 2012, the European Union won the Nobel Peace Prize. The Norwegian committee praised the EU and its forerunners for their contribution, 'for over six decades', 'to the advancement of peace and reconciliation, democracy and human rights in Europe'.[6] 'The dreadful suffering in World War II demonstrated the need for a new Europe,' ran its justification:

> Over a seventy-year period, Germany and France had fought three wars. Today war between Germany and France is unthinkable. This shows how, through well-aimed efforts and by building up mutual confidence, historical enemies can become close partners.

European Integration since the 1920s: Security, Identity, and Cooperation. Mark Hewitson, Oxford University Press.
© Mark Hewitson 2024. DOI: 10.1093/oso/9780198915942.003.0002

30 EUROPEAN INTEGRATION SINCE THE 1920s

> In the 1980s, Greece, Spain and Portugal joined the EU. The introduction of democracy was a condition for their membership. The fall of the Berlin Wall made EU membership possible for several Central and Eastern European countries, thereby opening a new era in European history. The division between East and West has to a large extent been brought to an end; democracy has been strengthened; many ethnically-based national conflicts have been settled.[7]

Predictably, much of the British right-wing press was outraged and sarcastic. The 'announcement caused widespread bemusement and derision, with critics pointing out that it comes as the eurozone battles the worst recession for nearly a century,' wrote Tim Shipman in the *Daily Mail* on 13 October 2012, adding that 'This week saw Greek citizens dressed as Nazis burn swastika flags to protest at a visit to Athens by German Chancellor Angela Merkel' before going on to quote Norman Lamont, the former Conservative Chancellor and well-known Eurosceptic: 'It would require a heart of stone not to die of laughter. It is the most ridiculous decision since the committee gave the peace prize to Barack Obama when he had been US President for two minutes.'[8] The same article repeated comments from Nigel Farage, the Tory Eurosceptic Bill Cash, and the financier Peter Hargreaves.[9] *The Times* remarked that the British Prime Minister, David Cameron, had refused to 'take up the suggestion from Herman Van Rompuy, the European Council President, that all 27 leaders should go to receive the award', commenting that enough people—three of the five EU presidents— would be going.[10] The left-leaning *Guardian* was more balanced, repeating the comments of Lamont, Farage, the Conservative leader in the European Parliament Martin Callanan ('it is downright out of touch'), and the Syriza spokesman Panos Skourletis ('we are experiencing what really is a war situation') alongside those of Jose Manuel Barroso ('At its origins, the European Union brought together nations emerging from the ruins of devastating world wars') and Herman Van Rompuy himself ('The EU is the biggest peacemaking institution ever created in human history').[11] Arguably, the hyperbole of supporters undermined the EU's credibility almost as much as the scorn of its detractors.

In Ireland, where support for the European Union has been more pronounced, journalists spent longer considering the merits of the award, at the same time as underlining the problems created by the eurozone crisis. 'That reality, that vision of a common political project and of shared political sovereignty, is too easily forgotten by those of us who did not live through military occupation by the Nazis, or see our families die in millions in the gas chambers, or by those of the yet-older generation for whom the inter-war years was not haunted constantly by the question of when, not if, France and Germany would again go to war,' recorded the *Irish Times* on 11 December: 'Or indeed, increasingly, by those of a younger generation for whom such trials are just "history", part of a long-distant past.'[12] Equally important, continued the same article, was 'what Brussels calls the

"European method", the exercise of "soft power"', which had made the union a 'vital engine for peace, not only inside the EU, but in the region'.[13] Using the 'carrot of accession and stick of its denial, with the rewards both of financial assistance and access to European markets', the European Union had managed successfully 'to cajole and encourage reconciliation and the embrace of the rule of law in the Balkans—most recently a landmark agreement between Serbia and Kosovo on border controls, inconceivable a few years ago—and the demilitarization and democratisation of the Turkish state'.[14] Peace-making in this fashion was a 'slow, imperfect and uneven process'—as the history of Turkish democratization has demonstrated—but the EU remained, as states in Africa and South America agreed, 'a model well worth emulating'.[15] The reaction to the award was generally positive elsewhere in Europe, with approving editorials in *Der Spiegel, Frankfurter Allgemeine Zeitung, Die Welt, Die Wiener Zeitung, Le Soir, Le Figaro, La Stampa, De Standaard*, and *Aftenposten*.[16]

Historians have been more sceptical about the diplomatic role of the European Communities and EU. For Tony Judt in *A Grand Illusion? An Essay on Europe* (1996), there were four aspects of 'the special context' out of which the European Community emerged, but none had anything to do with 'idealists for a united continent', who 'had no discernible real-world impact'.[17] First, the Second World War had allowed contemporaries to assume that, in peacetime, there would be comparably high levels of state involvement in all areas of policy, from social welfare to economic planning, making 'it easier to imagine pooling aspects of that [economic] control in a multinational authority'.[18] It had also led to the defeat of most European powers.[19] 'It is significant that ever since 1945 opinion polls across Western Europe show a consistent reluctance on the part of most people to express any confidence in their own state's military capacity, little support for high military expenditure, and no sustained inclination to treat military prowess as a measure of national greatness,' writes Judt: the war left Germans 'with nothing to be proud of in their recent past' and the Dutch, French, and Italians with a 'good reason to put recent history behind them'.[20] Second, the onset of the Cold War convinced the majority of European leaders that the Soviet Union posed 'a serious threat to Eastern Europe and that even if only for their own protection the states of Western Europe must come into some form of alliance with one another and with the United States', overcoming 'longstanding resentment of American power and suspicion of the motives of U.S. foreign policy' and averting the need for independent European rearmament.[21] Third, the creation of two hostile blocs on the continent permitted 'the rapid and uncontentious absorption of (western) Germany into the West European family'.[22] With the UK unable to pay for its own zone in Germany and the United States wanting 'a wealthy and loyal German state to play a role in the Western Alliance', the 'mistakes of 1919 were miraculously avoided—even though after 1945 there were altogether more convincing grounds than after the war of 1914–18 for treating Germany as a pariah state,

32 EUROPEAN INTEGRATION SINCE THE 1920s

guilty of crimes of war that the poor Kaiser had never imagined'.[23] Fourth, 'the disastrous recent economic history of the continent', culminating in the destruction of the Second World War, 'gave a special quality to the ensuing boom' and allowed—and seemed to call for—a greater degree of economic cooperation.[24] In Judt's verdict, this conjunction of events, including the chance 'to catch up on thirty years of economic stagnation' and 'rebuild after a disastrous war', was largely accidental.[25] In terms of its security, Western Europe had been 'bound together by the need to do so, or by the coincidence of Communist threat and American encouragement', the historian concludes: 'For good and ill the post-war circumstances, the midwife of mid-twentieth-century Western European prosperity, were unique; no one else will have the same good fortune.'[26] On this reading, the fact that a long-lasting peace was established had little to do with the European Communities.

Many historians of European integration disagree with Judt's analysis. Most notably, Walter Lipgens contended that federalism became much more significant within the various resistance movements of the Second World War and, subsequently, within the emerging European movements of the late 1940s and newly constituted post-war political elites.[27] Influential proponents of European integration were able, according to this account of events, to establish federal or supranational institutions such as the European Coal and Steel Community (1951), Euratom and the European Economic Community (1957) in the changed conditions of the late 1940s and 1950s, making use of the transnational networks of the resistance, the European movements, big business, and Christian Democracy.[28] Finding themselves in a hegemonic position 'by default' after the Second World War but fearing that 'the future belonged to socialism', Christian Democrats in particular sought to create and maintain transnational contacts, in part to counter similar efforts by right- and left-wing parties, as Josef Escher, the Swiss Conservative People's Party (SVKP) president, pointed out in March 1947 at the Lucerne meeting of Christian Democratic parties: 'When the political Right and Left organize themselves across borders, the Christian parties must not be left behind.'[29] Once European institutions were set up, they developed their own momentum, meaning—in Wolfram Kaiser's opinion—that 'national political actors and collective interests stand no realistic chance of influencing the policy-making process significantly unless they are well connected across borders in transnational networks, from the more formalised cooperation of EU-level political parties with a general stake in EU politics to highly informal expert networks within a specific policy sector, or what Peter M. Haas first called an "epistemic community"'.[30] Whereas Lipgens—a Catholic historian to whom 'the formation of a geographically limited core Europe...signified a morally superior attempt to overcome the nation-state'—'was not very concerned about, and failed to establish, causal links between these [European] movements' ideas and proposals and the actual process of core Europe formation', more recent historians have made this their main task.[31] By looking, in Christian Bailey's words, at 'how foreign and European policy shaped the domestic policy' of political parties and groups, 'rather than the other way around', scholars can reinterpret their principal stances: thus, for example, Kurt Schumacher and the SPD are usually seen to have chosen nationalism over internationalism during the late 1940s and 1950s in West Germany, yet part of their 'intransigent' disagreement with the CDU/CSU derived from their commitment to a Third Way via Europe, which was opposed to Adenauer's 'Westernizing' European policy.[32]

Most historians of the post-war era, even if they acknowledge that new transnational contacts complicated policy-making and tested allegiances, accept that the domestic agenda, usually resting on the need for reconstruction and reconciliation, and security policy, which seemed to require the involvement of the United States, were uppermost in politicians' minds for at least two decades after the Second World War. In this context, Adenauer was not unusual in characterizing foreign Christian Democrats as more or less 'aggressive' adversaries of Germany, rather than as party allies on the European level.[33] As Judt rightly claims, 'there was little talk of a "united Europe" in the first years after the defeat of Germany', for the terminology of unity was 'polluted' after Albert Speer's plans for a New European Order had found an echo 'in a thousand wartime speeches, where visions of a new Europe did sinister service as a synonym for anti-Bolshevism, collaboration with National Socialism, and rejection of the old liberal, democratic, and divided pre-war world'.[34] Instead, the makers of post-war Europe were driven 'by realistic, national motives of the most conventional and traditional kind—which is hardly surprising when one considers that most of them had grown up in a world of nation-states and alliances, their earliest adult memories dating back before the First World War'.[35]

Such conditions did not prevent European integration occurring in the 1950s, since they were accompanied—as Judt concedes—by an 'unrepeatable' special context, resting on the geopolitics of the Cold War and a corresponding shift in the 'German question', which made integration more likely.[36] Thus, Wilfried Loth has been able to argue from a different starting point that the Cold War—by highlighting the need for peace among sovereign states, for a resolution of the German question and for larger markets than the 'walled' economies of the interwar era, together with fear of US competition—made integration more likely, albeit within a *pax americana*.[37] For David Reynolds, integration likewise took place under the umbrella of NATO, which 'was not a coerced alliance', with the majority of European leaders pleased that Dwight Eisenhower's repeated insistence that American troops in Europe were 'a stop-gap operation' had metamorphosed into a continuing commitment because 'the defence of Western Europe was now dependent on nuclear weapons'.[38] Yet, when it did occur, despite being 'erratic' and 'faltering', European integration acquired its own momentum, turning the EEC into the 'focal point of Western Europe' within a few years: 'Those

34   EUROPEAN INTEGRATION SINCE THE 1920S

states left outside the Six were peripheral, both metaphorically and literally.'[39] With economics, politics, and diplomacy interlinked, questions about the EU's geopolitical role remain open.

Europe in a Bi-polar World

The EU became a model for the exercise of 'soft power', but it was established in the midst of hard power.[40] The process of European integration was affected by a broader, cross-continental division of the world into Soviet and American spheres of influence during the Cold War. Few historians defined what the 'Cold War' actually was, for, at the time, it seemed self-evident. With the end of the Cold War, this certainty has diminished, comparable in some respects to that concerning the nation-state, which was the object of competing definitions as it seemed to be disintegrating.[41] Here, I define the Cold War as an apparently insuperable enmity between two sides which could, at any time, trigger a hot war.[42] In effect, such enmity made Europe into a site, rather than an agent, of conflict. 'The Truman Doctrine treats those who are supposed to benefit by it as dependencies of the United States, as instruments of the American policy for "containing" Russia,' objected the journalist Walter Lippmann, author of the first book on the Cold War.[43] For Joseph Stalin, perusing a map of the new post-war borders of the USSR for the first time, it was 'okay to the West', in Europe: 'Finland has offended us, so we moved the border from Leningrad. Baltic states—that's age-old Russian land!—and they're ours again. All Belorussians live together now, Ukrainians together, Moldavians together.'[44] Likewise, 'Everything is all right to the North' and 'everything is in order' in the East: '"The Kurile Islands belong to us now, Sakhalin is completely ours—you see, good! And Port Arthur's ours, and Darien is ours"—Stalin moved his pipe across China—"and the Chinese Eastern railway is ours"'.[45] The Soviet Union was focusing on Asia and the wider world, not merely—or even largely—on Europe: '"But I don't like our border right here!" Stalin said and pointed to the Caucasus.'[46] For John Lewis Gaddis, what Moscow and Washington were doing after 1945 was constructing 'informal empires', creating 'a situation in which a single state shapes the behaviour of others, whether directly or indirectly, partially or completely, by means that can range from the outright use of force through intimidation, dependency, inducements, and even inspiration'.[47]

David Reynolds has argued that there were a series of Cold Wars in 1947–53, 1958–63 (from the Second Berlin Crisis to the Test Ban Treaty), and 1979–85 (from the Soviet invasion of Afghanistan to *glasnost* and *perestroika*).[48] Yet it seems more sensible to talk of peaks and troughs in a constant state of warlike enmity between the Soviet and Western blocs. From the standpoint of European history, it is also useful to divide the Cold War into two parts: a period of hostility up until

1963; and an era of détente after that date.[49] One of the central arguments in this chapter is that such periodization influenced the course of European integration, since the cooperation of continental states was required during the early period between 1945 and 1963 in the interests of security against a perceived Soviet threat.[50] It is intriguing to imagine what might have happened if the menace of the USSR had not existed or no pressure had been exerted on European states to cooperate by the USA: although it is likely, given the reaction of continental states to the events of the Second World War, that there would have been movement towards economic and political integration, it is by no means certain that such states would have been able to reconcile their varying security interests, as the failure of the European Defence Community in 1954 demonstrated.[51] As it turned out, the conflicting security interests of continental states were reconciled within the American-led and British-sponsored North Atlantic Treaty Organisation, and this effectively cleared the way for French-backed economic integration within Europe. Thus, by 1963, as overriding security needs began to diminish and as the foreign policies of European states started to become more independent, the foundations of a supranational and intergovernmental European Community had already been laid and proved strong enough to weather the storms of the 1970s and early 1980s.[52]

After 1945, the world was divided relatively quickly according to criteria of power, with the American and Soviet economies the largest in the world, and ideology, with a new and clearer-cut opposition between Communism and capitalism than had previously existed between fascism, liberal democracy, and Communism. 'One way of life is based upon the will of the majority, and is distinguished by free institutions, representative government, free elections, guarantees of individual liberty, freedom of speech and religion, and freedom from political oppression,' declared the American President in his 'Truman Doctrine' speech of March 1947: 'The second way of life is based upon the will of a minority forcibly imposed upon the majority. It relies upon terror and oppression, a controlled press and radio, fixed elections, and the suppression of personal freedoms.'[53] By July 1947, after Vyacheslav Molotov had walked out of the Marshall Plan talks in Paris, returning to Moscow to set up Eastern European trade agreements, to call for Western European Communist parties to organize strikes, to establish Cominform and to blockade Berlin, the United States and the Soviet Union realised that they could not work together to police a new world order, as Roosevelt had hoped. It should be recalled, however, that this opposition was not immediately apparent in the wake of the Second World War. Historians such as Reynolds and Anne Deighton are therefore correct to stress the contingency of the Cold War and the uncertainty of the transition towards it.[54]

Such contingency was manifested in different spheres. The first concerns postwar adjustment to a realignment of power: Britain was still a world power with its empire intact in 1945, and it was concerned to stay such. Thus, Winston Churchill

36 EUROPEAN INTEGRATION SINCE THE 1920s

opposed Roosevelt on free trade, spheres of influence agreements (with Stalin in October 1944), and the maintenance of a British special area of interest in the Middle East, Eastern Mediterranean, and India.[55] France, too, intended to reacquire its former colonies, bombarding Damascus and Madagascar, and sending troops to Indo-China.[56] Furthermore, in terms of technology, Britain and France seemed at first to be capable of keeping pace with the USSR, developing their own atomic bombs in 1952 (the UK) and 1960 (France), even if Churchill was convinced that the invention of the hydrogen bomb—tested by the USA and USSR in 1952–53—meant that 'we're now as far from the atomic bomb as the atomic bomb was from the bow and arrow'.[57] De Gaulle went as far as to claim that France and Britain were 'the two principal powers in the world' in 1945, although in private he, too, accepted that the United States was needed on the Continent to 'establish through their presence the conditions of a necessary balance of power in Europe'.[58] The importance of 'other powers'—in addition to the superpowers—is now widely accepted.[59]

Second, the ideological rift running through the European continent was not apparent immediately after the Second World War, confused in the United Kingdom by the wartime popularity of 'Joe Stalin', which prevented Ernest Bevin, the Labourite British Foreign Secretary, from publicly declaring his anti-Soviet policy.[60] For its part, the United States not only saw itself further from the class-based ideological antagonisms of the Old World, it also had had very little contact with the USSR during the interwar period (little trade and no borders), which meant that Soviet intentions were unclear to US planners.[61] Deighton shows that even the Labour government in the United Kingdom had a much steadier anti-Communist view than its American counterpart, fearing that the United States was not aware of the dangers of Communism spreading across Western Europe, if Washington were to delay any more.[62]

Third, the onset of the Cold War was obscured by economic disorder and uncertainty after the dislocation of the Second World War.[63] Germans were being kept alive by aid, and the Soviets and the French were confiscating German equipment as reparations (with the USSR claiming $20 billion of reparations).[64] Half of Britain's economy was inactive by 1946, preventing it from maintaining its supply of aid to Greece and Turkey, and prompting US intervention in the area, outlined in the 'Truman Doctrine' speech.[65] The United States' economy had grown by 90 per cent during the war, rendering its conversion into a peacetime economy hazardous.[66] It was difficult to plan when contemporaries did not know how different economies would adapt and grow during peacetime.[67] They expected, partly as a consequence of the lessons of 1918–19, that there would be rapid changes in the economic positions of states from this wartime starting point.

Lastly, there had been a switch during the war between international systems: before 1939, the United States had remained to a large extent isolated, despite economic links to Europe via the Dawes and Young Plans.[68] Most of the main events involving the League of Nations had been European; not least the entry and exit of powers such as Germany.[69] The principal focus of the international system had been the balance of power in Europe, even for many detached Americans. French governments were worried about finding a European counterweight to Germany; German governments looked to revise the Treaty of Versailles and the borders in Eastern Europe; Soviet leaders were concerned to protect the USSR against Germany on their western frontier.[70] By 1945, this pattern had changed, with a shift from a European balance of power to global power blocs and with talk of a 'Eurasian heartland' and 'rimland'. In particular, there was a concern in Washington that the Americas could be squeezed between Japan in the Pacific and the combination of the USSR's land mass and resources and Germany's industrial potential in Eurasia.[71] Yet Anton DePorte's new states' system had not yet been worked out, confused by the continuing existence of European empires, anti-colonial nationalisms, and established regional antagonisms—especially in Europe—which could not be moulded passively into a global design (see Map 1.1).[72] In 1945, some in the United States were anxious to leave Britain to work out Europe's difficulties and to re-establish a counterweight to the USSR. The Military Governor of the US zone, Lucius Clay, who was still refusing 'to be a pessimist' about working with the Russians in July 1946, threatened to pull out American troops from Europe in 1946 if a centralized administration failed to materialize in Germany.[73] Even during the negotiation of the Pleven Plan, John Foster Dulles reiterated his willingness to carry out 'an agonizing reappraisal' of the United States's commitment to European security, if the EDC were not passed.[74] All these shifts occurring in and after 1945 help to explain why the Cold War took so long to start and why it seems from archival material as if American and Soviet leaders were following, not dictating, events.

European capitals were following Washington and Moscow, however, with little capacity to guarantee their own security.[75] Over the longer term, the Cold War served to stabilize intra-European relations and allowed continental governments to concentrate on economic reconstruction and cooperation. Over the shorter term, its impact seemed less certain. The most salient change in Europe after 1945 concerned the role of the United States, yet it can be contended that US tutelage of European states worked both for and against continental integration. Few contemporaries challenged the assertion of the later German Chancellor Konrad Adenauer in January 1948 that 'The saving of Europe is only possible via the USA!'[76] The leaders of the defeated powers such as Germany and Italy were perhaps most reluctant to confront or alienate the United States because they were conscious of their own weakness, given the partial collapse of their respective states, and they were aware of their reliance on American forces of occupation, given the divisive social and political legacy of dictatorship.[77] Thus, although the presence of US soldiers and civilian authorities caused resentment, with majority support in Germany for de-Nazification and the Nuremberg trials shrinking to the

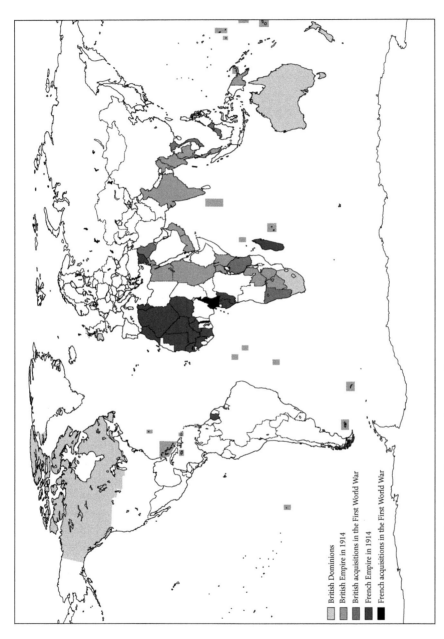

Map 1.1 The British and French empires between the wars
Source: J. Jackson (ed.), *Europe, 1900–1945* (Oxford, 2002), 222–3.

approval of a mere seventeen per cent of respondents to polls by 1949, it was seen to be an essential prop by West German political elites.[78] Even Christian proponents of Europe as a 'Third Force' such as Jakob Kaiser, the chairman of the CDU, and socialist advocates such as Carlo Schmid came by 1947–48, after the Soviet Union's rejection of the Marshall Plan (1947) and blockade of Berlin (1948), to accept the warnings of Adenauer and Kurt Schumacher about 'Eurasia swallowing Europe', in the words of the SPD leader.[79] Schumacher had already been chastened in January 1946 by the conduct of the Soviet Military Authority (SMAD) and its early efforts to force the merger of the KPD and SPD in the eastern zone, eventually creating the Socialist Unity Party (SED) in April 1946. With the partition of Germany apparently irreversible except on Soviet terms by 1948, Adenauer was adamant that 'our line is fixed in the field of foreign policy': 'It consists in the first instance of cementing a close relationship with our neighbouring states in the western world, in particular with the United States.'[80] Once the CDU-CSU was in office, after narrowly defeating the SPD by 31 to 29 per cent in the *Bundestag* election in 1949, Adenauer—whose SPD-inspired nickname of 'Chancellor of the Allies' proved an electoral asset—showed no sign of compromising the Federal Republic's relationship with the United States, which served as the country's main defence against the German Democratic Republic and the USSR.[81]

Likewise, in Italy, policy-makers such as Luigi Einaudi, Carlo Sforza, and Alcide De Gasperi, who was Prime Minister between December 1944 and June 1953, were cautious and deferential, unwilling to endanger their ties to the United States for the sake of the uncertain benefits of 'Europeanism', despite their federalist rhetoric and their backing of Article 11 of the 1947 constitution: 'Italy consents in the same way as other states to limits of sovereignty which are necessary for the safeguarding of peace and justice amongst nations.'[82] 'For we Italians, it is an historical hour,' wrote the Republican Foreign Minister Sforza in 1948: 'Starving, impoverished and having only escaped the abyss of pain and shame, into which fascism threw us, by a hair's breadth, we can regain honour, independence and well-being, if we become heralds of the new order in which the world will now move.'[83] The task for Christian Democrats was to convince a disoriented population and a sceptical left that 'we, like all the other countries of Europe, are no longer independent', as one ambassador put it, meaning that Italy was no more able to move towards the USSR than Poland was to enter 'the field of gravity' of the United States, while also lacking 'the power to carry out a policy on the basis of the idea of neutrality'.[84] Many contemporaries were largely ignorant of the United States or harboured anti-American sentiments fostered by the fascist regime, but they had little choice, contended Christian Democrats, but to accept the American international order.[85]

The United Kingdom was the principal champion of the USA in Europe after 1945. At the same time, its governments, both Labour (Clement Attlee, 1945–51) and Conservative (Winston Churchill, 1951–55), also proved the least receptive to European integration. Attlee and the Labour Foreign Secretary, Ernest Bevin, who dominated the formulation of foreign policy in the absence of a committee for foreign affairs, were closely involved in European politics, pursuing the wartime idea that Britain, with the backing of Europe and the Commonwealth, could be a third world power alongside the United States and the Soviet Union.[86] 'If we make every move in the realm of high policy contingent on American prior approval,' wrote Sir Orme Sargent, Deputy Under-Secretary of State at the Foreign Office, 'our prospects of being able to give a lead to Western Europe will vanish and we shall never attain what must be our primary objective *viz* by close association with our neighbours to create a European group which will enable us to deal on a footing of equality with our two gigantic colleagues, the USA and the USSR.'[87] In common with other Labour ministers, Bevin believed that 'Britain, like the other countries of Western Europe', was 'placed geographically and from the point of view of economic and political theory between these two great continental states', representing neither 'watered-down capitalism' nor 'watered-down Communism', but a genuine 'middle way'.[88] To this end, he courted Paris in late 1947 and early 1948 with a view to forming a European customs union on the ground, as he put it to the Foreign Minister Paul Ramadier, so that the British and French Empires could, 'if they acted together, be as powerful as either the Soviet Union or the United States'.[89] 'If some such union could be created, including not only the countries of Western Europe but also their colonial possessions in Africa and the East', he told the Cabinet on 8 January 1948, 'this would form a *bloc* which, both in population and productive capacity, could stand on an equality with the western hemisphere and Soviet *blocs*.'[90]

Underpinning such aspirations, however, was Bevin's fundamental commitment to the United States, which he had helped to convince not to withdraw from Europe in 1945–47.[91] British military planners were never in any doubt that US forces were needed to deter and resist the USSR in Europe, prompting the Foreign Office, too, to favour an Atlantic Pact—mooted from early 1948 onwards—and the establishment of NATO in 1949 (see Map 1.2).[92] What was more, the Treasury was always conscious that Britain was what Churchill had called 'the world's greatest debtor', obliging it, in the words of the Chancellor of the Exchequer Hugh Dalton, 'to maintain close economic ties with those countries which were able to supply our needs'—that is, the United States and the Commonwealth—'in pursuing the aim of closer economic cooperation in Western Europe'.[93] Because of its economic difficulties, the United Kingdom had been forced to merge its zone in Germany with that of the USA and to rely on US intervention in its spheres of interest in the Mediterranean and the Middle East, where 'in a major war the active partnership of the United States would be of supreme importance' and 'alignment of policy with the United States is accordingly essential'.[94] On no account should the UK be drawn into Europe, which seemed close to economic collapse, at the expense of its

Map 1.2 NATO and the Warsaw Pact, 1949–56

Source: https://en.wikipedia.org/wiki/North_Atlantic_Treaty#/media/File:Map_of_NATO_chronological.gif

42 EUROPEAN INTEGRATION SINCE THE 1920s

own economic well-being and its relationship with the United States, reiterated a joint paper by Bevin and Sir Stafford Cripps, Chancellor between 1947 and 1950, on 25 January 1949:

> We can...lay down firmly the principle that, while we must be ready to make temporary sacrifices in our standard of living, and to run some degree of risk in the hope of restoring Western Europe, we must do nothing to damage irretrievably the economic structure of this country. The present attempt to restore sanity and order in the world depends upon the United States and the British Commonwealth and the countries of Western Europe working together. If, however, the attempt to restore Western Europe should fail, this country could still hope to restore its position in cooperation with the rest of the Commonwealth and with the United States. But in these circumstances we could not look for continued United States military, political and economic support if, in the endeavour to re-establish Western Europe, our economic structure had been hopelessly impaired.[95]

Notwithstanding the shifting sands of European politics, there were significant pressures pushing towards the establishment of a bi-polar world in the late 1940s. Historians such as Gaddis have pointed to conflicts of interest and perception between the US and USSR, and to circumstances which led other states to accept their leadership.[96] Power in 1945, whatever its likely future distribution, was in the hands of the leaders of the Soviet Union and the United States: the former had ordered the occupation of areas that they were interested in and hoped to benefit from the popularity of Communism in times of dislocation; the latter offered material aid and support to fledgling or restored democracies, replacing the United Kingdom in the Near East (Greece and Turkey) and providing money for 'bizonia' in Germany. The USA had most power, as Admiral William Leahy had said on US radio, but the USSR occupied most territory, meaning that Washington actively had to threaten war—or, at least, give full support to Tehran—in order to force the removal of Soviet troops from Iran in 1946.[97] Such manoeuvres were complicated by the eagerness of the press and public in the United States to bring 'the boys home', leading to a reduction in troop numbers in Europe from 3.5 million at the end of the war to 400,000 by 1947. It was this historical moment between 1945 and 1947 which shaped the post-war settlement. If one of the two superpowers had withdrawn in this period, the other would have filled what amounted to a power vacuum.

Global bi-polarity was possible because of the transformation of warfare. In the interwar era, of the six Great Powers—Britain, France, Germany, Japan, the United States, and the USSR—only France and Germany seemed geographically vulnerable, with the capitals of the other powers having had no recent history of occupation. By 1945, all powers including the United States—after the Japanese attack on Pearl Harbor on 7 December 1941—assumed that they were exposed to attack. The invention of the atom bomb made this eventuality more likely, with American generals predicting the construction of intercontinental ballistic missiles (ICBMs) in the press immediately after the war.[98] Only the United States and the Soviet Union—by devoting approximately 20 per cent of GDP to military spending in the Soviet case—could produce large arsenals of nuclear weapons over the longer term, forcing France to remain in NATO under de Gaulle, despite leaving its integrated command structure in 1966.[99] Strategy and 'integration' were secondary, in the opinion of the Gaullist Foreign Minister Maurice Couve de Murville: what mattered was whether NATO would go nuclear in the event of war.[100] Isolationism no longer appeared to be a serious option, even for the United States. Although there were continuing disputes about funding, which Republicans wanted to reduce, no one put forward isolationist policies on the inter-war model.[101] The Soviet Union, too, had made preparations for the protection of its continental position, including the occupation of the Baltic states, part of Finland and the Polish-Belarussian corridor in 1939–41, and the creation of satellite states in Eastern Europe and the occupation of the Kurile and Sakhalin islands and part of Manchuria after 1945. Technology and trade, as well as the scope of the fighting in the Second World War, had promoted global theories of international relations, with both sides conceiving—in the manner of George Orwell's *1984* (1948)—of 'Eurasian', Pacific, and American blocs.[102]

Although he was convinced that the United States was 'greatly over-extended in our whole thinking about what we can accomplish' in the Far East, the Director of Policy Planning in the State Department, George F. Kennan, nevertheless split the world into strategic regions (the Middle East, Far East, Mediterranean, Western Europe, and the Soviet bloc), placing a premium—as he stated in February 1948—on the prevention of the 'Russians' from having 'further success in the coming months in their efforts at penetration and the seizure of political control of the key countries outside the iron curtain (Germany, France, Italy and Greece)': 'Some form of political, military and economic union in Western Europe will be necessary if the free nations of Europe are to hold their own against the people of the east united under Moscow rule.'[103] In Kennan's view, as the most influential advisor of Truman's Secretary of State, George C. Marshall, 'The only way in which a European union, embracing Britain but excluding eastern Europe, could become economically healthy would be to develop the closest sort of trading relationships either with this hemisphere (North America) or with Africa.'[104] Since 'We are still faced with an extremely serious threat to our whole security in the form of the men in the Kremlin', who were 'an able, shrewd and utterly ruthless group, absolutely devoid of respect for us or our institutions', the United States had to act—as Kennan had put it in an anonymous article ('X') in *Foreign Affairs* in July 1947—to contain 'the Soviet pressure against the free institutions of the western world' by 'the adroit and vigilant application of counter-force at a series of constantly shifting geographical and political points, corresponding to the shifts and maneuvers of Soviet policy'.[105] Western European states were recipients of US aid and a site of American military and diplomatic activity, rather than actors themselves.

Economic strategy reinforced this global bi-polarity. Washington's priority was to avoid a repetition of the 1920s and 1930s. Cordell Hull, who had been Secretary of the State Department since 1933, was mindful of the experiences of Herbert Hoover's administration during and after the Great Depression. His aim, shared by his successors, was to prevent states from withdrawing into protected zones and maintaining wartime measures, which had led to economic stagnation and military conflicts, partly based on economic interests, after the First World War. This American objective of keeping markets open ran counter to the command economies of COMECON countries, where the need to control production, wages, distribution, and demand necessitated strict limits on trade and more or less closed borders. The United States attempted to establish growing markets in the 'Third World' to stimulate demand for its own goods and guarantee a supply of raw materials, helping European reconstruction and aiding the transition of its own economy onto a peacetime footing.[106] For its part, the Soviet Union tried to entice countries of the Third World to supply materials and buy its goods.[107] 'In order to create an independent national economy and to raise the living standards of their peoples, these countries, though not part of the world socialist system, can benefit by its achievements,' declared Nikita Khrushchev to the 20th Congress of the CPSU in 1956: 'They now have no need to go begging to their former oppressors for modern equipment. They can obtain such equipment in the socialist countries.'[108] Competition between the two economic blocs, especially in the 1960s and 1970s, was exacerbated by the scarcity of critical resources, particularly uranium (Zaire) and oil (the Middle East). There was no middle way between the blocs, creating a rivalry which arguably became more intense as the Soviet bloc started to lag behind.[109]

Ideological rivalry between the United States and Soviet Union, though not immediately apparent, quickly came to overshadow other rivalries (see Map 1.3).[110] In Kennan's view, in his 'Long Telegram' from Moscow on 22 February 1946, 'we have here a political force committed fanatically to the belief that with [the] US there can be no permanent *modus vivendi*, that it is desirable and necessary that the internal harmony of our society be disrupted, our traditional way of life be destroyed, the international authority of our state be broken, if Soviet power is to be secure'.[111] Beyond the United States' championing of capitalism and liberal democracy, which was pitted against an absence of democracy and free markets under Communism, were opposing views of recent history.[112] Soviet leaders saw themselves as victims of capitalist states. Britain and France, after all, had backed the Whites in the Russian Civil War and prohibited the Bolsheviks from attending the Versailles Conference in 1919. The USSR had been treated as a pariah state in

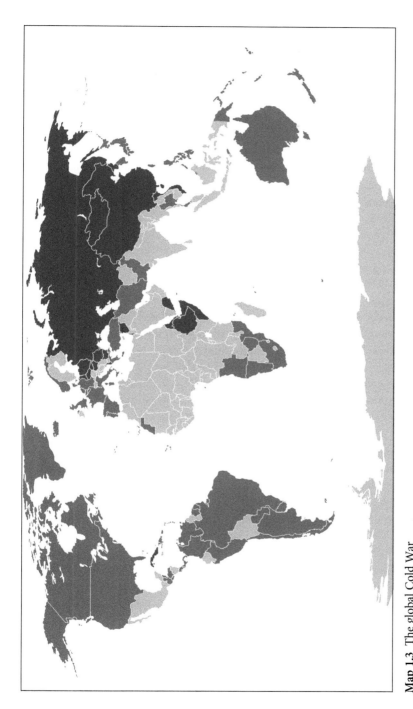

Map 1.3 The global Cold War

Source: https://en.wikipedia.org/wiki/Cold_War#/media/File:Cold_War_alliances_mid-1975.svg

the 1920s and 1930s, before being let down in 1938, as Neville Chamberlain and Edouard Daladier preferred to appease Hitler rather than work with Moscow, and in 1941–44, as Britain and the United States hesitated to open a second front in the world war, while millions of Soviet soldiers and civilians died.[113] These betrayals looked set to be repeated after 1945, as the United States especially began to label Western and Southern European Communist Parties anti-democratic and threatened to withhold Marshall Aid from France and Italy if the PCF or PCI assumed office.[114]

For its part, the Soviet administration had been justified, it was claimed, in creating its own buffer in Eastern Europe against Germany and in acting harshly against its old enemies: namely, Poland, which had opposed the USSR under Jósef Piłzudski; Romania, which had mobilized 500,000 troops against the Soviet Union; and Bulgaria, which had allowed Nazi Germany access to the Black Sea.[115] It had treated Finland leniently and had permitted elections in Hungary, despite their earlier enmity. Free elections in Czechoslovakia, whose government in exile had signed a pact with the USSR during the war, had resulted in Communists becoming the largest party in May 1946, with 38 per cent of the vote. The United States was deliberately thwarting Communism in Europe, confirming Moscow's belief 'in the basic badness of capitalism, in the inevitability of its destruction, in the obligation of the proletariat to assist in that destruction and to take power into its own hands', in Kennan's words in 'The Sources of Soviet Conduct' (1947): 'stress has come to be laid primarily on those concepts which relate most specifically to the Soviet regime itself'—particularly on 'the innate antagonism between capitalism and Socialism'—and 'to its position as the sole truly Socialist regime in a dark and misguided world, and to the relationships of power within it'.[116]

By contrast, the US government saw itself as fighting for freedom against repressive ideologies in the Second World War and spreading universal principles of national self-determination, a free market and democracy during the post-war era. Many in Washington saw the USSR as opportunistic, having signed a pact with Hitler in 1939, repressive, with the purges of the 'Terror' resulting in an estimated 4–5 million deaths, and expansionist, after a 'totalitarian' Communist regime had continued the policies of its tsarist predecessor. 'At bottom of Kremlin's neurotic view of world affairs is traditional and instinctive Russian sense of insecurity', resting on a history of self-defence 'on a vast exposed plain in neighbourhood of fierce nomadic peoples', wrote Kennan in the 'Long Telegram':

This thesis provides justification for that increase of military and police power which are together the natural and instinctive urges of Russian rulers. Basically this is only the steady advance of uneasy Russian nationalism, a centuries old movement in which conceptions of offence and defence are inextricably confused. But in new guise of international Marxism, with its honeyed promises to a desperate and war torn outside world, it is more dangerous and insidious than ever before.[117]

This level of mistrust between Washington and Moscow, when combined with the post-war bi-polarity of power and economic, technological and military globalization, was likely to lead to an enduring antagonism or, even, to a Cold War. The fact that such a 'war' was unexpected and slow to begin is proof, rather than disproof, of its likelihood: the threat of conflict became a policy in the new circumstances of 1945–47 as other options were ruled out one by one.

European states offered little resistance to the movement of world politics towards bi-polarity.[118] In truth, they had no means to oppose it, for Soviet and American dominance rested respectively on the overwhelming ground forces controlled by Moscow and on the nuclear deterrent of Washington. No single European state was strong enough to affect this balance of forces, as was manifest during a series of painful acts of separation between Eastern and Western Europe during the late 1940s, 1950s, and early 1960s. These acts included Britain's abandonment of an independent Polish state by July 1945, when it recognized the Communist provisional government of national unity in Poland and effectively gave up its aim, mooted at Yalta in February, that the Polish government in exile in London should also be given ministerial positions; West Germany's gradual realization—marked most notably by the thwarted strike of 1953 in East Berlin and by the building of the Berlin Wall in 1961—that partition was likely to be long-lived; and the stunned reaction of Western Europe as a whole to the Soviet Union's occupation of Budapest in 1956, by means of which it prevented the administration of Imre Nagy establishing a multi-party system of government. By the force of events, then, Western European states came to acknowledge that they were powerless to intervene in Eastern Europe.[119] What was more, the United States seemed to be the only real safeguard against Soviet intervention in their own domestic affairs, which they wanted to avoid at all costs. 'For my generation the Russian Revolution was one of the landmarks of our lives, whether we were for or against,' recalled the Belgian Socialist and later Secretary General of NATO, Paul-Henri Spaak (born in 1899), in his memoirs: 'As the First World War drew to its close and I began to take part in politics, I followed the ups and downs of the Revolution with passionate interest. I was opposed to Tsarism and to its system of political oppression, but I was not a Communist.'[120] In contrast to individual parties and social movements, European governments had little incentive to challenge the political preponderance of the USA before 1989.

There were specific reasons why individual European states were so ready to accept a bi-polar world in the period up until 1963: the first was that the strongest power in the region—the United Kingdom—still saw itself primarily as an imperial power, and was anxious, according to government correspondence, to maintain American involvement in Europe in order to free its own forces for imperial service, rightly anticipating problems in India, as it moved towards independence in 1947, and in Egypt, which eventually resulted in the Suez crisis of 1956.[121] By 1946, with Britain unable to meet the annual £80 million bill for its zone in Northern Germany, which led in turn to the merger of British and American zones, it was evident to British policy-makers that the United Kingdom was too weak economically to play a full military part in Central Europe.[122] Britain could only maintain a military presence 'commensurate with our economic power', the Foreign Office had warned in March 1945, alongside an economic balance sheet: 'if we enter into commitments which our economic strength will not bear we shall be exposed to another series of humiliations'.[123] By 1947, as the British were forced to withdraw troops and support from Greece and Turkey, it was not even clear that Britain was strong enough to meet traditional imperial commitments such as those connected to the Eastern question. The Foreign Office updated its assessment of the UK's position early in the same year: 'we have seldom been able to give sufficient economic backing to our policy; the present condition of the British zone in Germany is an obvious example of this, and the economic troubles of Greece are another'.[124] One by-product of such weakness was the increasing resolution of Washington to keep its forces in Europe. The danger of an American withdrawal, which had been present in 1945, seemed to be 'apparently over' by 1947, the same report continued: 'most Americans seem to feel now that the dangers of conflict between themselves and the Soviet Union are greater than between the Soviet Union and the British Commonwealth'.[125] Two years later, in March 1949, a Foreign Office memorandum on 'Third World Power or Western Consolidation' made it plain that a separate 'third' power headed by Britain and the Commonwealth in cooperation with other European states was no longer feasible, meaning that 'the immediate problem', 'in the face of implacable Soviet hostility and in view of our economic dependence on the United States', 'is to define the nature of our relationship with the United States'.[126] There was little likelihood of London resisting Washington's policy in Europe during the 1950s and 1960s.

The second European power which might have attempted to create a more independent, regional counterweight to the superpowers was France, whose leaders needed no reminding of the importance of controlling Germany and achieving reconstruction through the coordination of continental economies.[127] Yet France, too, remained dependent on the United States, as Jean Chauvel, the General Secretary of the Ministry of Foreign Affairs, admitted in April 1948 in a message to Henri Bonnet, the French ambassador in Washington, about the future of Germany:

> The French government, aware of the effect that its adherence to the Anglo-Saxon plan is bound to have on the Russians, measures the extent of its

responsibilities and worries about the means it has at its disposal to meet them. At this time these means, as you know, are nearly non-existent, or rather, they are in the hands of the Americans, and it is for the Administration in Washington to evaluate them and to dispose of them, in accordance with the policies it pursues.[128]

Like their counterparts in the United Kingdom, French governments in the 1940s and 1950s became preoccupied with empire and de-colonization.[129] French leaders under the Fourth Republic, it appeared, had been faced with a dilemma of their own making: after 1945, they had calculated that the country would only be strong enough to dominate European affairs through the leverage afforded by a strong empire; then, during the 1950s, French efforts to re-acquire and maintain colonies had led to costly wars in Indo-China between 1945 and 1954, and in Algeria between 1954 and 1962.[130] These conflicts were not mere skirmishes but major wars which scarred those soldiers and governments which were embroiled in them—up to half a million people, mainly Algerian, are estimated to have been killed in the latter conflict, for example.[131] While such bloodletting was going on— treated as a civil war by many French leaders, since Algeria formally had the status of a *département*—no French government, not even that of General de Gaulle after 1958, could devote time and energy to the creation of a semi-independent Europe.[132] Only after 'war and its humiliations came to an end', wrote Willy Brandt in his memoirs, did 'France have to come clean with itself' and decide where its interests lay.[133]

As a result, only Germany was left as a third possible source of European independence. Yet the Federal Republic was the least likely rallying point of all, despite the fact that its economy was expected by the United States and Britain to become the basis of a European market. Indeed, it was precisely because German economic strength was perceived to be necessary for continental reconstruction and defence that the Allies were so cautious in restoring political and military sovereignty to the Federal Republic. The relations between the powers were uncertain, but Germany's subservience to them was constant. Adenauer was unambiguous in a letter to Wilhelm Sollmann, a former SPD deputy who had emigrated to the United States, that the 'USA doesn't know Europe'.[134] 'I have got on very well with the officers of the American occupation forces here and again and again have had to learn that they do not know Europe,' he went on: 'That is also why the USA is not inclined to interest themselves in European affairs.'[135] As Chancellor, Adenauer was equally sure that Washington had to be convinced to keep its forces in Europe, not least because London refused to commit itself to the Continent. 'From the biological and economic point of view, France is not strong enough for this role,' he wrote on 8 April 1946: 'In my opinion, Europe has to be led by Britain and France and this makes necessary the integration of the economic interests of France, Britain and Germany. Like the British themselves, we,

50   EUROPEAN INTEGRATION SINCE THE 1920s

for our part, have the greatest interest that Britain should see itself as a European power.'[136] Yet the United Kingdom refused to play this role, as the Chancellor acknowledged: 'In my opinion, the British pursue a policy that runs entirely counter to their interests. After all, they can only maintain their position in the world as the leader of an economically united and politically reconciled Western Europe including at least the three Western Zones.'[137]

Given Britain's unreliability as a European partner and France's inability to fulfil the role as a European leader on its own, the United States remained Bonn's principal ally.[138] Since the US was the main occupying power, Bonn was obliged to work with Washington domestically as well as diplomatically, as Adenauer spelled out in the CDU-CSU government's first official statement in 1949: 'The only path to freedom is to try, in cooperation with the Allied High Commission, piece by piece to expand our freedoms and our authority.'[139] Germany did not regain full political sovereignty and control of foreign policy until 1955, after it had been integrated into NATO, subjected in effect to American military command, and had signed away its right to develop atomic, biological, and chemical weapons (ABC weapons). This policy of subordination to the Allies was willingly acceded to by Adenauer, Chancellor of the FRG between 1949 and 1963, in recognition of the German population's overriding need for security against Soviet Communism. Opinion polls in the 1950s showed that more than 60 per cent of Germans thought that security against the USSR was more important than German reunification, which in turn was considered by 75 per cent of *Bundesbürger* to be more significant than European integration.[140] The United States alone could provide such security, as Adenauer, blamed by the SPD but credited by the electorate for his pro-American policy, knew all too well.

The German Question

According to both Tony Judt and David Calleo, from divergent points of view, the prospects of European cooperation after the Second World War rested, above all, on the German question.[141] For the latter, who had argued that Germany—as the traditional buffer at the centre of a pentarchy of Great Powers—had been constrained within an unnecessarily restrictive European balance of power, the principal problem for the unstable continental system remained what to do with its most powerful, central state.[142] In 1939, Hitler had given the same geopolitical rationale as the Imperial Germans—namely, 'the need to acquire *Mitteleuropa* for Germany and to dominate the rest of Europe in order to create a global balance'— but he had carried out his plan with a 'lunatic racism, excluding most other Europeans' and mocking 'any collaborative pan-European vision'.[143] The British were especially mistrustful of Germany, their feelings mingling 'with pride in their own country's lonely heroism in the darkest days of World War II'.[144] The French, too, blamed the world wars on German aggression. It was the United States, in such circumstances, which seemed to offer Western Europe protection, not only against the Soviets, but against each other.[145] With Bevin himself doubting as late as December 1947 'whether Russia was as great a danger as a resurgent Germany might become', the British and French urged the United States to create an Atlantic Alliance as a way of containing Germany as well as the USSR.[146] Over the longer term, the governments of the United Kingdom and United States understood the failings of the European states' system in a different fashion from their continental counterparts, in Calleo's opinion: 'The Atlantic Alliance assumed Europe to be intrinsically unstable and therefore to require an external balancing power', whereas the 'European Union assumed that Europe was not irremediably unstable' and 'Europeans in general, and French and Germans in particular, were capable of reconciling their national interests and harmonizing them into a collective interest within a common institution.'[147] It was relevant that the French had sought but failed to receive US support against Germany after the First World War, pushing policy-makers after 1945 to pursue a direct relationship with Bonn, and that the 'racist horrors of the Nazi regime, once exposed, left the post-war Germans with a disabling burden of guilt whose effects last to the present day', making West German assertiveness unlikely.[148]

Judt agrees with much of Calleo's analysis, contrasting what George C. Marshall, the US Secretary of State, called France's 'outmoded and unrealistic' preoccupation with Germany as a major threat, with Washington's focus—by 1948—on the Cold War.[149] In the British historian's judgement, 'the French were successful beyond their wildest hopes in "Europeanizing" their historical difficulty by incorporating West Germany into a Francocentric community where France got what its leaders thought it needed without appearing to have done so by conventionally selfish means'.[150] French planners accepted 'the need for a revived West German economy and a unified West German state', as did the Benelux countries (which were 'willing to run the risks it entailed'), but they wished to hedge them in 'with international alliances, economic agreements, and other penumbra, while ensuring French access to its [West Germany's] potential wealth, vital for the success of the newly conceived Monnet Plan—a program for French industrial reconstruction that depended crucially upon available and affordable German raw materials'.[151] France was able to acquire, in Jacques Delors's words, 'that margin of liberty for a "certain idea of France"' in Europe, 'not only because Germany was in no position to object but also because, for special and contingent reasons, the authorities in Bonn wanted the same thing':[152]

> As the West German Chancellor Konrad Adenauer put it when he was first told of the Schuman Plan, 'This is our breakthrough.' Only through such a 'supernational' entity could the new Federal Republic of Germany hope to re-enter the international community on equal terms. From the beginning, West

52   EUROPEAN INTEGRATION SINCE THE 1920s

Germany (like France's other partners) would have preferred a broader union, one that included Britain, but acceded to the European Coal and Steel Community on French terms as a first step in obtaining French support for its own objectives—notably, increased sovereignty.[153]

These historical conjunctions and mutual benefits seemed to allow, in the context of the Cold War and an American system of security, a European solution to the German question. Yet such conditions were likely to change, not least in West Germany itself.

Normally, international events provide a backdrop to domestic politics. In Germany, because it was an occupied power, they were pivotal (see Map 1.4).[154] Many electoral triumphs and reversals were linked to foreign policy, including Adenauer's unexpected win in 1949 as a 'caretaker' Chancellor (he was seventy-three years old), and his next electoral success in 1953, just after the Soviet-backed suppression of the Eastern German workers' uprising of 16–17 June. Adenauer eventually resigned, along with the CSU leader Franz Josef Strauß, over the 'Spiegel Affair' in 1962–63, after the editor of the publication was arrested for having exposed the inadequacies of the German military.[155] In 1969, Willy Brandt inaugurated the first SPD-led government since 1930, in part by promising to pursue a policy of *Ostpolitik* and to conclude treaties to recognize the FRG's borders and relations with its eastern neighbours.[156] His successor Helmut Schmidt fell in 1982 as a consequence of the revolt of the left wing of the SPD over the stationing of US Pershing missiles.[157]

The international element of politics was so pronounced in Germany for varying reasons. Through the partition of the country, an external question had become an internal one. When Churchill gave his speech in Fulton, Missouri, about the 'Iron Curtain' in March 1946, he had been uncertain where it would eventually fall in Germany.[158] Berlin, he said, was currently behind the curtain, along with Warsaw, Prague, Vienna, Budapest, Belgrade, Bucharest, and Sofia, which were 'subject in one form or another, not only to Soviet influence but to a very high and, in many cases, increasing measure of control from Moscow'.[159] Yet, in Eastern Germany, Moscow's efforts were limited to an 'attempt...by the Russians in Berlin to build up a quasi-Communist party in their zone of Occupied Germany by showing special favours to groups of left-wing German leaders'.[160] If the Soviet government were to try, 'by separate action, to build up a pro-Communist Germany in their areas, this will cause new serious difficulties in the British and American zones, and give the defeated Germans the power of putting themselves up to auction between the Soviets and the Western democracies', but would the Soviets succeed and what would happen, if they did succeed, to the German territory in the East, from which the American and British armies had withdrawn 'in accordance with an earlier agreement'?[161]

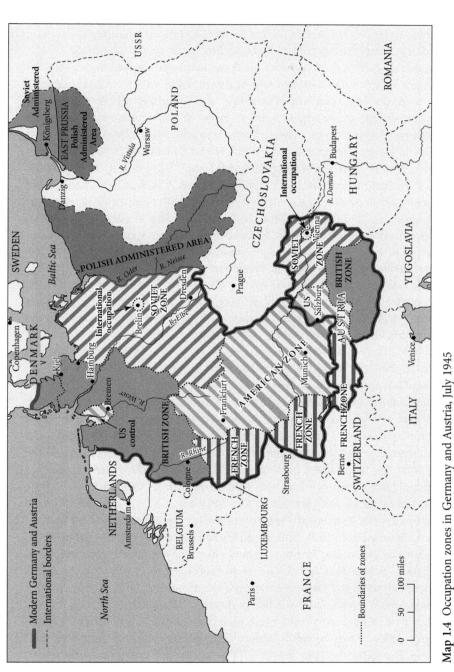

Map 1.4 Occupation zones in Germany and Austria, July 1945
Source: M. Allinson, *Germany and Austria, 1814–2000* (Oxford, 2002), 117.

54 EUROPEAN INTEGRATION SINCE THE 1920s

In 1946, such questions remained open. The division in Germany, which was created by 1948, at the latest, came to symbolize the Cold War, but it was also deepened by it, with the erection of the Berlin Wall in 1961 occurring after a long period of tension between the USSR and United States from 1958 onwards.[162] The absence of a peace treaty to regulate the German question served to heighten the importance of unconditional surrender and occupation, with the Allies remaining in Germany far longer than anticipated. Even during the Vietnam War, 'the Berlin thing is really more important, really, in terms of world peace than either the Mideast or in—in order of magnitude the least important is Vietnam', Richard Nixon told Henry Kissinger and the White House Chief of Staff, Bob Haldeman, in May 1971: 'It never, never has risked world war.'[163] 'Berlin is it,' he continued: 'Shit, if anything happens in Berlin, then you're at it.'[164] Given the American and Soviet military presence in each country, neither the FRG nor the GDR were fully sovereign states, finding it difficult to conceal their status as occupied territories and temporary entities. Until 1968, East and West German sportsmen and women competed in a joint German Olympic team, whose victories were rendered less uncomfortable by the adoption of Beethoven's 'Hymn of Joy' by both states as their national anthem.[165] The attempt by Adenauer's government to claim the status of the sole German state, threatening—in accordance with the 'Hallstein doctrine'—to break off diplomatic relations with any state which recognized the GDR, had failed by the late 1960s.[166]

Commentators maintained at the time that the FRG's foreign policy was frozen by the Cold War. The Allies appeared to be dictating the terms of the partition for power-political and ideological reasons, and the CDU-CSU and FDP accepted it out of fear of Communism and the USSR.[167] Washington had decided on a policy of containment by the spring of 1947, articulated publicly in the Truman doctrine's determination to stop Soviet expansion throughout the world. Germany was the most important flashpoint because it constituted the bridge between the industry of Western and Northern Europe and the territory and population—most of which was concentrated in its western lands—of the USSR. Given the forced merger of the SPD and KPD in the *Sozialistische Einheitspartei* (SED) in April 1946, together with the imposition of a Moscow-backed administration in Poland, it quickly became evident to US planners that the neutrality of a united Germany would permit Soviet interference and, even, occupation. Both Bevin and Adenauer worked hard to ensure that American forces remained in the western zones in order to prevent such interference. At the same time, they reinforced the partition.[168] 'Russia has in its hand the Eastern part of Germany' and most of Eastern Europe, Adenauer wrote in October 1945: 'Division into Eastern Europe, the Russian territory, and Western Europe is therefore a fact.'[169] 'The part of Germany not occupied by the Russians is an integral part of Western Europe,' he went on in the same letter: 'If it remains sick, that would have the most serious consequences for the whole of Western Europe, including Britain and France.'[170]

The Allies' desire of a German-led economic reconstruction of Europe—echoed in Churchill's insistence that Britons did not wish 'to be chained to a corpse'—seemed to necessitate continuing political weakness, underpinned by division without sovereignty.[171] The supposed quip of François Mauriac, the French novelist and journalist, which was probably apocryphal but was taken up by others, that he liked Germany so much that he was glad that there were two of them seemed to betray the Allies' policy.[172] Notwithstanding their public pronouncements, wrote Helmut Schmidt in his memoirs, none of the powers seriously wanted German reunification. There 'was hardly a government in Europe which genuinely regretted the partition of Germany' by the time he became Chancellor in 1974, he wrote: 'The world thus seemed to be quite content with the division of Germany; illogically, it was much less content with the division of Europe.'[173] The FRG's neighbours had no reason to elide the German and European questions, however, even if they accepted that they were closely connected. Judt's argument about an inverse relation, with the answer to the European question (integration) depending on the failure to resolve the German question (partition), is more convincing.

For a long time, it seemed as though West German political elites were willing to accede to Allied policy.[174] With Washington's support for the Christian Democrats contrasting with barely-concealed criticism of Schumacher's SPD, the CDU's appeal had long been based on 'no experiments', as its principal election slogan put it in 1957.[175] West German business and consumers had quickly come to see themselves as part of the 'West'.[176] In many respects, it appeared that the Christian politics and American-style consumerism of the FRG, which was pitted against the SED's socialist experiment in the East, was a smaller version of the opposition between Eisenhower's America and the USSR in the Cold War.[177] If West German opposition to the GDR were eliminated, it was not certain what would remain. More cynically, Christian Democrats were conscious that anti-Communism was a useful deflection—at home and abroad—from the Nazi past.[178] They also knew that there were nearly as many Catholics as Protestants in West Germany, which the largely Protestant populations of the East—together with working-class, SPD-strongholds in Saxony and Berlin—would overturn.

West Germans in general seemed to have become satisfied with the status quo, including partition.[179] By 1989, 70 per cent of them were worried about the prospect of unification, even if opinion polls registered support for it, on paper.[180] Eighty-five per cent of West Germans had thought unification unlikely or impossible in 1973 and 93 per cent thought so in 1983.[181] No more than one per cent of respondents from the mid-1970s onwards considered it the most important political issue facing the FRG, compared to 35–45 per cent in the 1950s and 1960s.[182] When David Marsh, the Bonn correspondent of the *Financial Times*, asked political and business leaders what they thought about reunification in 1988 and early 1989, he received a set of negative replies: 'I do not believe in reunification', declared Joachim Fest, editor of the conservative *Frankfurter Allgemeine Zeitung*; 'We gave up reunification as a solution thirty years ago,' agreed Werner Holzer of the left-leaning *Frankfurter Rundschau*.[183] Karl Otto Pöhl, the president of the *Bundesbank*, was anxious about the economic imbalance that a united Germany would create in Europe, and Edzard Reuter, chair of Daimler-Benz, replied that 'No one thinks of reunification.'[184] Willy Brandt, who later claimed that the two populations belonged together, declared in 1984 that 'All fruitless discussion about how open the German question is should be ended', and Helmut Schmidt confessed that 'I have not used the word "reunification" for thirty years.'[185] Many observers concluded that political elites and voters had become used to the division of Germany, which had been brought about by the Cold War. Only the end of the Cold War, combined with popular pressure exerted by East German citizens demonstrating in the streets of Leipzig, Dresden, and Berlin, pushed Helmut Kohl, brushing aside the anxieties of a majority of West Germans, to countenance unification. The stable domestic and foreign parameters of German politics did much to foster cooperation and integration in Europe before that date.

The Limits of Détente in Europe

Arguably, the overriding logic of security against Soviet interference ensured that all the states of Western, Central, and Southern Europe consented to American dominance.[186] Such dominance did not militate against a process of European integration, since the United States was in favour of a United States of Europe after 1947, but it did affect the speed and type of integration. In general, states such as the Netherlands, Germany, and Italy were prepared in the 1950s to leave the most awkward areas of military and foreign-policy coordination to the United States within NATO.[187] Consequently, with potential impediments to integration removed, the coordination of Europe's economies could proceed all the more quickly. During the 1960s, this division between European management of economic and, to a lesser extent, political integration, on the one hand, and American coordination of foreign policy and military strategy, on the other, began to break down.[188] Many reasons can be adduced to explain such a shift, including acts of youthful rebellion against the old order, which came to a head in 1968, most notably in Italy, France, and Germany; disillusionment with American foreign policy, which appeared to have become imperialist and immoral during the Vietnam War, with its use of napalm and its atrocities involving innocent civilians;

and, perhaps most significantly, a growing awareness, which eventually produced mass peace and disarmament movements, that a nuclear war waged by the two superpowers would initially destroy Europe, and might indeed be limited to the European continent in order to avoid Armageddon.[189] The three most important intra-European causes of détente after 1963 were related to changes in specific states: General de Gaulle's policy of a 'third force' during the 1960s; Willy Brandt's espousal of *Ostpolitik* during the late 1960s and 1970s; and a series of reform movements within the Eastern Bloc, from the Prague Spring of 1968 to the Solidarity movement, which began in 1980 in Poland. None of these shifts within Europe succeeded in overcoming the underlying Cold War division between Soviet and American spheres of influence, even though they did perpetuate a period of détente in Europe during the early 1980s, at a time of worsening relations between the USA and USSR as a consequence of the Soviet Union's invasion of Afghanistan in 1979 and the election of Ronald Reagan as President of the United States in 1980.[190]

De Gaulle's aim was to build a more independent Europe, which he attempted to implement after extricating France from the Algerian War in 1962.[191] 'Can France convince its [EEC] partners, by persuasion, initiatives or veto, that Europe is ready to claim and achieve its independence, i.e. that it must free itself from the US and Anglo-Saxon supremacy?' asked de Gaulle's advisor Jean Dromer on 7 January 1967.[192] The origins of the general's policy went back to the early years of the Second World War, when Britain and the United States had, at times, seemed to prefer to deal with the Vichy regime rather than with the French resistance.[193] But the policy also rested on the assumption that Germany, not the USSR, constituted France's main potential enemy and that European institutions now offered French ministers and bureaucrats a means of controlling Germany.[194] De Gaulle's independent foreign policy, which included open criticism of the Vietnam War, was popular in France, at least in part, because of the parochialism and anti-Americanism of the French public, which had included, in the immediate post-war period, an attempt to ban Coca-Cola, denouncing it as the vanguard of American cultural and economic imperialism—of 'coca-colonization' as one slogan put it.[195] In the mid-1960s, opinion polls showed that 60 per cent of the public were in favour of a policy of French independence, and only 15 per cent in favour of backing the United States; what was more, there were more than twice as many supporters of the idea of a united Europe independent of the USA than there were opponents of it.[196]

Unlike large sections of the public, however, de Gaulle himself knew that France still needed the backing of the United States, despite his diplomatic recognition of China in 1964 and his well-publicized visit to the Soviet Union in 1966. Thus, one of the general's first acts, on becoming president in 1958, was to call for a tripartite command structure—France, Britain, and the United States— for NATO's nuclear weapons. Only when President Eisenhower refused this

58   EUROPEAN INTEGRATION SINCE THE 1920s

request did de Gaulle remove the French Mediterranean fleet from the North Atlantic Treaty Organisation, press ahead with France's own nuclear weapons programme, which produced an atomic bomb by 1960, and withdraw from NATO's integrated command structure in 1966. Although Acheson complained that the French President had 'made the greatest imperial power the world has ever seen kiss de Gaulle's arse', it was evident to Francis Bator, Lyndon Johnson's advisor on European affairs, that 'de Gaulle has no real cards': 'If we play our hand skilfully, we can manage to carry on with NATO without him. In many ways, he is like a lightweight jujitsu artist. All his leverage comes from our over-exertion.'[197] France could not afford to leave NATO altogether, for it remained conscious, especially under right-wing Gaullist governments, of the dangers of Communism, and it realized that the United States alone could control Germany's military and foreign policies via the North Atlantic Treaty Organisation.[198] French policy-makers realized that, unless the Federal Republic of Germany gave up its primary allegiance to the United States, a stronger Europe would have to be subordinate to the logic of the NATO alliance. After the six member states of the EEC, together with the United Kingdom, had rejected a French initiative to reform the monetary system and destabilize the dollar in the spring of 1968, 'The France of General de Gaulle was brought back to its real dimensions,' noted Georges Pompidou: 'No more war against the dollar. No more lessons given to the mighty of this world. No more leadership of Western Europe.'[199]

During the late 1960s and early 1970s, it seemed to some observers that a reformulation of German foreign policy might have begun, as Willy Brandt and his coalition government of Social Democrats and liberals pursued *Ostpolitik* after 1969, seeking to come to a satisfactory arrangement with the Soviet Union over East Germany and Eastern Europe in general, at times without keeping the United States fully informed.[200] The British ambassador in Bonn remarked on the shift 'Towards a National Foreign Policy', according to the title of a memorandum in April 1969: 'Among its features are a greater self-reliance, a feeling that the period of atonement for the war is over, and impatience with restraints on German liberty of action.'[201] Brandt himself sought 'more self-reliance also with respect to the United States'.[202] A string of agreements followed in rapid succession: treaties with the USSR and Poland in 1970, with East Germany in 1972 (the Basic Treaty), and with Czechoslovakia in 1973. Yet all of these treaties were only conceived within the existing structure of eastern and western alliances. Indeed, they served to reinforce those alliances, by giving official West German recognition, which had previously been withheld, to Eastern European Communist states. 'We could not magic away the Wall', wrote Brandt in his memoirs.[203] Before the Basic Treaty with East Germany, the Christian Democrats, who had been in government from 1949 to 1969, had adopted the Hallstein doctrine, which attempted to deny diplomatic recognition by third parties. Now Willy Brandt, a former mayor of Berlin, signalled West Germany's acceptance of what had long been taken for granted elsewhere in the West: that the states of the Eastern Bloc were likely to endure.[204]

French diplomats, who were striving for greater détente against the wishes of Washington, were not alone in noting the juxtaposition of rapprochement and assertiveness towards the bloc in the FRG's new policy from the start, as Hervé Alphand, Secretary General of the Ministry of Foreign Affairs, remarked in October 1967: 'Everything is at a dead end—West Germany is not accepting either the post-war borders or the existence of East Germany, the Soviet Union prefers the status quo, and Brandt still persists with the search for détente with Eastern Europe.'[205] The Helsinki Accords of 1975, which resulted from the Conference on Security and Cooperation in Europe and which were presided over by the United States and the Soviet Union, completed the process of *Ostpolitik*, confirming borders in Eastern and Central Europe.[206] Although it is true that the treaties inaugurated an era of cooperation and even financial aid, which continued up until 1989, this had been achieved by moving further away from the prospect of reunification and, consequently, by consolidating the separation of Eastern and Western Europe and the alliance structures which were founded on that separation.[207] Initially, Richard Nixon had been reluctant to back Brandt, confiding to Kissinger that 'I don't want to hurt our friends in Germany [CDU-CSU politicians] by...catering to that son-of-a-bitch', but he had eventually accepted that Bonn's long-term goal of 'transformation' of East–West relations was compatible with Washington's objective of 'stability' and a recognition of the 'facts' of the Cold War, as the US diplomat and later ambassador to Germany Martin Hillenbrand recalled: 'until the late spring of 1971, they [Nixon and Kissinger] probably had grave reservations about *Ostpolitik* and the negotiations that led to the Berlin Agreement. Then they got on the bandwagon.'[208] Specifically European initiatives were only possible insofar as they kept within the bounds of American conceptions of stability.

Further proof of the brute fact of European partition came from those Warsaw Pact countries such as Czechoslovakia and Poland which tried to evade its logic. As in the West, these attempts at détente took account of the basic division between East and West, between capitalist democracy and a Communist one-party state. The new Czech Foreign Minister Jiří Hájek was hopeful, in light of *Ostpolitik*, that 'things might turn in the right direction', in the words of his political memoir.[209] Yet his advocacy of 'pan-European cooperation' to a parliamentary commission for foreign affairs in June 1968 was limited by his fear of 'doing anything that could be interpreted in the wrong way'.[210] Solidarity's programme of February 1981 was ambiguous, pointing out that the 'disappearance of democratic institutions is at the root of this crisis', whilst reassuring the authorities that 'we do not intend to replace the government in [carrying out its] tasks'.[211] Neither Alexander Dubček in 1968 nor Lech Wałęsa in 1980 intended to abandon socialism or introduce thorough-going parliamentary democracy, with Dubček

60   EUROPEAN INTEGRATION SINCE THE 1920S

wanting to increase the 'space' or 'scope' of the regime and Hájek telling Kissinger that he wanted to renovate Czechoslovak socialism in order to stabilize the community of the Eastern Bloc and consolidate peaceful co-existence.[212] For his part, Wałeşa—who had been involved in the strike movement of 1970 and had twice been fired for 'mouthing off' in the 1970s—continued to act as an unrelenting union leader.[213] Both Wałeşa and Dubček were primarily interested in reforming the existing system and counteracting the effects of economic failure—an overemphasis on heavy industry in Czechoslovakia and a $20,000 million debt to the West in Poland.[214] One million members of the Communist Party in Poland went on to join Solidarity.[215] 'We will not allow a return to the period before 1945, or even before 1948', Dubček had declared in 1968, ruling out the Communist-dominated multi-party system of the immediate post-war era.[216] This type of reform, like other forms of cooperation and foreign-policy initiatives, took place within the confines of a Cold War between extra-European superpowers.

Czechoslovak and Polish reformers' initiatives proved to be unacceptable to Moscow for two reasons: first, because the Communist Party of the Soviet Union was worried that further challenges to its own party line on economic affairs, in addition to those presented by China and Yugoslavia, would undermine its standing in the Communist bloc as a whole, with repercussions for Soviet foreign policy in the Third World; second, because the Brezhnev administration was anxious that a relaxation of censorship and limited authorization of opposition parties or unions, which were envisaged respectively in Czechoslovakia and Poland, might spiral out of control, as they seemed to have done in Hungary in 1956 and the USSR in the early 1960s under Khrushchev.[217] In general, Leonid Brezhnev and Alexander Kosygin rightly understood that only the threat of Soviet coercion guaranteed the durability of Communist regimes in Eastern Europe. The 'Brezhnev doctrine', which was enunciated in 1968 after the Prague Spring, stated that any movement away from Communism in Eastern European states would be treated as a menace to the Eastern Bloc in its entirety.[218] In short, that bloc, like the Western bloc, had become an alliance structure rather than an ideological experiment. The upshot for Europe was that any policies of détente on the part of continental states would be subordinated to the overarching policies of the United States and the Soviet Union: in the West, through anxiety about American isolationism; in the East, from fear of Soviet intervention.

The logic of the Cold War remained superimposed on Europe, but it was not inevitable. By 1960, the share of Western European economies in gross world product already stood at 26 per cent, the same as that of the United States, and substantially larger than that of the COMECON countries under the USSR, which stood at 19 per cent.[219] What was more, these Western European economies were actually coordinated within the EEC. In theory, Western Europe was economically powerful enough by the late 1960s to create a 'third force'. Why did it fail to do so? Partly, because European states, as capitalist democracies, could not afford in peacetime to devote in excess of 20 per cent of GNP to military expenditure, as occurred in the Soviet Union; mainly, though, because Western Europe had become accustomed to American coordination of continental foreign policies and military strategy. The European Communities had been predicated on this assumption, meaning that strict limits were placed on European foreign policy-making until 1989, since ideological oppositions and global power-political conflicts and tensions between the USA and USSR were now much more deeply entrenched than any residual divisions between Eastern and Western Europe. It was only after Mikhail Gorbachev had allowed the disintegration of the Warsaw Pact, by signalling the end of armed support for Communist regimes in Eastern Europe, that the countries of the European Community began to formulate more independent foreign policies and to reconsider the possibility of a joint European defence force.[220] This independence, in turn, has led to significant disagreements between the major European states, most notably over Yugoslavia, after Germany's unilateral recognition of Slovenia and Croatia, which was opposed by France and Britain.[221] The process of European integration was protected from such disagreements during the late 1940s and 1950s—at a time when they could have been extremely destructive—by the onset of the Cold War. By the 1960s, when some European states began to act more independently, and certainly by the 1990s, after the end of the Cold War, the habits and advantages of European cooperation and integration were already too well established to be threatened in their entirety.

Germany and the West during the Cold War

The imperatives of the Cold War were unavoidable in Germany after 1945, but they were not static, despite the immobile public faces of Walter Ulbricht or Leonid Brezhnev and the repeated rituals of military parades or exchanges of spies over the Glienicke Brücke in the spy films of the 1960s, 1970s and 1980s.[222] The image of a single, unending, overarching Cold War concealed significant shifts in the FRG's foreign policy and its international position, as the West German state regained powers and room for manoeuvre.[223] If citizens had the impression of stability and domesticity, it was—in part, at least—the product of the successful, sometimes soporific, rhetoric of politicians and a popular, make-believe world, contrasting with the violence of the Second World War, which had been created by public broadcasters, advertisers and the 'culture industry'.[224] In reality, West German policy-makers had to cope with a bewildering range of variables and the life-threatening situations of a nuclear confrontation, in which they had no control of the arsenal of weapons stationed on German soil.[225] Despite the appearance of an unchanging stand-off, the nuclear balance altered, forcing decision-makers to react.

62 EUROPEAN INTEGRATION SINCE THE 1920s

Two phases of the nuclear confrontation succeeded each other, with profound consequences for the German question. The first, from 1945 to the end of the 1950s, was characterized by Leahy's distinction between the US nuclear deterrent and Soviet land forces and occupation of territory. According to Acheson, the Soviet Union would not go to war with the United States 'unless they were absolutely out of their minds'.[226] Eisenhower continued this policy of 'massive retaliation' until 1959.[227] The second phase began at the end of the 1950s, as the USSR acquired the means—by 1957—to deliver nuclear warheads, which they had first developed in 1949, by intercontinental ballistic missiles (ICBMs). Momentarily threatened by a supposed 'missile-gap crisis', the United States increasingly began to concentrate on its own security, with Kissinger, the Secretary of State under Nixon in the early 1970s, declaring in 1979 that the US would not, and could not, protect Europe.[228] 'Don't you Europeans keep asking us to multiply assurances we cannot possibly mean and that if we do mean, we should not want to execute, and which if we execute, would destroy our civilization,' proclaimed the former Secretary of State in September, after pointing out that American use of nuclear weapons would risk exposing American cities to 'nuclear devastation'.[229] German policy-makers feared that the US policy of 'flexible response' might entail either the limitation of a nuclear war to Germany or a refusal to use nuclear weapons to defend the European mainland. Franz Josef Strauß was not alone, in 1965, in doubting that the United States would 'incinerate themselves in a nuclear holocaust for the sake of Europe's freedom'.[230] The 'risks associated with NATO strategy are not the same for the European allies as they are for the transatlantic parties,' noted the official German White Paper of 1975–76: 'By using strategic weapons the United States risks having its own territory exposed to similar effects from enemy weapons. By contrast, Western Europe and, above all, the Federal Republic of Germany would be a battlefield in any war, whether conducted with conventional or possibly even tactical nuclear weapons, even prior to escalation to the strategic nuclear stage.'[231]

West German policies changed markedly in response to the shift in Washington. Early hopes of gaining joint control of nuclear weapons, adumbrated by the creation in the early 1960s of a Multilateral Nuclear Force of submarines, were confounded when Lyndon Johnson scrapped the force and insisted on the Nuclear Planning Group, set up within NATO in 1966, remaining purely consultative.[232] Consequently, German planners concentrated on maintaining American troop deployments in Europe, since they served as 'hostages' likely to draw the United States into a limited European conflict, and on building up their own conventional force, with a target of 500,000 troops. 'Western nuclear weapons have only one single purpose—to deter the other side from using nuclear weapons both politically or militarily against us,' Helmut Schmidt wrote in *Die Zeit* in March 1989, tacitly admitting that the policy of the 1950s, when the government and *Bundeswehr* were sceptical of rearmament, had been abandoned.[233] 'Nuclear weapons must not be perceived as an instrument to deter limited war or even large-scale conventional attack,' he told the *New York Times* in April 1987: 'What we do need in order to discourage and deter an adversary... are credible conventional forces'.[234] While the strategic and diplomatic relations of the United States and USSR oscillated between a stand-off (1948–53, 1958–63, 1979–85) and détente (from the East German uprising in 1953 to the Second Berlin Crisis in 1958, and from the Test Ban Treaty in 1963 to the Soviet invasion of Afghanistan in 1979), the FRG's pursuit of détente—in common with that of other European powers—was more enduring.

In the 1950s, Adenauer had lived with a 'cauchemar de détente', mindful of the example of Potsdam, when the Allies had sought to do a deal with the USSR in their own interests, without involving German leaders.[235] With Churchill apparently taking Stalin's note in 1952 seriously for a time, the prospect of the 'neutralization' of a united Germany and the withdrawal of Allied troops still seemed to be real. By the late 1950s and early 1960s, even before the erection of the Berlin Wall, the Allies seemed to have altered course, looking to divide Germany for good. Now, the West German Foreign Minister, Heinrich von Brentano, noted 'a certain readiness in the free world to come to an understanding with the Soviet Union on the basis of the status quo', which clashed with the public, long-term commitment of the West German government to reunification.[236] Bonn's response in both cases—facing neutralization or partition—was to avoid doing anything that would deflect Washington from building up its nuclear arsenal and threatening massive retaliation. This stance had been reversed by the 1970s and 1980s, as West German leaders sought détente and arms control, after realizing that they could not rely on US support in a limited conflict and that they could no longer assume that the use of nuclear weapons in Europe would trigger a world war.

Accordingly, Brandt and Schmidt backed SALT I—the first strategic arms limitation treaty—in 1972 (Anti-Ballistic Missile Defence), SALT II in 1979 (long-range offensive systems), which was never ratified, and SALT III (short- and medium-range missiles in Europe), which remained a dead letter. Schmidt had discussed the question with Jimmy Carter, James Callaghan, and Valéry Giscard d'Estaing in January 1979 at a meeting in Guadeloupe:

> Jimmy Carter opened the meeting by saying, 'Well, Helmut has misgivings about the SS-20 [medium-range Soviet nuclear missiles], and we have thought it over and come to the decision that we will put medium-range weapons in Europe—and what do you, Helmut, think about it?' And I said, 'I will reserve my position—I represent a non-nuclear power, and the three of you are representing nuclear powers.'
>
> So Jim Callaghan answered first and said, 'This SS-20 problem must not be permitted to continue, but before you deploy American Eurostrategic weapons—

the name Pershing did not come up; the type of weapon was not really discussed, nor the name—before you do that, I would propose that you negotiate the weapon with the Russians.' Then came Giscard, who said, 'I think Callaghan is right, but the Russians will never negotiate seriously unless they are presented with the threat that if negotiations fail, the United States will unilaterally proceed and deploy their missiles.' And I was the last one to reply, and I said, 'I buy the combined solution of Callaghan and Giscard.' And in the end this is what Carter bought.[237]

Kohl's government permitted the stationing of 108 modernized Pershing and 96 cruise missiles in West Germany in 1983 as part of a 'dual track' policy, where the other track consisted of a continuing attempt to arrive at an arms-control settlement. In the 1950s, Bonn had feared détente and arms control, since a nuclear umbrella was the FRG's principal defence against Soviet intervention. By the 1980s, it pushed for arms control because it could no longer rely on the effective use of American nuclear weapons. What was evident throughout the negotiations was an unquestioned hierarchy of decision-making, with Washington initiating and Bonn (and Paris and London) responding.

Despite the appearance of increasing conformity, with the SPD claiming by the 1960s to be more ardent supporters of NATO than the CDU-CSU, West Germany's 'western' policy remained ambiguous, alternating between a 'European'—or pro-French—stance and an 'Atlanticist' one.[238] In the 1950s, this distinction was less salient, with France still a full member of NATO and the US backing a 'United States of Europe', which was designed to tie Germany to its neighbours and strengthen a continental bloc of states, eventually offering the prospect of an American withdrawal. Washington had initially backed the European Defence Community for this reason.[239] After the creation of the EEC, it had become more critical of the 'little Europe' of the 'Six', protecting its industries against US competition via a common external tariff (CET), and of de Gaulle, who used the development of a French atom bomb in 1960 to pursue a more independent defence and foreign policy, withdrawing from the integrated command structure of NATO in 1966 and calling for the establishment of a separate 'force de frappe' as part of a European third way between the United States and the Soviet Union. The French President visited Moscow in 1966—the first time a Western European leader had done so since 1945—and he vetoed British entry into the EEC in 1963 and 1967 on the grounds that the UK was an American 'Trojan horse'.[240] Increasingly, CDU-led governments seemed to have a choice between 'Europeanism', favoured by Adenauer, and 'Atlanticism', preferred by his successor as Chancellor Ludwig Erhard.[241] When the Franco-German 'Friendship Treaty' (the Elysée Treaty) was ratified in the Bundestag in 1963, deputies—including many Christian Democrats—felt obliged to attach a preface restating their allegiance to the United States. 'The Germans are behaving like swine,' declared de Gaulle: 'They are putting themselves completely at the disposal of the Americans.... And they are betraying Europe.'[242]

Initially, West German leaders had little choice but to support the United States, which was the principal occupying power and the provider of Marshall Aid. Washington had defied the blockade of Berlin in 1948–49, organizing airlifts, and it alone disposed of nuclear weapons, which could be used to deter Soviet aggression. In his memoirs, Adenauer spelled out that, in addition to cultural affinities with America, Germany was subject to the logic of the two power blocs:

> Soviet Russia was making it quite clear that for the time being it was not willing to release the German territory it had been allowed to take over, and that moreover it had every intention of gradually drawing the other part of Germany towards it as well.
>
> There was only one way for us to save our political liberty, our personal freedom, the way of life we had formed over many centuries and which was based on the Christian and humanist ideology: we must form firm links with the peoples and countries that shared our views concerning the state, the individual, liberty and property. We must resolutely and firmly resist all further pressure from the East.
>
> It was our task to dispel the mistrust harboured against us everywhere in the West.... The fundamental precondition for this, in my view, was a clear, steady, unwavering affirmation of identity with the West.[243]

Over time, the governments of the FRG gained greater leeway. The Occupation Statute came to an end in 1955; the Foreign Office was re-established in 1951, a Defence Ministry in 1955 and the *Bundeswehr* in 1956. Gradually, the experts who filled these ministries began to realize that the USSR's foreign policy was conservative, aiming to maintain existing borders and keep control of satellite states. Thus, Brandt's *Ostpolitik* strove to improve relations by recognizing borders (or 'the real situation in Europe', as *Time* magazine put it).[244] At the same time, West German policy-makers began to doubt the consistency and efficacy of US policy, criticizing—in private—the conduct of the Vietnam War, vacillation in the Middle East and the propping up of dictatorships in South America and the 'Third World'.[245] Ronald Reagan's rhetoric about an 'evil empire' and his sponsorship of the Strategic Defence Initiative—or so-called 'Star Wars' programme—in the 1980s introduced further uncertainty into a relationship which had already soured under Schmidt and Jimmy Carter. As Brandt wrote in his memoirs, the German Chancellor and Carter's security advisor, Zbygniew Brzezinski 'did not get on well, and did not bother to disguise the fact'.[246] As Washington began to pursue a harder line against the Soviet Union in the early 1980s, Kohl attempted to keep the FRG's relations with the GDR amicable and to heed public scepticism of the American president at home. With the rise of other powers and relative decline of

66   EUROPEAN INTEGRATION SINCE THE 1920s

the superpowers, international relations appeared to be less predictable, with the Federal Republic suddenly becoming a front-line state in a new sense, facing the collapse of the Soviet Union and an influx of refugees—with even Jürgen Habermas fearing tens of millions—from the East.[247]

Adenauer treated Europe and the United States as parts of the 'West'. Both 'our descent and our convictions root us in the West European world', he told the *Bundestag* in September 1949.[248] NATO served as a cover insofar as it allowed the Federal Republic to regain sovereignty over foreign and defence policy, and to be treated as a partner in specific areas in a way that was acceptable to other European states and the USSR, not least because of the reluctance of the public and the caution of ministers vis-à-vis German rearmament. It was for this reason that Eisenhower accepted 'we cannot take divisions out of Europe', for the 'effect on Adenauer would be unacceptably damaging'.[249] The principle of German funding for Allied troops in the FRG was quickly established.[250] For their part, the FRG's neighbours were reassured by the US policy of 'double containment', which applied to Germany as well as the Soviet Union, and they correctly assumed that Washington would not allow West Germany to conduct an independent foreign policy or initiate a nuclear programme.[251] For Mollet, at a meeting with Dulles in May 1957, it was important to reiterate that 'the European defence problem' required the 'Necessity of an American presence in Europe', which consisted of troops, not merely nuclear weapons, in part because of their role in tying the United States to Europe and in part because they guaranteed the American coordination of European defence policy in respect of Germany as well as the USSR.[252]

European institutions also provided cover for West German leaders to act, in Timothy Garton Ash's phrase, 'in Europe's name', with France gaining access to iron, coal, and German markets within the European Coal and Steel Community (1951) in return for acknowledging the FRG as an equal partner.[253] For Adenauer, the merger of German, European and Western goals and interests was not merely a matter of convenience or obfuscation. As a Rhinelander, he had believed since the 1920s that a Franco–German axis was central to Europe. As the person responsible for German foreign policy after 1949, precisely because the FRG was not sovereign and—initially—lacked a Foreign Office, he had worked closely with Allied High Commissioners and had quickly come to accept American dominance.[254] His desire for a 'European federation'—the word had a multiplicity of meanings, including '*Bund*' or confederation—was therefore multi-layered:

> Since its inception the CDU had always, from deep conviction, backed a European federation. In the creation of such a federation we saw and we still see the only possibility of saving the existence, the tradition, and the influence of Europe. The United States, too, emphatically desired a European federation.[255]

The FRG became the main sponsor of the unprecedented political and economic experiment of the European Community.[256] Arguably, the discomfort caused by the dominance of France, which was technically independent of NATO and in favour of a high CET against American goods, was offset by the advantages of integration, which proceeded rapidly from the ECSC in 1951 via Bonn's signature of the plan for a European Defence Community in 1952 to the ratification of the Treaty of Rome in 1957 and the phased removal of tariffs in the 1960s. Although successive German governments could not leave the European Communities (the ECSC, EEC, and Euratom), once the FRG had entered, since its equality of status and, increasingly, its political identity—with 'the division of Germany...simultaneously the division of Europe' (Helmut Kohl)—were so closely connected to them, there is little sign that they wanted to.[257]

Behind West Germany's movement towards European integration and gradual distancing from the United States was a metamorphosing economy. Many leaders favoured the language of economics abroad, not least because they were fearful of accusations of political assertiveness or meddling in military matters. The FRG's economic growth seems predictable but, given what happened in the Weimar years, its prospects seemed more mixed during the late 1940s: its Gross National Product was valued at 12.5 per cent of that of the United States in 1950 and 67 per cent of that of the UK.[258] In 1945, the US State Department's aim was the reconstruction and integration of the German economy, neither of which aims were easily attainable. 'Consequently, we must be prepared to take all possible steps in the initial phases of occupation to prevent [the] development of a chaotically unmanageable economic situation, since this is a prerequisite of the exercise of effective economic control,' ran one report: 'The eventual objectives imply the assimilation—on a basis of equality—of a reformed, peaceful and economically non-aggressive Germany into a liberal system of world trade.'[259] British planners agreed, rejecting the punitive Morgenthau Plan: 'Again it has been accepted that chaos and a starving and bankrupt Germany would not serve the interests of the occupying powers', with perceived harshness and dislocation threatening to 'weaken rather than strengthen the durability of the settlement, by the reactions it would provoke'.[260] Two decades later, the relative economic positions of the FRG and UK had been reversed, with consequences for European and foreign policy. After exceeding the growth rate of its neighbours (5.5 per cent per annum in 1953–73, compared to 4.3 per cent in Belgium and 3.0 per cent in the UK), the West German economy became the largest in Europe, overtaking that of the UK by the mid-1960s.[261] During the 1950s, its exports had increased at more than 10 per cent per annum, with the result that its volume of exports as a percentage of GDP had grown from 8.3 per cent in 1951 to 24.1 per cent in 1976.[262]

West Germany was now a competitor of the US, with the Bonn summit of the G7—the meetings of the West's largest economies which had begun in 1975—

signalling 'the full emergence' of the FRG 'from the shadow of the United States in international economic councils', in the words of the *New York Times*, and its metamorphosis into a 'world power', not just economically, but 'also increasingly politically', in the verdict of the *Wall Street Journal*.[263] 'Foreign policy today is... for us not just the specialist discipline of well-dressed, white-bearded, well-behaved diplomats, it is really world economic policy, world raw materials policy, world agrarian policy, world monetary policy, world development policy and world security policy,' wrote the new Chancellor in his paper on 'Guiding Thoughts on Our Foreign Policy' in January 1975: 'We live today in a universal system of dependent nations, marked by total interdependence of political and economic developments. This has so far not been understood by many foreign policy-makers. I mean not only in Germany but across the world.'[264] It was a paradox of West Germany's interdependence that it entailed greater freedom from the United States, not least because the linkages in the developing global system were unevenly distributed, with the bulk of the FRG's external manufacturing trade—70 per cent—with other EC member states by 1970, increasing to 79 per cent by 1990.[265] Whereas Germany exported DM 352,951 million to the EEC by 1989 (and DM 117,883 million to other European countries such as Sweden, Austria, and Switzerland), it exported DM 51,776 million to the United States and Canada.[266] This reciprocal relationship with the EEC—with West Germany's contribution making up 30 per cent of the European Community's budget and the Deutschmark forming the central currency in the European Monetary System (EMS)—inevitably pushed German leaders, both SPD (Schmidt) and CDU-CSU (Kohl), towards Europe and away from the United States.[267]

Europe as a whole had altered its position vis-à-vis Washington, largely following West Germany's lead, with monetary policy becoming the main bone of contention. Once Nixon had ended the Bretton Woods system of pegging European currencies to the dollar via gold, Bonn and Frankfurt had led European attempts to set up a regional system (the 'snake', EMS and ERM) to limit fluctuations of floating currencies, providing what Schmidt termed a 'monetary shield' and imposing—in effect—the *Bundesbank*'s priority of low inflation. Since US administrations had become accustomed to a low domestic savings ratio, budget deficits, and a large national debt in the 1960s, the introduction of floating currencies in the 1970s led to fluctuations in inflation and the value of currencies, heightening West German fears—which Schmidt expressed to Carter—of a financial crash resulting from the over-valuation and instability of the dollar. According to an interview with Schmidt in *Der Spiegel* on 6 January 1975, West Germany had been driven by economic imperatives, especially the need to maintain 'the monetary system of the free world economy', to become—in the title of the magazine issue—'a world power against its will'.[268] The FRG's role had increased during the course of the 1960s and the early 1970s, in Schmidt's view, because 'other partners in the North Atlantic Alliance [had] reduced their role as allies', because *Ostpolitik* had removed the weak point of 'the open flank of the German question and the threatened island status of Berlin' and, above all, because of 'the great success of German economic development and German economic policy'.[269]

After the Reagan administration had set high interest rates in order to bring down inflation, with real rates rising from 0 to 8 per cent in the early 1980s, foreign capital was drawn—artificially, in the *Bundesbank*'s opinion—to the United States, deepening the recession in Europe. The erratic, unreliable character of US monetary policy, from the point of view of West German policy-makers still mindful of the lessons of hyperinflation in the 1920s, not only pushed Bonn towards the European Community, it also helped to prepare the ground for Economic and Monetary Union. In Schmidt's opinion, this shift did not imply that the Federal Republic was 'the strongest power' in a 'multipolar system of several great and middle powers', which co-existed with the bipolar system of the USA and USSR: 'I can only accept this depiction, which you give, in a very limited way, since it implies that a bipolar system is underpinned or, even, overlaid— however you want to see it—by a multipolar one.'[270] 'In shaping the finance system of the world, we are a first-class partner', along with the US, Japan, France, and Britain, 'not just because of our weight, but also because of our specialized experience and expertise'; by contrast, when it came to 'nuclear testing, non-proliferation treaties, negotiations to limit strategic arms and mutual arms controls in the conventional sphere in Europe, in these fields the Federal Republic is a middling power'.[271]

Despite such military limitations, the growth and dynamism of the FRG's economy transformed 'German–German relations' and the European question, helping to bring about unification in 1989–90, with East German citizens—a quarter of whom crossed over into the West within days of the fall of the Wall—more anxious to visit KaDeWe than to explore other cultural and political affinities linking East and West Germany.[272] The Federal Republic's political independence vis-à-vis the United States and its centrality in the European Community also played a part. Whereas neither the FRG nor the GDR looked like permanent states in the 1950s, with the former having a temporary capital and Basic Law (*Grundgesetz*) instead of a constitution, their mutual recognition of borders and establishment of diplomatic relations in the Basic Treaty (1972) signalled their independent status, with *Ostpolitik* comprising an important component of détente in Europe after 1963, which cut across worsening relations between Washington and Moscow from 1979 to 1985. Bonn's provision of interest-free credit to the GDR, which had reached DM 800 million per annum by 1985, combined with a further easing of travel restrictions in 1985 and Erich Honecker's first state visit to the FRG in September 1987 to transform relations between the two states.[273]

70 EUROPEAN INTEGRATION SINCE THE 1920s

Few commentators predicted that the Soviet bloc would collapse in 1989, despite the advent of *glasnost* (openness) and *perestroika* (economic restructuring) in the mid-1980s under Mikhail Gorbachev, which Schmidt had claimed 'did nothing to change the fact that Moscow cast long shadows'.[274] Kohl himself had little inkling that unification was a possibility, not to mention an imminent one, and he initially seemed unsure how much freedom of manoeuvre he had. In late October 1989, when invited British journalists addressed 200 West German dignitaries in Bonn, the audience seemed 'somewhat taken aback that instead of expressing angst, we each of us, in our different ways looked forward to a united Germany', recorded Peregrine Worsthorne in the *Daily Telegraph*.[275] Kohl had, at first, preferred a two-state solution after the fall of the Wall, changing his mind during the course of November. The fact that the West German Chancellor was able to negotiate separately with Gorbachev and George Bush, using their hesitation and support to counter the panic and opposition of Margaret Thatcher and François Mitterrand, was an indication of how much the 'German question' had changed in the four decades since 1949 and how much it still relied on the foreign-policy stances of the superpowers, rather than on European neighbours.[276]

On 9 November 1989, Günter Schabowski, a government spokesman and party leader in East Berlin, announced at a press conference that permanent emigration from the GDR would be allowed 'immediately, without delay'.[277] His surprise announcement came after several months of events—the opening of the border between Hungary and Austria on 19 August, the flight of tens of thousands of East Germans via Czechoslovakia and Hungary to the West, demonstrations in Leipzig, Berlin and other cities in October—during which the old regime in the German Democratic Republic lost control. Gorbachev had already notified Warsaw Pact governments in July 1989 that they were free to carry out their own reforms without interference from Moscow—a policy which he made public on 26 October, when he declared that the 'Soviet Union has no moral or political right to interfere in the affairs of its East European neighbours.'[278] Honecker, facing growing numbers of demonstrators, was forced by Socialist Unity Party elites to stand down as General Secretary in favour of Egon Krenz on 18 October. Although he had no blueprint for unification, since an operative plan had been abandoned by Bonn with the building of the Wall in 1961, Kohl took the initiative and presented his Ten Point Programme on 28 November, in which he mentioned reunification after offering the prospect of economic support:

> We support the demand for free, equal and secret elections in the GDR, in which independent—and, of course, that also means non-socialist—parties participate. The SED must give up its monopoly on power.... We do not want to stabilize conditions that have become untenable. We know: there can only be an

economic upturn if the GDR opens itself up to Western investment, if it creates conditions for a market economy and enables private economic activity. I do not understand how one can raise the reproach of tutelage in this context. Every day, Hungary and Poland offer the GDR—likewise a COMECON member—examples that it could readily follow....

We are also prepared to take yet another decisive step, namely, to develop confederative structures (*konföderative Strukturen*) between both states in Germany, with the aim of creating a federation (*Föderation*), that is, a federal order (*bundesstaatliche Ordnung*), in Germany. However, that absolutely presupposes a democratically legitimized government in the GDR....If we find ourselves facing a democratically legitimized, that is, a freely elected, government as a partner, entirely new perspectives will open up. Step by step, new forms of institutional cooperation can emerge and be expanded....No one knows today what a reunified Germany (*ein wiedervereinigtes Deutschland*) will ultimately look like. That unity will come, however, when the people in Germany want it—of this, I am certain.[279]

Kohl realized, given the speed of events, that unification might occur quickly. The principal question here is how other states reacted and whether the Chancellor framed his plan primarily in European or 'Western' terms, in accordance with the imperatives of the Cold War.[280]

It is evident from available archival material and memoirs that the West German government viewed the acceptance of Washington and Moscow as a pre-requisite for unification.[281] Although their presence had become so familiar as to be almost invisible, the Four Powers—the US, Britain, France, and the USSR—retained a veto over German affairs (see Map 1.5). Kohl had intended to send a letter to George Bush explaining his position before he gave his speech on the Ten Point Programme at the end of November, but he was thwarted by technical difficulties.[282] The Chancellor and President's meeting at Laeken on 3 December 1989 demonstrated that their trust in each other remained intact, despite the Secretary of State James Baker's public setting of limits on unification on 29 November, when he had insisted that the FRG should avoid trading 'neutralism for unity' and that it should remain in NATO and the European Community: Bush reported as a friend and ally on his talk with Gorbachev on a Soviet warship off Malta on 2–3 December, noting that he had allayed the General Secretary's fear that 'Kohl is going too quickly' with an assurance that the 'Ten Point Plan of the Chancellor establishes three phases but no dates' and that 'He knows Kohl', who 'is cautious and will not rush into things'.[283] The President was reassured 'that developments are peaceful and without violence', but warned that Gorbachev should not be 'put under pressure', which would require the Allies—and mainly the US—to 'find a formula' including 'disarmament and every other topic'.[284]

Map 1.5 US military presence in Germany in 1990

Source: A. A. Holmes, *Social Unrest and American Military Bases in Turkey and Gemrany since 1945* (Cambridge, 2014), 159.

This pattern of consultation and collaboration with Washington in order to gain the agreement of Moscow continued throughout the complicated negotiations.[285] On 10 February 1990, Gorbachev agreed with Kohl during a meeting in Moscow, after a long discussion of NATO disarmament, that 'the decision for unity is a German affair'.[286] In protracted discussions about formal recognition of the Polish–German border (the Oder–Neisse line) and NATO membership for a unified Germany, which Bush negotiated on Kohl's behalf (after the Chancellor had offered a 'loan' of DM 5 billion) in early June, the superpowers remained uppermost in German calculations.[287] 'German–American friendship... is more important today than 30 or 40 years ago—it is existential,' said the Chancellor to the American President at Camp David on 24 February 1990:

> Massive changes are occurring in the Soviet Union. Even if Gorbachev is toppled, any successor would soon have to pursue similar policies in principle to those of Gorbachev—the force of events is pushing in this direction. There is no going back to Stalin—there is in Europe, especially, no place for a heavenly peace. It is, indeed, still possible theoretically that tanks roll into Dresden, Budapest or Warsaw—but this will have unforeseeable consequences. The world has gone beyond this. Not least, the media age has contributed to such a state of affairs.[288]

Given their history, it was 'psychologically very decisive and important for the relations of F[rance] / G[ermany] that we—in contrast to F—are not a nuclear power and will also not become one' and that 'the relations of G / USA remain intact—this helps, too, to counter anxieties'.[289] German–American relations must be 'as tight as possible', reiterated Kohl.[290] As Peter Hartmann, a section head in the Chancellery, pointed out to an East German delegation on 29 January 1990, 'we wish to embed German policy in an all-European process and in the East–West relationship'.[291] Arguably, '*West-Ost-Beziehungen*' were most important.

Thatcher and Mitterrand realized that they lacked a power of veto in 1989–90. The British Prime Minister made her objections to unification known at the time and in her memoirs, where she chides Mitterrand for having refused to enter into an anti-German Franco-British axis.[292] At the time, she had been more confident, after dining with the French President in Paris, that they stood 'on firm ground' together, even if 'everything was suddenly in motion', as Horst Teltschik put it to Kohl on 30 November 1989, reporting on a meeting between Thatcher and Genscher.[293] For the German Chancellor, however, there was no sense that the Prime Minister's position would alter his own, as he indicated to Bush at Laeken on 3 December: 'It is a pity that Mrs Thatcher is so unforthcoming. He wants to get along with her at the European Council meeting in Strasbourg at the end of next week.'[294] Mitterrand was a more significant actor, whose position the American President was eager to know, but he was also more guarded and pragmatic: 'President Bush asks whether Mitterrand has a problem with the 10 Point Plan. The Chancellor says no. He says the 10 Points are not an alternative to European union (*europäische Einigung*). On the contrary, European union is a precondition of his programme.'[295] Mitterrand does seem to have panicked in the autumn of 1989, fearing that events in Germany were moving too quickly.[296] He met Gorbachev on 6 December in Kyiv, hoping to slow down the movement towards unification and offering to meet with the Soviet leader again during a

74 EUROPEAN INTEGRATION SINCE THE 1920s

planned state visit to the GDR on the 20th of the same month. Shortly afterwards, the two leaders' advisors, Jacques Attali and Vadim Sagladin, met, with the former spelling out that France was Russia's traditional ally and that the two states should try to avert any historical repetition of German aggression.[297]

Two days later at the EU summit in Strasbourg, Kohl repeated his assurance that German unification and European integration were—and would continue to be—tied together. In private, over breakfast at the summit on 9 December, Mitterrand warned that 'what he could not yet foresee and grasp was how Gorbachev would react to a very rapid movement towards [German] unity'.[298] Kohl replied that he was 'in very close contact' with the General Secretary.[299] Neither mentioned European political and economic integration, which had already been agreed, with Kohl backing the Delors's report in spring 1989 and agreeing to an IGC on EMU before the fall of the Wall. Both concentrated on events in Central and Eastern Europe and in the USSR. The same was true of their meeting on 4 January 1990, which focused entirely on events in the East, with Mitterrand only alluding to 'the strengthening of the community of the twelve' and the eventual integration of 'the others' during the informal photo session after-wards: 'German–French relations have been of the greatest significance until now; in the nineties, they will be of even greater importance,' declared Kohl.[300] To the American President, who knew less about what had been agreed on a European level, the Chancellor was more explicit: 'He emphasized that we are a part of Europe and an integrative component of the EC. Without him, the *Bundeskanzler*, there would not have been progress in the development of the EC. He had done all that together with François Mitterrand and it is important that this is borne in mind.'[301] To the fear expressed by Giulio Andreotti, at a meeting of Christian Democrats in Salzburg, that 'the Federal Republic was drifting away from the EC or the Alliance [NATO]', Kohl retorted for Bush's benefit: 'This is nonsense. The Federal Republic of Germany is an integral part of the EC and the Alliance.'[302]

The German government was more than willing to accept further integration, leading to the creation of a European Union, but it kept the European question separate from the 'alliance question' and the security policies of the superpowers, on which unification continued to depend. American coordination of defence and foreign policy had allowed European wounds to heal. Kohl, who was fifteen in 1945, had expressed this desire to Mitterrand, who had been twenty-eight, at the European Council summit at Fontainebleau in March 1984:

> I would like to talk to you very openly, as a younger man to someone older whom he trusts. You are a man steeped in history and literature. I am, too....
> I want to tell you something. My grandfather had a son who died in the

War of '14....My father named his elder son after [him]. That son died in turn in the war in '45. My own son has the same name as my [dead] brother. He's now starting his military service. He knows very well the meaning of freedom. We want to meet the challenge which consists of having both freedom and peace.[303]

German *Wiedervereinigung* demonstrated that the overarching architecture of the *pax americana* remained in place. European integration had proceeded in the context of, and had been limited by, the terms of that peace. At the same time, however, critical shifts took place in intra-European relations, which—together with the changing terms of the German question and the diverging trajectory of détente on the Continent—helped to ensure that the European Union remained a haven of peace and security after the end of the Cold War. The next chapter examines these shifts.

Notes

1. Quoted in D. Reynolds, *One World Indivisible: A Global History since 1945* (London, 2000), 21.
2. Ibid.
3. *Economist*, 17 March 1945, quoted in D. W. Ellwood, *Rebuilding Europe: Western Europe, America and Postwar Reconstruction* (London, 1992), 29.
4. *New York Times*, 14 March 1945, quoted ibid.
5. Evaluations of such constraints differ, extending to Geir Lundestad's contention that the new order amounted to an 'empire by invitation': G. Lundestad, *'Empire' by Invitation: The United States and European Integration, 1945–1997* (Oxford, 1998).
6. https://www.nobelprize.org/prizes/peace/2012/press-release/.
7. Ibid.
8. T. Shipman, 'Ridicule as Nobel Peace Prize Is Given to the EU', *Daily Mail*, 13 October 2012.
9. Ibid. Nigel Farage claimed that, 'Rather than bring peace and harmony, the EU will cause insurgency and violence'; Bill Cash was quoted as saying, 'It is like giving an Oscar to a box office flop. It is thanks to NATO, the Marshall Plan and the help of the United States that Europe maintained peace after World War Two, certainly not the European Union'; and the financier Peter Hargreaves added, 'It's mad. It will be interesting to see if they take it back if Greece dissolves into martial law.'
10. Charles Bremner, 'EU Leaders Squabble over Their Peace Prize', *The Times*, 20 October 2012.
11. Luke Harding and Ian Traynor, 'Peace Prize: Ray of Light Pierces EU's Gloom as Nobel Committee Takes Long View', *Guardian*, 13 October 2012.
12. 'A Europe at Peace', *Irish Times*, 11 December 2012.
13. Ibid.
14. Ibid.
15. Ibid.
16. *Die Wiener Zeitung*, 12 October 2012; Agence France Presse, 'Nobel for EU Praised in European, not British, Press', 13 October 2012; the BBC reported that 'Europe's Press Has Mixed Response', but confirmed broad approval, with reservations: https://www.bbc.co.uk/news/world-europe-19,936,165.
17. T. Judt, *A Grand Illusion? An Essay on Europe* (1996), 4, 24.
18. Ibid., 25–6.
19. Ibid.
20. Ibid., 27.
21. Ibid., 28.
22. Ibid., 29.

76 EUROPEAN INTEGRATION SINCE THE 1920s

23. Ibid., 29–30.
24. Ibid., 30.
25. Ibid., 33. T. Judt, *Postwar: A History of Europe since 1945* (London, 2005), 7: the 'European model' emerged 'belatedly—and largely by accident'.
26. T. Judt, *A Grand Illusion?*33.
27. W. Lipgens, *Europa-Föderationspläne der Widerstandsbewegungen 1940–1945*; W. Lipgens, 'European Federation in the Political Thought of Resistance Movements during World War II', *Central European History*, 1 (1968), 5–19; W. Lipgens, A *History of European Integration*; W. Lipgens, *Die Anfänge der europäischen Einigungspolitik 1945–1950*; W. Lipgens and W. Loth (eds), *Documents on the History of European Integration* (Berlin, 1985–88), 3 vols; H. Halin, *L'Europe unie, objectif majeur de la resistance* (Paris, 1967); W. Loth, 'Explaining European Integration', *Journal of European Integration History*, 14 (2008), 12–16. For a study of pro-community federalism within French political elites, see C. Parsons, *A Certain Idea of Europe* (Ithaca, New York, 2003).
28. On transnationalism within postwar Christian Democracy, see especially W. Kaiser, *Christian Democracy and the Origins of European Union* (Cambridge, 2007); idem, 'Cooperation of European Catholic Politicians in Exile in Britain and the USA during the Second World War', *Journal of Contemporary History*, 35 (2000), 439–65; idem, 'No Second Versailles: Transnational Contacts in the People and Freedom Group and the International Christian Democratic Union, 1936–1945', in M. Gehler et al (eds), *Christdemokratie in Europa im 20 Jahrhundert* (Vienna, 2001); W. Kaiser and M. Gehler, 'Transnationalism and Early European Integration: The NEI and the Geneva Circle, 1947–1957', *Historical Journal*, 44 (2001), 773–98; W. Kaiser and B. Leucht, 'Informal Politics of Integration: Christian Democratic and Transatlantic Networks in the Creation of the ECSC Core Europe', *Journal of European Integration History*, 14 (2008), 35–50.
29. W. Kaiser, *Christian Democracy and the Origins of European Union* (Cambridge, 2007), 163, 198.
30. Ibid., 1.
31. Ibid., 5.
32. C. Bailey, *Between Yesterday and Tomorrow: German Visions of Europe, 1926–1950* (New York, 2013), 201. For an account of Schumacher's nationalism, see L. J. Edinger, *Kurt Schumacher: A Study in Personality and Political Behaviour* (Palo Alto, CA, 1965), 144–89, and P. Merseburger, *Der schwierige Deutsche. Kurt Schumacher* (Stuttgart, 1995), 505–30. Schumacher sometimes treated the powers as equivalent, complaining in the immediate post-war era that 'There is not a true democracy in any of the zones', since 'power is exercised by the military authorities': ibid., 385. According to Edinger, Schumacher believed that the occupying powers alone were preventing a revolution in Germany in the late 1940s.
33. W. Kaiser, *Christian Democracy and the Origins of European Union*, 238. Georges Bidault, the leader of the MRP, was classified as one of the more aggressive opponents.
34. T. Judt, *A Grand Illusion?*, 9.
35. Ibid., 9–10.
36. Ibid., 24.
37. W. Loth, 'Explaining European Integration', *Journal of European Integration History*, 14 (2008), 16–18; W. Loth, *The Division of the World, 1941–1955* (London, 1988), 15–33, 219–33.
38. D. Eisenhower, quoted in M. Trachtenberg, *History and Strategy* (Princeton, NJ, 1991), 163–4; D. Reynolds, *One World Divisible: A Global History since 1945* (London, 2000), 132.
39. D. Reynolds, *One World Divisible*, 129.
40. The distinction between hard and soft power was coined by Joseph Nye. It is not my intention here to return to those debates, but rather to accept that a distinction can be made between the use of military force and different forms of coercion and different types of persuasion and inducement: J. Nye, *Bound to Lead: The Changing Nature of American Power* (New York, 1990); J. Nye, *Soft Power: The Means to Success* (New York, 2004); J. Nye, 'Soft Power: The Evolution of a Concept', *Journal of Political Power*, 14 (2021), 196–208.
41. J. L. Gaddis, 'The Emerging Post-Revisionist Synthesis on the Origins of the Cold War', *Diplomatic History*, 7 (1983), 171–90; B. Cumings, '"Revising Postrevisionism," or, The Poverty of Theory in Diplomatic History', *Diplomatic History*, 17 (1993), 539–69. These debates barely touch on the definition of a Cold War, but concentrate on an orthodox revisionism, and post-revisionism which disagree about the origins and scope of the conflict. See also M. J. Hogan (ed.), *The End of the Cold War: Its Meaning and Implications* (Cambridge, 1992).
42. See H. Nehring, 'What Was the Cold War?', *English Historical Review*, 127 (2012), 920–49.

43. E. Edwards Spalding, *The First Cold Warrior: Harry Truman, Containment and the Remaking of Liberal Internationalism* (Lexington, KY, 2006), 74. W. Lippmann, *The Cold War: A Study in U.S. Foreign Policy* (New York, 1947).
44. J. L. Gaddis, *We Now Know: Rethinking Cold War History* (Oxford, 1997), 26, quoting Felix Chuev.
45. Ibid.
46. Ibid.
47. Ibid., 27.
48. D. Reynolds, 'Beyond Bipolarity in Space and Time', and W. LaFeber, 'An End to *Which* Cold War?' in M. J. Hogan (ed.), *The End of the Cold War*, 245–56, 13–20, and D. Reynolds, 'Introduction', in M. J. Hogan (ed.), *The Origins of the Cold War in Europe: International Perspectives* (New Haven, CT, 1994), 1–2. Also, F. Halliday, The Making of the Second Cold War, 2nd edn (London, 1986). Gottfried Niedhart, 'East–West Conflict: Short Cold War and Long Détente', in O. Bange and P. Villaume (eds), *The Long Détente: Changing Concepts of Security and Cooperation in Europe, 1950s–1980s* (Budapest, 2017), 19–30, takes issue with the term 'Cold War', wishing to replace it with 'East-West conflict', but much of what he says about détente relates specifically to Europe rather than the United States.
49. O. Bange and P. Villaume (eds), *The Long Détente*; R. G. Hughes, *Britain, Germany and the Cold War: The Search for a European Détente, 1949–1967* (London, 2007).
50. C. S. Maier (ed.), *The Cold War in Europe* (New York, 1991); W. Loth, 'Der "Kalte Krieg" in der historischen Forschung', in G. Niedhart (ed.), *Der Westen und die Sowjetunion* (Paderborn, 1983), 155–75.
51. K. Ruane, *The Rise and Fall of the European Defence Community: Anglo-American Relations and the Crisis of European Defence, 1950–55* (Basingstoke, 2000); E. Fursdon, *The European Defence Community: A History* (Basingstoke, 1980); R. Pastor-Castro, 'The Quai d'Orsay and the European Defence Community Crisis of 1954', *History*, 91 (2006), 386–400; P. Guillen, 'France and the Defence of Western Europe: From the Brussels Pact (March 1948) to the Pleven Plan (October 1950)', in N. Wiggershaus and R. G. Foerster (eds), *The Western Security Community* (Oxford, 1993), 125–48; J. van der Harst, *The Atlantic Priority: Dutch Defence Policy at the Time of the European Defence Community* (Brussels, 2003), 125–48.
52. P. Ludlow (ed.), *European Integration and the Cold War: Ostpolitik—Westpolitik, 1965–1973* (London, 2007); W. Loth and G. Soutou (eds), *The Making of Détente: Eastern Europe and Western Europe in the Cold War, 1965–75* (London, 2010); S. Kieninger, *Dynamic Détente: The United States and Europe, 1964–1975* (Cambridge, CT, 2016); A. Hofmann, *The Emergence of Détente in Europe: Brandt, Kennedy and the Formation of Ostpolitik* (London, 2007); L. Nuti, *The Crisis of Détente in Europe: From Helsinki to Gorbachev, 1975–1985* (London, 2008); K. Spohr and D. Reynolds (eds), *Transcending the Cold War: Summits, Statecraft and the Dissolution of Bipolarity in Europe, 1970–1990* (Oxford, 2016).
53. E. Edwards Spalding, *The First Cold Warrior*, 69–70.
54. A. Deighton, *The Impossible Peace: Britain, the Division of Germany and the Origins of the Cold War* (Oxford, 1990).
55. D. Reynolds, *From World War to Cold War: Churchill, Roosevelt and the International History of the 1940s* (Oxford, 2006), 267–330; R. Ovendale, *The English-speaking Alliance: Britain, the United States, the Dominions and the Cold War, 1947–1951* (London, 1985).
56. J. McDougall, 'The Impossible Republic: The Reconquest of Algeria and the Decolonization of France, 1945–1962', *Journal of Modern History*, 89 (2017), 772–811; T. Smith, 'The French Colonial Consensus and People's War, 1946–58', *Journal of Contemporary History*, 9 (1974), 217–47; A. Clayton, *The French Wars of Decolonization* (London, 2014).
57. W. Churchill to J. Colville, his private secretary, quoted in D. Reynolds, 'Great Britain', in D. Reynolds (ed.), *The Origins of the Cold War in Europe*, 91. Reynolds refers to this as the obsession of an ageing statesman. Bevin had been clear in 1947 that 'We have got to get this thing [the atom bomb] over here whatever it costs.... We've got to have the bloody Union Jack flying on top of it': D. Reynolds, *One World Indivisible*, 27.
58. De Gaulle's comments about power were made in a *Times* interview on 10 September 1945: R. Girault, 'The French Decision-Makers and Their Perception of French Power in 1948', in J. Becker and F. Knipping (eds), *Power in Europe?*, vol. 1, 49. C. de Gaulle, internal note Apr. 1945, in G.-H. Soutou, 'France', in D. Reynolds, 'Great Britain', in D. Reynolds (ed.), *The Origins of the Cold War in Europe*, 100.
59. An early essay, which focused on the UK but extended to other European powers, is D. Reynolds, 'The "Big Three" and the Division of Europe, 1945–48: An Overview', *Diplomacy*

78   EUROPEAN INTEGRATION SINCE THE 1920s

and Statecraft, 1 (1990), 118–23. See also A. Deighton (ed.), *Britain and the First Cold War* (Basingstoke, 1990).

60. A. Deighton, *The Impossible Peace*, 36–53.
61. See Joan Hoff Wilson, *Ideology and Economics: U.S. Relations with the Soviet Union, 1918–1933* (Columbia, MO, 1974); E. Mark, 'October or Thermidor? Interpretations of Stalinism and the Perception of Soviet Foreign Policy in the United States, 1927-1947', *American Historical Review*, 94 (1989), 937–62.
62. A. Deighton, *The Impossible Peace*, 54–80.
63. O. Appelqvist, 'Rediscovering Uncertainty: Early Attempts at a Pan-European Post-War Recovery', *Cold War History*, 8 (2008), 327–52.
64. N. Naimark, *The Russians in Germany: A History of the Soviet Zone of Occupation, 1945–1949* (Cambridge, MA, 1995); C. Defrance, *La Politique culturelle de la France sur la rive gauche du Rhin, 1945–1955* (Strasbourg, 1994).
65. R. Frazier, 'Did Britain Start the Cold War? Bevin and the Truman Doctrine', *Historical Journal*, 27 (1984), 715–27.
66. This growth was difficult to measure and was uneven, linked to the war economy: R. Higgs, 'Wartime Prosperity? A Reassessment of the US Economy in the 1940s', *Journal of Economic History*, 52 (1992), 41–60.
67. A. Shennan, *Rethinking France: Plans for Renewal, 1940–1946* (Oxford, 1989).
68. R. E. Hannigan, *The Great War and American Foreign Policy, 1914–1924* (University Park, PA, 2017), 274–89; M. Leffler, *The Elusive Quest: America's Pursuit of European Stability and French Security, 1919–1933* (Chapel Hill, NC, 1979); F. Costiglia, *Awkward Dominion: American Political, Economic and Cultural Relations with Europe, 1919–1933* (Ithaca, NY, 1987); Z. Steiner, *The Lights that Failed: European International History, 1919–1933* (Oxford, 2005).
69. Although Susan Pedersen, *The Guardians: The League of Nations and the Crisis of Empire* (Oxford, 2015), 394, aims to show the development of international organization and global negotiations, she, too, accepts that 'for most states, and indeed for the Secretariat, the war posed starkly the question of whether the League was something more than the handmaiden of the Allied powers'.
70. P. Jackson, 'France and the Problems of Security and International Disarmament after the First World War', *Journal of Strategic Studies*, 29 (2006), 247–80; A. Adamthwaite, *Grandeur and Misery: France's Bid for Power in Europe, 1914–1940* (1995); J.-B. Duroselle, *France and the Nazi Threat: The Collapse of French Diplomacy, 1932–1939* (New York, 2004); R. H. Haigh, D. S. Morris, and A. R. Peters, *Soviet Foreign Policy, the League of Nations and Europe, 1917–1939* (Aldershot, 1986); F. J. Fleron, E. P. Hoffmann, and R. F. Laird, *Classic Issues in Soviet Foreign Policy: From Lenin to Brezhnev* (New York, 1991).
71. C. Eisenberg, 'The Cold War in Europe', in J.-C. Agnew and R. Rosenzweig (eds), *A Companion to Post-1945 America* (Oxford, 2002), 414.
72. A. DePorte, *Europe between the Superpowers: The Enduring Balance* (New Haven, CT, 1979).
73. J. E. Smith, 'General Clay and the Russians: A Continuation of the Wartime Alliance in Germany, 1945-1948', *Virginia Quarterly Review*, 64 (1988), 27; J. E. Smith, 'The View from USFET: General Clay's and Washington's Interpretation of Soviet Intentions in Germany, 1945–1948', in H. A. Schmitt (ed.), *US Occupation in Europe after World War II* (Lawrence, KS, 1978), 64–85; J. H. Backer, *The Decision to Divide Germany* (Durham, NC., 1978); W. Krieger, 'Was General Clay a Revisionist? Strategic Aspects of the United States' Occupation of Germany', *Journal of Contemporary History*, 18 (1983), 165–84.
74. M. Charlton, *The Price of Victory* (London, 1983), 186.
75. See J. G. Giauque, *Grand Designs and Visions of Unity: The Atlantic Powers and the Reorganization of Western Europe, 1955–1963* (Chapel Hill, NC, 2002); M. J. Carley, 'Behind Stalin's Moustache: Pragmatism in Early Soviet Foreign Policy, 1917–1941', *Diplomacy and Statecraft*, 12 (2001), 159–74.
76. K. Adenauer to S. J. Vogel, 26 January 1948, in H.-P. Schwarz, 'Adenauer und Europa', *Vierteljahreshefte für Zeitgeschichte*, 27 (1979), 482.
77. Konrad Adenauer, *Erinnerungen 1953–1955* (Stuttgart, 1966), vol. 2, 303, noted in 1954: 'In this very pressing situation for us, it was certainly a relief for me that American policy coincided to a great degree with German policy.'
78. K. Jarausch, *After Hitler: Recivilizing Germans, 1945–1995* (Oxford, 2006), 55.
79. K. Schumacher, 3–4 January 1946, cited in W. Loth, 'German Conceptions of Europe during the Escalation of the East-West Conflict, 1945–1949', in J. Becker and F. Knipping (eds), *Power in Europe? Great Britain, France, Italy and Germany in a Postwar World, 1945–1950* (Berlin, 1986), 524.

HARD POWER 79

80. K. Adenauer private letter, 27 July 1949, in Schwarz, 'Adenauer und Europa', *Vierteljahreshefte für Zeitgeschichte*, 27 (1979), 479–80.
81. As Charles Williams, *Adenauer: The Father of a New Germany* (New York, 2000), 362–79, points out 'building Europe' was always linked to 'facing the bear', as was Adenauer's policy towards the USA.
82. E. Di Nolfo, 'Das Problem der europäischen Einigung als ein Aspekt der italienischen Aussenpolitik 1945–1954', *Vierteljahreshefte für Zeitgeschichte*, 28 (1980), 151.
83. Ibid., 156. See also M. Miller, 'The Approaches to European Institution-Building of Carlo Sforza, Italian Foreign Minister, 1947–51', in A. Deighton (ed.), *Building Postwar Europe: National Decision-Makers and European Institutions, 1948–1963* (Basingstoke, 1995), 55–69, which emphasizes both the adaptability and the traditionalism of Sforza's approach, rooted in the assumptions of the nineteenth century.
84. Ibid., 161.
85. See P. P. D'Attore, 'Americanism and Anti-Americanism in Italy', in Stirk and Willis (eds), *Shaping Postwar Europe*, 43–52. J. E. Miller, *The United States and Italy, 1940–1950* (Chapel Hill, 1986).
86. For the case against British isolation in Europe, see N. P. Ludlow, 'Paying the Price of Victory? Postwar Britain and the Ideas of National Independence', in D. Geppert (ed.), *Postwar Challenge*, 259–72.
87. V. R. Rothwell, *Britain and the Cold War, 1941–1947* (London, 1982), 435.
88. *The Times*, 5 January 1948, cited in G. Warner, 'Britain and Europe in 1948: The View from the Cabinet', in J. Becker and F. Knipping (eds), *Power in Europe?*, 34.
89. E. Bevin to P. Ramadier, 22 September 1947, ibid., 35.
90. Ibid.
91. On British anxiety about such withdrawal, see Deighton, *The Impossible Peace*; also, W. C. Cromwell, 'The Marshall Plan, Britain and the Cold War', *Review of International Studies*, 8 (1982), 233–49.
92. J. Baylis, *The Diplomacy of Pragmatism: Britain and the Formation of NATO, 1942–1949* (Basingstoke, 1993).
93. Cabinet Economic Policy Committee, 7 November 1947, Warner, 'Britain and Europe', in J. Becker and F. Knipping (eds), *Power in Europe?*, 36. Also, M. J. Hogan, *The Marshall Plan, Britain and the Reconstruction of Western Europe, 1947–1952* (Cambridge, 1987).
94. A paper on 'The Middle East' presented to the Cabinet in April 1949, cited in A. Adamthwaite, 'Britain and the World, 1945–1949: The View from the Foreign Office', in J. Becker and F. Knipping (eds), *Power in Europe?*, 19.
95. G. Warner, 'Britain and Europe', ibid., 43.
96. J. L. Gaddis, *The Long Peace: Inquiries into the History of the Cold War* (Oxford, 1987).
97. F. Scheid Raine, 'The Iranian Crisis of 1946 and the Origins of the Cold War', M. P. Leffler and D. S. Painter (eds), *The Origins of the Cold War*, 2nd edn (London, 2005), 93–111.
98. M. J. Sherwin, 'The Atomic Bomb and the Origins of the Cold War', in M. P. Leffler and D. S. Painter (eds), *The Origins of the Cold War*, 2nd edn (London, 2005), 58–71.
99. M. Trachtenberg, 'France and NATO, 1949–1991', *Journal of Transatlantic Studies*, 9 (2011), 184–94.
100. Ibid., 184.
101. Bear F. Braumoeller, 'The Myth of American Isolationism', *Foreign Policy Analysis*, 6 (2010), 349, challenges the notion, but accepts that 'isolationists played a role in the politics of the era' (1920s and 1930s). See also E. A. Nordlinger, Isolationism Reconfigured (Princeton, NJ, 1995); J. Dumbrell, 'Varieties of Post-Cold War American Isolationism', *Government and Opposition*, 24 (1999), 24–43; D. H. Dunn, 'Isolationism Revisited: Seven Persistent Myths in the Contemporary American Foreign Policy Debate', *Review of International Studies*, 31 (2005), 237–61.
102. Orwell referred to 'Eurasia', 'East Asia', and 'Oceania', fighting in Africa and India. The idea of Eurasia has a long history in Russia and the USSR: S. Wiederkehr, *Die eurasische Bewegung. Wissenschaft und Politik in russischen Emigration der Zwischenkriegszeit und im postsowjetischen Russland* (Cologne, 2007).
103. Memo by G. F. Kennan, 28 February 1948, in US Department of State (ed.), *Foreign Relations of the United States, 1948* (Washington DC, 1976), vol. 1, 509–29.
104. Ibid., 510.
105. Ibid., 528; 'The Sources of Soviet Conduct', *Foreign Affairs*, July 1947.

80 EUROPEAN INTEGRATION SINCE THE 1920S

106. Z. Karabell, *Architects of Intervention: The United States, the Third World and the Cold War, 1946–1962* (Baton Rouge, 1999); G. Kolko, *Confronting the Third World: United States Foreign Policy, 1945–1980* (New York, 1988).
107. O. A. Westad, *The Global Cold War: Third World Interventions and the Making of Our Times* (Cambridge, 2005), 39–72.
108. Ibid., 68.
109. M. Harrison, 'Coercion, Compliance and the Collapse of the Soviet Command Economy', *Economic History Review*, 55 (2002), 397–433; C. S. Maier, *Dissolution: The Crisis of Communism and the End of East Germany* (Princeton, NJ, 1997); J. Kopstein, *The Politics of Economic Decline in East Germany, 1945–1989* (Chapel Hill, NC, 2000).
110. For a discussion, see M. Kramer, 'Ideology and the Cold War', *Review of International Studies*, 25 (1999), 539–76; N. Gould-Davies, 'Rethinking the Role of Ideology in International Politics during the Cold War', *Journal of Cold War Studies*, 1 (1999), 90–109.
111. G. F. Kennan, 'Long Telegram', 22 February 1946, in US Department of State (ed.), *Foreign Relations of the United States, 1946* (Washington, DC., 1969), vol. 6, 696–709.
112. See R. Jervis, 'Identity and the Cold War', in M. Leffler and O. A. Westad (eds), *The Cambridge History of the Cold War: Crises and Détente* (Cambridge, 2010), vol. 2, 22–43.
113. M. McGwire, 'National Security and Soviet Foreign Policy', in M. P. Leffler and D. S. Painter (eds), *Origins of the Cold War*, 2nd edn (London, 2005), 53–76.
114. R. B. Levering, V. O. Pechatnov, V. Botzenhart-Viehe and C. E. Edmondson (eds), *Debating the Origins of the Cold War: American and Russian Perspectives* (Lanham, MD, 2001), 85–178.
115. V. Zubok and C. Pleshakov, *Inside the Kremlin's Cold War* (Cambridge, MA, 1996); V. Mastny, *The Cold War and Soviet Insecurity: The Stalin Years* (Oxford, 1996).
116. V. Mastny, 'The Sources of Soviet Conduct', *Foreign Affairs*, July 1947.
117. G. F. Kennan, 'Long Telegram', 22 February 1946, in US Department of State (ed.), *Foreign Relations of the United States, 1946* (Washington, DC., 1969), vol. 6, 696–709.
118. Historians have been keen to point out that even French policy-makers were realistic in this period: W. I. Hitchcock, *France Restored: Cold War Diplomacy and the Quest for Leadership in Europe, 1944–1954* (Chapel Hill, NC, 1998); D. Hüser, *Frankreichs 'doppelte Deutschlandpolitik'* (Berlin, 1996); C. Buffet, *Mourir pour Berlin: La France et l'Allemagne* (Paris, 1991).
119. J. Kofman, 'Failed Illusions: Moscow, Washington, Budapest and the 1956 Hungarian Revolt', *Polish Quarterly of International Affairs*, 15 (2006), 109–10; M. B. Smith, 'Peaceful Coexistence at All Costs: Cold War Exchanges between Britain and the Soviet Union in 1956', *Cold War History*, 12 (2012), 537–58.
120. P.-H. Spaak, *The Continuing Battle: Memoirs of a European* (Boston, MA, 1971), 402.
121. A. Adamthwaite, 'Overstretched and Overstrung: Eden, the Foreign Office and the Making of Policy', and G. Warner, 'Aspects of the Suez Crisis', in E. Di Nolfo (ed.), *Power in Europe? Great Britain, France, Germany and Italy and the Origins of the EEC, 1952–1957* (Berlin, 1992), vol. 2, 19–65.
122. A. Adamthwaite, 'Britain and the World, 1945–1949': The View from the Foreign Office', in J. Becker and F. Knipping (eds), *Power in Europe? Great Britain, France, Italy and Germany in a Postwar World, 1945–1950* (Berlin, 1986), vol. 1, 9–26.
123. Quoted ibid., 12.
124. Ibid., 14.
125. Ibid., 15.
126. Ibid., 17.
127. J. Young, *France, the Cold War and the Western Alliance, 1945–1949: French Foreign Policy and Post-War Europe* (Leicester, 1990); G. de Carmoy, *The Foreign Policies of France, 1944–1968* (Chicago, 1970); M. Harrison, *The Reluctant Ally: France and Atlantic Security* (Baltimore, 1981).
128. J. Chauvel to H. Bonnet, 15 April 1948, in R. Girault, 'The French Decision-Makers and Their Perception of French Power in 1948', in J. Becker and F. Knipping (eds), *Power in Europe?*, vol. 1, 48.
129. T. Smith, 'The French Colonial Consensus and People's War, 1946–58', *Journal of Contemporary History*, 9 (1974), 217–47; A. Clayton, *The French Wars of Decolonization* (London, 2014). Such preoccupations remained largely national, but there was also a European dimension to them: see especially Peo Hansen and Stefan Jonsson, *Eurafrica: The Untold History of European Integration and Colonialism* (London: Bloomsbury, 2014).
130. R. Girault, 'Decision-Makers, Decisions and French Power', in E. Di Nolfo (ed.), *Power in Europe?*, 78–9. J. McDougall, 'The Impossible Republic: The Reconquest of Algeria and the Decolonization of France, 1945–1962', *Journal of Modern History*, 89 (2017), 772–811.

131. More recent estimates range between 300,000 and 500,000. J. McDougall, *A History of Algeria* (Cambridge, 2017), 232–3; M. Thomas, *Fight or Flight: Britain, France and Their Roads from Empire* (Oxford, 2014), 289; M. Lazreg, *Torture and the Twilight of Empire: From Algiers to Baghdad* (Princeton, NJ, 2008), 53–4. Older estimates go up to three-quarters of a million deaths: M. S. Alexander and J. F. V. Keiger, *France and the Algerian War, 1954–1962: Strategy, Operations and Diplomacy* (London, 2002); M. S. Alexander and J. F. V. Keiger (eds), *The Algerian War and the French Army, 1954–1962: Experience, Image, Testimony* (Basingstoke, 2002); I. M. Wall, *France, the United States and the Algerian War* (Berkeley, CA, 2001); P. Dine, *Images of the Algerian War: French Fiction and Film, 1954–1992* (Oxford, 1994).
132. Although noting the unwillingness of *Le Monde* to report on the realities of the conflict, M. Khane, '*Le Monde's* Coverage of the Army and Civil Liberties during the Algerian War, 1954–58'; M. S. Alexander and J. F. V. Keiger (eds), *The Algerian War and the French Army, 1954–1962*, in 191, note 49, notes left-wing publications were more forthright.
133. W. Brandt, *Erinnerungen*, 254.
134. K. Adenauer to W. Sollmann, 16 March 1946, quoted in M. Overesch, 'Senior West German Politicians and Their Perception of the German Situation in Europe, 1945–1949', in J. Becker and F. Knipping (eds), *Power in Europe?*, vol. 1, 126.
135. Ibid.
136. K. Adenauer to U. Noack, 8 Apr. 1946, quoted in M. Overesch, 'Senior West German Politicians and Their Perception of the German Situation in Europe, 1945–1949', in J. Becker and F. Knipping (eds), *Power in Europe?*, vol. 1, 126.
137. K. Adenauer to H. Müller, 5 November 1946, quoted ibid.
138. See, especially, W. F. Hanrieder, *Germany, America, Europe: Forty Years of German Foreign Policy* (New Haven, CT, 1989), 27–106, 329–54.
139. Quoted in R. J. Ranieri, *The Ambivalent Alliance: Konrad Adenauer, the CDU/CSU and the West, 1949–1966* (New York, 2003), 29.
140. J. L. Richardson, *Germany and the Atlantic Alliance: The Interaction of Strategy and Politics* (Cambridge, CT., 1966), 11–12, 340–5.
141. See, for instance, David Calleo's *Europe's Future: The Grand Alternatives* (New York, 1965), which suggested that the status quo in Europe was more precarious than most imagined.
142. D. Calleo, *Rethinking Europe's Future* (Princeton, NJ, 2001), 25; see also D. Calleo, *The German Problem Reconsidered: Germany and the World Order, 1870 to the Present* (Cambridge, 1978).
143. D. Calleo, *Rethinking Europe's Future*, 25
144. Ibid., 18, 23.
145. Ibid., 4.
146. Ibid., 26. Bevin quoted in D. Reynolds (ed.), *The Origins of the Cold War in Europe*, 32.
147. D. Calleo, *Rethinking Europe's Future*, 27.
148. Ibid., 26.
149. George C. Marshall quoted in T. Judt, *Grand Illusion*, 14.
150. Ibid.
151. Ibid., 12, 16.
152. Ibid.; J. Delors, *La France par l'Europe* (Paris, 1988).
153. T. Judt, *Grand Illusion*, 15.
154. This does not mean that shifts in domestic politics had the potential to derail foreign-policy projects, as they had in the early 1930s. Kurt Schumacher not only was less willing to postpone the question of unification; he was also, to the astonishment of SPD colleagues, unwilling to give up large-scale nationalizations and state intervention in the economy: P. Merseburger, *Der Schwierige Deutsche. Kurt Schumacher* (Stuttgart, 1995), 401.
155. R. F. Bunn, *German Politics and the Spiegel Affair: A Case Study of the Bonn System* (Baton Rouge LA, 1968); D. Schoenbaum, *The Spiegel Affair* (Garden City, NY, 1968).
156. Brandt fell after his aide was exposed as an East German spy: E. Michels, *Guillaume, der Spion. Eine deutsch-deutsche Karriere* (Berlin, 2013).
157. J. Herf, *War by Other Means: Soviet Power, West German Resistance and the Battle of the Euromissiles* (New York, 1991), 113–63. There were also internal party reasons for the fall.
158. K. Larres, 'Churchill's "Iron Curtain" Speech in Context: The Attempt to Achieve a "Good Understanding on All Points" with Stalin's Soviet Union', *International History Review*, 40 (2018), 86–107; H. B. Ryan, 'A New Look at Churchill's "Iron Curtain" Speech', *Historical Journal*, 22 (1979), 895–920.
159. W. Churchill, 'Sinews of Peace' speech, 5 March 1946, National Archives, FO 371/51624.
160. Ibid.

82 EUROPEAN INTEGRATION SINCE THE 1920S

161. Ibid.
162. M. Wilke, *The Path to the Berlin Wall: Critical Stages in the History of Divided Germany* (New York, 2014).
163. Memorandum of a conversation between R. Nixon, H. Kissinger, and R. Haldeman, 28 May 1971, quoted in S. Kieninger, 'A Preponderance of Stability: Henry Kissinger's Concern over the Dynamics of *Ostpolitik*', *Journal of Transatlantic Studies*, 17 (2019), 51.
164. Ibid., 52.
165. M. H. Geyer, 'Der Kampf um nationale Repräsentation. Deutsch-deutsche Sportbeziehungen und die "Hallstein-Doktrin"', *Vierteljahreshefte für Zeitgeschichte*, 44 (1996), 55–86; K. Schiller and C. Young, *The 1972 Munich Olympics and the Making of Modern Germany* (Berkeley, CA, 2010), 157–86; L. Hillaker, 'Representing a "Better Germany": Competing Images of State and Society in the Early Cultural Diplomacy of the FRG and GDR', *Central European History*, 53 (2020), 372–92.
166. W. G. Gray, *Germany's Cold War: The Global Campaign to Isolate East Germany, 1949–1969* (Chapel Hill, NC, 2003).
167. J. Dülffer, '"No More Potsdam!" Konrad Adenauer's Nightmare and the Basis of His International Orientation', *German Politics and Society*, 25 (2007), 19–42.
168. H. A. Winkler, 'Rebuilding of a Nation: The Germans before and after Unification', *Daedalus*, 123 (1994), 109.
169. K. Adenauer to H. Weitz, 31 October 1945, translated in J. Dülffer, '"No More Potsdam!" Konrad Adenauer's Nightmare and the Basis of His International Orientation', *German Politics and Society*, 25 (2007), 21.
170. Ibid.
171. K. Sainsbury, *Churchill and Roosevelt at War: The War They Fought and the Peace They Hoped to Make* (Basingstoke, 1994), 152.
172. On its apocryphal nature, see F. Bozo, 'La France face à l'unification allemande', in J.-P. Cahn and U. Pfeil (eds), *Allemagne, 1974–1990. De l'Ostpolitik à l'unification* (Villeneuve d'Ascq, 2009), 285–301. The quotation was recycled by Walter Isaacson, 'Is One Germany Better than Two?', *Time*, 20 November 1989, and was used by Giulio Andreotti, among others: D. Cuccia, *There Are Two German States and Two Must Remain? Italy and the Long Path from the German Question to Reunification* (Hildesheim, 2019), 138.
173. H. Schmidt quoted in T. Garton Ash, *In Europe's Name: Germany and the Divided Continent* (London, 1993), 23. Even Gerhard Schröder, *Entscheidungen. Mein Leben in der Politik* (Hamburg, 2006), 328, still detected 'a certain, never fully banished, reserve vis-à-vis Germany in this Europe'.
174. A large public relations exercise was designed to show that Germans had changed and had become acceptable to the 'West': S. Wood, 'Das Deutschlandbild: National Image, Reputation and Interests in Post-War Germany', *Central European History*, 27 (2018), 651–73.
175. L. J. Edinger, *Kurt Schumacher*, 159–89. Willy Brandt, *Erinnerungen*, 271: 'With Adenauer it was "no experiments". The phrase reflected the need for peace of a people which was happy to leave the turmoil of the Nazi era and the war behind it.'
176. K. Jarausch, *After Hitler: Recivilizing Germans, 1945–1995*, 120–7; U. G. Poiger, *Jazz, Rock and Rebels: Cold War Politics and American Culture in a Divided Germany* (Berkeley, CA, 2000); H. Schissler, *The Miracle Years: A Cultural History of West Germany, 1949–1968* (Princeton, NJ, 2001); E. Carter, *How German Is She? Postwar West German Reconstruction and the Consuming Woman* (Ann Arbor, MI, 1997); V. R. Berghahn, 'The Debate on "Americanization" among Economic and Cultural Historians', *Cold War History*, 10 (2010), 107–30; V. R. Berghahn, *The Americanization of West German Industry, 1945–1973* (Cambridge, 1986); A. Doering-Manteuffel, *Wie westlich sind die Deutschen? Amerikanisierung und Westernisierung im 20. Jahrhundert* (Göttingen, 1999); H. Nehring, '"Westernization": A New Paradigm for Interpreting West European History in a Cold War Context', *Cold War History*, 4 (2004), 175–91.
177. K. H. Jarausch, and H. Siegrist (eds), *Amerikanisierung und Sowjetisierung in Deutschland, 1945–1970* (Frankfurt, 1997).
178. P. Major, *The Death of the KPD: Communism and Anti-Communism in West Germany, 1945–1956* (Oxford, 1998), 229–91.
179. G. Pridham, *Christian Democracy in Western Germany: The CDU/CSU in Government and Opposition, 1945–1976* (London, 1977).
180. K. H. Jarausch, *After Hitler*, 219: in 1979, 78 percent of West Germans polled thought that reunification was desirable, but 64 percent thought that the chances of it happening were minimal.

HARD POWER 83

181. E. Scheuch, *Wie deutsch sind die Deutschen?* (Bergisch-Gladbach, 1991), 201.
182. Timothy Garton Ash, *In Europe's Name*, 133–4, referring to the findings of the analyst of public opinion, Gebhard Schweigler.
183. D. Marsh, *The Germans* (London, 1989), 272–3.
184. Ibid. See also D. Schoenbaum and E. Pond, *The German Question and Other German Questions* (Basingstoke, 1996), 16–18.
185. D. Marsh, *The Germans*, 272–3, on Schmidt; A. J. McAdams, *Germany Divided: From the Wall to Reunification* (Princeton, NJ, 1993), 134, on Brandt. German intellectuals, on the whole, were even more certain: see Stephen Brockmann, *Literature and German Unification* (Cambridge, 2006), 46–7, on Peter Schneider, who became one of the most prominent German commentators on the unification question on American media.
186. There is an expanding literature on the degree to which this was the case. Angela Romano, 'Pan-Europe: A Continental Space for Cooperation(s)', in A. Romano and F. Romero (eds), *European Socialist Regimes' Fateful Engagement with the West: National Strategies in the Long 1970s* (London, 2021), 31, 43, has argued recently that 'studies on détente have revealed that European governments on the one hand and the superpowers on the other held different views on its meaning, scope and aim', and that several historians, since the early 2000s, 'have successfully challenged and qualified the long-lived understanding of Cold War Europe as a space of confrontation or separation'. The question concerns the degree and significance of such space. Few historians would disagree that a divergence between European governments and US administrations did occur, but its relevance is disputed, when gauged against the broader parameters and constraints of the Cold War. See also W. Loth, *Overcoming the Cold War: A History of Détente* (Basingstoke, 2002); W. Loth and G.-H. Soutou (eds), *The Making of Détente: Eastern and Western Europe in the Cold War, 1965–1975* (London, 2008); J. Hanhimäki, 'Détente in Europe, 1969–1975', in M. Leffler and O. A. Westad (eds), *The Cambridge History of the Cold War* (Cambridge, 2010), vol. 2, 198–218.
187. O. Croci, 'Not a Zero-Sum Game: Atlanticism and Europeanism in Italian Foreign Policy', *International Spectator*, 43 (2008), 137–55.
188. This shift created some space for European institutions to play a role: see A. Romano, *From Détente in Europe to European Détente: How the West Shaped the Helsinki CSCE* (Brussels, 2009). That role remained secondary to the part played by the principal member states, however. Angela Romano, 'Détente, Entente or Linkage? The Helsinki Conference on Security and Cooperation in Europe in US Relations with the Soviet Union', *Diplomatic History*, 33 (2009), 716, gives credence to this overarching balance of powers, despite highlighting the EC's role in her monograph. The shifts envisaged by European governments were long-term and, arguably, remained incomplete: 'First the Western European governments considered the CSCE to be a useful tool of their détente policy, whereas the United States did not. Secondly, Western European governments looked at détente as an opportunity to change the political scenario in Europe. They aimed a promoting a loosening of bipolar restraints and at deepening the two blocs' mutual interdependence.'
189. C. Becker-Schaum, P. Gassert, M. Klimke, W. Mausbach, and M. Zepp (eds), *The Nuclear Crisis: The Arms Race, Cold War Anxiety and the German Peace Movement of the 1980s* (New York, 2016); T. Geiger and J. Hansen, 'Did Protest Matter? The Influence of the Peace Movement on the West German Government and the Social Democratic Party, 1977–1983', in E. Conze, M. Klimke, and J. Varon (eds), *Nuclear Threats, Nuclear Fear, and the Cold War of the 1980s* (New York 2017), 290–315; A. S. Tompkins, *Better Active than Radioactive! Anti-Nuclear Protest in 1970s France and West Germany* (Oxford, 2016).
190. J. Hanhimauki, *The Rise and Fall of Détente: American Foreign Policy and the Transformation of the Cold War* (Washington, DC 2013); F. Bozo, M.-P. Rey, B. Rother and N. P. Ludlow (eds), *Visions of the End of the Cold War in Europe, 1945–1990* (New York, 2012); O. Bange and P. Villaume (eds), *The Long Détente: Changing Concepts of Security and Cooperation in Europe, 1950s-1980s* (Budapest, 2017); L. Nuti, F. Bozo, M.-P. Rey, and B. Rother (eds), *The Euromissiles Crisis and the End of the Cold War* (Washington, DC, 2015).
191. G. J. Martin, *General de Gaulle's Cold War: Challenging American Hegemony, 1963–68* (New York, 2013), 123–70; G. J. Martin, ' "Grandeur et dépendances": The Dilemmas of Gaullist Foreign Policy, September 1967 to April 1968', in N. P. Ludlow (ed.), *European Integration and the Cold War: Ostpolitik—Westpolitik, 1965–1973* (London, 2007), 36–52. See also F. Gloriant, 'To Adapt to the Cold War Bipolar Order? Or to Challenge It? Macmillan and de Gaulle's Rift in the Face of the Second Berlin Crisis', *Cold War History*, 18 (2018), 465–83.
192. G. J. Martin, *General de Gaulle's Cold War*, 128.

84   EUROPEAN INTEGRATION SINCE THE 1920s

193. See especially M. S. Neiberg, *When France Fell: The Vichy Crisis and the Fate of the Anglo-American Alliance* (Cambridge, MA, 2021). British policy was complicated, torn between distaste for the Vichy regime and the need to avoid a conflict with it, leaving open the possibility of the French Empire and navy joining forces with the Allies: R. T. Thomas, *Britain and Vichy: The Dilemma of Anglo-French Relations, 1940–42* (London, 1979), 118–37.

194. G.-H. Soutou, 'The Linkage between European Integration and Détente: The Contrasting Approaches of de Gaulle and Pompidou, 1965–1974', in N. P. Ludlow (ed.), *European Integration and the Cold War*, 11–35.

195. R. F. Kuisel, 'Coca-Cola and the Cold War: The French Face Americanization, 1948–1953', *French Historical Studies*, 17 (1991), 96–116.

196. S. H. Barnes and R. Pierce, 'Public Opinion and Political Preferences in France and Italy', *Midwest Journal for Political Sciences*, 15 (1971), 648. M. Winock, 'U.S. Go Home. L'antiaméricanisme français', *L'Histoire*, 50 (1982), 7–20; E. Morse, *Foreign Policy and Interdependence in Gaullist France* (Princeton, NJ, 1973).

197. Quoted G. J. Martin, *General de Gaulle's Cold War*, 102, 117.

198. E. J. Mahan, *Kennedy, de Gaulle and Western Europe* (Basingstoke, 2002).

199. G. J. Martin, *General de Gaulle's Cold War*, 189.

200. G. Niedhart, '*Ostpolitik*: Transformation through Communication and the Quest for Peaceful Change', *Journal of Cold War Studies*, 18 (2016), 14–59; N. D. Cary, 'Reassessing Germany's Ostpolitik: From Détente to Refreeze', *Central European History*, 33 (2000), 235–62; N. D. Cary, 'Reassessing Germany's Ostpolitik: From Refreeze to Reunification', *Central European History*, 33 (2000), 369–90; J. v. Dannenberg, *The Foundations of Ostpolitik* (Oxford, 2008).

201. R. W. Jackling to FCO, 9 Apr. 1969, in G. Niedhart, '*Ostpolitik*: Transformation through Communication and the Quest for Peaceful Change', *Journal of Cold War Studies*, 18 (2016), 21.

202. W. Brandt note, 3 Jan. 1967, ibid., 22.

203. W. Brandt, *Erinnerungen*, 233.

204. On the origins of Brandt's stance, see W. Schmidt, 'Die Wurzeln der Entspannung. Der konzeptionelle Ursprung der Ost- und Deutschlandpolitik Willy Brandts in den fünfziger Jahren', *Vierteljahreshefte für Zeitgeschichte*, 51 (2003), 521–63; A. Hofmann, *The Emergence of Détente in Europe: Brandt, Kennedy and the Formation of Ostpolitik* (London, 2007); A. Daum, *Kennedy in Berlin* (Cambridge, 2008).

205. H. Alphand, diary entry, 22 October 1967, in G. J. Martin, *General de Gaulle's Cold War*, 159.

206. O. Bange and G. Niedhart (eds), *Helsinki 1975 and the Transformation of Europe* (New York, 2008). This is not to argue that Washington's position did not shift as a result of German initiatives and European support: see Stephan Kieninger, 'Transformation or Status Quo: The Conflict of Stratagems in Washington over the Meaning and Purpose of the CSCE and MBFR, 1969–1973', ibid., 67–82. See also S. Kieninger, *Dynamic Détente: The United States and Europe, 1964–1975* (Lanham, MD, 2016); S. Kieninger, 'A Preponderance of Stability: Henry Kissinger's Concern over the Dynamics of *Ostpolitik*', *Journal of Transatlantic Studies*, 17 (2019), 42–60.

207. Washington, accordingly, did not try to block *Ostpolitik*: G. Niedhart, 'U.S. Détente and West German *Ostpolitik*: Parallels and Frictions', in M. Schulz and T. A. Schwartz (eds), *The Strained Alliance: U.S.-European Relations from Nixon to Carter* (Cambridge, 2010), 23–44.

208. R. Nixon to H. Kissinger, 29 May 1971, and M. J. Hillenbrand diary, 30 December 1972, in S. Kieninger, 'A Preponderance of Stability: Henry Kissinger's Concern over the Dynamics of *Ostpolitik*', *Journal of Transatlantic Studies*, 17 (2019), 50.

209. Quoted in C. Domnitz, 'Overcoming Bloc Division from Below: Jiří Hájek and the CSCE Appeal of Charter 77', in F. Bozo, M.-P. Rey, B. Rother and N. P. Ludlow (eds), *Visions of the End of the Cold War in Europe*, 179.

210. Ibid.

211. A. Paczkowski, *Revolution and Counterrevolution in Poland, 1980–1989: Solidarity, Martial Law and the End of Communism in Europe* (Rochester, NY, 2015), 19. Jadwiga Staniszkis, *Poland's Self-Limiting Revolution* (Princeton, NJ, 1984), used the term 'self-limiting', which has been widely adopted.

212. C. Domnitz, 'Overcoming Bloc Division from Below: Jiří Hájek and the CSCE Appeal of Charter 77', in F. Bozo, M.-P. Rey, B. Rother and N. P. Ludlow (eds), *Visions of the End of the Cold War in Europe*, 179. On Dubček, see K. Williams, *The Prague Spring and Its Aftermath: Czechoslovak Politics, 1968–1970* (Cambridge, 1997), 3.

213. A. Paczkowski, *Revolution and Counterrevolution in Poland*, 139–54.

214. On economic failure in Czechoslovakia, see ibid., 20–5.

215. A. Paczkowski, *Revolution and Counterrevolution in Poland*, 17.
216. Quoted in K. Williams, *The Prague Spring and Its Aftermath*, 13. Mary Heimann, 'The Scheming Apparatchik of the Prague Spring', *Europe-Asia Studies*, 60 (2008), 1717–34, presents Dubček, convincingly, as an insider.
217. Given that there were no Soviet army units in Czechoslovakia, the First Secretary 'thought that we were much freer than we were', as he put it later: K. Williams, *The Prague Spring and Its Aftermath*, 11. On the rationale behind the Soviet stance, see M. Kramer, 'The Kremlin, the Prague Spring and the Brezhnev Doctrine', in V. Tismaneanu (ed.), *Promises of 1968: Crisis, Illusion and Utopia* (Budapest, 2011), 285–370.
218. M. J. Ouimet, *The Rise and Fall of the Brezhnev Doctrine in Soviet Foreign Policy* (Chapel Hill, NC, 2003).
219. R. Wegs and R. Ladrech, *Europe since 1945*, 65, 206–8. The figures for the Soviet bloc are unreliable. The State Department estimated that Soviet GNP per capita was 41 per cent of the US level by 1987.
220. G. R. Chafetz, *Gorbachev, Reform and the Brezhnev Doctrine: Soviet Policy toward Eastern Europe, 1985–1990* (Westport, CT, 1993).
221. See Chapters 2 and 7.
222. J. M. Mushaben, *From Post-War to Post-Wall Generations: Changing Attitudes towards the National Question and NATO in the Federal Republic of Germany* (Boulder, CO, 1998).
223. T. Banchoff, *The German Problem Transformed: Institutions, Politics and Foreign Policy, 1945–1995* (Ann Arbor, MI, 1999).
224. T. W. Adorno, 'The Culture Industry Reconsidered' (1963), *New German Critique*, 6 (1975), 12–19; D. Cook, *The Culture Industry Revisited: Theodor W. Adorno on Mass Culture* (New York, 1996).
225. See F. Biess, *German Angst: Fear and Democracy in the Federal Republic of Germany* (Oxford, 2020), 95–129, 290–330; E. Conze, M. Klimke, and J. Varon (eds), *Nuclear Threats, Nuclear Fear, and the Cold War of the 1980s* (New York 2017).
226. R. L. Beisner, *Dean Acheson: A Life in the Cold War* (Oxford, 2009), 70.
227. P. Nash, 'Eisenhower, Nuclear Weapons and Arms Control', in C. J. Pach (ed.), *A Companion to Dwight Eisenhower* (New York, 2017), 329.
228. This sense of the situation on the part of US planners was not continuous or constant, but cumulative. In 1970, Kissinger was convinced that 'American weight and leadership were still needed' in Europe 'because for all their economic progress the Europeans plainly had not developed the cohesion, the internal stability, or the will to match the power of the Soviet Union': H. Kissinger, *The White House Years* (Boston, 1979), 382.
229. *New York Times*, 2 September 1979.
230. F. J. Strauß, *The Grand Design: A European Solution to German Reunification* (New York, 1966), 50.
231. Quoted in W. F. Hanrieder, *Germany, America, Europe*, 77–8.
232. Ibid., 46–9.
233. 'Ein Gesamtkonzept, aber wie', *Die Zeit*, 3 March 1989.
234. 'If the Missiles Go, Peace May Stay', *New York Times*, 29 April. 1987.
235. J. Dülffer, '"No More Potsdam!" Konrad Adenauer's Nightmare and the Basis of his International Orientation', *German Politics and Society*, 25 (2007), 19–42.
236. Quoted in W. F. Hanrieder, *West German Foreign Policy, 1949–1963: International Pressure and Domestic Response* (Palo Alto, 1967), 174. See also B. Heuser and K. Stoddart, 'Difficult Europeans: NATO and Tactical/Non-strategic Nuclear Weapons in the Cold War', *Diplomacy and Statecraft*, 28 (2017), 454–76.
237. 'A Talk with Helmut Schmidt', *New York Times Magazine*, 16 September 1984.
238. D. C. Large, *Germans to the Front: West German Rearmament in the Adenauer Era* (Chapel Hill, NC, 1996).
239. M. Creswell and M. Trachtenberg, 'France and the German Question, 1945–1955', *Journal of Cold War Studies*, 5 (2003), 5–28, make this point on the basis of Dulles's pronouncements.
240. S. Hoffmann, 'De Gaulle, Europe and the Atlantic Alliance', *International Organization*, 18 (1964), 14.
241. H. Kohl, *Erinnerungen 1930–1982* (Munich, 2004), vol. 1, 181, claimed that this 'dispute' was 'completely incomprehensible' and was 'artificial', dreamt up by competing political groups. He also admitted, however, that 'This nonsense weighed us down practically throughout Erhard's period of office.'
242. A. Peyrefitte, *C'était de Gaulle* (Paris, 1997), vol. 2, 270.

243. K. Adenauer, *Memoirs, 1945–53* (Chicago, 1966), 79.
244. *Time*, 4 January 1971.
245. W. Schmidt, 'A Prophet Unheard: Willy Brandt's North-South Policy and Its Reception in the United States' and A. M. Fonseca, 'From the Iberian Peninsula to Latin America: The Socialist International's Initiatives in the First Years of Brandt's Presidency', in B. Rother and K. Larres (eds), *Willy Brandt and International Relations: Europe, the USA and Latin America, 1974–1992* (London, 2019), 67–84, 179–94.
246. W. Brandt, *My Life in Politics* (London, 1992), 322.
247. J. Habermas, *Staatsbürgerschaft und nationale Identität*, 25.
248. K. Adenauer, 20 September 1949, in H. Haftendoorn, *Coming of Age: German Foreign Policy since 1945* (Lanham, MD, 2006), 17.
249. H. Zimmermann, *Money and Security: Troops, Monetary Policy and West Germany's Relations with the United States and Britain, 1950–1971* (Cambridge, 2013), 93.
250. Ibid., 11–44, 87–120.
251. J. G. Hershberg, '"Explosion in the Offing": German Rearmament and American Diplomacy, 1953–1955', *Diplomatic History*, 16 (1992), 512, states that 'Recently declassified archival sources...show that there was considerable tension in U.S.–West German relations during 1953 and 1954, in particular over the question of German rearmament, and some uncertainty in Germany about the contours and aims of American Cold War strategy'. Ralph Dietl, 'In Defence of the West: General Lauris Norstad, NATO Nuclear Forces and Transatlantic Relations, 1956–1963', *Diplomacy and Statecraft*, 17 (2006), 347–92, shows how France struggled to act on its own, against the United States and UK. The FRG did not figure as an independent actor.
252. H. Zimmermann, *Money and Security*, 93.
253. T. Garton Ash, *In Europe's Name*, 21: 'For Adenauer, the enterprise of building Europe clearly had two sides. On the one hand, the Germans, whose capacity to steer their own course he sometimes doubted, were to be bound into a larger European community, to which they might yield some of the traditional authority and powers of a nation-state. On the other hand, participation in a (West) European community was a way for (part of) Germany to recover such authority and powers.'
254. T. W. Maulucci, *Adenauer's Foreign Office: West German Diplomacy in the Shadow of the Third Reich* (Ithaca, NY, 2012).
255. Ibid.—section on Europe.
256. For Garton Ash, *In Europe's Name*, 16–27, the FRG's role came to seem natural because of the conflation of the German and European 'questions'.
257. Ibid., 19. Kohl argues in his memoirs that 'I comprehend the relationship of Germany and Europe in the same as the family and society', which stand 'in an indivisible relationship of exchange and mutual influence': 'Germany without Europe can just as little be understood as Europe without Germany.' H. Kohl, *Erinnerungen 1982–1990* (Munich, 2005), vol. 2, 377. Hans-Dietrich Genscher, *Erinnerungen* (Berlin, 1995), 225, continued to talk the opportunity which Europe offered to a country such as Germany—for example, in 1974, as the FRG took over the presidency for six months, which he took as a 'good omen, and as a symbol, too. European union was, in my view, the particular task of my generation which had experienced, suffered and survived the Second World War in a conscious state. To have Germany as a member of the community of European democracies—that was our hope and longing!'
258. P. M. Kennedy, *The Rise and Fall of the Great Powers: Economic Change and Military Conflict from 1500* (London, 1989), 369.
259. 'Economic Policies towards Germany', annexe to J. Dunn to J. McCloy, 23 January 1945, in J. C. Van Hook, *Rebuilding Germany: The Creation of the Social Market Economy, 1945–1957* (Cambridge, 2004), 31. See also T. A. Schwartz, *America's Germany: John J. McCloy and the Federal Republic of Germany* (Cambridge, MA, 1991).
260. J. Troutbeck, 'The German Settlement', 23 January 1945, in J. C. Van Hook, *Rebuilding Germany*, 32.
261. A. Boltho (ed.), *The European Economy: Growth and Crisis* (Oxford, 1982), 10. See also European Commission, *European Economy* 46, December 1990.
262. Economist, *Europe's Economies: The Structure and Management of Europe's Ten Largest Economies* (London, 1978), 3. See L. Lindlar and C.-L. Holtfrerich, 'Geography, Exchange Rates and Trade Structures: Germany's Export Performance since the 1950s', *European Review of Economic History*, 1 (1997), 217–46.

HARD POWER   87

263. *New York Times* and *Wall Street Journal* in July 1978, quoted in K. Spohr, *The Global Chancellor: Helmut Schmidt and the Reshaping of the International Order* (Cambridge, 2016), 29.
264. H. Schmidt, 'Guiding Thoughts on Our Foreign Policy', 17 January 1975, ibid., 17–18.
265. OECD Outlook 64 (1998), 154.
266. M. Balfour, *Germany: The Tides of Power* (London, 1992), 257.
267. M. Haeussler, 'A "Cold War European"? Helmut Schmidt and European Integration, c. 1945–1982', *Cold War History*, 15 (2016), 427–47.
268. *Der Spiegel*, 6 January 1975.
269. Ibid.
270. Ibid.
271. Ibid.
272. L. Kettenacker, *Germany 1989: In the Aftermath of the Cold War* (London, 2009), 111.
273. H. Schmidt, 'Einer unserer Brüder', *Die Zeit*, 24 July 1987.
274. Ibid.
275. *Daily Telegraph*, 25 October 1989.
276. W. Weidenfeld, *Außenpolitik für die Deusche Einheit. Die Entscheidungsjahre 1989/90* (Stuttgart, 1998), 131–3 on Thatcher, 153–8 on Mitterrand; R. Biermann, *Zwischen Kreml und Kanzleramt. Wie Moskau mit der deutschen Einheit rang* (Paderborn, 1997), 352, and H. Adomeit, *Imperial Overstretch: Germany in Soviet Policy from Stalin to Gorbachev* (Baden-Baden, 1998), 459–60, on the Soviet view of Mitterrand's actions.
277. V. Sebestyen, *Revolution 1989: The Fall of the Soviet Empire* (New York, 2009), 352.
278. *New York Times*, 26 October 1989.
279. V. Gransow and K. Jarausch (eds), *Die Deutsche Vereinigung: Dokumente zu Bürgerbewegung, Annäherung und Beitritt* (Cologne, 1991), 101–4.
280. For an excellent summary, see K. Spohr, 'German Unification: Between Official History, Academic Scholarship and Political Memoirs', *Historical Journal*, 43 (2000), 860–88.
281. K. Spohr, 'Precluded or Precedent-Setting? The "NATO Enlargement Question" in the Triangular Bonn-Washington-Moscow Diplomacy of 1990–1991', *Journal of Cold War Studies*, 14 (2012), 4–54; K. Spohr, 'Germany, America and the Shaping of Post-Cold War Europe: A Story of German International Emancipation through Political Unification, 1989–90', *Cold War History*, 15 (2015), 221–43.
282. P. Zelikow and C. Rice, *Germany Unified and Europe Transformed: A Study in Statecraft* (Cambridge, MA, 1997), 122–3; W. Weidenfeld, *Außenpolitik für die Deusche Einheit*, 126–9.
283. H.Teltschik memo to H. Kohl, 30 November 1989, and talk between H. Kohl and G. Bush, 3 December 1989, in Bundesministerium des Inneren unter Mitwirkung des Bundesarchivs (ed.), *Deutsche Einheit: Sonderedition aus den Akten des Bundeskanzleramtes 1989/90* (Munich, 1998), 574, 600.
284. Ibid., 603.
285. Ibid., 574–1367. H.-D. Genscher and the Auswärtiges Amt tended to concentrate on Moscow, leaving US relations to the Chancellery: see H.-D. Genscher, *Erinnerungen* (Berlin, 1995); H. Teltschik, *329 Tage. Innenansichten der Einigung* (Berlin, 1993).
286. Talk between H. Kohl and M. Gorbachev, 10 February 1990, Bundesministerium des Inneren unter Mitwirkung des Bundesarchivs (ed.), *Deutsche Einheit*, 801.
287. G. Bush to H. Kohl, 4 June 1990, ibid., 1178–80.
288. Talk between H. Kohl and G. Bush, 24 February 1990, ibid., 860.
289. Ibid., 861.
290. Ibid.
291. P. Hartmann memo, 29 January 1990, ibid., 727.
292. M. Thatcher, *The Downing Street Years* (London, 1993), 789–99.
293. H. Teltschik to H. Kohl, 30 November 1989, Bundesministerium des Inneren unter Mitwirkung des Bundesarchivs (ed.), *Deutsche Einheit*, 575.
294. Talk between H. Kohl and G. Bush, 3 December 1989, ibid., 603.
295. Ibid., 602.
296. F. Bozo, 'Mitterrand's France, the End of the Cold War and German Unification: A Reappraisal', *Cold War History*, 7 (2007), 455–78, has done much, on the basis of his investigation of archival material in France, to dispel the myth that Mitterrand was opposed to unification, but he does not prove that the President was not worried by events and sought to slow down unification.
297. W. Weidenfeld, *Außenpolitik für die Deusche Einheit*, 156–7.

88 EUROPEAN INTEGRATION SINCE THE 1920s

298. Meeting of H. Kohl and F. Mitterrand, 9 December 1989, Bundesministerium des Inneren unter Mitwirkung des Bundesarchivs (ed.), *Deutsche Einheit*, 630.
299. Ibid.
300. Talk between H. Kohl and F. Mitterrand, 4 January 1990, ibid., 682–90.
301. Talk between H. Kohl and G. Bush, 3 December 1989, ibid., 602.
302. Ibid., 603.
303. H. Kohl to F. Mitterrand, March 1984, quoted in P. Short, *Mitterrand*, 383.

2
Soft Power

The German question, although still technically open in 1989–90, did not escalate as some commentators predicted, not least because the European Community—and the North Atlantic alliance—had become what Karl Deutsch, in 1957, had termed a 'security community'.[1] Although the political scientist conceded that pluralism, amalgamation, and integration overlapped, with leaders often using broader symbols such as 'union' to cover the different possibilities, he saw Western Europe as a 'pluralistic security community', retaining the legal independence of separate governments, contrasting with the United States as an 'amalgamated security community', having seen the 'formal merger of two or more previously independent units into a single larger unit, with some type of common government'.[2] Despite the existence of such governments, 'the achievement of a security community would involve something like the crossing of a threshold, from a situation where war between the political units concerned appeared possible and was being prepared for, to another situation where it was neither', when the community could be considered 'integrated'.[3]

The sense of 'community that is relevant for integration', Deutsch continues, 'turned out to be rather a matter of mutual sympathy and loyalties; of "we-feeling", trust and mutual consideration; of partial identification in terms of self-images and interests; of mutually successful predictions of behaviour, and of cooperative action in accordance with it—in short a matter of a perpetual dynamic process of mutual attention, communication, perception of needs and responsiveness in the process of decision-making', guaranteeing 'peaceful change'.[4] A 'sense of community' and 'integrative behaviour' were the result of social learning 'in the face of background conditions which change only slowly, so that they appear at any moment as something given—as political, economic, social or psychological facts that must be taken for granted for the purposes of short-range politics'.[5] The apparent fixity of conditions depended on the interplay of background conditions with moving political events, with 'larger, stronger, more politically, administratively, economically and educationally advanced political units' forming 'the cores of strength around which in most cases the integrative process developed'.[6] In pluralistic security communities, states could be 'of markedly unequal power, but their existence always implied acceptance by both parties of a political situation between them which neither side expected to change by force'.[7] As long as members behaved predictably, shared 'major values relevant to political decision-making', communicated with each other regularly, possessed

---

European Integration since the 1920s: Security, Identity, and Cooperation. Mark Hewitson, Oxford University Press.
© Mark Hewitson 2024. DOI: 10.1093/oso/9780198915942.003.0003

90   EUROPEAN INTEGRATION SINCE THE 1920s

'a great many established political habits and functioning political institutions', states could co-exist in peace and security.[8] Few of these conditions seemed to obtain in Europe during the late 1940s, with the most powerful states—Germany, France, the United Kingdom, and Italy—having the longest and most destructive histories of violence.

According to Ole Waever, who adapts Deutsch's model, Western Europe became a security community in the post-war era, not by establishing common security structures or institutions, as contemporary theorists expected, 'but primarily through a process of "desecuritization", a progressive marginalization of mutual security concerns in favour of other issues'.[9] Although Monnet looked back in his memoirs on security as one of the main reasons for the founding of the European Communities, this objective only became relevant over the longer term. 'Twenty-five years ago, the urge to have done with our violent past left us no choice but to advance towards a common goal,' he wrote in 1976: 'What was decided on then is still just as vital; and now it is part of the everyday of our lives.'[10] In fact, contends Waever, the period of which Monnet was writing (the late 1940s and early 1950s) was characterized by a level of insecurity—the Soviet threat, the menace of Communism at home, the German question—that could only be dealt with by the United States as a superpower: the prospect of a Soviet intervention provoked 'the greatest social affect' and 'legitimized a wide array of activities and contributed to defining the identity of what was first of all a Western or North Atlantic community', leaving European identity 'naturally secondary and instrumental in relation to that of *the West*'.[11] Likewise, in this period, the dominant answer to the German question within West Germany and among American and European countries was one of '*Einbindung* into NATO as well as (what became) the EU', in that order.[12]

During the era of détente between 1960 and 1985, such considerations became more routine, 'increasingly a ritual for securing a continued upholding of the deterrence order'.[13] As the leader of the CSU, Franz Josef Strauß, put it, 'In the present European situation there is no possibility of changes through war, but neither through revolution or civil war.'[14] With the 'drama taken out of security', as governments and publics focused on détente, Western European states did not think in terms of security and insecurity, but tried to think of other things, especially economic policy and political cooperation within Europe, which had been secondary matters of security during the 1940s and 1950s.[15] 'Desecuritization' had proceeded to such an extent in the 1960s, 1970s, and 1980s that when 'Europe after the Cold War faced the basic choice of whether to return to traditional power balancing or to create enough concentration of power to achieve a centred development (as, e.g., North America—and a long list of historical cases from other regions)', it seemed to many leaders to be possible 'to construct a narrative of state, nation and Europe that makes sense in relation to the national tradition of political thought', generating 'Europe in the plural' or Europes which are politically compatible internally, and that allowed the coordination of a security policy on a European level in order to deal with external threats.[16] Neo-realists were perhaps correct to stress the importance of the geopolitical context in the early stages of European unity, writes Andrew Hurrell, 'and yet wrong in ignoring the degree to which both informal integration and successful institutionalization altered the dynamics of European international relations over the ensuing forty years'.[17] The habits created by informal integration and institutionalization affected European security, in the broad sense, over the long term.

European Cooperation and the Superpowers

What was striking about the immediate post-war era in Europe was its uncertainty. Leaders' acceptance of a *pax americana* ruled out conflict but it did not reconcile historical enemies or transform contemporaries' views of the world. For its part, Washington did not attempt to restructure European politics. In some respects, the United States' role in Europe after 1945 was comparable to that of the interwar era. Although the State Department came to support the idea of a United States of Europe, it did little to bring it about. As in the 1920s, the US provided capital to European states, allowing their economies to recover from the war. It is true that Washington had created a much more comprehensive apparatus for free trade and mutual support during the Second World War, setting up the World Bank and the International Monetary Fund and requiring formal commitments at Bretton Woods in 1944, which it consolidated and mitigated through the negotiation of the terms of the Marshall Plan (1947).[18] It is also true, however, that US-style industrial production, productivity, regulation of markets and state intervention had been widely discussed in Europe since the 1920s, attracting both support and opposition. Those who agreed with many of the terms of the new economic order, such as Ludwig Erhard and the 'ordo-liberals' in Germany, could view European organizations, many of which—the Organisation for European Economic Cooperation (OEEC) and the European Payments Union, for instance—had been created by Washington or London, as interim measures on the path to global trade. They remained resistant to the idea of a continental customs union or common market, fearing protectionism and a high external tariff.[19] Those who disagreed, including most Social Democrats and the majority of parties in France, had little option but to work within the American framework and to ensure that any continental customs, currency, or industrial union conformed to that framework, given their reliance on $19 billion of Marshall Aid and on American coordination of European security (see Map 2.1).[20] The military commitment of the United States to Western Europe eventually stabilized the region, calcifying into more or less static opposition between the two superpowers. Yet the depth and duration of Washington's commitment was not immediately apparent, and its

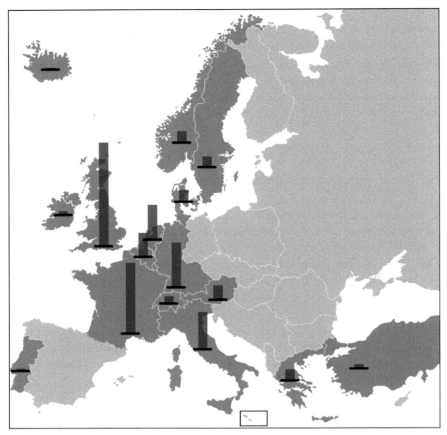

Map 2.1 The OEEC and Marshall Aid
Source: adapted from https://en.m.wikipedia.org/wiki/File:Blank_map_of_Europe_1956–1990.svg
Members: Austria, Belgium, Denmark, Greece, Ireland, Iceland, Italy, Luxembourg, Netherlands, Norway, Portugal, Sweden, Switzerland, Turkey, United Kingdom, West Germany

opposition to the USSR seemed precarious, not least because of the obscure designs of the Soviet leadership and its possession of increasingly destructive nuclear weapons. Whether such superpowers would succeed in pacifying Europe, preventing a reversion to internal strife and dictatorship at the same time as overcoming the external enmities and radical nationalism of European populations (during the 1930s and early 1940s) was a moot point in the late 1940s and 1950s.

For post-war elites in Europe, it seemed necessary to avoid the mistakes of the interwar era. The fact that attempts at European 'integration' and 'cooperation' failed during the interwar era and succeeded in the post-war years has tended to obscure important similarities between the two periods. The idea that 'realists' had taken over in the post-war era from 'utopians' at once underestimates the viability of attempts to cooperate on a European level in the 1920s and overestimates the role of pro-Europeans and their likelihood of success in the 1950s.'It is partly in reaction to the ideology of "Europeanism" in the interwar era that actions in favour of European unity came about in the aftermath of the Second World War', contends Jean-Luc Chabot, one of a number of scholars who have sought to excavate and re-evaluate the legacies of the interwar years: 'Drawing their lessons from the relative failure of the intellectualism of the European current prior to 1939, and benefitting equally from the self-destruction of nationalism in a totalitarian guise with the end of the second global conflict, the movements for the unity of Europe took, with Jean Monnet, paths which were mindful of the efficacy of neo-liberal technocracy.'[21] Contrasts between the cultural assumptions and political utopianism of the Pan-European and other movements founded in the 1920s and the political pragmatism of the founders of the ECSC and EEC after 1945 are largely misplaced. Part of the case for contrasting the two periods— before and after the Second World War—rests on the proven failure of the European movements of the interwar years either to agree on a realistic programme of European cooperation or to convince governments to carry out their ideas.[22] Another part of the case hinges on the inability of the different governments either to impose their will on their neighbours—especially in respect of France, which had occupied the Ruhr in 1923 and had stood down in 1925—or to overcome national rivalries and longstanding hostilities in order to achieve a degree of economic and political cooperation.[23] However, important policy-makers were affected by discussions of 'Europe' and continental cooperation after each world war, with Aristide Briand, Gustav Stresemann, Austen Chamberlain, and others creating a 'Locarno system'—guaranteeing the western border between France, Germany, and Belgium, and underwritten by Britain and Italy in 1925— within which European cooperation could have occurred.[24] The speed with which this system collapsed, once the German government ceased to cooperate after 1930, served as a warning to post-war political leaders. The lack of a European 'security community' in the late 1940s and early 1950s could easily have permitted a rapid worsening of relations, as in the pre-Nazi era between 1930 and 1933, without the coordination of the United States.

By the mid-1930s, dictatorships outnumbered democracies on the Continent, leaving the Versailles 'system', including the League of Nations, apparently powerless to prevent Germany's remilitarization of the Rhineland, Italy's invasion of Abyssinia and the outbreak of the Spanish Civil War, all of which occurred in 1936 (see Map 2.2).[25] The French writer Georges Duhamel summarized a common point of view before the Paris conference of *Le comité français de cooperation européenne*: 'An enormous, terrible silence has fallen on the genius of Europe. We have all had the impression that a European spirit has been struck by stupefaction, that the workers for a future Europe have been infinitely discouraged.'[26] After the Nazi seizure of power in 1933, there was little opportunity to unite Europe politically or economically. Even earlier, with Heinrich Brüning's nomination as

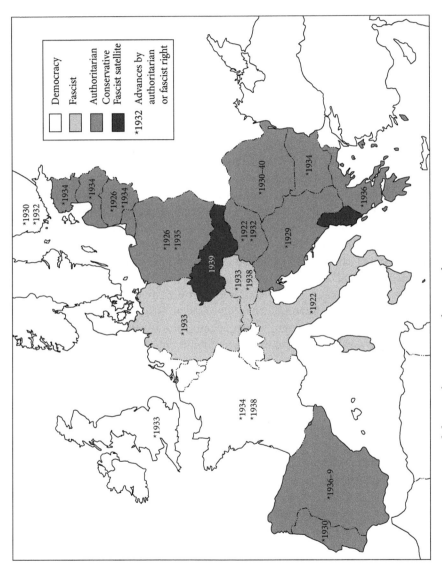

Map 2.2 Democracy and dictatorship in Europe between the wars
Source: J. Jackson (ed.), *Europe, 1900–1945* (Oxford, 2002), 225.

Reich Chancellor in March 1930, Franco-German reconciliation—and therefore attempts at European cooperation—had been deprived of much of their impetus. The German government's response to Briand's memorandum about a European Union in May 1930 was privately hostile, with Bernhard Wilhelm von Bülow, who was about to take over as Secretary of State at the Foreign Office, accusing France of wanting 'to impose new fetters on us' and with the Chancellor suspecting the Quai d'Orsay of trying to restrict Germany's claim to 'sufficient natural living space'.[27] Robert Curtius, the new Minister of Foreign Affairs was more cautious, but he was urged by the cabinet to give the memorandum 'a first-class burial'.[28] By April 1931, Bülow had decided to conclude a German–Austrian customs union, which eventually came to nothing, rather than pursue a European customs union founded on an agreement between France and Germany.[29] In effect, the Brüning government had decided to bring the Locarno era of Stresemann to an end. French elites and public opinion subsequently lost hope in a European solution to the German question.[30]

The principal difference between the interwar and post-war eras in Europe was the external threat posed by the USSR, which seemed to stabilize European politics—largely by ensuring a US military presence in Europe—but which in other respects perpetuated ideological differences of opinion and a sense of precariousness among contemporaries. The threat of Communism, which had been evident since 1917 but which seemed to the majority of onlookers to have increased with the victory of the USSR in 1945, was perhaps the overriding impulse behind European leaders' 'Atlanticism'. In Germany, after the effective partition of the western and eastern zones in 1946–49, the menace was most visible, associated with the barbarity of fighting on the Eastern Front during the Second World War, the feared and resented presence of Soviet troops throughout East Germany, the imprisonment of German soldiers in Soviet camps, the increasingly forlorn question of reunification, and a growing sense of insecurity, heightened by Moscow's blockade of Berlin in 1948, its acquisition of the atom bomb in 1949, its suppression of the workers' rising in the German Democratic Republic in 1953 and its replacement by force of the reformist government of Imre Nagy in Hungary in 1956. According to opinion polls, international 'security' remained the dominant political issue in Germany until the 1960s, taking precedence over reunification, which itself was seen by most respondents to be much more important than 'Europe'.[31] On the left, the battle against Communism derived especially from the SPD leadership's experiences of the forced merger of the KPD and SPD in the eastern zone in 1946–47.[32] In the centre and on the right, attitudes to the USSR were strongly ideological, combined with long-standing stereotypes of the 'Slavs' and the 'East'. For Adenauer, the Soviet Union was 'an Asian power', 'a vast power governed by a genius and a way of thinking totally different from our West European conditions'.[33] 'Asia stands on the Elbe', wrote the future Chancellor in March 1946 to Sollmann.[34] Although such a fact necessitated 'an economically and spiritually regenerated Western Europe under British and French leadership', which alone could 'check the further advance of this Asian spirit and power', it was accepted among CDU and CSU leaders—as Pascual Jordan put it—that 'our security... is guaranteed only by the presence of US troops'.[35] This calculus of power underlay the decision-making of the German government between 1949 and the 1960s.

Such calculations should not be confused with the seemingly static analyses of the later Cold War, however. Adenauer is a good example, altering his position fundamentally between the 1920s and the 1950s. The main danger after 1945, it seemed, was not that European states would fail to cooperate, but that the United States would withdraw or pursue its own interests to the detriment of its European partners, as it had done at various points—failing to ratify the Versailles Treaty in 1919 and repatriating capital in 1929—in the interwar period. Adenauer's fear, as he explained in an interview with Ernst Friedländer just after the Soviet-backed suppression of the workers' uprising in East Germany in June 1953, was that the United States might use Germany as a bargaining counter in a Cold War deal with the Soviet Union, as it had done at the Potsdam conference in 1945, when the country was divided into zones irrespective of German wishes: 'Bismarck spoke of his nightmare of coalitions against Germany. I have my nightmare, too. It is called Potsdam. The danger of a common policy of the Great Powers to the disadvantage of Germany has existed since 1945 and has continued to exist since the founding of the Federal Republic. The foreign policy of the federal government was directed from then onwards at coming out of this danger zone.'[36] Although, of course, the German Chancellor looked to European cooperation as a means of averting the danger of abandonment, his priority remained Germany's relationship with the United States.[37] Thus, when the French Assembly failed to ratify the European Defence Community in 1954, Bonn showed little hesitation in joining NATO in 1955, in spite of Paris's reservations. Other European statesmen seem to have adopted a similar strategy, spending much of their energy cultivating ties with Washington in order to persuade it to remain in Europe and relying on American-backed economic and security structures in the event that supplementary European ones failed to materialize.

Adenauer's foreign policy was founded on the notion that Europe's and the United States' positions had been transformed since the First World War. The Chancellor, born in Imperial Germany and the mayor of Cologne in the 1920s, had adapted to such circumstances and had fashioned the Federal Republic's European policy accordingly, as he conceded in his inaugural address to the first conference of the CDU in October 1950:

Until 1914, the world looked as follows; Germany was the strongest military power, England was the strongest sea power in the world, its fleet was bigger than the two next largest fleets put together. France was an economically and militarily powerful Great Power. The same was true of Italy. As a further Great Power, Austria-Hungary combined the national forces of the earlier Greater Austria, Hungary and Czechoslovakia, and it bound almost all the Balkan states to Europe. Russia was a Great Power, but it saw itself as part of Europe, belonging to its culture. This politically and economically strong European states' system, which on the whole was in equilibrium, could lead the rest of the world politically and economically, as a consequence of its strength and its balance of power: the United States of North America was a debtor country in 1914—which is not believed when it is said today. Its military forces were relatively small... Europe decided the fate of the world.

And now? Germany violently split into two parts, politically and economically badly damaged, diplomatically a vacuum. France has not yet been able to recover from the deep wounds which it received in both wars. The same is true of Italy. England has relinquished much of its economic and political influence and has partially lost its world standing, although the diplomacy of its leaders has kept intact, to a considerable extent, its old imperial connections.

Soviet Russia no longer feels a European, but a Bolshevik power... Yet it is in a position to have a decisive influence on the political fate of other European countries because of its expansion into *Mitteleuropa* and by means of its fifth column.

The United States of North America has developed into a world power of the first rank since 1914. One can say, without exaggerating, that no country since the time of the Roman Empire under Emperor Augustus has ever had such power in its hands as the United States does now. It is the strongest military power, the strongest economic power in the world... Whereas Europe since 1914 had a decisive influence on the political and economic workings of the world, it has now fallen into a lame state, which doesn't allow it to intervene decisively in the course of events.[38]

Despite, as a Rhinelander, having a vaguely defined interest in Franco-German reconciliation and European cooperation, Adenauer had become more 'Atlantic' in his definition of priorities as a consequence of the rise of the United States as a world power.[39] At no stage—including his signature of the Elysée Treaty with France in 1963, which incorporated a reaffirmation of support for the USA in its preamble—was the German Chancellor willing to put Europe before America, since he had long recognized the reversal of their positions in the global balance of power. The fact that Washington was prepared to coordinate the continent's security and to prop up its economy after 1945 at times seemed to ease the process of European integration by removing difficult subjects—especially defence—from the negotiating table, yet at other times it made such integration or cooperation seem less necessary or pressing than during the 1920s.

Adenauer's assessment of the Soviet threat and those of his opponents were characterized by an openness which went back to the interwar era.[40] The Chancellor was unusual in opting for the 'West'—primarily the United States, but also Western Europe—so quickly after 1945. On his right, national-minded conservatives such as Heinrich Brüning, the former Chancellor and Centre Party politician, criticized Adenauer for endangering not merely 'the German Reich', but 'the entire nation (*Volk*)': the Federal Republic should not commit itself, recognizing that 'time is working for us' and using 'narrower ties between European states' for 'particular purposes' such as the regaining of economic and political autonomy instead of risking 'an enduring partition of Germany' by adopting 'French' and 'Western' policies, including the founding of the ECSC and the attempt to set up a European parliament.[41] On the Chancellor's left, liberals such as Karl-Georg Fleiderer and Reinhold Maier, together with Paul Sethe, Richard Tüngel, and Rudolf Augstein from *Der Spiegel* and *Die Zeit*, also blamed him for entering into western alliances which prevented reunification and for rejecting Stalin's offer of neutrality for the whole of Germany in 1952.[42] Even Theodor Heuss, the liberal-democratic President of the FRG, distanced himself from Adenauer's western policy until 1948, at the earliest, contending that Germany could be a 'bridge' between East and West: 'We, the German people, must not be forced to "opt" either for the East or the West', he had declared in January 1947, 'though many of our countrymen may, in their hearts, be so inclined, but by ignoring the permanent existence of the areas of German settlement'.[43] The unresolved national question in Germany made it difficult to opt definitively for a French, European, or western system which seemed to prolong partition. In this respect, Adenauer himself, despite discounting the possibility of reunification within an unreliable system of collective—rather than American—security or as a result of a Soviet deal, was unwilling to give up the idea of a successful reconstitution of Germany. In the Chancellor's opinion, the USSR would either recognize that it could not win against a united and strong West, as it was overwhelmed by the cost of the arms race, global intervention, and the maintenance of its system of satellite states, or it would become preoccupied by the menace of China in the East, causing it to reduce its commitments in the West.[44] With such apparently shifting points of view, even of the Soviet threat, the German government's commitment to Europe often seemed subordinate either to its relationship with the United States or its longer-term goal of reunification.

Many French policy-makers had a similarly shifting view of the USSR and the international order in the late 1940s and early 1950s, which recalled the unpredictable alliances and agreements of the interwar years.[45] Thus, pragmatic economic planners such as Monnet were subject to radical oscillation between practical objectives and nightmarish fears of war and collapse, predicting a nuclear conflagration in 1950—'They are going to drop it, the atom bomb, and then . . .'—even before the outbreak of the Korean War: 'People have latched on to a simple and dangerous aim.... The Cold War, the basic aim of which is to make the adversary yield, is the first stage in the preparation of war. This is breeding a rigidity of mind characteristic of fixation on a single goal.... We are already at war.'[46] For Monnet, as for other French statesmen, the international system seemed to be characterized by instability after 1945, with earlier hopes—from 1943—of 'transforming the European epicentre of two world wars into an ensemble pacified by the creation of a "European federation or entity"' was by no means certain in the emerging global order.[47] Thus, although 'it was axiomatic' in the late 1940s for the head of the French *Commissariat Général au Plan*, in the opinion of the US Under-Secretary of State George Ball, that 'lasting peace could be achieved only by bringing France and Germany together and exorcising the demons of the past', it was also necessary to work towards 'a real Federation of the West', to include the British dominions and the United States.[48] Without such British participation, Europe would remain a vacuum between the dynamism of Communism and US capitalism, Monnet maintained.[49] Yet he found it difficult to escape the logic of the American ambassador in Paris in April 1950 that 'there will be no real European integration without whole-hearted participation by the UK, ... the UK will not whole-heartedly participate ..., ergo there will be no purely European integration'.[50]

Monnet's contemporaries were likewise uncertain of the relationship between European cooperation and world politics. Many, like de Gaulle in June 1947, wanted France to create a 'Europe' which was in a position 'to meet any possible claim of hegemony and to establish a balance of power between both rival masses which is necessary for the maintenance of peace', but there was little agreement about how to achieve such a goal.[51] De Gaulle's Commissioner for Foreign Affairs during the Second World War, René Massigli, who became the French ambassador in London in August 1944, had envisaged not only a US-led collective security organization, but also a Franco-British alliance and an anti-German Franco-Soviet treaty, which was actually signed in December 1944. Among the parties, the Communists, together with the Christian Democratic *Mouvement Républicain Populaire* (MRP) and the Socialists (SFIO) until 1947, were in favour of a Soviet pact, while the Gaullists (RPF) and Radicals quickly gave up the idea. Even between the latter parties, however, there was still disagreement about whether a French-led 'European federation' could constitute a third bloc between the superpowers, as the RPF's Jacques Soustelle contended, or whether 'a continental force leaning upon that of the two great powers whose civilization and political ideas are like ours'—namely, that of the United States—was the best that could be hoped for, as the Radical Jean Coutard proposed.[52] As late as 1957, the Socialist premier Guy Mollet was still worried that the USSR might be able to 'blackmail' the Federal Republic of Germany, with the likely election of an SPD government after the death of the ageing Adenauer, into cooperation with Moscow at the expense of Europe, in exchange for 'the mirage of reunification'.[53] In spite of the Cold War,

100 EUROPEAN INTEGRATION SINCE THE 1920s

relations between European states remained unstable. The role of the French Empire in European and global politics added a further element of confusion to such debates.[54]

Franco-German Friendship

The Franco-German axis quickly became central to European integration and to France's role on the Continent and beyond it.[55] Although the United States and NATO had ruled out the possibility of a military conflict, the prospects of a political rapprochement between Paris and Bonn were more fraught and depended on cooperation on a European level. The 'German problem', as Spaak revealed in 1963, could have resurfaced at any time: 'I do not believe that there is a solution which would command unanimous acceptance. If this problem were suddenly to be placed in the forefront again, the sceptics, and those who prefer to wait and see, would regain the ground they have lately lost, and this would be a great pity.'[56] The historical portents were poor, with European cooperation having rested and then foundered on the relationship between France and Germany in the 1920s and early 1930s. At the time, the relationship had relied to an extent on the structure of the League of Nations, which Germany eventually entered in 1926, and on a tangle of bi-lateral arrangements between France, Belgium, the Netherlands, and the new states of Central and Eastern Europe. It also existed within parameters which were set by the United States and the United Kingdom, both of which were reluctant to enforce the payment of reparations or to broker agreements between continental states.

As Peter Krüger rightly points out, the Locarno system of European security, which Briand's project for a European union (1929–30) sought to extend, was threatened and undermined largely by internal conditions, disputes about domestic policy, electoral shifts and changes of government between 1930 and 1933 within Germany itself, all of which had relatively little to do with foreign policy, despite the recurring question of 'revision'.[57] Thus, even after the accession of Brüning's right-wing government to office in March 1930, Curtius and the Foreign Office began to waver in their response to Briand's memorandum during the summer, when the Reich's ambassadors—especially Leopold von Hoesch in Paris, who had previously urged resistance against France's occupation of the Ruhr in 1923—reported that the French Minister of Foreign Affairs was not committed to existing borders in the East or to the precedence of political over economic affairs, but merely wanted to treat them in conjunction with each other rather than handing them over entirely to experts.[58]

Curtius's hesitation, in the face of his Chancellor's expressed desire to bury Briand's project, betrayed the extent to which the Locarno system, economic cooperation and a rhetoric of Europeanism had been accepted by significant political constituencies, commanding a majority of the vote until at least 1930, in Weimar Germany and elsewhere. According to the German embassies there, both the press and the governments of Poland, Czechoslovakia, Estonia, Latvia, Lithuania, Romania, and Yugoslavia—the new states created, or refashioned, by Versailles and allied to France—were almost wholly in favour of Briand's memorandum.[59] There was a similar reaction in the neutral states of Scandinavia, which saw the memorandum, in the words of one diplomat, as 'proof of the depth of the feeling that a way must be found of escaping the disputes which hinder the progress of Europe'.[60] The Austrian and Belgian governments, although mindful of the position of Berlin, supported the project, with Brussels, like The Hague, reiterating its unwillingness to subordinate economic cooperation to security. Such willingness did not prevent the failure of European cooperation and the Continent's descent into war.

Although European politics after 1945 were simplified by the Cold War, at least in terms of allegiances, they continued—as was the case after 1918—to be complicated by the German question, with many politicians and ministers as mindful of the legacy of the 1930s and the Second World War as they were of the growing antagonism of the superpowers (see Map 2.3). With the exception of the SFIO, which nonetheless advocated the internationalization of the industry of the Ruhr, majorities in all political parties in France until 1948 seem to have perceived Germany as their principal enemy.[61] Although such continental anxieties eventually pushed many French, German, Belgian, and Dutch decision-makers, as in the 1920s, to view European cooperation as a means of guarding against a revival of German nationalism, they could easily and rapidly work in the opposite direction.[62] The French could only have confidence in the Marshall Plan, declared Monnet in July 1947, 'if the development of German resources is coupled with safeguards to ensure that they will not, one day, be used again by the Germans to make war'.[63] When Dean Acheson, the US Secretary of State, asked Paris and London to consent to German rearmament at the start of the Korean War in September 1950, the French Foreign Minister Robert Schuman—who was still denigrated by French diplomats 'for having fought in German uniform', as a native of Lorraine, in the First World War—retorted that 'Germany's malady dates too far back to have been permanently cured.'[64] To Mollet in 1956, 'the risk of a revival of German nationalism' was still 'no myth'.[65] The problem, to which there was a bewildering range of solutions on offer during the late 1940s and early 1950s, was how to control Germany. When Schuman was requested by Acheson to prepare a policy towards Germany for the United States, the UK, and France in September 1949, 'the bald top of his head went red, as always when he was embarrassed', wrote his chief of staff: 'Back in Paris, hardly a week passed without Schuman pressing me: "What about Germany? What do I have to do to meet the responsibility put upon me?" It became an obsession with him.'[66]

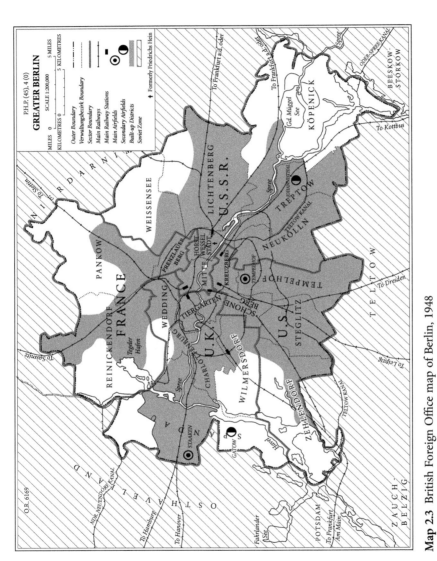

Map 2.3 British Foreign Office map of Berlin, 1948

Source: https://www.nationalarchives.gov.uk/education/coldwar/G4/cs1/cwar.pdf

Schuman was confronted by changing conditions and conflicting advice. Initial hopes of a re-agrarianized Germany, along the lines of the Morgenthau plan, or a loose confederation of individual German states, as in de Gaulle's prediction of 1944 that 'there would no longer be "one" Germany but several', were quickly replaced by a desire in Paris to control the reconstruction of the German economy, state and military, which was being pursued progressively between 1945 and 1950 by the United States, faced with the need to reduce its spending in the Allied zones, to refloat the European economy, to create a strong enough political structure in Germany to resist the Soviet-backed SED regime in the eastern zone, and to allow the transfer of US troops to the war in Korea (1950–54).[67] As after 1924, 'The system of domination of Germany, through the Saar and the Ruhr, could not be maintained forever, but no one wanted to be responsible for the decision to bring it to an end', wrote Robert Mischlich, a member of Schuman's staff at the Quai d'Orsay.[68] When the Minister of Foreign Affairs had decided on Monnet's limited policy of 'settling the German problem in a...European steel pool in which French and Germans would be equally represented', influential members of the ministry such as the Political Director Maurice Couve de Murville and the Secretary-General Jean Chauvel advised that 'France had to keep a free hand', in Mischlich's words: 'If there were to be a military or economic alliance, it should in no way foreclose France's political freedom, notably to withdraw from any alliance.'[69]

French diplomats continued to try to tie the ECSC, after it had been established in 1951–52, to the Council of Europe by insisting—unsuccessfully—on a shared secretariat, and they had nothing to do with the relaunching of European talks—proposed by Monnet and the Belgian Minister of Foreign Affairs Paul-Henri Spaak at Messina in 1955, which led to the founding of the EEC in 1957. Even to figures like Hervé Alphand, who had been Director of Economic Affairs at the Quai d'Orsay after the Second World War, before becoming ambassador to NATO between 1952 and 1954, such economic integration was unlikely on its own to bind the FRG to France, leaving the European Defence Community as 'the last chance to impose on Germany a regime offering guarantees of limiting German militarism'.[70] For his part, de Gaulle, who remained influential in the realms of diplomacy and the military, opposed the EDC in a press conference in February 1953, since it entailed a renunciation of French national interests and 'contains not only equality, but also a route to the hegemony of the Germans', reopening the prospect of 'a Reich'.[71] Adenauer was portrayed in the interview as the 'Chancellor of the Reich' and was accused by implication of harbouring hegemonic designs.[72] In such circumstances, any movement towards European integration, based on Franco-German reconciliation, was neither certain nor separate from policies involving the United States. Formally, the sanction of the US and the UK, as the other two occupying powers with Allied High Commissions in Germany, was needed for any negotiation involving the FRG to take place at all.

The Franco-German axis has continued to be the basis of a wider European security community, not only because France and Germany had been pivotal in previous European conflicts (1870–71, 1914–18, and 1939–45), but also because they remained the largest and most powerful continental states, some of whose leaders and citizens felt animosity towards each other. Nicolas Sarkozy, like his predecessors, 'had become, over the years, a militant of the Franco-German axis'.[73] 'Retrospectively, I can measure the depth of vision of the architects of this reconciliation better' and 'the veritable revolution that this represented' for de Gaulle and Adenauer.[74] On 22 January 1963, the Franco-German Treaty of Friendship was signed by de Gaulle and Adenauer in Paris, to the surprise of German officials, who had not brought treaty paper or a leather folder with them, having to buy them hurriedly in the Rue Faubourg St. Honoré.[75] It provided for the French and German heads of government to meet twice a year and foreign ministers every three months, with the two countries pledging to 'consult each other, prior to any decision, on all important questions of foreign policy ... with a view to arriving, in so far as possible, at a similar position'.[76] There was also provision for regular meetings of ministers and officials responsible for youth affairs, education, and defence, with the French and German high commands to harmonize tactics and strategy and to organize joint procurement.

The meetings became an enduring feature of European politics, yet they were the product of a bi-lateral treaty which, deputies in the *Bundestag* felt obliged to add, in a preamble, should not lead to decisions incompatible with EEC treaties (or those with the USA). The signing of the treaty came a week after de Gaulle's press conference, on 14 January, announcing his government's decision to veto the UK's application to join the European Economic Community, and nine months after his decision to scrap the Fouchet Plan to introduce a European Political Commission, made up of civil servants, to deal with defence, foreign policy and economic matters, as part of the French President's attempt to replace supranational EEC institutions with intergovernmental committees. 'To be effective, to draw on the sentiment and support of its peoples, to not lose itself in the coulds of theories, "Europe" currently can only consist of a cooperation organized among states', de Gaulle had written to Adenauer in July 1960: 'To adopt this conception is to admit that the "supranational" organisms that had been constituted among the Six, which tend inevitably and abusively to become irresponsible superstates, will be reformed, subordinated to the governments and employed for the normal tasks of technical advice.'[77] The French President torpedoed the Fouchet Plan because he believed that his own negotiators had compromised to too great an extent. The Franco-German Treaty was partly an admission that he had been unable to achieve what he wanted within the EEC. Adenauer signed the treaty, effectively sanctioning de Gaulle's vetoing of British entry and his abandoning of the Fouchet Plan, in part because he recognized its long-term significance for Franco-German reconciliation and partnership, and partly because he had come to know and trust the French leader, who had hailed him as 'a great German, a great European, a great man who is a great friend of France' during the German Chancellor's state visit in July 1962.[78]

De Gaulle's willingness to work outside the European Community, although often linked to his character or historical experiences, in fact corresponded to the shifting positions of the majority of French power-brokers in the 1950s. For Pierre Mendès France and other proponents of a 'confederal track' (Craig Parsons), the cooperation of the major European powers, including the United Kingdom, was essential, with the Western European Union (WEU) at once binding them together and permitting West Germany's entry into NATO. 'Franco-German reconciliation is a condition of political stability in Europe, and of its economic and social development', declared the Radical premier in September 1954, after allowing the failure of the bill to ratify the European Defence Community: 'But the birth of a loyal, real and durable understanding would have difficulty in a tête-à-tête between the two nations; it is necessary to associate the neighbouring countries, notably Britain.'[79] The creation of the WEU and the Federal Republic of Germany's membership of NATO ensured the stationing of British troops on the Continent, which would not have occurred within what Churchill called 'the sludgy amalgam' of the EDC.[80] The French ambassador in the UK reportedly wept, having waited fifty years for such a commitment.[81] An internal discussion of the SFIO concluded that the WEU released France from an over-reliance on the European Community: the 'Accords deliver us from the Europe of Six and the risks of German hegemony, which it contained; today is the Europe of Seven.'[82]

Arguably, what such politicians desired in the mid-1950s was intergovernmental cooperation. 'Traditionalists', including de Gaulle himself (four years before he assumed the presidency), likewise favoured cooperation, as well as bi-lateral ties to Germany, which were also supported by much of French business. Their only objection was that the WEU was too 'Anglo-Saxon'.[83] With very little backing in French political and business circles for a common market, in addition to the existence of intergovernmental cooperation on security, the British observer on the Spaak Committee, which was tasked with assessing the possibility of creating such a market, was happy to leave the talks early, in November 1955, assuring London that the treaty had 'no chance of being concluded; if it is concluded, it has no chance of being ratified; and if it is ratified, it has no chance of being applied'.[84] In 1957–58, a treaty to create a European common market was, indeed, concluded, ratified and applied, partly because Guy Mollet, a socialist supporter, happened to be premier.[85] It did not rule out bi-lateral agreements and intergovernmental cooperation, but it did, over time, alter officials' and ministers' expectations of collaboration within European institutions. Eventually, the meetings of French and German leaders, agreed by de Gaulle and Adenauer in 1963 as an alternative to the 'community track', came to precede meetings of the European

Council and they were seen as an opportunity to prepare common positions within the EU.

In 1989–90, as the pillars of the Cold War began to crumble, tensions between French and German decision-makers resurfaced. Mitterrand was worried, according to Attali, that the incorporation of—or uncertainty about—East Germany could create a Federal Republic which was 'too Prussian'.[86] The French President's solution was to tie the FRG to a political European union, as he explained to Kohl on 24 October 1989: 'Your problem can only be resolved within the European framework.'[87] On the next day, the Chancellor did not 'even pretend to listen', in Attali's opinion, as the French leader laid out his plan for a German confederation and for a bank for Eastern Europe.[88] Kohl's only concern, it seemed, was to be granted direct access to East German interlocutors in the coming negotiations. When Michel Rocard rejoiced that 'a rediscovered peace' had been created for Europe after the fall of the Wall, the President exploded in private: 'Peace! How can he talk of peace? It is quite the contrary that awaits us!'[89] Gorbachev had assured Mitterrand on the phone that Kohl had said that he would resist calls for unification but, at a dinner of European leaders at the Elysée on 18 November, the German Chancellor had begun to talk of an old NATO agreement to unification dating back to 1970. Thatcher had objected publicly: 'You see, you see what he wants.'[90] Mitterrand's answer was to stress Europe more, as he reportedly scribbled on a piece of paper before facing the press after the dinner: 'The German question is a European question.'[91] When Gorbachev changed his position on 27 November, allowing the FRG to do what it wanted with the GDR (within existing treaty commitments), the French President warned Genscher, who had agreed to talks about political and monetary union on the 30th, that,

> If German unification came before European unification (*l'unité*), then you will find the triple alliance [France, Britain and Russia] against you, exactly as in 1913 and 1939. You will have 90 million inhabitants, certainly, but the USSR will turn against you, you will be encircled, and that will end in a war in which all the Europeans will again be in league against the Germans. Is that what you want? If, in contrast, German unification comes after progress on European unification, we shall help you.[92]

In Attali's judgement, there were four possibilities for Germany: neutrality (Gorbachev's preference), independence (supposedly Kohl's position), Atlanticism (Bush), and Europeanism (Mitterrand).[93] Europeanism—Mitterrand's preference—won out.

Such an outcome was not a coincidence. The French and German governments had experienced colder relations under Ludwig Erhard, who was more sympathetic to the economic and foreign policies of the UK and the US than his predecessor, and during the 'empty chair' crisis in 1965–66. Under Georges

Pompidou, Valéry Giscard D'Estaing, and Mitterrand during the early 1980s, together with Willy Brandt, Helmut Schmidt, and Kohl, Bonn and Paris worked closely together, despite difficulties over monetary policy.[94] Giscard, in particular, pushed for the establishment of a European Council, at which the leaders of member states met away from the pressures of domestic policy, and he backed the European Monetary System (EMS), set up in 1979. In Parsons's view, the French President's 'ideas about Europe—framed in the community model he adopted under the Fourth Republic—selected the strategy that led him to the EMS instead of maintaining the status quo'.[95] This decision on EMS locked in Mitterrand, his successor, who was faced with capital flight and a run on the franc after his election in May 1981, since it affected how the new president reacted to the pressures of a global recession and increasing economic interdependence: 'In 1981, Mitterrand believed that his policies would succeed and be consistent with the EMS; to the extent that he doubted this, the short-term costs of EMS exit led him to risk it. As his policies failed, however, the difficulty of straddling domestic-political and EMS commitments grew. The longer he defended the franc in the EMS, the more exit entailed a jump from heights he had never meant to climb.'[96] Rather than leave the EMS, Mitterrand decided to abandon the experiments of the Fifth Republic's first Socialist government under Pierre Mauroy. The President's turn towards Europe after the Socialist U-turn at home had little public support, with the left gaining only 35.7 per cent of the vote for the European Parliament elections of June 1984, compared to 57.6 per cent for the right, including 19 per cent of Mitterrand's voters from 1981. Rather, it was a decision made from above, as the French diplomat Gabriel Robin spelled out: 'the doctrine was well secured—no new treaty, no questioning of the Luxembourg Compromise, no flight forwards in an institutional sense'.[97] Kohl helped Mitterrand by shoring up the franc within the EMS.[98] The question is whether this type of collaboration among elites fostered further cooperation and created a wider sense of 'security'.

A European Security Community?

The European Community gradually acquired an apparatus for the discussion of foreign and defence policy. The failure of the EDC in 1954 was a major setback, even in France, whose Assembly was responsible for non-ratification. By 1952, most officials at the Quai d'Orsay were against the initiative, but French parties remained divided: about two-thirds of the SFIO were in favour of the final treaty deal in May 1952, as were centrists in the Radical Party and Union Démocratique et Socialiste de la Résistance.[99] Mollet remained 'fanatically attached to the EDC, which he saw as an extension of the ECSC, a step towards European unity', in the opinion of his fellow Socialist, Jules Moch.[100] Much of the Christian Democratic Mouvement des Républicains Populaires continued to back the defence

108 EUROPEAN INTEGRATION SINCE THE 1920S

community plan, at least in theory, and a large rump of conservative Independents and Peasants wavered between support and rejection. The failure to ratify the treaty deal left many parties in disarray. According to commentators such as Raymond Aron, traditional domestic priorities and foreign-policy positions had collided with a clash of principle on the European level:

> The difficulty seems to me to have been that for the theoreticians of Europe, the whole meaning of the EDC was in its supranationality. They were more attached to this principle than to reality. On the other hand, the EDC opponents were more against the principle than against the reality. The former dreamed about a European State of the Six growing out of the EDC; the latter imagined this with horror.[101]

Others in Belgium, the Netherlands, and West Germany, which had ratified the treaty, were distraught. Paul-Henri Spaak, the ECSC president and former Belgian premier, considered it a 'very heavy blow for the supporters of a united Europe'.[102] The US Secretary of State John Foster Dulles thought it a 'tragedy', which might 'endanger the whole of Europe'.[103] Although the EDC treaty has been labelled 'the largest single cession of sovereignty made by the countries of Western Europe until the Treaty on European Union in 1992', it also underwrote American day-to-day control by declaring—in Article 18—that 'the competent supreme commander responsible to NATO', who would be an American, 'be empowered to satisfy that the European Defence Forces are organized, equipped, trained and prepared for their duties in a satisfactory manner'.[104] The European Defence Community would have both necessitated a pooling of European sovereignty in foreign and defence policy-making and tied Europe's forces to the United States.

The EDC was quickly replaced by the Western European Union (WEU), which retained the council of ministers of the Brussels Pact (1948), added a consultative assembly and, critically, committed four British divisions and tactical air forces to the Continent. Not everyone was convinced by the replacement, with the Dutch Minister of Foreign Affairs, Johan Willem Beyen, calling it a form of 'fake integration'.[105] Many on the French Right felt, like de Gaulle, that the union was an 'Anglo-Saxon' attempt to limit France to a European role. Similarly, former supporters of the EDC refused to back it, abstaining in such large numbers in the Assembly that it, too, ran the risk of non-ratification. Schuman called it a 'little entente', relating to an unimportant 'platonic Europe'.[106] Monnet dismissed it as a 'weak coordination structure', likely to 'vegetate'.[107] All the same, less committed French politicians and opponents of the EDC were supportive of the WEU, with the Independent Jacques Bardoux typical of many in preferring it to a 'Europe of castrated states' in a European Defence Community.[108] Formally separate from the European Coal and Steel Community and, later, the EEC, the WEU served (along with the Organization for European Economic Cooperation) as a location for the meetings which led to the Treaty of Rome in 1957. It acted as a bridge between European institutions and a forum for the discussion of defence. Until the establishment of direct elections for members of the European Parliament in 1979, many politicians continued to serve in the assemblies of the WEU, the Council of Europe and the European Economic Community.[109] In 1967, the West German government proposed that the union be strengthened and expanded.[110] Little came of the proposal, not least because it was overshadowed by the plan for European Political Cooperation (EPC) in 1970.

EPC was an intergovernmental mechanism which provided for summits of EC leaders—and the British before the UK entered the EEC in 1973—and for cooperation in the field of foreign policy. It marked a generational shift from the era of de Gaulle and Adenauer to that of Georges Pompidou and Willy Brandt, who helped to consolidate a specifically European form of détente, including bilateral agreements between the FRG and Eastern European states (*Ostpolitik* from 1969 to 1974) and the establishment of a common position during the 'Helsinki Process' of the American-led Conference on Security and Co-operation in Europe (CSCE) between 1972 and 1975.[111] 'On CECE—we never wanted it but we went along with the Europeans', Kissinger, Nixon's Secretary of State, told the incoming President, Gerald Ford, in August 1974 during a long conversation in the Oval Office about national security: 'It is meaningless—it is just a grandstand play to the left. We are going along with it.'[112] In Kissinger's opinion, the process had little impact on the Cold War, compared to the US policy of being 'brutal when they [the Soviets] step out of line', but it did demonstrate that EC governments were beginning to coordinate their efforts and act semi-independently of Washington: 'My guess is the Europeans will decide on a summit. We have positioned with the Soviet Union, so we look like we are ahead of the Europeans.'[113] One year previously in November 1973, European Community foreign ministers had outlined their own plan—the first time that they had put forward a unified position in foreign policy—for peace in the Middle East.[114]

The 'essential aim' of peace was one of the aims of the 'Declaration on European Identity', which was adopted by member states early in December 1973 and which sought to achieve a better definition of their responsibilities, relations with other countries, and 'the place which they occupy in world affairs':

> The Nine [member states] might have been pushed towards disunity by their history and by selfishly defending misjudged interests. But they have overcome their past enmities and have decided that unity is a basic European necessity to ensure the survival of the civilization which they have in common.... Although in the past the European countries were individually able to play a major role on the international scene, present international problems are difficult for any of the Nine to solve alone. International developments and the growing concentration of power and responsibility in the hands of a very small number of great powers

110 EUROPEAN INTEGRATION SINCE THE 1920s

mean that Europe must unite and speak increasingly with one voice if it wants to make itself heard and play its proper role in the world.... The Nine intend to play an active role in world affairs and thus to contribute, in accordance with the purposes and principles of the United Nations Charter, to ensuring that international relations have a more just basis; that the independence and equality of states are better preserved; that prosperity is more equitably shared; and that the security of each country is more effectively guaranteed. In pursuit of these objectives the Nine should progressively define common positions in the sphere of foreign policy.[115]

The member states vowed to strengthen their ties to other European countries via the Council of Europe, to 'industrialized countries, such as Japan and Canada', to the USSR and East European countries, with whom they had contributed 'to the first results of a policy of détente and cooperation', to Latin America, with which they had traditional, 'friendly links', and to China and the rest of the world.[116] At the heart of the document was an assurance 'that in present circumstances there is no alternative to the security provided by the nuclear weapons of the United States and by the presence of North American forces in Europe'.[117] Given the 'relative military vulnerability of Europe, the Europeans should, if they wish to preserve their independence, hold to their commitments and make constant efforts to ensure that they have adequate means of defence at their disposal', ran Paragraph 8: these commitments were to the United States, not least to show that European states were serious about defence.[118] European commitments to peace overlaid American safeguarding of European security, but they at once established habits of diplomatic cooperation and allowed for limited divergence from Washington.

The London Report of October 1981 introduced a rapid crisis procedure under the auspices of EPC. On 19 June 1983, the Stuttgart Declaration of EC leaders—formally entitled the 'Solemn Declaration on European Union'—reiterated their desire to speak 'with a single voice in foreign policy, including political aspects of security', in order to 'contribute to the preservation of peace', in part by strengthening 'European Political Cooperation through the elaboration and adoption of joint positions and joint action, on the basis of intensified consultations'.[119] By bringing together Heads of State or Government and the President of the Commission, assisted by foreign ministers and a member of the Commission, the European Council was singled out as the principal means of expressing a 'common position in questions of external relations' and issuing 'general political guidelines for the European Communities and European Political Cooperation'.[120] In the previous year, EPC had allowed member states to adopt a common policy towards Poland, after General Jaruzelski's imposition of martial law in 1981, imposing milder sanctions than those of the United States. Sanctions were also imposed on the Soviet Union, after it had backed the crackdown on Solidarity in Poland, and on Argentina in April 1982, for its invasion of the Falklands. On the former occasion, Moscow was 'completely indifferent', in the words of one *Spiegel* report, since the sanctions were ineffective and slow to come into effect.[121] On the latter occasion, the EC's unanimous imposition of economic and military sanctions—despite the fact that approximately 10 million Italian nationals were living in Argentina—had a significant effect, not least because about one-fifth of Argentinian exports were to the EEC. The US ambassador to the European Community commented in private that he had been 'very struck by the complete solidarity' of the member states.[122] Although Ireland, Italy and West Germany began to balk at them before the Falklands War ended in June, the imposition of sanctions constituted the first time that the European Community had used this mechanism on a security matter in a unified way.[123]

Within the territory of the bloc, the European Community succeeded in defusing tensions. Greece joined the EEC in 1981, just seven years after the end of the regime of the colonels (1967–74), which had collapsed after the Turkish invasion of Cyprus in July 1974 (see Map 2.4).[124] Whereas NATO had failed to prevent hostilities between two of its members (Greece and Turkey), with the United States backing the military dictatorship in Athens, the process of accession and later membership of the EC served to consolidate democracy in Greece and, eventually, helped to prevent an escalation of conflict on Cyprus, which joined the

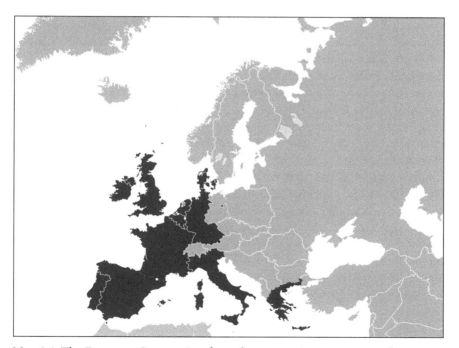

Map 2.4 The European Community after enlargements in 1973, 1981, and 1986
Source: https://en.wikipedia.org/wiki/European_Economic_Community#/media/File:Expansion_of_the_European_Communities_1973-1992.png

European Union in 2004, with the *acquis communautaire* (EU law) suspended in Turkish-backed Northern Cyprus.[125] Despite US mediation, which included the presence of American negotiators on the island in 1974, relations between Greece, Turkey, Britain—which had ruled Cyprus as a colony since 1925, retaining military bases after the island's independence in 1960—and France, whose President Giscard D'Estaing was a close friend of the post-dictatorship Prime Minister of Greece Konstantinos Karamanlis, were confused and unpredictable.[126] Arguably, they became more predictable as Greece prepared to enter the European Community.[127]

The same was true of Spain, where the first elections after Franco had taken place on 15 June 1977, and Portugal, where the 1974 Carnation Revolution had dislodged the post-Salazar dictatorship under Marcello Caetano and inaugurated a period of political and economic turmoil.[128] Portugal witnessed another military coup on 25 November 1975, as voters and parties shifted to the left. Spain experienced its last attempt at a military coup on 23 February 1981. Although the relationship between democratization and accession is complex, few—if any—commentators deny that Spain's and Portugal's application for membership helped to stabilize democracy.[129] As Mario Soares, the Portuguese Prime Minister, had put it during his speech at the European Commission on 11 March 1977, after handing in Portugal's application for membership, the step posed a challenge for Portugal, 'since we are not unaware of our weaknesses or of our present difficulties', and for 'Europe', 'since in knocking on Europe's door we feel we are giving expression to the meaning and to the truly European dimension of the political and social changes that have taken place in the recent past and are indeed still proceeding in southern Europe'.[130] As the President of the European Commission, Roy Jenkins, spelled out at the opening of the Spanish negotiations on 5 February 1979, the application was going ahead only because of 'the remarkable and peaceful way in which Spain has undergone profound consti-tutional change in such a short time': 'The new institution of parliamentary democracy in Spain and your respect for human rights have together created the conditions for Spanish membership of the Community.'[131] With the United States discredited in sections of the population for its cooperation with Franco, Salazar and the military junta in Greece, Washington accepted that the EC had the potential to be a 'stabilizing factor' in Southern Europe.[132] The de-escalation of the long-standing dispute between the United Kingdom and Spain over Gibraltar, which took place from the 1980s onwards, was a by-product of enlargement.[133]

The role of the EU in easing or containing violence on the part of the leaders and followers of minority nationalisms remains a contested one. Many are wary of claims such as those of Wolfgang Danspeckgruber that the European Union is 'the most successful integration experiment in diplomatic history', at once encour-aging 'communal activities and responsibilities and even devolution, as in the case of Scotland, and further struggles for self-governance, as in the case of Catalonia'.[134] Does the EU contribute 'to new understandings of community related to authority above and below the state', with individuals adopting 'multiple identities'?[135] Cross-border 'Euro-regions' in the Basque country or in the South Tyrol have been limited by the reluctance of member states to pool resources, coordinate their activities and dismantle their borders, even within the Schengen area.[136] It can be argued that the peace process in Northern Ireland was largely bilateral, resting on the Anglo-Irish Agreement of 1985, which gave the Irish government consultative rights on all matters not devolved to the Northern Ireland Assembly, and the Good Friday Agreement of 1998, which set up all-Ireland political institutions and recognized the right of self-determination.[137] Opinion polls showed that Protestants had become more 'British'—39 per cent in 1967, with 32 per cent claiming an Ulster identity and 20 per cent an Irish one, compared to 67 per cent in 1978, with 20 per cent opting for Ulster and 8 per cent Irish—and that Catholics had remained largely 'Irish' (76 per cent in 1967 and 69 per cent in 1978).[138]

A poll in Northern Ireland in 2002 revealed that 8 per cent of respondents always thought of themselves as European (7 per cent of Catholics, 6 per cent of Protestants, 15 per cent of no religion), 23 per cent sometimes thought of themselves as European (27 per cent of Catholics, 19 per cent of Protestants, 29 per cent of no religion) and 67 per cent never thought of themselves as European (64 per cent of Catholics, 73 per cent of Protestants, and 54 per cent of no religion), which was roughly in line with results elsewhere in the United Kingdom.[139] However, party leaders had altered their stance towards the EU, with the Catholic Social and Democratic Labour Party (SDLP) coming to support the EU and cross-border cooperation by the late 1970s and Sinn Féin doing the same by the late 1980s.[140] Although the Protestant Democratic Unionist Party (DUP) and the larger, more moderate Ulster Unionist Party (UUP), both opposed cross-border cooperation and the European Parliament's Haagerup Report (1984), which aimed to establish joint British–Irish responsibilities and eventual devolution, they lobbied the EC together with Irish nationalist parties in matters relating to the Common Agricultural Policy (CAP) and Structural Funds. As the UUP MEP Jim Nicholson admitted, 'It is possible to use the [European] Parliament to benefit the people of Northern Ireland.'[141] What mattered most was an acceptance among political elites in Dublin and London and among Northern Ireland's leaders and citizens that cooperation was possible, including within the institutions of the EU. Even critics of the claims made for European integration such as John McGarry and Brendan O'Leary concede that 'it has led to a number of improvements for at least some divided nations', since 'the borders that divide states are now less rigid and impermeable' and 'an overarching European rights regime based primarily on the ECHR [European Convention on Human Rights] and partly linked to EU "conditionality"' have made 'it more difficult for European

114   EUROPEAN INTEGRATION SINCE THE 1920s

states coercively to assimilate the minority segments of divided nations'.[142] Critically, leaders of minority nationalities have avoided violence.

It is true that the record of the European Union is more uneven in Central and Eastern Europe. After Fidesz's electoral victory in May 2010, Viktor Orbán's new government immediately eliminated the residency requirement for Hungarian citizenship, appealing to national minorities—'external kin'—in Romania and Slovakia.[143] Even here, however, expectations of ethnic and national conflict, which were commonplace in 1989–90, have not been fulfilled. The EU's record in creating security communities beyond its borders has been less successful, as the wars in Yugoslavia in the 1990s and Ukraine from 2014 onwards have made plain.[144] 'In any crisis the Europeans are like jackals', Kissinger had told Ford on 23 August 1974, with reference to the earlier conflict beyond its borders in Cyprus: 'You know what the French did in Greece. Now Wilson is saying we didn't stop the Turks so we could get credit for the new administration. When they behave like this on Greece, what they would do in a Middle East crisis would be brutal.'[145] By 1990–91, confronted with Slovenian and Croatian steps towards independence and the prospect of a bloodier war than in Cyprus in 1974, the member states failed to act in unison. In December 1990, Erhard Busek, the leader of the conservative Österreichische Volkspartei promised to back a Slovenian declaration of independence. By May 1991, the Danish Foreign Minister Uffe Elleman-Jensen was also expressing his sympathy, along with Giulio Andreotti, Italy's Christian Democrat Prime Minister, in June: 'When you will proclaim independence, in two minutes we will recognise you.'[146] The Italian Foreign Minister, the Socialist Gianni De Michelis, was less eager—'He was very harsh and very blunt but very sincere'—but, with the Yugoslav National Army close to deployment in late June, he changed his mind: 'You will be an independent state. Croatia, on the other hand, is a more complicated issue.'[147] Early in July, the German government admitted in public that it was considering recognizing the two states.[148]

The French Minister of Foreign Affairs, Roland Dumas, disagreed a couple of days later: 'Tomorrow what we have done for Yugoslavia would be applied to other cases.'[149] The British Foreign Secretary, Douglas Hurd, was also more reluctant, though conceding that the 'integrity of Yugoslavia', which he supported, could not be maintained by force.[150] The European Community did not recognize Slovenia and Croatia until 16 December 1991, at a Council of Ministers meeting in Brussels, subject to them meeting standards governing human rights, guarantees for minorities, democracy and the peaceful resolution of border disputes. Shortly beforehand, the UK and France had threatened to block German recognition of the two states by means of a UN Security Council resolution warning states not to act on their own in a way that might upset the political balance in Yugoslavia. On 23 December, Bonn nonetheless unilaterally recognized Slovenia and Croatia, which might—under Franjo Tudzman's HDZ (Croatian Democratic Union) government—have failed to meet the EC's conditions. Given the high stakes, with the death toll in the Croatian War mounting to approximately 20,000 and in the Bosnian War to 100,000, member states found it difficult initially to present a common front and impossible to limit or stop the war.[151] All the same, they were able to prevent a crisis, not to mention a conflict, occurring within the European Community itself.

The Gulf War between 2 August 1990 and 28 February 1991, in which only France and Britain of the EC states had played a major part, had demonstrated to Jacques Delors that, 'once it became obvious that the situation would have to be resolved by armed combat, the Community had neither the institutional machinery nor the military force to allow it to act as a community'.[152] Delors's solution was to reinforce the WEU in order to allow the EC to 'shoulder its share of the political and military responsibilities of our old nations', yet Washington remained unconvinced, warning that any European defence initiative should not weaken NATO by creating a European group within it or by marginalizing non-EC members such as Turkey and Norway. In the event, the WEU became a 'bridge' to NATO, where 'out-of-area' operations (such as the Gulf War) could be discussed.[153] The 'pillar' structure of the European Union, which Paris and London insisted on, ensured the intergovernmental basis of a Common Foreign and Security Policy, which was a matter for the European Council, not the Commission or European Parliament.[154] As the United States stood back at the start of the Yugoslav conflict, given—as the Secretary of State James Baker noted in his memoirs—that 'all the talk was of an emerging European superpower', the EC found it hard to coordinate member states and proved incapable of maintaining peace in its borderlands.[155] The Luxembourg Foreign Minister Jacques Poos's statement, in his capacity as the President of the Council of Ministers, that 'This is the hour of Europe...not the hour of the Americans', soon sounded preposterous.[156] Yet the first large-scale European war since 1945 also showed citizens on the other side of the EU border how alien military conflict had become.

In Michael Winterbottom's film *Welcome to Sarajevo* (1997), based on the ITN reporter Michael Nicholson's *Natasha's Story* (1994), the journalist's experiences in the war zone—'the worst place on earth'—are juxtaposed with silent scenes in his garden in London, where no one understands what is happening only two-and-a-half hours away by plane.[157] Just over forty years earlier, Western Europeans would have had no difficulty imagining a descent into war. It was not merely the long absence of war, which had also marked out the period before 1914, but cooperation on the European level, in supranational and intergovernmental settings, that had created a sense of security on the Continent. Thus, as late as 2018, German and French respondents to a large-scale Eurobarometer poll, together with those of five other member states, continued to maintain that the EU's greatest achievement was 'peace among the member states'.[158] Cooperation had eventually ruled out conflict.

Notes

1. K. W. Deutsch, *Political Community and the North Atlantic Area* (Princeton, NJ, 1957).
2. Ibid., 6–7.
3. Ibid., 82.
4. Ibid., 36.
5. Ibid., 37.
6. Ibid., 38.
7. Ibid., 66.
8. Ibid., 66–7.
9. O. Waever, 'Insecurity, Security and Asecurity in the West European Non-War Community', in E. Adler and M. Barnett (eds), *Security Communities* (Cambridge, 1998), 69.
10. J. Monnet, *Memoirs* (1976), ibid., 79.
11. O. Waever, 'Insecurity, Security and Asecurity in the West European Non-War Community', in E. Adler and M. Barnett (eds), *Security Communities*, 81.
12. Ibid., 82.
13. Ibid., 84.
14. Quoted ibid., 85.
15. Ibid., 85–6.
16. Ibid., 90.
17. A. Hurrell, 'Explaining the Resurgence of Regionalism in World Politics', *Review of International Studies*, 21 (1995), 358.
18. C. Spagnolo, 'Reinterpreting the Marshall Plan: The Impact of the European Recovery Programme in Britain, France, Western Germany and Italy, 1947–1955', in D. Geppert (ed.), The Postwar Challenge, 1945–1958 (Oxford, 2003), 275–98.
19. S. Lee, 'German Decision-Making Elites and European Integration: German "Europolitik" during the Years of the EEC and Free Trade Area Negotiations', in A. Deighton (ed.), *Building Postwar Europe*, 43–4.
20. See I. M. Wall, *The United States and the Making of Postwar France* (Cambridge, 1991).
21. J.-L. Chabot, *Origines*, 325.
22. Karl Holl, 'Europapolitik um Vorfeld der deutschen Regierungspolitik. Zur Tätigkeit proeuropäischer Organisationen in der Weimarer Republik', *Historische Zeitschrift*, 219 (1974), 33–94, and Jürgen Hess, 'Europagedanke und nationaler Revisionismus. Überlegungen zu ihrer Verknüpfung in der Weimarer Republik am Beispiel Wilhelm Heiles', *Historische Zeitschrift*, 225 (1977), 572–622, disagree about the relative likelihood and significance of 'Europeanism' in the interwar era, with Hess emphasizing the inevitability of national interest, but they agree about the potential significance of the movements, their damaging inability to cooperate with each other, and their failure to enlist the German government.
23. Some scholars argue that a successful French strategy after 1919 was the only chance of a durable peace, in opposition to British and American appeasement of Germany, but the Quai d'Orsay was unable to impose a stronger and consistent policy because of internal failings and the weakness of France's economic and military position; see J. Jacobson, 'Strategies of French Foreign Policy after World War I', *Journal of Modern History*, 55 (1983), 78–95, for a summary. For a criticism of France's and Belgium's inability to overcome their national differences and cooperate economic-ally, see E. Bussière, *La France, la Belgique et l'organisation économique de l'Europe* (Paris, 1991).
24. For arguments in favour of a 'shift' of international system after 1919, and especially after 1924, see P. Krüger, 'Das doppelte Dilemma: Die Aussenpolitik der Republik von Weimar zwischen Staatensystem und Innenpolitik', *German Studies Review*, 22, (1999), 247–67, and P. Krüger, *Die Aussenpolitik der Republik von Weimar* (Darmstadt, 1985). For scepticism about Locarno's signifi-cance, given different interpretations of it by various governments, see J. Jacobson, *Locarno Diplomacy: Germany and the West* (Princeton, 1972).
25. See S. Payne, *A History of Fascism, 1914–1945* (London, 1996), 245–327; S. Payne, *Falange: A History of Spanish Fascism* (Palo Alto, CA, 1961).
26. E. du Réau, 'La France et l'Europe d'Aristide Briand à Robert Schuman. Naissance, déclin et redéploiement d'une politique étrangere (1929–1950)', *Revue d'histoire moderne et contemporaine*, 42 (1995), 561.
27. Cited in J. Wright, *Gustav Stresemann: Weimar's Greatest Statesman* (Oxford, 2002), 485.
28. A. Rödder, *Stresemanns Erbe. Julius Curtius und die deutsche Aussenpolitik 1929–1931* (Paderborn, 1996), 113–19.

SOFT POWER   117

29. K. Holl, 'Europapolitik', *Historische Zeitschrift*, 219 (1974), 39.
30. E. du Réau, 'La France et l'Europe', *Revue d'histoire moderne et contemporaine*, 42 (1995), and E. du Réau, *Edouard Daladier, 1884–1970* (Paris, 1993); J.-B. Duroselle, *La Décadence, 1932–1939* (Paris, 1979); Y. Lacaze, *L'Opinion française et la crise de Munich* (Berne, 1991).
31. J. L. Richardson, *Germany and the Atlantic Alliance: The Interaction of Strategy and Politics* (Cambridge, CT., 1966), 11–12, 340–5.
32. D. Staritz and A. Sywottek, 'The International Political Situation as Seen by the German *Linksparteien* (SPD, SED and KPD) between 1945 and 1949', in J. Becker and F. Knipping (eds), *Power in Europe?*, vol. 1, 213–24.
33. Cited in M. Overesch, 'Senior West German Politicians and Their Perceptions of the German Situation in Europe, 1945–1949', in J. Becker and F. Knipping (eds), *Power in Europe?*, vol. 1, 125.
34. Ibid.
35. Adenauer ibid.; Jordan cited in W. Becker, 'Views of the Foreign Policy Situation among the CDU Leadership, 1945–5', in E. Di Nolfo (ed.), *Power in Europe?*, vol. 2, 365–6.
36. K. Adenauer to E. Friedländer, 13 June 1953, quoted in H.-P. Schwarz, 'Adenauer und Europa', *Vierteljahreshefte für Zeitgeschichte*, 27 (1979), 480. Also, G. Schmidt, 'Divided Europe—Divided Germany, 1950–63', *Contemporary European History*, 3 (1994), 155–92.
37. D. C. Large, 'Grand Illusions: the United States, the Federal Republic of Germany and the European Defence Community, 1950–1954', in J. M. Diefendorf et al. (eds), *American Policy and the Reconstruction of West Germany* (Cambridge, 1993), 375–94; H. E. Volkmann and W. Schwengler (eds), *Die Europäische Verteidigungsgemeinschaft* (Boppard, 1985).
38. H.-P. Schwarz, 'Adenauer und Europa', *Vierteljahreshefte für Zeitgeschichte*, 27 (1979), 516.
39. According to Andreas Rödder, 'Der Mythos von der frühen Westbindung. Konrad Adenauer und Stresemanns Aussenpolitik', *Vierteljahreshefte für Zeitgeschichte*, 41 (1993), 543–73, Adenauer had little knowledge of foreign policy, despite being embroiled in the Ruhr dispute as mayor of Cologne, and he remained opposed to Stresemann's policy of understanding in the West.
40. Adenauer was unusual insofar as he had already, by 1930, had 'half of his life', carrying out 'important political offices as the Mayor of Cologne and President of the Prussian Staatsrat', in Franz Josef Strauß's words: F. J. Strauß, *Die Erinnerungen*, 149. Many in the FRG's political elites had first experienced 'a certain political and historical consciousness around 1930'.
41. Brüning in 1950–51, cited in H.-P. Schwarz, 'Adenauer und Europa', *Vierteljahreshefte für Zeitgeschichte*, 27 (1979), 500–1.
42. Ibid., 502–5. Franz Josef Strauß's view, *Die Erinnerungen*, 152, was that 'Many had still not understood that that we had declared a total war and had lost this total war totally. We were powerless and without rights.'
43. Cited in M. Overesch, 'Senior West German Politicians', in J. Becker and F. Knipping (eds), *Power in Europe?*, vol. 1, 129.
44. Schwarz, 'Adenauer und Europa', *Vierteljahreshefte für Zeitgeschichte*, 27 (1979), 512.
45. See, in general, J. W. Young, *France, the Cold War and the Western Alliance* (Leicester, 1990).
46. J. Monnet, mid-April and the start of May, 1950, quoted in F. Duchêne, *Jean Monnet: The First Statesman of Interdependence* (New York, 1994), 198.
47. Monnet, 5 Aug. 1943 (Algiers), cited in E. du Réau, 'Integration or Cooperation? Europe and the Future of the Nation-State in France, 1945–1955', in D. Geppert (ed.), *Postwar Challenge*, 241.
48. F. Duchêne, *Monnet*, 187–8.
49. Ibid., 188.
50. D. Bruce, 25 Apr. 1950; F. Duchêne, *Monnet*, 189.
51. De Gaulle, 29 June 1947, in Loth, 'De Gaulle und Europa', *Historische Zeitschrift*, 253 (1991), 637.
52. Cited in S. Berstein, 'French Power', in Becker and Knipping (eds), *Power in Europe?*, vol. 1, 180–1.
53. Cited in P. Guillen, 'Europe as a Cure for French Impotence? The Guy Mollet Government and the Negotiation of the Treaties of Rome', in E. Di Nolfio, *Power in Europe?*, vol. 2, 507. For Franz Josef Strauß, *Die Erinnerungen*, 292, the SPD continued to a pursue an unrealistic and dangerous 'pseudo foreign policy', even after Schumacher's death—for example, opposing the European Defence Community in 1952–4.
54. See S. Berstein, 'The Perception of French Power by the Political Forces' and P. Milza, 'Public Opinion and Perception of Power in France at the End of the Fourth Republic', in E. Di Nolfio, *Power in Europe?*, 333–50, 462–76; M. Newman, 'Léon Blum, French Socialism and European Unity, 1940–1950', *Historical Journal*, 4 (1981), 189–200.
55. To Robert Marjolin, *Le travail d'une vie. Mémoires 1911–1986* (Paris, 1986), 262, 'For de Gaulle, as for Jean Monnet, Europe—the angular rock on which Europe had to rest—was essentially Franco-German rapprochement.'

118 EUROPEAN INTEGRATION SINCE THE 1920S

56. Spaak's letter of thanks to Khrushchev, whom he had visited in the USSR. In part, he was trying to convince the Soviet leader not to bring Germany back into play. P.-H. Spaak, *The Continuing Battle*, 431.
57. Krueger, 'Das doppelte Dilemma', *German Studies Review*, 22, (1999), 247–67. Also, H. Ashby Turner, Jr, 'Continuity in German Foreign Policy? The Case of Stresemann', *International History Review*, 1 (1979), 509–21.
58. P. M. R. Stirk, *European Integration since 1914*, 37. W. Lipgens, 'Europäische Einigungsidee 1923–1930 und Briands Europaplan im Urteil der deutschen Akten', *Historische Zeitschrift*, 203 (1966), 334–7.
59. Ibid., 324–8, for these countries and those below.
60. Cited ibid., 325.
61. S. Berstein, 'French Power', in J. Becker and F. Knipping (eds), *Power in Europe?*, vol. 1, 176.
62. From the German point of view, articulated by Franz Josef Strauß, *Die Erinnerungen*, 483–5, many Europeans' fears of a resurgent German military power were chimerical: 'It is not a question of dreams of world power. Germany has failed twice in a fundamental way on this course, to its own misfortune and that of many other peoples.' Germany did, however, have to 'escape the valley of impotence', which entailed 'a maximization of the available possibilities of power of the Federal Republic of Germany', including science and the economy, which had the potential to create significant foreign-policy tensions. Germany had to become 'capable of action', in the CSU leader's view, in order to challenge Communism and the USSR in Europe.
63. J. Monnet, 22 July 1947, in F. Duchêne, *Monnet*, 184.
64. Ibid., 206; E. du Réau, 'Integration or Cooperation?', in D. Geppert (ed.), *Postwar Challenge*, 248.
65. P. Guillen, 'Europe as a Cure for French Impotence?', in E. Di Nolfio, *Power in Europe?*, vol. 2, 507.
66. F. Duchêne, *Monnet*, 191.
67. Cited in W. Loth, 'De Gaulle und Europa', *Historische Zeitschrift*, 253 (1991), 631.
68. F. Duchêne, *Monnet*, 199. The Saar question was important for Adenauer: R. Irving, *Adenauer* (London, 2002), 115–23.
69. Monnet note of 13 Dec. 1948, and Mischlich memoirs, in F. Duchêne, *Monnet*, 206.
70. H. Alphand, 9 Feb. 1953, in G. Bossuat, 'Les hauts fonctionnaires français et le processus d'unité en Europe occidentale d'Alger à Rome, 1943–1958', *Journal of European Integration History*, 1 (1995), 101.
71. Loth, 'De Gaulle und Europa', *Historische Zeitschrift*, 253 (1991), 645–6. The argument here counters that of Loth, who emphasizes de Gaulle's willingness to consider supranational solutions.
72. Ibid.
73. N. Sarkozy, *Le Temps de tempêtes* (Paris, 2020), vol. 1, 24.
74. Ibid., 25.
75. H.-P. Schwarz, *Konrad Adenauer*, vol. 2, 672.
76. Quoted in M. Gilbert, *European Integration: A Political History*, 2nd edn (Lanham, MD, 2021), 95.
77. C. de Gaulle to K. Adenauer, July 1960, quoted in C. Parsons, *A Certain Idea of Europe*, 133.
78. M. Gilbert, *European Integration*, 95.
79. C. Parsons, *A Certain Idea of Europe*, 92, referring to the paraphrasing of Pierre Guillen, 'Pierre Mendès France et l'Allemagne', in R. Girault (ed.), *Pierre Mendès France et le role de la France dans le monde* (Grenoble, 1991), 39–54.
80. F. Mérand, *European Defence Policy: Beyond the Nation-State* (Oxford, 2008), 48–9; W. Rees, 'Preserving the Security of Europe', in A. Dorman, S. Croft, W. Rees, and M. Uttley, *Britain and Defence, 1945–2000* (London, 2001), 49–68. Anthony Eden agreed to station four divisions and an airforce in Europe for fifty years in part to persuade France to accept the FRG's membership of NATO. The British Foreign Secretary still wanted, as he had stated in 1952, to maintain close ties between Paris and Bonn: 'on balance I had rather see France and Germany in a confused but close embrace, than at arm's length': Roger Bullen and M. E. Pelly (eds), *Documents on British Policy Overseas*, series ii, vol. I, *The Schuman Plan, the Council of Europe and Western European Integration 1950–1952* (London, 1986), 846–7.
81. C. Parsons, *A Certain Idea of Europe*, 93.
82. J. Hauriou, early Oct. 1954, in G. Cophornic, 'SFIO et UEO: La recherche d'une unité', in R. Girault and G. Bossuat (eds), *Europe brisée, Europe retrouvée* (Paris, 1994), 257–82.
83. C. Parsons, *A Certain Idea of Europe*, 95; C. de Gaulle, *Mémoires d'espoir* (Paris, 1970–71), vol. 2, 621.
84. Quoted in J.-F. Deniau, *La découverte de l'Europe* (Paris, 1994), 54.
85. C. Parsons, *A Certain Idea of Europe*, 102–16.
86. J. Attali, *Verbatim* (Paris, 1993), vol. 1, 305.

87. Ibid., 311.
88. Ibid.
89. Ibid., 315.
90. Ibid., 316.
91. Ibid., 317.
92. Ibid., 321.
93. Ibid., 323.
94. C. Parsons, *A Certain Idea of Europe*, 147–201, argues that monetary policy remained a point of disagreement. Other authors argue that the dynamic and logic of monetary policy eventually helped integration: A. Moravcsik, *The Choice for Europe: Social Purpose and State Power from Messina to Maastricht* (Ithaca, NY, 1998); M. Loriaux, *France after Hegemony: International Change and Financial Reform* (Ithaca, NY, 1991); T. Oatley, *Monetary Politics: Exchange Rate Cooperation in the European Union* (Ann Arbor, 1997); J. B. Goodman, *Monetary Sovereignty: The Politics of Central Banking in Western Europe* (Ithaca, NY, 1992).
95. C. Parsons, *A Certain Idea of Europe*, 175.
96. Ibid., 175–6.
97. G. Robin, *La diplomatie de Mitterrand, ou le triomphe des apparences 1981–1985* (Paris, 1985), 219.
98. H. Kohl, *Erinnerungen,* vol. 2, 111.
99. C. Parsons, *A Certain Idea of Europe*, 77–8.
100. J. Moch, *Une si longue vie* (Paris, 1976), 477.
101. R. Aron, 'Historical Sketch of the Great Debate', in R. Aron and D. Lerner (eds), *France Defeats EDC* (New York, 1957), 20.
102. Quoted in K. K. Patel, *Project Europe*, 62.
103. Ibid.
104. M. Gilbert, *European Integration*, 50–1.
105. E. Calandri, 'The Western European Union Armaments Pool: France's Quest for Security and European Cooperation in Transition, 1951–55', *Journal of European Integration History*, 1 (1995), 56.
106. C. Parsons, *A Certain Idea of Europe*, 97.
107. J. Monnet, *Mémoires*, 466.
108. N. Leites and C. de la Malène, 'Paris from EDC to WEU', *World Politics*, 8 (1955), 193–219. See also G.-H. Sotou, *L'alliance incertaine. Les rapports politico-stratégiques franco-allemands, 1954–1996* (Paris, 1996), 28.
109. K. K. Patel, *Project Europe*, 41.
110. Ibid., 43.
111. Willy Brandt, *Erinnerungen* (Frankfurt, 1989), 240–60, marked the change of tone in a chapter of his memoirs entitled 'Der große Charles und das kleine Europa'.
112. H. Kissinger, G. Ford, and B. Scowcroft, memorandum of a conversation, 15 Aug. 1974, Collection 036600162, National Archives and Records Administration.
113. Ibid. See A. Romano, 'Détente, Entente or Linkage? The Helsinki Conference on Security and Cooperation in Europe in US Relations with the Soviet Union', *Diplomatic History*, 33 (2009), 703–22.
114. For the development of this trend during the Helsinki negotiations, see A. Romano, *From Détente in Europe to European Détente: How the West Shaped the Helsinki CSCE* (Brussels, 2009); and A. Romano, 'The EC Nine's Vision and Attempts at Ending the Cold War', in F. Bozo, M.-P. Rey, B. Rother, and N. P. Ludlow (eds), *Visions of the End of the Cold War, 1945–1990* (New York, 2012), 134–46.
115. 'Declaration on European Identity', *Bulletin of the European Communities*, 12 (1973), 118–22.
116. Ibid.
117. Ibid.
118. Ibid.
119. 'Solemn Declaration on European Union', *Bulletin of the European Communities*, 6 (1983), 24–9.
120. Ibid.
121. *Der Spiegel*, 22 Mar. 1982, quoted in K. K. Patel, *Project Europe*, 75.
122. Quoted in K. K. Patel, *Project Europe*, 75.
123. Kiran Patel, *Project Europe*, 75, states, on the basis of German records, that 'When actual fighting broke out in the South Atlantic a number of governments—including Dublin and Bonn —argued for the sanctions to be lifted.' See also L. L. Martin, 'Institutions and Cooperation: Sanctions during the Falkland Islands Conflict', *International Security*, 16 (1992), 163, and N. P. Ludlow,

120 EUROPEAN INTEGRATION SINCE THE 1920S

'Solidarity, Sanctions and Misunderstanding: The European Dimension of the Falklands Crisis', *International History Review,* 43 (2021), 508–24, which is based largely on British records.

124. C. M. Woodhouse, The Rise and Fall of the Greek Colonels (London, 1985).

125. J. Ker-Lindsay, *EU Accession and UN Peacemaking in Cyprus* (Basingstoke, 2005), and J. Ker-Lindsay, *The Cyprus Problem: What Everyone Needs to Know* (Oxford, 2011); N. Tocci, *EU Accession Dynamics and Conflict Resolution: Catalysing Peace or Consolidating Partition in Cyprus?* (Aldershot, 2004). As Tozun Bahcheli and Sid Noel, 'Ties That No Longer Bind: Greece, Turkey and the Fading Allure of Ethnic Kinship in Cyprus', in T. J. Mabry and J. McGarry (eds), *Divided Nations and European Integration* (University Park, PA, 2013), 337, point out, the EU was seen to have failed in 2004, yet the fading allure of ethnic kinship in Cyprus is arguably also connected to the system of inducements in the EU and aspirations of 'European' lifestyles.

126. See, for instance, A. Nafpliotis, *Britain and the Greek Colonels: Accommodating the Junta in the Cold War* (London, 2012).

127. E. Karamouzi, *Greece, the EEC and the Cold War, 1974–1979: The Second Enlargement* (Basingstoke, 2014).

128. P. Preston, *The Triumph of Democracy in Spain* (London, 2001); J.-F. Jiménez-Diaz and S. Delgado-Fernández (eds), *Political Leadership in the Spanish Transition to Democracy, 1975–1982* (New York, 2016); K. Maxwell, 'Portugal: "The Revolution of the Carnations", 1974–75', in A. Roberts and T. Garton Ash (eds.), *Civil Resistance and Power Politics: The Experience of Non-Violent Action from Gandhi to the Present* (Oxford, 2009), 144–61.

129. Thus, Robert Fishman, 'Shaping, not Making, Democracy: The European Union and the Post-Authoritarian Political Transformations of Spain and Portugal', *South European Society and Politics,* 8 (2003), 31–46, seeks to qualify earlier claims—for example, by Jonathan Story and Benny Pollack, 'Spain's Transition: Domestic and External Linkages', in G. Pridham (ed.), *Encouraging Democracy: The International Context of Regime Transition in Southern Europe* (New York, 1991), 45–61—that the transition and EEC membership were two sides of the same coin, but he accepts that accession and membership played a significant part.

130. 'Portugal's Application for Accession to the Communities', *Bulletin of the European Communities,* 3 (1977), 8.

131. 'Speech by the Right Hon. Roy Jenkins, President of the European Communities, on the Occasion of the Opening of the Spanish Negotiations, Brussels, 3 Feb. 1979, *Archive of European Integration,* http://aei.pitt.edu/id/eprint/11312.

132. 'US and Allied Security Policy in Southern Europe', 15 Dec. 1975, quoted in K. K. Patel, *Project Europe,* 77.

133. Peter Gold, *Gibraltar: British or Spanish?* (London, 2005), 51–169, stresses the ups and downs, but the overall defusing of tension is also clear.

134. W. Danspeckgruber, 'Self-Determination in Our Time: Reflections on Perception, Globalization and Change', in J. Fisch (ed.), *Die Verteilung der Welt. Selbstbestimmung und das Selbstbestimmungsrecht der Völker* (Munich, 2011), 313–14. See also W. Danspeckgruber, 'Self-Determination and Regionalization in Contemporary Europe', in W. Danspeckgruber (ed.), *The Self-Determination of Peoples: Community, Nation and State in an Interdependent World* (Boulder, CO, 2002), 165–200.

135. W. Danspeckgruber, 'Self-Determination in Our Time: Reflections on Perception, Globalization and Change', in J. Fisch (ed.), *Die Verteilung der Welt,* 313–14.

136. Zoe Bray and Michael Keating, 'European Integration and the Basque Country in France and Spain', in T. J. Mabry and J. McGarry, *Divided Nations and European Integration,* 150–1: 'The border has not disappeared under the impact of European integration, but it has been transformed and has become a new factor in local politics. Europe has permitted new ways of constructing Basque identity, but these are always negotiated by actors in multiple ways, and Europe itself has not gained consensual meaning. Cross-border cooperation themes have proliferated, but it would be a mistake to group these under a heading of "uniting" the Basque Country just as it was a mistake in the 1990s to imagine that the European Commission had a plan to subvert the state and transform the continent into a "Europe of the Regions".'

137. John McGarry and Brendan O'Leary, 'The Exaggerated Impact of European Integration on the Politics of Divided Nations', in T. J. Mabry, J. McGarry, M. Moore, and B. O'Leary (eds), *Divided Nations and European Integration* (Philadelphia, PA, 2013), 350–1.

138. J. McGarry, 'Globalization, European Integration and the Changing International Order', in M. Keating and J. McGarry (eds), *Minority Nationalism and the Changing International Order* (Oxford, 2001), 301–2.

139. E. Tannam, 'The Divided Irish', in T. J. Mabry and J. McGarry, *Divided Nations and European Integration*, 270.
140. Ibid., 264.
141. E. Tannam, 'The European Union and the Politics in Northern Ireland', *Ethnic and Racial Studies*, 18 (1995), 812.
142. John McGarry and Brendan O'Leary, 'The Exaggerated Impact of European Integration on the Politics of Divided Nations', in T. J. Mabry and J. McGarry, *Divided Nations and European Integration*, 382.
143. Z. Csergö and J. M. Goldgeier, 'Kin-State Activism in Hungary, Romania and Russia: The Politics of Ethnic Demography', in T. J. Mabry and J. McGarry, *Divided Nations and European Integration* (Philadelphia, PA, 2013), 109–10.
144. Carsten Sander Christensen (ed.), *Analyzing Political Tensions between Ukraine, Russia and the EU* (Hershey, PA, 2020); A. Paul, 'The EU in the South Caucasus and the Impact of the Russia-Ukraine War', *The International Spectator*, 50 (2015), 30–42.
145. Memorandum of a conversation between G. Ford, H. Kissinger and B. Scowcroft, 23 Aug. 1974, National Security Adviser Collection 036600070, National Archives and Records Administration, Washington DC.
146. Interview with Lozje Peterle, quoted in R. Caplan, *Europe and the Recognition of New States in Yugoslavia* (Cambridge, 2009), 100.
147. Interview with Dimitrij Rupel, ibid., 102.
148. 'Some Western Nations Split off on Yugoslavia', *New York Times*, 3 July 1991. *The Independent*, 5 July 1991, reported that Kohl had declared: 'The peoples of Yugoslavia must be free to choose their own future. Free Europe must stand beside them.... The importance of the principle of self-determination is that much more evident for Germans because by means of self-determination our nation was able to regain its unity.'
149. 'European Community Freezes Arms Sales and Aid', *New York Times*, 6 July 1991.
150. 'First Test for New Europe', *The Independent*, 28 June 1991.
151. G. Fink (ed.), *Stress of War, Conflict and Disaster* (Oxford, 2010), 469; 'New War Demographics', UN International Criminal Tribunal for the Former Yugoslavia, 29 Mar. 2011.
152. Quoted in George Ross, *Jacques Delors and European Integration* (Cambridge, 1995), 97–8.
153. A. Forster, *Britain and the Maastricht Negotiations* (Basingstoke, 1999), 113.
154. Ibid.
155. J. Baker, *The Politics of Diplomacy* (New York, 1995), 636–7.
156. *New York Times*, 29 June 1991.
157. M. Nicholson, *Natasha's Story* (London, 1994).
158. Sam Pryke, 'National and European Identity', *National Identities*, 22 (2020), 100, quoting the findings of the large-scale Eurobarometer poll of 27,000 respondents: in 20 member states, 'the free movement of people, goods and services within the EU' was seen as the Union's greatest achievement.

3

European Stories

Historically, European integration appears likely, given the breadth of support for diplomatic and economic cooperation after 1918, and improbable, if one bears in mind the absence of an institutional framework for cooperation before the First World War and the failure of governments to cooperate after it.[1] International organizations and inter-state conflicts had co-existed in Europe in the first half of the twentieth century.[2] In the second half of the century, it seemed as though the imperatives of the Cold War would at once reduce the number of inter-state conflicts in the rim around the Soviet Union, with the exception of 'proxy' wars, and push governments to participate in US-backed, 'Western' organizations rather than specifically European ones. However, although they continue to belong to a panoply of international organizations, European states have cooperated most fully on the European level and have delegated more powers to European institutions than to their international counterparts, begging a series of questions about how and why they have done so. In this institutional context, how far have citizens come to identify with the European Union? The next two chapters investigate overlapping processes of identification and allegiance on which the EU as a political and legal order has come to rely. They re-examine the relationship between citizenship, belonging, politics, and culture, which has long characterized the study of nationalism, in order to discover whether affiliations and loyalties have been transferred from national to European institutions. To what extent does the EU need citizens—'Europeans'—to identify with Europe?

For Alan Milward, allegiance—or 'all those elements which induce citizens to give their loyalty to institutions of governance, whether national, international, or supranational'—is more important than identification.[3] It 'excludes repression', since 'few would doubt the validity of the generalization that all in all the member states of the successive European Communities' government has been in its essentials government by consent'.[4] The model of the nineteenth-century nation-state, which sought to protect citizens from internal and external threats, has been partly displaced since 1945 by a much more broadly defined need for 'security' in an economic and symbolic sense.[5] 'Except in moments of perceived danger, or when issues relating to one dominant personality have emerged, personal and family income and the perspective of future income through the life-cycle have been the major determinants of voting,' Milward writes: 'This may mean that they are also major determinants of allegiance.'[6] Citizens agreed to pay ever higher taxes in the post-war period, which issued in tax rates double those of

---

European Integration since the 1920s: Security, Identity, and Cooperation. Mark Hewitson, Oxford University Press.
© Mark Hewitson 2024. DOI: 10.1093/oso/9780198915942.003.0004

the 1930s—in order to pay for welfare and other public services, all of which provided security.[7] Yet it would be 'absurdly mechanistic to suppose that the disposition of allegiance between the different forms of governance on offer has been—or will be—determined by accurate materialistic calculations or even solely by materialistic perspectives'.[8] Rather, the 'symbolic role of "Europe" in political rhetoric and the changing way in which it enters into national political discourse' also affect citizens' loyalty, even if we know little—in Milward's judgement—about how they came about.[9] Earlier theorists had assumed that 'popular support for the idea of a united Europe' rested on the belief that it was 'something better than the nation-state'.[10] Milward, though, insists that 'there has been no diminution in national allegiance, even though there has been a growth of secondary allegiance to "Europe"'.[11] 'The assumption that there is a fundamental antithesis between the nation-state and the Community was set in circulation by academic discourse' and it 'has lain at the heart of virtually all attempts to construct comprehensive theoretical explanations of the evolution of the European Community, as well as of the early attempts to write its history', he declares in *The European Rescue of the Nation-State* (1992).[12] This chapter explores such discourse, which was produced by commentators at the time and, subsequently, by academics.

The task for historians is to balance, evaluate, and explain shifting loyalties and affiliations on local, national, European, and international levels. It also involves questions about the objects of citizens' affiliation and loyalty, which, in turn, necessitates an assessment of mediators'—that is, intellectuals' and journalists'— perceptions of and stories about European history and a European culture.[13]

Is There a European Culture?

Debates about the geography and history of a European continent or culture have proved to be enduring but inconclusive. 'Europe', claimed Simone de Beauvoir in the memoirs which she published in 1963, was a myth, used by the United States as it sought to restore the power of Germany as a counterweight to that of the USSR.[14] A coherent and credible story about Europe, to which citizens can feel an attachment, is necessary insofar as political authority and allegiance require loyalty beyond mere adherence to justifiable rules of democratic deliberation or a calculation of self-interest. Functionalists contended that 'in a given transnational community citizens would, through experiencing socio-economic benefits from cooperation, transfer their primary loyalties away from nation-states to an apolitical, supranational, functionally specific authority, and that from citizens within the community would come the impetus for further cooperation and integration', writes Juliet Lodge.[15] Neo-functionalists concentrated on elite loyalties. Yet what 'remains rather unclear' is 'the process by which supranational loyalties are to be generated and, more importantly, how loyalties, to use Haas's metaphor, are transferred from one setting to another'.[16] Loyalty, here, implies not 'mere emotion', but 'the *willing* engagement of a man in pursuit of a cause'.[17] Proponents of integration added a functional aspect, based on 'perceived and concrete utilitarian interests', to 'more diffuse and affective responses'.[18] Given the distance between citizens and the European Community, together with 'the "facelessness" of its institutions', it has proved difficult to generate loyalty resting on 'accountability and responsiveness'.[19] It is, therefore, all the more important to generate loyalty deriving from a shared, desirable, or defensible history and feeling of belonging. The problem for the European Union is that its forerunners were established to avert the 'self-destruction' of Europe carried out, in two world wars, in the name of 'culture'.[20]

Most components of a putative European identity are contentious. The significance and role of antiquity, Christianity, the Enlightenment, science, industrialization, and imperialism have been interpreted in a variety of ways. Some authors such as the German playwright Gerhart Hauptmann believed that these traditions had been destroyed by the First World War, turning 'Europe's pride' into 'its shamelessness'.[21] Europe's 'most shameless lies are Christianity, love of mankind, the rule of reason, international law, the League of Nations, humanity, culture', he wrote in 1923: 'Instead of this, they must be called bestiality, hatred of mankind, the rule of unreason, international lawlessness, the persecution of nations, inhumanity and, instead of the word "Kultur", theft, robbery, arson, murder and plunder must stand.'[22] Observers such as Paul Valéry, who seemed to agree with the German writer in his well-known essay on 'The Crisis of the Spirit' in 1919, in fact continued to presume that European science and technology were superior to those of the rest of the world and should not be exported overseas.[23] Yet other intellectuals questioned whether Hauptmann's apparently indisputable grounds for European pride had ever existed. Albert Demangeon, whose *Déclin de l'Europe* (1920) enjoyed a success in France redolent of that of Oswald Spengler's *Der Untergang des Abendlandes* (1918–22) in Germany, accounted for the continent's decline largely in economic and political terms, as the rest of the world was able to carry out a process of 'de-Europeanization'.[24] In much the same way, the editor of *Die Zukunft* Maximilian Harden prophesied in 1923 that 'Europe would be the sphere of economically more unified states or it would lose its ascendancy and submit to an honourable calcification'.[25] For his part, Spengler saw Western—or Central and Western European—decline largely in cultural terms, albeit mixed with a determining form of materialism, and he predicted that it was irreversible, as part of the inevitable rise and fall of monadic world cultures.[26]

Many commentators continued this tradition after the Second World War, echoing T. S. Eliot's anxiety that 'our entire culture' could collapse.[27] Only a minority placed much hope, as Eliot did, in 'our Christian legacy' of morality and its mediation of the 'ancient civilizations' of Greece and Rome.[28] As the British poet Stephen Spender announced to a meeting of European intellectuals—including Karl Jaspers, Georg Lukacs, Georges Bernanos, Denis de Rougement, and Julien Benda—in Geneva in 1946, Europe could no longer find its cultural unity in the idea of Europe, since this was characterized by 'nihilism, nationalism, destruction and hatred'.[29] What would hold Europe together politically? Hannah Arendt had argued that totalitarianism had created a rupture in European history which would force Europeans to re-evaluate their political principles and reconstruct their political institutions. Her cultural diagnosis of the condition of Europe was not optimistic, however. In an essay on 'Nightmare and Flight' (1945), she proposed that 'the problem of evil will be the fundamental question of postwar intellectual life in Europe—as death became the fundamental problem after the last war'.[30] Given that 'totalitarianism' remained in place in Eastern Europe and authoritarian dictatorships in Southern Europe, it was not obvious how specifically European political traditions could be identified and refashioned. Few found, like Klaus Mann in his posthumously published essay on 'Europe's Search for a New Credo' (1949), cause for celebration in the fact that 'everyone in Europe' was 'tortured and unsettled', ignorant and fearful of what was to come.[31] Despair, nostalgia, or utopianism—in the manner of Jean-Paul Sartre's call for 'a united, socialist European Community' in 1949—were more common responses.[32] As in the years after the First World War, confusion was widespread.

In general, right-wing authors such as Spengler tended to stress the continent's cultural collapse to a greater degree, emphasizing the lapsed legacy of Christianity and criticizing the impact of the Enlightenment, science, and industrial transformation. Liberal and left-wing observers were often more optimistic about 'rationality' and economic progress, and they were more willing to condemn Christian obscurantism, but there were many exceptions. German commentators across the political spectrum were arguably more suspicious of 'Zivilisation', or the assimilation of quantifiable methods and material technologies, and they were more receptive to the Romantic irrationality of 'Kultur'—a proclivity which can even be detected in Max Horkheimer and Theodor Adorno's iconoclastic Dialektik der Aufklärung (1944)—than were their French counterparts, who frequently equated 'civilization', humanitarianism, enlightenment, and culture.[33] The nationalist right in countries defeated in the First World War was more likely to espouse technology in the name of a new European order and to rail against an old order associated with the Paris peace conferences than was its equivalent in the victorious powers. From a standpoint of formal neutrality in the First and Second World Wars, an observer like José Ortega y Gasset was perhaps especially eclectic but nonetheless indicative in his selection of European attributes, discounting antiquity and downgrading Christianity—'men have not lived exclusively by faith in God, but... faith in science, in reason'—in his identification of the origins of 'Europe' in the eighth century, as Islam destroyed the civilization of the Mediterranean and the centre of the continent was established in the North by Charlemagne with the emergence of 'Germanism', or the duality of Roman-inspired law and states, on the one hand, and Germanic freedom, science, and vitality, on the other.[34] The bewilderment caused by such heterogeneity was visible in the mixed response of some contemporaries to the Nazis' use of many of the same tropes, as part of their plan for a 'New Europe' or a 'European confederation'.[35] Although indicating that it was misguided, John Maynard Keynes's fear in November 1941 that Hitler stood a chance of getting 'his new Europe going properly' hinted at contemporaries' uncertainty about what Europe was or what it stood for (see Map 3.1).[36]

In the post-war era, the leaders and proponents of the European Communities and the EU have struggled with the concept of culture, with the EC largely ignoring it and the European Union espousing cultural diversity.[37] The Maastricht Treaty 'was the first time the community had taken for itself significant powers in the cultural field', writes Enda O'Doherty:

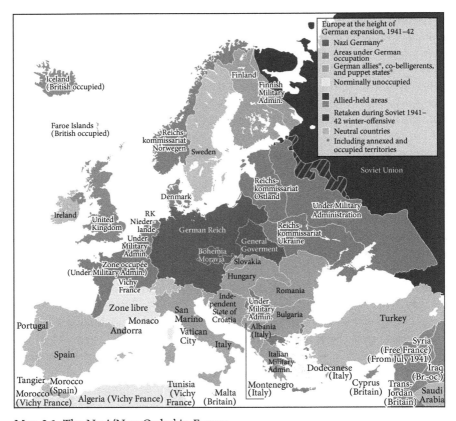

Map 3.1 The Nazi 'New Order' in Europe
Source: https://en.wikipedia.org/wiki/New_Order_%28Nazism%29#/media/World_War_II_in_Europe, _1942.svg.

European *cultures* (note the plural), the relevant article stated, were to be understood as requiring 'respect'—by which one understands freedom from too much supranational interference ('The Community shall contribute to the flowering of the cultures of the member states, while respecting their national and regional diversity'). At the same time, the Community was to be entrusted with the task of 'bringing the common cultural heritage to the fore'.[38]

In O'Doherty's view, there is 'a compromise lurking here, or possibly a contradiction', since 'cultures are to be understood as national (and grudgingly, just a little bit regional)', and 'they are even perhaps what define nations' (as 'the particular set of practices and inheritances which the Dutch, or the Germans, or the Portuguese have by virtue of their nationality, the thing that they have and no other nation has'), 'yet it seems, according to Maastricht, that there is also a common cultural heritage which belongs equally to the Dutch and the Germans and the Portuguese'.[39] What is this heritage—'Is it something made up of a little bit of everywhere sort of tacked together ("the Europe of Dante, Shakespeare and Goethe" perhaps, to which statesmen like to pay obeisance in their speeches before quickly passing on to more important matters)' or 'could it be something more mysterious, something actually European?' asks O'Doherty.[40] The Hungarian philosopher Agnes Heller's contention that a European culture does not exist but can be created is 'the wrong way round', borne out by the EU's disastrous 'cultural record since Maastricht': 'there certainly has been a European culture, while it seems now rather doubtful if a new or renewed one can be created, least of all perhaps by our European institutions'.[41] However, if the American notion of *e pluribus unum* (out of the many one) is not possible, not least because it requires European citizens 'to leave behind much of what they have been', is 'a *unitas multiplex*, in which difference, diversity and complexity and a Babel of languages are accorded a positive value', a sufficient grounding for political allegiance and authority?[42]

Historically, there are reasons to doubt that culture alone—or, more narrowly, a shared set of values—provides sufficient grounds to convince the leaders of nation-states to give up powers or to contemplate, in Simon Glendinning's words, 'a "decision" that would be a willed act of giving up the will to act'.[43] Few nineteenth-century commentators disagreed with the idea that a common European culture existed, but they did not contemplate political or economic cooperation, for the most part. As the interwar and postwar eras demonstrated, commentators were only likely to advocate greater cooperation between European states or, even, integration in certain spheres of state activity because of a specific set of beliefs about recent history, Europe's place in the world, economic prosperity, nationalism, and the nation-state.[44] This insufficiency of culture does not mean that it became irrelevant after the Second World War, displaced by planning and technocracy in practice and by neo-functionalism in theory, as some scholars have claimed.[45] There was no 'zero hour' in 1945 which made projects for Europe seem more realizable and significant, to the exclusion of long-established ideas of Europe and at the expense of tradition 'as a legitimizing force'.[46] Many earlier conceptions of and projects for Europe, which were informed by a barely challenged set of cultural assumptions, persisted after the Second World War.[47] The French intellectual Julien Benda was not unusual in maintaining that 'the war has exercised no influence either way on my ideas or on my conception as to the manner of expressing them'.[48] Partly as a consequence, thinkers continued to countenance and disseminate heterogeneous views about the future of Europe, some of which influenced decision-makers.

Commentators continued to disagree about the foundations of Europe's cultural identity, although few doubted that it existed.[49] In Germany, the terms '*Abendland*', '*Mitteleuropa*', '*Paneuropa*', 'Reich', and '*Großraum*' all subsumed or impinged on the meaning of 'Europe', but they all had different connotations, linked to the domestic disputes of political parties.[50] Was Europe principally a territory or geographical region and, if so, where were its borders? For Richard von Coudenhove-Kalergi, the founder of the *Paneuropa* movement, the United Kingdom was not sufficiently European to be included in his designs for the continent, at least until 1938, whereas for Wilhelm Heile, the head of the *Verband für europäische Verständigung*, Britain was an indispensable part of Europe, on which the future of the continent was likely to depend (see Map 3.2).[51] Many observers were sceptical that geography defined Europe at all, preferring to think of it as a culture or civilization with a shared history. Yet these definitions, too, were marked by ambiguity and contradiction. Europeans in the interwar era, remarked Ortega y Gasset, had seen their fundamental beliefs replaced by doubts as a consequence of the onslaught of new ideologies and forms of dictatorship, leaving them little sense of the continent's position in the world: 'One part of Europe advocates principles which it considers "new"; the other part tries to defend traditional principles. Now this is the best proof that neither set of principles is in force at the moment, and either they have lost, or have not reached, the status of accepted norms.'[52] After the Second World War, 'each people' in Europe was 'introverted in spite of the visibly gigantic worldwide intercourse' taking place.[53] In both the interwar and post-war years, it was hard to distinguish values, ideas, practices, or institutions which could unite the continent. Europe after the First World War, went on the Spanish intellectual, had had an 'ignoble vegetative existence . . . , its muscles flabby for want of exercise, without any plan of the new life', meaning that even a culturally backward event such as the Russian Revolution, which was reminiscent of 1817 rather than 1917, risked attracting Europeans to its cause: 'It is simply a misunderstanding of the European to expect that he can hear unmoved that call to new action when he has no standard of a cause as great to unfurl in opposition.'[54] Many observers repeated 'daily' and 'with moving sanctimony that Western civilization must be saved', but it was unlikely

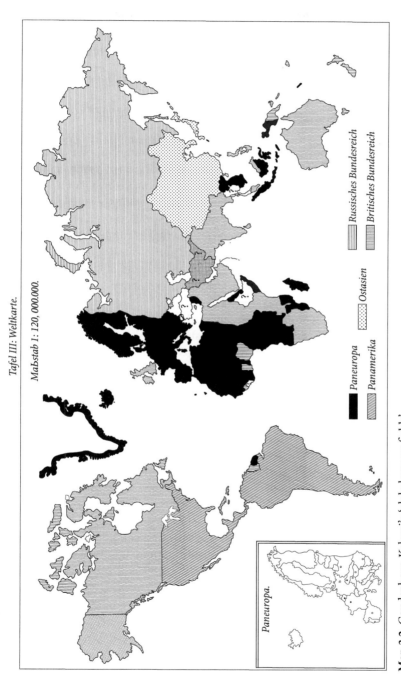

Map 3.2 Coudenhove-Kalergi's 'global power fields'
Source: R. N. Coudenhove-Kalergi, *Pan-Europa* (Vienna, 1923), Fig. 3.

130 EUROPEAN INTEGRATION SINCE THE 1920S

that such an endeavour would be unifying or worthwhile: its proponents, declared Ortega, 'seem to me like dissectors who tire themselves out trying to resurrect a mummy. Western civilization has died a beautiful and honourable death. It died alone; its enemies did not kill it.'[55] What, though, was to replace that civilization and to unite the continent? Many commentators have replied 'history'.

Intellectuals and the History of the Present

Europe was an 'invention', in Gerard Delanty's formulation, insofar as it was 'constructed in a historical process', 'a historically fabricated reality of ever-changing forms and dynamics'.[56] As such, it was the product of history's divisions and frontiers, both internal and external, 'interpolated in concrete configurations of power and their geo-political complexes'.[57] Ideas in this sense rarely dictated political actions, but they were connected to an evolving historical context, which comprised the interplay of events and contemporaries'—and later scholars'— understanding of those events. 'Europe', as a construction of ideas, has been subject to constant contestation and transformation, as different interested parties sought to adapt it to existing or perceived conditions, or to prevent its adaptation, for their own purposes. In these circumstances, the 'origins' or enduring elements of a purported European idea or identity—'crystallisations', in Delanty's phrase— are less significant than shorter-term relationships between participants in public debates, politics and the making of public policy in given but changing conditions.[58] Individuals' motivations and actions are incomprehensible without reference to their assumptions, ideas, and beliefs, but they are not to be understood merely as their corollary. Advocates and opponents of diverse projects for Europe appear to have had very different reasons for acting, as a consequence of their varying national and political perspectives, traditions, and interests, not least because any European project required the establishment of new practices and institutions, in conjunction with a shift away from existing levels and spheres of government. Actors had many motives for supporting, opposing, or ignoring a particular conception of or project for Europe. The converse is also true, however: the same actors were limited by specific sets of historical conditions and cultural discourses. What they expected of European institutions was shaped by these circumstances.

Press reports tended to follow events, linking Europe to the onset of the Cold War.[59] For *The Times*, Churchill's speech in Fulton, Missouri, in March 1946 was critical, locating the Continent between Communist and democratic ideological blocs.[60] For the German press, this realization came later, in 1948, with journalists such as Erich Kuby, the editor of the liberal *Süddeutsche Zeitung*, noting that the Oder was the 'border of Europe'.[61] The signature of the Treaty of Brussels by the UK, France, and the Benelux countries on 17 March 1948, which provided for economic, social, cultural. and, especially, military cooperation, establishing a Western Union and forming the basis of NATO (from 1949 onwards), was hailed by the *Süddeutsche* as a 'call towards the West', 'a cornerstone of European reconstruction' and a 'bulwark' against the Soviet Union.[62] The conservative *Frankfurter Allgemeine Zeitung* treated the Pact and the later founding of NATO more superficially, until West Germany joined the alliance in 1955, but it, too, located the FRG unambiguously in an anti-Communist 'West'.[63] The creation of the European Coal and Steel Community in 1951 and the EEC in 1957, together with the failure to ratify the European Defence Community in 1954, were all represented in the German, British, and Dutch press as part of a wider struggle against Communism.[64] The *FAZ* remained more ambivalent about the 'West', viewing the European Defence Community and NATO as 'unnatural', but it also saw them as complementary and necessary organizations of defence against 'the Russian colossus':

> The idea of a European Union is an illegitimate child of the Cold War, whose father is Stalin. Europeans have discovered that this child has such adorable features, which remind them of the lost values of their western (*abendländisch*) past, that they want to forget its suspect origins and are ready to care for it...as their own. They are disappointed to learn that Great Britain does not object to such care, but it has pledged its own love for another illegitimate offspring of the Cold War, the North Atlantic Community.[65]

In the pressured conditions of the Cold War, even the conservative journalists of the *Frankfurter Allgemeine Zeitung* had quickly accepted the primacy of the United States.[66] For British newspapers such as *The Times*, the need to court the USA and to defend 'Western civilization' had been long-standing aims.[67] The left-leaning *Manchester Guardian* had likewise recycled Bevin's official line on America and the West.[68] By contrast, newspaper coverage of other European states and governments was still marked by a certain degree of suspicion.[69]

In accordance with contemporary commentary, the actions of European statesmen and politicians in both the interwar and post-war eras were largely defensive, reacting to the menace of extra-European powers such as the USSR and United States and to conflict and a crisis of confidence in Europe itself after the First World War—facts which seemed to have been confirmed by the Second World War, the onset of the Cold War, and shocking revelations about the Holocaust. The 'German question' and the Franco-German axis remained central to most European policy-makers in both postwar periods, with even semi-detached British observers like Hastings Ismay—Winston Churchill's chief military assistant in the Second World War and later Secretary General of NATO—admitting that the North Atlantic Treaty Organisation was not merely designed to keep the United States in Europe and the USSR out, but also to keep Germany down.[70] At the same

132 EUROPEAN INTEGRATION SINCE THE 1920S

time, many European ministers continued to combine fear and hubris with regard to the wider world, with the Quai d'Orsay attempting to rebuild its empire—including major campaigns and loss of life in Syria, Madagascar, Indo-China, and Algeria—until the late 1950s and the British Foreign Office attempting to maintain a global role until the Suez crisis of 1956.[71] Such uncertainty about the role of European powers was similar in some respects to that of the 1920s. It helped to produce a bewildering array of prognoses for Europe's recovery in the late 1940s and 1950s, as in the 1920s, which clashed with plans for the 'rescue' of individual nation-states and reconstruction of national economies. Such plans were put forward in tumultuous conditions, militating towards limited, predominantly economic reform on the European level rather than political or military integration.[72] What is surprising, it could be held, is the precariousness of decisions for and against 'Europe' both in the 1920s and early 1930s, and in the late 1940s and early 1950s. History, agreed the liberal, 'positivist' Austrian émigré Karl Popper and the ex-socialist, conservative-minded Spanish liberal Ortega y Gasset, had no intrinsic direction.[73] What would happen in and to Europe was, as historians of the Cold War have begun to acknowledge, difficult to predict.[74]

In the immediate post-war years, few writers doubted that 'Europe' existed, even though they disagreed about its character and purpose, and many proposed that there was a case for cooperation between European states. There was broad agreement that European economies would benefit from integration. The interwar era had witnessed the establishment of increasingly protected markets in Germany, Italy, the USSR and the United States in accordance with the dictates of all-embracing ideologies—save in the case of the US—and against the advice of the majority of experts.[75] As a consequence, many economists and other commentators had called for economic cooperation or integration in the 1920s and 1930s.[76] By 1945, even a 'national planner' such as Keynes, who vigorously opposed Friedrich Hayek's notion of market-driven distribution and social organization, accepted that European economies needed greater coordination beyond the level of the nation-state, as he spelled out in an early plan for an International Clearing Bank during the Second World War:

> A view of the post-war world which I find sympathetic and attractive and fruitful of good consequences is that we should encourage *small* political and cultural units, combined into larger, and more or less closely knit, economic units. It would be a fine thing to have thirty or forty capital cities in Europe, each the centre of a self-governing country entirely free from national minorities (who would be dealt with by migrations where necessary) and the seat of a government and parliament and university centre, each with their own pride and glory and their own characteristics and excellent gifts. But it would be ruinous to have thirty or forty entirely independent economic and currency unions.[77]

Few of Keynes's contemporaries concurred with his preference for a 're-medievalized Europe', an idea which he omitted from later drafts, but most agreed with his economic prescriptions.[78] Ortega y Gasset, for instance, warned in the late 1940s that 'we shall continue with national economies on the defensive, which is the saddest and most dangerous attitude for an economy', unless a European structure could be created.[79] 'Today, production itself, in the forefront of collective life with everything depending on it, is the new form from which could be expected only the politics of grand design,' he went on: 'In these last thirty years, as the need has steadily become more evident, so the numbers have grown of those who advocate supernational institutions matching the gigantic size to which production problems have increased.'[80] Nation-states had not been able since the First World War to find 'a healthy, natural and viable solution to economic problems'.[81] In Ortega's opinion, European economic integration was a commonly shared goal.

Like Keynes, Ortega was less confident that his demand for some sort of juridical and political structure for Europe would find support, hinting that many of his contemporaries believed that the 'idea of a European economy' alone would be 'an effective standard', which would regulate its own workings and which would resolve disputes between nation-states.[82] There was, however, a broad commitment among intellectuals—and post-war politicians—to human and political rights, pluralism, constitutionalism, political parties, parliaments, liberal democracy, a market or mixed economy, and a welfare or social state, which could—in the right circumstances—facilitate political cooperation or limited integration on a European level.[83] The most salient reason for such qualified consensus was opposition to 'totalitarianism' and dictatorship, whether authoritarian, fascist, or Communist, which extended back into the interwar period.[84] This opposition helped to ensure in Italy that liberal socialists such as Carlo Rosselli (*Liberal Socialism*, 1930) and Gramscian Marxists, reading the *Prison Notebooks* as they were published between 1948 and 1951, remained committed to individual liberties and a democratic path to socialism or Communism, joining liberals such as Guido De Ruggiero (*History of European Liberalism*, 1924) and Benedetto Croce, who had revised his formerly Hegelian view of freedom in response to fascism during the 1930s (*History as Thought and Action*, 1938).[85] In Germany, too, despite many individual points of contention, virtually all legal and political theorists had been converted to the necessity of a democratic order, even Carl Schmitt, who conceded in 1963 that his 'concept of the political' in the interwar period had been flawed, since its distinction between friend and foe as the basis of political action had failed to differentiate between 'conventional, real and absolute enemies', permitting an unlimited escalation of political conflict.[86] Pupils of Schmitt such as Werner Weber, in spite of criticism of oligarchical party structures and a call for a strong

134 EUROPEAN INTEGRATION SINCE THE 1920S

executive and civil service to fill the 'authority vacuum' of the FRG, claimed that they accepted the need for mass, party democracies.[87]

In France, the political debate of intellectuals after 1945 was marked by a division between Communists and existentialists on the left, who—like Maurice Merleau-Ponty—were committed in theory to revolution, and 'moderates' in the centre and on the right such as Raymond Aron, Emmanuel Mounier, Jacques Maritain, Bertrand de Jouvenel, Maurice Duverger, and René Capitant, who sought to entrench the four fundamental democratic principles of autonomy, equality, secularism, and sovereignty.[88] Aron's attempt to combine bourgeois citizenship, technological efficiency, and the right of individuals to choose their own way of life was typical in its negotiation of the potential perils of a technocratic and industrial society and in its renunciation of 'the abstractions of moralism and ideology', together with the pursuit of 'the true content of possible choices, limited as they are by reality itself'.[89] In his lecture to the Congress of Cultural Freedom— later revealed to be in receipt of CIA funding—in West Berlin in June 1960, Aron argued that the industrial societies which had emerged in Europe after the Second World War had become 'stabilized and pacified democracies', with representative institutions and guarantees of personal freedoms which stood in contrast to the ideological, social, and ethnic conflicts of the earlier twentieth century.[90] In Britain, the main debate was between liberal intellectuals, defending 'negative' liberty (Isaiah Berlin) and the 'open society' (Karl Popper), advocates of capitalism (Hayek) and proponents of 'social' citizenship and welfare (T. H. Marshall), yet all supported the need for a balanced constitution and a parliamentary democracy.[91] Throughout the continent, the dangers of the European 'crisis', it seemed, had reinforced intellectuals' belief—detectable well before 1945—in the merits of liberal democracy, social protection, and economic cooperation. Post-war European projects were associated with, and benefited from, these reactions.

Such domestic preferences, which were framed against a history of dictatorship on the Continent, did not address questions about competition and antagonism between nation-states, which seemed to have caused the crisis in the first half of the twentieth century, and about the relationship between national and European institutions. The means by which persisting national allegiances were to be reconciled with attachments to 'Europe' were often left undiscussed in the relevant post-war literature, echoing the French publicist Bertrand de Jouvenel's admission in 1930 that 'the reconciliation of nationalism and internationalism, let's be frank, is a fairy tale'.[92] 'The truth is that we have to choose,' he went on: 'If we wish to maintain full and complete sovereignty, a United States of Europe remains a dead letter.'[93] In Germany, which had the most destructive history of nationalism in Europe, Friedrich Meinecke, the liberal historian and well-known critic of the Nazi dictatorship, had argued in *Die deutsche Katastrophe* (1946) that only those recognizing the 'internal alien domination' of 'a criminal club' of National

Socialists would discover 'a solution to the national problem of duty', making 'the era of external, alien domination' of the Allies after 1945 palatable.[94] In other words, Germans who failed to understand that the Allied occupation was a direct consequence of Nazi crimes would not be able to identify and carry out their national responsibilities. Yet Meinecke went on to suggest that National Socialism was not a specifically German phenomenon, but an extension of modern European pathologies resulting—in an echo of Ortega y Gasset and other contemporary thinkers—from the transition to mass society, which had served to simplify notions of national belonging, loyalty and interest, and to pervert the dominant nineteenth-century movements of nationalism and socialism. Germany, according to this reading, was not a special case but a European problem.[95] References to 'Europe' here were, in part, designed to relativize and make comprehensible Germans' feelings of guilt and actual culpability for the catastrophe of the Second World War.[96]

To many observers, the European project was still obstructed by the tradition and actuality of the state. Was the nation-state compatible with Europeanism? Some, like Benda, denounced nationalism altogether after the Great War, arguing that it had replaced the egotism of the individual with the egotism of the group.[97] The 'treason of the clerks', identified by the French writer in the 1920s, consisted in an 'attachment, more ferocious, conscious and organised than ever, to the *purely temporal*, and contempt for all genuinely ideal and disinterested values', leaving humanity with only two 'religions'—'Nation' or 'Class'.[98] Europe would only be a moral act, 'if morality consists in Being ceasing to think of itself under the mode of the real, of the distinct, of the finite, [in order] to think of itself under the mode of the infinite or divine'.[99] This 'passion for reason', intrinsic to Benda's aspirations for Europe, would banish nationalism: 'You will only vanquish nationalist passion by another passion.'[100] Few of Benda's contemporaries imitated such flights of fancy. Most depicted some sort of accommodation between nationalism and 'Europeanism', which extended as far as Pierre Drieu La Rochelle on the far right. The French fascist maintained his belief in a 'United States of Europe' from the 1920s, when he put his faith in big business, to the latter stages of the Second World War, when he continued to champion Hitlerism as the 'last rampart of some liberty in Europe'.[101] Nationalism, in Drieu's opinion, was one of the 'great doctrinal systems of modern times', along with socialism, but it was 'anti-human' and deterministic, based on notions of soil and climate. It impeded, at least in the form of the narrow chauvinism of the masses, a necessary transition to a more dynamic and economically successful European federation.[102] The French writer and journalist continued to conceive of Europe as a collective of nation-states, with nationalism constituting a stage of fascism, which was itself justified—in *With Doriot* (1937)—as a means of bolstering the French state in order to make it unassailable, leaving the relationship between nations and Europe undefined.[103] How were such nation-states to be combined within a European federation?

136 EUROPEAN INTEGRATION SINCE THE 1920s

Most intellectuals agreed that nation-states and national affiliations were inescapable. In France after the Second World War, Aron, who had been a close friend and associate of Sartre but who was moving towards the centre-right, oscillated between calls for greater European cooperation—both political and economic—and warnings that national obstacles, especially in the UK and France, could not be overcome, making a Western European federation a 'pure utopia', as he put in *L'Age des empires et l'avenir de la France* (1945).[104] Although he was sure by 1948 that 'only an authority to which states have transferred part of their sovereignty will be capable of substituting the unity of a great economic area for the multiplicity of national economies, each enclosed within its own frontiers, regulations, and monetary and fiscal policy', he continued to doubt 'that ancient nations, intensely conscious of their uniqueness and history and laden with the memory of their secular rivalries, should voluntarily renounce their unconditional sovereignty'.[105] Aron supported the supposedly moderate and limited European Coal and Steel Community in 1950, partly on the grounds that 'Europe cannot afford the luxury of disappointing its peoples and accepting the failure of such an undertaking', but he opposed—in 1954—the European Defence Community, which had allegedly occasioned 'the greatest ideological and political debate France has known since the Dreyfus Affair', because it implied—or would be seen to imply—'an abandonment of sovereignty'.[106] For the *Le Figaro* journalist, it was unrealistic to think of a 'European government' akin to a national one.[107] Such an institution could only be a long-term goal not a short-term expectation.

Aron's position was shared by the majority of commentators in other countries, even after the discrediting of extreme, or fascist, nationalism in the Second World War. In Britain, some prominent intellectuals, especially exiles such as Hayek and Popper, had come to abhor nationalism as a revival of tribalism, but few saw Europeanism as a plausible alternative.[108] Most continued to assume, like the Oxford philosopher and Russian émigré Isaiah Berlin, that national belonging underpinned citizenship and political participation, taking precedence over other identities and values.[109] In Spain, where authoritarian nationalism persisted under Franco, Ortega y Gasset was the principal advocate of Europe. He, too, however, contended that the nation could be defined as a 'society led by the state'.[110] In Ortega's opinion, it was not defined by geography, language or culture, but by a vision of the future which extended to all groups, meaning that the nation was 'at all times something that comes from and goes forward'.[111] The nation was 'always doing something in common: conquering other peoples, founding colonies, aligning itself with other peoples; that is to say that at any moment it is exceeding what appeared to be the basic principle of union, that is, kinship, language, natural boundaries'.[112] Since the Middle Ages, aristocracies, states, and nationalities had vied for supremacy, leading in much of Northern and Western Europe to the establishment of powerful, elite-led, more or less democratic nation-states during the third stage of civilization from 1848 onwards, after earlier traditional-mythical and individualistic-rationalistic stages. These 'vertebrate' nation-states—Britain, France, and Germany—had created 'that mode of human existence in accordance with which the world has been organized', Ortega had declared in 1929.[113] Spain remained 'invertebrate', since the state had developed too early (in the sixteenth century) and the vernacular traditions of the people had been allowed to weaken the aristocracy—and other elites—permanently. In this context, nationalism was a necessary corrective, to be adopted by all Spanish parties, including the socialists: 'The less developed their respective nations are, the more national socialist parties have to be.'[114] After the imposition of Franco's dictatorship in the Spanish Civil War and the destructive force of national conflicts in the Second World War, it could seem that nationalisms were 'so many blind alleys', which had a 'positive value' in 'periods of consolidation', but which were 'nothing but a mania, a pretext to escape from the necessity of inventing something new', in a Europe where 'everything is more than consolidated'.[115] Yet it was still difficult to discern from Ortega's post-war writings how the existing, 'basically national structure' would 'be replaced by a basically European one'.[116]

The championing of Europeanism and the reaction against nationalism went furthest in Germany after 1945, where open support for the idea of the nation had been tarred by the brush of racism under the National Socialists. 'The thought of a merger of Europe had found an extraordinarily receptive audience in Germany, especially amongst our youth,' wrote Adenauer in his memoirs: 'it was not only affirmed by the heart, but also by reason'.[117] Academics and publicists, especially resurfacing liberals, criticised Germany under, and prior to, the Nazi dictatorship, emphasizing either the moral failings of unreflective nationalism, Romanticism and other forms of utopianism—as philosophers such as Karl Jaspers and literary figures such as Thomas Mann were inclined to do—or the institutional short-comings of Weimar democracy and German liberalism, which became favourite subjects of social scientists such as Karl Dietrich Bracher, whose *Die Auflösung der Weimarer Demokratie* was published in 1955.[118] Their calls, respectively, for re-education and for a re-founding of democracy usually proposed the reconstruction of an acceptable German state, after the unacceptable extremes of the National Socialist regime. They generally assumed the continuing existence of a German national identity, notwithstanding the early appearance of what Dirk A. Moses has termed 'non-German Germans' on the left.[119] When the exiled Austrian constitutional lawyer Hans Kelsen, the most prominent legal commentator of the interwar and postwar periods, asserted in 1945 that Germany was no longer a state in international law, since the 'supreme authority' of the Allies contradicted the definition of a state as 'a certain population ... living on a definite territory under an independent government', the majority of political and legal theorists rejected his argument in favour of a continuing tradition of statehood and nationality.[120]

The many points of disagreement among academics in the late 1940s and early 1950s about the nature of the state, democracy, political parties, and politics, from Carl Schmitt and his followers on the right to Otto Kirchheimer and the Frankfurt School on the left, frequently betrayed uncertainty or scepticism about the national sentiments of significant sections of the German population. For politicians such as Willy Brandt, recalling Adenauer's position of 'no experiments', it seemed that 'the slogan matched the need for tranquility on the part of a *Volk* which was happy to have the aberrations of the Nazi era and the war behind it and which did not want to look backwards'.[121] The sociologist Helmut Schelsky opposed Schmitt's—and, indeed, Max Horkheimer's—critiques of an apolitical, administered, technocratic society with the argument that such a society created stability in spite of alienation from the modern democratic order on the part of a 'sceptical generation' after 1945.[122] Political abstractions and a rapid transformation of institutions risked a reversion to authoritarianism and nationalism, as had occurred under the Weimar Republic, contended Schelsky, citing the revised edition of Arnold Gehlen's *Der Mensch* (1950) in his support.[123] Likewise, defenders of different versions of the 'modern democratic state' (Gerhard Leibholz), purportedly based on well-organized political parties and an implied concept of French-inspired direct democracy, and supporters of 'traditional, liberal-representative parliamentary democracy' (Ernst Fraenkel), resting on British notions of representation and a strong parliament, were interested in harnessing, educating, and controlling a German public that had so recently turned against parties and democracy in the name of a national and racial *Volksgemeinschaft*.[124] The attempt of the liberal journalist and political scientist Dolf Sternberger from the late 1940s onwards to salvage the idea of 'patriotism', as an attachment to laws and *patrie*, explicitly acknowledged the public discrediting of the term 'nationalism', but failed to resolve the problem, which the Heidelberg academic conceded was 'a very remarkable situation', that the Basic Law included as citizens millions of 'Germans' who lived outside the territory of the Federal Republic.[125] The reluctance of many commentators openly to discuss the national question did not mean that it had disappeared in Germany or elsewhere.

The Adenauer government's aim after 1949 was to reacquire sovereignty, as the German Chancellor struggled to persuade the Federal Republic's neighbours in the 1950s that (West) Germany had changed and as the Cold War order in Europe came to depend on the partition and diplomatic weakness of the two German states.[126] The European continent provided an arena, only partly controlled by the two superpowers, in which reconstruction and the regaining of limited independence could be pursued. In the most extreme interpretation, Carl Schmitt's *Der Nomos der Erde* (1950), Europe was seen as a continental bloc, limiting warfare internally and guarding against the escalation of enmity towards its absolute form, as would be the case under the aegis of maritime powers like Britain and the United States.[127] Most authors were much more guarded than Schmitt, doubting that a European bloc could, or should, be restored. The diplomatic historian Ludwig Dehio was typical: the final success of the European international order, the defeat of Nazi Germany, 'cost the system its life, just as the *Reich*, the assailant, paid for its defeat with its existence'.[128] Nevertheless, the past of the European states' system was presented as a series of bids for continental hegemony on the part of individual Great Powers, and its future was left open. Even progressive lawyers such as Ulrich Scheuner and Wilhelm Grewe, who had described limited transfers of sovereign powers to international organizations, balked at applying such principles to the superpowers, which seemed to be engaged in a traditional struggle for power and to have restricted international law, at most, to the regulation of inter-state relations.[129]

Despite internationalization, the tradition of the state, it appeared, remained intact after 1945, complicating any transition towards a European sphere or level of government.[130] To an extent, nationalism and racism had undermined the state, challenging the principle of equality before the law and creating 'an anarchic mass of over- and underprivileged individuals', as Arendt had pointed out in *The Origins of Totalitarianism* (1951).[131] Within National Socialist ideology, the state was subordinate to the movement and party, serving as a guarantor and sponsor of the race rather than as a source of justice or a provider of services, which were deemed to interfere with a legitimate struggle of individuals and groups for supremacy and survival.[132] Although state structures persisted within and were commonly associated with authoritarian and fascist dictatorships, it is possible that the reaction against radical nationalism and a widespread desire for impartiality and an end to political conflict after the Second World War aided the rebuilding of states which had collapsed or which had been dismantled (in West Germany, Austria, Italy, France, Belgium, the Netherlands, Denmark, and Norway).[133] The repressive instruments or corrupt practices of particular regimes had been discredited, not the idea of the state itself.[134]

The re-establishment of legal and constitutional states seemed to many onlookers to be the only way to protect the private sphere from the possible recrudescence of 'totalitarian' ideologies and to recreate a public sphere in which genuine political debate could take place. The conditions for a reversion to dictatorship and totalitarianism still appeared to be in place: comprehensive ideologies explaining and promising to replace chaotic conditions retained their appeal (Arendt); the malfunctioning of markets and threat of revolution promoted the reimposition of monopoly capitalism, of which fascism had been an extension (Franz Neumann); the proclivity towards bureaucratization and technocratic rationalization remained unchecked (Friedrich Pollock, Herbert Marcuse); the means of communication had been concentrated and had become more invasive (Adorno, Horkheimer); and the state had become an impersonal, value-neutral and disposable 'machine', unable to defend itself against seizure and abuse by a single mass party willing to install an 'official ideology' and acquire a monopoly

140 EUROPEAN INTEGRATION SINCE THE 1920s

over communication and the military, enforced by a 'system of terroristic police control' (Carl J. Friedrich).[135] Against such a background, it appeared that the liberal democratic states of the interwar period—the Weimar Republic, the Third Republic, the Italian monarchy—had been too weak and now needed to be strengthened. At the same time, they needed to intervene, becoming planned, welfare, or social states, in order to avert the type of social and economic dislocation—and subsequent political radicalization—experienced by citizens during the interwar era. Economic planning and social intervention, even though they threatened to breach some of the barriers between state and society re-erected by the *Rechtsstaat*, were believed to be necessary by most observers, including conservative lawyers such as Ernst Forsthoff.[136] This type of intervention, which went alongside the creation of a 'social market economy' in Germany and alongside various forms of Keynesianism and planning elsewhere, gave governments a greater duty of care towards their own citizens and made them at once more energetic and inward-looking, as they grappled with the problems of reconstruction.[137] It was not obvious to observers like Aron how such internal reconstruction, together with different national perspectives and disorienting disputes about executives, parties, parliaments, and judicial systems in the context of widespread anxiety about 'totalitarianism', technocracy, and radicalism, could be reconciled with a new political structure for Europe, which would not, of necessity, be like those of re-emerging nation-states.[138]

For the majority of intellectuals, Europe was of secondary importance, frequently eclipsed by domestic affairs and national interests. After the Treaty of Versailles in 1919, Keynes had been appalled by the cynicism of the participants, 'where men played shamelessly, not for Europe, or even England, but their own return to Parliament in the next election'.[139] The worst consequences of the peace, however, as far as he was concerned, were closer to home: 'No more does he believe...in the stability of the things he likes. Eton is doomed; the governing classes, perhaps Cambridge too.'[140] In the early 1930s, the historian Arnold Toynbee was certain that the 'catastrophe' which 'Western minds were contemplating' was 'not the destructive impact of any external force but a spontaneous disintegration from within'.[141] Of course, in the defeated and occupied states of mainland Europe after 1945, commentators' insularity was less pronounced than among their pre-war British counterparts. Nonetheless, most Continental, post-war advocates of 'Europe' continued to prioritize the affairs of their own state. Thus, French intellectuals, for example, devoted most of their attention to the consequences of the Liberation and the politics of the Fourth Republic. Inasmuch as they looked beyond metropolitan France, it was to the United States and the USSR at the start of the Cold War, and to French colonies and colonial wars—although even these received relatively little coverage, with Aron writing only eighteen articles on Indochina (out of a total of 162) between 1947 and 1954, Albert Camus only four, and Georges Bernanos none (out of seventy-eight).[142]

Aron was unusual in the consistency and intensity of his interest in the European project in the post-war era, partly as a consequence of the time he spent in Germany between 1930 and 1933, yet even he considered Franco-German reconciliation, which he placed at the centre of attempts at European cooperation and integration, in terms of national advantage and necessity:

> Obsessed as we are by our own disparate anxieties, we end up by forgetting the essential: the indispensable effort towards the reconciliation of the two peoples. I know that some of my readers will be surprised and shocked. And yet, if the French and Germans are ever to put an end to a secular conflict which the transformation of the world has turned into an anachronism, could a moment ever be more propitious than this? Will Germany ever be weaker or more amenable (*disponible*) than she is today?
>
> I am certainly not claiming that the Germans have once and for all renounced aggressive nationalism or that they have become good 'democrats'. But what Germany is tomorrow depends partly on what we do. The frank and resolute resumption of humane relations with the Germans is a not unworthy contribution that it is within our power to make to the restoration of the West.[143]

For the dominant coteries of French Marxists, either in the Communist Party or in existentialist circles around Sartre and de Beauvoir, the events of the 1930s, 1940s, and 1950s appeared, in spite of the discomfort occasioned by the discovery of Stalin's purges and gulags, to have confirmed the frailties of the bourgeois order at home and the logic of capitalist imperialism abroad.[144] 'The war and the occupation alone have taught us that values remain nominal and indeed have no value without an economic and political infrastructure to make them participate in existence', wrote the Marxist philosopher and journalist Maurice Merleau-Ponty in the first issue of *Les Temps modernes* in 1945.[145] 'Europe' was significant mainly as an area of contention for the superpowers and their opposing ideologies, leading left-wing French intellectuals to a detailed and convoluted calculus of American and Soviet criminality.[146] 'I cannot turn my moral values solely against the USSR,' declared Sartre in 1946: 'While it is true that the deportation of several million people is more serious than the lynching of a black man, the lynching of a black man is the result of a situation which has been going on for more than a hundred years.'[147] French colonialism and conflicts on the periphery of Europe were seen to be part of this international ideological struggle, but the focus of French writers—and allegedly that of the targets of their criticism—was usually France itself, which was supposedly subject to the same ideological conflicts as the wider world: it was therefore natural that the bourgeoisie should be 'perfectly indifferent to the 40,000 people killed at Sétif, the 80,000 murdered Madagascans, the famine and the misery in Algeria, the burned-out villages in Indochina, the Greeks dying in the camps, the Spaniards shot by Franco', since such killing was

142   EUROPEAN INTEGRATION SINCE THE 1920S

the result of a capitalist system, wrote de Beauvoir in her autobiography, but 'the bourgeoisie was suddenly heart-broken when faced with the misfortunes of the Soviet prisoners'.[148] Despite—and sometimes because of—their internationalism, French Marxists had comparatively little to say about Europe. The European bourgeoisie was in crisis after the Second World War, rejoiced Sartre, having lost its power to the 'non-European' and 'non-bourgeois' giants, the Soviet Union, and the United States.[149]

Like Marxists, Catholic intellectuals, whose writings underpinned the varying projects of 'Christian Democracy', also appear to have alternated between global and national politics, leaving little room for the regional sphere of Europe.[150] Jacques Maritain's argument that the future would be dominated by Christian-democratic or totalitarian systems, for instance, derived from an adaptation of his earlier horror at the lapse of European civilizations into barbarism in the 1930s (*Ransoming the Times*, 1938) to the new circumstances of the United States' victory in the Second World War, which seemed to have confirmed the vitality of America's Christian-inspired democracy (*Christianity and Democracy*, 1943).[151] The coming of the Cold War appeared to have demonstrated the menace of Communist totalitarianism and the need for pluralism and moral, socially responsible citizens, rather than the selfish, autonomous individuals promoted by liberalism. Other French Christian-democratic thinkers such as Emmanuel Mounier, whose 'personalism' was close to the 'integral humanism' of Maritain, concentrated more exclusively on domestic politics after 1945, drawing their lessons from the failure of the French bourgeoisie and the fall of France in 1940, after initial cooperation with the Vichy regime and a brief flirtation with the idea of a new conservative or authoritarian European order at the start of the Second World War.[152] 'Europe', as far as it was mentioned at all, was depicted as a purportedly decadent culture—or 'bourgeois Pharisaism', in Maritain's phrase—which had gradually unmasked the 'respectable conventional man' or independent individual of the nineteenth century, through exposure to the theories of Marx, Nietzsche, and Freud, to leave a man who 'has lost track of his soul', 'having given up God so as to be self-sufficient'.[153] The continent, contended Maritain during the war, had witnessed the collapse of democracy and 'the twilight of civilization'.[154] The only way to reinvigorate European culture seemed to be the importation of Christian democracy and, even, capitalism from the United States, but such imports would take place, it was assumed, on a national rather than a European level.

Geopolitics and the European Project

The debate about 'Europe' changed gradually after the founding of the European Coal and Steel Community in 1951 and the European Economic Community in 1957. Imperceptibly, the pathos which surrounded many discussions of a declining and self-destructive continent began to dissipate, insofar as commentators were able to separate developments in Western Europe from the maintenance of an 'Iron Curtain' between East and West.[155] At certain junctures, the trend seemed to have been reversed, as generational misunderstandings were exacerbated and historical conflicts were reignited. 'Europe will no longer be what we have known for half a century,...dependent on the two superpowers', declared Mitterrand in his address to the nation on 31 December 1989:

> she will return to her own history and geography, as one returns to one's own home. Either the tendency to break apart, to split into small pieces, will grow stronger and we will find again the Europe of 1919..... Or Europe will be built. She can do it in two stages. First, thanks to the Community of the Twelve, which it is absolutely essential to strengthen....The second stage remains to be invented. I expect to see in the 1990s the birth of a European Confederation in the true sense of the term which will associate all the states in our continent in a common permanent organization for trade, peace and security.[156]

The European Union became Mitterrand's 'confederation'. What was striking, however, was Mitterrand's rhetoric, which harked back to the heroic, or pathos-laden, period of European politics before 1951.[157] Once the European Communities were established—and during the negotiations which preceded them—they became the preserve of experts from the disciplines of political science and international relations, even if a range of intellectuals from other fields, from philosophers such as Habermas, Jean Baudrillard, Étienne Balibar, Slavoj Žižek, and Norberto Bobbio to sociologists like Anthony Giddens, Zygmunt Bauman, Ralf Dahrendorf, Pierre Bourdieu, and Ulrich Beck, continued to write about Europe.[158] One exception has been the discussion of federalism, which was championed by politicians and intellectuals—particularly from Italy and the United Kingdom—at the same time as remaining a matter of interest to political scientists.[159] Like other post-war approaches to integration, however, federalism has narrowed the field of enquiry, losing sight of the historical circumstances which led to the formation of European institutions in the first place.[160]

The circumstances from which the European Communities emerged were dominated by the geopolitics of the Cold War (see Map 3.3). Initially, it seemed to pro- and anti-Communist commentators that the ideological opposition of the superpowers left no room for Europe.[161] Contemporary intellectuals' oscillation between national priorities and a global struggle of ideologies worked against the idea that Europe was a separate—potentially semi-independent—region between the two superpowers. Instead, the continent appeared to be threatened by the incursions of one power and to be protected—in prospect—by the influence and presence of the other. At least until the Soviet intervention in Hungary in 1956, a significant part of the French left remained unapologetic in its support of the

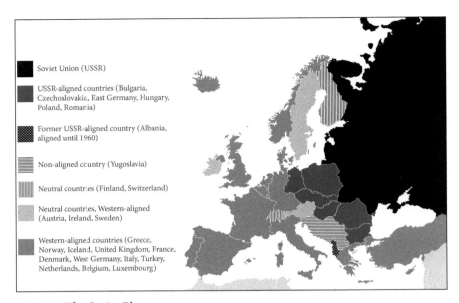

Map 3.3 The Soviet Bloc
Source: https://en.wikipedia.org/wiki/Eastern_Bloc#/media/File:Europe-blocs-49-89x4.svg

USSR, in the spirit of Pierre Courtade's retort to Edgar Morin: 'I was right to be wrong, while you and your kind were wrong to be right.'[162] Another part of the left was more sceptical, with Merleau-Ponty writing that 'one cannot be anti-Communist, one cannot be Communist', but they were prepared to excuse or relativize the excesses of Stalinism and to justify the Soviet occupation of Eastern Europe as a defensive shield against capitalism, to the disgust of exiles such as Mircea Eliade, who accused them of giving up the rest of Europe: 'all these countries *are* in Europe, all these peoples belong to the European community.'[163] To French Communists, and to others on the left, Eastern Europe had not been given up or excluded as much as the Soviet Union had been included in the affairs of Europe, not least because it still seemed a lesser evil compared to the United States, which—Sartre asserted—had 'gone mad'.[164] The West, contended the French existentialist in the 1950s, had nothing to offer in place of Communism.[165]

Much of the centre and right disagreed. To Camus, who had attacked 'progressive' violence in *L'Homme révolté* (1951), it would be necessary 'to choose between Russia and America', probably in favour of the latter. The former Communist and future Gaullist André Malraux, to whom the author was speaking in 1945, replied that the choice was not between Russia and America but 'between Russia and France', for 'when a weak France finds itself confronted by a powerful Russia, I no longer believe a word of what I believed when a powerful France was confronted by a weak Soviet Union. A weak Russia wants popular fronts, a strong Russia wants popular democracies.'[166] When, by the late 1940s, it became evident that the USSR was powerful and wanted to install its own satellite states in Europe, the majority of Gaullist, Christian Democrat and liberal intellectuals had already turned against it. 'Stalin's enterprise is of the same kind as Hitler's', wrote Aron in 1949: 'Soviet expansion has come to a halt. In no country to the west of the Iron Curtain does the Communist Party still have a serious chance of seizing power either through elections or through a *coup d'état*. And it has been acknowledged, since 1945, that by crossing the line of demarcation, the Red Army would set the world on fire.'[167] Faced with such an enemy, most centrist and right-wing commentators, notwithstanding their continuing complaints, accepted American influence and military assistance. 'This nation...is more foreign to me than any other', wrote the Catholic novelist François Mauriac in 1959, before admitting that US culture had already permeated Europe: 'I've never been there.... what is the point? It has done more than just visit us; it has transformed us.'[168] Even to Mauriac, who had called the United States 'this great exterminating nation' after the Suez crisis in 1956, Europe had voluntarily become part of an American-dominated 'West'.[169]

Most commentators perceived Europe's subordination to the United States and the USSR after the Second World War as the latest stage in a long-running crisis, extending back to the First World War. They interpreted the crisis in divergent ways, from Drieu La Rochelle's description of the conflict as a 'war of religions' between incompatible 'Asian' and 'European' cultures to the Nobel-Prize-winning chemist Frédéric Joliot-Curie's championing of a war for Communism, of which 'the Party is bound to have a better understanding than each of us'.[170] Some were more pessimistic than others, from the doom-laden pronouncements of Spengler and his followers to the tentative hopes of Croce for 'the birth of a new consciousness, a new [European] nationality' to replace nations and restore 'liberal ideals', but virtually all were defensive, seeking to protect Europe from a series of internal and external threats.[171] Perceived menaces after 1918 included the recurrence of what Coudenhove-Kalergi referred to as a European 'civil war' akin to the First World War, the decadence of European culture, an increasing population and inadequate territory (Ortega y Gasset), economic collapse (Keynes), the existence of destructive nationalisms and obstructive nation-states, the threat of left-wing revolutions and right-wing coups d'états.[172] The list of threats to 'Europe' also included the imposition of ideological dystopias and authoritarian or totalitarian dictatorships, invasion or domination by expanding extra-European powers such as the United States and the USSR, the proximity—given the spread of globe-shrinking means of communication—of 'a non-European humanity which has become dangerously closer and easily superior in terms of material force' (Hermann von Keyserling), and the failure of the states' system and international organisations such as the League of Nations, which had not done 'great things', as the left claimed, but which had 'not perished', as the right maintained (Bertrand de Jouvenel).[173]

146 EUROPEAN INTEGRATION SINCE THE 1920s

Few of these dangers and threats had diminished as a result of the Second World War. Indeed, many observers thought that things had got worse. To Ortega y Gasset, the conflict had confirmed the movement towards state tutelage and mass society, and a transition from 'open' to 'closed nationalism' or *nationalisme rentré*, where 'each people would live according to its private style' and 'feels that its way of life clashes with others'.[174] To Keynes, the war was 'a dreadful confirmation of Hobbes's diagnosis of human nature and of what is required to preserve civilization': 'From one point of view we can regard what is now happening as the final destruction of the optimistic liberalism which Locke inaugurated.'[175] In *L'Homme contre les tyrans* (1944), Aron went even further, predicting the end of the belief in 'progress':

> In the last century, the most popular philosophies of history, and even the consciousness of ordinary people, were dominated by the doctrine of progress, according to which a kind of parallelism or interdependence was said to exist between the accumulation of knowledge, increased mastery over nature, and the moral improvement of humanity. In other words, an indisputable fact—the development of knowledge and technology—was broadened into a naively confident vision of historical development as a whole. The catastrophes of the twentieth century have provoked a complete reversal of attitudes and brought into being a doctrine which is the exact opposite of the doctrine of progress. The same deterministic interpretation has been preserved, whereby the movement which is dragging capitalism to its death and the economy towards a planned regime is held to be irresistible. But instead of linking these transformations with the liberation of man, they are associated with tyranny, wars of conquest and fanaticism.... What gives the current pessimism its debilitating poignancy is that it asserts an interdependence between ineluctable necessities and detestable phenomena.[176]

The creation of a European community in such circumstances, if it were to happen, would occur for many different—and largely defensive—reasons and would correspond to varying sets of expectations. Yet, to many intellectuals, it still appeared at once possible and desirable.

'Imagining Europe' proved difficult in a post-war world of extra-European superpowers, the end of empire and globalization.[177] One of the problems faced by proponents of an 'official' political identity for the EU, which was inaugurated in 1992, was the fact that it was an '(increasingly awkward) continuation of the circumstances in which the first phase of the construction of a political Europe took place: an East–West confrontation (culminating in the "victory" of the West), and decolonization', neither of which were specifically European.[178] Although contemporaries viewed the partition of Europe during the Cold War with a mixture of fear and pathos, comparable to their predecessors' responses to the

First World War, their perspectives were divided. In Poland, Timothy Garton Ash writes of his conversations as a journalist with post-Communist political elites, 'their general attitude was: let bygones be bygones; no trials, no recriminations; look to the future, to democracy and "Europe", as Spain had done'.[179] In part, new elites could not imagine a reconstructed Communist Party being successful at the polls and, in part, their attention was drawn to the pressing challenges of economic and political reconstruction in the future. In Czechoslovakia, Václav Havel's attitude could likewise be described as 'one of pre-emptive forgiveness'.[180] By contrast, the conservative government of József Antall in Hungary, lacking experience of front-line opposition to Communism, adopted 'a vivid rhetoric of reckoning', as did East German dissidents in a unified Federal Republic.[181] The Gauck authority was set up to give the public access to their own Stasi files, revealing which of their neighbours, friends, and relatives had spied on them. By the turn of the century, about 500,000 East Germans had seen their records.

East Germans' western counterparts had quite different memories of the Cold War and varying attitudes to Communism, frequently viewing 'Easterners with mistrust and suspicion' and 'seeing them as authoritarian and self-pitying "Jammer-Ossis" (Eastern moaners) without a democratic mentality or any aptitude for working in a free-market society', in the judgement of Alexander von Plato's oral history of 'an unfamiliar Germany'.[182] Similarly, disparate experiences and histories of the Second World War and the Holocaust seemed to undermine any sense of a common 'memory' or shared remembrance as components of a common European identity.[183] 'Fifty years after the catastrophe, Europe understands itself more than ever as a common project, yet it is far from achieving a comprehensive analysis of the years immediately following the Second World War,' wrote Hans-Magnus Enzensberger in the 1990s: 'The memory of the period is incomplete and provincial, if it is not entirely lost in repression or nostalgia.'[184] In the post-war decades, politicians' wariness of their citizens' experiences of violence, trauma, conflict, guilt, vengeance, and forgetting helped to stifle appeals to a shared European identity or set of values and to render practical acts of European cooperation attractive (see Map 3.4).[185] As a consequence, it appeared that 'output-oriented' and 'indirect forms of legitimacy', which derived from the 'EU as an essentially intergovernmental body' made up of lawful nation-states, had come to obscure the role of identification and allegiance in European integration.[186]

In some respects, outputs and indirect forms of legitimacy seemed to be worthy of attention, generating political discussion and filling newspaper columns. From The Hague congress onwards, journalists had asked themselves what a future European 'union' would look like.[187] Coverage of the European question differed from country to country, ranging from the external perspective of many British journalists, who doubted that 'western Europe as a unifying cultural conception' existed for 'the great majority of all classes', to the eager adoption of a continental perspective on the part of Germans, nearly all of whom were 'Europeans', in the

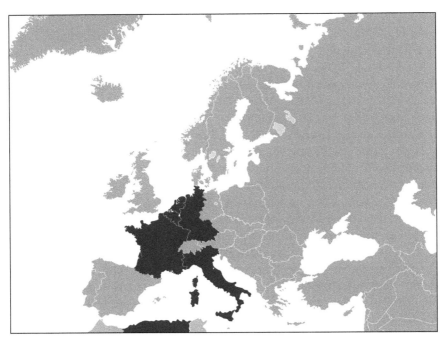

Map 3.4 The European Economic Community in 1957
Source: https://en.wikipedia.org/wiki/Enlargement_of_the_European_Union#/media/File:EC-EU-enlargement

opinion of the SPD politician and first president of the Europa-Union, Carlo Schmid.[188] In the United Kingdom, the Europe of the 'six' was treated separately from Europe as a whole: in the words of a *Times* leader in July 1952, the member states of the European Coal and Steel Community were not 'the whole of Europe; they are "little Europe"'.[189] Nonetheless, British newspapers continued to chart the progress of the European Community, conceding that Britain had lost ground to it economically.[190] During the 1960s, *The Times* backed the UK's application for membership of the EEC.[191] The *Manchester Guardian* was more cautious, articulating the doubts of union leaders and Labour MPs, but it, too, gave extensive coverage to the European Community as an economic organization, reporting on Macmillan's speech to the Assembly of the Western European Union on 30 May 1961 under the heading, 'Mr Macmillan: "Goal within Grasp"—Unity in Europe and Beyond':

> The Prime Minister...said that the goal ahead—in spite of the difficulties in creating new systems—was clear and within our grasp: it was to create the maximum unity in Europe and beyond. He did not doubt that they would succeed—'and succeed perhaps sooner than some pessimists may believe.'...
> There were, of course, difficulties. In Britain there was our agricultural problem, which had been organised for many years on a wholly different system of

support than in Europe. Above all, there was the Commonwealth—not merely a point of honour and tradition and interest to the British people, but a vital element of strength and stability to the whole free world....

Britain must play a full part in the new community or 'we must resign ourselves to becoming a sort of offshore island of this new dynamic movement'.[192]

In common with newspapers elsewhere, British publications treated the EC as an expanding, increasingly complex economic organization. Growth, in itself, had diplomatic effects, as Erich Kobbert pointed out in June 1962—contending that 'the European Economic Community, as the largest trading power on earth, unsettles the entire world', provoking enmity with the USSR and, more destabilizing, bringing it 'an excess of love', including from Eastern European states—but journalists usually concentrated on how and why growth had occurred.[193] In German publications such as the *Frankfurter Allgemeine Zeitung*, it was widely accepted that economics raised political questions about the nature of 'European union' or 'unity' (*Einigung*), which remained open-ended, not least because of de Gaulle's plans for 'l'Europe des patries' and a 'third force'.[194] *The Times*, too, asked 'What kind of a Europe is Britain proposing to join?'[195] The debate continued in the 1970s, with David Spanier, the paper's Europe editor, confessing that 'I still believe in the idea of a united Europe, Brussels' style. That is, a community of like-minded nations, seeking by common action and common policies to shape their destiny together, and pushed and prodded, as necessary, by an independent European Commission. My reason is that the present Community has already achieved so much.'[196] Unnoticed, though, even supportive journalists such as Spanier had shifted their focus from Europe's place in the world to the internal workings of the European economy and polity.

From the 1950s onwards, exponents of international relations sought to explain how and why integration was happening, treating the process as a form of regionalism (neo-functionalism) or the European Community as an international organization (liberal intergovernmentalism).[197] It was striking in both instances that IR specialists treated the EC in isolation from, or, at least, with relatively little reference to, the geopolitics of the Cold War.[198] Neo-functionalists posited that 'Converging economic goals embedded in the bureaucratic, pluralistic and industrial life of modern Europe provided the crucial impetus,' in the words of Ernst Haas: 'The economic technician, the planner, the innovating industrialist and trade unionist advanced the movement, not the politicians, the scholar, the poet, the writer.'[199] Haas compared the European Community with nine other regional blocs, only to conclude that the EEC was unique, alone offering the possibility of 'automatic politicization'.[200] For their part, liberal intergovernmentalists concentrated on the formation of state preferences in a 'two-level game' (Robert Putnam), where national governments look to garner support, create coalitions, and put forward policies as well as to negotiate simultaneously in the 'information-rich

150 EUROPEAN INTEGRATION SINCE THE 1920s

setting' of the European Community and EU, which have been entrusted with varying types of low politics, but not high politics (following Stanley Hoffmann).[201] The formation and negotiation of domestic interests are technical, leaving the relationship between high and low politics largely untouched. Andrew Moravcsik's claim that the European Community is the 'most successful example of institutionalized policy coordination in the world' betrays the focus of liberal intergovernmentalists on bargaining and economic interdependence, using the models of (international) political economy.[202] 'National governments employ EC institutions as part of a "two-level" strategy with the aim of permitting them to overcome domestic opposition more successfully,' writes Moravcsik: 'The EC fulfils this function in two ways; by according governmental policy initiatives greater domestic political legitimacy and by granting them greater domestic agenda-setting power.'[203] Rational actors take part because it is in their interest to do so, not as a consequence of political decisions taken in uncertain historical conditions. As for neo-functionalists, the limits, incursions, and uncertainties of the Cold War play little part in the account of intergovernmentalists.

In the 1980s and 1990s, political scientists began to focus on governance and to compare the institutions of the EU to those of other polities, not least because the party politicians who set up and ran the European Communities had many domestic and foreign objectives in addition to those of 'integration'.[204] Some political scientists compared European institutions to those of nation-states.[205] Others have emphasized the uniqueness of the European Union, rejecting the idea that politics in liberal-democratic nation-states is the norm. For proponents of 'multilevel governance', decision-making takes place on different levels, with the boundaries between them less clear-cut than in sovereign systems of government.[206] 'Governance is synthetic,' write Peterson and Bomberg: 'it results from a mix of factors, including political leadership, state-society relations, institutional competition, electoral politics, and so on. The EU's existence as an extra level or layer of governance that has been "fused" on the nation-state (Wolfgang Wessels) makes the mix unusually eclectic in Europe compared to other parts of the world.'[207] Scholars who examine path dependencies, policy networks, and the adoption of European norms, or 'Europeanization', largely work within the paradigm of overlapping levels of governance.[208] Although such political scientists pay attention to the diachronic and normative context of decision-making, eschewing rational-choice theory, they are interested primarily in how decisions are made, and with what consequences, rather than why they are made and how they change over a long period of time. Discourse theory and social constructivism have extended such analysis to communicative interaction and the creation of 'epistemic communities', aiming to 'evaluate empirically whether "Europeanness" is part of... collective identity' and 'whether a sense of Europeanness has any impact on... actual policies toward the EU', but they concentrate on genealogy—or on the origins and roots of concepts—rather than on the history of decision-making and decision-makers in a wider geopolitical context. The historical role of the European Communities has, accordingly, been lost from view.[209]

To what extent has the narrower, technical focus of political scientists on how European institutions work affected—or reflected—the ways in which the EU is viewed by intellectuals, journalists, and the public? Over time, the romance of the European project appears to have diminished and the hopes which citizens invested in 'Europe' seem to have subsided, yet such hopes were also often the product of the same citizens' uncertainty and anxieties in the aftermath of war and dictatorship.[210] 'Again I was aware that the past was done for, work achieved was in ruins, Europe, our home, to which we had dedicated ourselves had suffered a destruction that would extend far beyond our life,' wrote the Austrian novelist Stefan Zweig at the end of *Die Welt von Gestern* (1942), just before committing suicide in Brazil: 'Something new, a new world began, but how many hells, how many purgatories had to be crossed before it could be reached!'[211] It is difficult to recreate such pathos decades later, although it is evident that many politicians—including Winston Churchill, as he made plain in his Zurich speech of October 1946—were animated by similar feelings at the time.[212] With Europe divided during the Cold War, occupied, threatened, and defended by two ideologically antithetical superpowers, intellectuals especially continued to project Europe's future and to lament its present.[213] In November 1956, the director of the Hungarian News Agency sent a telex to 'the entire world', shortly before his office was hit by Soviet artillery, 'with a desperate message announcing that the Russian attack against Budapest had begun', wrote Milan Kundera in his essay on 'The Tragedy of Central Europe', which appeared in the *New York Review of Books* in April 1984:

> The dispatch ended with these words: 'We are going to die for Hungary and for Europe.'…What did this sentence mean? It certainly meant that the Russian tanks were endangering Hungary and with it Europe itself. But in what sense was Europe in danger? Were the Russian tanks about to push past the Hungarian borders and into the West? No…. 'To die for one's country and for Europe'— that is a phrase that could not be thought in Moscow or Leningrad; it is precisely the phrase that could be thought in Budapest or Warsaw.[214]

The Hungarian, Czech, and Polish nations had 'belonged to the part of Europe rooted in Roman Christianity' for a thousand years, according to Kundera: consequently, for them, 'the word "Europe" does not represent a phenomenon of geography but a spiritual notion synonymous with the word "West"'.[215] The notion of a 'geographical Europe', extending from the Atlantic to the Ural Mountains, 'was always divided into two halves which evolved separately: one tied to ancient Rome and the Catholic Church, the other anchored in Byzantium and the Orthodox Church'.[216] After 1945, Poles, Czechs, and Hungarians, who

152 EUROPEAN INTEGRATION SINCE THE 1920s

'had always considered themselves to be Western woke up to discover that they were now in the East', since the border between the two Europes during the Cold War had moved several hundred kilometres to the West.[217] 'As a result,' Kundera continued, 'three fundamental situations developed in Europe after the war: that of Western Europe, that of Eastern Europe, and, most complicated, that of the part of Europe situated geographically in the centre—culturally in the West and politically in the East.'[218]

Western intellectuals and citizens, in contrast to their Central European counterparts, had become accustomed to the boundaries of the Cold War, implied Kundera, quietly jettisoning 'Europe' as a point of cultural or rhetorical reference.[219] In Western Europe, no intellectual would have contemplated making the case for European culture, identity, and politics in Kundera's terms by the 1980s. Habermas's *Staatsbürgerschaft und nationale Identität. Überlegungen zur europäischen Zukunft* in 1990, for example, was filled with foreboding at the impact of nationalism and mass migration from the collapsing Eastern Bloc and it looked to the European Community as a means of limiting the impact of identity politics in unexpectedly unstable times.[220]

Given the conflicts, divisions, and extremes of the twentieth century, it was unlikely that intellectuals or journalists would discover or write compelling stories about Europe which would serve to unite its citizens. Modernity had destroyed the very idea that social collectivities could pass on narratives about the world from one generation to the next, wrote Pierre Nora in 1989. 'We have seen the end of societies that had long assured the transmission of and conservation of collectively remembered values, whether through churches or schools, the family or the state; the end too of ideologies that prepared a smooth passage from the past to the future or that had what the future should keep from the past—whether for reaction, progress, or even revolution,' he went on: 'Indeed, we have seen the tremendous dilation of our very mode of historical perception, which, with the help of the media, has substituted for a memory entwined in the intimacy of a collective heritage the ephemeral film of current events.'[221] Europe was never a 'society', with churches, schools, and a state to transmit its collectively remembered values or create 'memory'. What it has, in Nora's terms, is a history; namely, a 'critical discourse that is antithetical to spontaneous memory', or 'life, borne by living societies founded in its name'.[222] Whereas memory 'takes root in the concrete, in spaces, gestures, images, and objects', history 'binds itself strictly to temporal continuities, to progressions and to relations between things'.[223] History can only conceive what is relative, but by the same token it can relate individuals' actions and ideas to historical processes and conditions. It cannot create 'memory', but it can investigate memories. To what extent have historians of 'Europe' managed to find continuities and to trace the relations between a panoply of individual memories and collective but fragmentary *lieux de mémoires* in order to contextualize, assess, and explain processes of integration?

Critics have accused historians of failing to devise theories, resting on the description and evaluation of relations, to challenge those of political science.[224] Although it is inevitable that historical theories of integration remain 'under the sign of the interim' (Perry Anderson), exponents of narrative histories of integration attempt to do without theories altogether, '"like children on a crowded beach, building separate small sand castles", lacking theoretical foundations or structural support, "all of which look very vulnerable to the incoming tide"', in John Gillingham's view.[225] They have also wrongly equated '"integration" with the single set of institutions headquartered at Brussels and today known as the European Union', diverting attention away from 'other trends and tendencies which have contributed to the integration process', Gillingham goes on: they have credited 'the EU undeservedly as the sole source of change'; they have overlooked 'the importance of context as a parameter for policy-making'; and they have neglected 'impacts', conflating process and policy and ascribing unintended consequences 'merely to mistakes or oversights of human agents rather than to the operation of factors beyond their control'.[226] The attempts of advocates of the European Union to construct narrative accounts of its genesis are bound to backfire, since they leave the principal questions unanswered. How can scholars explain the EU's history of 'zigs, zags—and lags'?[227] Even if the 'main accomplishments of the EU are evident' insofar as 'it has ended the economic division of Europe into national markets, defused conflict between neighbours, promoted democracy and good government, and restored the confidence of Europeans in the values and vitality of their civilization', how can we account for its trajectory, given that it is 'neither on a one-way track to federal union (as professed by its champions)' nor 'closer to having its own armed forces today than it was over fifty years ago when the European Defence Community was first proposed'.[228] 'The European Social Model is still mere political rhetoric' and the 'ruinous Common Agricultural Policy cannot be eliminated'.[229] For Gillingham, 'negative integration', or the provision of 'thou-shalt-not' rules to economic activity, has been more successful than 'positive integration', or the 'creation of new institutions to overcome "market failure"', but historians have 'largely left the economics of integration to others'.[230] On this reading, 'Whig' histories of political integration lack credibility because they have forsaken the constant questioning of critical discourse, which is intrinsic to 'history' as opposed to 'memory'.[231]

In theory, historians have found it easier to explore the memories, experiences, mentalities, and ideas of decision-makers, including their conceptions of 'Europe', than have political scientists. In practice, though, historical approaches to integration have rarely connected Delanty's inventions of Europe to other constructs, to policy-making and wider historical processes and sets of conditions. One approach, associated with the voluminous and detailed work of Walter Lipgens, investigates blueprints for a European federation put forward by a network of pro-European groups in the interwar and post-war eras and by resistance movements during the Second World War, but it is less successful in demonstrating their significance—or that of transnational contacts within business, unions, and circles of Social and Christian Democrats—for national governments.[232] Another approach, established by Alan Milward, starts by examining the decisions and policies of national governments.[233] To the British historian, 'the process of integration was deliberately conceived and developed to preserve the nation-state by supporting a range of new social and economic policies whose very purpose was the resurrection of the nation-state after its collapse between 1929 and 1945'.[234] For Gillingham, the notion that European integration was conceived to offer support to nation-states under reconstruction is 'fanciful', with little evidence to support the proposition that '"the Union exists because it has been a response by national governments to popular demand" and that it "buttressed the nation-state in the pursuit of income, welfare, family security and employment"'.[235] More importantly, Milward's approach, though paying attention to decision-makers' perceptions of national interest, does little to recreate the mental worlds and points of reference—including European points of reference—of decision-makers.

Histories of the 'idea of Europe' regularly overlook the significance of discourses in decision-making, with intellectuals acting as intermediaries.[236] If 'European economic and political integration has proceeded in a technocratic fashion' during the Cold War at a time of 'permissive consensus' about Europe, as Jeffrey Checkel and Peter Katzenstein claim, 'these attempts to de-politicize politics, to create Europe by stealth, have produced a political backlash that has increased over time'.[237] The connections between politicians, officials, commentators, and the public in European matters are now harder to ignore, but they were always relevant. The decision-making of governments depended on ministers' and officials' reading of public opinion and their conception of 'national interest', which in turn were informed by discussion in the press and other media. The intersection of these domestic preferences with policy-making, negotiations, deals, and compromises on the European level was also affected—in addition to the primary concerns of domestic politics—by the positions of other states and policy-makers' cultural and historical understanding of 'Europe'. It is conceivable that Europe has provided a stable framework for the maintenance of nation-states, as Azar Gat has contended, with nationalism having had both emancipating and aggressive or violent aspects for those espousing the values of the Enlightenment. The 'ostensible weakening of national sentiments in the developed world' is, according to Gat, 'a direct result of the triumphant materialization and secure prevalence of the national principle, in a liberal and defensive, seemingly "banal," form'.[238] From such a vantage point, European affiliations and interests could co-exist with, and even reinforce, national identities and objectives. It 'is now obvious to all that Germany in an integrated Europe is less fear-inducing and, therefore, appears tamer', writes Gerhard Schröder in his memoirs, reassuring 'all of its neighbours', including those in Prague, Warsaw, Bucharest, and Moscow, that 'this European centre' lives with them in 'peaceful relations secured by agreements'.[239] Yet, at various times, European affiliations have appeared to clash with national sentiments and identities. To what extent were leaders willing to give way or cede powers in such circumstances for the sake of 'Europe'?[240] Their calculations rested, not only on their relations with other member states and anticipation of opposition at home, but also on their understanding of European history and their identification with the European Community. The next chapter explores the tensions between and consolidation of these competing allegiances on the part of leaders and citizens.

Notes

1. Z. Steiner, *The Lights that Failed: European International History, 1919–1933* (Oxford, 2005); Z. Steiner, *The Triumph of the Dark: European International History, 1933–1939* (Oxford, 2010). William Mulligan, *The Great War for Peace* (New Haven, CT, 2014), has made the case for the role of the First World War in creating a new, potentially peaceful, international order, but given the manifest disorder of inter-state relations and markets in Europe (and elsewhere), it is difficult to avoid the conclusion that organizations such as the League of Nations and International Labour Organization were ineffective.
2. G. Sluga, *Internationalism in the Age of Nationalism* (Philadelphia, PA, 2013); G. Sluga and P. Clavin (eds), *Internationalisms: A Twentieth-Century History* (Cambridge, 2016).
3. A. S. Milward, 'Allegiance: The Past and the Future', *Journal of European Integration History*, 1 (1995), 14.
4. Ibid.
5. See also P. Lagrou, *The Legacy of Nazi Occupation: Patriotic Memory and National Recovery in Western Europe, 1945–1965* (Cambridge, 2000).
6. A. S. Milward, 'Allegiance: The Past and the Future', *Journal of European Integration History*, 1 (1995), 15.
7. Ibid., 16.
8. Ibid.
9. Ibid.
10. Ibid.
11. Ibid. A. Milward, *The European Rescue of the Nation-State*, 2nd edn (London, 2000), 4: 'The development of the European Community, the process of European integration, was, so runs the argument of this book, a part of that post-war rescue of the European nation-state, because the new political consensus on which this rescue was built required the process of integration, the surrender of limited areas of national sovereignty to the supranation. The history of that surrender is but a small part of the post-war history of the nation-state, though it may eventually seem to have been the most significant.'
12. A. Milward, *The European Rescue of the Nation-State*, 4.
13. See J. Habermas, 'An Avantgardistic Instinct for Relevances: The Role of the Intellectual and the European Cause', in J. Habermas, *Europe: The Faltering Project* (Cambridge, 2009), 49–58.
14. S. de Beauvoir, *La force des choses* (Paris, 1963), 340.
15. J. Lodge, 'Loyalty and the EEC: The Limitations of the Functionalist Approach', *Political Studies*, 26 (1978), 232.
16. Ibid.
17. Ibid., 233.
18. Ibid.
19. Ibid., 242.

156 EUROPEAN INTEGRATION SINCE THE 1920S

20. See, for instance, P. M. Lützeler, *Die Schriftsteller und Europa* (Munich, 1992); J. Elvert, 'The "New European Order" of National Socialism: Some Remarks on Its Sources, Genesis and Nature', in D. Gosewinkel (ed.), *Anti-Liberal Europe: A Neglected Story of Europeanization* (New York, 2015), 105–27; F. Greiner, *Wege nach Europa. Deutungen eines imaginierten Kontinents in deutschen, britischen und amerikanischen Printmedien, 1914–1945* (Göttingen, 2014), 179–223.

21. Gerhard Hauptmann's appeal 'To the Conscience of the World' in 1923, quoted P. M. Lützeler, *Die Schriftsteller und Europa*, 287.

22. Ibid.

23. Ibid., 301–2.

24. Ibid., 279–80.

25. Ibid.

26. O. Spengler, *Der Untergang des Abendlandes*, revised edn (Munich, 1923), 746–83.

27. T. S. Eliot, 'The Unity of European Culture' (1946), in M. Lützeler, *Die Schriftsteller*, 408. Intellectuals in Britain were particularly preoccupied with the question of decline: I. Hall, *Dilemmas of Decline: British Intellectuals and World Politics, 1945–1975* (Cambridge, 2012).

28. M. Lützeler, *Die Schriftsteller*, 408.

29. Ibid., 410.

30. Quoted in J.-W. Müller, *Contesting Democracy: Political Ideas in Twentieth-Century Europe* (New Haven, CT, 2011), 126.

31. Ibid., 417.

32. Ibid., 416.

33. M. Horkheimer and T. W. Adorno, *Dialektik der Aufklärung* (Amsterdam, 1947). The work was first published unofficially in 1944. Paul Betts, *Ruin and Renewal: Civilising Europe after the Second World War* (London, 2020), 15–16, reassesses the notion of 'civilization': 'What distinguished the twentieth-century notion of civilization from its predecessors was the explicit linkage to cultural crisis. It was no accident that the most serious commentators on the idea of civilisation—Lucien Febvre, Joachim Moras, Norbert Elias, Toynbee and, of course, Sigmund Freud in his late work—were writing in the 1930s. . . . Civilization in trouble became a central theme of European political commentary after both wars, though comparatively little attention has been paid to the post-1945 story. . . . Postwar Europe played host to competing custody battles over what civilization was and could be after Nazism, the war and empire.'

34. H. C. Raley, *José Ortega y Gasset: Philosopher of European Unity* (Alabama, 1971), 62–76. These views were stated in *Revolt of the Masses* in 1929 and in *Meditation on Europe*, published after the Second World War.

35. Mention of a 'European confederation' was made by Joachim von Ribbentrop, Germany's Foreign Secretary, in March 1943: M. Salewski, 'Europa: Idée und Wirklichkeit in der nationalsozialistischen Weltanschauung und politischen Praxis', in O. Franz (ed.), *Europas Mitte* (Göttingen, 1987), 85–106; P. Krüger, 'Hitlers Europapolitik', in W. Benz. H. Buchheim, and H. Mommsen (eds), *Der Nationalsozialismus. Studien zur Ideologie und Herrschaft* (Frankfurt, 1993), 104–32; P. M. R. Stirk, 'Authoritarian and National Socialist Conceptions of Nation, State, and Europe', in P. M. R. Stirk (ed.), *European Unity in Context: The Interwar Period* (London, 1989), 125–48. J. Laughland, *Tainted Source: Undemocratic Origins of the European Idea* (New York, 1997), has attempted to extend this idea, examining parallels between the Nazi New Order, German industrialists' discussion of a European economic community during the Second World War and post-war plans for Europe.

36. J. M. Keynes to 'Sigi' Waley, 11 November 1941, in R. Skidelsky, *John Maynard Keynes* (London, 2000), vol. 3, 197.

37. See O. Calligaro, *Negotiating Europe: EU Promotion of Europeanness since the 1950s* (Basingstoke, 2013), whose focus on the 'Jean Monnet Action' in universities, cultural heritage programmes, and iconography of the euro betrays the limitations of EU activity in this sphere.

38. E. O'Doherty, 'Does European Culture Exist?', *Dublin Review of Books*, 1 July 2013.

39. Ibid. On the EU's struggles with this notion, see O. Calligaro, 89–104.

40. E. O'Doherty, 'Does European Culture Exist?', *Dublin Review of Books*, 1 July 2013.

41. Ibid. A. Heller, 'Europe: An Epilogue', in B. Nelson, D. Roberts, and W. Veit (eds), *The Idea of Europe* (Oxford, 1992), 12–25. On the 'teleology' and 'essentialism' of such representations of Europe, 'advocated not only by the European Commission, but also by MEPs, representatives of national governments, and non-institutional actors', see O. Calligaro, *Negotiating Europe*, 182. The EU's and Council of Europe's policies in this field have been different: O. Calligaro, 'Which

Culture(s) for Europe? The Contrasting Conceptions of the Council of Europe and the European Union from 1949 to the Present Day', *Cambio*, 13 (2017), 67–83.

42. E. O'Doherty, 'Does European Culture Exist?', *Dublin Review of Books*, 1 July 2013.

43. S. Glendinning, 'Europe Should Reject Jürgen Habermas's Vision of a Federal European State and Instead Create an Enduring Association between Sovereign Nations', *EUROPP blog* (LSE), 3 September 2013.

44. See especially E. du Réau, *La construction européenne au XXe siècle. Fondements, enjeux, defies* (Nantes, 2007), 15–32, and E. du Réau, *L'idée d'Europe au XXe siècle. Des mythes aux réalités* (Brussels, 1996), 17–70; and J. L. Chabot, *Aux origines intellectuelles de l'Union européenne* (Grenoble, 2005).

45. See, for instance, O. Waever, 'Europe since 1945: Crisis to Renewal', in K. Wilson and J. van der Dussen (eds), *History of the Idea of Europe* (London, 1993), 13–82. Elisabeth du Réau, *L'Europe en construction. Le second vingtième siècle*, 2nd edn (Paris, 2007), explores the enduring cultural context. For more on neo-functionalist theories of European integration, see A. Wiener and T. Diez, *European Integration Theory* (Oxford, 2003) and B. Rosamond, *Theories of European Integration* (Basingstoke, 2000).

46. O. Waever, 'Europe since 1945: Crisis to Renewal', in K. Wilson and J. van der Dussen (eds), *History of the Idea of Europe*, 152; other works emphasizing an historical shift around 1945 are W. Lipgens, *A History of European Integration, 1945–1947* (Oxford, 1982), W. Lipgens, *Die Anfänge der europäischen Einigungspolitik 1945–1950* (Stuttgart, 1977), and W. Lipgens, *Europa-Föderationspläne der Widerstandsbewegungen 1940–1945* (Munich, 1968), notwithstanding his studies of the 1920s and 30s; D. W. Urwin, *The Community of Europe: A History of European Integration since 1945* (London, 1991); A. Bachoud, J. Cuesta, and M. Trebitsch (eds), *Les intellectuals et l'Europe de 1945 à nos jours* (Paris, 2000).

47. Elisabeth du Réau makes the point about continuities from the 1920s and early 30s to the late 40s and early 50s in *L'idée d'Europe*, 72.

48. Quoted in R. Nichols, *Treason, Tradition and the Intellectual: Julien Benda and Political Discourse* (Lawrence, 1978), 155.

49. Ariane Brill, *Abrgrenzung und Hoffnung. 'Europa' in der deutschen, britischen und amerikanischen Presse 1945–1980* (Göttingen, 2014), 174–263, makes the case that there were more consistent and regular references to a shared, European high culture in German newspapers such as the *Frankfurter Allgemeine Zeitung* than in the British *Times*. Such references were intermixed with stereotypes and fresh discoveries on the part of travel correspondents, who charted the rise of mass tourism in Europe.

50. V. Conze, *Das Europa der Deutschen* (Munich, 2005), 1. These debates also took place in the mainstream press. See, for instance, 'Synthesis Europa', *Frankfurter Allgemeine Zeitung*, 13 May 1950: 'Insofar as Europe has a form, it stems from Rome, and that which stems from Rome is called *Abendland*.'

51. P. M. R. Stirk, *European Unity in Context: The Interwar Period* (London, 1989), 12.

52. Cited in Raley, *Ortega y Gasset*, 141.

53. Ibid.

54. J. Ortega y Gasset, *Revolt of the Masses*, 185–6.

55. In Raley, *Ortega y Gasset*, 175.

56. G. Delanty, *Inventing Europe*, 3.

57. Ibid.

58. Ibid., 13.

59. A. Brill, *Abrgrenzung und Hoffnung*, 40–93.

60. 'Britain and America in Peace', *Times*, 6 March 1946; 'Russia and Her Allies', *Times*, 9 March 1946; 'The Three Powers', *Times*, 14 March 1946.

61. 'Ein Ausflug an die Ostgrenze Europas', *Süddeutsche Zeitung*, 1 May 1948, in A. Brill, *Abgrenzung und Hoffnung*, 46.

62. 'Eckstein des europäischen Wiederaufbaus', *Süddeutsche Zeitung*, 20 March 1948; 'Der Ruf nach Westen', *Süddeutsche Zeitung*, 9 March 1948; 'Kriegspsychose', *Süddeutsche Zeitung*, 20 March 1948, in A. Brill, *Abgrenzung und Hoffnung*, 47.

63. Ibid., 48.

64. S. de Roode, *Seeing Europe through the Nation: The Role of National Self-images in the Perception of European Integration in the English, German and Dutch Press in the 1950s and 1990s* (Stuttgart, 2012), 185–218.

65. 'Elastische Europapolitik Großbritanniens', *FAZ*, 23 April 1952, in A. Brill, *Abgrenzung und Hoffnung*, 54–5.

158   EUROPEAN INTEGRATION SINCE THE 1920S

66. See, for instance, 'Amerikanische Garantie für Europa', *FAZ*, 17 April 1954; 'Wir und der "New Look"', *FAZ*, 26 April 1954, 'Amerika setzt Paris und Rom unter Druck', *FAZ*, 25 May 1954, in A. Brill, *Abgrenzung und Hoffnung*, 66.

67. For instance, 'Headway in the West', *The Times*, 6 March 1948.

68. Thus, 'Mr. Bevin's Statement on the Pact: "No Ganging Up" against any Country', *Manchester Guardian*, 19 March 1949; 'Today's Signature of Atlantic Treaty: Arms for the West; Mr Acheson's Explanations to Eager Statesmen', *Manchester Guardian*, 2 April 1949; 'Lessons of the Brussels Treaty: Framework for Atlantic Defence Organization', *Manchester Guardian*, 5 April 1949.

69. S. de Roode, 'Changing Images of the Nation in England, Germany and the Netherlands: A Comparison', *History Compass*, 7 (2009), 894–916.

70. See A. Deighton, *The Impossible Peace: Britain, the Division of Germany, and the Origins of the Cold War* (Oxford, 1990). More generally, D. Calleo, *The German Problem Reconsidered* (Oxford, 1978).

71. D. K. Fieldhouse, *Western Imperialism in the Middle East, 1914–1958* (Oxford, 2008), 245–348; I. M. Wall, *France, the United States and the Algerian War* (Berkeley, CA, 2001); A. Shaw, *Eden, Suez and the Media* (London, 2009); B. Turner, *Suez 1956: The Forgotten War* (London, 2006); D. M. Anderson and D. Branch, *Allies at the End of Empire: Loyalists, Nationalists and the Cold War, 1945–76* (London, 2017); W. Ward, *British Culture and the End of Empire* (Manchester, 2001); J. M. MacKenzie, *Propaganda and Empire: The Manipulation of British Public Opinion, 1880–1960* (Manchester, 1986). A major part of P. Betts, *Ruin and Renewal*, 223–428, concerns the ramifications of the end of empire for Europe and for the rest of the world.

72. A. Milward, *The European Rescue of the Nation-State* (London, 1992). The view expressed here is, of course, highly contested.

73. See, for instance, Jeremy Shearmur's commentary on Popper's *The Poverty of Historicism* (1957) in *The Political Thought of Karl Popper* (London, 1996), 41–3; also, H. C. Raley, *José Ortega y Gasset: Philosopher of European Unity* (Alabama, 1971), 11, R. Gray, *The Imperative of Modernity: An Intellectual Biography of Ortega y Gasset* (Berkeley, 1989), and A. Dobson, *An Introduction to the Politics and Philosophy of José Ortega y Gasset* (Cambridge, 1989).

74. Especially D. Reynolds (ed.), *The Origins of the Cold War in Europe* (New Haven, 1994), D. Reynolds, *From World War to Cold War* (Oxford, 2006), and D. Reynolds, *One World Divisible* (London, 2000).

75. In the German case, see H. James, *The German Slump* (Oxford, 1986).

76. I have written more on this in M. Hewitson and M. D'Auria (eds), *Europe in Crisis*, 15–34, 63–81.

77. Cited in R. Skidelsky, *Keynes*, vol. 3, 218. On 'national planning' and 'market restoration', see A. Gamble, *Hayek* (Cambridge, 1996), 164. On Keynes's gradually softening attitude to capitalism, see A. Fitzgibbons, *Keynes's Vision* (Oxford, 1988), 167–80.

78. R. Skidelsky, *Keynes*, vol. 3, 218.

79. J. Ortega y Gasset, *Meditation on Europe* (1949), in H. C. Raley, *Ortega*, 177.

80. Ibid.

81. Ibid.

82. Ibid.

83. See, above all, M. Conway, *Western Europe's Democratic Age, 1945–1968* (Princeton, NJ, 2020), 98–198; M. Conway and V. Depkat, 'Towards a European History of the Discourse of Democracy: Discussing Democracy in Western Europe, 1945–1960', in M. Conway and K. K. Patel (eds), *Europeanization in the Twentieth Century* (Basingstoke, 2010), 132–56. Jan-Werner Müller, *Contesting Democracy*, 126–9, claims that Ortega himself, who held 'the cataclysms of the twentieth century to have originated in the rise of "the masses"', was partly to blame, but he also underlines a widely felt need for stability: 'In other words, in post-war Western Europe a new, chastened, Weberian politics triumphed: not charismatic, but firmly centred on the executive and pragmatic leaders; not geared towards generating meaning, but based on more than economic success (namely, moral foundations, such as natural law); not animated by a comprehensive liberal vision, but attempting to integrate citizens through shared values in a rejection of the fascist past and the Communist threat from the East in the present.'

84. See, above all, M. Conway, 'The Rise and Fall of Western Europe's Democratic Age, 1945–1973', *Contemporary European History*, 13 (2004), 67–88; S. Levsen, 'Authority and Democracy in Postwar France and West Germany, 1945–1968,' *Journal of Modern History*, 89 (2017), 812–50; J.-W. Müller, *Contesting Democracy*, 125–70.

85. S. M. Di Scala and S. Mastellano, *European Political Thought, 1815–1989* (Boulder, Colorado, 1998), 186–8, 197. Also, D. R. Roberts, *Croce and the Uses of Historicism* (Berkeley, 1987), 238–9; N. Bobbio, *Ideological Profile of the Twentieth Century in Italy* (Princeton, 1995).

EUROPEAN STORIES 159

86. C. Schmitt, Preface to *Der Begriff des Politischen*, new edn (Berlin, 1963). See Stirk, *German Political Thought*, 135–64, on the democratic basis of political debates in Germany after 1945.
87. P. Stirk, *German Political Thought*, 143, 150.
88. The reference to 'moderation' comes from N. O'Sullivan, *European Political Thought since 1945* (Basingstoke, 2004), 79–85.
89. Ibid., 83.
90. R. Aron, 'Les institutions politiques de l'occident dans le monde du XXe siècle', in R. Aron et al., *La démocratie à l'épreuve du XXe siècle* (Paris, 1960), quoted in M. Conway, *Western Europe's Democratic Age, 1945–1968*, 1.
91. Ibid., 20–3, 28–35.
92. B. de Jouvenel, *Vers les Etats-Unis d'Europe* (1930), in J. L. Chabot, *Aux origines intellectuelles de l'Union européenne* (Grenoble, 2005), 158.
93. Ibid.
94. F. Meinecke, *Die deutsche Katastrophe* (Wiesbaden, 1946), 151–2.
95. See also G. Ritter, *Europa und die deutsche Frage* (Munich, 1948).
96. Meinecke discussed the war, as the main 'catastrophe', more than the Holocaust. His account, and many other accounts which used the passive form, confronted much more uncompromising accusations and analyses of guilt; for example, K. Jaspers, *The Question of German Guilt* (New York, 1947).
97. R. Nichols, *Treason, Tradition and the Intellectual*, 127.
98. Benda interview in *Nouvelles littéraires* in 1925, cited in M. Winock, *Le siècle des intellectuelles* (Paris, 1997), 238.
99. R. Nichols, *Treason, Tradition and the Intellectual*, 128.
100. Ibid., 129.
101. R. Soucy, *Fascist Intellectual: Drieu La Rochelle* (Berkeley, 1979), 93.
102. Ibid., 65–6.
103. Ibid., 176–7.
104. Cited in R. Colquhoun, *Raymond Aron* (London, 1986), vol. 1, 419.
105. Ibid., 420.
106. Ibid., 429, 433.
107. Ibid., 432.
108. J. Gray, *Isaiah Berlin* (London, 1995), 99.
109. Ibid., 98–121.
110. Quoted in H. C. Raley, *Ortega*, 58.
111. Ibid.
112. Ibid.
113. Ortega y Gasset, *Revolt*, 135.
114. Quoted in Dobson, *Ortega*, 51.
115. H. C. Raley, *Ortega*, 144–5.
116. J. Ortega y Gasset, *Meditation on Europe* (1949), quoted in Raley, *Ortega*, 177.
117. K. Adenauer, *Erinnerungen 1953–1955* (Stuttgart, 1966), vol. 2, 302.
118. See especially P. O'Brien, *Beyond the Swastika* (London, 1996); also, D. A. Moses, *German Intellectuals and the Nazi Past* (Cambridge, 2007); M. Fulbrook, *German National Identity after the Holocaust* (Cambridge, 1999); J. Herf, *Divided Memory: The Nazi Past in the Two Germanys* (Cambridge, Mass., 1997); K. H. Jarausch, *After Hitler: Recivilizing Germans, 1945–1995* (Oxford, 2007); S. Berger, *The Search for Normality. National Identity and Historical Consciousness in Germany since 1800* (Oxford, 1997); and N. Frei. *Adenauer's Germany and the Nazi Past: The Politics of Amnesty and Integration* (New York, 2002).
119. D. A. Moses, 'The Non-German German and the German German: Dilemmas of Identity after the Holocaust', *New German Critique*, 101 (2007), 45–94.
120. H. Kelsen, 'Is a Peace Treaty with Germany Legally Possible and Politically Desirable?', *American Political Science Review*, 41 (1947), 1188. See Peter Stirk's excellent study of *Twentieth-Century German Political Thought* (Edinburgh, 2006), 154–5, for commentary on this and many of the points below.
121. W. Brandt, *Erinnerungen* (Berlin, 1989), 271.
122. H. Schelsky, *Die skeptische Generation* (Düsseldorf, 1957).
123. P. Stirk, *German Political Thought*, 138–9.
124. The quotation comes from Leibholz, a judge and academic. G. Leibholz, 'Der Strukturwandel der modernen Demokratie' (1952), and G. Leibholz, *Das Wesen der Repräsentation* (Berlin, 1929),

160 EUROPEAN INTEGRATION SINCE THE 1920S

and E. Fraenkel, *Der Doppelstaat* (Oxford, 1941), and E. Fraenkel, *Military Occupation and the Rule of Law* (Oxford, 1944), cited in Stirk, *German Political Thought*, 144–6.

125. D. Sternberger, 'Begriff des Vaterlandes' (1947) and 'Das Problem der Loyalität' (1956), ibid., 155–6.
126. T. Garton Ash, *In Europe's Name: Germany and the Divided Continent* (London, 1993).
127. V. Cotesta, 'Rosenzweig, Schmitt and the Concept of Europe', in M. Hewitson and M. D'Auria (eds), *Europe in Crisis*, 169–82.
128. L. Dehio, *The Precarious Balance* (London, 1948), cited in Stirk, *German Political Thought*, 156.
129. W. Grewe, 'Die auswärtige Gewalt der Bundesrepublik' (1954), ibid., 157.
130. K. Dyson, *The State Tradition in Western Europe* (Oxford, 1980), 155–204; G. Poggi, *The State: Its Nature, Development and Prospects* (Cambridge, 1990).
131. H. Arendt, *The Origins of Totalitarianism* (New York, 1951), 290.
132. A. Hitler, *Mein Kampf* (Berlin, 1925–6), vol. 1, 280–323; vol. 2, 9–22, 82–91.
133. Müller, *Contesting Democracy*, 130–2, argues that the 'decent state' in post-war Britain was the exception, 'vindicated by the victory over Nazism—when almost everywhere else in Europe state authority had been eroded by the war'. At the same time, the state traditions of continental Europe were more entrenched than in the United Kingdom: see, for instance, J. Harris, 'Political Thought and the State', in S. J. D. Green and R. C. Whiting (eds), *The Boundaries of the State in Modern Britain* (Cambridge, 2002), 15–28; G. Poggi, *The Development of the Modern State: A Sociological Interpretation* (Palo Alto, CA, 1978); G. Poggi, 'The Constitutional State of the Nineteenth Century: An Elementary Conceptual Portrait', *Sociology*, 11 (1977), 311–32.
134. See, for instance, K. Dyson, 'The Ambiguous Politics of Western Germany: Politicization in a "State" Democracy', *European Journal of Political Research*, 7 (1979), 375–96.
135. C. J. Friedrich, 'The Unique Character of Totalitarian Society', in C. J. Friedrich (ed.), *Totalitarianism* (New York, 1953); F. Neumann, *Behemoth* (London, 1942) and C. J. Friedrich, *The Democratic and the Authoritarian State* (New York, 1957); F. Pollock, *Automation. Materialien zur Beurteilung der ökonomischen und sozialen Folgen* (Frankfurt, 1956); H. Marcuse, *Reason and Revolution* (Oxford, 1941) and H. Marcuse, *Eros and Civilization* (London, 1956); Horkheimer and Adorno, *Dialektik der Aufklärung*.
136. E. Forsthoff, 'Begriff und Wesen des sozialen Rechtsstaates' (1954), in P. Stirk, *German Political Thought*, 152–3.
137. A. J. Nicholls, *Freedom with Responsibility: The Social Market Economy in Germany, 1918–1963* (Oxford, 1994); P. Nord, *France's New Deal: From the Thirties to the Postwar Era* (Princeton, NJ, 2010).
138. R. Colquhoun, *Aron*, vol. 1, 431–2.
139. J. C. Smuts to a friend, 7 May 1919, in R. Skidelsky, *Keynes*, vol. 1, 378.
140. Ibid.
141. Cited in P. Stirk, *European Unity*, 10.
142. D. Drake, *Intellectuals and Politics in Postwar France* (Basingstoke, 2002), 100.
143. Aron in 1946, cited in R. Colquhoun, *Aron*, vol. 1, 422.
144. M. Winock, *Le siècle des intellectuelles*, 487–754, calls the 1940s, 50s and 60s 'les années Sartre'.
145. Cited in A. Rabil, Jr, *Merleau-Ponty: Existentialist of the Social World* (New York, 1967), 90.
146. M. Conway, *Western Europe's Democratic Age*, 143, claims that 'European ambitions for a new democratic order retreated from the global to the European level', faced with the failure of the UN. It was understood that 'internationalism', of which much had been expected with the founding of the United Nations, had failed because of the Cold War, but this did not necessarily work in Europe's favour, since intellectuals could side with each of the superpowers and their version of 'international' organizations (for example, NATO) and aspirations. See also M. Mazower, *No Enchanted Palace: The End of Empire and the Ideological Origins of the United Nations* (Princeton, NJ, 2009).
147. Ibid., 64–5.
148. Cited ibid., 69.
149. Quoted in M. Poster, *Existential Marxism in Postwar France: From Sartre to Althusser* (Princeton, 1975), 137.
150. On the centrality of Maritain to the 'Christian Democratic moment', see J.-W. Müller, *Contesting Democracy*, 132–9; S. Moyn, 'Personalism, Community, and the Origins of Human Rights', in S.-L. Hoffmann (ed.), *Human Rights in the Twentieth Century* (Cambridge, 2010), 86–106.
151. M. S. Power, *Jacques Maritain, Christian Democrat, and the Quest for a New Commonwealth* (Lampeter, 1992).

EUROPEAN STORIES 161

152. Maritain watered down his championing of the common good over individual rights in *Integral Humanism* (1936) as a result of his assessment of the National Socialist dictatorship. On Mounier, see J. Hellmann, *Emmanuel Mounier and the New Catholic Left, 1930–1950* (Toronto, 1981), and R. W. Rauch, Jr, *Politics and Belief in Contemporary France: Emmanuel Mounier and Christian Democracy, 1932–1950* (The Hague, 1972).
153. J. Maritain, *Scholasticism and Politics* (1927), cited in M. S. Power, *Maritain*, 124.
154. This is the title of one of Maritain's books, published in 1943.
155. For an older generation of intellectuals, including Aron, some of their older fears began to resurface in the late 1960s and 1970s, which the French sociologist compared to Weimar: R. Aron, *Plaidoyer pour l'Europe décadente* (Paris, 1977). He continued to pit liberal democracy against the repressive state socialism of the USSR. On the shift in Germany, see V. Conze, *Das Europa der Deutschen*, whose study of the concept of a European *Abendland* ends in 1970. For Delanty, old appeals to European culture rang hollow after the interwar era of dictatorships, two world wars and the Holocaust and in the midst of superpower dominance and the failures of de- and re-colonization. 'America's myth of Europe' was a pastiche, unlikely to win over Europeans themselves: G. Delanty, *Inventing Europe*, 100–55.
156. F. Mitterrand, 31 December 1989, quoted in P. Short, *Mitterrand*, 482.
157. Ole Waever, 'Europe since 1945: Crisis to Renewal', in K. Wilson and J. van der Dussen (eds), *The History of the Idea of Europe*, 178–87, notes that different versions of 'Europe' started to emerge in the 1980s, from Milan Kundera's drawing of a cultural border between Central and Eastern Europe in the *New York Review of Books* in April 1984 and Mikhail Gorbachev's reference to a the 'idea of a common European home' in a speech at the Council of Europe in Strasbourg on 6 July 1989 to Timothy Garton Ash's discussion of *Mitteleuropa* from the perspective of Czech, Polish, Hungarian, and German commentators in 1990: T. Garton Ash, '*Mitteleuropa?*', *Daedalus*, 119 (1990), 1–21; M. Gorbachev, 'Europe as a Common Home', 6 July 1989, at https://digitalarchive. wilsoncenter.org/document/speech-mikhail-gorbachev-council-europe-strasbourg-europe-common-home. See also R. Dahrendorf and T. Garton Ash, 'Die Erneuerung Europas', *Süddeutsche Zeitung*, 4–5 July 2003, for the later evolution of this debate. According to Waever, there was a *de facto* establishment of cross-border contacts and networks of businesses and regional governments, partly to avoid the impression of German domination. W. v. Bredow and R. H. Brocke, *Das deutschlandpolitische Konzept der SPD* (Erlangen, 1986). These discussions were different in kind from the laments for a lost or destroyed European culture which were articulated in the interwar era. Intellectuals such as E. Morin, *Penser l'Europe* (Paris, 1987) and Hans Magnus Enzensberger, *Ach Europa* (Frankfurt, 1987) drew attention to Europe's diversity. This theme was taken up by Margaret Thatcher in her Bruges speech at the *Collège d'Europe* on 20 September 1988, at https://www.cvce.eu/education/unit-content/.
158. See U. Liebert, 'Contentious European Democracy: National Intellectuals in Transnational Debates', in J. Lacroix and K. Nicolaïdis (eds), *European Stories*, 51–77; A. Bachoud, J. Cuesta and M. Trebitsch (eds), *Les intellectuels et l'Europe de 1945 à nos jours* (Paris, 2000), 11. Most of the new literature on 'Europe' dates from the period after 9/11, after rifts had emerged between the a neo-conservative USA and 'old Europe' (Donald Rumsfeld). Sociologists have tended to concentrate on the European Social Model, admitting that this remains a competence of member states: A. Giddens, *Europe in the Global Age* (Cambridge, 2007), 1–29, 164–98; G. Therborn, European Modernity and Beyond: The Trajectory of European Societies, 1945–2000 (London, 1995), 85–99. Ulrich Beck and Edgar Grande, *Cosmopolitan Europe* (Cambridge, 2007), 6, 242, although seeing Europe as a potential answer to Beck's notion of a 'risk society', also present a vision of a 'cosmopolitan Europe', where 'Europe is another word for variable, variable national interests, variable involvement, variable internal-external relations, variable statehood and variable identity', and where political and cosmopolitan integration are combined, pre-supposing the continuing existence of nation-states and 'resting on the principle that diversity is not the problem but the solution'. The institutional and other implications of such cosmopolitan integration are not clear, but they should be set alongside the revival of interest in the EU among left-leaning philosophers such as Étienne Balibar and Jürgen Habermas as a potential site of rights-based, transnational citizenship and democratic deliberation: E. Balibar, *We, the People of Europe? Reflections on Transnational Citizenship* (Princeton, NJ, 2004); J. Habermas, 'European Politics at an Impasse: A Plea for a Graduated Integration', in J. Habermas, Europe: *The Faltering Project* (Cambridge, 2009), 78–105; J. Habermas, *The Crisis of the European Union* (Cambridge, 2012). It is notable that these calls for cosmopolitan, graduated or differentiated integration tend to reject the idea of a shared European 'culture'—Beck and Grande assume a diversity of national cultures—and to assume that 'Europe' is on the defensive or, in Habermas's

162   EUROPEAN INTEGRATION SINCE THE 1920S

description, 'faltering'. Beck's discussion of a 'social contract for Europe' in *German Europe* (Cambridge, 2013), 5–79, starts with a discussion of the Euro crisis and 'the blindness of economics', before going on posit that Europe is 'under threat' within a wider 'crisis of politics'. See also G. Delanty and C. Rumford, *Rethinking Europe: Social Theory and the Implications of Europeanization* (London, 2005).

159. R. Harrison, *Europe in Question: Theories of Regional Federalism* (New York, 1974), 44. J. H. H. Weiler, *The Federal Vision: Legitimacy and Levels of Governance in the United States and the European Union* (Oxford, 2003); M. Burgess, *Federalism and the European Union: The Building of Europe, 1950–2000* (London, 2000); M. D'Auria, 'The Ventotene Manifesto: The Crisis of the Nation-State and the Political Identity of Europe', in M. Spiering and M. Wintle (eds), *European Identity and the Second World War* (Basingstoke, 2011), 141–58; M. Spiering and M. Wintle, 'Junius and the "President Professor": Luigi Einaudi's European Federalism', in M. Hewitson and M. D'Auria (eds), *Europe in Crisis: Intellectuals and the European Idea, 1917–1957* (New York, 2012), 289–304.

160. This trajectory can be traced in M. Burgess, *Federalism and the European Union: The Building of Europe, 1950–2000* (London, 2000). Ole Waever, 'Europe since 1945: Crisis to Renewal', in K. Wilson and J. van der Dussen (eds), *History of the Idea of Europe* 151–210, suggests that separate French, German, Russian, and British discourses about Europe accompanied this narrowing of the field, but expositions by intellectuals and journalists were rarer and less visible. In France, 'neo-Tocquevillian' or 'liberal' commentators such as Pierre Manent and Marcel Gauchet argued for the necessity of institutions, a democratic framework and political community, which the EU lacked: J. Lacroix, 'Borderline Europe : French Visions of the European Union', in J. Lacroix and K. Nicolaïdis (eds), *European Stories: Intellectual Debates on Europe in National Contexts* (Oxford, 2010), 111–13. See P. Manent, *Democracy without Nations? The Fate of Self-Governance in Europe* (Wilmington, DE, 2007); M. Gauchet, *La démocratie contre elle-même* (Paris, 2002); M. Gauchet, *La condition politique* (Paris, 2005); M. Gauchet, 'Comment l'Europe divise la France', *Le débat*, 136 (2005), 4–19. For a reading of the re-emergence of a 'liberal' strand in France, see M. Lilla, *New French Thought* (Princeton, NJ, 1994).

161. See Justine Lacroix, 'Borderline Europe: French Visions of the European Union', in J. Lacroix and K. Nicolaïdis (eds), *European Stories*, 105–21, on Sartre and Aron.

162. Cited in T. Judt, *Past Imperfect: French Intellectuals, 1944–1956* (Berkeley, 1992), 290.

163. M. Merleau-Ponty, *Humanisme et terreur* (1947), cited in Rabil, Jr, *Merleau-Ponty*, 94; M. Eliade, 'Examen leprosum' (1952), in Judt, *Past Imperfect*, 280.

164. T. Judt, *Past Imperfect*, 198.

165. See, for instance, J.-P. Sartre, 'Le fantôme de Staline', *Les Temps modernes*, 129–31 (1956–7), 678.

166. Cited in C. Cate, *André Malraux* (London, 1995), 353.

167. R. Colquhoun, *Aron*, vol. 1, 424.

168. Mauriac in *L'Express*, 29 August 1959, in T. Judt, *Past Imperfect*, 197.

169. Ibid., 198. See also A. Doering-Manteuffel, 'Perceptions of the West in Twentieth-Century Germany'; R. Bavaj, 'Germany and "Western Democracies": The Spatialization of Ernst Fraenkel's Political Thought'; M. Steber, '"The West", Tocqueville and West German Conservatism from the 1950s and 1970s'; and D. Geppert, 'Bridge over Troubled Water: German Left-Wing Intellectuals between "East" and "West", 1945–1949', in R. Bavaj and M. Steber (eds), *Germany and 'the West': The History of a Modern Concept* (New York, 2015), 81–96, 183–99, 230–47, 262–76.

170. Drieu saw the Second World War as a struggle between ideologies, not countries, in his novel *Straw Dogs* (1944). See Soucy, *Fascist Intellectual*, 90–105. On Joliot-Curie, see D. Drake, *Intellectuals*, 41.

171. B. Croce, *Storia d'Europa nel secolo decimonono* (1932), cited in J.-L. Chabot, *Origines*, 140–1; F. F. Rizi, *Benedetto Croce and the Birth of the Italian Republic, 1943–1952* (Toronto, 2019).

172. R. von Coudenhove-Kalergi, *L'Europe unie* (1938); J. Ortega y Gasset, *Revolt of the Masses* (1929); J. M. Keynes, *The Economic Consequences of the Peace* (1919).

173. H. von Keyserling, *Das Spektrum Europas* (1928), B. de Jouvenel, *Vers les Etats d'Europe* (1930). See J.-L. Chabot, *Origines*, 221, 139, 157.

174. In H. C. Raley, *Ortega*, 144–7.

175. Keynes to S. P. Lamprecht, at the start of the war, in R. Skidelsky, *Keynes*, vol. 3, 74.

176. Quoted in R. Colquhoun, *Aron*, vol. 1, 273.

177. See C. Bottici and B. Challand, *Imagining Europe: Myth, Memory and Identity* (Cambridge, 2013), which is mainly concerned with the need for some form of European identity and legitimacy in the absence of a credible European mythology.

EUROPEAN STORIES 163

178. E. Balibar, *Europe, constitution, frontière* (Bordeaux, 2005), 15.
179. T. Garton Ash, 'Trials, Purges and History Lessons: Treating a Difficult Past in Post-Communist Europe', in J.-W. Müller (ed.), *Memory and Power in Post-War Europe: Studies in the Presence of the Past* (Cambridge, 2002), 267–8.
180. Ibid., 268.
181. Ibid.
182. A. v. Plato, 'An Unfamiliar Germany: Remarks on the Past and Present Relationship between East and West Germans', *Oral History*, 21 (1993), 37–8.
183. For varying evaluations, see L. Probst, 'Founding Myths in Europe and the Role of the Holocaust', and D. Diner, 'Restitution and Memory: The Holocaust in European Political Cultures', *New German Critique*, 90 (2003), 36–58; H. Rousso, 'Das Dilemma eines europäischen Gedächtnisses', *Zeithistorische Forschungen*, 1 (2004), 363–78; J.-W. Müller, 'On "European Memory": Some Conceptual and Normative Remarks'; S. Berger, 'Remembering the Second World War in Western Europe, 1945–2005'; and H. Karge, 'Practices and Politics of Second World War Remembrance: (Trans-) National Perspectives from Eastern and South-Eastern Europe', in M. Pakier and B. Stråth (eds), *Contested Histories and Politics of Remembrance* (New York, 2010), 25–37, 119–46.
184. Quoted in T. Judt, 'The Past Is Another Country: Myth and Memory in Post-War Europe', in J.-W. Müller (ed.), *Memory and Power in Post-War Europe*, 157. Judt's own argument is that individuals' memories of perpetration were concealed by more general myths of victimhood, but these differed radically from one country (or political constituency) to another.
185. M. Pakier and B. Stråth, 'Introduction: A European Memory?', in M. Pakier and B. Stråth (eds), *Contested Histories and Politics of Remembrance*, 1–20; B. Stråth, 'Methodological and Substantive Remarks on Myth, Memory and History in the Construction of a European Community', *German Law Journal*, 6 (2003), 255–71. There were marked differences of opinion and practice in individual countries. Helmut Kohl, *Erinnerungen 1982–1990*, vol. 2, 380, quotes Theodor Heuss in November 1945, who argued that those who died in the camps deserved—and 'the voice of the dead searches for'—a hearing. Willy Brandt, *Erinnerungen*, 271, who was better known for his acknowledgement of feelings of guilt and indebtedness, pointed to the tendency of West German citizens to forget the past and look forwards.
186. C. Bottici and B. Challand, *Imagining Europe*, 21, summarizing Andrew Moravcsik's position, by and against which their own arguments are framed.
187. Because of the close involvement of Churchill, Bevin, Duncan Sandys, and others, the British press had also taken an interest in the various European movements: 'European Unity', *Times*, 11 March 1948; 'Unity to Retain Freedom', *Times*, 22 April 1948; 'Mr. Churchill's Call to Europe', *Times*, 8 May 1948.
188. 'Western Europe', *Times*, 30 March 1948; C. Schmid, *Europa und die Macht des Geistes* (1973), cited in A. Brill, *Abgrenzung und Hoffnung*, 99. See also S. de Roode, *Seeing Europe through the Nation*; S. Seidendorf, *Europäisierung nationaler Identitätsdiskurse? Ein Vergleich französischer und deutscher Printmedien* (Baden-Baden, 2007); J. Díez Medrano, *Framing Europe: Attitudes to European Integration in Germany, Spain and the United Kingdom* (Princeton, NJ, 2003).
189. 'The Six Powers', *Times*, 22 July 1952.
190. 'Urgent Problems of the Six and the Seven', *Times*, 17 March 1960; 'Problems for Britain in Links with the Six', *Times*, 30 June 1960.
191. 'Britain Drawn by Grip of Europe', *Times*, 3 May 1962; 'Britain Puts New Proposals to E.E.C.', *Times*, 12 April 1962; 'No Opposition to Britain on E.E.C', *Times*, 15 May 1962; 'Mr. Wilson Ready for Europe—On Terms', *Times*, 19 March 1966; 'Mr. Heath Stakes All on Europe Link', *Times*, 29 March 1966.
192. *Manchester Guardian*, 30 May 1961. The last part of the text quotes John Hynd, the Labour MP for Attercliffe in Sheffield.
193. 'Ertrinkt die EWG in toter Liebe?', *FAZ*, 25 June 1962, in A. Brill, *Abgrenzung und Hoffnung*, 127.
194. Ibid., 134.
195. 'Counting the Forces of Federalism', *Times*, 26 March 1962.
196. 'Viewpoint', *Times*, 7 May 1974.
197. On intellectuals' neglect of 'Europe', see A. Bachoud, J. Cuesta, and M. Trebitsch (eds), *Les intellectuels et l'Europe de 1945 à nos jours* (Paris, 2000); and J. Lacroix and K. Nicolaïdis (eds), *European Stories: Intellectual Debates on Europe in National Contexts* (Oxford, 2010), 1–29. The latter put forward three reasons for intellectuals turning away from the European project: first, 'perversity', or the idea that 'European unity had been tainted beyond redemption by the most lethal plan yet for European unification, namely Hitler's New European Order'; second,

164 EUROPEAN INTEGRATION SINCE THE 1920s

'diversion', or the notion that, 'at least from the late 1950s onwards, Europe had become a diversion from the two great causes of the era'—the Cold War and decolonization; and, third, 'disillusion', with the EEC identified with a Europe of 'tradesmen' and technocracy, 'devoid of the kind of commitment to values and spiritual uplifting with which they had identified Europe in the interwar period'.

198. K. Deutsch, *Political Community and the North Atlantic Area* (Princeton, NJ, 1957), constituted an exception.

199. E. B. Haas, *The Uniting of Europe* (Notre Dame, Indiana, 1968), xix.

200. E. B. Haas and P. Schmitter, 'Economics and Differential Patterns of Political Integration', *International Organization*, 18 (1964), 718.

201. S. Hoffmann, *The European Sisyphus: Essays on Europe, 1964–1994* (1995), 9–136; A. Moravcsik, *The Choice for Europe* (1998); A. Moravcsik, 'Negotiating the Single European Act: National Interests and Conventional Statecraft in the European Community', *International Organization*, 45 (1991), 19–56. R. D. Putnam, 'Diplomacy and Domestic Politics', *International Organization*, 42 (1988), 427–61.

202. A. Moravcsik, 'Preferences and Power in the European Community: A Liberal Intergovernmentalist Approach', *Journal of Common Market Studies*, 31 (1993), 474.

203. Ibid., 515.

204. See especially S. Hix, *The Political System of the European Union*, 2nd edn (Basingstoke, 2005) and S. Hix and C. Lord, *Political Parties in the European Union* (Basingstoke, 1997).

205. Following, for example, J. G. March and J. P. Olsen, 'The New Institutionalism: Organizational Factors in Political Life', *American Political Science Review*, 78 (1984), 734–49; P. Hall, *Governing the Economy: The Politics of State Intervention in Britain and France* (Oxford, 1986), 19.

206. J. Peterson and E. Bomberg, *Decision-Making in the European Union* (Basingstoke, 1999), 4–30.

207. Ibid., 5; W. Wessels, 'An Ever Closer Fusion? A Dynamic Macropolitical View on Integration Processes', *Journal of Common Market Studies*, 35 (1997), 267–99.

208. A. Stone Sweet and W. Sandholtz, 'European Integration and Supranational Governance', *Journal of European Public Policy*, 4 (1997), 297–317; H. Kassim, 'Policy Networks and European Union Policy-Making: A Sceptical View', *West European Politics*, 17 (1994), 15–27; T. Börzel and T. Risse, 'Conceptualizing the Domestic Impact of Europe', in K. Featherstone and C. Radaelli (eds), *The Politics of Europeanization* (Oxford, 2003), 57–80.

209. T. Christiansen, K. E. Jørgensen, and A. Wiener (eds), *The Social Construction of Europe* (London, 2001), 203; D. Howarth and J. Torfing (eds), *Discourse Theory in European Politics: Identity, Policy and Governance* (Basingstoke, 2005), 1–32.

210. V. Conze, *Das Europa der Deutschen*, which compares two strands of thought (Catholic conceptions of an *Abendland* and broader orientations towards Western Europe and the 'West' in general), ends her study in 1970. See also C. Bailey, *Between Yesterday and Tomorrow: German Visions of Europe, 1926–1950* (New York, 2013), which examines the 'lost Europes' of the Internationaler Sozialistischer Kampfbund and Das Demokratische Deutschland, together with the periodical *Merkur. Deutsche Zeitschrift für Europäisches Denken*.

211. S. Zweig, *The World of Yesterday* (London, 1953), 436.

212. R. Toye, '"This Famous Island Is the Home of Freedom": Winston Churchill and the Battle for "European Civilization"', *History of European Ideas*, 46 (2020), 666–80.

213. For more on this topic, see J. Vermeiren and M. Hewitson (eds), *Europe and the East* (London, 2023).

214. M. Kundera, 'The Tragedy of Central Europe', *New York Review of Books*, 7 April 1984.

215. Ibid.

216. Ibid.

217. Ibid.

218. Ibid.

219. See also J. Rupnik, *The Other Europe* (London, 1988), for a rare warning from the West. Rupnik is a French academic born in Prague in 1950. Likewise, Zygmunt Bauman, *Europe: An Unfinished Adventure*, 35, was willing to consider culture and identity, especially in opposition to the politics of the USA, when considering 'Europe', although deriding—for example—the Europa-Union's attempts to give substance to Vaclav Havel's call in the European Parliament for a 'A Charter of European Identity' on 8 March 1994.

220. J. Habermas, *Staatsbürgerschaft und nationale Identität. Überlegungen zur europäischen Zukunft* (St Gallen, 1990).

221. P. Nora, 'Between Memory and History: *Les Lieux de Mémoire*', *Representations*, 26 (1989), 7–8.

222. Ibid., 8.

223. Ibid., 9.
224. One recent attempt to address this shortcoming is W. Kaiser and A. Varsori (eds), *European Union History: Themes and Debates* (Basingstoke, 2010).
225. J. Gillingham, 'A Theoretical Vacuum: European Integration and Historical Research Today', *Journal of European Integration History*, 14 (2008), 27, quoting A. Milward.
226. Ibid, 28.
227. Ibid., 31.
228. Ibid., 30.
229. Ibid.
230. Ibid., 31, 27.
231. On 'Whig' or progressive histories of European integration, see M. Gilbert, 'Narrating the Process: Questioning the Progressive Story of European Integration', *Journal of Common Market Studies*, 46 (2008), 641–8.
232. W. Lipgens, *Europa-Föderationspläne der Widerstandsbewegungen 1940–1945*; W. Lipgens, 'European Federation in the Political Thought of Resistance Movements during World War II', *Central European* History, 1 (1968), 5–19; W. Lipgens, A *History of European Integration*; W. Lipgens, *Die Anfänge der europäischen Einigungspolitik 1945–1950*; W. Lipgens and W. Loth (eds), *Documents on the History of European Integration* (Berlin, 1985–88), 3 vols.; W. Loth, 'Explaining European Integration', *Journal of European Integration History*, 14 (2008), 12–16. For a study of pro-community federalism within French political elites, see C. Parsons, *A Certain Idea of Europe* (Ithaca, New York, 2003).
233. A. S. Milward, *The European Rescue of the Nation-State*; A. S. Milward, *The Reconstruction of Western Europe, 1945–51* (London, 1984); A. S. Milward and V. Sorensen (eds), *The Frontier of National Sovereignty: History and Theory, 1945–1992* (Routledge, 1993).
234. A. S. Milward, 'Allegiance: The Past and the Future', *Journal of European Integration History*, 1 (1995), 11–12.
235. J. Gillingham, 'A Theoretical Vacuum: European Integration and Historical Research Today', *Journal of European Integration History*, 14 (2008), 29. A. S. Milward, 'The Social Basis of Monetary Union', in P. Gowan and P. Anderson (eds), *The Question of Europe* (London 1997), 152, 160.
236. Justine Lacroix and Kalpypso Nicolaidis (eds), *European Stories*, 1, rely on Stefan Collini's definition of intellectuals as figures 'regarded as possessing some kind of "cultural authority", that is who deploy an acknowledged intellectual position or achievement in addressing a broader, non-specialist public'. S. Collini, *Absent Minds: Intellectuals in Britain* (Oxford, 2006), 46.
237. J. T. Checkel and P. J. Katzenstein, 'The Politicization of European Identities', in J. T. Checkel and P. J. Katzenstein (eds), *European Identity* (Cambridge, 2009), 2.
238. A. Gat, *Nations: The Long History and Deep Roots of Political Ethnicity and Nationalism* (Cambridge, 2012), 387.
239. G. Schröder, *Entscheidungen. Mein Leben in der Politik* (Hamburg, 2006), 82. His comments about Russia, and indeed his own role in respect of Russia, have not stood the test of time, revealing the difference between relations in the EU and outside of it.
240. Those in charge of European institutions have attempted to use prizes and other appeals to symbols in order to influence this debate, albeit in ways which remain secondary to the parallel efforts of national leaders: F. Foret and O. Calligaro, 'Governing by Prizes: How the European Union Uses Symbolic Distinctions in Its Search for Legitimacy', *Journal of European Public Policy*, 26 (2019), 1335–53.

4

Identity

Citizens' feelings of affiliation with and allegiance to the European Union and to the nation-state rarely come into conflict with each other, not least because the two sets of institutions operate in different, well-defined spheres. There remain, however, powers and competencies open to dispute, political disagreements about the future, and competition for popular support and loyalty. Leaders have been guided by divergent views of sovereignty and identity, as Margaret Thatcher's speech on 20 September 1988 to the Collège d'Europe in Bruges underlined:

> My first guideline is this: willing and active cooperation between independent sovereign states is the best way to build a successful European Community. To try to suppress nationhood and concentrate power at the centre of a European conglomerate would be highly damaging. . . . Europe will be stronger precisely because it has France as France, Spain as Spain, Britain as Britain, each with its own customs, traditions and identity.[1]

On the same day, the Danish Prime Minister, Poul Schlüter, addressed the America-European Community Association in London:

> The nation-state was the twin of the industrial society, and like industrial society it is becoming outworn. . . . The evolution of Europe in the next decades will be shaped by the phasing in of the information society to replace the industrial culture and industrial technology which have served us so well for almost two hundred years.[2]

For Schlüter, the first Conservative Prime Minister in Denmark since 1901, the territorial and political claims of the nation-state were being undermined or made redundant by new forms of social organization, which were based on the collection and transfer of information rather than the extraction of resources and the production of goods. For Thatcher, who had been one of the principal sponsors of the Single European Act in 1986, the bonds of allegiance between citizens and nation-states remained intact, despite the fact that states—in her opinion, as a neo-liberal Conservative—were reducing the scope of their activities and individuals were increasingly defining themselves within markets.

European Integration since the 1920s: Security, Identity, and Cooperation. Mark Hewitson, Oxford University Press.
© Mark Hewitson 2024. DOI: 10.1093/oso/9780198915942.003.0005

Deconstructing Europe

The contrasting positions of the two prime ministers hinged on diverging judgements of the nation-state as a repository of identity and power, with implications for the future of the European Community. The intellectual historian J. G. A. Pocock reflected on these differences of opinion one year later, as he watched the revolutions of 1989 in Eastern Europe from his vantage point as a New Zealander in Italy: 'One was close enough, at all events, to experience a sensation that we were witnessing the end of a European era forty years long, and of a definition of "Europe" predicated on the partition collapsing before one's eyes.'[3]

On the one hand, European societies seemed to be moving towards 'a state of affairs in which political communities had been effectively reduced to insignificance, and humans could identify themselves only as existing in market communities, engaged in no other self-defining activities than the manufacture, distribution and consumption of goods, images and the information (if that is the right word) relating thereto'.[4] Because the EEC was above all a market composed of post-industrial states, it was associated with this form of 'post-modernity'. 'What took a much more visible shape was an ideology of "Europeanness" which enjoined the rejection of previously distinct national histories without proposing a synthetic or universal history to take their place,' wrote Pocock in his essay on 'Deconstructing Europe' at the end of 1991: 'When the British are enjoined to consider themselves "European", it is usually with the implication that they should not consider their history as in any way distinctive; and though this injunction has not been notably effective, it has strengthened the tendency toward the kind of post-modernism in which any *Lebensform* is presupposed an act of hegemony, an imposition to be deconstructed.'[5] 'Europeanization' in this sense did not imply a transfer of allegiances and affiliations: '"Europe" could therefore become the ideology of a post-historical culture, in which varyingly affluent and varyingly alienated masses—there is an alienation of the consumer as well as an alienation of the deprived—float from one environment to another with no awareness of moving from one past, and one commitment to it, to another.'[6]

On the other hand, the revolutions of 1989 and the end of the Cold War had reunited Europe, confronting the European Community with nationalism and history, as Tatyana Tolstaya had pointed out in 1991, referring to 'western Eurasia not far beyond Europe': '"in the West the sense of history has weakened or completely vanished; the West does not live in history; it lives in civilization (by which I mean the self-awareness of transnational technological culture as opposed to the subconscious, unquestioned stream of history)"'.[7] In Russia and, by extension, other areas of Eastern Europe, 'there is practically no civilization, and history lies in deep, untouched layers over the villages, over the small towns that have reverted to near wilderness, over the large uncivilized cities, in those places where

168 EUROPEAN INTEGRATION SINCE THE 1920s

they try not to let foreigners in, or where foreigners themselves don't go'.[8] By 'history', Tolstaya meant 'the experience and memory of the past unprocessed, in the nature of raw sewage: an unmediated, uninterpreted, uncriticised and (incidentally if not centrally) unsanitised present but not controlled, unimpeded in its capacity to drive humans to unspeakable things'.[9] This reunion of the two Europes posed questions of the European Community and its member states.[10]

Until 1989, Europeans had believed that their post-national states within the EEC had been harbingers of a universal future, visible elsewhere in the 'West'. 'The mystique of "Europe", which has often made it possible to use the word as an incantation with which there can be no argument, may have been the product of a turn toward a post-historic consumer culture, but it has also been a product of the Community's singular success in creating a common economy, elements of a common culture, and some institutions of a shared administrative—it seems too soon to call it "civic"—political structure,' Pocock claimed: 'All these were the connotations of "Europe" as it was being used down to 1989, and as it is still used as it looks toward 1992.'[11] The collapse of the Wall and the opening of the Iron Curtain, however, had 'deprived "Europe" of its partition along the militarized and policed frontier which had defined its identity as opposed to the presumed alternative culture of late Leninism'.[12] Western Europeans were obliged to ask, precisely at the point when American commentators such as Francis Fukuyama were proclaiming the end of history, whether their own predictions of a post-historical and post-national future were not mistaken, transforming the European Community from a post-modern space (and market) into a potential 'empire'.[13]

With the Communist system of late Leninism little more than a hollow shell, the 'liberal-democratic capitalism of the Community was faced with the task, not of transforming a counter-culture, but of filling a vacuum and tidying up a gigantic mess', wrote Pocock: 'The collapse extended beyond the Central and Eastern Europe occupied in 1944–5, deep into the Soviet Union itself and the heartlands of northern Eurasia, where what collapsed in 1991 was not only an economic and political order but a system of states possessing sovereignty distributed among themselves, so that the ideological transformation of the continent instantly took on a geopolitical dimension.'[14] Europe, continued Pocock, 'came face to face with a Central Europe, an Eastern Europe, and a Eurasia extending through Siberia, which had not been integrated into its post-modern culture and did not belong with any simplicity to its history', since these regions were at once 'ethnically diverse and politically indeterminate'.[15] The challenge that they posed was not merely temporary, in the historian's opinion, but raised the question once more of whether 'one of the aims of the state is to exercise some control over its own history, defining its past and seeking to determine its future', with the individuals in liberal states acting 'as citizens in the determination of their own historicized identities' and exercising freedom, in history as in politics, within 'an autonomous and sovereign political community'.[16]

The practical inequality and diverging attitudes of citizens within the two Europes had begged questions about individual autonomy, political power, and the relationship between politics and economics:

> Is the supra-national community we look at in the double perspective of this essay—the European Community, since no Pacific community is in process of formation—a species of empire, in which ultimate political control belongs to some institutions rather than others, to some national communities rather than others? The problems placed before the Community by the changes taking place in Central and Eastern Europe seem to make this a reasonable question; there are said to be differing German, French and British policy preferences regarding the future of the states of Eastern Europe. If we answer the question in the affirmative, we return 'Europe' to the domain of reason of state. 'Empire' and 'confederation' are not mutually exclusive terms, but are ranged along a spectrum of meanings: it may be said, however, that if there is to be a 'Europe' commanding its political present, there must be a political structure capable of defining its own past and writing its own history. On the other hand, the 'mystique of Europe' that has taken shape does not seem to offer a political history, which as far as can be seen would have to be that of a plurality of states acting in their own history and never yet confederated or incorporated in a lasting imperial structure. This opens the way to the reply that the question has been wrongly posed, and that the community being shaped is not a political community in the sense of a redistribution of the sovereignty possessed by states, but a set of arrangements for ensuring the surrender by states of their power to control the movement of economic forces which exercise the ultimate authority in human affairs. The institutions jointly operated, and/or obeyed, by member states would then not be political institutions bringing about a redistribution of sovereignty, but administrative or entrepreneurial institutions designed to ensure that no sovereign authority can interfere with the omnipotence of a market exercising 'sovereignty' in a metaphorical because non-political sense.[17]

In such circumstances, 'an uneasy hybrid, an "empire" of the market in which residual political authority was unequally distributed between the political entities subject to its supra-political authority' might result, or 'a more benign, at least a more familiar, scenario in which confederated nations successfully operated shared institutions designed to allow market forces that freedom of operation which it had been agreed should belong to them'.[18] Pocock's preference was clearly the latter solution, but the former remained a possibility, with the relationship between the European Union and the nation-state unresolved.

Recent studies of national identification and solidarity have tended to emphasize the persistence and resilience of ethnic, symbolic and cultural ties.[19] To Azar Gat, 'nationalism is one particular form of political ethnicity', with ethnicity denoting 'a population of shared kinship (real or perceived) and culture'.[20] The field has been 'marked by a great fault line' since the 1980s: on one side 'stand those who regard the nation as a creation of modernity', emerging in Europe during the nineteenth century after the French and industrial revolutions as a result of 'processes of social integration and political mobilization, which have welded together large populations hitherto scattered among parochial and loosely connected small rural communities spanning extensive territories'.[21] Here, it was only with 'the advent of print technology, wide-scale capitalist economies and, later, industrialization, urbanization, mass education, and mass political participation that such social integration and mobilization became possible, with active solicitation by the state'.[22] On the other side 'stand those who defend, adapt, and develop the more traditionalist view of the nation (labelled "primordial" or "perennial")', maintaining that 'nationhood, as a reality and sentiment, is older, existed before modernity (even if not universally), perhaps as far back as antiquity, and not only in Europe but throughout the world'.[23]

Gat rightly points out the difference between 'nations as "imagined" (in Anderson's sense of collective consciousness) and "invented"' entities, with Tom Nairn—a 'modernist'—reminding scholars that 'the inherently fanciful processing and reprocessing of tradition did not mean fabrication *ex nihilo*'.[24] For the Israeli historian, 'One cannot begin to comprehend the enormous appeal of nationalism, its "spell" and combustive nature..., unless it is understood as the tip of an iceberg', with ethno-political formations 'permeating political history and history in general' and springing from 'deep within the human psyche'.[25] Such findings rest on earlier research by scholars such as Anthony Smith and Walker Connor. 'The dichotomy between the realm of national identity and that of reason has proven vexing to students of nationalism,' writes Connor: 'With the exception of psychologists, people trained in the social sciences tend to be uncomfortable in confronting the non-rational.'[26] For Sigmund Freud, 'the emotional wellsprings of national identity defied articulation'.[27] Feelings of kinship are extended to those within the group, but not to those outside it: 'The fault lines that separate nations are deeper and broader than those separating non-kindred groups, and the tremors that follow those fault lines more potentially cataclysmic.'[28] For this reason, in Connor's opinion, 'when nationalism and patriotism are perceived as in conflict, it is nationalism that customarily proves the more powerful allegiance', despite the 'many effective means', including control of public education and history courses, available to states.[29]

In Europe, the disintegration of Yugoslavia into ethnic hatred and civil war shocked political leaders and public opinion alike, raising the question of national allegiance and the possibility of transfer to, or coexistence with, the European Union. In Jack Snyder's verdict, liberal optimism, which seemed—with the fall of the Wall in 1989—finally to have triumphed against Communism and fascist nationalism, had to confront the realities of a nationalist revival. The hope that 'democratization was sweeping formerly authoritarian countries in Latin America, Southern Europe and Eastern Europe, and even making inroads in East Asia', with states everywhere adopting market economies and permitting 'liberal, American-based mass news media and popular culture', had led some commentators to believe that 'war was becoming obsolete' and nationalism 'was rapidly heading into the dustbin of history'.[30] Such hopes were quickly dashed:

> War has been endemic since the collapse of the Berlin Wall. Nor have these been trivial wars at the periphery of the international order: the world's oil supply was at risk in the 1991 Gulf War; in June 1991 the Yugoslav army battled Slovenian separatists scarcely a hundred miles from Vienna, and NATO's air forces mounted a sustained bombing campaign throughout Serbia during the 1999 Kosovo conflict.... In civil wars from Somalia to Bosnia, the armed forces of the liberal international community were bedevilled, attacked, held hostage by local thugs....As a result, the conventional wisdom was soon turned on its head: *The Atlantic Monthly* relabelled the post-Communist world as 'the coming anarchy' and the eminent Harvard political scientist Samuel Huntington announced that the future would hold in store a 'clash of civilizations'.... even those who retained the vision of spreading liberal democracy to unaccustomed corners of the globe considered age-old ethnic prejudices to be liberalism's major foe. President Clinton, in his 1993 presidential inauguration speech, remarked that 'a generation raised in the shadows of the Cold War assumes new responsibilities in a world warmed by the sunshine of freedom but threatened still by ancient hatreds'.[31]

In Snyder's opinion, 'the good news is that this view is largely incorrect': 'Most of the globe's recent strife is not due to ancient cultural hatreds', with Serbs and Croats, for example, never having fought each other until the twentieth century, 'and then largely because the Nazis installed an unrepresentative regime of murderers in Zagreb'.[32] The bad news is that 'the very trends that liberals saw as bringing the end of history have in many instances fuelled the revival of nationalism', with the end of the Soviet Union spurring the 'aspiring leaders of many of its intermingled nations to establish their own national states, whose conflicting claims to sovereignty and territory often gave rise to disputes'.[33] Nationalist leaders exploited the freedom of the press and stoked up resentments resulting from 'painful adjustments to a market economy'.[34] Democratization produced the immediate stimulus for nationalism, Snyder contends, but the question remains whether 'long-standing popular nationalist rivalries precede' it or whether 'nationalism is usually weak or absent among the broad masses of the population', escalating during the course of democratic disputes.[35]

172 EUROPEAN INTEGRATION SINCE THE 1920S

Nationalism in East and West

The descent of Yugoslavia into civil war forced observers to reconsider the relationship between nationalism, federalism, and Europeanism during an era of post-Communism and European enlargement. How could the explosive forces of ethnic nationalism and the end of the Cold War be contained by a post-national, federal (or confederal) political structure? What lessons did the disintegration of Yugoslavia offer to proponents and critics of the EU? Did it, as the Czech-born, French political scientist Jacques Rupnik claimed, fundamentally challenge 'the comfortable but empty Europe, reduced to the Common Market, to compensatory payments and to agricultural surpluses'?[36]

Many commentators, including Snyder, considered that the bloody disintegration of Yugoslavia proved that nationalist antagonism and armed conflict could arise unexpectedly and rapidly from democratization itself. The component parts of Yugoslavia—Slovenia, Croatia, Serbia, Bosnia, Montenegro, and Macedonia— had co-existed in a single state, with the exception of the Nazi-backed Ustaše regime, since the First World War.[37] *Jugosloventsvo* (the doctrine of South Slav unity), the commonality of the Serb and Croat languages (separated only by Cyrillic and Roman script), past opposition to the Ottoman Empire and a shared history of Communism, outside the Soviet sphere, seemed to have created ties between the populations of the republic, bolstered by the formal institutions—the Yugoslav army (JNA), the League of Communists of Yugoslavia (LCY), a federal constitution, and the Yugoslav state presidency, with its rotation of chairs—and continuing economic links between the republics and Western Europe, where one million Yugoslavs worked, sending back foreign currency to their families.[38] Although the economy lacked balance, with the wealth ratio between the richest part of the federation (Slovenia) and the poorest (Kosovo) increasing from 4:1 in the 1950s to 6:1 in the 1980s, GDP had grown by 5.5 per cent per annum in the 1970s, making the country the most prosperous in the Eastern Bloc and leaving some professionals feeling better off than their friends in Western Europe, even if their position deteriorated during the 1980s, as average growth slumped to 0.5 per cent per annum and real wages decreased by 24 per cent.[39] The 1974 constitution had given extensive powers to the republics' governments, including some competence in foreign policy, but they remained tied to Belgrade financially, constitutionally, militarily, and politically (through the LCY).[40] When the League of Communists began to lose control, as the Communist governments of Slovenia and Croatia backed multi-party elections in 1989 and the Slovene delegates walked out of the LCY congress in January 1990 (after the other delegates had refused to establish a fully confederal party), commentators asked what would replace the 'party' as a cohesive force in a multi-party democracy, which had been granted in 1990. These difficulties of a post-Communist transition, however, were not unique to Yugoslavia.[41]

Western observers were, therefore, taken by surprise as the Serbs of Knin began to arm themselves and set up roadblocks, the Slovenian and Croatian governments sought to build up their 'police' forces and the Serbian government put pressure on the JNA to intervene militarily during the course of 1990.[42] Snyder's thesis that peaceable, mixed populations had been radicalized during a fraught process of democratization, as newspaper readers and TV viewers who were unfamiliar with an uncensored press were fed with rumours by opposing publications and channels, found support in Mark Thompson's detailed analysis of the escalation of atrocity stories and historical myths during the Bosnian War (April 1992–November 1995). His conclusion is unequivocal:

Media were and are indispensable conduits for disinformation, propaganda, half-truths and so forth. They promoted certain information and opinions while suppressing or marginalizing others. And the result? 'The public is not able to inform itself about the actions of government. Lacking elementary information about the motives and intentions of its leaders, it has been kept blindfolded and disoriented.' (L. Tindemans et al., *Unfinished Peace: Report of the International Commission on the Balkans*, 153) As for the effect of ethnic propaganda on public perceptions, it can be measured. Research into the 'perception of other ethnic groups' among students at Zagreb university in May 1992 and June 1993 has indicated the power of the media to influence these attitudes. In May 1992, when the first sample was taken, 'the distance towards the Muslims was the lowest in comparison with that expressed towards other ex-Yugoslav ethnic groups'. The second sample showed a dramatic change: now the Muslims 'were classified in the same manner and in the same category as Serbs and Montenegrins'. The researchers noted that the change 'would not be so striking if the respondents had actually experienced Muslim misdeeds or atrocities personally. In this case, when the entire war was perceived through the media, it can be concluded that the same media, at least partially, induced an increase in the social distance.' Between May 1992 and June 1993, 'Croats from Croatia read in their daily newspapers about their new enemy—the Muslims.' (They also, of course, watched and heard the same message on their television sets and radios.) In sum, the media 'thus served as an instrument for the legitimization of the actions of the Croatian political elite'.[43]

Television, in particular, appeared to have helped, by creating myths and juxtaposing them with reality, to convert history into nature.[44] It also relied on fear, 'including the thrill and pang of public fears funnelled ethereally into private homes'.[45] '"Ethnic hatred" has mistakenly (often self-servingly) been accepted by the outside world as the cause of war'—as 'an expression of deeply ingrained animosity'—yet this 'hatred was implanted and cultivated'.[46] 'What we witnessed was violence-provoking nationalism from the top down, inculcated primarily

174 EUROPEAN INTEGRATION SINCE THE 1920s

through the medium of television,' recalled Warren Zimmermann, the American ambassador in Belgrade.[47] There seemed, on this reading, little reason that a radicalization of nationalism could not occur in other parts of Central and Eastern Europe and, indeed, in Southern and Western Europe.

There are reasons to doubt the applicability of the Yugoslav case, however. Journalists such as Tim Judah, who had seen what had occurred with his own eyes, have pointed to the many profound divisions between Serbs, Croats, and Albanians; Catholics, Orthodox Christians, and Muslims; Communists and democrats; villagers and city-dwellers; each resting on a series of legends and more recent memories (for example, the killing of the Second World War).[48] As the 'Memorandum' of the Serbian Academy of Arts and Sciences had underlined in 1986, in one of the acts of an escalation of dissent and intellectual opposition, 40 per cent of Serbs lived outside 'inner Serbia', in Vojvodina, Bosnia, Croatia, Kosovo, and elsewhere (see Table 4.1).[49] Slobodan Milošević—an outsider whose parents had both committed suicide, but whose wife Mirjana Marković belonged to one of Serbia's leading political families and whose sponsor was the President of Serbia, Ivan Stambolić, a friend from university—used nationalism to gain popular support and convert the old League of Communists into the Socialist Party of Serbia, which was voted into government in the first Serbian elections of December 1990.[50] He forged links with Serbs in Kosovo, Bosnia, and Croatia, helping to arm them and planning to keep them in a single state, both of which objectives frightened other groups (Bosnian Muslims, and Kosovan Albanians

Table 4.1 Yugoslav Census of 1981 and 1988

	Yugoslavia (No.)	Yugoslavia (%)	Serbia	Croatia	Bosnia
Serbs	8,140,000	36.3	6,181,000	532,000	1,321,00
Croats	4,428,000	19.8	140,000	3,455,000	758,000
Muslims*	2,000,000	8.9	211,000	24,000	1,630,000
Slovenes	1,754,000	7.8	—	25,000	—
Albanians	1,730,000	7.7	1,299,000	—	—
Macedonians	1,340,000	6.0	29,000	—	—
'Yugoslavs'	1,219,000	5.4	439,000	179,000	326,000
Montenegrins	579,000	2.6	147,000	—	—
Hungarians	427,000	1.9	385,000	25,000	—
Others**	811,000	3.6	148,000***	—	—
Total	22,428,000	100	9,750,000 (1988)	4,680,000 (1988)	4,440,000 (1988)

* 'Muslims as an ethnic group', mostly Bosnian and Sandzak Muslims.

** Including Turks, Romanians, Roma etc.

*** Slovaks, Romanians, and Bulgarians only.

Source: adapted from B. Denitch, *Ethnic Nationalism: The Tragic Death of Yugoslavia* (Minneapolis, 1994), 29, and A. Sellier and J. Sellier, *Atlas des peuples d'Europe centrale* (Paris, 1991), 143–66.

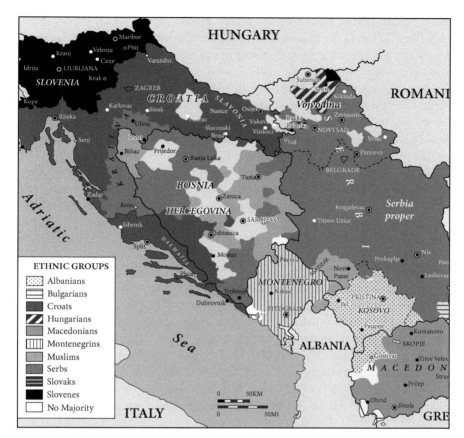

Map 4.1 Ethnic structure of the population of Yugoslavia (1981)
Source: https://en.wikipedia.org/wiki/Ethnic_groups_in_Yugoslavia#/media/File:EtnickaKartaSFRJMZ.jpg

especially, but also Croats and Montenegrins), since they would become targets or minorities in a Serbian-dominated rump Yugoslavia (see Map 4.1).[51]

According to the diary of Borisav Jović, one of Milošević's allies, on 28 June 1990, the Serbian leadership was already contemplating the expulsion of Slovenia and Croatia from Yugoslavia, with the exception of Croatian territories inhabited by Serbs. 'I don't expect war because Croats would have no chance of winning,' boasted the Serbian propaganda chief in Krajina (Croatia), Lazar Macura: 'You must have bloodshed to make a country.'[52] Yet the Croats did risk war, which raged between March 1991 and January 1992, with the fall of Vukovar to the Serbs, propelled by the Croatian Democratic Union (HDZ) under Franjo Tudjman (a former general in the JNA who had been imprisoned in 1972 for his part in the 'Croatian Spring'), who had been voted into office in April 1990. In statements likely to anger and panic Croatia's 600,000 Serbs, Tudjman declared that the Ustaše regime was 'not only a quisling organization and a fascist crime, but was

176 EUROPEAN INTEGRATION SINCE THE 1920s

also an expression of the Croatian nation's historic desire for an independent homeland'.[53] During the Bosnian War, which ended with a death toll of approximately 100,000 and 2.2 million displaced out of a population of 4.4 million, such statements—about the number of Serbs who died in the Ustaše concentration camp at Jasenovac (said to be between 350,000 and one million, rather than 80,000) or about the atrocities committed by Serb Cetniks against 200,000 Croats who died in the Second World War—multiplied in a context of long-standing mutual suspicions and false rumours.[54] Some of these divisions were specific to Yugoslavia, others were common elsewhere in Europe.

The sociologist Rogers Brubaker explains why cultural and national divisions can lead to radicalization. He identifies a 'triadic nexus' of national minorities, nationalizing states and external national 'homelands', which can easily lead to a heightening of national tension, with each set of actors provoking intended and unintended reactions.[55] In Yugoslavia, the Croatian republic quickly became a nationalizing state, not just a secessionist movement, replacing Serbs, who were traditionally overrepresented in administrative posts (including the police), with Croats, adopting the red-and-white chequered flag of the medieval Croatian state and Ustaše regime, 'Croatianizing' the language and claiming 'full state sovereignty' for the 'Croatian nation'.[56] Members of the Serbian national minority in Croatia responded defensively to the challenges issued and drew on both memories and myths of Croatian atrocities during wartime, supported by propaganda from Belgrade.[57] 'Efforts by nationalist radicals in Serbia to mobilize grievances and fears among Croatian Serbs were indeed an important part of the process,' writes Brubaker: 'But the bulk of the work of mobilizing grievances and fears was undertaken locally by Croatian Serbs', calling 'on memories and stories about the murderous wartime Independent State of Croatia, and especially about the gruesome fate of many Croatian and Bosnian Serbs'.[58] These events coincided with the 'revival of Serbian homeland politics', initially focusing on Kosovo, which seemed to be undergoing a gradual process over decades of 'Albanianization'.[59] The 'mutually alienating encounters between the nationalizing and increasingly independent Croatian state and the fearful and increasingly radicalized Serb borderland minority' intersected with 'homeland stances' involving 'identification with, assertions of responsibility for, and demands to support or even "redeem" and incorporate ethnic Serbs outside Serbian state territory'.[60]

The different triadic relationships in Kosovo and Bosnia, which had a larger Serbian minority (1.3 million, compared to 1.6 million Muslims and 758,000 Croats) and more forceful political organization in the Serbian Democratic Party (SDS) of the former psychiatrist and ecologist Radovan Karadžić, became entangled with those in Croatia, with unpredictable effects. Unlike in the Soviet Union, where Russians constituted a majority (51.4 per cent in 1989) and where 25 million Russians outside the Russian Republic could rely on the hegemonic position of their 'homeland' for protection after the end of the Cold War, Serbs remained a minority in 'their' state of Yugoslavia (36.3 per cent in 1981) and feared that Serbia on its own would not be able to counter a Western-backed coalition of Croatia, Slovenia and, possibly, Bosnia-Hercegovina, with a joint population of 11 million, compared to 9.75 million in Serbia (or 5.85 million in Central Serbia, without Vojvodina and Kosovo). Although Brubaker argues that nationalism, as an institutionalized political and cultural form and as a 'set of "nation"-oriented idioms, practices and possibilities', is 'continuously available or "endemic"' in modern conditions, he outlines series of interactions and relations, leading to war in Yugoslavia but not in Czechoslovakia or the Baltic states, which are specific and unlikely to be replicated elsewhere in Europe.[61]

The contention that there has been a resurgence of nationalism in Europe since the late twentieth century, undermining the idea of supranationalism, is largely illusory. It derives from three separate developments. The first concerns the states emerging from the disintegrating Soviet bloc in the 1990s. Here, an overlapping series of special conditions obtained after the end of the Cold War, some of which remained unresolved.[62] Most Central and Eastern European nation-states were recent creations, dating back to the Treaties of Versailles, St Germain-en-Laye, Trianon, Neuilly-sur-Seine, and Sèvres in 1919–20. In cases such as that of Poland, they were also linked to nationalist dictatorships which had failed to integrate segmented societies.[63] The existence of diaspora after the collapse of multinational empires in 1917–21 and of the USSR in December 1991 left a patchwork of ethnic groups: 25 million Russians scattered across the lands of the former Soviet Union; 3 million ethnic Hungarians in Romania, Slovakia, Serbia, and Ukraine; 2 million Albanians in Serbia, Montenegro and Macedonia, 2 million Serbs in Croatia and Bosnia, and 1 million Turks in Bulgaria. Many national issues had not been worked out in the interwar period, before being suppressed (rather than frozen completely) under Communism. Most Communist regimes had paid lip service to nationality and national differences. In practice, some states had functioned as empires for the dominant national groups (most notably, Russians and Serbs), with deals struck with nationalities in the early years before being institutionalized territorially as republics—fifteen in the USSR and six in Yugoslavia—and ethnically, with 'nationality' recorded in passports and used to distinguish between citizens, storing up ethnic and political tensions.[64] Relatively weak civic traditions, economic backwardness, intellectual-dominated opposition movements, uprooted populations in large cities, a wide audience for television combined with a lack of critical discussion could all lead to simplifying nationalist solutions with broad appeal.[65] Yet, to the surprise of commentators at the time, Eastern Europe did not descend into a series of civil wars, acts of persecution or ethnic cleansing, despite the economic and social dislocation of the 1990s, including impoverishment, inequality, and corruption.[66]

The appeal of long-standing foundation myths and national opposition to Communist states and the USSR, which made nationalism appear emancipatory, help to explain why states avoided civil unrest. The 'lack of normal access to the national past was a form of deprivation', wrote Timothy Garton Ash in 1988: 'the recovery of it [is] a form of emancipation'.[67] The legitimacy of democracy, 'Europe' and the 'West' in the early 1990s, the crucial years of the transition, together with the economic transformation and urbanization of Eastern European societies under Communism, meaning that they were no longer segmented and were relatively well educated, provided further reasons.[68] Poland, the Czech Republic, Slovakia, and Hungary had 'already undergone a vast "unmixing of peoples" in the twentieth century', in Snyder's words, and they had few national minorities as a result, after expulsions and migration at the end of the Second World War (see Table 4.2).[69] Nationalism had seemed to be a danger to the fledgling democratic states of Eastern Europe and to the EU, but it had been contained, albeit resurfacing in the political programmes of later populists.[70]

Populism seemed to have been involved in the re-emergence of minority nationalisms (Basque, Catalan, Breton, Corsican, Scottish, and Tyrolean)—a second type of late-twentieth-century nationalist revival—which cut across the national identities of the larger states of Western and Southern Europe (Spain, France, Britain, and Italy). With few exceptions, however, these nationalisms have not been separatist or, at least, have been prepared to limit their demands for independence.[71] Even in the Basque country, the majority has favoured a greater

Table 4.2 Ethnic geography of East Central Europe, 1991–92

	Total population	Largest minorities (%)	Minorities (approx. no.)
Poland	38,419,603	Ukrainian 0.78	300,000
		Belarussian 0.52	200,000
		German) 0.52	200,000
Hungary	10,375,323	Roma 3.9	404,461
		German 1.69	175,000
		Slovak 1.06	110,000
Czech Republic	10,298,731	Moravian 13.2	1,359,432
		Slovak 3.0	308,962
		Roma 0.49	50,000
Romania	22,760,449	Hungarian 7.12	1,620,199
		Roma 1.8	409,723
Bulgaria	8,472,724	Turkish 9.7	822,253
		Roma 3.4	287,732
Slovakia	5,268,935	Hungarian 10.76	566,741
		Roma 1.53	80,627
		Czech 1.01	53,422

Source: M. A. Vachudova, Europe Undivided: Democracy, Leverage and Integration after Communism (Oxford, 2005), 53.

degree of autonomy within Spain rather than complete separation.[72] In most places, minority nationalism has been associated with advanced societies, rather than regional backwaters, and established cultures, many of them—such as Catalan, Basque, and Scottish cultures—dating back to inventions and re-discoveries of the eighteenth and nineteenth centuries and resting on language, folklore, religion, or political institutions, as in the case of Scotland, with its separate legal and educational systems.[73] Arguably, it was because of the increased interventions of regenerated nation-states during the 1950s and 1960s that such cultures came to form the kernel of minority nationalisms. It was no coincidence that it was the large, technocratic, and distant states, like France and Britain, which suffered most from revived minority nationalisms.[74] Often such states had set up regional programmes in order to maximize economic development, but then insisted on administering them from Paris or London—as in the case of the French Delegation for Regional Development and Planning and the British Regional Economic Planning Boards. The Franco regime in Spain, in particular, found it difficult to grant any autonomy to the regions, given the legacy of the Spanish Civil War.[75] Until the 1950s, there were fines for anyone even overheard speaking Catalan or Basque; during the 1940s, Catalan and Basque leaders had been executed or driven into exile.[76] In general, those who challenged these states have come from the managerial, technical, and administrative sections of the middle classes or from the young, mobile, and skilled sections of the working classes. They have tended to view minority nationalism as a source of greater prosperity—for example, in Catalonia or Scotland, with its North Sea oil reserves—or as a repository for protest votes.[77] It is for this reason that the nationalist parties have tended to be unstable, since their voters are relatively sophisticated, weighing up options according to circumstances. Although minority nationalism has occasionally issued in violence—most notably in Northern Ireland and the Basque country—populations have normally been satisfied with cultural recognition, autonomy statutes, devolution or, in Northern Ireland, with consociational government.[78] Separatist parties in the Basque country, Catalonia, Scotland, and Wales have sought to create a triangular relationship between devolved governments, the multi-national state and the European Union, aiming to retain EU membership after independence.[79] In this respect, nationalism reinforced Europeanism.

Throughout Europe, radical right-wing nationalism has constituted a third apparent instance of a resurgence of nationalism. At various points, the press has decried the rise of the far right, with *The Economist* directing attention to 'Europe's tea parties' in early 2014, for instance, in the wake of the eurozone crisis.[80] In that year's European Parliament elections, in which far-right-wing parties regularly benefit from proportional representation and the potential for protest voting, the *Front National* (FN) in France gained 24.9 per cent of the vote, UKIP in the United Kingdom 26.8 per cent, the Danish People's Party (DF) 26.6 per cent, the *Freiheitspartei Österreichs* (FPÖ) 19.7 per cent, and Jobbik in Hungary 14.7 per cent.[81] In Poland and Hungary, the respective governing parties, Law and Justice and Fidesz, have both moved to the right, using racist and nationalist symbols and discourse to appeal to voters.[82] Most of the literature, however, emphasizes the limits of support for the far right, with ten out of twenty-eight member states having no far-right-wing party in the period between 2004 and 2013, four out of twenty-eight experiencing a fall of more than 5 per cent in the vote for far-right-wing parties (Romania, Slovakia, Italy, and Belgium) and four seeing a rise of more than 5 per cent (Hungary, France, Austria, and Latvia).[83] Over the longer term, the vote of the far right has remained around 10–15 per cent in most cases: in legislative and presidential elections, the FN gained between 4.3 per cent (2007 presidential) and 21.3 per cent (2017 presidential), hovering between 9.7 per cent (1986 and 1988) and 14.9 per cent (1997) in legislative elections between 1986 and 2017, with the exception of 2007 (4.3 per cent).[84]

Sociologically, manual workers (30 per cent in 1995) and the unemployed (25 per cent) have comprised a major part of the *Front National*'s electorate.[85] In the presidential election of 2002, support in some polls was as high as 30 per cent for manual workers, 32 per cent for shopkeepers, artisans, and the self-employed and 38 per cent for the unemployed.[86] There is some evidence that this limited, predominantly male constituency is larger in wealthier European countries, where economic disparities are greater.[87] Historically, far-right-wing electors' concerns about immigration—with just under three-quarters of FN voters recording this as the reason for their vote in 1997—have not been shared by the voters of other parties, for less than one-quarter of whom immigration figured as a priority in 1997.[88] 2013 was not 1933, as David Art put it: 'Given the percentage of Europeans who identify themselves as very racist or somewhat racist—upwards of 40 per cent, according to the most recent Eurobarometer, the public opinion agency of the European Union—perhaps the more interesting question is why the radical right has not won more votes and exerted more political influence.'[89] Cas Mudde's answer is that such questions are 'normal', but they have been pursued by the far right in an extreme or 'pathological' way, serving to perpetuate radical right-wing parties' isolation, even if there are signs that their agenda (immigration and Euroscepticism) is being 'normalized'.[90] Such parties have generally been unwilling to undermine or challenge democracy itself—in contrast to their criticism of venal politicians—or to advocate violence, distinguishing them from their counterparts in the interwar era. Unlike in the early 1930s, far-right-wing nationalism has been neither popular nor ruthless enough to derail the European project.

The National Question since 1945

For the majority of the electorate, the duties and rights of national citizenship seem relatively straightforward. 'Every country depends for its sense of identity on a story about itself, a narrative that draws on history and reminds us of who we are and why we belong together,' wrote Gordon Brown in his memoirs, but, given that 'our sense of who we are is becoming more localised and inward-looking, even as our range of experience is becoming more and more global', what does such a narrative consist of?[91] Why do citizens feel similar to each other and to their governments, and why do they wish to establish or submit themselves to a common state? These questions can be answered abstractly in terms of three ideal-types, which distinguish between a political nation, in which citizens choose to remain because they calculate that it is in their interests to do so, an ethnic nation, where citizens feel that their belonging to the group is determined by race or kinship, and a cultural nation, in which citizens feel that they can choose between nations, but believe that their choice is limited by various cultural considerations, such as language, religion and so on.[92] Such definitions are relevant because they determine the ease with which loyalties might be transferred from nation-states to European institutions. It is at least arguable that most federalists, particularly in the 1940s, 1950s, and 1960s, adopted the model of a political nation, assuming that economic self-interest and an acceptance of value-neutral rules of the political game would allow a transfer of loyalty from individual nation-states to 'Europe'. This assumption was easier to make because, as John Plamenatz pointed out, Western Europe had tended well before 1945 to favour political models of the nation, following France's example, whereas Eastern Europe had tended to favour ethnic or, even, racial versions of the nation.[93] In part, the geographical division between Western and Eastern Europe rested on the prior existence of strong states in the West, which then became nation-states like France and Britain, and the existence of multi-ethnic empires in the East, where there was no coincidence of language or religious groups, on the one hand, and already existing political institutions, on the other.

The similarity between governments and citizens, and consent to a common national state, do not need to be treated via ideal-types, but can be understood historically. Three major theses have been put forward to explain why nation-states began to emerge from the late eighteenth century onwards and why they became the central focus of political loyalty, with the right to demand the sacrifice of citizens' lives in war, and with the right, in Max Weber's phrase, to exercise a monopoly of violence.[94] The first thesis, which has been put forward by Benedict Anderson, rightly points out that a nation-state is an 'imagined community'. The way in which citizens imagine it depends, to a large extent, on how they experience it and on the means of communication available to them.[95] To Anderson, the nation-state is distinguished from other forms of imagined

182 EUROPEAN INTEGRATION SINCE THE 1920s

community by the existence of a fixed territory, a known population and a direct relationship between rulers and the ruled. Previous imagined communities such as churches and nobilities had been open-ended hierarchies without finite borders or numbers, where what mattered were relations within the hierarchical web between master and servant, lord and liege, priest and parishioner.[96] One critical step on the path to imagining the nation-state, in Anderson's opinion, was the advent of the newspaper and, later, film, radio and television, for they gave subjects direct access both to other subjects and to those in power.[97] Only in a world of daily news from the rest of the nation was direct loyalty to government and direct sympathy with other citizens likely. 'Hegel observed that newspapers serve modern man as a substitute for morning prayers,' notes Anderson: 'Yet each communicant is well aware that the ceremony he performs is being replicated simultaneously by thousands (or millions) of others of whose existence he is confident, yet of whose existence he has not the slightest notion.'[98]

The second thesis has been formulated by Ernest Gellner and involves necessary increases in communication—and therefore the standardization of language and growth of education—during the transition from agrarian to industrial societies.[99] His argument is that the complex division of labour, which is required by industrialization, has meant that all citizens have had to be given similar types of elementary and, later, secondary education so that they can communicate quickly and efficiently with other individuals in other occupations, other industries, and in government: 'the mutual relationship of a modern culture and states is something quite new, and springs, inevitably, from the requirements of a modern economy'.[100] It is no coincidence, then, that our age, as he puts it, is one of 'universal high culture': a whole series of cultural assumptions need to be made, he claims, in order to enable effective communication and this sense of shared assumptions underpins a sense of common nationhood.[101] The question for supporters of the EU concerns the speed with which a universal high culture on the European level will develop in the wake of a European division of labour.

The third and final thesis is associated with John Breuilly and concerns the growth of monarchical states well before the emergence of self-conscious cultural nations.[102] Cultures were formed and defined as national cultures, Breuilly argues, primarily in response to the incursions of state bureaucracies.[103] If Breuilly were to re-write Anderson's thesis, he might claim that states undermined and abolished other hierarchies and corporations, helping to create a direct relationship between rulers and citizens.[104] If he were to refashion Gellner's arguments, he would perhaps contend that states coordinated economies and systems of education. 'When Anderson writes of "imagining", Gellner of the transformed role of culture as identity in industrial society, and Weber of "orientation to the state", one problem is identifying the agency involved,' writes Breuilly: 'The orientation of nation to state, or more generally to organized political action, involves a two way interaction between leaders and followers', which in turn is 'framed by the various networks of nationally framed affiliations that modernity has created'.[105] In powerful nation-states, many networks 'will be framed in national terms' because the state is a 'focus of loyalty', provides services (for instance, education) and holds social orders 'together within a strong territorial frame'.[106] Although their reciprocal relations were complex, states—and those who opposed state intervention—created nations: 'Nationalism was more important as a product than as a cause of national unification.'[107] In respect of the ease with which loyalty might be transferred from national to European institutions, it can be posited that, according to Breuilly, the concentration of power in Brussels and Strasbourg might in itself start to undermine national political cultures to the net gain of Europe; Gellner and Anderson, on the other hand, might argue that any shift of loyalty would have to be accompanied by a broader movement towards a common European culture, the foundations of which would rest on economic organisation and the means of communication.[108] 'In themselves, market zones, "national"-geographic or politico-administrative, do not create attachments,' Anderson reminded his readers in 1983: 'Who will willingly die for Comecon or the EEC?'[109]

To put it another way, national cultures had been constructed—through literature, the press and a shared history—during the two centuries or so before 1945.[110] Moreover, they had also come to legitimize the state, to the point where Weber, just before the First World War, could say that nation and state were now interchangeable concepts.[111] Given these facts, any movement away from the nation-state after the Second World War was likely to be gradual and incomplete. The interwar period was marked by a pronounced shift towards nation-states: Versailles redrew the map of Europe along lines of national self-determination; economies were protected by increasing tariffs and subjected to greater state intervention; state welfare and expenditure increased, together with a rhetoric which emphasized government responsibility for the nation's well-being; and states continued to pursue their own national interests abroad, leading ultimately to the failure of the League of Nations and the outbreak of war.[112] Above all, fascist and authoritarian governments promoted different forms of radical nationalism, aiming to create self-sufficient nation-states and to merge the individual within a national community, a state of affairs which had seemed to exist briefly at the start of the First World War.[113] A priori, it would seem unlikely that such a pronounced proclivity towards the consolidation of nation-states before 1939 would not only have been reversed, but actually negated by the events of the Second World War. For a child of the interwar era such as Jacques Chirac, born in 1932, the 'destiny of the nation' remained an unquestioned point of reference.[114] 'Every new presidency carries with it a hope and legitimate desire for change, but it also has the duty of ensuring a necessary continuity and the preservation of the values, principles and traditions that have forged our people's identity, and which remain the best guarantors of its unity.'[115]

Rather, it was more probable that many of the national foundations of states would be retained and reinforced after 1945, in spite of the destruction of particular regimes, such as those in Germany, Italy, and France, and the annexation, occupation, and subjugation of the majority of European states by the Axis powers and, then, by the Allies.[116] Milward's case about the rescue of nation-states after 1945 has to be set against this backdrop: ten out of the twenty-six European states in 1938 had been occupied by the end of 1940, three had been annexed, one occupied by friendly powers, four divided by hostile powers, and two reduced to the status of satellites.[117] Given that the tasks of economic and political reconstruction were so great, it seemed sensible to retain the borders of the 1919 Versailles Treaty, with the exception of the Baltic states and the borders of Poland and the GDR (see Maps 4.2 and 4.3). Why endanger the priorities of prosperity and democratization in the West, or nationalization and Communism in the East, by breaking up the old territorial and cultural units, which had existed before the war? It was noteworthy that established national symbols, like the Polish eagle or the black-red-and-gold flag of liberal Germany, were willingly retained and exploited even in the Eastern Bloc. What was more, as restored nation-states began to make amends for the disorder and suffering of the Second World War, they invariably resorted to a new level of social and economic interventionism.[118] Almost everywhere, industries were nationalized, government economic plans were formulated and publicized, and welfare states were constructed.[119] Even in states like the Federal Republic of Germany, where other expressions of national pride were carefully avoided, opinion polls registered considerable identification with the country's social security system and economic success—so-called 'Deutschmark nationalism'.[120] At the same time, nation-states regained their political sovereignty. This pattern could be distinguished, too, in the Soviet sphere. Poland, for example, had had a Communist government imposed on it in 1945, after the Soviet armies had allowed German soldiers to slaughter much of its non-Communist resistance movement in the struggle for Warsaw between August and October 1944.[121] By 1956, the national-minded Communist government of Wladyslaw Gomulka had replaced that of the Stalinists and survived the threat of Soviet intervention. Gomulka had been dismissed and arrested during the immediate post-war period because of alleged 'nationalist deviation'.[122]

Although he shows that nation-states did not simply disappear in the years after 1939, Milward does not prove that nationalism and national aspirations were restored to their pre-war intensity.[123] In fact, both internal and external constraints continued to operate on nation-states, and actually increased during the post-war era, to the point where historians like Tom Nairn and Eric Hobsbawm began to talk of such states' disintegration.[124] Internally, nationalism became a taboo subject—distinguished from 'patriotism' in the scholarly literature, for example—in the Federal Republic of Germany, with its outlawing of the Nazi

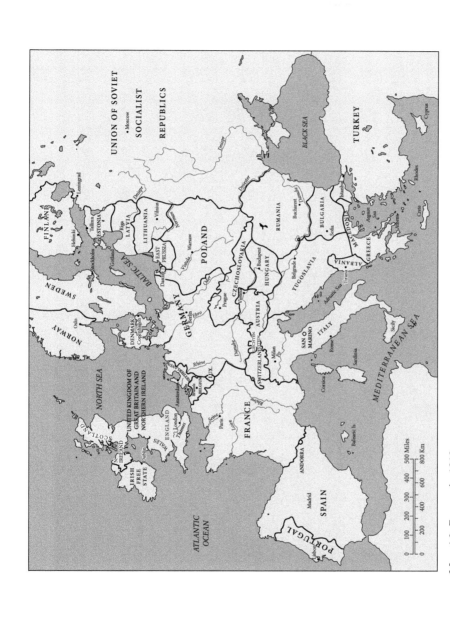

Map 4.2 Europe in 1919

Source: R. Gerwarth (ed.), *Twisted Paths: Europe, 1914–1945* (Oxford, 2007), 384–5.

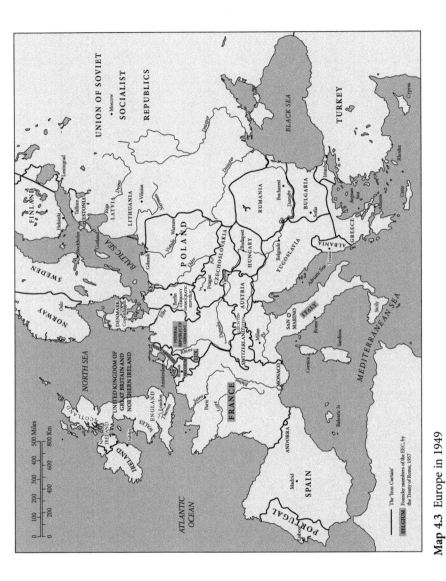

Map 4.3 Europe in 1949
Source: M. Fulbrook (ed.), *Europe since 1945* (Oxford, 2001), 304–5

salute and its proscription of extreme nationalist parties like the Socialist Reich party in 1952, and it remains controversial in many other countries, including Austria, where the Hitler salute is also illegal.[125] In the International Values Survey of 1981–82, only 35 per cent of Germans said that they were 'very proud' of their nationality, and about 30 per cent professed that they were not proud to be German.[126] In other states such as Italy, it has been claimed that nation-building had been insufficient and nationalism remained inchoate, despite citizens' experiences of fascism.[127] After 1945, the combination of Christian Democracy's 'occupation of the state', from where it dispensed favours to its supporters, its association with the clientelism and criminality of the South, and its amnesty for fascists all helped to create deep cynicism in the Italian public—or sections of the public—about the existing nation-state. One corollary of such cynicism was the success at the polls during the 1980s and 1990s of the Northern League under the leadership of Umberto Bossi.[128] Whatever its leaders' motives, the League—which represented the rich, industrial North against the poor, agrarian South—seemed to signal the beginning of the disintegration of the Italian nation.[129]

Externally, all European states had to accept a certain level of superpower tutelage and interference. This was the case across Western Europe, where American funding, including Marshall Aid, was made dependent on the acceptance of freer trade and opposition to Communism (especially in France and Italy).[130] It was also true of the Eastern Bloc, where Communist governments were imposed on more or less resistant populations between 1945 and 1948. Even in Czechoslovakia, which had elected a Communist-led government in 1946, with the Communists gaining more than twice as many votes as any other single party (38 per cent), the coalition government was replaced in the spring of 1948, with the Foreign Minister Jan Masaryk pushed out of a window of the Foreign Office in Prague.[131] In the East, the threat of Soviet armed intervention remained the paramount counterweight to nationalism right up until 1989. In the West, a more important counterweight, which marked out the period after 1973, has been that of globalization, which has worked in two separate spheres. Economically, as obstacles to the free movement of capital were removed and multinational companies began to spread across Europe and the world, governments like that of Pierre Mauroy under the new presidency of François Mitterrand in 1981 found that they could no longer pursue policies of nationalization, economic planning and social welfare, such as had been possible under the system of exchange controls and protectionism which had existed in the 1950s.[132] 'You remember what they called the "honeymoon period" in 1981,' Mitterrand reminisced with a friend: in his daydreaming of 'utopia' and 'a kind of collectivism', he imagined 'shaking up the country.... I would have nationalized everything. Why not! I know why I did not do it. You can guess.'[133] Without an actual revolution, the new president was bound to take France's position in European and global markets into account. The other sphere of globalization concerns a revolution

188   EUROPEAN INTEGRATION SINCE THE 1920s

in the means of communication through the advent of television, which reached mass audiences from the 1960s onwards, and de-regulation in the production and scheduling of programmes, which has taken place during the 1980s and 1990s.[134] Together with the arrival of mass tourism during the 1970s, television made it more difficult to distinguish clear national limits to experiences and culture.

There is every indication, however, that manifold, routine, banal acts of national identification (Michael Billig) continued to occur in countries across Europe, confounding left-wing commentators in Germany, who had argued that the FRG was 'post-national', and post-modern and other critics elsewhere, who contend that national identity has come under attack from the processes of economic and communicative globalization, from 'depthless', de-centred citizens, with multiple identities, and from people feeling 'lost in the fluid conditions of the post-modern world'.[135] The latter are likely to favour 'an older, fiercer psychology of identity', or 'tribalism', producing polarization, in the opinion of post-modernists such as Kenneth Gergen and Fredric Jameson, between authoritarians in need of a sense of order and hierarchy, and those subverting distinctions and playing with the idea of 'liminality' (Gergen); between the brittle, emotionally intense psyche of the authoritarian, which is dominated by affect and rigid stereotypes, and the ironic detachment of the post-modernist, which relies on 'cognitive mapping' (Jameson) rather than affect; and between those fixated on a single identity (usually a race or nation), rejecting outsiders in order to shore up a sense of self, and those without an investment in particular identities and conscious of interdependence, whose expansion causes the 'distinction between self and other, mine and yours' to wither (Gergen).[136] These psychological effects, which at once undermine, polarize, and radicalize citizens' attachments to nation-states, are produced by a broader shift from a 'world system' (Immanuel Wallerstein) of separate, bounded societies and states, to a world in which financial transactions and the flow of information are international, fragmenting and weakening existing states as containers of power and points of political identification.[137] Citizens who adapt to globalization, with the 'ironic detachment and the shifting depthlessness of the de-centred ego', in Michael Billig's words, are alienated from 'the fascist thug or the ethnic cleanser, both of whom are being washed up on the beach of "tribalism" in the post-modern world'.[138] Whereas the post-modern citizen has been seen as a 'nomad wandering between unconnected places', the disorientated see themselves faced with the 'collapse of old boundaries, the loss of certainty and the blurring of a sense of place', causing 'ontological insecurity' (Anthony Giddens).[139] The EU would be caught, if this characterization were true, between a cosmopolitan, global elite and disaffected tribal nationalists.

Such a scheme—in which one set of psychological dispositions and economic circumstances destabilize existing states from above (in accordance with 'the playful uncertainties of the de-centred ego') and the other from below (assaulted by 'the fierce furies of an ego centred upon a single identity')—appears to have eroded the 'banal identity of nationhood', causing the nation-state to wither away, yet it is too neat, in Billig's opinion.[140] The sociologist's survey of a single day's newspapers in the United Kingdom on 28 June 1993 indicates how they 'constantly flag the world of nations', using a 'deixis of little words'—'here', 'us', 'the'— and situating us 'in the homeland within a world of nations'.[141] The lead story for most publications, with the exception of the *Star* (fans overheating at an open-air concert in London) and the *Sun* ('Rock star's Mum of 70 has a toyboy, 29') was the bombing of Baghdad by American war-planes on the orders of President Bill Clinton.[142] Much of the coverage depicted events from the US point of view, as an ally: 'Clinton warns Saddam—don't try to hit us back' (*The Times*); 'Fight back and we smash you, warns Clinton' (*Star*), with the 'we' referring to the collective of 'America'.[143] It also featured Britain prominently, with papers which supported the Conservative government placing the UK 'at the head of an international chorus'.[144] The *Daily Mail* recorded that 'John Major led international support for the raid'.[145] Publications which were critical of the attack focused on the situation of three British citizens imprisoned there: 'What hope for them now', ran the headline of *Today*, going on to note that 'Families of Britons imprisoned by Saddam Hussein say their men have been condemned to more years in jail by the US attack on Iraq.'[146] An international news story was thus framed for a British audience, with individual citizens mentioned as well as the UK government. It was surrounded by a thicket of national stories, from 'Britain basked in 79° temperatures yesterday' (*Sun*) and 'Brits in passport scam' (*Today*) to 'worst places in Britain to be without a job' (*Guardian*) and 'Martin Hoyle on a new British voice' (*Times*).[147]

Benedict Anderson is correct, according to Billig, in emphasizing the significance of newspapers in 'the reproduction of nationality' by direct means, operating 'through their messages, stereotypes and deictics, rather than by setting up what Freud called "secondary identification", or a perceived feeling of similarity'.[148] Readers unthinkingly consume home news with greater interest than foreign news.[149] However, why bother to notice direct 'signs which are not struggling for our attention and which often provide the means for directing awareness to much more interesting things?' Billig's answer is 'that by noticing the flaggings of nationhood, we are noticing something about ourselves', including the 'depths and mechanisms of our identity, embedded in routines of social life'.[150] In this way, we forget that we are being reminded, but nevertheless indicate to ourselves 'that we are "us"', different from 'them'.[151] Nation-states continue to rest on 'a banal mysticism, which is so banal that all the mysticism seems to have evaporated long ago', but which 'binds "us" to the homeland—that special place which is more than just a place, more than a mere geophysical area', and which is 'made to look homely, beyond question and, should the occasion arise, worth the price of sacrifice'.[152] There are reasons to doubt whether citizens would 'fight to the end for Britain', as one of Billig's interviewees—an anti-royalist

190 EUROPEAN INTEGRATION SINCE THE 1920s

'patriot'—maintained, but not to deny that their commitments and loyalties to the nation-state are persistent and real.[153] The next section examines how such commitments affect citizens' 'Europeanism'.

Europeanism and Nationalism

The question of whether Europeanism and nationalism are compatible partly relates to the claims of historians such as Milward that nation-states were 'rescued' or reconstructed after the Second World War. Milward himself contended that such national reconstruction was tied to cooperation on the European level, yet other historians have pointed out that the particularity and insularity of nation-states—even if they did not succumb to radical forms of nationalism, as had occurred during the interwar era—increased after 1945, as welfare states intervened more and offered greater benefits, making immigration appear costlier.[154] Left-wing parties and unions were often less well disposed to the EEC than right-wing parties. It was for this reason that the Labour Party voted by 2:1 to leave the European Economic Community in April 1975.[155]

Although European and national identities are not exclusive, 'Europeanism' sits uneasily alongside citizens' affiliations with and allegiances to nation-states.[156] It is, therefore, relevant that expressions of national pride have become more fragmented and conditional over recent decades. In the opinion of many commentators, European nation-states were beginning to break up or to be eclipsed by the 1970s and 1980s, with citizens more and more sceptical of national sentiment.[157] When asked how proud they were to be Dutch in 1995, just over 20 per cent responded 'very proud'. Asked the same question in 2003, under a quarter of Czechs, about a third of Swedes and well under a half of Britons, Spaniards, and Hungarians were very proud of their nationality, compared to 80 per cent of Americans and 75 per cent of Indians.[158] More than half of Italian, Spanish, Irish, Danish, Dutch, Belgian, and Portuguese respondents claimed that they felt attached to the EU at roughly the same time (see Table 4.3).[159] Although under 30 per cent of Britons reported such an attachment, the EU-15 average stood at just under 50 per cent. By 2011, in spite of the eurozone crisis, well over 60 per cent of respondents from most member states felt themselves to be citizens of the European Union.[160] It is evident from such surveys that citizens could feel national and European at the same time, but had European sentiment increased as national pride had diminished? Despite polls showing that the two sets of ideas and affiliations could coexist, with majorities in many countries professing sentiments of national and European belonging, this fact did not exclude the possibility that there was a weak, inverse correlation over time.[161]

It seems unrealistic to expect a majority of citizens to renounce or, simply, no longer feel their sentiments of affiliation and allegiance to existing nation-states.

Table 4.3 Judgement on EU membership by country

	2003			2011		
	Good thing	Bad thing	Neither	Good thing	Bad thing	Neither
Luxembourg	77	6	15	72	13	13
Ireland	73	6	15	63	12	18
Greece	62	7	30	38	33	28
Spain	62	7	27	55	17	22
Netherlands	62	12	23	68	12	19
Italy	58	10	28	41	17	36
Denmark	57	22	19	55	16	28
Belgium	56	12	29	65	11	23
Portugal	56	11	26	39	26	30
Germany	46	10	34	54	16	26
France	44	17	27	46	19	33
Sweden	40	32	27	56	17	25
Finland	39	22	37	47	19	33
Austria	36	20	42	37	25	36
UK	28	30	29	26	32	37
Romania	—	—	—	57	11	28
Poland	—	—	—	53	10	33
Slovakia	—	—	—	52	10	37
Estonia	—	—	—	49	9	40
Lithuania	—	—	—	49	16	31
Bulgaria	—	—	—	48	10	38
Malta	—	—	—	42	18	37
Slovenia	—	—	—	39	21	39
Cyprus	—	—	—	37	25	36
Hungary	—	—	—	32	22	44
Czech Rep	—	—	—	31	19	48
Latvia	—	—	—	25	21	51
EU	48	15	31	47	18	31

Source: Eurobarometer 60, 2003, First Results, 8; Eurobarometer 75, 2011, 37.

Even in the supposedly post-national Federal Republic of Germany, there has been a broad acknowledgement of the relevance of national belonging in the wake of unification in 1990.[162] The novelist Patrick Süskind's reaction to the events of 1989 and 1990 put into words the more cautious or muted responses of others, as he leaped from a feeling, on the opening of the East German border, that 'there was still order in the world' and that the tempo of European events was 'swift' but 'entirely rational and calculable' to a sense, as he listened to the speech of Walter Momper, mayor of Berlin, at midnight on 9 November, that he was displaced and falling 'out of time':

> 'Tonight the German people are the happiest in the world!' I was thunderstruck. I thought I must have heard wrong.... Was this guy playing with a full deck? Was

he drunk? What did he mean by the German people? The citizens of the Federal Republic or the GDR? West Berliners or East Berliners? All of them together? Possibly even us Bavarians? Maybe ultimately me? My God, Walter Momper, I thought, how could you be so far off the mark?[163]

Süskind's playful assumption was that everyone would jump on Momper for his careless remark, which he would regret for the rest of his life. To his mock surprise, it became the motto of 1989, as the novelist watched agog, attributing Willy Brandt's comment about 'what belongs together is growing together' to the onset of Alzheimer's.[164] Helmut Kohl's toast to Germany in February 1990, standing in front of journalists in the aisle of an aeroplane, left him 'flabbergasted': 'Until that moment, I had never seen anyone toast Germany.'[165] Other writers were more sombre, but their conclusions were similar, resting on years of atonement and a premonition of a 'post-conventional' or 'post-industrial' future. Günter Grass, who had called publicly for a two-state solution rather than unification in 1989–90, argued that Auschwitz should rule out the re-constitution of a German nation-state:

> We should be aware—as our neighbours are—of how much grief this unified state caused, of what misfortune it brought to others and to ourselves as well. The crime of genocide, summed up in the image of Auschwitz, inexcusable from whatever angle you view it, weighs on the conscience of this unified state.
>
> Never before in their history had the Germans brought down upon themselves such terrifying shame. Until then, they were no better and no worse than other peoples. But the megalomania born of their complexes led them to reject the possibility of being a cultural nation within a federation and insist instead on the creation of a unified state in the form of a Reich—by any and all means. The state laid the foundation for Auschwitz. It formed the power base for the latent anti-Semitism that existed in other places as well. It helped provide an appallingly firm foundation for the racial ideology of National Socialism.[166]

It is notable that such moral teleologies retained 'we Germans' as a subject, switching from 'ourselves' to 'themselves' and back again.[167]

For Jürgen Habermas, as for the political philosopher Dolf Sternberger, who coined the term 'constitutional patriotism' at the same time as recognizing that 'we' are still 'in mourning for the division of the nation', there is a tension between a critical awareness that a majority of contemporaries continued to harbour national sentiments, which had been necessary for the formation of nation-states, and an expectation, and a barely concealed hope, that such feelings, which had caused so much suffering in the world wars and the Holocaust, could be dispensed with in a future 'post-national constellation'.[168] Nation-state and democracy had seemed to be 'twins' as they emerged from the French Revolution, with both standing, 'culturally, in the shadow of nationalism', wrote Habermas in *Staatsbürgerschaft und nationale Identität* (1991): 'The meaning of "nation" had metamorphosed from a pre-political quantity to a point of reference which was constitutive of the political identity of a citizen of a democratic community (*Gemeinwesen*).'[169] Although nationalism had supplied a useful 'collective identity' for citizens in the late eighteenth and nineteenth centuries, further consolidated by Romanticism and history as a burgeoning discipline, it was not connected intrinsically to citizenship.[170] 'The nation-state had only created a temporarily close connection between "ethnos" and "demos",' he writes: 'As far as the concept was concerned, citizenship (*Staatsbürgerschaft*) was always independent of national identity.'[171]

The communicative interaction, civic participation and democratic deliberation of citizens would itself produce Charles Taylor's requisite of 'political and cultural anchoring', in Habermas's view: 'Democratic citizenship does not need to be rooted in the national identity of a people; irrespective of the multiplicity of different cultural ways of life, it requires the socialization of all citizens in a common political culture.'[172] As the 'institutionalization' of the democratic process 'via nation-states came increasingly under pressure from globalization from the 1970s onwards', given that such states could no longer control the internationalization of 'networks' through the technology of satellites and digital communication ('whether it concerns means of transport for goods and people, the flow of wares, capital and money, the electronic transfer and deciphering of information or circulation between humans, technology and nature'), there was a need to establish forms of 'international cooperation' which replicated the 'legitimacy' of 'institutionalized processes of nation-states', not least to counter internal 'ethnocentric reactions of indigenous populations against everything foreign', as workers began to fear for their own social security and systems of welfare.[173]

The European Union, legitimized by 'European constitutional patriotism', is Habermas's main hope of protecting welfare states and democracy against the effects of globalization.[174] Over time, however, the philosopher—although still advocating a federal union, a European constitution, a harmonization of tax and alignment of social policies—has come to separate the normative possibility of democratic deliberation on a European level from the actual absence of a European public sphere and the continuing presence of legitimate nation-states.[175] During the eurozone crisis, Habermas encouraged European governments— especially the German government, as the largest net contributor—to reform the EU and bridge the gap between European institutions and national public spheres, 'dethroning' the Council and moving from intergovernmentalism to the community method.[176] The member states were no longer to be the 'sovereign subjects' of the treaties.[177] Nation-states would supposedly retain their statehood by continuing to implement European laws and safeguarding their citizens' civil liberties. Critics have rightly objected that such roles would amount to little, compared to the policy-making power of the European Union.[178] Historians such as Hanna

Schissler have seen such statements as expressions of the 'generational phenomenon' of 'West German postnationality', especially prevalent amongst intellectuals of a 'middle generation' born between 1940 and 1955, who had combined criticism of the hyper-nationalism of the Third Reich, a 'Holocaust-identity' (Bernhard Giesen), a 'penitent attitude concerning the division of Germany' (Wolf Lepenies), a belief in 'postnational democracy among nation-states' (Karl Dietrich Bracher), acceptance of a 'post-material search for meaning and orientation' (Lutz Niethammer) and vocal pro-Europeanism.[179] For Heinrich August Winkler, this 'leap into being a European or into cosmopolitanism is wishful thinking and might in fact veil a flight from history and from the responsibility that emerges from this history'.[180] In general, such historians have recognized that a majority of German citizens continue to identify with varying versions of a German nation-state.[181]

Throughout much of the post-war era, notwithstanding US policies of de-Nazification and the incremental advances of *Vergangenheitspolitik*, West German political leaders, with the exception of Kurt Schumacher's opposition to partition in the late 1940s and early 1950s, had largely avoided the 'national question', mindful of opinion polls—for example, one in 1955 which found that 48 per cent thought 'Hitler would have been one of the greatest statesmen ever', had it not been for the Second World War—suggesting that citizens had not dealt with the National Socialist past and remained wedded to the idea of a reunified German nation-state.[182] From the Hallstein doctrine, according to which the FRG would break off relations with any state recognizing the GDR, to the refusal of successive governments to reform German citizenship, which rested on *jus sanguinis* following the provisions of a law in place since 1913 and which referred to the borders of 1937 (Article 116 of the *Grundgesetz*), it was evident that German 'reunification' remained on the political agenda.[183] Although decreasing numbers of respondents thought that reunification was likely (7 per cent by 1983), about three-quarters still thought that it was desirable.[184] In 1963, 53 per cent of West Germans had agreed that the division of Germany was 'an intolerable situation'.[185]

With official backing of the idea that the FRG was 'not a country of immigration' (*kein Einwanderungsland*), despite an influx of 18 million, mainly German-speaking, immigrants by the 1960s and a large population of 'foreigners', or *Ausländer* (8.4 per cent by 1990), the existence of a German national identity— or 'Germanness' (*Deutschtum*)—was rarely brought into question by politicians, visible in their unwillingness to change the status of the children and grandchildren of 'guest workers' (*Gastarbeiter*).[186] The 1965 Aliens Law, enacted by the government of the liberal-minded Christian Democrat Ludwig Erhard, allowed the expulsion of foreigners for injury to 'the interests of the FRG' (Section 2) or 'the free democratic order' (Section 6). The 'consolidation policy' (*Konsolidierungspolitik*) of the Social Democratic government of Helmut Schmidt in the 1970s paid premiums to *Gastarbeiter* willing to return to their country of origin (so-called 'get lost' payments) and endeavoured to revoke the residence permits of foreign workers in receipt of social assistance, at the same time as barring foreigners from living in areas which were supposedly already 'overloaded' (*überbelastet*).[187] Such policies were in part a response to polls showing that 62 per cent of West Germans thought—in 1982—that there were 'too many foreigners in the country' and 50 per cent wanted them to be 'sent back to their own country'.[188] In 1980, 44 per cent had said that foreigners should only marry within 'their own group', 51 per cent that they should be denied political activity and 66 per cent (dropping to 51 per cent by 1990) that they should adapt their lifestyles to 'German standards'.[189] In such respects, the FRG was no more 'post-national' than other EU member states.[190]

In the EU as a whole, 44 per cent of citizens polled thought themselves to be 'national only' in 2004, 43.3 per cent felt themselves to be national and, secondarily, European; 8.8 per cent primarily European, but also national; and 3.9 per cent solely European.[191] In other words, although 87.3 per cent believed themselves to be mostly national, 56 per cent thought of themselves as 'European' to some degree.[192] Some populations, such as that of Ireland, are both patriotic—with 75 per cent saying that they were 'very proud' to be Irish in 2003—and pro-European: 44 per cent thought themselves national and European, 2 per cent European and national, 3 per cent exclusively European, and 2 per cent did not know.[193] 83 per cent of Irish respondents had believed that membership of the EU was a 'good thing' in 1997 and just under 70 per cent thought themselves citizens of the EU in 2011.[194] By contrast, in the UK, 62 per cent thought themselves to be British alone in 2004, with 27 per cent national and European, 4 per cent European and national, and 4 per cent only European (together with 3 per cent who did not know).[195] About 45 per cent were 'very proud' to be British, placing them in the mid-range of the national pride ratings (2003), above the Czech Republic and the Netherlands (under 25 per cent), but well below Austria, Slovenia, and Portugal (50–60 per cent), and Nigeria and Brazil (60–70 per cent).[196] These results seem to show that most Britons were not particularly proud to be British, yet did not consider themselves to be European. Even when they were asked whether they felt themselves to be citizens of the EU, irrespective of their feelings about the UK, only 40 per cent replied—in 2011—that they did.[197]

In Gordon Brown's view, 'Today's battle for Britain is not being fought out on the old terrain of empire, the Industrial Revolution, two world wars, or a country that once confidently felt it was sufficient unto itself.'[198] Instead, 'Britain has been, and is being, reshaped by three great forces: wave after wave of globalization; the neoliberalism with which our economy was managed, or more accurately mismanaged; and the struggle of progressive politics to offer an alternative.'[199] For Brown, writing about the 1980s, 1990s, and 2000s with the hindsight of Brexit, 'international cooperation' was New Labour's answer to 'the Conservatives' turn from Europe towards isolationism'.[200] Europe plays no part in the former Prime Minister's discussion of identity, other than as a foil for 'nationalist parties across

196 EUROPEAN INTEGRATION SINCE THE 1920s

the continent' to make 'their claims for greater self-government'.[201] Unusually, Blair—writing in 2010—agrees with his Chancellor, conceding that Europeanism has little hold over the majority of the UK's population:

> My theory—but this may be total nonsense—is that our problem with Europe is that we didn't invent it; or at least weren't a founding member. Then when Harold Macmillan sensibly decided we should join, de Gaulle said, 'Non'. This, combined with strong imperial feelings that still lurked beneath the surface of the British psyche—part superiority complex, part insecurity complex—gave us a national narrative about the EU that was deeply unhelpful.[202]

Six years later, 51.9 per cent of British voters chose to leave the European Union, and 48.1 per cent to remain in it, with a turnout of 72 per cent. Seventy-one per cent of 18–24 year olds elected to remain and 64 per cent of those over 65 chose to leave.[203] There were also correlations between the vote and party, education, ethnicity, and region.[204] Even in the UK, feelings about Europe and the nation were not clear-cut.

In other countries, there was a more obvious inverse relationship between national pride and European sentiment. In Belgium, 39 per cent thought of themselves as solely Belgian, 44 per cent as national and European, 8 per cent as European and national, and 7 per cent as European only (see Table 4.4).[205] In total, 59 per cent admitted that they felt 'European' to some degree. Just under 70 per cent thought of themselves as citizens of the EU.[206] In France, only 29 per cent felt French alone, 54 per cent French and European, 8 per cent European and French, and 6 per cent European only.[207] Likewise, the corresponding figures for Germany were 38 per cent (German only), 46 per cent (German and European), 6 per cent (European and German), and 2 per cent (European only), with considerably more 'Europeans' in Western Germany than in the East.[208] As Gerhard Schröder points out in his memoirs, the FRG had long been the EU's main net contributor, with 'no other member of the European Union' having 'a similar burden to shoulder as Germany with the costs of unification' since 1990, yet such a burden had not led political elites or citizens to question their membership.[209] Although it is often said that German politicians and citizens prefer to speak 'in Europe's name', this claim is not borne out by indices of Europeanness, where the FRG occupies a central position.[210] The country's history of Nazism and *Vergangenheitspolitik* has meant that citizens have been warier of talking in Germany's name, at least in public. National pride ratings in the Federal Republic were consistently low, with 21 per cent 'extremely proud' and 41 per cent 'not at all proud' or 'not very proud' to be German in the 1980s, and 17 per cent 'very proud' and 26 per cent 'not at all' or 'not very proud' in 2000.[211] Notwithstanding exceptions, citizens have been less willing over time to admit to pride in their nation and more willing to call themselves 'Europeans'.

Table 4.4 National identity by country in 2004 (%)

	National only	National and European	European and national	European only	Don't know
UK	62	27	4	4	3
Finland	60	37	2	1	0
Sweden	57	37	3	1	1
Greece	55	39	3	2	1
Austria	50	36	7	4	3
Ireland	49	44	2	3	2
Netherlands	48	43	5	2	1
Portugal	46	46	5	2	1
Denmark	43	51	4	1	0
Belgium	39	44	8	7	2
Germany (West)	38 (35)	46 (48)	6 (8)	2 (6)	2 (2)
Spain	32	58	4	3	3
France	29	54	8	6	3
Italy	28	56	8	33	5
Luxembourg	27	39	12	18	4
EU-15	41	46	6	4	3

Source: Eurobarometer 61, April 2004, B. 106.

What makes citizens feel European? Some scholars have asked whether a common set of conceptions of Europe—shared beliefs about what Europe is—actually exists, re-evaluating older studies of the idea of Europe and investigating whether there are continuities and an evolution of ideas or, indeed, ruptures.[212] Other scholars have enquired whether there are grounds for a common conception of Europe, examining the evidence for shared sets of values or attitudes.[213] Thus, John McCormick has pointed out that Europeans tend to favour welfare—with well over 60 per cent of British, French, and Italian respondents stating that they preferred their governments to cater to the needs of all rather than ensuring that individuals were free to pursue their goals without government interference, compared to about one-third of Americans (2003)—and they tend to be more secular than citizens in other regions of the world: less than half of Germans, Hungarians, Bulgarians, Britons, French, Danish, and Estonians believe in God, compared to more than 70 per cent of Americans (in 2005).[214] While 'committees adopt symbols, and leaders develop policies and approve laws', citizens' and leaders' 'Europeanism' actually rests on the idea that they share a common set of interests, norms, and values, which underpin policy-making and distinguish Europe from other areas of the world, writes McCormick: 'The foundations of Europeanism lie in the evolving identities of Europeans, whose home has long been afflicted by crisis and conflict, who have had to adapt to the repeated redefinition of their political, social, and religious communities, and who have been repeatedly obliged to reconsider their affiliations accordingly.'[215] On this reading, commonality has emerged from conflict and difference.[216] 'Paradoxically, few Europeans are actively aware of what they have in common, the focus of their conscious self-identification remaining with the nation, the state, or a combination of the two,' writes the political scientist: 'only a small minority think of themselves as European', even though they have become more similar.[217] The significance of such unrecognized similarities is not obvious.

A large number of Europeans, clustering in specific social groups, do seem to be aware of commonalities. There is some evidence for a weak correlation between education, occupation, travel, language use, and Europeanism. The 'people most likely to interact with other Europeans are those who are educated and who hold higher-status occupations,' writes Neil Fligstein, referring to his research into the occupation, income, age, and political preference data of the Eurobarometer polls: 'older people and more conservative people are less likely to interact with people from other countries'.[218] Those who feel that they are well informed about the EU tend to think that it has a positive reputation (59 per cent in 2004) and that membership is 'a good thing' (61 per cent), whereas those who feel that they know least are less positive about its image (31 per cent 'positive', 22 per cent 'negative') and about membership (36 per cent thinking it 'a good thing', 35 per cent 'a bad thing').[219] Men are more positive than women about the image of the EU (47: 40 positive), membership (52: 43) and benefits deriving from membership (52: 43).[220] Fifty-two per cent of managers thought the image of the EU quite or very positive in 2004 and 17 per cent quite or very negative, compared to 38 per cent and 22 per cent of manual workers, and 32 per cent and 23 per cent of the unemployed.[221] The same managers were much more positive about membership of the EU (59 per cent thought it a 'good thing', 12 per cent a 'bad thing') than manual workers (42: 18) and the unemployed (38: 21).[222] They also believed that their country benefited (59: 30) more regularly than did workers (40: 38) or the unemployed (38: 39).[223]

The young—52 per cent of the 15–24 age group—had a very or fairly positive image of the EU and 57 per cent thought membership a good thing, compared to 40 per cent of those over 55 having a positive image and 43 per cent thinking membership a good thing.[224] As Fligstein notes, far more of the young speak a second language—82.4 per cent of 15–24 year-olds, compared to 34.1 per cent of over sixty-fives—albeit largely English (82.4 per cent of Germans and 75.0 per cent of French).[225] 64.3 per cent of Britons did not speak a second language in 2000, compared to around 13 per cent of those in Denmark, Sweden, and the Netherlands.[226] Partly as a result of such varied conditions, the difference between countries is pronounced. In Belgium, 78 per cent of managers and professionals and of the young (15–24) thought that membership was a good thing in 2004, compared to 39 per cent of those leaving school at 15 and 47 per cent of the unemployed and of the over fifty-fives.[227] Only 42 per cent of managers and 52 per cent of those with higher education in the UK thought membership a good thing, compared to 25 per cent of those with the lowest incomes and 19 per cent who left school at fifteen.[228] In other words, a higher percentage of older and unemployed respondents in Belgium thought that membership of the EU was a good thing than did managers in the UK: the most Europhile social groups in Britain had a similar opinion of the European Union as the most sceptical Belgians.

To what extent can such findings be related to acts of identification and feelings of allegiance on the part of European citizens? The European Community first declared its interest in the subject in 1973, when the Foreign Ministers of the nine member states adopted the 'Document on European Identity', which concentrated on representative democracy, the rule of law, social justice and human rights, in an effort to 'unite and speak increasingly with one voice if [the EC] wants to make itself heard and play its proper role in the world'.[229] Although there are sudden shifts, the long-term trends are consistent. The Treaty on European Union in 1992 added European citizenship to this list of aspirations, declaring that 'Citizenship of the Union is hereby established' and that 'Citizenship of the Union shall complement and not replace national citizenship'.[230] Practically, the treaty's provisions entitled Europeans to travel through and live in any member state, to vote and stand in municipal and European Parliament elections there, to be given diplomatic protection by any member state when travelling beyond the EU, and to petition the European Parliament and appeal to the European Ombudsman. Both the Maastricht (1992) and Lisbon Treaties (2007) sought to define the competencies of the EU and member states, assuming—with some justification—that affiliations and loyalties were not in direct competition and that support for the European Union would continue to grow. Those who identify themselves as solely national constituted 33 per cent in 1994, rising to 46 per cent by 1996, which was also the case in 2010, whereas those calling themselves national and, secondarily, European has fluctuated between 41 per cent (1997, 2010) and 48 per cent (1992, 2001, 2005), with notable increases in Sweden (from 36 to 50 per cent over the period 1992–2010) and Hungary (34–53 per cent) after accession, for example.[231] Overall, those thinking of themselves sometimes or often as not only national but also European rose from 45 to 54 per cent between 1990 and 2006, despite Maastricht in 1992 and the controversial enlargement of the EU in 2004.[232]

The eurozone crisis damaged the image of the EU, with 52 per cent having a positive image and 15 per cent a negative one in 2007, falling to 30 per cent positive and 29 per cent negative in 2012–13, before rising to 45 per cent positive and 17 per cent negative in 2019 (see Table 4.5 for other 2007 results).[233] Whereas 23 per cent felt themselves 'definitely' to be citizens of the European Union in 2011, and 62 per cent definitely or 'to some extent', the combined total had dropped to 37 per cent by 2015 (see Table 4.6).[234] Such polling results begged questions about the depth and consistency of citizens' feelings for and loyalty to the European Union. In 2010, 53 per cent had said that they were very or fairly

Table 4.5 Is membership in the EU a good thing, by group, 2007 (%)

	A good thing	A bad thing	Neither good nor bad	Don't know
EU-27	58	13	25	4
Gender				
Male	62	12	23	3
Female	55	13	27	5
Age				
15–24	65	7	24	4
25–39	60	12	25	3
40–54	59	13	25	3
55+	54	15	26	5
Education (up to)				
15	46	18	30	6
16–19	55	13	29	3
20+	74	8	17	1
Occupation				
Manager	71	9	18	2
Employee	62	12	24	2
Self-employed	61	11	26	2
Manual worker	55	14	27	4
Housewife/husband	53	13	28	6
Unemployed	51	13	30	6
Retired	52	16	27	5
Student	71	6	20	3

Source: Eurobarometer 68 (2007), First Results, 25.

attached to the EU, but more than 90 per cent had said the same of their own nation-state.[235] What matters, according to Jonathan White, are 'practices of identification' and depth of feeling, yet there are few instances 'when people express mutual sympathies to one another as "Europeans" and undergird this with an appeal to signs and discourses that refer to Europe'.[236] Interviews tend to show 'that "Europe" rarely provokes an emotional response, instead being a point of indifference or resignation', with the limited exception of mobile elites.[237] It is worth noting in this context that Billig's study of acts of national identification would be less noticeable than White suggests, relying on a deixis of small words and increased coverage in the media.[238] Here, European Union actors are mentioned in 40 per cent of relevant articles in France and Spain, 33 per cent in Germany, Italy, and the Netherlands, and 15 per cent in the UK prior to Brexit.[239] The difference between shallow and profound feelings is difficult to gauge. A majority of citizens surveyed have remained optimistic about the future of the EU throughout, even during the eurozone crisis.[240] Their affiliations and allegiances have rarely, if ever, been separable from their perceptions of what is at stake.

Table 4.6 Image, citizenship, trust in the EU, 2006–18*

	2006	2009	2012	2015	2018
Image					
Positive	48.0	46.5	30.5	39.0	44.0
Negative	33.0	35.5	39.0	38.0	36.5
Neutral	16.0	15.5	28.5	21.0	20.5
Don't know	2.5	2.5	2.0	2.0	1.5
Citizenship					
Yes			62.0	65.5	70.5
No			37.0	32.5	28.5
Trust					
Tend to trust	46.5	47.5	32.0	36.0	42.0
Tend not to trust	39.5	40.5	58.5	48.0	48.0
Don't know	13.5	12.0	9.5	13.5	10.0
Future					
Optimistic		65.0	49.5	55.5	58.0
Pessimistic		28.0	45.5	38.5	36.5

* Average of two results for given years.

Source: Eurobarometer 92 (2019), First Results, 11; 'European Citizenship', Eurobarometer 92 (2019), 28; 'Public Opinion in the EU', Eurobarometer 92 (2019), 75.

For the British sociologist Anthony Smith, who has studied the cultural under-pinnings of national identity, nations have been based on 'the territorial bound-edness of separate cultural populations on their own "homelands"', shared myths of origin and historical memories of the community, 'the common bond of a mass, standardized culture', a common territorial division of labour and a shared set of legal rights and duties under common laws and institutions, all of which make the replacement of nation-states by the EU impossible over the short and medium term.[241] The idea of the nation defines and legitimates politics in cultural terms, with the nation 'a political community only insofar as it embodies a common culture and a common social will'.[242] National identifications possess distinct advantages over the idea of a unified European identity, since they are 'vivid, accessible, well established, long popularized, and still widely believed, in broad outline at least', Smith writes: '"Europe" is deficient both as idea and as process' because 'it lacks a pre-modern past—a "pre-history" which can provide it with emotional sustenance and historical depth'.[243] The difficulty of defining and evaluating the significance of a common European culture and the lack of other bases for a European identity poses a problem for the EU. There is 'no pan-European system, only *national* systems' of education, 'and what they teach, or omit to teach, is determined by *national*, not European priorities'; in the media, 'news stories tend to be relayed or at least interpreted from a national standpoint', and 'drama, comedy shows, children's tales, even the weather reports accord the national state and its literature and outlook first place'.[244] As far as rituals and symbols are concerned, 'there is no European analogue to Bastille or Armistice Day, no European ceremony for the fallen in battle, no European shrine of kings or saints', and no European equivalent of a national or religious community.[245] Similarly, the absence of external 'others' seems to deprive the European Union of self-definition through opposition: until 1990, the European Community's significant others were the protagonists of the Cold War. Now it appears more likely that 'an increasingly affluent, stable, conservative but democratic European federation' will face and protect itself from the demands and needs of groupings of states in Africa, Asia, and Latin America, pursuing 'not just economic exclusion, but also cultural differentiation and with it the possibility of cultural and racial exclusion', which are unappealing and hard to justify.[246]

However, it also possible that the contradiction between a European identity and existing national identities may be more apparent than real, Smith continues, for if 'we accept a more voluntaristic and pluralistic conception and regard the nation as a rational association of common laws and culture within a defined territory', which is 'the one generally accepted in Western countries', 'individuals may choose to which nation they wish to belong, and there is ... room for competing focuses of identity', making the conflict between the claims of the nation and those of a looser European identity 'more situational and pragmatic'.[247] The cultural history of humanity has been 'a successive differentiation (but also enlargement) of processes of identification', from the simplest and earliest societies in which the scale and number of identities were relatively limited via more complex agrarian societies to the modern era of industrial capitalism and bureaucracy, when 'the number and in particular the scale of possible cultural identities have increased yet again', leaving people with a multiplicity of allegiances and multiple identities.[248]

Whereas, for individuals, identity is usually situational, since they 'identify themselves and are identified by others in different ways according to the situations in which they find themselves', collective identities tend to be pervasive and persistent, less subject to rapid changes, 'even when quite large numbers of individuals no longer feel their power'.[249] Under the pressure of globalization, with the rapid growth of transnational companies, the rise and fall of large power blocs (the superpowers) and a vast increase in the scale and density of the means of communication, collective identities have undergone 'adaptive Westernization', with the 'global diffusion of some aspects of modern Euro-American culture, especially popular music, films, videos, dress and some foods'.[250] In these conditions, there is no reason to believe in a dichotomous view of national and European identities.[251] 'We have already seen that, sociologically, human beings have multiple identities, that they can move between them according to context and situation, and that such identities may be concentric rather than conflictual,' writes the sociologist: 'None of this is to deny the cultural reality and vivid meanings of these identities, which, transmitted through successive generations, are not exhausted by the often fickle volitions and changing perceptions of individuals. At the same time, there is plenty of historical evidence for the coexistence of concentric circles of allegiance.'[252] Just as it was possible to be Athenian, Ionian, and Greek in the ancient world, or Ibo, Nigerian, and African in the contemporary one, one can feel simultaneously Catalan, Spanish, and European, with the latter at once a family of cultures and a history in the making.[253]

It is tempting either to underplay or to overstate the contrast between 'depthless' cosmopolitans and 'tribal' authoritarians during an era of globalization. In some respects, citizens' national and European affiliations have existed uneasily along-side each other or have come into conflict. The far right, in particular, has sought to profit from such tensions, becoming more markedly Eurosceptical since the 1990s.[254] At the same time, many citizens evidently have had multiple attachments to the nation-state, the European Union and to other groups and institutions. Most voters were 'less concerned about Europe' than politicians were, remarked John Major as he struggled to ratify the Maastricht Treaty in parliament, facing opposition from a small minority of Conservative MPs (and a number of 'bas-tards', as he had called ex-ministerial colleagues off-air).[255] Since the spheres in which the EU and member states operate are distinct and well-defined, there have been relatively few clash points, when parties and individuals have had to choose between the position of their own government and that of 'Brussels'. National governments themselves are responsible for the 'history-making decisions' of the EU in the European Council, which generally works by minimizing differences between member states.[256] Such cooperation and compromise on an intergovern-mental level within the European Union has not prevented national leaders from blaming Brussels, often for decisions which they themselves have sanctioned, nor has it dampened down criticism of the EU in the press (especially in right-wing tabloids), but it has reduced the number of occasions on which citizens have had to decide whether to support their own government or the European Union.[257] In these circumstances, a majority of citizens in most member states (except the UK, Austria, and Scandinavia, at different points in time) have maintained national and European affiliations and allegiances, notwithstanding the fluctuation of events, over a long period.[258] The next chapters ask how far such affiliations are connected to instances of economic and social convergence.

Notes

1. W. Wallace, 'Rescue or Retreat? The Nation-State in Western Europe, 1945–93', in P. Anderson and P. Gowan (eds), *The Question of Europe* (London, 1997), 21.
2. Ibid.
3. J. G. A. Pocock, 'Deconstructing Europe', *London Review of Books*, 19 December 1991.
4. Ibid.

204 EUROPEAN INTEGRATION SINCE THE 1920s

5. Ibid.
6. Ibid.
7. Ibid.
8. Ibid.
9. Ibid. See also M. Glenny, *The Rebirth of History: Eastern Europe in the Age of Democracy* (London, 1990).
10. In a similar fashion, Zygmunt Bauman, *Europe: An Unfinished Adventure* (Cambridge, 2004), 124–5, claims that Tzvetan Todorov was 'well placed to the job' of defining a European identity by referring to sets of values, since he had 'a biography that spanned both sides of what some people view as Europe's outer frontier—while some others see it as Europe's two-millennia-old yet now outdated "great divide"'. See also T. Todorov, *The New World Disorder: Reflections of a European* (Cambridge, 2005).
11. J. G. A. Pocock, 'Deconstructing Europe', *London Review of Books*, 19 December 1991.
12. Ibid.
13. F. Fukuyama, *The End of History and the Last Man* (London, 1992).
14. J. G. A. Pocock, 'Deconstructing Europe', *London Review of Books*, 19 December 1991.
15. Ibid. For broader reflections on this question, extending well beyond these regions, see L. Donskis, *Troubled Identity and the Modern World* (Basingstoke, 2009).
16. J. G. A. Pocock, 'Deconstructing Europe', *London Review of Books*, 19 December 1991.
17. Ibid.
18. Ibid.
19. U. Özkirimli, *Theories of Nationalism: A Critical Introduction*, 3rd edn (New York, 2017), 154–227; P. Lawrence, *Nationalism: History and Theory* (London, 2005), 180–97; J. Hearn, *Rethinking Nationalism: A Critical Introduction* (Basingstoke, 2006), 170–250.
20. A. Gat, *Nations: The Long History and Deep Roots of Political Ethnicity and Nationalism* (Cambridge, 2012), 3.
21. Ibid., 1.
22. Ibid.
23. Ibid.
24. Ibid., 17.
25. Ibid.
26. W. Connor, *Ethnonationalism: The Quest for Understanding* (Princeton, NJ, 1994), 203.
27. Ibid.
28. Ibid., 207.
29. Ibid.
30. J. Snyder, *From Voting to Violence: Democratization and Nationalist Conflict* (New York, 2000), 8.
31. Ibid., 9–10.
32. Ibid., 10.
33. Ibid., 11.
34. Ibid.
35. Ibid., 33–4. Snyder holds the latter view.
36. J. Rupnik, *L'Autre Europe. Crise et fin du communisme* (Paris, 1993), 12. For American leaders such as James Baker, the Secretary of State, the problems were distant, regional ones, akin to the those of Gulf, on which—along with 'turmoil in the Soviet Union—he had been concentrating in 1991. 'And I thought the Middle East was complicated,' he had uttered after one meeting in June: J. Major, *The Autobiography* (London, 1999), 532. For Major himself, the conflict was 'horrific and proximate'. P. Short, *Mitterrand: A Study in Ambiguity* (London, 2013), 547: Mitterrand told Warren Christopher that 'Europe has always lived under empires.... Now every ethnic group thinks it should have its own special status. We haven't seen that since the start of the Middle Ages.'
37. J. R. Lampe, *Yugoslavia as History: Twice There Was a Country*, 2nd edn (Cambridge, 2000), 101–331.
38. Ibid., 241–64; S. A. Sofos, 'Culture, Politics and Identity in Former Yugoslavia', in B. Jenkins and S. A. Sofos (eds), *Nation and Identity in Contemporary Europe* (London, 2003), 252–63.
39. S. Radošević, 'The Collapse of Yugoslavia: Between Chance and Necessity' and V. Bojičić, 'The Disintegration of Yugoslavia: Causes and Consequences of Dynamic Inefficiency in Semi-command Economies', in D. A. Dyker and I. Vejvoda (eds), *Yugoslavia and After* (London, 1996), 28–47, 65–83.
40. B. Denitch, *Ethnic Nationalism: The Tragic Death of Yugoslavia*, revised edn (Minnesota, 1996), 1–21, 51–126, makes the case for the validity of Yugoslav institutions and ties. Many authors are less sanguine: A. Pavković, *The Fragmentation of Yugoslavia: Nationalism and War in the Balkans*,

2nd edn (Basingstoke, 2000), 61–74, argues that the state was a 'semi-confederation under Tito's personal rule'.

41. Sabrina P. Ramet, *Thinking about Yugoslavia: Scholarly Debates about the Yugoslav Breakup and the Wars in Bosnia and Kosovo* (Cambridge, 2005), 35–53, gives a useful summary of this literature on post-Communism in the Yugoslav context.

42. The best account of this descent into violence is the BBC documentary, 'The Death of Yugoslavia', which includes interviews with the main protagonists. It was accompanied by L. Silber and A. Little, *The Death of Yugoslavia*, revised edn (London, 1996).

43. M. Thompson, *Forging War: The Media in Serbia, Croatia, Bosnia and Hercegovina* (Luton, 1999), 292–3. See also E. D. Gordy, *The Culture of Power in Serbia: Nationalism and the Destruction of Alternatives* (University Park, PA, 1999), 61–102.

44. M. Thompson, *Forging War*, 298.

45. Ibid., 297.

46. Ibid.

47. W. Zimmermann, *Origins of a Catastrophe: Yugoslavia and Its Destroyers* (New York, 1996), 121.

48. T. Judah, *The Serbs: History, Myth and the Destruction of Yugoslavia* (New Haven, CT, 1997), 168–258. Other journalists' accounts along similar lines include the BBC's Misha Glenny, *The Fall of Yugoslavia: The Third Balkan War*, 3rd edn (London, 1996), and the Neue Zürcher Zeitung and FAZ's Viktor Meier, *Yugoslavia: A History of Its Demise* (London, 1999). See S. P. Ramet, *Balkan Babel: The Disintegration of Yugoslavia from the Death of Tito to the War for Kosovo* (Boulder, CO, 1999) for a good academic analysis of cultural divisions; on mythology, see B. Anzulovic, *Heavenly Serbia: From Myth to Genocide* (London, 1999).

49. J. Dragović-Soso, *'Saviours of the Nation': Serbia's Intellectual Opposition and the Revival of Nationalism* (London, 2002), 177–95.

50. R. Thomas, *Serbia under Milošević: Politics in the 1990s* (London, 1999), 44–106.

51. For the responses of Kosovan Albanians, see N. Malcolm, *Kosovo: A Short History* (Basingstoke, 1998), 334–56.

52. Quoted in T. Judah, *The Serbs*, 181.

53. M. Tanner, *Croatia: A Nation Forged in War* (New Haven, CT, 1997), 223.

54. D. B. MacDonald, *Balkan Holocausts? Serbian and Croatian Victim-Centred Propaganda and the War in Yugoslavia* (Manchester, 2002); D. Rieff, *Slaughterhouse: Bosnia and the Failure of the West* (New York, 1995).

55. R. Brubaker, *Nationalism Reframed: Nationhood and the National Question in the New Europe* (Cambridge, 1996), 55.

56. Ibid., 71.

57. See N. Caspersen, *Contested Nationalism: Serb Elite Rivalry in Croatia and Bosnia in the 1990s* (New York, 2010).

58. R. Brubaker, *Nationalism Reframed*, 72.

59. Ibid., 73.

60. Ibid.

61. Ibid., 10.

62. Sabine Rutar, 'Nationalism in Southeastern Europe, 1970–2000', in J. Breuilly (ed.), *The Oxford Handbook of the History of Nationalism* (Oxford, 2013), 516, comments that 'The national, or better, nation-state master narrative continues to exercise a powerful influence.' See J. Bugakski, *Nations in Turmoil* (Boulder, CO, 1995); I. Bremmer and R. Taras (eds), *Nations and Politics in the Communist Successor States* (Cambridge, 1993); C. Kupchan (ed.), *Nationalism and Nationalities in the New Europe* (Ithaca, NY, 1995); A. Pavcovic, H. Koscharsky, and A. Czarnota (eds), *Nationalism and Post-Communism* (Aldershot, 1995).

63. I. Budge and K. Newton, *The Politics of the New Europe: Atlantic to Urals* (London, 1997), 104; G. Schöpflin, 'Nationalism and Ethnicity in Europe, East and West', in C. A. Kupchan (ed.), *Nationalism and Nationalities in the New Europe*, 37–65.

64. G. I. Mirsky, *On Ruins of Empire: Ethnicity and Nationalism in the Former Soviet Union* (Westport, CT, 1997); R. G. Suny, *The Revenge of the Past: Nationalism, Revolution and the Collapse of the Soviet Union* (Palo Alto, CA, 1993); D. P. Gorenburg, *Minority Ethnic Mobilization in the Russian Federation* (Cambridge, 2003).

65. L. Holmes, *Post-Communism: An Introduction* (Oxford, 1997), 296–8, lists the following factors as exacerbating nationalism: historical tradition; official and unitarist nationalism; rapid modernization or revolutionary change; the imposition of political structures from above; a permissive, liberal political climate; poor regime performance; perceptions of unequal or unjust treatment; perceived subjugation to a foreign power; the creation of transnational networks of nationalists;

206   EUROPEAN INTEGRATION SINCE THE 1920s

the ability to create an organized movement. See also G. Schöpflin, 'Nationalism and Ethnicity in Europe, East and West', in C. A. Kupchan (ed.), *Nationalism and Nationalities in the New Europe*, 37–65; I. Budge and K. Newton, *The Politics of the New Europe*, 101–19; T. Gallagher, 'Nationalism and Romanian Political Culture in the 1990s', in D. Light and D. Phinnemore (eds), *Post-Communist Romania: Coming to Terms with Transition* (Basingstoke, 2001), 104–26; M. Neuburger, *The Orient Within: Muslim Minorities and the Negotiation of Nationhood in Modern Bulgaria* (Ithaca, NY, 2004).

66. For an emphasis on the descent into violence, see C. King, *Extreme Politics: Nationalism, Violence and the End of Europe* (Oxford, 2010). He, too, distinguishes between Hungary, Poland, and other Central European states, and Serbia, Georgia, Ukraine, Russia, and other Eurasian and Eastern European states. Sabine Rutar, 'Nationalism in Southeastern Europe, 1970–2000', in J. Breuilly (ed.), *The Oxford Handbook of the History of Nationalism*, 529, concludes that 'The weaker the system and the more insecure the social vision and reality, the more successful was the appeal of nationalism.' J. Stein, 'National Minorities and Political Development in Post-Communist Europe', in J. Stein (ed.), *The Politics of National Minority Participation in Post-Communist Europe* (New York, 2000), 1–30. Citizens' belief in official corruption proved enduring, with the New Europe Barometer (2004), for instance, showing that only 12 per cent of Bulgarians, 15 per cent of Romanians, 20 per cent of Slovakians and twenty-six Poles felt that the majority of public officials were not corrupt.

67. T. Garton Ash, *The Uses of Adversity* (London, 1989), 242. Gerhard Schröder, *Entscheidungen*, 344, was aware that, 'For the Poles, their national identity derives from a long, painful history of struggles of liberation.'

68. Z. Jičinský, a signatory of the dissenting Charter 77 and the person entrusted to draft a federal constitution for post-Communist Czechoslovakia, was not unusual in thinking that 'at the moment Czechoslovakia, if it wishes successfully to attach itself to the processes of European integration, must do so as a whole, as a relatively strong state': quoted in M. Glenny, *The Rebirth of History: Eastern Europe in the Age of Democracy* (London, 1990), 42. 10 per cent of 18–24 year olds in Hungary were going to university in 1989 and 14 per cent in Poland, rising to 30 and 38 per cent, respectively, by 2004, compared to an EU-15 average of 23 per cent: I. T. Berend, *From the Soviet Bloc to the European Union: The Economic and Social Transformation of Central and Eastern Europe since 1973* (Cambridge, 2009), 229.

69. J. Snyder, *From Voting to Violence*, 32.

70. J.-W. Müller, *What Is Populism?* (London, 2017), 3. See also C. Mudde, *Populist Radical Right Parties in Europe* (Cambridge, 2007).

71. Montserrat. Guibernau, 'Nationalism without States', in J. Breuilly (ed.), *The Oxford Handbook of the History of Nationalism*, 592, points out that the main Catalan, Galician, Welsh, and Corsican parties 'have not been secessionist'. The SNP's call for independence, which did not find majority support until Brexit, is contrasted by John. Breuilly, *Nationalism and the State* (Manchester, 1985), 326, with Wales, where cultural nationalism has been 'much stronger' and there has been a higher level of 'peripheral sectionalism', yet calls for independence have been less popular, with Plaid Cymru getting less than 8 per cent of the vote in 1983 and 1987. See also D. Balsom, 'Wales', in M. Watson (ed.), *Contemporary Minority Nationalism* (London, 1990), 8–23.

72. J. Diez Medrano, *Divided Nations: Class, Politics and Nationalism in the Basque Country and Catalonia* (Ithaca, NY, 1995); L. Mees, *Nationalism, Violence and Democracy: The Basque Clash of Identities* (Basingstoke, 2003); J. M. Beck, *Territory and Terror: Conflicting Nationalisms in the Basque Country* (London, 2004); A. Perez-Agote, *The Social Roots of Basque Nationalism* (Reno, NV, 2006); J. L. Sullivan, *ETA and Basque Nationalism: The Fight for Euskadi, 1890–1986* (London, 2015).

73. J. Brand, *The National Movement in Scotland* (London, 1978), 65–7, calls this a Scottish political 'sub-system'.

74. M. Keating, 'Minority Nationalism and the State: The European Case', in M. Watson (ed.), *Contemporary Minority Nationalism*, 174–94; M. Keating, *Nations against the State: The New Politics of Nationalism in Quebec, Catalonia and Scotland*, 2nd edn (London, 2001).

75. Ibid.

76. M. Guibernau, *Catalan Nationalism: Francoism, Transition and Democracy* (London, 2004); A. Balcells, *Catalan Nationalism* (London, 1996).

77. See, for instance, C. Harvie, *Scotland and Nationalism: Scottish Society and Politics, 1707 to the Present*, 3rd edn (London, 1998), 169–257.

78. M. Guibernau, 'Nationalism without States', in J. Breuilly (ed.), *The Oxford Handbook of the History of Nationalism*, 606–11. See also M. Guibernau, *Nations without States* (Cambridge, 1999).

79. M. Guibernau, 'Nationalism without States', in J. Breuilly (ed.), *The Oxford Handbook of the History of Nationalism*, 609.
80. Quoted in C. Mudde, 'The Far Right and the European Elections', *Current History*, 113 (2014), 98. See also M. Berezin, *Illiberal Politics in Neoliberal Times: Culture, Security and Populism in the New Europe* (Cambridge, 2009).
81. D. Halikiopoulou and S. Vasilopoulou, 'Support for the Far Right in the 2014 European Parliament Elections: A Comparative Perspective', *Political Quarterly*, 85 (2014), 285–8.
82. K. Polynczuk-Alenius, 'At the Intersection of Racism and Nationalism: Theorising and Contextualising the "Anti-immigration" Discourse in Poland', *Nations and Nationalism*, 27 (2021), 766–81; S. Kim, '"Because the Homeland Cannot Be in Opposition: Analysing the Discourses of Fidesz and Law and Justice (PiS) from Opposition to Power', *East European Politics*, 37 (2021), 332–51.
83. C. Mudde, 'The Far Right and the European Elections', *Current History*, 113 (2014), 101.
84. See P. Davies, *The National Front in France* (London, 2012); J.-Y. Camus and N. Lebourg, *Far-Right Politics in Europe* (Cambridge, MA, 2017).
85. These results come from SOFRES exit polls in the presidential election of 1995.
86. J. Shields, 'The Far Right Vote in France: From Consolidation to Collapse?', *French Politics, Culture and Society*, 28 (2010), 29.
87. G. Lucassen and M. Lubbers, 'Who Fears What? Explaining Far-right-wing Preference in Europe', *Comparative Political Studies*, 45 (2012), 547–74.
88. M. A. Shain, 'The Extreme-Right and Immigration Policy-Making: Measuring Direct and Indirect Effects', *West European Politics*, 29 (2006), 277.
89. D. Art, 'Why 2013 Is Not 1933: The Radical Right in Europe', *Current History*, 112 (2013), 93.
90. C. Muddle, 'The Populist Radical Right: A Pathological Normalcy', *West European Politics*, 33 (2010), 1175–7; C. Muddle, *The Far Right Today* (Cambridge, 2019), 3, on 'normalization' and mainstreaming.
91. G. Brown, *My Life, Our Times* (London, 2017), 22.
92. I have discussed this at greater length in M. Hewitson, 'Conclusion: Nationalism and the Nineteenth Century?', in T. Baycroft and M. Hewitson (eds), *What Is a Nation? Europe, 1789–1914* (Oxford, 2006), 312–55.
93. J. Plamenatz, 'Two Types of Nationalism', in E. Kamenka (ed.), *Nationalism: The Nature and Evolution of an Idea* (London, 1970), 22–36. See also V. A. Spencer, 'Rethinking Cultural and Political Nationalism', *Politics, Groups and Identities*, 2 (2014), 666–73.
94. M. Weber, *Wirtschaft und Gesellschaft* (Tübingen, 1921), 29; Z. Norkus, 'Max Weber on Nations and Nationalism: Political Economy before Political Sociology', *Canadian Journal of Sociology*, 29 (2004), 389–418.
95. B. Anderson, *Imagined Communities: Reflections on the Origin and Spread of Nationalism* (London, 1983).
96. Ibid., 1–38.
97. Ibid., 39–84.
98. Ibid., 35.
99. E. Gellner, *Nations and Nationalism* (Oxford, 1983).
100. Ibid., 140. See also ibid., 19–37, 62–84, 110–17.
101. Ibid., 34–7.
102. J. Breuilly, *Nationalism and the State* (Manchester, 1985).
103. Ibid., 81–148.
104. This is not to argue that he would seek to reframe Anderson's arguments. See, in particular, Breuilly's summary of Anderson in J. Breuilly, '*Imagined Communities* and Modern Historians', *Nations and Nationalism*, 22 (2016), 643: 'He uses the idea of print capitalism, in particular the impact of specific kinds of writing, such as newspapers and novels, to argue that these inadvertently generated new ways of envisioning social ties—as a series of parallel, "horizontal" communities co-existing in "empty" time and space.'
105. J. J. Breuilly, 'Nation, Nation-state and Nationalism', in E. Hanke, L. Scaff, and S. Whimster (eds), *The Oxford Handbook of Max Weber* (Oxford, 2020), 199–200.
106. Ibid.
107. J. Breuilly, *Nationalism and the State*, 65.
108. Laura Cram, 'Does the EU Need a Navel? Implicit and Explicit Identification with the European Union', *Journal of Common Market Studies*, 50 (2012), 78, points out that 'the statement that the EU is an "imagined community" underestimates the degree of "deep, horizontal comradeship" implied by Anderson (1991, p. 6) in his reference to community. It also overestimates the

208 EUROPEAN INTEGRATION SINCE THE 1920s

existence, in any community, of a single imagining of what that community is and what membership of the community means. There is no single imagining of the EU and no single understanding of what it means for an individual to identify with it.... What it means to an individual to be Scottish, Greek or European today may not be the same tomorrow. Likewise, for any given individual at any given time, both the meaning and utility of identifying as Scottish, Greek or European may not be the same as that for any other individual at that particular time.'

109. B. Anderson, *Imagined Communities*

110. Cram also pays attention to Michael Billig's 'day to day reinforcement of national consciousness', which can take place over long periods, with cumulative effects: L. Cram, 'Identity and European Integration: Diversity as a Source of Integration', *Nations and Nationalism*, 15 (2009), 113.

111. D. Beetham, *Max Weber and the Theory of Modern Politics*, 2nd edition (Cambridge, 1985), 63–94; R. Bellamy, 'Liberalism and Nationalism in the Thought of Max Weber', *History of European Ideas*, 14 (1992), 499–507.

112. Z. Steiner, *The Lights That Failed: European International History, 1919–1933* (Oxford, 2005), 256–313; R. Boyce, *The Great Interwar Crisis and the Collapse of Globalization* (Basingstoke, 2009), 77–424; M. M. Payk and R. Pergher (eds), *Beyond Versailles: Sovereignty, Legitimacy and the Formation of New Polities after the Great War* (Bloomington, Indiana, 2018); J. Rothschild, *East Central Europe between the Two World Wars* (Seattle, 1974); R. Bideleux and I. Jeffries, *A History of Eastern Europe* (London, 1998), 405–516; R. Okey, *Eastern Europe, 1740–1985: Feudalism to Communism*, 2nd edn (London, 1992); N. Davies, *God's Playground* (Oxford, 2005), 291–321.

113. O. Zimmer, *Nationalism in Europe, 1890–1940* (Basingstoke, 2003), 80–106; H.-U. Wehler, 'Radikalnationalismus und Nationalsozialismus', in J. Echternkampf and S. O. Müller (eds), *Die Politik der Nation. Deutscher Nationalismus in Krieg und Krisen 1760 bis 1960* (Munich, 2002), 203–17.

114. J. Chirac, *My Life in Politics* (Basingstoke, 2009), 141.

115. Ibid.

116. For a figure such as Helmut Kohl, *Erinnerungen 1982–1990* (Munich, 2005), vol. 2, 375–82, who was attacked for his striving to re-establish a '*Normalnation*' in Germany in the 1980s, it had always been obvious that 'the German nation, like every other *Volk*, is shaped by its historical, cultural and social development'. He was, he stressed in his memoirs, mindful not only of the 'highs', but also the depths', of that history.

117. A. Milward, *The European Rescue of the Nation-State*, 2nd edn (London, 2000), 3–4.

118. Ibid., 24: 'It was the broader post-war political consensus and the political machinery by which it was operated which led to the economic and social policies to which growth theorists point as part of their explanation for the high rates of growth of the period. The reassertion of the nation-state, because it required the satisfaction of so many demands if it were to succeed, was the start of the higher growth rates of the post-war world. This does not mean that government policy was the chief cause of those high growth rates. But as long as they were achieved they strengthened the reassertion of the nation-state, so that from its collapse in 1940 it had achieved in twenty years a degree of power and a legitimacy founded successfully without the process of integration, for that proved necessary to make some of its responses effective.'

119. Ibid., 26–9.

120. D. Haselbach, '"Soziale Marktwirtschaft" als Gründungsmythos. Zur Identitätsbildung im Nachkriegsdeutschland', in D. Mayer-Iswandy (ed.), *Zwischen Traum und Trauma—Die Nation* (Tübingen, 1994), 255–66; W. Meyer, *Mythos Deutsche Mark. Zur Geschichte einer abgeschafften Währung* (Berlin, 2001). In Willy Brandt's view, *Erinnerungen*, 271, 'The gaze forwards was good for economic reconstruction'. At the time, few Germans wanted to look back to the Nazi era, in Brandt's view.

121. J. K. M. Hanson, *The Civilian Population and the Warsaw Uprising of 1944* (Cambridge, 1982); N. Davies, *Rising '44: The Battle for Warsaw* (New York, 2004).

122. R. Taras, 'Gomulka's "Rightist-Nationalist Deviation", the Postwar Jewish Communists and the Stalinist Reaction in Poland, 1945–1950', *Nationalities Papers*, 22 (1994), 111–27; A. Werblan, 'Wladyslaw Gomulka and the Dilemmas of Polish Nationalism', *International Political Science Review*, 9 (1988), 143–58.

123. A. Milward, *The European Rescue of the Nation-State*, 18–40.

124. T. Nairn, *The Break-up of Britain: Crisis and Neo-Nationalism*, 2nd edn (London, 1981); E. J. Hobsbawm, *Nations and Nationalism since 1780* (Cambridge, 1990).

125. Otto Dann, *Nation und Nationalismus in Deutschland*, 3rd edn (1993), 16, draws a sharp distinction between nationalism, which is predicated on feelings of superiority, and patriotism,

which denotes civic activism and a sense of the common good (*Gemeinwohl*). See D. Art, *The Politics of the Nazi Past in Germany and Austria* (Cambridge, 2006).

126. M. Dogan, 'The Decline of Nationalisms within Western Europe', *Comparative Politics*, 26 (1994), 287. Only 28 per cent of Italians said they were 'very proud' and 15 per cent 'not proud'.

127. N. Doumanis, *Inventing the Nation: Italy* (London, 2001), 155: 'Overall, it is not very clear how many Italians were "made" by Fascism, but Italian society certainly did not enter the Second World War as a nation of patriots.'

128. Ibid., 162–70. P. Ginsborg, *Italy and Its Discontents, 1980–2001* (London, 2001), 174–8.

129. Doumanis, *Inventing the Nation: Italy*, 170, maintains that this impression is mistaken, though understandable: 'Particularist, as opposed to national, loyalties appear to retain greater emotional weight among Italians than they do among many other European nations, yet for all the talk of regional devolution and for all the enthusiasm for European integration, the political crisis of the 1990s revealed that Italians do recognize their nation as the essential political unit.'

130. Benn Stiel, *The Marshall Plan: Dawn of the Cold War* (Oxford, 2018), 179–217, shows the complexity of the negotiations, in which supporters of Marshall also pointed to the danger of Communism in Western Europe, if funding were withheld.

131. C. Sterling, *The Masaryk Case* (New York, 1969).

132. P. McCarthy, *The French Socialists in Power, 1981–1986* (New York, 1987); A. Cole, *François Mitterrand: A Study in Political Leadership* (London, 1994), 32–52.

133. Quoted in P. Short, *Mitterrand*, 373.

134. C. v. Hodenberg, *Television's Moment: Sitcom Audiences and the Sixties Cultural Revolution* (New York, 2015); M. Hilmes, *The Television History Book*, 3rd edn (London, 2004); R. Lorimer, *Mass Communications: A Comparative Introduction* (Manchester, 1994), 228–86.

135. M. Billig, *Banal Nationalism* (London, 1995), 136.

136. Ibid., 137–8. K. J. Gergen, *The Saturated Self* (New York, 1991); F. Jameson, *Postmodernism, or the Cultural Logic of Late Capitalism* (London, 1991).

137. M. Billig, *Banal Nationalism*, 129–34. I. Wallerstein, *The Modern World-System* (New York, 1974–2011), 4 vols.

138. M. Billig, *Banal Nationalism*, 136.

139. Ibid.; A. Giddens, *The Consequences of Modernity* (Cambridge, 1990); the reference to nomads comes from Zygmunt Bauman, 'Soil, Blood and Identity', *Sociological Review*, 40 (1992), 675–701.

140. M. Billig, *Banal Nationalism*, 138. See also M. Skey and M. Antonsich (eds), *Everyday Nationhood: Theorising Culture, Identity and Belonging after Banal Nationalism* (Basingstoke, 2017).

141. M. Billig, *Banal Nationalism*, 174.

142. Ibid., 111–12.

143. Ibid., 112.

144. Ibid.

145. Ibid.

146. Ibid., 112–13.

147. Ibid., 113.

148. Ibid., 125.

149. Ibid.

150. Ibid., 175.

151. Ibid.

152. Ibid.

153. Ibid., 138; M. Billig, *Talking of the Royal Family* (London, 1992). J. Stoetzel, 'Defeatism in Western Europe: Reluctance to Fight for the Country', in M. Dogan (ed.), *Comparing Pluralist Democracies: Strains on Legitimacy* (Boulder, CO, 1988), 169–80.

154. M. Kros and M. Coenders, 'Explaining Differences in Welfare Chauvinism between and within Individuals over Time: The Role of Subjective and Objective Economic Risk, Economic Egalitarianism and Ethnic Threat', *European Sociological Review*, 35 (2019), 860–73; F. Hjorth, 'Who Benefits? Welfare Chauvinism and National Stereotypes', *European Union Politics*, 17 (2016), 3–24; M. A. Eger, 'Even in Sweden: The Effect of Immigration on Support for Welfare State Spending', *European Sociological Review*, 26 (2010), 203–17; J. van der Waal et al., '"Some Are More Equal than Others": Economic Egalitarianism and Welfare Chauvinism in the Netherlands', *Journal of European Social Policy*, 20 (2010), 350–63; P. Scheepers, M. Gijsberts, and M. Coenders, 'Ethnic Exclusionism in European Countries: Public Opposition to Civil Rights for Legal Migrants as a Response to Perceived Ethnic Threat', *European Sociological Review*, 18 (2002), 17–34; D. Oesch, 'Explaining Workers' Support for Right-wing Populist

210 EUROPEAN INTEGRATION SINCE THE 1920s

Parties in Western Europe: Evidence from Austria, Belgium, France Norway and Switzerland', *International Political Science Review*, 29 (2008), 349–73.

155. BBC report, 'Labour Votes to Leave the EEC', 26 April 1975. See R. Saunders, *Yes to Europe! The 1975 Referendum and Seventies Britain* (Cambridge, 2018).

156. See Laura Cram, 'Identity and European Integration: Diversity as a Source of Integration', *Nations and Nationalism*, 15 (2009), 109–28, for an interesting set of reflections on cases of complementarity, including in 'stateless nations', divided nations, and in diaspora (allowing 'virtual unification').

157. T. Nairn, *The Break-up of the United Kingdom* remains a classic text: see also W. Matthews, *The New Left, National Identity and the Break-Up of Britain* (Leiden, 2013); B. Wellings and M. Kenny, 'Nairn's England and the Progressive Dilemma: Reappraising Tom Nairn on English Nationalism', *Nations and Nationalism*, 25 (2019), 847–65; J. White, 'The Spectres Haunting Europe: Reading Contemporary Catalan Nationalism through the Break-up of Britain', *European Review*, 26 (2018), 600–15.

158. World Values Survey, 2003/4, at http://www.wordvaluessurvey.org.

159. Eurobarometer 60, 2003, First Results, 8.

160. Eurobarometer 75, Spring 2011, 188.

161. On such co-existence and complementarity, see Laura Cram, 'Identity and European Integration: Diversity as a Source of Integration', *Nations and Nationalism*, 15 (2009), 109–28.

162. J.-W. Müller, *Another Country: German Intellectuals, Unification and National Identity* (New Haven, CT, 2000); M. Geyer (ed.), *The Power of Intellectuals in Contemporary Germany* (Chicago, 2001), 221–393.

163. P. Süskind, 'Deutschland, eine Midlife-Crisis', *Spiegel*, 36 (1990), translated in H. Schissler, 'Postnationality—Luxury of the Privileged? A West German Generational Perspective', *German Politics and Society*, 15 (1997), 10.

164. Ibid., 11.

165. Ibid.

166. G. Grass, 'Short Speech of a Rootless Cosmopolitan' (1990), in *Two States—One Nation?* (New York, 1990), 6.

167. See A. D. Moses, 'The Non-German German and the German German: Dilemmas of Identity after the Holocaust', *New German Critique*, 101 (2007), 45–94; A. D. Moses, *German Intellectuals and the Nazi Past* (Cambridge, 2007).

168. D. Sternberger, 'Verfassungspatriotismus' (1979), in *Schriften* (Frankfurt, 1992), vol. 10, 13–14. J. Habermas, *Die postnationale Konstellation. Politische Essays* (Frankfurt, 1998).

169. J. Habermas, *Staatsbürgerschaft und nationale Identität* (St. Gallen, 1991), 7–9.

170. Ibid., 9.

171. Ibid., 10.

172. Ibid., 15–16.

173. J. Habermas, 'Die postnationale Konstellation und die Zukunft der Demokratie', in *Die postnationale Konstellation*, 102–3, 110–12.

174. J. Habermas, *Staatsbürgerschaft und nationale Identität*, 24.

175. See J. Habermas, 'European Politics at an Impasse: A Plea for a Policy of Graduated Integration', in *Europe: The Faltering Project* (Cambridge, 2009), 78–105.

176. J. Habermas, 'Democracy, Solidarity and the European Crisis', in A.-M. Grozelier, B. Hacker, W. Kowalsky, J. Machnig, H. Meyer, and B. Unger (eds), *Roadmap to a Social Europe* (Falkensee, 2013), 7.

177. Ibid.

178. See, for instance, Simon Glendinning, 'Europe Should Reject Jürgen Habermas' Vision of a Federal European State', *LSE European Politics and Policy (EUROPP) Blog*, 3 September 2013.

179. H. Schissler, 'Postnationality—Luxury of the Privileged?', *German Politics and Society*, 15 (1997), 8–27; B. Giesen quoted in K. H. Jarausch, 'Postnationale Nation. Zum Identitätswandel der Deutschen 1945–1995', *Historicum*, 30 (1995), 30; W. Lepenies, *Folgen einer unerhörten Begebenheit. Die Deutschen nach der Vereinigung* (Berlin, 1992), 86; K. D. Bracher in J. Hess, 'Westdeutsche Suche nach nationaler Identität', in W. Michalka (ed.), *Die Deutsche Frage in der Weltpolitik* (Stuttgart, 1986), 11; L. Niethammer, 'Konjunkturen und Konkurrenzen kollektiver Identität. Ideologie, Infrastruktur und Gedächtnis in der Zeitgeschichte', *PROKLA: Zeitschrift für kritische Sozialwissenschaft*, 3 (1994), 398. On historians, see S. Berger, *The Search for Normality: National Identity an Historical Consciousness in Germany since 1800* (Oxford, 1997), 77–229.

180. H. A. Winkler, 'Für den Westen—ohne Vorbehalt', *Die Zeit*, November 1993, quoted in H. Schissler, 'Postnationality—Luxury of the Privileged?', *German Politics and Society*, 15

IDENTITY   211

(1997), 20; also H. A. Winkler, 'Rebuilding of a Nation: The Germans before and after Unification', *Daedalus*, 123 (1994), 107–27.

181. H. A. Winkler, *Der lange Weg nach Westen. Deutsche Geschichte vom 'Dritten Reich' bis zur Wiedervereinigung* (Munich, 2000), vol. 2, 638–9; T. Raithel, 'The German Nation and the 2006 FIFA World Cup', in S. Rinke and K. Schiller (eds), *The FIFA World Cup, 1930–2010: Politics, Commerce, Spectacle and Identities* (Göttingen, 2014), 353–71.

182. E. Noelle and E. P. Neumann (eds), *Jahrbuch der öffentlichen Meinung 1947–1955* (Allensbach, 1956), quoted in I. Kershaw, 'The "Hitler Myth": Image and Reality in the Third Reich', in D. Crew, *Nazism and German Society, 1933–1945* (London, 1994), 210. See also J. Herf, *Divided Memory: the Nazi Past in the Two Germanys* (Cambridge, MA, 1997), 267–372; D. Art, *The Politics of the Nazi Past in Germany and Austria* (Cambridge, 2006), 1–144. Lewis Edinger, *Kurt Schumacher*, 87, rightly points out that the SPD was, in his own words, driven by 'a sense of duty toward Social Democracy and the German people', which made his position on the national question much more forthright. If he had pursued such policies in office, it was likely to have had a significant effect on the FRG's foreign policy and on post-war discussions of a German nation.

183. R. Brubaker, *Citizenship and Nationhood in France and Germany* (Cambridge, MA, 1998). Peter O'Brien, *Beyond the Swastika* (London, 1996), argues that there were liberal components to these policies, which were combined with one of the most generous laws on asylum in the world. See also N. Frei, *Vergangheitspolitik. Die Anfänge der Bundesrepublik und die NS-Vergangenheit* (Munich, 2012), and K. H. Jarausch, *After Hitler: Recivilizing Germans, 1945–1995* (Oxford, 2006).

184. See P. H. Merkl, *German Unification in the European Context* (Palo Alto, CA, 1993), 119–31.

185. Ibid., 120.

186. R. Chin, *The Guest Worker Question in Postwar Germany* (Cambridge, 2009). Willy Brandt's position, *Erinnerungen* (Berlin, 1989), 132–4, was guided by his feeling during the Second World War of uncertainty of 'What would become of Germany?', once the Allies had won. In deciding on the terms of the peace, the Allies were driven in part, an 'emotional enmity towards Germans', even 'an inverted racism'. To counter the possible refusal of a future for Germany was Brandt's 'self-evident duty'.

187. P. O'Brien, *Beyond the Swastika*, 51.

188. M. Fulbrook, 'Aspects of Society and Identity in the New Germany', in M. Mertes, S. Muller, and H. A. Winkler (eds), *In Search of Germany* (New Brunswick, NJ, 1996), 245; M. Fulbrook, *German National Identity after the Holocaust* (Cambridge, 1999). *Die Zeit* had run an article about 'Fear of the Foreigners' in January 1982: R. Chin, *The Guest Worker Question in Postwar Germany*, 147. See R. Münch, 'German Nation and German Identity: Continuity and Change from the 1770s to the 1990s', in B. Heurlin (ed.), *Germany in the Nineties* (Basingstoke, 1996), 13–43.

189. German Allbus surveys, in M. Hoskin, *Understanding Immigration: Challenges in an Era of Mass Population Movement* (Albany, NY, 2017), 132. Also H. Kurthen, W. Bergmann, and R. Erb (eds), *Antisemitism and Xenophobia in Germany after Unification* (Oxford, 1997).

190. For a summary, see S. Berger, *Inventing the Nation: Germany* (London, 2004), 165–256. There was a widely shared sense, expressed in Helmut Schmidt's last speech to the Bundestag in 1986 (and quoted by Franz Josef Strauß in his memoirs), that 'We Germans remain an endangered *Volk* which needs political orientation.' F. J. Strauß, *Die Erinnerungen*, 150: 'This sentence needs further commentary. We are already endangered by our geo-strategic or geo-political position; we are endangered by our history; we are perhaps also endangered on the grounds of our national character, which Churchill once summarized, with some exaggeration but not entirely falsely, in the phrase that the Germans are either at your throat or they are prostrate before you on their knees.'

191. Eurobarometer 61, April 2004, in N. Fligstein, *Euroclash*, 141.

192. Ibid. Some commentators have interpreted such figures in a negative fashion, implying an expectation that there could be a transfer from national to largely European sets of affiliations: see E. Bonino, A. King, C. Larass, A. Matutes, N. Notat, and A. Pelinka, *How Much Popular Support Is There for the EU?* (Brussels, 1997), which contains essays on this question from different points of view.

193. Eurobarometer 61, April 2004, in N. Fligstein, *Euroclash*, 143; World Values Survey (2003–4), in J. McCormick, *Europeanism*, 83.

194. Eurobarometer 48, 1997; ibid., 75, 2011, 52.

195. Eurobarometer 61, 2004, in N. Fligstein, *Euroclash*, 143.

196. World Values Survey (2003–4), in J. McCormick, *Europeanism*, 83.

212 EUROPEAN INTEGRATION SINCE THE 1920S

197. Eurobarometer 75, 2011, 52. Conservative Eurosceptics have been able to exploit this lack of 'Europeanness', but as John Major, *The Autobiography* (London, 1999), 346, points out, MPs' own positions were fickle: Maastricht 'commanded a great majority on all sides of the Commons, and within the parliamentary Conservative Party'. What had changed was the Conservative majority, which had been reduced in the 1992 election to 21, leaving the small group of Eurosceptics with a disproportionate amount of leverage, since 'there were many more than twenty-one sceptics on the Tory benches'. In the run-up and aftermath of Brexit, the 'European Research Group' of Eurosceptics were also a minority within the Conservative Party.
198. G. Brown, *My Life, Our Times*, 23.
199. Ibid.
200. Ibid., 29.
201. Ibid., 407.
202. T. Blair, *A Journey*, 534.
203. Peter Moore, 'How Britain Voted at the EU Referendum', YouGov, 27 June 2016.
204. S. B. Hobolt, 'The Brexit Vote: A Divided Nation, A Divided Continent', *Journal of European Public Policy*, 23 (2016), 1259–77; M. Carreras, '"What Do We Have to Lose?" Local Economic Decline, Prospect Theory, and Support for Brexit', *Electoral Studies*, 62 (2019), online; S. O. Becker, T. Fetzer, and D. Novy, 'Who Voted for Brexit? A Comprehensive District-Level Analysis', *Economic Policy*, 32 (2017), 601–50.
205. Eurobarometer 61, 2004, in N. Fligstein, *Euroclash*, 143.
206. Eurobarometer 75, 2011, 52.
207. Eurobarometer 61, 2004, in N. Fligstein, *Euroclash*, 143.
208. Ibid.
209. G. Schröder, *Entscheidungen*, 88.
210. T. Garton Ash, *In Europe's Name: Germany and the Divided Continent* (London, 1993).
211. E. A. Tiryakian, 'Coping with Collective Stigma: The Case of Germany', in D. Rothbart and K. V. Korostelina (eds), *Identity, Morality and Threat* (Lanham, MD, 2006), 339.
212. See above: for instance, Gerard Delanty, *Inventing Europe* (1995); Anthony Pagden (ed.), *The Idea of Europe* (2002); R. Girault (ed.), *Identité et conscience européenne au XX. siècle* (2004), which look back to J-B. Duroselle, *L'Idée d'Europe* (1965); H. Brugmans, *L'Idée européenne* (1970); F. Chabod, *Storia dell'idea europa* (Bari, 1961); D. Hay, *Europe: The Emergence of an Idea* (1957); G. Barraclough, *European Unity in Thought and Action* (1963).
213. Two of the main works are: N. Fligstein, *Euroclash: The EU, European Identity and the Future of Europe* (2008) and J. McCormick, *Europeanism* (2010).
214. J. McCormick, *Europeanism*, 127, 177.
215. Ibid., 216.
216. Others have made similar points: see C. Bottici and B. Challand, *Imagining Europe: Myth, Memory and Identity* (Cambridge, 2013), 15–40; J-W. Müller, *Constitutional Patriotism* (Princeton, NJ, 2009), 93–140; J-W. Müller, 'Introduction: The Power of Memory, the Memory of Power and the Power over Memory', in J-W. Müller (ed.), *Memory and Power in Post-War Europe: Studies in the Present of the Past* (Cambridge, 2002), 1–35.
217. J. McCormick, *Europeanism*, 220.
218. N. Fligstein, *Euroclash: The EU, European Identity and the Future of Europe* (Oxford, 2008), 154, 158–9.
219. Eurobarometer 61 (2004), Bericht, 21.
220. Ibid., Annexes: Tables, 40–4.
221. Ibid., 44.
222. Ibid., 40, 42.
223. Ibid.
224. Ibid., 44, 40.
225. N. Fligstein, *Euroclash*, 149–50.
226. Ibid., 148.
227. Eurobarometer 61, 2004, Belgium Report, 48.
228. Eurobarometer 61, 2004, UK Report, 32.
229. U. Liebert, 'The Emergence of a European Identity', in H. Zimmermann and A. Dür (eds), *Key Controversies in European Integration* (Basingstoke, 2012), 97.
230. Quoted in J. McCormick, *Europeanism*, 79.
231. Ibid., 100–1.
232. Ibid., 101.
233. Eurobarometer 92 (2019), First Results, 8.

234. H. Zimmermann and A. Dür, 'Can There Be a Common European Identity?', in H. Zimmermann and A. Dür (eds), *Key Controversies in European Integration*, 95.
235. J. McCormick, *Europeanism*, 101.
236. J. White, 'A Common European Identity is an Illusion', in H. Zimmermann and A. Dür (eds), *Key Controversies in European Integration,*, 107; J. White, *Political Allegiance after European Integration* (Basingstoke, 2011); A. Favell, *Eurostars and Eurocities: Free Moving Urban Professionals in an Integrating Europe* (Oxford, 2007).
237. J. White, 'A Common European Identity', in H. Zimmermann and A. Dür (eds), *Key Controversies in European Integration*, 107.
238. L. Cram, 'Does the EU Need a Navel? Implicit and Explicit Identification with the European Union', *Journal of Common Market Studies*, 50 (2012), 71–86, makes this point.
239. T. Risse, *A Community of Europeans? Transnational Identities and Public Spheres* (Ithaca, NY, 2010), 29, referring to articles in EU policy areas. In the UK, two-thirds of EU stories in the press only mention UK actors.
240. Peter. Katzenstein and Jeffrey. Checkel, 'Conclusion: European Identity in Context', in P. Katzenstein and J. Checkel (eds), *European Identity* (Cambridge, 2009), 216, suggest that 'European identities are supported by factors too weak or inchoate to replicate processes of nation-state identity formation', which might well be true, but they give little indication how they would prove this case.
241. A. Smith, 'National Identity and the Idea of European Unity', *International Affairs*, 68 (1992), 60.
242. Ibid., 62.
243. Ibid.
244. Ibid., 73.
245. Ibid.
246. Ibid., 76. See also G. Delanty, *Inventing Europe*, 149–55.
247. A. Smith, 'National Identity and the Idea of European Unity', *International Affairs*, 68 (1992), 56.
248. Ibid., 58–9.
249. Ibid., 59.
250. Ibid., 66.
251. One of the main questions concerns how they are linked. In Ulrich Beck and Edgar Grande's opinion, there are 'two radical counter-proposals' to modern ways of dealing with difference (universalism, nationalism and cosmopolitanism): an 'essentialistic hierarchy of difference, which is by no means restricted to the premodern period', and a 'postmodern incommensurability of difference', where 'cosmopolitanism should not be confused with postmodernism or interpreted as a variant of the latter (as in Smith 1995, for example)', since the 'postmodern strategy of tolerating difference consists in absolutizing otherness without a supportive framework of common substantive and procedural norms'. See U. Beck and E. Grande, *Cosmopolitan Europe*, 15.
252. Ibid., 67.
253. Ibid., 67–74.
254. R. Harmsen and M. Spiering (eds), *Euroscepticism: Party Politics, National Identity and European Integration* (Amsterdam, 2004).
255. J. Major, *The Autobiography*, 343, 354; Alaistair Campbell, *The Alistair Campbell Diaries: Power and Responsibility, 1999–2001* (2011), vol. 3, 39–40, that he was urging New Labour to capitalize on William Hague's scepticism in June 1999 by using the phrase 'leading Europe, or leaving Europe'. We 'were heading for pretty bad results in the European elections and we had to build up to the last few days painting the Tories as wanting to take us out of Europe. GB [Gordon Brown] was worried that was not credible, but I felt Hague's recent line about renegotiating the Treaty of Rome—which needs unanimity—could get us there.'
256. See Chapter 8.
257. For instance, C. Galpin and H.-J. Trenz, 'Converging towards Euroscepticism? Negativity in News Coverage during the 2014 European Parliament Elections in Germany and the UK', *European Politics and Society*, 20 (2019), 26–76.
258. N. Fligstein, A. Polykova, and W. Sandholtz, 'European Integration, Nationalism and European Identity', *Journal of Common Market Studies*, 50 (2012), 106–22.

5

Trade Blocs

During the eurozone crisis of 2010–12, there was speculation in the press about the disintegration of the European Union. Such speculation was most pronounced in English-speaking publications, but it also affected coverage and the commentary of politicians on the Continent.[1] In a speech at a prize-giving ceremony in Aachen in May 2010, Angela Merkel had warned European leaders that 'We have a common currency, but no common political and economic union.'[2] With the EU facing its 'greatest test...since the collapse of Communism', the German Chancellor detected an 'opportunity' in the crisis of reforming the union.[3] Inactivity or mistakes, however, would have unforeseeable consequences, with the collapse of the euro carrying the risk that 'Europe and the idea of the European union will fail.'[4] Donald Tusk, the Polish Prime Minister and later President of the European Council who was being awarded the Charlemagne Prize, replied that he, too, 'paradoxically', saw an opportunity in the crisis to strengthen and further develop Europe, yet he also acknowledged that 'The bell is tolling for Europe.'[5] His later partner in the Brexit negotiations, Jean-Claude Juncker, the future President of the European Commission and ex-President of the Eurogroup, went even further, declaring in March 2013 that Europe could be in a position analogous to that of 1913, when no one had anticipated how close the Continent was to a catastrophic world war.[6] Although less hyperbolic, other European leaders made similar points.[7]

The eurozone crisis compounded the financial crash of 2007–08, which had already led to the collapse—or near-collapse—of British, Irish, Belgian, and Dutch banks. On 14 September 2007, Northern Rock, the UK's fourth largest and highly leveraged lender, had had to close its doors, after a disclosure that it had been propped up by the Bank of England. News about the US sub-prime mortgage scandal continued to leak out in late 2007 and the first half of 2008, with the federal takeover of Freddie Mac and Fannie Mae, government-sponsored mortgage corporations, on 6 September. Nine days later, on 15 September 2008, Lehman Brothers—which had a large European office in London—had gone bankrupt after the Federal Reserve had refused to guarantee its loans. By 7 October, the British government was struggling to cope. 'I was at a meeting of European finance ministers when I took a call from the chairman of RBS', which was nominally Europe's largest banking group, recalled the Chancellor of the Exchequer Alistair Darling: 'He said the bank was in danger of running out of money. I said, "okay, we have plans in place, how long have you got?" And he said,

---

European Integration since the 1920s: Security, Identity, and Cooperation. Mark Hewitson, Oxford University Press.
© Mark Hewitson 2024. DOI: 10.1093/oso/9780198915942.003.0006

"a few hours". That was chilling.'[8] The UK government announced a £500 billion bank rescue package on the next day, buying £20 billion of Royal Bank of Scotland shares and £17 billion of HBOS and Lloyds TSB shares, followed by a £50 billion second rescue package on 12 January 2009. The Belgian group Fortis, which had bought the Dutch bank ABN AMRO along with RBS and Santander in October 2007, collapsed and was bought out by the Dutch and Belgian governments on 3–5 October 2008. In Dublin, the Irish government had issued a two-year unlimited guarantee of the debts of six banks in order to try to stabilize a system exposed to the effects of a bursting property bubble, but it had subsequently been forced to nationalize the Anglo Irish Bank by late December, going on to plough €12.7 billion into the group by early 2010.

The shock waves of the 2007–08 crisis helped to produce balance-of-payments crises in the eurozone as Northern European banks sought to reduce their exposure to indebted governments, after years of speculative investment in Southern Europe under the low-interest regime of the European Central Bank (ECB).[9] By April 2010, the Greek government, whose budget deficit was 15 per cent and national debt was 127 per cent of GDP in 2009, was no longer able to borrow on international markets and had to request a loan of €45 billion from the EU and International Monetary Fund (IMF). The First Economic Adjustment Programme for Greece, which was agreed by the eurozone finance ministers (the Eurogroup), the ECB and IMF on condition of the implementation of government austerity measures, provided a further €107.3 billion on 1–2 May 2010 and a Second Adjustment Programme lent €130 billion on 21 February 2012. By the end of 2011, Greek national debt stood at €356 billion, or 171.4 per cent of GDP.[10] Facing similar, if more limited pressures, the Irish government signed a €67.5 billion bailout agreement with the EU and IMF on 29 November 2010 and the Portuguese government requested €78 billion in April 2011. Three member states with a combined population of 26.25 million—or 5 per cent of the EU as a whole—had taken out €427.8 billion of loans—or €16,300 per capita—within two years. The 'PIGS'—Portugal, Ireland, Greece, and Spain—appeared to be threatening the collapse of the entire eurozone, as well as their own economies and the banking systems of Western and Northern Europe, which held the bulk of debtor governments' bonds. The European Financial Stability Facility (EFSF), set up on 9 May 2010 with €440 billion from the EU and €250 billion from the IMF, was designed to ward off speculation against government bonds. It was replaced by the European Stability Mechanism in September 2012, which went on to lend €273 billion over the next five years to Cyprus, Greece, Ireland, Portugal, and Spain. The political effects of such borrowing and austerity were damaging, with the *Bild-Zeitung* in the EU's largest creditor state—the FRG—asking why Greeks had lived beyond their means and had not made the same sacrifices as Germans.[11] For their part, Greek demonstrators—where GDP had shrunk by 9 per cent by May 2011, compared to 2008—labelled Merkel and other German leaders Nazis.[12]

The old debates about the relationship in Europe between an economic and political union were difficult to ignore.

To John Gillingham, the most trenchant economic opponent of the EU's political project, the 'faulty design of the European Monetary Union' had 'raised the spectre of institutional collapse'.[13] EMU had been 'hammered out against an atmosphere of intense political pressure, but without the benefit of independent outside opinion', with many economists pointing out its flaws at the time: the lack of a 'natural customs area', unsuited to 'a one-size-fits-all policy'; a European Central Bank which 'lacked the authority to make fiscal or macro-economic policy'; adherence to 'rigid and unsuitable rules' as the sole means of enforcement; and no provision made 'for coping with failure'.[14] With relatively cheap and easy currency conversion by the 1980s and the growth of a Euro-capital market based on the ecu—a currency unit coexisting with national currencies—in the 1990s, the leaders of the European Union had no good economic reason to remove the beneficial devaluation effects of individual currencies, Gillingham contended in 2003.[15] 'If exchange rates are abandoned as an economic tool, something else must take their place,' wrote the German-American economist Rudi Dornbusch: 'Maastricht's promoters have carefully avoided spelling out just what that might be. Competitive labour markets is the answer, but that is a dirty word in social welfare Europe.'[16] In Gillingham's opinion, the eurozone crisis, which had begun with the 'collapse of the American housing bubble on Wall Street' but which would last longer and be more profound than in the United States, had exposed such flaws, which could be traced back to the very inception of the European Communities, as Jean Monnet had realized that 'the public of his day was not ready to countenance the idea of European political union and could not be trusted to support it'.[17] Consequently, to advance his project, the French head of planning and later President of the High Authority of the ECSC, 'operated by stealth and championed policies in the name of economic reform whose underlying purpose was a European federation':

> To this end, he staged a sequence of *faits accomplis* calculated to produce irreversible outcomes. This approach, followed also by his successors, has made it nearly impossible to un-do what already has been done. Monnet's methods have exacted a heavy toll in bad governance and faulty institutional design, maladies that very much still afflict today's EU. They have, furthermore, deprived it of democratic legitimacy and also, therefore, of sovereign power.
>
> The European Commission was the centrepiece of Monnet's scheme. The agenda-setting power vested in this executive authority built an elitist bias into the EU, according to Majone, which henceforth stifled policy making from the bottom up and by popular consensus. Although the Commission has been forced to share power with competing governance institutions over time, it has never lost its fundamental prerogatives.[18]

In Gillingham's view, the three-term President of the European Commission in the 1980s and early 1990s, Jacques Delors, ensured that Monnet's legacy remained relevant.

With the breakdown during the early 1970s of the Bretton Woods system, which 'rested on a peg of major currencies to the US dollar [and] which, bolstered by national capital controls, provided buffers that insulated domestic economies from international competition', the 'compatibility between the mixed-economy welfare state and the European Community (and eventual EU)' was brought into question, with increased capital mobility and new flows of liquidity imperilling 'corporatist business arrangements', undermining 'the resistance of entrenched state bureaucracies', loosening the bonds between the state, industry, commerce and finance, and setting the stage for the 'dramatic growth of the European enterprise'.[19] Liberalization, which had been intrinsic to the post-war global financial and commercial settlement but whose impact in Europe had been limited by remaining restraints on capital mobility, now transformed the European Community from 'a customs union with an attached farming programme' into 'something powerful, controversial and operational', exposing the confrontation between two contesting principles of organization underpinning the history of the EU: one was 'the gradual but steady expansion of the international market economy and its increasing influence on national development'; the other, associated with Monnet, 'aimed at framing the structures of a future European state'.[20]

Delors opted for a 'misconceived state-building policy' on the European level in order to protect an 'insufficiently productive and no longer affordable mixed economy welfare state—and the so-called "European social model"'—backed by 'deepeners' such as Mitterrand and Kohl, who 'was determined to slay the European fear of German domination', contends Gillingham.[21] The Treaty on European Union (1992) signed at Maastricht not only established the 'so-called three-pillar system of the EU—a grotesque structure wobbling on unstable compromises'—with only the 'first upright', the single market, able to support anything and the others, a Common Foreign and Security Policy and Justice and Home Affairs, 'nothing but hollow tubes erected in the vague hope that they could be filled in the future by the ambitions of bureaucratic state builders'.[22] It also created a system in the form of EMU and a single currency which was designed at once to symbolize European unity and to offset the risks in a free-trade area with floating currencies (alongside the ecu) and devaluations of individual currencies leading to the export of foodstuffs from 'cheap' member states to expensive ones (and thus undermining the Common Agricultural Policy), at the same time as protests at devaluations—understood as 'exchange dumping'—prompted calls for protectionism. These political decisions had subjected some members of the eurozone, deprived of the possibility of devaluation, to a logic of lower wages and cuts to public services. It had left the zone as a whole exposed to the danger of 'a systemic shock'.[23]

218   EUROPEAN INTEGRATION SINCE THE 1920s

Change, for Gillingham, 'took place more easily by means of "negative" integration—that is, by applying "thou-shalt-not" rules to economic activity—rather than "positive integration"—the creation of new institutions to overcome market failure'.[24] Other scholars—even champions of a European 'superpower' such as John McCormick—have been less willing to separate politics and economics or, at least, to discount political cooperation in the EU as 'state-building'.[25] Yet the eurozone crisis has obliged them, too, to re-assess the relationship between political and economic integration. Whereas McCormick had earlier been confident that the European Union had played an important part in creating a 'European economic colossus', as 'the world's biggest capitalist marketplace, the world's biggest trading power and the world's biggest magnet for—and source of—foreign direct investment', he was more guarded by 2012, singling out Europe's role as a peacemaker, a global power, and an institutional model as the principal benefits of the European project.[26] The EU was still 'the most effective force in the world today for the peaceful promotion of democracy and capitalism', but the latter was mainly used to induce states which sought 'access to the vast European marketplace' to spread democracy.[27] The single currency had long been seen 'as the essential first step in completing the single market', yet it had not worked out as intended: 'the euro lacked a mechanism for centralized control over borrowing and spending'; Greece had been allowed to join, 'even though it had not met all the stability criteria for entry'; and France and Germany 'broke their own rules on budget deficits'.[28] The creation of the euro was, in the words of the German Minister of Foreign Affairs Joschka Fischer, 'a profoundly political act, because a currency is not just another economic factor but also symbolizes the power of the sovereign who guarantees it'.[29] Despite the 'wild ride' of the eurozone crisis after 2010, however, the populations of eurozone countries continued to support the currency, with 52 per cent in favour in the spring of 2012 and 40 per cent against.[30]

McCormick's list of economic benefits of political union remains a long one, including the opening of markets and dismantling of monopolies, a reduction in the complexity of national standards and regulations as a result of harmonization, the building of common infrastructure and transport (Trans-European Networks, or TENs), economies of scale and the pursuit of comparative advantage in a larger market, and the removal of discriminatory laws. The 'psychological effect of making the foreign more accessible and familiar' has been matched by actual market integration: more than 70 per cent of exports from EU members go to other member states, which is a far higher percentage than amongst contiguous economies in other trade areas.[31] 'Speculating on how matters might have unfolded without the European Union is not easy,' the Anglo-American scholar notes: 'Market pressures would have led to some of the changes brought by the single market, but the example of other parts of the world with close economic and trading ties suggests that such changes would have taken longer to achieve or would not have gone so far', not least because the protection of national companies and markets 'has strong appeal for voters, business and unions'.[32] Although the EU has not produced large, innovative companies such as Apple, Google, and Amazon, with its tally of twelve comparing unfavourably with fifty-one big new firms in the US and forty-six in emerging markets between 1950 and 2000, it has gained an increased share of the world's largest corporations: 238—or almost 60 per cent—of the *Fortune* 400 were American and 108 (27 per cent) were European in 1969, whereas 176 (35 per cent) of the *Fortune* Global 500 were American and 158 (32 per cent) were European in 2005.[33] Citizens and consumers were more likely to base their judgements on the range and price of products, job security, public services, and 'serendipitous' benefits of integration such as progress on environmental cooperation; most notably, reductions in air and water pollution, the disposal of waste and use of renewable energy, all of which proved easier in a single market.[34] Partly as a consequence, 67 per cent of respondents in twelve member states avowed that membership of the EU had benefited their economies, even at the height of the eurozone crisis in the summer of 2011.[35] McCormick's reading of such statistics points to widespread acceptance of the economic advantages of political cooperation. Yet how much difference did the ECSC and EEC make and how much political integration was necessary?[36] This chapter re-examines the relationship between such institutional integration and economic convergence, which has underpinned the European project from the start.

Neo-Functionalism and Economic Growth

After more ambitious plans for a supranational political community had come to nothing, 'fervent Europeans' turned their attention to technocratic designs for sectoral economic integration, which was later described by 'neo-functionalist' theorists such as Ernst Haas as the main form of European unity.[37] During the Second World War, Monnet had been hopeful that European trade and currencies could be coordinated under the auspices of a strong League of Nations. He predicted in an interview in *Fortune* magazine in August 1945 that there would be 'a true yielding of sovereignty' to 'some kind of central union', together with a large European market without customs barriers, not least to prevent the recrudescence of nationalism, 'which is the curse of the modern world'.[38]

In the event, integration took place more slowly than Monnet had anticipated. Attempts to set up extensive supranational institutions within the Council of Europe (1949) and European Defence and Political Communities (1950–54) failed. To federalists such as Pierre Uri, a professor at the new *Ecole nationale d'administration* and one of the architects of the EEC, the European Coal and Steel Community, established in 1951, 'was two things at once', 'a common basis of development' and 'a prototype for general integration', yet the former—as a practical means of developing western European industry—seemed to have taken precedence over the latter.[39] After the 'defeat' of the EDC, Uri recalled that most members of the High Authority—or supranational executive—of the ECSC agreed that 'we will have to be modest', trying 'to extend the powers of the High Authority' from coal to oil, gas, electricity and transport, since 'it plays a major role in coal, iron ore and steel'.[40] Monnet, too, was cautious, preferring to concentrate on the new industry of nuclear energy—which became the European Atomic Energy Community (Euratom) in 1957—because it was closely linked to the state and lacked entrenched vested interests: 'We started with Euratom because we didn't dare go to a Common Market.'[41] To Monnet in November 1955, after the matter had been discussed by foreign ministers at Messina in June, a common market, which was an extension of a customs union with its common external tariff, also implied 'federal social, monetary and conjuncture policies' to ensure that internal tariffs were removed or retained.[42] Other measures such as competition policy were designed which would allow different national markets and industries to coalesce and grow. 'Our ambitions were modest,' Spaak wrote in retrospect: 'So were our hopes. It seemed important to us to advance on solid ground where we had real chances of success, leaving bigger plans till later. Above all, we had to avoid another rebuff.'[43]

This cautious, incremental approach was described by neo-functionalist theorists, whose works became the principal guide to integration in the late 1950s and 1960s. Haas, who became the best-known exponent of neo-functionalism, made his name by observing the European Coal and Steel Community at close quarters and showing 'the common market in operation', as the heading of one chapter put it.[44] His purpose was 'merely the description of major policy measures undertaken by the High Authority in cooperation with the Council of Ministers, the reactions to these measures expressed in the Common Assembly and the opposition voiced by governments and private groups through the medium of lawsuits in the Court of Justice'.[45] Although there had been no tariffs on coal, iron ore and scrap metal, 'certain transport discriminations and double pricing practices' had existed, which came to an end on 10 February 1953.[46] Since German taxes were lower than French ones, the German government argued that producers should be taxed at local rates, whilst the French government contended that competition in a common market dictated that taxes should be levied where the product was sold, with French producers being taxed at lower German rates on sales in the FRG. The High Authority of the ECSC referred the matter to a commission of economists, which ruled in favour of the French position. 'The preceding months had been taken up not only with harmonising the policies of six governments in simultaneously removing trade barriers, but also in identifying the firms subject to the ECSC, working out new price rules, assessing the production tax as well as collecting it and making transitional arrangements with respect to certain transport questions, subsidies, rebates and temporary tariffs in the case of Italy,' Haas went on, demonstrating in detail what a supranational pooling of sovereignty, even in a restricted economic sector, actually entailed.[47]

By the spring of 1953, the French government had taken the High Authority itself to the Court of Justice, complaining that the price set for Belgian coal was too low, undercutting companies in France. Despite the High Authority's subsequent raising of Belgian prices, 'the French proceeded to establish a discriminatory coal barge compensation fund for canal-carried coal in northern France, in an effort to burden imported Belgian coal', which in turn prompted the Belgian government to sue.[48] For Haas, 'these fragmentary efforts at resistance to the Treaty' hinted at how unlikely a full freeing of trade would be in the absence of formal treaty obligations and supranational institutions.[49] Once the common market had 'become a reality' and the 'growing interpenetration of formerly protected national markets' had occurred, however, the benefits were undeniable, with the volume of trade in iron ore and coal between member states increasing by 40 per cent between 1952 and 1955, and in steel and scrap by 151 per cent and 357 per cent respectively.[50] Given the advantages of such cooperation, Haas expected that there would be 'spill-over' effects and that the model would be extended, with 'friends and critics' agreeing that 'economic integration in the long run cannot rest on supranational rules and institutions for one economic sector alone, no matter how vital that sector may be in the total scheme of life'.[51]

The High Authority of the ECSC was the main supranational body, funded by the proceeds of a common external tariff and disposing of the power to impose fines on individual companies, set up re-training programmes, raise finance in capital markets and make loans for the purposes of investment. It was composed of nine members nominated by the six participating states, with France and Germany each putting forward two members, plus a president—the first being Monnet himself—chosen by the eight nominees. It was advised by a Consultative Committee of fifty representatives from industry, unions, and consumer groups and it was checked by a Council of Ministers, which controlled the budget and sanctioned new initiatives, by an Assembly made up of seventy-eight deputies from national parliaments, which had the power to remove the High Authority by a two-thirds vote, and by a Court of Justice, composed of seven judges serving for six years, which heard cases brought by member states or the Council. Clement Attlee dismissed the ECSC during a House of Commons debate in late June as 'an irresponsible body that is appointed by no one and [is] responsible to no one'.[52]

Haas asked why the Benelux countries, France, Germany, and Italy had transferred vital economic interests to such an organization. His investigation of political parties in the six states at the time of ratification suggested that 'a common dedication to European principles' was not discernible 'as a unifying element': 'Only in Holland was the essence of "Europeanism" accepted without dissent, thus becoming actually part of the content of Dutch nationalism.'[53] More convincing was the argument that there had been 'a possibly temporary

222 EUROPEAN INTEGRATION SINCE THE 1920S

convergence of party motives and ideologies, and emphatically not in terms of a clear, permanent and united majority'.[54] 'Europeanism, even after five years of successful ECSC operations, continues to be a mixture of frequently opposing aspirations,' Haas wrote.[55] Over time, union organizations became more favourably disposed to the ECSC, but in industry 'Fragmentation was and is typical.'[56] Governments were more decisive in 1950, even if French leaders had 'purely economic aims', but their long-term positions were less clear-cut, with the Netherlands, Belgium, and Luxembourg preferring 'more integration at the earliest possible moment', and with France, Italy, and Germany—for different reasons—being more circumspect.[57] Only 'processes of integration at the supranational level', which was the heading of Haas's third and final section of *The Uniting of Europe*, explained the momentum behind integration and the transition from the ECSC to the EEC.[58]

What was critical, claimed Haas, were the habits of cooperation and compromise fostered by supranational organizations. Why did the ECSC Council of Ministers, which 'is an intergovernmental organ', act differently from the Council of the Organization for European Economic Cooperation (OEEC), which was one of more than twenty other international organizations that had 'sprouted in Western Europe during the first fifteen years after the Second World War', according Kiran Klaus Patel?[59] The OEEC's Council included 'the same persons who are active in Luxembourg [in the ECSC], it is subject to the unanimity rule, possesses a self-conscious and active secretariat, and is, in principle at least, concerned with European integration', yet, apart from 'slicing up the pie' of the Marshall Plan funds, 'the basic fact concerning OEEC activity is its failure to contribute to long-term integration', remarked Haas.[60] The channelling of funds to poorer regions in Europe, the coordination of investment, the modernization of machinery, coordinated monetary policies, the creation of sectoral and general markets, and the free movement of capital and labour 'were all suggested and discussed, but never fully implemented' because of national vetoes and the absence of any supranational body able to pursue such goals consistently.[61] Short-term goals such as the abolition of quantitative restrictions—or quotas—and the introduction of currency convertibility were pursued more consistently, pushed by Washington, but they, too, were subject to vetoes, escape clauses, and annual authorizations.

As a French former official of the OEEC confessed,

OEEC experience should be carefully considered. It demonstrates that a simple international organization, paralyzed by the right to use the veto, is unable to create a common market in Europe: national particularism and private interests are too powerful. An organic tie is necessary to limit the sovereignty of nation-states. It also demonstrates that Britain is not disposed to accept an organic union with the Continent.[62]

By contrast, the members of the ECSC Council were 'firmly "engaged" to maintaining the common market for coal and steel and to extending it', meaning that they could not 'indefinitely oppose meeting to some extent the maximalist demands put forward by one of their treaty partners, thus begetting a compromise pattern going beyond the minimalist position perhaps desired'.[63] What was more, governments knew 'that binding opinions could be made in some situations despite their negative vote and that some agreement is called for in any case', making them unwilling 'to be forced into the position of being the single hold-out, thus to be isolated and exposed as "anti-European"'.[64] As a consequence, 'even in situations calling for unanimity, the Council pattern of compromise is far more federal in nature than would be indicated by the customary practices of intergovernmental conferences'.[65] With compromise and cooperation developing their own momentum in a supranational organization and spill-over effects of the coordination of coal, iron, and steel being felt in other sectors (for instance, transport), economic integration seemed, to Haas, to have become self-perpetuating, without encountering significant resistance, precisely because it had not required broad party and public approval. Leon Lindberg and others produced similar accounts of the European Economic Community.[66]

Lindberg's, Scheingold's, and Haas's models of beneficial cooperation, economies of scale, and spill-over effects seemed convincing because they came into being during a period of economic growth. Although European institutions were widely associated with such growth, the gradual removal of tariffs in the EEC, which took place in three four-year-long phases during the 1960s and which the *Economist* had parodied in 1957 (promising Italians that they would be able to buy a Volkswagen at German prices 'in twelve years' time, if things go well, or seventeen years, if not'), played a belated, secondary role in the initial period of reconstruction and 'supergrowth' between 1945 and the early 1970s, celebrated in France as '*les trente glorieuses*' and in West Germany as the '*Wirtschaftswunder*'.[67] The peculiarity of post-war growth in Europe is obvious from a comparison with the interwar era, notwithstanding the fact that it rested on the same foundations. Reconstruction was based on types of production and goods which had been available in the 1920s and 1930s, if not before, from the automobile and the aeroplane—both produced in the 1900s—to strip-mill steel production and large-scale chemical plants.[68] Radios, television, refrigerators, nylon, plastics, and vacuum cleaners all date from the period before 1945. More importantly, key sectors of industry for reconstruction remained those which had dominated the interwar era, with 'other manufactures' only exceeding traditional areas of production in the UK—such as the food, textiles, and engineering industries—by the 1970s, for example.[69]

The fact that traditional sectors of industry and already-extant technologies formed the core of reconstruction in the late 1940s and 1950s allowed Eastern Europe to outstrip Western Europe after 1948, helping to explain why a country

224 EUROPEAN INTEGRATION SINCE THE 1920s

Table 5.1 GDP and per capita GDP by region, 1950–92 in international dollars (1950 index)

	1950	1973	1980	1992
Western Europe*				
GDP	1,396,188 million	4,096,456 million	4,849,409 million	6,202,870 million
Index	100	293	347	444
Per capita GDP	4,579	11,416	13,197	16,256
Per capita index	100	249	288	355
Eastern Europe**				
GDP	185,023 million	550,756 million	675,819 million	559,611 million
Index	100	298	365	302
Per capita GDP	2,111	4,988	5,786	4,591
Per capita index	100	236	274	217
USSR				
GDP	510,243 million	1,513,070 million	1,709,174 million	1,592,084 million
Index	100	297	335	312
Per capita GDP	2,841	6,059	6,426	5,451
Per capita index	100	213	226	192

*Western Europe denotes all countries (except micro-states) outside the Soviet Bloc, including Greece, Spain, Portugal, Norway, and Switzerland.
**Including Yugoslavia.
Source: derived from A. Maddison, *The World Economy: Historical Statistics* (Paris, 2003), 233–4.

such as the GDR—with a population of 17 million inhabitants—could be believed to be the tenth largest industrial economy in the world by the 1970s, given the strength of its optics, chemicals, and steel industries.[70] In the Eastern Bloc, it appeared, planning, targeted investment, the production of capital goods, quotas, wage and price controls all permitted rapid re-industrialization, just as they had benefited the Soviet Union in the 1930s (see Table 5.1).[71] Problems in the Eastern Bloc arose when production switched to high-quality consumer goods, confounding the hopes of COMECON governments of selling their wares in western markets. They had also become visible during a new phase of industrialization, resting on computers and electronics, which took place from the 1970s onwards. The result was that a state such as Poland under Edward Gierek, whose 1971–75 plan had used western credit and technology transfers for the production of exports destined for the West, found that it could not compete, leaving it saddled with a $24 billion debt to western states and banks by 1980, rising to $48 billion by 1990.[72] 'Do you really believe that the Communist regime can succeed in developing the Polish economy?' Giscard had asked Gierek, who—as the son of a migrant Polish miner—had been educated in France during the interwar era.[73] By the turn of the century, the EEC and the Single market, which had been created by the Single European Act (1986), had helped to facilitate economic integration and the consolidation of large European multinationals.[74] Yet such effects should not be confused with the more limited impact of the ECSC and common market in the 1950s and 1960s.

The defining characteristics of the post-war era in Western Europe, which used the products of reconstruction for novel ends and distinguished the post-war from the interwar years, were related to consumption. The 1950s and 1960s witnessed mass consumerism such as only the United States had experienced before 1945. The car became the symbol of this consumer culture, with 9 million vehicles being produced annually in Europe by the 1970s, compared to 0.5 million in 1940.[75] The demand for such goods required consumers, with increasing disposable incomes: in West Germany, for example, citizens were spending almost half of their incomes, on average, on cars, furniture, leisure, and travel by 1957, compared to one-third in the late 1940s (see Table 5.2). The constant quest to improve the range and quality of products for new consumers, with the quick adaptation of technological innovations, helped to produce a novel electronic and computer-based phase of the industrial revolution.[76] By the mid-1960s, IBM Deutschland and IBM UK had already begun to develop their 360-series computer, at a total cost of $5.7 billion.[77] By the 1980s, smaller, more powerful computers and robots were being used in manufacturing plants in Japan, the United States and Europe. The consumer goods which they produced, in conjunction with further improvements of 'Fordist' production lines, displaced or marginalized older forms of production and marked out Western Europe (and the 'West') from the Eastern Bloc.[78] Such innovations, in addition to an increasingly unwieldy Common Agricultural Policy (CAP), formed the basis of economic convergence within the EEC, even if they were not directly attributable to the existence of a common market.[79]

The reasons why economic 'supergrowth' and consumerism occurred in Europe were closely connected to—but were not necessarily caused by—the durability of the European Community.[80] At the time, the EEC was widely credited with growth, as the committee of Sir Frank Lee, a supporter of British accession, spelled out in April 1960. Although only 14 per cent of British exports

Table 5.2 Expenditure of average disposable income in West Germany, 1957–85

	1957	1967	1977	1985
Food	36.6	29.3	23.0	17.4
Clothing	12.5	9.4	8.2	6.5
Housing	9.3	13.5	14.4	15.6
Furniture, cars, travel, Leisure, etc.	33.6	36.1	40.7	47.8
Savings	8.0	11.7	13.7	12.7

Source: W. Voß, *Die Bundesrepublik Deutschland. Daten und Analysen* (Stuttgart, 1980), 135; *Die Zeit*, 23 May 1986; V. R. Berghahn, *The Americanization of West German Industry, 1945–1973* (Cambridge, 1986), 292.

226   EUROPEAN INTEGRATION SINCE THE 1920s

went to the European Community, 'great economic benefits' would accrue from membership of the trading bloc or 'near identification' with it.[81] Harold Macmillan's 'Grand Design' memo arrived at a similar conclusion at the end of 1960, warning of the 'economic damage' of 'economic exclusion'.[82] There was a good chance, concluded another committee in 1960, that 'a new world power will have come on the scene', which the UK would have refused to join, leaving its 'position vis-à-vis both the United States and Western Europe' in 'decline'.[83] Notwithstanding contemporaries' perceptions, the connections between growth, consumption, and the establishment of the EEC are not straightforward, not least because they coincided with the increasing interventions of welfare states, whose economic effects were varied, and the re-organization and expansion of international trade, which was led by the United States and was accompanied by the inauguration of COMECON.[84] Such developments explain why the Eastern Bloc had higher rates of GDP per capita growth—at least on paper—in the 1950s than did the 'West'. They also explain why Western Europe experienced unprecedented rates of growth, of a different order from those of the nineteenth and earlier twentieth century: income per capita increased at 4.5 per cent between 1950 and 1970, compared to approximately 1 per cent per annum between 1800 and 1950, meaning that the generation entering the workforce in the 1940s and 1950s saw their real incomes rise more in two decades than over the previous 150 years.[85] US income per capita increased at 2.2 per cent per annum, or only half the Western European rate, during these years. Why, exactly, did European economies grow so rapidly between 1950 and the early 1970s, creating a foundation for the European Economic Community and confounding the expectations of many contemporaries, who had feared that recovery might be replaced by recession, as had happened after the First World War?[86] How, asked Robert Marjolin, the first Secretary-General of the OEEC, was it that 'the re-establishment' of the European economy 'did not stop when Europe reattained its pre-war position, but was transformed during the 1950s and 1960s into a powerful movement of expansion, which led it to a level of prosperity that it had never known in its history' and which contrasted to such an extent with the years between 1919 and 1939?[87]

Europe after the Second World War had the potential for one-off, catch-up gains, with levels of production artificially low after the rearmament programmes of the 1930s and transfer to war industries between 1939 and 1945: the Gross National Product of the United States was $381 billion in 1950, compared to $71 billion in the United Kingdom, $50 billion in West Germany and France, and $29 billion in Italy (see Table 5.3).[88] The principal components of growth were already in place in these European states in 1945, producing unprecedently high growth figures from a low starting point.[89] 'Suddenly, after 1945, all the conditions favourable to the flourishing of individual initiatives were reunited,' recalled Marjolin.[90] Although the receptiveness of European governments to economic cooperation in the 1920s suggests that European integration could have occurred

Table 5.3 Total GNP and per capita GNP of the powers in 1950 (in 1964 dollars)

	Total GNP	Per capita GNP	GNP as a percentage of US GNP
United States	381 billion	2,536	100
USSR	126	699	33.0
UK	71	1,393 (1951)	18.6
France	50	1,172	13.1
West Germany	48	1,001	12.6
Japan	32	382	8.4
Italy	29	626 (1951)	7.6

Source: adapted from P. M. Kennedy, *The Rise and Fall of the Great Powers: Economic Change and Military Conflict from 1500 to 2000* (London, 1988), 475.

in the 1950s, even without such favourable conditions, it would, without question, have been more difficult. It was critical that economic conditions in the late 1940s were better than those of the early 1920s.

First, European states had populations with comparatively high levels of secondary education and they had an adequate number of trained university graduates. Second, they benefited from a high level of technical knowledge, with most of the important industrial technologies and business techniques already familiar to European officials, managers, and technicians before 1945.[91] In the ultimate test of such know-how—namely, the invention of the atom bomb—German scientists had played a major role at the end of the war in the United States, Russian scientists followed suit in 1949 (admittedly with the help of Soviet spies), and their British counterparts in 1952.[92] Third, European states possessed a large amount of industrial plant, despite the destruction wrought by the war.[93] Even war-torn West Germany had one-tenth more stock in 1945 than it had had in 1939.[94] The Economics Minister Ludwig Erhard, the architect of German reconstruction, was so confident that the FRG's supply side was in place by 1949 that he removed price controls and a centralized allocation of resources.[95] Fourth, there was sustained demand for materials and capital goods in Europe to repair the damage done during the war and for consumer goods, after the Depression in the early 1930s and wartime deprivation between 1939 and 1945. Fifth, there was a plentiful supply of labour as a result of migration and expulsions, with the FRG absorbing 12 million German refugees—7 million of whom joined the workforce—fleeing from the East.[96] Over the longer term, they were joined by the post-war generation of 'baby boomers'—symbolized by the '*beaux bébés*' of General de Gaulle—who had increased Western Europe's population from 264 million to 320 million between 1940 and 1970. France's population had grown from 42 million to 50 million between 1950 and 1966, which matched the demographic increase of the previous 150 years.

228 EUROPEAN INTEGRATION SINCE THE 1920s

Lastly, there was a drift away from agriculture, where productivity growth was low, to industry and services, where it was higher. In the immediate post-war years, the agricultural population was declining at a rate of 3.5 per cent per annum in countries such as Finland and France. Whereas the UK had an agricultural workforce of less than 5 per cent of the total in 1950 and its level of productivity was 62 per cent of that of the United States, Italy's productivity was only 34 per cent of the US level and its agricultural population accounted for 37 per cent of its workforce.[97] It has been estimated that 42 per cent of Italian growth between 1950 and 1962 resulted from the movement away from agriculture.[98] Because Italy's population continued to drift from rural regions to cities and industry, keeping unemployment there high and industrial wages low, its economy continued to register high rates of growth—3.7 per cent per annum compared to 1.5 per cent in the UK and 2.4 per cent in the FRG—throughout the 1970s.[99]

What effect did such sustained economic growth have on citizens' and politicians' attitudes to the European Community? There is considerable evidence that Europeans value the economic benefits of integration (see Table 5.4 for GDP per capita growth).[100] Yet functionalists and neo-functionalists had also assumed that citizens in a transnational community would transfer their primary loyalties from nation-states to a supranational authority on the basis of recognized benefits accruing from cooperation in a self-perpetuating cycle, explained Juliet Lodge in 1978, shortly before the first direct elections

Table 5.4 GDP per person in 1990 international dollars

	1950	1973	1992
Switzerland	8,939	17,953	21,036
UK	6,847	11,992	15,738
Sweden	6,738	13,494	16,927
Denmark	6,683	13,416	19,351
Netherlands	5,850	12,763	16,898
Belgium	5,346	11,905	17,165
France	5,221	12,940	17,959
Norway	4,969	10,229	17,543
FRG	4,281	13,152	19,351
Finland	4,131	10,768	14,646
Austria	3,731	11,308	17,160
Italy	3,425	10,409	16,229
Spain	2,397	8,739	12,500
Portugal	2,132	7,568	11,130
Greece	1,558	6,229	8,238
Japan	1,873	11,017	19,425
USA	9,573	16,607	21,558

Source: adapted from A. Maddison, *The World Economy: Historical Statistics* (Paris, 2003), 63–9.

to the European Parliament in the following year, but they had been proved wrong, since transfers of allegiance were not so straightforward:

> In the past macro-level loyalty building has been associated with the integration of the masses into a common political form ranging from Plato's city-state to the modern nation.... Where national-level political loyalties are concerned, it is traditionally assumed that men owe allegiance to a national-level organization *qua* nation-state in exchange for the latter undertaking to safeguard their security.[101]

The question in the immediate post-war years concerned the nature of 'security', which had come to include economics and was associated with the EEC, but which remained, at the same time, military and diplomatic, resting on the nation-state and, above all, the United States. More recent 'post-functionalist' accounts of European integration have tended to emphasize the 'politicization' of integration, with 'closed shops of government leaders, interest groups and Commission officials...bypassed as European issues have entered party competition'.[102] Not only has public support for the EU been lower than support among elites, from a 12 per cent gap in Ireland and 18 per cent in the Netherlands to 54 per cent in Germany and 57 per cent in Sweden in 1996, populist parties, stressing tradition, authority and nationalism, have emerged which cut across existing right-left cleavages based on redistribution.[103]

Philippe Schmitter's reply on behalf of neo-functionalists to such objections accepts that 'politicization has occurred since the mid-1980s', partly because the European Union 'had a tough time dealing with Eastern Enlargement and its own institutional re-definition', and partly because 'identity politics' at the European level is not likely to prove 'epiphenomenal or episodic'.[104] Neo-functionalists' expectations that 'mass publics would be aroused to protect the *acquis communautaire* against the resistance of entrenched national political elites determined to perpetuate their status as guarantors of sovereignty' have been confounded.[105] 'What was not predicted was that this mobilization would threaten rather than promote the integration process', Schmitter concedes. 'In the post-functionalist version, the inverse has occurred—opening up a gap between elites, by and large favourable to expansion of EU tasks and decisional autonomy, and masses resistant to both.'[106] European parties, which might have acted as a 'plausible mechanism for responding to the elite-mass gap in expectations and for re-fashioning multiple collective identities according to different levels of political aggregation', had not emerged to replace national parties, which themselves were in decline, leaving the politics of the European Union 'to pass through and be distorted by the conflicts and aspirations of national party politicians for whom the European level is of secondary importance'.[107] Looking back, neo-functionalists acknowledged, despite perceived linkages between 'supergrowth' and the EEC, that economic integration had become more political and problematic.

The Politics of Economic Integration

Despite appearances, economic integration was never automatic. It took place within clearly defined political parameters, which governments had fought for at the outset and continued to negotiate in the 'club' of a common market, with its mixture of supranational and intergovernmental agencies.[108] Calls for the revival of 'Europe' after 1945, which was a necessity widely accepted by intellectuals and politicians alike, made the securing of vital national interests, especially on the part of France and the FRG, easier to justify, yet politics and economics remained difficult, if not impossible, to disentangle on the European level.[109] This state of affairs extended back into the interwar era. 'In 1919, Europe was confronted by problems similar to those which it got to know a quarter of a century later,' rendering a comparison of the two post-war periods 'fascinating', recalled Marjolin, the first Secretary General of the OEEC.[110] Such problems were at once political and economic.

There was always an economic component to Franco-German cooperation. Behind French ministers' desire for a rapprochement with Germany in the 1920s were complicated negotiations concerning France's economy and currency.[111] The need to strengthen the franc had been connected from the start to the question of German reparations, with French policy-makers preferring to capitalize the Reich's future payments through the floating of reparation bonds, which could be sold to the City of London and Wall Street in order to create liquidity in France and in Europe generally. Observed from this historical vantage point, the preference of post-war policy-makers for Franco-German economic cooperation amounted to taking up the policies of the 1920s, when the United States seemed to have contributed to the destabilization of the franc and to have offered little prospect of industrial collaboration. For its part, the French Ministry of Foreign Affairs had granted economics precedence over security from the early 1920s onwards. The policy was opposed by the military, which gave support to the separation of the Rhineland from Germany and to what Marshal Ferdinand Foch, the supreme commander of the Allied armies at the end of the First World War, termed—in 1925—the 'surrounding' of Germany with a strong network of alliances' and a refusal 'to let anyone tamper even an iota with the Treaty of Versailles'.[112] Some ministers, such as the Minister of Finance between 1922 and 1924 Charles de Lasteyrie du Saillant, believed as a consequence that 'a certain opposition between the two aims pursued by France'—'on the one hand to be paid and on the other to assure its security'—had emerged, yet few of their colleagues in the Quai d'Orsay appear to have been convinced by their arguments.[113] It was much more common in the Ministry of Foreign Affairs to assume that the Treaty of Versailles, in dismantling the Ottoman, Habsburg, Russian and German Empires, had led to what Jacques Seydoux implied was an unsustainable 'fragmentation of states' and to the alienation of most parties, even the democratic and republican ones, in Germany, which had left much of Eastern Europe in an exposed position between a revisionist German state and the unknown quantity—outside the League of Nations—of the Soviet Union.[114]

To the Quai d'Orsay in the 1920s, it had seemed that an economic agreement with Germany would bring in its train better diplomatic relations between Paris and Berlin, securing the position of France's Eastern European allies, even though their borders, which had been defined by the Paris Peace Conferences, would be subject to arbitration by the League of Nations. 'I know that our smaller allies in the East are rather disturbed by what has happened in Geneva and at Thoiry,' wrote Seydoux in autumn 1926: 'If there is Franco-German collaboration, and the signature of the steel cartel is one of the most important indicators, this means that we will talk to Germany before we act, that we will come to an agreement with her, that we will do nothing against her. This radically changes our attitude to the countries on which our policy has until now relied. Basically it is a question of a complete reversal, one which should lead to peace much more surely than the old policy.'[115] Economic reconciliation between France and Germany would allow the rewriting of European history, the diplomat continued in a memorandum of February 1925:

> What we all want in Europe is peace: to succeed at making peace, we must put Germany back into circulation, bring it into the League of Nations and search for...a formula which will allow Germany to find its equilibrium in Europe and to pursue, in concert with the Allies, the work of economic and financial reconstruction which, alone, will allow the binding up of the wounds of war and the avoidance of new conflicts.[116]

Briand's plan for a European union, although also reflecting his own evolving political priorities, constituted the continuation of a well-entrenched diplomatic and economic strategy during the 1920s. It is relevant here because it reveals the long-standing centrality of a Franco-German economic agreement. Since raising the question of the capitalization of reparations in his Thoiry meeting with Stresemann in September 1926, the socialist former Minister of Foreign Affairs had promoted the economic reconciliation of France and Germany, building on the successful negotiation in 1926 of the International Steel Cartel between France, Germany, and Luxembourg, which was initiated by the pro-European manufacturer and founder of the Franco-German Study Committee Emile Mayrisch. Briand's commitment extended the scope of the Franco-German trade treaty signed in 1927 and supported the ongoing efforts of the entrepreneur and ex-minister Louis Loucheur, who had presented a plan for the cross-border sectoral cooperation of industry and the eventual creation of a customs union to the League of Nations in September 1925. For Loucheur, speaking at the League in May 1927, it was likely that cooperation had to proceed 'following the so-called horizontal method'—'that is, by industry'—but this would subsequently 'allow the creation of the necessary profound transformations' and would 'resolve, in part, the question of tariff barriers' and 'present the possibility of a parallel and simultaneous raising of salaries, in order to return to post-war Europe the power of consumption of pre-war Europe'.[117]

Despite tensions between different lobbies wishing, respectively, to prioritize the concentration of industry, to form a customs union and to rebuild the financial structure of post-war Europe, many commentators, industrialists, financiers, officials, and ministers in France and elsewhere assumed that such objectives complemented rather than contradicted each other.[118] Accordingly, the economic section of Briand's memorandum of May 1930 emphasized 'the possibilities of an expansion of the economic market, attempts at the intensification and improvement of industrial production and, in the same way, all possible guarantees against crises of work, sources of political as well as social instability', echoing the expectation of the President of the *Chambre de commerce internationale* that 'a European commercial league would constitute a free internal market of a fertility at least the equal of that of the United States and its production could then compete with that of this vast country of commercial exchanges on equal terms'.[119] Initially, in his speech introducing the project of a 'United States of Europe' to the Assembly of the League of Nations in September 1929, Briand had been unequivocal in asserting that 'the association will act chiefly in the economic domain: it is the most pressing question'.[120] He also mentioned an accompanying European political apparatus, vaguely alluding to 'a sort of federal link', which recalled his reference to a 'kind of European federation' in a private conversation with Stresemann a few months earlier, but also reassuring his listeners that no participating state would lose its sovereignty.[121] The terms of this debate paralleled those of the late 1940s and early 1950s.

By the time that Briand put forward his 'Memorandum on the Organisation of a Regime of European Federal Union' to the League of Nations in May 1930, he gave a much fuller description of the institutions of the union and spelled out 'the necessary subordination of the economic to the political', after lobbying by other states and in response to Stresemann's call for a clarification of the political ideas in the plan.[122] As on the occasion of his speech to the League in September 1929, when he had expressed disappointment that Stresemann had only welcomed the economic aspects of his project, Briand was seeking to ensure that the new powers being granted to Germany were counterbalanced by binding political commitments. 'The contrary order would not only be useless,' the memorandum stated, 'it would appear to the weaker nations to be likely to expose them, without guarantees or compensation, to the risks of political domination which might result from an industrial domination of the more strongly organised states.'[123]

Stresemann's response on 9 September 1929 welcomed Briand's project as 'a great idea', which—like other great ideas—might seem 'crazy at first'.[124]

He rejected the scepticism of 'pessimists in principle' and criticized proponents of autarky and protectionism.[125] The European economy was excessively fragmented, akin to Italy before unification or Germany before the *Zollverein* and made worse by the Treaty of Versailles, he continued: 'Where is the European currency, the European postage stamp?'[126] Economic integration would improve Europe's ability to resist US penetration and strengthen the position of European statesmen in negotiations. The economy and the conquest of nature would better occupy the continent's youth than dreams of a future war, in which technology would produce slaughter not heroism. The Locarno Treaties and other similar endeavours were designed to foster greater international understanding and avert conflict, Stresemann suggested. Such German support went back to the Genoa Conference in 1922, which had mooted the eventual formation of a European customs union and which had rejected a Central European bloc in favour of 'European free trade'.[127] It also recalled Berlin's backing of Loucheur's plan in 1925, urged on by most German unions, many politicians—especially SPD deputies—and much of German business, and the government's hailing of the Franco-German trade treaty of 17 August 1927 as a 'European event'.[128] Although Stresemann was principally interested in Germany's national interests, as leader of the *Deutsche Volkspartei* (DVP) and a prominent advocate of the war effort prior to 1918, he had long been interested in economic integration in Europe, as a former spokesman of German big business. As he put it in a newspaper article in 1925, he was looking beyond the imminent security pacts of Locarno to the development of an 'economic understanding between the great industrial nations of Europe and beyond that something like the structure of a European community, in comparison to the present system which has created a Europe reminiscent of the old Germany with its dozens of states and customs barriers'.[129]

For French administrations after 1945, cooperation with Germany was essential, not simply as a means of addressing the German question and controlling the neighbouring state, but also as a way of regenerating French industry, particularly by giving steel manufacturers in Alsace and Lorraine favourable access to supplies of coke in the Ruhr and Saarland. To many ministers, Allied, bilateral or multilateral arrangements, like the International Steel Cartel of the 1920s, would probably have been sufficient, but they were prevented by the insistence of the United States and the UK on the rapid reconstruction of the German economy, which entailed the incorporation of the Ruhr and Rhineland in the FRG (not their 'internationalization'), by France's desire to break up German coal and steel cartels, against the wishes of West German industrialists, and by the German government's determination to reacquire the Saarland, undermining Paris's plans to maintain its separation or keep control of its industry.[130] It was only after the failure of 'traditional' and 'confederal' policies between 1945 and 1949 that the supranational European solution of the European Coal and Steel Community—first outlined by Monnet in a meeting with Spaak, the Belgian

234 EUROPEAN INTEGRATION SINCE THE 1920s

Foreign-Minister-in-exile, in 1941—was actually taken up by the French *Commissaire Général au Plan* and accepted by Schuman and other ministers, permitting the implementation of American-inspired anti-trust clauses in the Treaty of Paris, overcoming a Franco-German impasse over the Saarland and reassuring the governments of the Benelux countries, which were anxious that their interests would be overlooked in a bilateral Franco-German treaty.[131] Schuman's declaration of 9 May 1950, which initiated the founding of the ECSC, did not mention supranationality and talked, instead, of an authority 'whose decisions would tie together France and Germany'.[132]

Arguably, the main reason for the existence of an organization like the European Coal and Steel Community, from Paris's point of view, was the perceived decline of the French economy, which had been a matter of discussion since the nineteenth century—heightened in the interwar era—and on which all parties agreed.[133] 'From the very moment when armies are no longer the essence of the nations, it is the ability to cope with life, the capacity for work and production that become at once the essential preconditions for the independence and influence of our country,' declared de Gaulle in a radio broadcast on 25 May 1945, days after Germany's capitulation: 'Yesterday there was no national duty that had precedence over the duty to fight. But today there is none that can take precedence over that to produce.'[134] Although de Gaulle later bewailed France's exclusive fixation under the Fourth Republic on 'its standard of living', he continued to emphasize the theme of decline and to connect it to international influence and power. 'Decadence,' he confided in 1957: 'It is not that we are moving towards it, we are there, we are rolling in it.... France no longer has any national ambition.'[135]

The only way for the French right and centre to improve on what one commentator, sceptical of policies of *grandeur*, called France's 'folding seat beside the Big Three' seemed to be to rebuild its economy, maintaining access to raw materials and markets, increasing its production of capital goods, and avoiding an immediate and destructive conversion—urged by the United States— to free trade and fully convertible currencies.[136] Failure to cooperate with Germany, probably—by 1949–50—within a European structure, would not entail the perpetuation of the status quo, given Bonn's changing attitudes and Washington's desire to reconstruct and rearm the FRG, but competition against Germany in an unfavourable world market. In respect of steel production, Monnet wrote to Schuman on 1 May 1950, 'Germany has already asked to be allowed to increase its output from 10 to 14 million tons', meaning that the myth of Franco-German parity—with French production standing at 9 million tons— would have been exploded:

> We will refuse, but the Americans will insist. Finally, we will make reservations and give way.... There is no need to describe the consequences in any detail: German export dumping; pressure for protection in France; a halt in the freeing

of trade; the revival of pre-war cartels;...France back in the rut of limited, protected production.[137]

In the critical sphere of coal, iron, and steel production, which underpinned both reconstruction and rearmament, France—it was widely agreed—needed to cooperate with Germany.[138]

Against such a background, with de Gaulle himself conceding to Coudenhove-Kalergi in 1948 that no one was 'more convinced of the necessity of creating Europe'—which would mean delegating 'part of [each state's] sovereignty'—than he was, in order to arrive at a 'regulation of the German question', the slow and incremental nature of European integration is almost as striking as the unprecedented establishment of supranational forms of governance.[139] On 7 July 1944, Monnet had admitted to Macmillan that Europe's future depended on Germany and that a United States of Europe was out of the question. Agreement proved possible by the mid-1950s because the mechanisms of a common market, outlined by the Dutch Foreign Minister Johan Beyen, promised to allow the protection of French agriculture and German transfer payments to France's *départements* and *territoires d'outre-mer* in return for free access to the markets of the DOMs-TOMs, together with a wider, controlled movement towards freer trade in Europe favoured by Bonn, Brussels, The Hague, and Rome. The supranational institutions of the European Economic Community—the European Parliamentary Assembly and the Commission of the EEC—were weaker than those of the ECSC, without a veto and dependent on a Council of member states' ministers for the approval of legislation. What was more, they were, as Beyen had spelled out, designed principally to facilitate 'general economic integration'.[140] This aim, it could be held, had long been shared by political leaders in Belgium and the Netherlands, who had signed the Treaty of Ouchy regulating tariffs between the two countries in 1932. It had also enjoyed broad support in France and Germany during the 1920s and early 1930s. Other objectives, such as de Gaulle's initial desire for a French-led, 'European' integration of military command structures or Adenauer's demand for 'equal rights' for the FRG as it sought to regain sovereignty, met with much greater resistance.

Out of office, de Gaulle had summarily dismissed German calls for 'equality' in a radio broadcast of November 1949, despite the fact that he had come to champion a 'direct agreement between the French and German people', resting at first on economic integration and cultural exchange, and later on 'defence and politics'.[141] For his part, Adenauer was 'unable completely to conceal a degree of mistrust' during the negotiation of a European Coal and Steel Community, because 'he could not believe that we were really proposing full equality', recalled Monnet.[142] Mutual mistrust in areas other than the field of economic integration was common and inhibiting, with the chances of reaching agreement correspondingly reduced. 'Europe' was a popular cause and rallying point, founded on a widespread sense of relative decline and perceptions of historical self-destruction. Many contemporary leaders—perhaps the majority—believed that it was essential for European states to cooperate and to grow in order to avoid eclipse and a lapse back into conflict. The interwar question was how to achieve pragmatic, economic cooperation in the face of historical mistrust, nationalism, and ideological division. By the late 1940s, diplomatic and military cooperation appeared to have been safeguarded by the United States and ideological divisions, although not disappearing, had been focused on the Iron Curtain separating East and West.

European leaders had learned the most important lesson of the disastrous first post-war era after 1918; namely, that international cooperation was essential. In the interwar era, there was a 'lack of any international cooperation', wrote Marjolin: '*Each country strove to resolve its difficulties as if it was alone in the world.* There were, of course, certain international contacts; occasionally, one country tried to help another; but no government recognized in a relatively clear fashion the state of interdependence in which all the participants in the global economic game actually existed.'[143] Without a realistic assessment of such interdependence, the actions of one state often had a 'boomerang effect', creating unexpected consequences for each actor.[144] 'There was no international organization where responsible statesmen could meet regularly and discuss their problems,' Marjolin continued.[145] Given that the United States had refused to join the League of Nations, the United Kingdom had refused to play a leading economic and monetary role in Europe for 'anachronistic reasons', and France 'was not an economic power of the first rank', interwar international organizations and diplomacy 'rapidly lost all credit', since they were 'unable to take decisions'.[146] By contrast, the United States had taken up a leading role in the period after 1945 and had created credible international organizations. With the signature of the Bretton Woods agreement and the approval of Marshall Aid, Washington had helped to re-establish economic cooperation in Europe.[147] Yet, here, European statesmen, even in the UK, had more reservations about US leadership and saw greater advantages accruing from a regional pooling of resources and the founding of common institutions, which could set, enforce, and alter mutually agreeable regulations and restrictions.[148] To advocates of state planning, a social market economy or Keynesian economics, the simultaneous freeing and controlling of trade within a common market proved more attractive than the alternatives of protectionism or US-led laissez faire and currency convertibility.[149] In this context, Franco-German reconciliation and European cooperation made sense in the late 1940s and 1950s, just as they had done in the 1920s.

After the Second World War, France—with its need to adapt to the world market and its long-standing desire to gain access to German coal, steel, and markets—and West Germany—with its supply of critical raw materials (coke), its high technology industries (electricity, chemicals, transport) and its manufacture of machines and consumer goods—seemed to have much to gain from the concentration of industry, the negotiation of production quotas, the creation of liquidity, and the lowering of tariffs within an emerging common market. That economic objectives came to constitute the motor of European integration after the Second World War, once fascist Italy and Nazi Germany had been defeated, seemed natural to many contemporaries.

Commerce and the Common Market

Economic growth, which was widely associated with the EEC, had allowed political integration to take place during the 1950s, helping to establish a series of myths about—or distortions of—the relationship between economics, politics and the European Community. In the first two decades of their existence, the ECSC and EEC constituted a semi-protected European enclave in a US-dominated global—or 'Western'—market, easing the transition to freer trade and allowing member states to defend special interests and develop their own welfare systems.[150] There seemed to be relatively little friction between burgeoning welfare states, the European common market and global trade outside the Communist bloc. According to Paul-Henri Spaak, the Foreign Ministers meeting at Messina in June 1955 had resolved to create 'a European common market free from tariff barriers and all quantitative restrictions on trade' as an 'aim in the economic sphere', as if they 'were unaware of the significance and extraordinary audacity of their views'.[151] In part, their lack of awareness derived from the freeing of trade which had already occurred. The 'work of establishing a united Europe must be accompanied by developing common institutions, by a gradual amalgamation of the various national economies, the creation of a common market and the progressive coordination of their social policies', wrote Spaak, allowing Europe 'to retain its present position in the world', to restore 'its influence and radiance', and to ensure 'the standard of living of its people'.[152] By the 1970s and 1980s, however, the connections between such states, the EEC and the world market had become a matter of contention. Economic transformation, and shifting political understandings of that transformation, appeared to pose questions about the role of the European Community. What were the actual achievements and what was the purpose of the common market?

It is plausible to attribute the much more rapid and sustained economic growth of Western Europe after 1945, compared to the pre-war and interwar eras, to an expansion of international commerce, rather than to the creation of the European Communities. 'In truth, the contrast between the two post-war eras, which one can detect in all areas, was due principally to the policy of the United States,' wrote Marjolin, who became one of France's first European Commissioners in 1958–67 after serving as Secretary-General of the OEEC.[153] Through the provision of Marshall Aid, the US had prevented the repetition of a politics of debt and

238   EUROPEAN INTEGRATION SINCE THE 1920S

reparations, which 'had literally poisoned the relations between Europe and America from 1919 to the start of the 1930s'.[154] It had also provided the international infrastructure of economic cooperation, with the OEEC becoming 'the centre of Europe for several years' and ensuring that there was no relapse 'into the illusion of thinking that the different governments would act together in the function of a European interest' without external coordination.[155]

Commerce after the Second World War was much more open and cooperative than during the interwar period, both of which circumstances were—and are—held to have underpinned greater increases in industrial production after 1945 than during the nineteenth and early twentieth century.[156] In the post-war era, all European economies except that of the United Kingdom, experienced a growth in exports of more than 5 per cent per annum, with Italy and West Germany reaching double digits. In other words, it is possible that growth was export-led, with external trade increasing faster than domestic demand.[157] The main structures regulating such trade were international rather than European, formed as a consequence of American, British, and Soviet discussions at Bretton Woods in July 1944 and linked to the establishment of the Marshall Plan in 1947, the signing of the General Agreement on Tariffs and Trade (GATT) in the same year, the setting up of the Organization of European Economic Cooperation (OEEC) in 1948 and the founding of the European Payments Union in 1950.

Such organizations and structures corresponded to the American aims of establishing Europe as a market and a reliable set of trading partners, ending the era of European empires, and protecting European economies from collapse and the spectre of Communist revolutions.[158] They were designed—in the form of shorter-term Marshall Aid and longer-term aid from the International Monetary Fund and World Bank—to provide liquidity to European governments, businesses, and consumers in a period of dollar shortages after 1945, which had resulted from states' trade deficits with the United States; to establish more or less constant exchange rates, at least until 1971, when Richard Nixon severed the link between the dollar and the price of gold and obliged European currencies to float in international markets; and to work towards freer trade as a stipulation of the Bretton Woods agreement and as a condition of American loans, with the gradual removal of quantitative restrictions in Europe under the auspices of the OEEC.[159] By 1955, 84 per cent of quotas had already been removed.[160]

Compared to American-backed international organizations, European institutions were less important in the 1950s and 1960s, with the ECSC covering a relatively small proportion of economic activity and the EEC's abolition of internal tariffs between member states taking place gradually over three separate phases within twelve years.[161] Scandinavian economies in EFTA and the Spanish economy outside it achieved levels of growth comparable to those of the EEC (see Table 5.5).[162] The most visible consequences of this economic transformation, however, were continental, with the bulk of external trade

Table 5.5 Per capita real GDP growth 1870–1992 (annual average compound growth rates)

	1950–73	1973–92	1950–92	1870–1913	1913–50
Spain	5.8	1.9	4.0	1.2	0.2
Portugal	5.7	2.1	4.0	0.5	1.2
Sweden	3.1	1.2	2.2	1.5	2.1
Denmark	3.1	1.6	—	1.6	1.6
Norway	3.2	2.9	—	1.3	2.1
FRG	5.0	2.1	3.7	1.6	0.3
France	4.0	1.7	3.0	1.3	1.1
Italy	5.0	2.4	3.8	1.3	0.8
Belgium	3.5	1.9	2.8	1.0	0.7
Netherlands	3.4	1.4	2.6	0.9	1.1
UK	2.5	1.4	2.0	1.0	0.8

Source: adapted from A. Maddison, 'Macroeconomic Accounts for European Countries', in B. van Ark and N. Crafts (eds), *Quantitative Aspects of Post-war European Economic Growth* (Cambridge, 1996), 32, and A. Maddison, *Monitoring the World Economy* (Paris, 1995), 62.

Table 5.6 Foreign trade in France and the FRG, 1952–89 (% shares in total)

	1952–54	1958–60	1968–70	1977–79	1989
France: imports					
From the franc area	24.7	18.2	9.8	2.8	—
From the EEC	21.2	30.4	54.6	50.4	—
From othercountries	54.1	51.4	35.6	46.8	—
France: exports					
To the franc area	38.4	26.2	12.0	5.1	—
To the EEC	25.3	32.6	52.5	52.1	—
To othercountries	36.3	41.2	35.3	42.8	—
FRG: exports					
To the EEC	—	—	—	—	55.0
Other European countries	—	—	—	—	18.4
USA and Canada	—	—	—	—	8.1
Developing countries	—	—	—	—	9.6
Communist bloc	—	—	—	—	4.6
Other	—	—	—	—	4.3

Source: adapted from A. Boltho (ed.), *The European Economy: Growth and Crisis* (Oxford, 1982), 454; M. Balfour, *Germany: The Tides of Power* (London, 1992), 257.

becoming intra-European. Even former imperial powers such as France, just under 40 per cent of whose exports had gone to colonies and former colonies during the early 1950s, had come to rely on Europe by the early 1970s (see Table 5.6). The same pattern was more pronounced in economies such as that of West Germany. In these circumstances, the Conservative government of Harold Macmillan and the Labour government of Harold Wilson saw little alternative but

240 EUROPEAN INTEGRATION SINCE THE 1920s

to apply for membership of the EEC, which had become the dominant European trading bloc.[163] For his part, Mitterrand found that he was effectively locked into the European market and the European Monetary System, when he came into office in 1981.[164] Faced with a run on the franc, he briefly toyed with the idea of leaving the EMS and allowing the French currency to float. Although business was divided (with the head of Schlumberger in favour and that of L'Oreal against) and a meeting for economists at the Elysée turned into 'bedlam' ('Everyone had a different opinion'), his Prime Minister Pierre Mauroy and Finance Minister Jacques Delors were opposed, believing—in Mauroy's words—that 'Leaving the EMS would be a catastrophe'.[165] Even Delors's deputy, the young Socialist hopeful Laurent Fabius, who had earlier urged the President to leave the EMS, quickly changed his mind when he was called into the Treasury and told that the franc would lose at least 20 per cent of its value and interest rates would rise to unprecedented levels, crippling investment: 'I saw Fabius suddenly change colour,' reported Michel Camdessus, Permanent Secretary to the Treasury.[166]

A desire to expand trade was a cause, rather than a consequence, of European integration in the 1950s, even if it left open what form 'unity' should take.[167] Protectionism before 1945 had meant that small European economies had enjoyed only limited access to other markets and had benefited little from mutual cooperation to prevent recessions. 'The truth is that nothing can finally compensate continental Europe for the loss of its largest market [Germany], and the impact of this is likely to be felt by the Dutch sooner than any other people,' reported the *Economist* in 1946.[168] Three years later, the 'Germany memorandum' of Max Kohnstamm and Max Hirschfeld, who worked at the Dutch Ministry of Foreign Affairs and who were responsible for distributing Marshall Aid, concluded, largely on economic grounds, that 'A future for Western Europe without West Germany [is] unthinkable'.[169] The weakness of Germany would have potentially disastrous diplomatic consequences, but the solution seemed to be economic:

> The danger of a Germany that turns against Western Europe—if not on its own, then as an ally of Russia—remains. If this were to materialise, Western Europe would no longer have a future. The only policy that offers any future prospects for Western Europe is one aimed at making Germany stronger and, at the same time, absorbing it into Western Europe. Thus is our objective clear.[170]

It was the convergence of the Dutch and Belgian governments with the German government which convinced the ministry of the right-wing Radical Edgar Faure in 1956–57 that a common market was possible without too much damage to—or resistance from—reluctant sectors of the French economy. On the flight to Messina, the French Minister of Foreign Affairs Antoine Pinay was still expecting to say 'yes to Euratom and no to the Common Market' until Olivier Wormsier, the Director of Economic Relations at the Quai d'Orsay explained that 'it is not quite like that': 'France has already said no to the EDC. It cannot cast an outright veto a second time.'[171] Bonn's position was quite different, with Erhard 'against' Euratom, not least because the United States and Britain enjoyed 'a lead in this field', as Pierre Uri accepted.[172] By contrast, 'The German government would agree completely and Erhard would not hold out against' the pursuit of 'both approaches at the same time, Euratom on one hand and a general common market on the other', since the establishment of a European market could be seen as a staging-post on the way to the gradual and qualified freeing of global—or, at least, western—trade favoured by the German Economics Minister.[173]

A similar set of arguments were rehearsed within the Dutch and Belgian governments, where Spaak's own deputy, the Socialist Minister for Commerce and Vice-Minister for Foreign Affairs in Brussels, Victor Larock, had proposed sectoral Free Trade Areas (FTAs), including the UK, within the OEEC on two separate occasions, in November 1954 and March 1955. In The Hague, too, most ministers were sympathetic to the traditions of free trade, Atlanticism, and even neutrality associated with a maritime and imperial power. The Chamber of Commerce in Rotterdam was not alone, recalled Charles Rutten, in the European Directorate of the Dutch Foreign Office in 1956, in fearing that, 'if we get into a customs union with the French, it will be high tariffs, it will be the Continental system all over again. Where Napoleon did not succeed, Mollet will succeed and grass will grow on the quays of Rotterdam.'[174] Beyen, who had moved from the International Monetary Fund to the Foreign Ministry in 1952 as a compromise candidate of the Labour and Catholic parties, was unusual in rejecting 'the general opinion' that a common market 'would only be possible on an intergovernmental basis, and cooperation on a supranational basis only... for specific sectors'.[175]

Earlier, after the collapse of the EDC, Beyen had warned that 'we should not place much hope on further supranational organisation in western Europe' and he had seriously considered the idea of an FTA within the OEEC.[176] Yet, by 1955, he was sure that 'the OEEC does not offer the degree of control western European countries need to make sure their economies are not at loggerheads' and that 'sectoral integration does not reinforce the sense of solidarity and unity in Europe to the same degree as general economic integration': 'To strengthen these sentiments, it is vital that a feeling of joint responsibility of the European states for the common welfare should be embodied in an organisation which follows the general interest, with an executive which is answerable not to the national governments but before a supranational parliament.'[177] Spaak, who—although 'scared'—was eventually convinced by Beyen's 'daring' plan, wondered 'if the policy you propose has much chance of success... in particular if the French government can accept it.'[178] Shortly afterwards, in May, the Benelux Memorandum, which Beyen and Spaak had drafted, was toned down, removing references to 'treaties', a 'common authority' and 'European Assembly' in favour of further 'studies' in order to determine what was acceptable to Paris and Bonn.[179]

Such steps were tentative but successful. They derived from a widely held belief in The Hague, Brussels, and Bonn in the advantages of international trade. The creation of a European common market made sense in this wider context of internationalization, led by the United States. It offered governments the chance, over the longer term, to diverge from Washington in particular respects, but it also presupposed an acceptance of Bretton Woods and openness towards American companies and government initiatives. In other words, the external limits of the European economic project were maintained by European leaders themselves, partly for internal reasons.

Faith in international commerce left other questions about economic growth unanswered. The extent to which government planning and state intervention affected growth has been contested more in retrospect than it was at the time. Nevertheless, even if few contemporaries denied that a mixed economy, with an increased role for the state, was beneficial against the backdrop of a perceived failure of economic liberalism in the interwar years and the necessity of state control of the economy during the Second World War, the precise form they should take was less certain. John Maynard Keynes's *General Theory of Employment, Interest and Money*, which had been published in 1936, found a receptive audience, with its conclusions adapted to national circumstances, for example by the 'ordo-liberals' around Erhard in West Germany.[180] For Adenauer, quoting from a CDU/CSU pamphlet from July 1949 in his memoirs, 'The "social market economy" stands in sharp opposition to the system of a planned economy (*Planwirtschaft*), which we reject', but it 'also stands in opposition to the so-called "free-market economy" of a liberal cast'.[181] The idea that governments could intervene—spending, cutting taxes and making credit more easily available in order to counter economic slowdowns and raising taxes and restricting credit to control inflation—was widely accepted: post-war welfare states comprised more than 40 per cent of GDP by the 1970s, compared to less than 25 per cent in the interwar era, meaning that governments had bigger budgets—and therefore levers—at their disposal.[182]

Yet what should such levers be used for? Some governments prioritized price stability and an external balance of payments (West Germany) while others concentrated on full employment (the UK, at the cost of regular balance of payment crises).[183] Although all Western and Northern European states created mixed economies, based on varying forms of intervention and planning, levels and types of investment varied significantly, with a lower proportion of GDP invested in the UK between 1955 and 1975 (13.6 per cent)—and disproportionately in nationalized industries—than in the Netherlands and West Germany (around 18 per cent).[184] Governments had to decide what their objectives were and how best to achieve them, recalled Helmut Schmidt in his memoirs, since the market alone 'does not create social justice, social insurance, monetary reason, fiscal solidity or measured tax and budget policies'.[185] However, it was also tempting to overestimate what was achievable. Given public ignorance of economics, governments can 'awaken illusory expectations in their own people (and in their own ranks) in respect of the results of their economic policies', creating 'general economic calamity' despite 'the best intentions', Schmidt continued.[186] Although economic divergences between Europe and the USA were discernible in the immediate post-war era, there was little agreement within Europe between the governments of member states about what a European economic project should consist of, beyond a phased freeing of trade.[187]

The policies of European states, whether inside or outside the European Community, had become more and more managerial during the 1950s and 1960s, coinciding with increasing international trade, reconstruction, and growing domestic consumer demand. The EEC had benefited from this nexus. By the 1970s, national economic management was in crisis as states found that they could not buy their way out of stagnation, since attempts at reflating the economy created inflation, not growth.[188] As Brandt recalled, this shift had occurred quickly and remained mixed up with the hope of social and economic reform, which marked out the late 1960s and early 1970s: 'I said—have no fear of experiments, and we are creating a new Germany', but the oil crisis and the 'lack of responsibility of the United States' also demonstrated to progressive leaders their 'dependency on international economic occurrences'.[189] 'Stagflation' appeared to prove that inflation and growth were not necessarily connected, contradicting policymakers' assumptions that state-led growth and adjustments to taxes, credit and wages could be continued in perpetuity. The past advantages of European economies had come to an end, with productivity in France 90 per cent of that of the United States by the 1970s.[190] The productivity hike from a movement to industry and services was unlikely to be repeated: even in Italy, only 12 per cent of the workforce remained on the land by 1973, contributing 8 per cent of GDP, compared to 37 per cent of the labour force in the early 1950s.[191] European currencies, many of which had been undervalued during the 1950s and 1960s, were forced to float after 1971–73, increasing the price of exports. What was more, educational reforms, which took place in the 1950s and 1960s, had little effect on labour markets until the late 1970s and 1980s, and state intervention seemed, in many cases, to have led to budget deficits, inefficiencies and rigidities over the longer term, with nationalized companies sheltered from competition and failing to innovate.

Critics of 'Eurosclerosis'—or, in the UK, of the 'British disease'—asked whether European economies were flexible enough to adapt to the use of computers and robots and to compete with lower-wage economies in East Asia.[192] Lower rates of growth in the 1970s—2.7 per cent per annum in West Germany and 3.2 per cent per annum in France compared to 4.5 and 5.5 per cent in the 1960s—suggested that they were not.[193] 'At present European vitality is low,' admitted the President of the Commission, Roy Jenkins, in a speech at Nuremberg in December 1980: 'By comparison with our major industrial partners, we have been relatively unsuccessful in renewing existing industries and in introducing new industries based on advanced technologies.'[194] In its report of 1980–81, the Commission confirmed that 'the Community's economy has...been losing ground in world markets'.[195] Most commentators blamed national governments for the slowdown more than the EEC.[196] In France, for example, the economy had 'not adapted to international competition', in Mitterrand's opinion, expressed at a news conference in April 1984: 'Either France will show itself capable of meeting [this challenge] and, in doing so, will ensure its independence and prosperity, or it will be dragged down and head into decline.'[197] All the same, the question remained: could anything be done on the European level to make things better? Was the EEC being circumvented by global corporations and patterns of trade by the 1970s and early 1980s, creating rivalries between defensive member states, and was the formation of a single market in the late 1980s an adequate response? Many, including Thatcher, thought that the European Community could be part of the solution, as she indicated to a dinner of Conservative MEPs on 8 March 1984:

> I want to solve [the current problems] so that we can set about building the Community of the future. A Community striving for freer trade, breaking down the barriers in Europe and the world to the free flow of goods, capital and services; working together to make Europe the home of the industries of tomorrow; seizing the initiative on world problems, not reacting wearily to them; forging political links across the European divide and so creating a more hopeful relationship between East and West; using its influence as a vital area of stability and democracy across the world.
>
> That is my vision.[198]

According to the British Prime Minister's vision, 'politics' corresponded largely to external relations, but they rested on the continuing expansion of a successful European economy.

Globalization and Regionalism

Economic changes in Europe took place against the backdrop of 'globalization', a term first coined in the interwar period but passing into common usage in the 1980s and 1990s.[199] By the turn of the twenty-first century, despite regular deployment in the media, meaning that the word was 'in danger of becoming, if it has not already become, the cliché of our times', the term remained contested.[200] The political scientists David Held, Anthony McGrew, David Goldblatt, and Jonathan Perraton distinguish between 'hyperglobalizers', for whom 'peoples everywhere are increasingly subject to the disciplines of the marketplace', 'sceptics', for whom 'globalization is essentially a myth' concealing 'the reality of an international economy increasingly segmented into three major regional blocs in which national governments remain very powerful', and 'transformationalists', for whom 'contemporary patterns of globalization are conceived as historically unprecedented such that states and societies across the globe are experiencing a process of profound change as they try to adapt to a more interconnected but highly uncertain world'.[201] What did economic convergence mean in this world?

Usually, globalization described a system of interconnected economies and a level of trade which appeared to be creating convergence and a degree of uniformity in the political decision-making of implicated governments and in the daily preferences and choices facing ordinary citizens. The 'new commercial reality' was 'the emergence of global markets for standardized consumer products on a previously unimagined scale of magnitude', wrote the economist Theodore Levitt in his seminal article on 'The Globalization of Markets' in 1983.[202] 'A powerful force drives the world toward a converging commonality, and that force is technology', which had 'proletarianized communication, transport and travel' and had 'made isolated places and impoverished peoples eager for modernity's allurements', he continued: whereas the multinational company 'operates in a number of countries, and adjusts its products and practices in each, at high relative costs', the global corporation 'operates with resolute constancy—at low relative cost—as if the entire world (or major regions of it) were a single entity; it sells the same things in the same way everywhere'.[203] The main question seemed to be whether European companies and economies had adapted to these new conditions. In reality, the consolidation of regional European markets was more marked during the 1980s and 1990s than globalization, with European states trading more with each other and less with the rest of the world in 2003 than they had in 1993.[204]

At the time, many of the principal economic reversals appeared to be domestic, connected to narratives about strikes, 'overmanning', state intervention and wastefulness.[205] Giscard d'Estaing, who was President of the Republic from 1974 to 1981, described his 'enduring struggle to modernize the economy' and indicated 'the great priorities of government action' largely in domestic and global terms—'to maintain the rank and role of France in the world, to pursue economic rebalancing, to accentuate social progress, and to increase liberties and responsibilities'—alongside other objectives, 'which I kept to myself' because they were less relevant for his Prime Minister Raymond Barre: 'to organize Europe, which is starting to take shape, and to consolidate French culture, such a precious and fragile support for our threatened identity'.[206] Giscard's main opponent on the right, Jacques Chirac, who led the *Rassemblement pour la République* (RPR) and who wished to distance it from the Independent Republicans, was not so charitable, indicating in 1981 that he 'personally' intended to vote against the incumbent President:

> What choice do we have?...The result of his seven years in power can be summed up in three phrases: record unemployment, galloping inflation, and

246 EUROPEAN INTEGRATION SINCE THE 1920S

the weakening of French influence in the world. Are we going to continue for seven more years to drain our country of its substance, to drive our youth to despair, to paralyse our democracy,...to dilapidate the heritage of General de Gaulle and Georges Pompidou,...to tie a rope around our necks?...I appeal to you without hesitation to vote for François Mitterrand. [His] election does not carry the risk of a change of social system or a threat to our freedoms....It is the condition for the renewal of our country.[207]

What is striking, apart from the political volte face precipitated by the crises of the 1970s, is the inward-looking narrative of domestic failure. 'Europe' was something that Giscard had sought to organize on the side, not a solution to France's ills.

Falls in the rate of economic growth were regularly tied to inflation, but they had been brought about by more profound, structural causes. Inflation merely exacerbated such structural deficiencies, storing up problems and encouraging higher wage claims, lower investment and habits of indebtedness, which would not be wiped from the ledger in times of low inflation. Growth was not prevented by inflation: Italy's economy continued to grow at 3.8 per cent per annum during the 1970s, despite inflation of more than 20 per cent per annum in 1974 and 1976, because of a continued movement away from agriculture (17 per cent of the labour force) and continuing unemployment in the South (10 per cent higher than in the North), which kept down wages.[208] With productivity in Italy 66 per cent of the US level, there was still an opportunity for catch-up gains. Nonetheless, the 1970s appeared to show that European economies still depended on the position of Europe in the world market, with attempts to protect industries over the longer term seeming to have failed.[209] To some commentators, the decade also seemed to have demonstrated that states could grow too large, taking up to 50 per cent of GDP and threatening to destabilize whole economies through their own budget deficits or mismanagement. In Italy, notwithstanding the strong fundamentals of its economy, government mismanagement appeared to endanger economic stability, with the budget deficit having increased from 3 per cent of GDP in 1969 to 7 per cent in 1973.[210] Although the government found it easy to fund the deficit because of inflation, with creditors and taxpayers footing the bill, it did so at the cost of longer-term difficulties, with wage demands rising by 20 per cent per annum by the late 1970s and with cuts in investment because of the unpredictability of conditions and the uncertainty of returns in a period of balance of payments crises and high interest rates.

Many governments had accepted by the 1980s that openness was necessary for growth. This assumption fitted in with common practice in Europe after 1945, but it had been obscured by defensive policies and rhetoric, especially after the 1973 oil crisis.[211] As Margaret Thatcher recalled of her meeting in 1979 with Helmut Schmidt (the first visit of a foreign leader during her term of office), she 'had developed the highest regard for him' during her time in Opposition, despite their more obvious political differences: 'He had a profound understanding of the international economy on which—although he considered himself a socialist—we were to find ourselves in close agreement.'[212] When the new British Prime Minister stressed these similarities in the joint press conference after their meeting, Schmidt intervened: 'Don't go too far, Prime Minister, and do not spoil my relations with my own Party, please!'[213] All the same, they could agree on many aspects of monetary policy and they were both concerned to expand external trade.

It seemed that an expansion of trade could still work, with economies growing by approximately 3 per cent per annum by the late 1980s—a much higher equilibrium than before 1945 (see Table 5.7). The passing of the Single European Act (SEA) in 1986 was designed to stimulate such expansion. There had been earlier attempts to remove non-tariff barriers, such as the European Court of Justice ruling in 1979 against the German government over the sale of *Cassis de Dijon*, which helped to establish the principle that any legal product in one member state could be sold in another, even if it did not meet all the technical requirements. Yet the fact that the case was brought in the first place, with German regulators arguing that *cassis* was too strong to be a wine and not strong enough to be a spirit, also revealed the inventiveness of businesses and governments in

Table 5.7 Average growth rates per period in the EU, US, and Japan, 1960–2000

	1960–70	1970–80	1980–90	1990–2000
Greece	8.55	4.71	0.70	2.32
Spain	7.36	3.55	3.01	2.44
Portugal	6.48	4.80	3.19	2.55
Italy	5.72	3.62	2.23	1.49
France	5.57	3.31	2.47	1.95
Netherlands	5.08	2.98	2.20	2.88
Belgium	4.91	3.39	2.05	2.08
Finland	4.84	3.50	3.09	2.08
Austria	4.72	3.64	2.31	2.09
Sweden	4.65	1.98	2.02	1.69
Denmark	4.50	2.18	1.58	2.17
FRG	4.47	2.74	2.26	1.90
Ireland	4.21	4.74	3.59	6.62
UK	2.92	1.97	2.69	2.18
EU	4.86	3.02	2.42	2.02
USA	4.25	3.28	3.2	3.21
Japan	10.17	4.47	4.01	1.27

Source: adapted from EUROSTAT data and A. Rodriguez-Pose, *The European Union: Economy, Society and Polity* (Oxford, 2002), 33.

devising barriers to trade.[214] Germany banned imports of foreign beer which did not meet its long-standing beer purity regulations; Italy refused to allow entry to pasta not made from *grano duro*; and Belgium required margarine to be sold in cubes, not rectangular slabs, as was the case elsewhere.[215] The SEA was designed to abolish such barriers, with Jacques Delors's draft, which drew on the Philips CEO's 'Europe 1990' plan, promising that 'The Union shall have exclusive competence to complete, safeguard and develop the free movement of persons, services, goods and capital within its territory.'[216] Liberalization, or the removal of regulation for safe products in the expectation that free movement would prevail automatically, was added to 'mutuality', or recognition of other member states' regulatory standards (as in the case of *Cassis*), and 'approximation', involving the imposition of European standards on potentially dangerous products.[217]

As the European Commission's White Paper on 'Completing the Internal Market' put it in 1985, non-tariff barriers had, during the recessions of the 1970s, 'multiplied as each member state endeavoured to protect what it thought was its short-term interest': 'Member states also increasingly sought to protect national markets and industries through the use of public funds to aid and maintain non-viable companies.'[218] The author of the White Paper was Arthur Cockfield, the commissioner responsible for the internal market and a former minister for trade and industry under Margaret Thatcher. The former Prime Minister later accused Cockfield of having gone 'native', moving from 'deregulating the market to re-regulating it under the rubric of harmonization', yet she remained positive about the single market:

> I had one overriding positive goal. This was to create a single common market.... British businesses would be among those most likely to benefit from an opening up of others' markets.... The price which we would have to achieve a single market with all its benefits, though, was more majority voting in the Community.[219]

The SEA gave the Council a qualified majority vote on all European legislation required to achieve free movement of goods, persons, and capital, with the exception of fiscal provision, immigration and the rights of the unemployed. The report written for Mitterrand in December 1985, prior to signature, was more grudging but still supportive:

> An Anglo-German front has formed against French positions on three essential subjects—the internal market, monetary policies, social policies. At Luxembourg, you are not certain to be able to count on German support, as has been the case so far.... In terms of the creation of a great internal market, our positions in favour of a rapprochement of policies in all areas—fiscal, monetary, social— are still running into the free-trade approach of our British and German partners.[220]

The renewed espousal of openness imposed restrictions on policy-makers, who had to maintain full convertibility and free movement of capital: it became increasingly difficult to control capital flows or to withstand them, given that it seemed impossible in the 1980s and 1990s to re-peg currencies. Policy-makers accepted that they could not run up large state budget deficits without weakening their national currency, which floated on international markets. Italian governments were obliged to raise interest rates because banks and traders were reluctant to buy a currency which was prone to inflation.[221] Correspondingly, limits on budget deficits (3 per cent per annum) and national debt (60 per cent of GDP) were incorporated as a condition for economic and monetary union (EMU). Under these conditions, the renationalization of companies proved challenging and privatization attractive because it offered governments the prospect of reducing their budget deficits. European Community competition policy and the leverage of multinational companies prevented the sheltering of nationalized firms or areas of an economy, especially in open economies such as that of Belgium, in which 59 per cent of the value added to goods derived from direct foreign investment by 1990, compared to 22 per cent in 1968.[222]

The opening of European economies had been in train since the 1950s, with exports as a percentage of GDP increasing from 24.1 to 59.8 per cent in Belgium between 1951 and 1976, and from 8.3 to 24.1 per cent in West Germany (see Table 5.8).[223] Whether the effects of further liberalization during the 1980s were positive or not remained a matter of debate: inflation was brought under control through large increases in interest rates, raising the cost of borrowing; productive investment and profitability rose; exports increased from approximately 2 to 5 per cent of GDP per annum; wage restraint returned, but partly because of the emergence of structural employment of 10 per cent or more in

Table 5.8 Volume of exports as a percentage of gross domestic product, 1951–76

	1951	1960	1970	1976
Belgium	24.1	29.5	48.4	59.8
Netherlands	16.2	23.6	37.2	47.8
UK	14.1	13.2	15.9	19.6
Switzerland	13.3	16.9	24.3	30.4
Sweden	12.7	15.2	20.6	23.1
FRG	8.3	12.6	18.2	24.1
France	8.2	9.8	12.8	15.9
Austria	7.4	12.4	20.0	23.6
Italy	4.4	7.3	14.2	18.2
Spain	3.2	4.8	6.5	8.7

Source: adapted from The Economist, *Europe's Economies: The Structure and Management of Europe's Ten Largest Economies* (London, 1978), 3.

250 EUROPEAN INTEGRATION SINCE THE 1920S

Belgium (11.3), Ireland (12.6), the Netherlands (10.1), Spain (16.6) and the UK (10.5) between 1980 and 1985.[224] Facing international competition, mechanization and the expansion of the workforce, with the inclusion of a larger number of female workers, governments found it difficult to reduce unemployment during the 1980s and 1990s. They also struggled to reduce public sector deficits, since social expenditure—in particular, unemployment benefits and pensions for an ageing population—remained high. Even in West Germany, noted Kohl, admittedly with a political agenda to justify retrospectively, 'a deep pessimism had spread through business and the population'.[225] There was 'a lack of trust in politics and a lack of confidence in the future'.[226] In the FRG, 149,000, or 0.7 per cent of the workforce, had been unemployed in 1970 compared to 2.3 million, or 9.1 per cent in 1983. The economy had grown by 7.5 per cent in 1969 and had shrunk by 1 per cent in 1982, recalled Kohl.[227] By the 1980s, how to cope with globalization—for example in the development of hi-tech industries and the restructuring of sheltered companies such as the French electronics companies Bull and Thomson—had become the principal economic question of European integration.[228]

Because of the creation of the ECSC and EEC, together with an increased flow of information between liberal democracies, the reconstruction, and liberalization of European economies followed similar trajectories, compared to the interwar era. Even during the 1950s and 1960s, when exchange controls and continuing restrictions on trade made it easier to experiment and intervene, economies experienced comparable patterns of diversification, with the development of heavy industry in Southern Europe and chemical industries in the Netherlands and Belgium, for example.[229] During the 1980s and 1990s, with the advent of the single market and the increased market share of multinational companies, a standardization of goods and, even, services occurred. In general, the periphery and accession states of the European Union have grown more rapidly than older member states. Spain and Portugal's economies grew at 3.0 per cent per annum in the 1980s, compared to 2.4 per cent per annum in the EU-12, and they continued to grow more quickly in the early 1990s.[230] By 1995, the Czech Republic had an estimated annual growth rate of 5.2 per cent and Poland 7.0 per cent.[231] Over time, these rates of growth have led to significant changes in the incomes and living standards of citizens in Southern, Central, and Eastern Europe. In 1985, before entering the EEC, Spain's GDP per capita had been 53.8 per cent of the EC average (or a PPS of 70.5) and Portugal's had been 29.1 per cent (or 55.1), but these figures had risen to 68.4 (83.0) and 50.0 (75.7), respectively, by 2000. Ireland's GDP per capita had increased from 65.9 to 118.9 over the same period, transforming Irish citizens into one of the wealthiest populations in the European Union.[232] GDP per capita in the Czech Republic, Slovakia, Poland, Hungary, and Slovenia increased from 7,903 ECU in 1990 to an estimated 20,539 in 2015, compared to a doubling of income from 14,609 to 27,005 in the EU-15.[233] The standardization of products and the convergence of economic activities and standards of living at once facilitated and was brought about by integration, which had focused—at the policy-making level—on the removal of tariffs within the EEC and non-tariff barriers in the single market (SEA).

The main consequence of such overlapping processes was an increase in intra-European trade. For John Major, who was 'a friendly agnostic' rather than 'a starry-eyed supporter' of the European Union, it was obvious, given that 'Half our trade was with our immediate neighbours', that 'our economic self-interest was inextricably linked to the Continent', not to the United States', with which 'we shared a language' and 'our instincts and outlook were more often in tune'.[234] In 1938, the nine Western European countries of an expanded EEC had exported 53 per cent of goods to each other; by 1973, exports within the EEC had risen to 75 per cent of a much larger volume.[235] EEC states' trade with each other had expanded more than sixfold in the 1950s and 1960s, and fourteenfold, in absolute terms, by the end of the 1980s, compared to its level in 1958.[236] The significance of such shifts could be read from the trade statistics of each country: in 1952/4, 38.4 per cent of French exports went to the Franc Area, 25.3 per cent to the nine members of an expanded EEC, 36.3 per cent to the rest of the world; by 1968/70, 12 per cent went to the Franc Area, 52.5 per cent to the EEC, and 35.5 per cent to other countries.[237] The transformation of commerce was partly explained by weakening ties with former colonies, with French exports to the Franc Area dropping from 38.4 per cent to 26.2 per cent between 1952/4 and 1958/60, and partly by regional consolidation under the Bretton Woods and OEEC regime, with exports to the nine Western European economies (including the UK) rising from 25.3 per cent to 32.6 per cent. During the 1970s, trade with France's former colonies continued to diminish, but commerce with Europe—as a percentage—did not increase.

The Single European Act (1986) provided a further fillip to the integration of trade. By the early 1980s, the intra-European exports of the EU-15, including Sweden, Finland, and Austria, as a percentage of all those states' exports, plateaued at around 60 per cent, but grew between 1985 and 1992 to over 70 per cent, around which they hovered for the rest of the decade and beyond.[238] In 1995, intra-EU trade accounted for 79.9 per cent of Dutch, 66.7 per cent of Danish, 63.0 per cent of French, 59.8 of British, and 57.1 per cent of German exports.[239] 73.2 per cent of Western European merchandise exports went to other Western European economies in 2003, compared to 68.9 per cent in 1993.[240] At the same time, 55.8 per cent of exports from North America stayed in the same region, compared to 35.6 per cent in 1993. In other words, regionalization was occurring within an overall expansion of global trade. Intra-EU merchandise exports have remained at a similar level between the financial crash of 2008 and 2017, declining slightly from 67 per cent of the total to 64 per cent, together with stable trade with the rest of Europe (6 per cent).[241] Most European economies have witnessed stable levels of exports in the last two decades, despite the enlargements of 2004 and

Table 5.9 Intra-EU exports

	1995	2004	2009	2016
Austria	65.4	73.5	71.8	71
Denmark	66.7	70.6	67.4	62
France	63.0	66.0	62.1	59
Germany	57.1	64.6	63.0	59
Greece	59.1	64.2	62.5	56
Netherlands	79.9	79.9	77.4	76
Spain	68.4	74.4	68.8	67
United Kingdom	59.8	58.8	55.1	47

Source: Eurostat, *External and Intra-European Union Trade*, various years.

2007, the financial crash in 2007–08 and eurozone crisis in 2010–12, with the exception of the United Kingdom, whose EU exports were disrupted during the 'Great Recession' after 2007–08, decreasing from 62.9 per cent of total exports in 2006 to 47 per cent in 2016 (see Table 5.9).

This process of regional economic integration, in which all member states participated, initially took place under American auspices, with the Chair of the Foreign Affairs Committee of Congress reminding the new President, Dwight Eisenhower, on 16 June 1953, that 'It was in 1949 that the Economic Cooperation Act was amended to state that it was the policy of the "people of the United States to encourage the unification of Europe"'.[242] Yet it had increasingly become a European affair, encouraged by large European companies. By the early 1970s, Washington was more likely to see European firms and the EEC as competitors, with John McCloy—one of the architects of the post-war order in Europe, in his position as US High Commissioner for Germany—agreeing with Richard Nixon by 1973 that, 'from an American point of view, additional European unity was no longer desirable'.[243] What 'we had to do adroitly is to throw a monkey wrench into the Common Market machinery, for European unity in economic areas would definitely work against US interests', Henry Kissinger admitted to the Chairman of the Federal Reserve, Arthur Burns.[244] Such competition continued throughout the 1980s, with Mitterrand berating the Americans at the G7 in Bonn in May 1985 for attempting to dictate economic policy: 'It's not healthy. Just as it's not healthy that Europe's affairs should be judged by countries which are far from Europe. If this goes on, I am ready to start a public debate.'[245]

As European growth rates began to fall in the 1970s, commentators began to worry—in the words of one Reuters report in 1970—that 'companies in the European Economic Community are incapable of competing with giant American corporations under present conditions', but there is little evidence that such competition altered the balance or longer-term trajectory of European markets.[246] The number of European corporations amongst the world's largest companies rose from 108 out of 400—or 27 per cent—in 1969 to 158 out of 500—or 32 per cent—in 2005.[247] Multinationals outside the EU—taken from the 450 largest companies in the world—had about two-thirds of their sales and assets in their home country, with most of the rest—about a quarter—in the EU, increasing their sales in the European single market from 19 to 24 per cent and their assets from 20 to 24 per cent during the decade of 'globalization' between 1987 and 1997.[248] European multinationals had 78–9 per cent of their employees, 81–2 per cent of their assets, and 70–2 per cent of their sales in the EU throughout the decade. By contrast, the same firms had moved assets, staff and sales from their home countries to other member states, where 25 per cent of assets (compared to 17 per cent in 1987), 32 per cent of staff (25), and 35 per cent of sales (30) were now located.[249] Large national corporations had become more European, with a quarter of their assets and about a third of sales and employees in other EU states. The bulk of Foreign Direct Investment (FDI) came from such companies and from European banks and investment funds: in 2002, 94 per cent of FDI in Slovakia, 89 per cent in France, and 77 per cent in Germany came from within the European Union.[250] Although it is true that supply chains and networks of affiliates had become more complex (with 45 per cent of global trade taking place within companies by the early 1970s) and FDI had increased (from 6.5 per cent of global GDP in 1980 to 32 per cent by 2006), the bulk of activity remained regional.[251]

European multinationals and the business organizations representing small and medium-sized enterprises (SMEs) lobbied for the extension, consolidation, and protection of the common market.[252] By 2009, there were an estimated 15,000–20,000 interest group organizations operating in Brussels, compared to 654 registered organizations in 1985, with large multinationals such as British Telecom—one of 300 firms with their own offices in the Belgian capital—having daily contact with the European Commission 'from formal written papers to informal "chats" at all levels from Commissioner to lower DG staff', according to BT's internal records.[253] The Anglo-Dutch multinational Unilever—the twelfth largest company in the world, with 318,000 employees in 75 countries—shows how large European corporations have pursued the goal of economic integration.[254] In the early post-war era, more than a half of the firm's capital was invested outside Europe, with its twenty businesses in Africa still making one-fifth of its profits by the mid-1970s.[255] This pattern changed markedly during the period from 1955 to the end of the 1970s, when its capital investments in Europe increased from 48 to 72 per cent and its sales from 59 to 74 per cent.[256]

The bulk of Unilever's staff—200,000 by the late 1950s—and its sales had been based in the UK and on the Continent since the Second World War, accounting for one-third of the total market for detergents in Western Europe in the 1960s, but this concentration became more marked as colonial markets declined and the EEC came into being.[257] In 1957, the board welcomed the common market 'for the

254 EUROPEAN INTEGRATION SINCE THE 1920s

part it seems about to play in raising the standards of living in the member countries'.[258] With headquarters in Rotterdam and London, together with a work-force in the UK of 95,621 and 99,760 on the Continent by the 1970s, Unilever had much to gain from the entry of the United Kingdom into the EEC, with its British Chairman, George Cole, already declaring that '[we] are wholeheartedly supporters of European integration' in 1963.[259] 'I can only regret that the United Kingdom was not part of the community from the start and I hope we do not miss our present opportunity,' Cole's successor wrote to The Times in July 1971.[260] Under pressure from the American multinational Proctor and Gamble, which manufactured a smaller range of products in the company's core detergents market (186 compared to Unilever's 665 products in the late 1970s), Unilever rationalized and began to sell off factories in the rest of the world—about 70 in total—in order to concentrate its production in Europe, with 188 larger factories there, including in Southern Europe, by 1988.[261] As one internal report had stated in 1986, 'it was impossible to continue to operate the detergents business in Europe on the basis of a series of sixteen associated companies because it denied us the advantages of economies of scale which proved to be such a powerful weapon for the competition'.[262] Within the single market, abetted by its levelling of different sets of standards as impediments to trade, Unilever slowly integrated its varied groupings of companies and standardized its range of products. Integration and the creation of global corporations—in Europe—appeared to be mutually reinforcing.

The difficulties encountered by large corporations—as the bridgehead of globalization—in restructuring themselves and adapting to market conditions are revealing. Governments were slow, even within a common market, to remove non-tariff barriers, and multinational companies—even Unilever, which claimed to have been a European entity before the existence of the European Community—were slow to change. Small and medium-sized enterprises were not usually able to buy and establish affiliates in other markets, as multinationals such as France Telecom were. By the turn of the century, the company was the ninth largest non-financial transnational corporation in the world and had 102,016 employees and $73,454,000,000 of assets outside France.[263] Yet it was precisely for this reason that SMEs needed the single market, for they could not afford to circumvent non-tariff barriers and cut through a tangle of different regulatory regimes. In the EU-28, small and medium-sized enterprises accounted for 38 per cent of exports of goods by 2018, most of which stayed within the EU.[264] In Estonia, this figure was 76 per cent; in the Netherlands 64 per cent; and in the UK 42 per cent. SMEs accounted for 41 per cent of exports of goods within the EU in 2018 and 32 per cent outside it, indicating that they found it harder to sell goods outside the single market.[265]

In services, which accounted for 70 per cent of total value added in the EU-15 by 2000, compared to 50 per cent in 1970, businesses found it harder to export: in 2017, despite making up more than three-quarters of GDP across the European

Table 5.10 Exports of goods and services as a share of GDP (%)

	Goods intra-EU	Goods rest of the world	Services intra-EU	Services rest of the world
Austria	27.3	12	12.6	3.8
Belgium	42.9	16.9	15.7	7.1
Czech Republic	55.2	10.8	8.3	4.1
Estonia	37.6	11.2	18.2	7.2
France	12.7	9.3	5.9	4.7
Germany	22.8	15.8	4.5	4.2
Italy	14.3	11.3	3.4	2.5
Poland	35.7	8.0	8.2	3.6
Portugal	21.1	6.8	11.6	4.5
Spain	16.2	8.0	7.1	3.8
Sweden	19.8	12.2	7.0	6.4
United Kingdom	8.0	8.3	5.8	8.5

Source: European Commission, 'Trade in Goods and Services' (2018).

Union, exports of services accounted for only 31.7 per cent of the total, with agricultural and manufactured goods comprising 68.3 per cent.[266] With the exception of the UK, the value of exports of services was typically between one-quarter and a half of that of goods exports, with most service exports going to other EU states (see Table 5.10). Although the freedom to offer services throughout Europe is stated in Article 59 of the Treaty of Rome (1957) and in all subsequent treaties, most regulation of services occurs on a national level, creating barriers to trade.[267] An attempt by Frits Bolkestein, the Dutch Commissioner for the Internal Market, to introduce a Services Directive in 2006—nicknamed the 'Frankenstein Directive' by its opponents—was watered down after meeting resistance.[268] Nonetheless, proximity, the operations of national corporations in other EU countries and the familiarity of the European marketplace ensured that substantially more services were exported to the European Union—in many cases more than two times more—than to the rest of the world.[269] Providers of services and SMEs, as well as transnational corporations, had come to rely on, and had been integrated within, a European single market.

The existence of a Common External Tariff (CET) distinguishes a customs union from a free trade area, where external tariffs differ country-by-country. The creation of the apparatus of a common market in 1951 and 1957 allowed member states to alter the CET at short notice and in a strategic fashion. By 1971, the EEC's average Common External Tariff was 8.5 per cent, but its tariff on British commercial vehicles was 22 per cent, chemicals 18 per cent, and on plastics 16–18 per cent.[270] One of the reasons a common market was acceptable to the

256 EUROPEAN INTEGRATION SINCE THE 1920s

French and Italian governments, in particular, was its capacity to protect certain sectors—foodstuffs above all—from external competition. 'The Community's internal tariffs on goods had been abolished by July 1968,' wrote Thatcher in her memoirs: 'At the same time, it had become a customs union, which Britain had fully accepted' by July 1977 , now that the UK was on the inside.[271] The GATT rounds, which became the World Trade Organization, and trade deals between the EU and other states, have reduced the importance of tariffs: the average CET by 2019 was 1.3 per cent, yielding €26.7 billion of customs duties on €2.05 trillion of imports, even though individual tariffs can be far higher, including a 10 per cent tariff on cars and 12.8 per cent on beef.[272] Since the Single European Act (1986) at the latest, however, non-tariff barriers and variable regulations have been the main concern of the EU as a 'regulatory state'.[273] 'What remained were the so-called "non-tariff barriers",' recalled Thatcher: 'These came in a great variety, ranging from safety to health, regulations discriminating against foreign products, public procurement policies, delays and over-elaborate procedures at customs posts— all these and many others served to frustrate the existence of a real Common Market.'[274] Since 1986, the European Commission, Council and Parliament have sought to abolish, modify, or replace a multiplicity of national rules, standards, labour laws, and environmental legislation, which could be used to hinder trade.

The regulation of the market remains the European Union's primary competence, where most major policy decisions are taken at the EU level, with other competencies—taxation, education, health, welfare, justice, defence, and foreign policy—either shared with or belonging to national governments.[275] Even though EMU has threatened at different junctures to merge them, high politics remain separate from economic regulation, but economic integration and exclusion have occurred precisely because they have been largely a regulatory matter.[276] What this separation has meant for the wider question of convergence is the subject of the next chapter.

Notes

1. See, for instance, 'Fraying at the Edges', *New York Times*, 4 February 2010, which began with Benjamin Franklin's comment on the colonies in America: 'We must hang together. Else, we shall most assuredly hang separately.' For a summary of this response, ranging from the *Daily Telegraph* and *Economist* in the UK to the historian Walter Laqueur in the United States, see I. T. Berend, *The History of European Integration: A New Perspective* (London, 2016), 234–8.
2. *Der Spiegel*, 13 May 2010.
3. Ibid.
4. Ibid.
5. Ibid.
6. H-W. Sinn, *The Euro Trap: On Bursting Bubbles, Budgets and Beliefs* (Oxford, 2014), 2, quoting a *Spiegel* interview with Juncker on 11 March 2013. Sinn's own verdict was that 'this comparison is largely overblown'.
7. See, for example, Nicolas Sarkozy: 'EU Risks Being Split Apart, Says Sarkozy', *Irish Times*, 9 December 2011.
8. '"That Was Chilling": Ten Years since the Financial Crash', BBC News, 9 August 2017.

9. M. Copelovitch, J. Frieden, and S. Walter, 'The Political Economy of the Euro Crisis', *Comparative Political Studies*, 49 (2016), 811–40.
10. Eurostat, 12 (2012).
11. M. Gilbert, *European Integration*, 243–52.
12. Ibid.
13. J. Gillingham, 'The End of the European Dream', in H. Zimmermann and A. Dür (eds), *Key Controversies in European Integration* (Basingstoke, 2012), 29.
14. Ibid., 26–7. Towards the end of her tenure, Thatcher linked membership of the ERM and the project of EMU to 'the federalist express' of Jacques Delors and his Christian Democratic and Socialist supporters: M. Thatcher, *The Downing Street Years*, 742. However, the Chancellor at the time, John Major, *The Autobiography*, 660, is adamant that the recession of the early 1990s 'was caused by the unwinding of the late 1980s boom, and not by our membership of the Exchange Rate Mechanism, which did not begin until October 1990.... The high interest rates which flung the housing market and many other sectors of the economy from boom to bust came in 1989. The impact of the ERM was not the cause of a recession that became inevitable long before our membership.'
15. J. Gillingham, *European Integration, 1950–2003: Superstate or New Market Economy* (Cambridge, 2003), 269–78.
16. R. Dornbusch, 'Euro Fantasies', *Foreign Affairs*, 75 (1996), 110–25, quoted by Gillingham, *European Integration*, 269.
17. J. Gillingham, 'The End of the European Dream', in H. Zimmermann and A. Dür (eds.), *Key Controversies*, 29, 20.
18. Ibid., 20–1, referring to Giandomenico Majone, *Europe as the Would-be World Power: The EU at Fifty* (Cambridge, 2009).
19. J. Gillingham, 'The End of the European Dream', in H. Zimmermann and A. Dür (eds), *Key Controversies*, 22.
20. Ibid. Gillingham, 'A Theoretical Vacuum: European Integration and Historical Research Today', *Journal of European Integration History*, 14 (2008), 32, quotes Perry Anderson, 'Depicting Europe', *London Review of Books*, 20 September 2007, 23–41, as proof of the predominance of liberalization, viewed from the left (in contradistinction to his own neo-liberal vantage point): 'What was originally the least prominent strand of the weave of European integration had become the dominant pattern. Federalism stymied, inter-governmentalism corroded, what had emerged was neither the rudiments of a European democracy controlled by its citizens, nor the formation of a European directory guided by its powers, but a vast zone of increasingly unbound market exchange, much closer to a European "catallaxy" as Hayek had conceived it.'
21. J. Gillingham, 'The End of the European Dream', in H. Zimmermann and A. Dür (eds), *Key Controversies*, 22–3. In this context, Gillingham takes issue with A. Milward, *The European Rescue of the Nation-State* (London, 1993) and A. Milward, *Reconstruction of Western Europe, 1945–1951* (London, 1984): 'He argued that the eventual EU was part and parcel of a triumphant European social democracy; that the two were complementary and their development thus went hand-in-hand in a mutually reinforcing and progressive process. Milward's thesis puts the cart before the horse: the historical roots of the welfare state run far deeper than the negotiations which led to the eventual EU.' Although true, the point at issue here is the relationship between a desire to maintain welfare and and pursue the liberalization of European (and global) markets.
22. J. Gillingham, *European Integration*, 272. See also B. Eichengreen, 'European Monetary Unification: A Tour d'horizon', *Oxford Review of Economic Policy*, 14 (1998), 24–51.
23. J. Gillingham, 'The End of the European Dream', in H. Zimmermann and A. Dür (eds), *Key Controversies*, 24.
24. J. R. Gillingham, 'A Theoretical Vacuum: European Integration and Historical Research Today', *Journal of European Integration History*, 14 (2008), 31.
25. J. McCormick, *The European Superpower* (Basingstoke, 2007). Gillingham, 'The End of the European Dream', in H. Zimmermann and A. Dür (eds), *Key Controversies*, 31, recommends 'radical surgery', including the abolition of the European Parliament and removal of the Commission's agenda-setting powers, after which 'What was once expected to be a *Bundesstaat* should devolve into a *Staatenbund* of revived states. The authority of the new confederation should arise from a network of individual multinational treaties of demonstrated utility drafted to deal with specific problems. Thus reconstituted, a future EU can promote the ever-closer union that its peoples, at heart, may still want. It cannot survive in its present form.'
26. J. McCormick, *The European Superpower*, 84. He includes a positive evaluation of EMU: 'At the time, eurodoubters made much of the practical and political difficulties involved in completing the single market and building the single currency, but in retrospect it is remarkable just how much

progress was made once the right combination of political support and economic opportunity came along.' (87); J. McCormick, 'Why Europe Works', in H. Zimmermann and A. Dür (eds), *Key Controversies*, 11–19.

27. J. McCormick, 'Why Europe Works', in H. Zimmermann and A. Dür (eds), *Key Controversies*, 18.
28. J. McCormick, *Why Europe Matters: The Case for the European Union* (Basingstoke, 2013), 49.
29. Joschka Fischer, 'From Confederacy to Federation: Thoughts on the Finality of European Integration', speech given at the Humboldt University, 12 May 2000, ibid., 61.
30. Eurobarometer 77 (2012), First Results, 15.
31. J. McCormick, *Why Europe Matters*, 53.
32. Ibid., 59.
33. Ibid., 58; J. McCormick, *The European Superpower*, 103–4.
34. J. McCormick, *Why Europe Matters*, 47–8.
35. Ibid., 51, citing a German Marshall Fund survey, Transatlantic Trends (Washington, DC, 2011), of Bulgaria, France, Germany, Italy, the Netherlands, Poland, Portugal, Romania, Slovakia, Spain, Sweden, Turkey, and the UK.
36. Orfeo Fioreto, *Reconstructions: Multilateralism and European Varieties of Capitalism after 1950* (Oxford, 2010), pays relatively little attention to European economic integration in his analysis of the development of the German, British, and French economies, alternating instead between national policy-makers and global conditions; for approaches which integrate national and European constraints, see Emmanuel Mourlon-Druol, *A Europe Made of Money: The Emergence of the European Monetary System* (Ithaca, NY, 2012); and L. Warlouzet, *Governing Europe in a Globalizing World: Neoliberalism and Its Alternatives Following the 1973 Oil Crisis* (London, 2018).
37. E. B. Haas, *The Uniting of Europe: Political, Social and Economic Forces, 1950–1957* (Notre Dame, IN, 1958).
38. Duchêne, *Monnet*, 187.
39. Ibid., 269.
40. Ibid., 264.
41. Ibid., 270.
42. Ibid.
43. Ibid.
44. E. B. Haas, *The Uniting of Europe*, 60–112.
45. Ibid., 60.
46. Ibid.
47. Ibid., 61.
48. Ibid., 63.
49. Ibid.
50. Ibid.
51. Ibid., 103.
52. E. Dell, *The British Abdication of Leadership in Europe* (Oxford, 1995), 176.
53. E. B. Haas, *The Uniting of Europe*, 153.
54. Ibid., 155.
55. Ibid.
56. Ibid., 162.
57. Ibid., 241, 268.
58. Ibid., 283–527.
59. Ibid., 520. K. K. Patel, *Project Europe*, 15: these included the Council of Europe, United Nations Economic Commission for Europe, the European Payments Union, EFTA, and the Western European Union.
60. E. B. Haas, *The Uniting of Europe*, 520.
61. Ibid.
62. Guy de Carmoy, *Fortune de l'Europe* (Paris, 1953), 179–80, quoted ibid., 521.
63. E. B. Haas, *The Uniting of Europe*, 523.
64. Ibid.
65. Ibid., 524.
66. L. N. Lindberg, *The Political Dynamics of European Economic Integration* (Palo Alto, CA, 1963); L. N. Lindberg and S. A. Scheingold (eds), *Regional Integration: Theory and Research* (Cambridge, MA, 1963); Lindberg and Scheingold, *Europe's Would-be Polity: Patterns of Change in the European Community* (Englewood Cliffs, NJ, 1970).

67. *Economist*, 30 March 1957. On the construction of connected myths, see Kai Krüger, *Wirtschaftswunder und Mangelwirtschaft. Zur Produktion einer Erfolgsgeschichte in der deutschen Geschichtskultur* (Bielefeld, 2020); S. Grüner, *Geplantes 'Wirtschaftswunder'? Industrie- und Strukturpolitik in Bayern 1945 bis 1973* (Berlin, 2009); R. H. Dumke, 'Reassessing the Wirtschaftswunder: Reconstruction and Postwar Growth in West Germany in an International Context', *Oxford Bulletin of Economics and Statistics*, 52 (1990), 451–91; R. Pawin, 'Retour sur les "Trente Glorieuses" et la périodisation du second XXe siècle', *Revue d'histoire modern et contemporaine*, 60 (2013), 155–75.
68. See the histories of the 'people's car' or *Volkswagen* in Nazi and post-war Germany, for instance: B. Rieger, *The People's Car: A Global History of the Volkswagen Beetle* (Cambridge, MA, 2013); S. Tolliday, 'Enterprise and State in the West German Wirtschaftswunder: Volkswagen and the Automobile Industry, 1939–1962', *Business History Review*, 69 (1995), 273–350.
69. T. O. Lloyd, *Empire to Welfare State: English History, 1906–1967* (Oxford, 1970), 446–7.
70. See H. Berghoff and U. A. Balbier (eds), *The East German Economy, 1945–2010: Falling Behind or Catching Up?* (Cambridge, 2013), 1–50.
71. The figures produced by Eastern Bloc regimes were unreliable, but they continue to be used, with appropriate adjustments: see, for instance, Jeffrey Kopstein, *The Politics of Economic Decline in East Germany, 1945–1989* (Chapel Hill, NC, 1997).
72. J. R. Wegs and R. Ladrech, *Europe since 1945*, 4th edn. (New York, 1996), 251; M. Myant, 'Poland—the Permanent Crisis', in R. A. Clarke (ed.), *Poland: The Economy in the 1980s* (London, 1989), 1–28.
73. V. Giscard d'Estaing, *Le Pouvoir et la vie* (Paris, 2004), vol. 1, 158–9.
74. See, for example, Ivan Berend, *The History of European Integration*, who traces the effects of market integration on large European companies. On the history of Unilever, examined below, see G. Jones and P. Miskell, 'European Integration and Corporate Restructuring: The Strategy of Unilever, c. 1957–c.1990', *Economic History Review*, 58 (2005), 113–39.
75. See B. Rieger, *The People's Car: A Global History of the Volkswagen Beetle* (Cambridge, MA, 2013).
76. P. Marsh, *The New Industrial Revolution: Consumers, Globalization and the End of Mass Production* (New Haven, CT, 2012), 1–20.
77. H. James, 'The Fall and Rise of the European Economy in the Twentieth Century', in T. C. W. Blanning (ed.) *The Oxford History of Modern Europe* (Oxford, 2000), 202.
78. W. Brus, 'Evolution of the Communist Economic System: Scope and Limits', in D. Stark and V. Nee, *Remaking the Economic Institutions of Socialism: China and Eastern Europe* (Palo Alto, 1989), 255–77.
79. On CAP, which came to absorb most of the EC's budget and with which the EEC became associated by European publics, see A.-C. L. Knudsen, *Farmers on Welfare: The Making of Europe's Common Agricultural Policy* (Ithaca, NY, 2009); K. K. Patel, *Europäisierung wider Willen: Die Bundesrepublik Deutschland in der Agrarintegration der EWG 1955–1973* (Munich, 2009); N. P. Ludlow, 'The Making of the CAP: Towards a Historical Analysis of the EU's First Major Policy', *Contemporary European History*, 14 (2005), 347–71.
80. This historical evaluation contrasts with later accounts which emphasize the impact of integration on growth: A. Rodriguez-Pose, *The European Union: Economy, Society and Polity* (Oxford, 2002), 7–33; A. J. Marques Mendes, 'The Contribution of the European Community to Economic Growth: An Assessment of the First 25 Years', *Journal of Common Market Studies*, 24 (1986), 261–77. See B. Balassa (ed.), *European Economic Integration* (Amsterdam, 1975); A. Sapir, 'European Integration at the Crossroads: A Review Essay on the 50th Anniversary of Bela Balassa's *Theory of Economic Integration*', *Journal of Economic Literature*, 49 (2011), 1200–29. Balassa argues that the EEC had an impact on growth, but his account is more mixed in respect of actual growth rates.
81. The phrases are taken from the report, which was balanced: A. Moravcsik, *The Choice for Europe*, 171, 174.
82. Ibid., 165. These economic arguments were tied deliberately to strategic ones. Britain was 'harassed with countless problems: the narrow knife-edge on which our economy is balanced; the difficult task of changing an Empire into a Commonwealth…, the uncertainty about our relationships [with] the new economic, and perhaps political, state which is being created by the Six countries of continental Western Europe; and the uncertainty of American policies towards us': see S. Wall, *The Reluctant European*, 54.
83. J. W. Young, 'British Officials and European Integration, 1944–60', in A. Deighton (ed.), *Building Postwar Europe: National Decision-Makers and European Institutions, 1948–63* (London, 1995), 98. S. Wall, *Reluctant European*, 103, notes that the UK's and EEC's situation had changed by the early 1970s, prompting the economist Geoffrey (Lord) Crowther to declare in the House of Lords in July 1971 that 'You do not haggle over the subscription when you are invited to climb into a lifeboat. You scramble aboard while there is still a seat for you.'

84. A. Maddison, *Economic Growth in the West* (London, 1964); S. Pollard, *Peaceful Conquest: The Industrialization of Europe, 1760–1970* (Oxford, 1981); D. S. Landes, *The Unbound Prometheus: Change and Industrial Development in Western Europe from 1750 to the Present* (Cambridge, 1969).
85. R. C. O. Matthews, C. H. Feinstein, and J. C. Odling-Smee, *British Economic Growth, 1856–1973* (Oxford, 1982); C. H. Feinstein (ed.), *The Managed Economy: Essays in British Economic Policy and Performance since 1929* (Oxford, 1982); F. Caron, *An Economic History of Modern France* (London, 1979).
86. M. M. Postan, *An Economic History of Western Europe, 1945–1964* (London, 1967), 11–21, emphasizes growth, created by states and planners. The short recession in the United States was viewed anxiously in Europe.
87. R. Marjolin, *Le travail d'une vie. Mémoires 1911–1986* (Paris, 1986), 229.
88. M. Abramovitz, 'Catching Up, Forging Ahead and Falling Behind', *Journal of Economic History*, 46 (1986), 385–406; M. Abramovitz, 'The Catch Up Factor in Postwar Economic Growth', *Economic Inquiry*, 38 (1990), 1–18; S. Dowrick and D.-T. Nguyen, 'OECD Comparative Economic Growth 1950–1985: Catch-Up and Convergence', *American Economic Review*, 79 (1989), 1010–30. Nicholas Crafts and Terence C. Mills, 'Europe's Golden Age: An Econometric Investigation of Changing Trend Rates of Growth', in B. van Ark and N. Crafts (eds), *Quantitative Aspects of Post-War European Growth* (Cambridge, 1996), 415–31, stress that there were other endogenous factors at play beyond mere 'catch-up'.
89. N. Crafts and G. Toniolo, 'Postwar Growth: An Overview' and B. Eichengreen, 'Institutions and Economic Growth: Europe after World War II', in N. Crafts and G. Toniolo (eds), *Economic Growth in Europe since 1945* (Cambridge, 1996), 1–72.
90. R. Marjolin, *Le travail d'une vie*, 235.
91. N. Crafts and G. Toniolo, 'Reflections on the Country Studies', *Le travail d'une vie*, 578–9.
92. M. Jones, 'Great Britain, the United States, and Consultation over the Use of the Atomic Bomb', *Historical Journal*, 54 (2011), 797–828; W. L. Kohl, *French Nuclear Diplomacy* (Princeton, NJ, 1971); J. Chace, 'Sharing the Atom Bomb', *Foreign Affairs*, 75 (1996), 129–44; A. M. Hornblum, *The Invisible Harry Gold: The Man Who Gave the Soviets the Atom Bomb* (New Haven, CT 2010).
93. Mary O'Mahoney, 'Measures of Fixed Capital Stocks in the Post-war Period: A Five-country Study', in B. van Ark and N. Crafts (eds), *Quantitative Aspects of Post-War European Growth* (Cambridge, 1996), 165–214, shows how that capital stock was subsequently replaced at different speeds.
94. K. Larres and P. Panayi, *The Federal Republic of Germany since 1949: Politics, Society and Economy before and after Unification* (London, 1996), 5.
95. A. C. Mierzejewski, *Ludwig Erhard: A Biography* (Chapel Hill, NC, 2004), 43–120.
96. I. Connor, *Refugees and Expellees in Post-war Germany* (Manchester, 2007), 18–57.
97. The Economist, *Europe's Economies: The Structure and Management of Europe's Ten Largest Economies* (London, 1978), 3.
98. D. H. Aldcroft and S. Morewood, *The European Economy since 1914*, 5th edn. (London 2013), 199. See N. Crafts and M. Magnani, 'The Golden Age and the Second Globalization in Italy', and S. N. Broadberry, C. Giordano, and F. Zollino, 'Productivity', in G. Toniolo (ed.), *The Oxford Handbook of the Italian Economy since Unification* (Oxford, 2013), 69–107, 187–226.
99. R. Ranieri, 'Italy: After the Rewards of Growth, the Penalty of Debt', in B. J. Foley (ed.), *European Economies since the Second World War* (Basingstoke, 1998), 78–9.
100. This question is addressed by surveys of those believing that they derived 'benefits' from membership of the EU, which remained at 50–60 per cent in the 2000s, despite enlargement and the eurozone crisis: Eurobarometer, 75 (2011), 34.
101. J. Lodge, 'Loyalty and the EEC', *Political Studies*, 26 (1978), 232, 234–5.
102. L. Hooghe and G. Marks, 'A Postfunctionalist Theory of European Integration: From Permissive Consensus to Constraining Dissensus', *British Journal of Political Science*, 39 (2009), 8–9.
103. Ibid., 9, 15–18.
104. P. C. Schmitter, 'On the Way to a Post-Functionalist Theory of European Integration', *British Journal of Political Science*, 39 (2009), 212.
105. Ibid., 211.
106. Ibid., 212.
107. Ibid., 214.
108. S. Wall, *Reluctant European*, 107: this remained the case at the time of the accession of the UK and was made explicit in the communiqué documenting the meeting of the accession states with member states in Paris in October 1972: 'The Member States of the Community...affirm their

intention to transform before the end of the present decade the whole complex of their relations into a European Union.' 'The Heads of state or of Government reaffirm the determination of the enlarged Communities irreversibly to achieve the economic and monetary Union,' which had been laid out in the Werner Report (1970), the text continued: 'The necessary decisions should be taken in the course of 1973 so as to allow the transition to the next stage of the economic and monetary Union on 1 January 1974, and with a view to its completion not later than 31 December 1980.' Alec Douglas-Home commented in the subsequent Commons' debate about the possibility of a 'European Union', 'This is something that has to be worked out in each sphere of the Community's activity over the years. Nobody was anxious at the conference to use labels like "confederation" or "federation" and therefore "union" is a word which will gradually become defined over the years.'

109. For Spaak, 'it became increasingly difficult...to go along with the British' in 1955–57, since 'Success in the Common Market negotiations was virtually certain, and I was not prepared to sacrifice such an achievement to a much more modest enterprise which offered no prospect of a European political union': P.-H. Spaak, *The Continuing Battle: Memoirs of a European, 1936–1966* (Boston, CT, 1971), 236.

110. R. Marjolin, *Le travail d'une vie. Mémoires 1911–1986* (Paris, 1986), 147.

111. See D. Artaud, *La question des dettes interalliees et la reconstruction de l'Europe, 1917–1929* (Lille, 1978), D. Artaud, 'A propos de l'occupation de la Ruhr', *Revue d'histoire moderne et contemporaine*, 17 (1970), 1–21, D. Artaud, 'Die Hintergründe der Ruhrbesetzung 1923: Das problem der Interallierten Schulden', *Vierteljahreshefte für Zeitgeschichte*, 1979, 241–59, and D. Artaud, 'La question des dettes interalliées et la reconstruction de l'Europe', *Revue historique*, 530 (1979), 375; G. Soutou, 'Problèmes concernant le rétablissement des relations économiques franco-allemandes après la premiere guerre mondiale', *Francia*, 2 (1974), 580–96, and G. Soutou, 'Die deutschen Reparationen und das Seydoux-Projekt 1920–21', *Vierteljahresheft für Zeitgeschichte*, 23 (1975), 237–70.

112. N. Jordan, 'The Reorientation of French Diplomacy', *English Historical Review*, 117 (2002), 885.

113. Ibid., 877–8.

114. Ibid., 871.

115. Ibid., 885.

116. Ibid., 882. The quotation refers to a comment by Seydoux to Edouard Herriot before his meeting in June 1924 with Ramsay MacDonald.

117. Quoted in E. Bussière, 'Premiers schemas européens et économie internationale Durant l'entre-deux-guerres', *Relations internationales*, 123 (2005), 62.

118. See, especially, C. Fischer, *A Vision of Europe. Franco-German Relations during the Great Depression, 1929–1932* (Oxford, 2017).

119. E. du Réau, 'La France et l'Europe', *Revue d'histoire moderne et contemporaine*, 42 (1995), 560; Bussière, 'Schemas européens', 63.

120. In P. Stirk, *European Integration since 1914*, 35.

121. Ibid.

122. Ibid., 35–6.

123. Ibid., 36.

124. Ibid., 484.

125. Ibid.

126. Ibid.

127. P. Krüger, 'European Unity and German Foreign Policy in the 1920s', in P. M. R. Stirk (ed.), *European Unity in Context: The Interwar Period* (London, 1989), 90.

128. Ibid., 96.

129. J. Wright, 'Stresemann and Locarno', *Contemporary European History*, 4 (1995), 130.

130. On Paris's various attempts and setbacks in the coordination of coal and steel production in the Belgian, French, and German borderlands, see F. M. B. Lynch, *France and the International Economy, from Vichy to the Treaty of Rome* (London, 1997); G. Bossuat, *La France, l'aide américaine et la construction européenne 1944–1954* (Paris, 1992); S. Lefèvre, *Les relations économiques franco-allemandes de 1945 à 1955* (Paris, 1998).

131. See Frances Lynch's criticism of Craig Parsons's emphasis on pro-community decision-makers in 'France and European Integration: From the Schuman Plan to Economic and Monetary Union', *Contemporary European History*, 13 (2004), 117–20. Also, C. Parsons, 'Showing Ideas as Causes: The Origins of the European Union', *International Organization*, 56 (2002), 47–84.

132. Cited in G. Trausch, 'Der Schuman-Plan zwischen Mythos und Realität', in R. Hudemann (ed.), *Europa im Blick der Historiker*, 109.

262 EUROPEAN INTEGRATION SINCE THE 1920s

133. S. Berstein, 'French Power', and R. Frank, 'The French Dilemma: Modernistion with Dependence or Independence and Decline', in Becker and Knipping (eds), *Power in Europe?*, vol. 1, 163–84, 263–82.
134. Quoted in Frank, ibid., 264.
135. Berstein, 'French Power', in Di Nolfo (ed.), *Power in Europe?*, vol. 2, 335.
136. André Philip, 1–2 September 1946, *Le Populaire*, cited in Berstein, ibid., vol. 1, 166.
137. Quoted in F. Duchêne, *Monnet*, 198.
138. Franz Josef Strauß, *Die Erinnerungen*, 152, pointed out that 40 per cent of German industry was to be found in the Ruhr, under Allied control and subject to dismantling. Germany had therefore agreed to the Petersburg Agreement on 22 November 1949, modifying but also perpetuating the Occupation Statute, which set the terms of American and British control.
139. De Gaulle to Coudenhove-Kalergi, 30 December 1948, in W. Loth, 'De Gaulle und Europa', *Historische Zeitschrift*, 253 (1991), 637; on the delegation of sovereignty, de Gaulle to G. Palewski and R. Triboulet, 28 December 1951, *Historische Zeitschrift*, 253 (1991), 641.
140. F. Duchêne, *Monnet*, 274, 279.
141. De Gaulle, 14 November 1949, in W. Loth, 'De Gaulle und Europa', *Historische Zeitschrift*, 253 (1991), 638.
142. Duchêne, *Monnet*, 207.
143. R. Marjolin, *Le travail d'une vie*, 160.
144. Ibid.
145. Ibid.
146. Ibid.
147. M. Holm, *The Marshall Plan: A New Deal for Europe* (London, 2016).
148. See the contributions to A. Deighton (ed.), *Building Postwar Europe: National Decision-Makers and European Institutions, 1948–63* (Basingstoke, 1995).
149. J. Eatwell and M. Milgate, *The Fall and Rise of Keynesian Economics* (Oxford, 2011), 1–19; M. Bleaney, *The Rise and Fall of Keynesian Economics: An Investigation of Its Contribution to Capitalist Development* (Basingstoke, 1985), 92–198.
150. Lucia Coppolaro, 'In Search of Power: The European Commission in the Kennedy Round Negotiations, 1963–1967', *Contemporary European History*, 23 (2014), 40, examines how the negotiation between the European Commission and member states occurred during the Kennedy round of GATT in the mid-1960s, concluding that governments kept a tight grip on negotiations in the early stages, 'pragmatically [setting] limits to the actions of the Commission', guided by the principle of how they could enhance their trade interests: 'In the end, they allowed the Commission to strengthen its role because this was in line with their interests.' The Tokyo round in the 1970s witnessed a similar dynamic of negotiations between member states: L. Coppolaro, 'In the Shadow of Globalization: The European Community and the United States in the GATT Negotiations of the Tokyo Round, 1973–1979', *International History Review*, 40 (2018), 752–73.
151. P.-H. Spaak, *The Continuing Battle*, 228.
152. Ibid.
153. R. Marjolin, *Le travail d'une vie*, 230.
154. Ibid., 229.
155. Ibid., 234.
156. On the difference between Southern Europe, which had access to 'Western' trade, and Central and Eastern Europe in the restricted trading sphere of COMECON, see Bart von Ark, 'Convergence and Divergence on the European Periphery: Productivity in Eastern and Southern Europe in Retrospect', in B. van Ark and N. Crafts (eds), *Quantitative Aspects of Post-War European Growth* (Cambridge, 1996), 271–326.
157. The thesis of export-led growth is contested, but the close relationship between exports and growth, with causality working both ways, is less contestable: A. Boltho, 'Export-led Growth or Growth-led Exports? Western Europe in the "Golden Age"', *European Journal of Comparative Economics*, 17 (2020), 185–203.
158. M. J. Hogan, *The Marshall Plan: America, Britain and the Reconstruction of Western Europe, 1947–1952* (Cambridge, 1987).
159. The plan of full convertibility of currencies in Europe had been achieved by 1958. The United Kingdom's attempt at full convertibility in 1946, under pressure from Washington, had failed. Over the longer term, the IMF was to provide funds to governments, tiding over imbalances in the external accounts of individual states and averting devaluations. The regime did not prevent devaluations altogether; for example, in the UK in 1946 and 1967. M. J. Bordo, R. Macdonald, and

M. J. Oliver, 'Sterling in Crisis, 1964–1967', *European Review of Economic History*, 13 (2009), 437–59.

160. D. S. Landes, *The Unbound Prometheus*, 504–13.
161. This was the plan. In the event, tariffs were removed slightly ahead of schedule.
162. The assessment of the early effects of membership of the ECSC and EEC on trade and economic growth is complicated, depending on domestic policy-making and the varying starting points of members and non-members. Between 1950 and 1973, Spain and Portugal had the highest growth rates of real GDP per capita (5.7–5.8 per cent per annum), but from a completely different starting point, compared to France (4.0), for example. Denmark and Sweden had growth rates of 3.1 per cent per annum, compared to 3.4 per cent in the Netherlands, but even in these cases there were significant differences: both Sweden and Denmark started with a higher GDP per person (6,738 and 6,683 1990 international dollars) than the Netherlands (5,850), which they maintained until 1973 and beyond (13,494 for Sweden in 1973, 13,416 for Denmark, and 12,763 for the Netherlands). See the relevant tables in this chapter, based on A. Maddison, *The World Economy: Historical Statistics* (Paris, 2003). Also, T. Wieser and E. Kitzmantel, 'Austria and the European Community', *Journal of Common Market Studies*, 28 (1990), 431–49; L. Lundberg, 'European Economic Integration and the Nordic Countries' Trade', *Journal of Common Market Studies*, 30 (1992), 157–73; R. Bailey, *The European Connection: Implications of EEC Membership* (Oxford, 1983).
163. A. Milward, *The Rise and Fall of a National Strategy: The UK and the European Community* (London, 2002), vol. 1; S. Wall, *The Official History of Britain and the European Community: From Rejection to Referendum, 1963–1975* (London, 2012), vol. 2. S. Wall, *Reluctant European*, 67, notes that Wilson had claimed in a speech that, 'if there has to be a choice, we are not entitled to sell our friends and kinsmen down the river for a problematic and marginal advantage in selling washing machines in Düsseldorf', but his position changed once in office.
164. On the dynamics of this process, which corresponded to longer-term shifts of opinion among a 'transnationally connected monetary elite' and the shorter-term decision-making of governments in the European Council, see E. Mourlon-Druol, *A Europe Made of Money*, 132–282.
165. F. Mitterrand and P. Mauroy, quoted in P. Short, *Mitterrand*, 368–9.
166. M. Camdessus, quoted ibid., 370.
167. In the FRG, the ordo-liberal Ludwig Erhard was widely credited, as 'the father of well-being', with helping the population to 'arrive, from a catastrophic starting point after 1945, to arrive at a better situation and be able to achieve things', in Helmut Kohl's view in *Erinnerungen, 1930–82*, vol. 1, 183. Yet, as an economic liberal, Erhard often found himself closer to US and UK positions.
168. Quoted in M. Segers, *The Netherlands and European Integration, 1950 to the Present* (Amsterdam, 2020), 62.
169. Quoted ibid., 66.
170. Ibid., 66–7.
171. Ibid., 281.
172. Ibid., 269.
173. Carl-Friedrich Ophüls, 6 April 1955, cited by Uri, ibid.
174. Ibid., 272.
175. Ibid.
176. Ibid.
177. Beyen to Spaak, 4 April 1955, ibid, 273. Also, R. T. Griffith and A. Asbeek Brusse, 'The Dutch Cabinet and the Rome Treaties', in E. Serra (ed.), *Il Rilancio dell'Europa e i trattati di Roma*, Giuffrè, Milan 1989, 461–93, and R. T. Griffiths (ed.), *The Netherlands and the Integration of Europe* (Amsterdam, 1990).
178. Spaak to Beyen, 7 April 1955, ibid., 274.
179. Ibid., 274, 279.
180. A. J. Nicholls, *Freedom with Responsibility: The Social Market Economy in Germany, 1918–1963* (Oxford, 1994), 151–8, 178–205. Helmut Kohl, *Erinnerungen, 1982–1990* (Munich, 2005), vol. 2, 261, noted that the theory of Keynes had been 'taken on in many western countries', including West Germany.
181. K. Adenauer, *Erinnerungen*, vol. 1, 209.
182. P. Flora, and A. J. Heidenheimer (eds), *Development of Welfare States in Europe and America* (London, 1981).
183. The UK experienced balance-of-payments crises in 1947 and 1949, 1951, 1955, 1957, 1960–1, 1964–5 and 1967–8. See J. Tomlinson, 'Managing the Economy, Managing the People', in

264 EUROPEAN INTEGRATION SINCE THE 1920S

F. Carnevali and J.-M. Strange (eds), *Twentieth-Century Britain: Economic, Cultural and Social Change*, 2nd edn (London, 2007), 233–46.

184. M. Larkin, *France since the Popular Front: Government and People, 1936–1986* (Oxford, 1988), 391.

185. H. Schmidt, *Weggefährten*, 186.

186. Ibid., 182.

187. The different responses of European governments had become clear by the 1980s, with British Conservatives representing American-style neo-liberalism in Europe, yet it should also be borne in mind that European models remained relevant points of reference, even if ultimately rejected. Before descending into stereotypes, Thatcher, *The Downing Street Years*, 94, recalled that 'Some people offered what they thought of as the "German model". We were all conscious of Germany's economic success.... However, what might work for Germany would not necessarily work for us. The German experience of hyperinflation between the wars meant that nearly everyone there was deeply conscious of the need to keep inflation down, even at the expense of a short-term rise in unemployment. German trade unions were also far more responsible than ours, and of course German character is different, less individualistic and more regimented. So the "German model" was inappropriate for Britain.'

188. See A. Andry, E. Mourlon-Druol, H. A. Ikonomou, and Q. Jouan, 'Rethinking European Integration History in Light of Capitalism: The Case of the Long 1970s', *European Review of History*, 26 (2019), 553–72, for a qualification of the idea of the 1970s as a rupture. By 1982, when the CDU-CSU came to power again in West Germany, bankruptcies, debt, cutbacks, and social tensions all showed that Keynesianism had 'long ago reached its limits': H. Kohl, *Erinnerungen 1982–1990*, vol. 2, 262.

189. W. Brandt, *Erinnerungen*, 271–7.

190. B. J. Foley, 'France: A Case of Eurosclerosis?', in B. J. Foley (ed.), *European Economies since the Second World War*, 54.

191. *The Economist, Europe's Economies*, 3.

192. T. Abe, 'The "Japan Problem": The Trade Policy between the European Countries and Japan in the Last Quarter of the 20th Century', *Entreprises et histoire*, 80 (2015), 13–35.

193. European Commission, *European Economy*, 46 (December 1990).

194. Roy Jenkins, 4 December 1980, quoted in I. T. Berend, *The History of European Integration*, 112–13.

195. Ibid., 113.

196. D. Clayton and D. M. Higgins, '"Buy British": An Analysis of UK Attempts to Turn a Slogan into Government Policy in the 1970s and 1980s', *Business History*, 64 (2020), 1260–80.

197. F. Mitterrand, Apr. 1984, quoted in P. Short, *Mitterrand*, 395. See also J. Chirac, *My Life in Politics*, 147, recalling his feelings in 1995: 'The deleterious notion was spreading, among both the ordinary public and the elite, that France had become a minor power and was fated to inevitable decline.'

198. M. Thatcher, *The Downing Street Years*, 537.

199. P. James and M. B. Steger, 'A Genealogy of "Globalization": The Career of a Concept', *Globalizations*, 11 (2014), 417–34.

200. R. Robertson, *Globalization: Social Theory and Global Culture* (London, 1992). Robertson claims to have first used the term in 1979: 'Interview with Roland Robertson', *Globalizations*, 11 (2014), 447.

201. D. Held, A. McGrew, D. Goldblatt, and J. Perraton, *Global Transformations: Politics, Economics and Culture* (Oxford, 1999). The main hyperglobalizer cited is K. Ohmae, *The Borderless World: Power and Strategy in the Interlinked Economy* (New York, 1990); K. Ohmae, *The Evolving Global Economy: Making Sense of the New World Order* (Cambridge, MA, 1995); the main sceptics are P. Hirst and G. Thompson, *Globalization in Question: The International Economy and the Possibilities of Governance* (Cambridge, 1996); the main transformationalists are A. Giddens, *The Consequences of Modernity* (Cambridge, 1990), and J. Rosenau, *Along the Domestic-Foreign Frontier: Exploring Governance in a Turbulent World* (Cambridge, 1997).

202. T. Levitt, 'The Globalization of Markets', *Harvard Business Review*, 61 (1983), 92–102.

203. Ibid.

204. N. Fligstein, *Euroclash*, 75.

205. On the UK, see B. Supple, 'Fear of Failing: Economic History and the Decline of Britain', *Economic History Review*, 47 (1994), 441–58; J. Tomlinson, 'Inventing "Decline": The Falling Behind of the British Economy in the Postwar Years', *Economic History Review*, 49 (1996), 731–57.

206. V. Giscard d'Estaing, *Le Pouvoir et la vie. Choisir* (Paris, 2007), vol. 3, 136. Barre was Prime Minister from 1976 to 1981.
207. J. Chirac, quoted in P. Short, *Mitterrand*, 309–10.
208. R. Ranieri, 'Italy: After the Rewards of Growth, the Penalty of Debt', in B. J. Foley (ed.), *European Economies since the Second World War*, 90.
209. B. Harrison, *Finding a Role? The United Kingdom, 1970–1990* (Oxford, 2010), 7–19; B. W. E. Aldford, *British Economic Performance, 1945–1975* (1988).
210. R. Ranieri, 'Italy: After the Rewards of Growth, the Penalty of Debt', in B. J. Foley (ed.), *European Economies since the Second World War*, 90–3.
211. See especially Lucia Coppolaro, 'In the Shadow of Globalization: The European Community and the United States in the GATT Negotiations of the Tokyo Round, 1973–1979', *International History Review*, 40 (2018), 752–73, who shows how successive French and British governments were more resistant to calls for liberalization, whereas German and US administrations were better disposed, believing their national economies to be stronger and better able to withstand globalization. For a longer-run analysis of the same, L. Warlouzet, *Governing Europe in a Globalizing World: Neoliberalism and Its Alternatives Following the 1973 Oil Crisis* (London, 2018); and L. Warlouzet, 'Britain at the Centre of European Co-operation, 1948–2016', *Journal of Common Market Studies*, 56 (2018), 955–70, on the twists and turns of UK economic policy in respect of the EC/EU.
212. M. Thatcher, *The Downing Street Years*, 34.
213. Ibid., 35.
214. Kiran Klaus Patel, *Project Europe*, 190–6, places much emphasis on this and other ECJ measures.
215. K. Middlemas, *Orchestrating Europe* (London, 1995), 92–3.
216. Quoted in I. T. Berend, *The History of European Integration: A New Perspective* (London, 2016), 159.
217. L. Buonanno and N. Nugent, *Policies and Policy Processes of the European Union*, 146–50; J. Pelkmans, 'Mutual Recognition in Goods and Services: An Economic Perspective', in F. Kostoris and P. Schioppa (eds), *The Principles of Mutual Recognition in the European Integration Process* (Basingstoke, 2005), 83–128.
218. I. T. Berend, *The History of European Integration*, 159.
219. M. Thatcher, *Downing Street Years*, 547, 553. S. Wall, *Reluctant European*, 183–5, recalls that Thatcher's 'Bruges speech' in September 1988 had been encouraged by Geoffrey Howe', 'looking forward to the single market'. Although critical of the EC as an 'end in itself' in the speech, the Prime Minister was also positive about 'British involvement in Europe, cooperation with Europe and contribution to Europe', which 'is today as strong as ever.... Britain does not dream of some cosy, isolated existence on the fringes of Europe. Our destiny is in Europe, as part of the Community.'
220. Quoted in C. Parsons, *A Certain Idea of Europe*, 194.
221. A. J. Tooze, 'Who Is Afraid of Inflation? The Long Shadow of the 1970s', *Journal of Modern European History*, 12 (2014), 53–60; N. Crafts and M. Magnani, 'The Golden Age and the Second Globalization in Italy', in G. Toniolo (ed.), *The Oxford Handbook of the Italian Economy since Unification* (Oxford, 2013), 88–92.
222. P. M. Solar and H. J. de Jong, 'The Benelux Countries', in B. J. Foley (ed.), *European Economies since the Second World War* (Basingstoke, 1998) 105.
223. The Economist, *Europe's Economies*, 3.
224. R. Layard, S. Nickell and R. Jackman, *Unemployment: Macroeconomic Performance and the Labour Market* (Oxford, 1991), 398.
225. H. Kohl, *Erinnerungen 1982–1990*, 261, speaking of 1982, as he took over.
226. Ibid.
227. Ibid., 263.
228. 'IBM, Groupe Bull of France Form Alliance: Paris Moves to Help State-owned Firm Meet Japanese Competition', *Washington Post*, 29 January 1992; 'Bull? Or Albatross', *Forbes*, 30 March 1992; 'Bull's Story Is a Tear-Jerker', *Wall Street Journal*, 29 June 2000.
229. N. Crafts and G. Toniolo, ' "Les Trente Glorieuses": From the Marshall Plan to the Oil Crisis', in D. Stone (ed.), *The Oxford Handbook of Postwar European History* (Oxford, 2012), 356–78.
230. The Economist, *Europe's Economies*, 3: Spain and Portugal's growth rates were around 2.2 per cent versus 1.5 percent in the EU-12 in 1991, and around 3.1 per cent versus 2.8 per cent in 1995.
231. *European Economy*, 6 (1995); *Economics of Transition*, 4 (1996), 282–94.
232. A. Rodríguez-Pose, *The European Union: Economy, Society and Polity* (Oxford, 2002), 36.

266 EUROPEAN INTEGRATION SINCE THE 1920S

233. ECU at Purchasing Power Parity: I. T. Berend, *From the Soviet Bloc to the European Union: The Economic and Social Transformation of Central and Eastern Europe since 1973* (Cambridge, 2009), 262. See G. Fischer and R. Strauss (eds), *Europe's Income, Wealth, Consumption and Inequality* (Oxford, 2020).
234. J. Major, *The Autobiography* (London, 1999), 578.
235. I. T. Berend, *The History of European Integration*, 80–1.
236. Ibid., 80.
237. A. Boltho (ed.), *The European Economy: Growth and Crisis* (Oxford, 1982), 454.
238. United Nations, *Annual Trade Statistics* (New York, 1980–2000).
239. European Communities, *External and Intra-European Union Trade: Statistical Yearbook,* (Luxembourg, 2003), 89–170.
240. World Trade Organization, *Annual Report* (1996, 2006), quoted in N. Fligstein, *Euroclash*, 74.
241. World Trade Organization, *World Trade Statistical Review 2019* (Geneva, 2019), 57.
242. Alexander Wiley to Dwight Eisenhower, 16 June 1953, quoted in I. T. Berend, *The History of European Integration*, 33.
243. Quoted ibid., 102.
244. L. A. Nichter, *Richard Nixon and Europe: The Reshaping of the Postwar Atlantic World* (Cambridge, 2015), 123–4.
245. F. Mitterrand, May 1985, quoted in P. Short, *Mitterrand*, 402.
246. Reuters, Aug. 1970, quoted in I. T. Berend, *The History of European Integration*, 112.
247. Ibid., 58; J. McCormick, *The European Superpower*, 103–4.
248. N. Fligstein, *Euroclash*, 80.
249. Ibid., 79, referring to the database in Stafford and Purkis. The proportion had been reduced from 64 per cent of assets, 53 per cent of employees, 42 per cent of sales in the home countries of multinationals in 1987 to 57 per cent, 47 per cent and 35 per cent in 1997.
250. Ibid., 81.
251. I. T. Berend, *The History of European Integration*, 135.
252. G. Ballor, 'Agents of Integration: Multinational Firms and the European Union', *Enterprise and Society*, 2 (2020), 886–92.
253. I. T. Berend, *The History of European Integration*, 148. See D. Coen and J. Richardson (eds.), *Lobbying the European Union: Institutions, Actors and Issues* (Oxford, 2009), 6.
254. See D. K. Fieldhouse, *Unilever Overseas: The Anatomy of a Multinational, 1895–1965* (London, 1978); W.J. Reader, *Fifty Years of Unilever, 1930–1980* (London, 1980); G. Jones, *Renewing Unilever: Transformation and Tradition* (Oxford, 2005).
255. I. T. Berend, *The History of European Integration*, 126.
256. Ibid., 127.
257. G. Jones and P. Miskell, 'European Integration and Corporate Restructuring: The Strategy of Unilever, c. 1957–c.1990', *Economic History Review*, 58 (2005), 116.
258. Ibid., 117.
259. Ibid.
260. Ibid.
261. G. Jones *Renewing Unilever*, 102.
262. G. Jones and P. Miskell, 'European Integration and Corporate Restructuring', *Economic History Review*, 58 (2005), 127.
263. United Nations Conference on Trade and Development, *World Investment Report: The Shift towards Services* (New York, 2004), 276.
264. Eurostat, 'International Trade in Goods by Enterprise Size' (2020): small enterprises made up 17 per cent and medium-sized enterprises 21 per cent.
265. Ibid.
266. I. T. Berend, *The History of European Integration*, 132–3. Eurostat, 'World Trade in Goods and Services: An Overview' (2019).
267. G. Majone, *Europe as the Would-be World Power*, 116–17.
268. Ibid., 122–3; K. Nicolaïdis and S. K. Schmidt, 'Mutual Recognition "On Trial": The Long Road to Services Liberalization', *Journal of European Public Policy*, 14 (2007), 717–34.
269. Once again, the UK, with its large service sector—especially financial services—and its access to English-speaking markets, was the exception, but also had most to gain from continuing attempts to liberalize services in the EU. See H. Badinger and N. Maydell, 'Legal and Economic Issues in Completing the EU Internal Market for Services: An Interdisciplinary Perspective', *Journal of Common Market Studies*, 47 (2009), 693–717; A. Lejour, 'Economic Aspects of the Internal Market for Services', in J. Pelkmans, D. Hanf, and M. Chang (eds), *The EU Internal Market in Comparative Perspective: Economic, Political and Legal Analyses* (Brussels, 2008), 115–37.

270. M. J. Dedman, *The Origins and Development of the European Union, 1945–95* (London, 1996), 113.
271. M. Thatcher, *The Downing Street Years*, 553.
272. European Commission, 'EU Customs Union: Facts and Figures' (2019); 'Brexit: How Will the New Tariff System Work', BBC News, 13 March 2019.
273. On the regulatory state, see G. Majone, 'The Rise of the Regulatory State in Europe', *West European Politics*, 17 (1994), 77–101; G. Majone, *Regulating Europe* (London, 1996), 9–82; P. Genschel and M. Jachtenfuchs, *Beyond the Regulatory Polity? The European Integration of Core State Powers* (Oxford, 2013).
274. M. Thatcher, *The Downing Street Years*, 553.
275. L. Buonanno and N. Nugent, *Policies and Policy Processes of the European Union* (Basingstoke, 2013), 13.
276. British Conservatives especially have felt threatened by this possibility. Thatcher, *The Downing Street Years*, 690–1, recalled, with considerable hindsight, that the 'anchoring' of the pound to the deutschmark, even before pound sterling's entry into the ERM, was a 'strangely appropriate' metaphor: 'for if the tide changes and you are anchored, the only option to letting out more chain as your ship rises is to sink by the bows; and in an ERM where revaluations were ever more frowned upon there was no more chain to let out. Which leads on to EMU.' In opposing EMU, Nigel Lawson and Thatcher 'were at one', with Lawson's lecture at Chatham House in January 1989 'the most powerful critique of the whole concept': 'It is clear that economic and monetary union implies nothing less than European government—albeit a federal one—and political union: the United States of Europe.' 'That is simply not on the agenda now, nor will it be for the foreseeable future,' Lawson had declared. Control of monetary policy was a central tenet of Thatcherism, but there is little indication, here, why such a policy could not be run in a joint, limited fashion. Lawson himself had earlier argued for entry into the ERM precisely because pound sterling was linked to the deutschmark and other European currencies, despite 'floating', in theory.

6

Living Europe

To what extent do Europeans feel, or believe, that their outlook and lived experiences are similar? This question, on which political integration depends, is difficult to answer, not least because emotions and attitudes are elusive and varied.[1] Many scholars have attempted to answer it. 'Europe is not just a cluster of symbols,' writes John McCormick: 'arguably more telling as an indicator of "Europe" has been the growth of a European consciousness, and of a sense that there is a set of political, economic and social norms, interests and values that define Europe and the European experience, that explain European public preferences and proclivities, that drive the attitudes of Europeans towards each other and towards others, that guide European views about their place in the world, and that collectively might be understood as Europeanism.'[2] For McCormick, changing attitudes to the state, nationalism and citizenship, a shared political culture, welfare, similar family structures, multiculturalism, secularism, rights, and 'working to live' are common points of reference for contemporary Europeans, helping to unite them 'in diversity'.[3]

Historians have been keen to provide proofs of convergence. 'Is a European society emerging before our very eyes?' asked Hartmut Kaelble in 1987: 'Does it have different structures and ways of life from industrial societies in America and Asia?'[4] His conclusion was that there had been social convergence, 'beyond the economic integration of markets and a political integration of institutions', in eight respects: the history of the family, patterns of employment, big business, social mobility and education, social equality and inequality, urbanization, the welfare state and labour conflict.[5] By 2009, Kaelble was more cautious, admitting that he lacked 'adequate empirical research on the identification with European diversity', with some trends reinforcing and others undermining 'identification with European norms and lifestyles'.[6] What could still be said was, first, that there remained significant instances of social integration 'in important fields such as work, health, migration, education, urban life, social welfare programs and media'; second, 'European lifestyles have become increasingly internationalized' since the 1950s and 1960s, with 'more consumer goods...imported from other European countries' rather than the United States or East Asia and with more citizens travelling, studying, working, marrying, and retiring elsewhere in Europe; and, third, 'the representation of other European countries has changed', given the gradual erosion of citizens' experiences and memories of war.[7] For the French historian René Girault, it has proved possible on this basis to distinguish

European Integration since the 1920s: Security, Identity, and Cooperation. Mark Hewitson, Oxford University Press.
© Mark Hewitson 2024. DOI: 10.1093/oso/9780198915942.003.0007

between a *Europe vécue* (norms, lifestyles, solidarity), *Europe pensée* (debates about Europe) and *Europe voulue* (European institutions in the future).[8]

The sociologist Zygmunt Bauman has been more sceptical about a shared set of values, experiences, and social conditions, quoting the avant-garde Polish poet Alexander Wat, 'who was shuffled between the revolutionary barricades and the gulags that spattered the continent of Europe in his lifetime and [who] had ample opportunity to taste in full the sweet dreams and the bitter awakenings of the past century—notorious for its abundance of hopes and wretchedness of frustrations'.[9] As he 'scanned the treasure boxes and rubbish bins of his memory to crack the mystery of the "European character"', asking 'What would a "typical European" be like?', he fashioned an ironic reply: '"Delicate, sensitive, educated, one who won't break his word, won't steal the last piece of bread from the hungry and won't report on his inmates to the prison guard..." And then added, on reflection, "I met one such man. He was an Armenian."'[10] In the absence of shared values, ways of life or social solidarity could have bound Europeans together, but they had been hollowed out:

> Modern fears were born during the first bout of deregulation-cum-individual-ization, at the moment when the kinship and neighbourly bonds between people, apparently eternal or at least present since time immemorial, were loosened or broken. The solid-modern mode of fear management tended to replace the irreparably damaged 'natural' bonds with their artificial equivalents in the form of collectives unified by shared daily routines; *solidarity* took over from *belonging* as the main shield against an increasingly hazardous life.
>
> The dissipation of solidarity spelled the end of the solid-modern fashion of fear management. The turn has now come for the modern, artificial, adminis-tered protections to be loosened, dismantled or otherwise broken. Europe, the first to undergo the modern overhaul and the first to run the whole spectrum of its sequels, is now going through 'deregulation-cum-individualization mark two'—though this time not of its own choice, but succumbing to the pressure of global forces it can no longer control or hope to check.[11]

Xenophobia and racism, rather than multiculturalism, were more likely to be the result of this 'deregulation-cum-individualization' under the pressure of global-ization: 'Paradoxically, the more that is left locally of the "cradle to grave" protections now everywhere under assault, the more attractive become xenopho-bic outlets for the gathering feelings of imminent danger', for example in Scandinavia.[12] Unemployment, which affected a minority but threatened many, left individuals feeling superfluous, useless, and disposable, likely to fall into 'the black hole of the underclass'.[13] By the mid-1970s, 'blissful unconcern about life risks' gave way to the issue of 'insecurity', as citizens foresaw their own exclusion, possibly for good: 'there is nowadays no line separating the included from the

270 EUROPEAN INTEGRATION SINCE THE 1920s

(potentially) excluded, and most certainly no tight and impermeable (secure) border keeping the two categories apart'.[14] The question, here, is where did these changes leave the idea of the welfare state? To what extent have Bauman's bleak predictions about the effects of individualization, deregulation, and globalization been borne out by events? This chapter investigates the putative bases of social convergence, shared experience, and solidarity, which have been put forward as a corrective to economic inequalities and as a key to political integration.

The European Social Model

The British sociologist Anthony Giddens agrees that the 'welfare state is embattled', even though the idea of a 'golden age' in the 1960s and 1970s, 'when there was good economic growth, low unemployment, social protection for all' and a feeling of security on the part of citizens, is misleading.[15] For Spain, Portugal, Greece, and the accession states of Central and Eastern Europe, 'there was no golden age at all' and, for states with advanced welfare systems, there was mass production and bureaucratic hierarchies, 'where management styles were often autocratic and many workers were in assembly-line jobs', few women had careers and only a small minority went to university.[16]

The notion of a 'European Social Model' (ESM)—characterized by 'a developed and interventionist state, funded by relatively high levels of taxation', 'a robust welfare system, which provides effective social protection, to some degree for all citizens, but especially for those most in need', and 'the limitation, or containment, of economic and other forms of inequality'—gained credence during the post-war era and served as a point of reference for all European states.[17] However, it has been put under strain by globalization, which has highlighted the need to be competitive in world markets and has pushed down wages; by a changing social structure, including the rise of new classes (with 'Big Mac' and 'Apple Mac' workers making up more than 20 per cent of the workforce in both cases) and immigration (with 5.3 per cent of the population in Spain, 8.3 per cent in the UK, and 10 per cent in France and the Netherlands born abroad in 2002); and by the perceived cost of social spending.[18] The 'trilemma' facing Gøsta Esping-Andersen's 'three worlds of welfare capitalism'—the Nordic type (high taxation and extensive public-sector employment), the conservative or corporatist type in Germany, France, and Italy (payroll contributions) and the liberal or 'Anglo-Saxon' type ('residual' welfare and lower taxation)—is how to attain balanced budgets, economic equality, and a high level of employment.[19] The Nordic countries have achieved equality and employment, but at the expense—in Esping-Andersen's view—of high levels of public-sector borrowing. The UK has created private-sector jobs and maintained fiscal discipline but failed to avoid widespread poverty. France, Italy, and—around the turn of the century—Germany experienced poor growth of employment, even though they have limited inequality and more or less balanced their budgets. In 2004, 93 million adults under the age of 60—out of the EU's population of 455 million—were economically inactive and 70 million (20 per cent of the population) were over 60.[20] GDP per capita was 70 per cent of the US level, with one-third of the shortfall resulting from shorter hours, one-third from lower levels of employment, and one-third from lower productivity, which had lagged behind the United States' rate of growth by 1 per cent per annum over the previous decade.[21] In these circumstances, could the welfare state survive and could a European Social Model be said to exist?

In Giddens's judgement, Esping-Andersen's 'trilemma' is chimerical: 'The recent history of Scandinavia shows that it is in fact possible to have sound public finances, low inequality and high levels of employment at the same time.'[22] The Nordic states experienced average rates of economic growth of 2.9 per cent during the 1990s and early 2000s, close to that of the United States, and productivity growth of 2.4 per cent, compared to between 0.5 and 1.6 per cent in Germany, France, and Italy, which the sociologist labelled 'blocked societies', where the need for reform was widely recognized but prevented by 'natural conservatism' or vested interests.[23] The former also had an employment rate of 71 per cent, compared to 62 per cent in the 'blocked' group. Sweden, Denmark, and Finland have embraced reform, adopting a policy of 'flexicurity' (flexibility and security), providing re-training and social security for the unemployed, who are obliged to take jobs offered if their 'job search is unsuccessful after a certain period', while maintaining family-friendly policies and the highest level of income equality in the world.[24] The records of other EU member states, measured by the criteria of the Lisbon Agenda (2000), which had emphasized economic growth, productivity, flexibility, employment, and the knowledge economy, were much patchier: Italy's economy, which had been the same size as the UK's in 1987, was about 80 per cent of its size by 2005, with knock-on effects for its social security system, which lacked comprehensive unemployment insurance and channelled large sums to pensioners (retiring on average at the age of fifty-seven); France spent 'virtually as much as Sweden does on social policy but has three to four times as much poverty', in part because of high unemployment (hovering around 10 per cent since 1983) and a divided labour market, with legal protections for those already in jobs—leading to 25 per cent of redundancies going to court—and with 70 per cent of new entrants on fixed-term contracts, without such protection.[25] Sixty-three per cent of French respondents said that they were 'worried' by globalization in 2002.[26] Ten per cent were 'confident' and 2 per cent 'enthusiastic'.[27]

Such anxieties and struggles have not led to the abandonment of the welfare state, which continues to exist in a variety of forms throughout the continent, even in the UK, whose supposedly 'residual' system drew on a level of taxation equivalent to that of Germany by 2005 and included, in the form of the NHS, 'the most "socialized" system of medicine in Europe'.[28] Indeed, writes Giddens,

272   EUROPEAN INTEGRATION SINCE THE 1920s

'The *social model* (in its diversity) is a basic part of the reason for the existence of the EU', which sounds odd insofar as 'Europe's welfare systems largely developed independently of the EU institutions and the EU still lacks power over them', yet 'Europeans as a whole, as surveys show, see the care and protection offered by welfare provisions as central to their lives', in contrast to the United States, where 'quite different attitudes' predominate.[29] The challenge is to transform a Keynesian system, ignoring its own economic effects and resting on traditional patterns of work and family life, into a more flexible basis for 'competitiveness in a post-industrial context'.[30] A right-wing Gaullist politician such as Jacques Chirac, who became President of the Republic in 1995 and resolved, along with his Prime Minister Alain Juppé, to remove the 'bottomless' hole in France's social budget, was nonetheless convinced that, since 1945, 'the system had been part of the identity of France and the heritage of the French'.[31] 'Neither the slowing of economic growth that had occurred from 1974 nor the inexorable growth of unemployment had impeded social progress,' he went on, even though the social system—'with 3 million unemployed, 5 million victims of social exclusion, and 6.5 million people living in troubled neighbourhoods'—had been put under pressure and faced 'bankruptcy'.[32] The task which Chirac and Juppé set themselves was to restore the system, not dismantle it, albeit by 'attacking' the causes of poverty: 'the fight against social fracture ... arose out of a vision of man and of society. I reject intransigent individualism and liberalism just as much as I reject passively giving support to people in a way that enshrines poverty in statute.'[33] Their emphasis on creating a new 'social model', which emphasized employment, housing, access to schooling and medical care, and aid to troubled neighbourhoods, was consistent with an historical attachment to a welfare or social state.[34]

There is considerable evidence indicating majority support in Europe for social spending and equality. One poll conducted by a US magazine in 1990 found that 80 per cent of Italians and Austrians, and 60–70 per cent of Britons and Germans thought that it was necessary for their government to reduce disparities of income, compared to 29 per cent of Americans.[35] This difference has persisted, with French approval for a welfare safety net increasing from 51 to 64 per cent (1991–2011), German approval from 41 to 62 per cent, British approval fluctuating between 55 and 62 per cent, and American approval remaining at around 35 per cent (see Table 6.1). It is worth noting that these evaluations had little or no relation to citizens' views of the workings of the market, their own country's economy or their own circumstances. In 2007, between 55 and 75 per cent of Europeans 'completely' or 'mostly' agreed that they were better off in a free market economy.[36] Even after the financial crash of 2007–08 and the eurozone crisis of 2010–12, 74 per cent of Germans polled in 2012 thought that their personal economic situation was good, up from 67 per cent in 2008.[37] 65 per cent of French and 64 per cent of British respondents thought the same, compared to 68 and 72 per cent, respectively, in 2008, which contrasted with greater pessimism

Table 6.1 Attitudes to government intervention and equality: safety net vs freedom

	1991 Safety net*	2002 Safety net	2011 Safety net	2002 Freedom**	2011 Freedom	1991 Care***	2002 Care
FRG	41 (67 GDR)	57	62	39	36	45 (64 GDR)	45
France	51	62	64	36	36	62	50
UK	59	62	55	33	38	62	59
Italy	64	71	—	24	—	66	48
Czech Republic	35	58	—	40	—	67	57
Poland	73	64	—	31	—	56	69
Bulgaria	60	67	—	29	—	81	67
USA	36	34	35	58	58	23	29
Canada	—	52	—	43	—	—	—
Japan	—	50	—	45	—	—	—
South Korea	—	71	—	27	—	—	—

* Safety net: 'The government guarantees no one is in need.'

** Freedom: 'Free from government interference to pursue goals.'

*** Care: 'Government has a responsibility to care for the poor.'

Source: Pew Global Attitudes Project, 'Views of a Changing World' (Washington, DC, 2003), 105–6; Pew Global Attitudes Project, 'The American-Western European Values Gap' (Washington, DC, 2011), 1.

274 EUROPEAN INTEGRATION SINCE THE 1920s

in Poland (45 per cent, down from 63 per cent in 2008), the Czech Republic (50 per cent), Spain (57 per cent, down from 68 per cent), and Greece (17 per cent).[38] These figures differed from the same respondents' assessment of the national economic situation, which only a minority believed to be good by 2012.[39] Although the percentage of respondents who thought that 'the government has a responsibility to care for the poor' diminished during the 1990s—from 62 to 50 per cent in France, 66 to 48 per cent in Italy, 62 to 59 per cent in the UK, and 67 to 57 per cent in the Czech Republic—it was still much higher than that of the USA (23–9 per cent). By contrast, those believing that individuals should be free to pursue their goals without government interference was lower in Europe (36–9 per cent in the FRG, 36 per cent in France, 33–8 per cent in the UK) than in the United States (58 per cent). A majority of Europeans thought—in 2002—that the government should be responsible for ensuring that older people had sufficient income to maintain their standard of living in retirement (81 per cent in Spain, 57–64 per cent in the UK, France, FRG, and Italy), but only a minority of Americans thought so (44 per cent).[40] Given such attitudes, it is not surprising that European governments allocate a larger proportion of GDP to social spending (Table 6.2).

There have been varying patterns of social spending in Europe. Some high-income states with long traditions of social expenditure, such as Sweden, Austria, and the Federal Republic of Germany have maintained a more or less constant level of spending at around 25 per cent of GDP. Others, such as France, Denmark, and Belgium, have increased their social spending by 5 per cent or more since 1990, hovering around 30 per cent by 2019. The UK and Italy, whose GNI per capita has declined relative to high-income countries, have followed different trajectories, with the former increasing spending under Labour governments before cutting it under the Coalition and Conservative governments after 2010, and with the latter increasing its social expenditure, in common with other Mediterranean countries (Spain, Portugal, Greece), whose incomes have risen more rapidly. The same is true of Central European states such as Poland and the Czech Republic, which kept their social budgets low in the uncertain decade after 1990 but then increased the proportion of GDP allocated to health, pensions, sickness, and unemployment benefits as their economies continued to catch up with the EU average: Poland had a GNI per capita of $10,003 in 2000, devoting only 14.2 per cent of GDP to social expenditure, contrasting with 21.3 per cent of a much larger GDP ($32,433 per capita) by 2019. The United States's social budget increased to 18.7 per cent by 2019, but from a lower starting point (13.2 per cent). Together with Canada and Australia, it spends up to 10 per cent less than equivalent states in the EU. Japan's social spending—as a percentage of GDP—is currently at the same level as that of the UK, Poland, and Portugal, but it was only 10.9 per cent in 1990, or roughly the same level as South Korea now. Most middle and low-income states allocate far lower proportions of GDP to social

LIVING EUROPE 275

Table 6.2 Public social spending (% of GDP) and gross national income ($ per capita)

	1990 Social spend	2000 Social spend	2000 GNI	2010 Social spend	2019 Social spend	2019 GNI
France	24.4	27.7	26,518	31.1	31.0	50,246
Finland	23.3	22.6	26,629	27.4	29.1	51,869
Belgium	24.6	23.7	28,514	28.4	28.9	55,375
Denmark	21.9	23.8	28,026	29.6	28.3	62,090
Italy	20.6	22.6	26,981	27.0	28.2	44,749
Austria	23.1	25.7	29,133	27.6	26.9	58,957
Germany	21.4	25.5	27,308	26.0	25.9	57,411
Sweden	26.9	26.5	29,649	25.9	25.5	56,664
Spain	19.1	19.5	21,446	24.9	24.7	42,275
Greece	15.7	17.8	—	24.8	24.0	30,616
Portugal	12.2	18.5	18,579	24.5	22.6	35,911
Poland	14.2	20.2	10,003	20.7	21.3	32,433
UK	14.9	16.9	26,523	23.3	20.6	47,650
Czech Rep	14.0	17.9	15,900	19.6	19.2	40,370
USA	13.2	14.1	36,770	19.1	18.7	66,022
Canada	17.5	15.7	28,593	17.6	18.0	50,011
Australia	13.1	18.2	27,460	16.6	—	51,960
Japan	10.9	15.4	27,225	21.2	22.3	43,919
S. Korea	2.6	4.4	18,415	4.9	12.2	43,099
Mexico	3.1	4.4	9,942	7.4	7.5	20,143

Source: OECD, Gross National Income and Social Expenditure Database (1990–2019).

spending—between 3.1 and 7.5 per cent in Mexico, for instance. The European Social Model is to be understood in this context: it has endured despite the different economic trajectories of Mediterranean, Scandinavian, Western, Central, and Eastern European states.

Welfare states in Europe have deep, entangled roots. Industrialization had begun in Britain, Belgium, Northern France, and parts of Germany in the late eighteenth and early nineteenth centuries, fifty years or so before the United States and almost a century before Russia. Partly as a consequence, only Western and Central European countries became industrial economies in the full sense, where the industrial sector (extractive industries, manufacturing, construction) was larger—between the mid-nineteenth century and 1970—than the tertiary sector (commerce, banking and insurance, transport and communication, social and personal services, public administration, and the military).[41] In Britain and Belgium, industry occupied 48 and 32 per cent and the service sector 28 and 13 per cent of the workforce, respectively, by the 1840s (see Table 6.3).[42] By 1961, services (49 per cent) had surpassed industry (48 per cent) in the UK, and they were on the verge of doing so in Belgium (45 per cent versus 47 per cent). In France, the industrial sector had exceeded the size of the tertiary sector by the 1840s and remained roughly the same size until the early 1960s and, in Germany, services only became the largest sector by the 1970s. In countries such as Sweden,

Table 6.3 Industrial and service sectors in selected countries (% of workforce)

	1840s		1880/81		1920/1		1950/1		1960/1		1970/1		1980/1	
	Ind.	Serv.	Ind.	Serv.	Ind.	Serv.	Ind.	Serv.	Ind.	Serv.	Ind.	Serv.	Ind.	Serv.
Belgium	32	13	36	24	47	32	49 (1949)	39	47	45	44	50	35	62
Denmark	26 (1855)	18	26	22	29	38	35	41	36	47	37	52	29	63
France	26	22	26 (1886)	27	29	29	34 (1954)	33	38 (1962)	38	40	46	36	55
Germany	24	20	34 (1882)	23	41 (1925)	28	45	33	48	39	49	43	45	49
Greece	—		—		19	24	18	25	19	25	25	35	31	41
Italy	—		25	13	25	19	32	26	40	31	44	37	38	48
Netherlands	25	30	31 (1889)	36	36	40	37 (1947)	42	42	46	39	54	32	62
Portugal	—		25 (1890)	10	18 (1930)	31	25	27	29	28	33	37	36	36
Spain	—		11 (1877)	19	22	20	27	26	33	27	37	34	36	45
Sweden	—		17	15	35	21	41	39	45	41	40	52	32	62
UK	48	28	52	33	49	44	49	43	48	49	45	52	38	59
USA	—		20	33	32	45	33	55	32	60	33	61	31	66
Canada	—		—		29	37	34	46	32	54	—		29	66
Australia	—		29 (1890)	40	34 (1926)	42	38 (1948)	45	39	48	37	55	31	62
Japan	—		7	11	21	24	22	30	29	38	35	34	35	54

Source: H. Kaelble, 'Was Prometheus Most Unbound in Europe?', *Journal of European Economic History*, 15 (1986), 75–8.

Denmark, Spain, and even Portugal, there were periods when industry was the largest sector. Although the USA, Canada, and Australia all had large industrial workforces by the 1920s, these occupational groups remained significantly smaller than the service sector. Japan followed a different trajectory: its industrial sector briefly surpassed the service sector around 1970, but agriculture, industry, and services each occupied about one-third of the labour force, at a time when agriculture employed less than 5 per cent in the industrialized regions of Europe. The social and political consequences of shifts in the occupational structure were not straightforward, given the heterogeneity of the service sector and overlapping effects of confession, urban geography (small towns and large cities), regional affiliations and gender, with the franchise only extended to women between 1918–19 (in the UK and Germany, for instance) and 1945 (in France). Nonetheless, they created class affiliations and political cleavages, on which the 'social question' and support for the welfare state were based and which were less relevant elsewhere in the world.[43] In 1950, one survey found that 27 per cent of respondents in France called themselves 'working-class', 23 per cent 'middle-class' (classes moyennes), 8 per cent 'bourgeois', and 14 per cent 'peasant'; in the United States in the same year, 45 per cent thought themselves 'middle-class', 10 per cent 'working-class', and 5 per cent 'upper-class'.[44]

Class consciousness, even in the 1950s and 1960s, proved difficult to define. Marx's references to capital and means of production remained influential, but most observers added Weberian criteria of status, party organization, and life chances, education and skills in a market.[45] In the section of his memoirs entitled 'Das ökonomische Sein bestimmt das Bewußtstein', which he had adapted from Marx, Helmut Schmidt went on to concede that, 'In truth, all kinds of factors have an effect on our consciousness and on public opinion', even if it was also true that 'our political predilections and dislikes are in fact strongly influenced by our economic situation'.[46] Liberal intellectuals such as Ralf Dahrendorf, in *Class and Conflict in Industrial Society* (1957) and Raymond Aron, in *La Lutte des classes* (1964), continued to treat class consciousness seriously, partly to prevent their left-wing counterparts—inspired by reform-minded Communists, such as the Yugoslav writer and politician Milovan Djilas, whose *New Class* was published in English in 1957—dominating the field.[47] Yet how likely were citizens to conceive of themselves, their position in society and their politics in class terms? For many Western Europeans, it was hard to work out what was going on in the Eastern Bloc, but the egalitarian nature of society seemed undeniable: one study from 1963, published by the historian J. P. Nettl, revealed that cabinet ministers in the USSR earned $9,125, factory managers $6,240, a master foreman $5,028, and technician $3,724, more than a lawyer ($1,376) or a doctor ($1,260), whose salaries were similar to those of coal miners ($1,092).[48] In the West, greater inequality and class consciousness prevailed. Studies of the UK in the 1950s, 1960s, and 1970s showed that as much as 93 per cent of the population thought

278 EUROPEAN INTEGRATION SINCE THE 1920S

that class existed.[49] Twenty-five per cent believed that a class system was inevitable, 58 per cent thought that wealth was the main determinant of class, 15 per cent education. A series of studies by the Oxford sociologist John Goldthorpe in the 1960s and 1970s—*The Affluent Worker* (1968–69), *The Social Grading of Occupations* (1974), *Social Mobility and Class Structure in Modern Britain* (1980)—showed that such beliefs were tied to social immobility and a lack of opportunity, with the Nuffield Social Mobility Study demonstrating in 1972 that sons of workers stood four times less chance of reaching top positions than the sons of those in such positions.[50] In France, studies discovered similar obstacles and class-based advancement. In 1953, 78 per cent of senior managers were themselves sons of middle and senior managers, white-collar workers, or professionals (see Table 6.4).[51] By 1977, the figure had risen to 94 per cent, according to another survey.[52] In this context, most citizens seem, with some justification, to have believed in the existence of a class 'system'. Even in Sweden, with its longer history of Social Democratic governments and an emphasis on egalitarianism, 97 per cent of respondents surveyed in the early 1970s thought that class was relevant in a social, economic, and cultural sense, albeit with a higher percentage (38 per cent) deeming education to be crucial.[53]

Although social mobility was greater in many European countries during the 1950s and 1960s than it was after the 1970s, because of the drift away from agriculture, the enduring nature of the class system and the long history of the formation of working-class milieux in towns, cities, and industrial areas continued to have an impact on politics. Notwithstanding movement from the land in France, with 62 per cent of farmers' sons leaving the farm and 35 per cent becoming workers by 1977, there was relatively little mobility out of the working class, with 14 per cent of workers' sons becoming white-collar workers (and 17 per cent moving the other way) and 11 per cent becoming middle managers, but 58 per cent remaining in similar jobs to their fathers (62 per cent in 1953—see Table 6.4). Intermarriage between workers and other groups was much lower in Europe than in the USA: whereas 40 per cent of marriages in the United States in 1951–77 were between workers and the free professions, only 7 per cent were in France and 2 per cent in Germany and the UK.[54] 41 per cent of US marriages were between employees and workers, while only 18 per cent in Germany and 9 per cent in the UK were. Because industrialization had begun earlier, urbanization had proceeded much more slowly in Europe, with the creation of working-class districts in cities, typically in the south and east, where the wind blew the smoke from factories and workshops. The number of city-dwellers in Europe doubled between 1900 and 1970, but it rose fivefold in the USA (and the same in Canada between 1900 and 1950) and sevenfold in the USSR (and the same in Japan between 1900 and 1950), leaving urban populations more mobile and fragmented in the rest of the world, with less time for distinct working-class districts, social milieux, and identities to develop.[55] By contrast, the 1950s and 1960s have been

Table 6.4 Patterns of social mobility in France, 1953–85

Fathers		Sons (aged 40–59)						
		1)	2)	3)	4)	5)	6)	7)
1) Farmers	1953	**60**	8	1	2	2	5	17
	1977	**38**	6	2	3	4	9	35
	1977*	**33**						
	1985	**34**						
2) Artisans, shopkeepers	1953	4	**48**	3	3	6	8	26
	1977	3	**22**	6	12	10	14	32
	1977		—					
	1985							
3) Liberal professions, businessmen	1953	3	10	**43**	12	7	7	17
	1977	1	14	**21**	26	12	10	16
	1977			—				
	1985							
4) Senior management	1953	4	16	6	**41**	17	14	2
	1977	2	4	10	**43**	22	9	10
	1977				**58**			
	1985				**60**			
5) Middle management	1953	0	16	12	16	**16**	19	21
	1977	1	4	6	30	**30**	11	18
	1977					**36**		
	1985					**31**		
6) White-collar	1953	5	10	4	12	14	**17**	38
	1977	1	7	2	16	21	**17**	35
	1977						**15**	
	1985						**14**	
7) Workers	1953	3	11	1	1	9	11	**62**
	1977	1	7	2	6	11	14	**58**
	1977							**52**
	1985							**48**

*Taken from D. Merllié and J. Prévot, *La Mobilité sociale* (Paris, 1991), 62, using different categories (removing artisans and shopkeepers, and liberal professions).

Source: adapted from C.Thélot, *Tel père, tel fils?* (Paris, 1982), 46, and D. Merllié and J. Prévot, *La Mobilité sociale* (Paris, 1991), 62.

depicted as the high water mark of working-class cultures in Europe, even in countries such as France, where the working classes remained heterogeneous and compartmentalized.[56] At the same time as the peasantry—'the supposed traditional backbone of conservative parties' (Donald Sassoon)—shrank by up to 48 per cent (in France), manufacturing industries had taken on workers, with increases of 1.9 per cent in the manufacturing workforce in the UK, 13.3 per cent in Austria, 25.5 per cent in Italy, and 37.2 per cent in West Germany

280 EUROPEAN INTEGRATION SINCE THE 1920s

during the 1950s.[57] The welfare state came into being and, with it, a distinct European Social Model against this backdrop.

It was one of the oddities of post-war history in Europe that the welfare state was more commonly inaugurated or administered by Christian Democrats or Conservatives than by Social Democrats, with the latter frequently in government in 1945 but only in charge in the UK, Sweden, and Norway over the longer term. There were many reasons for the left's failure to retain power: in France and Italy, moderate Socialists were squeezed between powerful Communist and Christian Democratic parties; in West Germany, they narrowly lost to the CDU/CSU in 1949, in part because they were associated with nationalization, regimentation and—unfairly—the Socialist Unity Party (SED) in the East; in Belgium, the Netherlands, Austria, and Denmark, they entered into coalition governments. Nevertheless, their electorates were large and the influence of 'social democracy' in the broad sense extended well beyond the ranks of the parties (see Table 6.5). Although there was always an 'economic' and a 'social' wing in the CDU-CSU, in Helmut Kohl's opinion, they were both supportive of the 'social state'.[58] In the United Kingdom, the effects of the Second World War and the promises made to—or feelings of indebtedness towards—soldiers were instrumental in the creation of a welfare state via the National Insurance Act (1946) and the creation of the National Health Service (1948) under the Labour government of Clement Attlee in 1945–51. 800,000 people had bought the first Beveridge report in 1942, on *Social Insurance and Allied Services* (the second was on *Full Employment in a Free Society*, coming out in 1944), because they were interested in its vision of a new social order.[59] If the Conservatives had been elected in 1945, it seems likely that they would have introduced a watered-down version of the same: Churchill had promised on 21 March 1943 that state ownership would be extended after the war, unemployment abolished, and compulsory national insurance established 'for all purposes from the cradle to the grave'.[60]

The UK's spending on the welfare state was unprecedented in Europe during the late 1940s and early 1950s, with total public expenditure in 1952 reaching 32.9 per cent of GNP, compared to 22.4 per cent in Denmark, and 27.1 per cent in the Netherlands.[61] The other big spender was Sweden, with 37.5 per cent of GNP devoted to public expenditure by 1960. These two social models were arguably most influential during the 1950s, as European governments sought to reconstruct their economies and refashion their public services. The more conservative, 'corporatist' insurance model of France and Germany came into being more slowly. The Croizat Law of 1945—bearing the name of Ambroise Croizat, the Communist Minister of Labour—established the principle that everyone would be covered, but initially it only applied to wage-earners and their families, not the self-employed, and it provided only for sickness, temporary disability, family allowances, and maternity, not unemployment. Coverage for everyone was not provided until 1967. In the FRG, Adenauer pushed through pension reform,

Table 6.5 Socialist, Social-Democratic and Labour parties' share of the vote, 1945–60 (%)

	1945	1946	1947	1948	1949	1950	1951	1952	1953	1954	1955	1956	1957	1958	1959	1960
Au	44.6	—	—	—	38.7	—	—	—	42.1	—	—	43.0	—	—	44.8	—
Be	32.4	—	—	—	29.8	35.5	—	—	—	38.7	—	—	—	37.1	—	—
Dk	32.8	—	40.0	—	—	39.6	—	—	40.4 41.3	—	—	—	39.4	—	—	42.1
Fi	25.1	—	—	26.3	—	—	26.5	—	—	26.2	—	—	—	23.2	—	—
Fr	23.8	21.1 17.9	—	—	—	—	14.5	—	—	—	—	14.9	—	22.8	—	—
Ne	—	28.3	—	25.6	—	—	—	29.0	—	—	—	32.7	—	—	30.4	—
It	—	20.7	—	31.0	—	—	—	—	12.7	—	—	—	—	14.3	—	—
Sw	46.7	—	46.1	—	45.7	—	—	46.0	—	—	—	44.6	—	46.2	—	47.8
UK	48.3	—	—	—	—	46.1	48.8	—	—	—	46.4	—	—	—	43.9	—
Ge	—	—	—	—	29.2	—	—	—	28.8	—	—	—	31.8	—	—	—

* Italy in 1948 was joint with the Communists.

** Sweden held elections in 1944 rather than 1945.

Source: adapted from D. Sassoon, *One Hundred Years of Socialism: The West European Left in the Twentieth Century* (New York, 1996), 118, 191.

against opposition from Ludwig Erhard, as late as 1957, after a report two years earlier had revealed that pensions only covered 30 per cent of the average wage. Reform within the insurance model was piecemeal and belated, pursued by Christian Democrats who were wary of raising costs or wages. Their parties had, though, accepted the basic principles underpinning the welfare state, as the CDU's Ahlen Programme (1947) intimated, declaring that 'the period of uncurtailed rule by private capitalism is over'.[62] In Italy, the Christian Democrats had backed the inclusion of Article 38 in the constitution of the new republic, stating that 'workers have a right to insurance provisions necessary to meet their needs in case of accident, sickness, disability, old age, and involuntary unemployment'.[63] Constitutional declarations did not amount to practical legislation, with the DC alternating between the centre-right and centre-left throughout the 1950s and 1960s and with the Italian national health service established only in 1978.[64] The terms of the debate had been established, however, and a pattern of high social spending set in train.

The Christian Democrats, who came to lead coalition governments in Italy, West Germany, the Netherlands, Belgium, Austria, and France and who were closely associated with European integration, adopted varying policies, with Adenauer following Erhard's 'ordo-liberalism' in the establishment of a 'social market', for example, but they had accepted the need for social policies and a 'social state'.[65] The bulk of their voters were Catholic and rural: the Dutch Katholieke Volkspartij (KVP) represented 80–90 per cent of Catholic voters, gaining 30.8 per cent in 1946, compared to 28.3 per cent for the Social Democrats, with whom they governed in a coalition until 1958; the Italian Democrazia Cristiana (DC), for its part, gained 48.5 per cent of the vote in 1948, with the majority of its deputies coming from the rural regions of the South and the Veneto, in parts of which—the province of Vicenza, for instance—the party gained two-thirds of the vote in 1953 and 1958.[66] According to the electoral analyses of the Cattaneo Institute, there was a correlation between rural small-holdings and the DC vote, with the *Coldiretti*—the main association of smallholders, with 1.8 million members by the early 1960s—ensuring a direct connection with the Catholic Church and the party.[67] Until the early 1960s, more than two-thirds of those who attended church regularly voted for the DC and, as late as 1975, 64 per cent of regular churchgoers still did so, compared to 13 per cent of those who attended church only irregularly.[68]

The Christian Democrats had to pander to such voters. 'The alternative is this,' Alcide De Gasperi had written to Pius XII in early 1952: 'either to concentrate around the most reliable and active Catholics a large grouping which can resist the still extremely strong grouping of the enemy; or to create a sort of Christian Labour Party which is more systematic and programmatic and which, by rationalizing method, doctrine and action, would proceed to social reform in a most ample manner.'[69] He opted for the former, but he never fully gave up his earlier notion of a 'centre party looking toward the left'.[70] According to Sassoon, DC-led governments of national unity characterized the period of 1944–47, centrist administrations in 1947–62, and 'organic', centre-left governments in 1963–68, with an alternation of centrist and centre-left administrations during the 1970s.[71] Christian Democrats in Italy and elsewhere knew that their electorate was changing, with the rural workforce in Italy shrinking from 44 per cent in 1951 to 17 per cent in 1971, and with 'secular' points of view expressed within Catholic circles, as the 1974 referendum vote against reversing the recently passed divorce law had demonstrated.[72] Across Europe, the war itself had produced a seismic shift amongst voters, prompting Christian Democrats to distance themselves from discredited right-wing parties and to offer a mixture of apolitical, technocratic competence and the prospect of reconciliation, stability, and protection to society as a whole (hence the term 'Christian Democracy', not 'Political Catholicism'). With a long-standing preference for families and social groups rather than 'individualism', they proved willing—encouraged by John XXIII's blessing of social rights in 1961—to take over the administration of the welfare state.[73] Such positioning made it easier for Christian Democrats to countenance—and even promote—a European Social Model.[74]

The uneasy political consensus about the management of the economy and the delivery of public services, embodied in 'Butskellism' in the UK (as the compound of the Conservative Chancellor Rab Butler and the Leader of the Opposition, Hugh Gaitskell) and 'grand coalitions' in the Netherlands, Austria, and, in the 1960s, West Germany, broke down in the 1970s and 1980s.[75] The causes of political unrest were varied, with many relating directly or indirectly to 'welfare' or the 'state', which no longer seemed capable—through the Keynesian devices of A. W. H. Phillips's 'machine', directing the flow of national income around the economy (with taxes, savings, and foreign trade as siphons)—of maintaining economic growth and avoiding inflation.[76] In part, the shift was generational. Those who had no experience of dictatorship or the Second World War were unwilling to accept the low wages and limited prospects of the post-war generation. Average hourly earnings in 1965 were still low: the equivalent of just 30 cents in Spain, 60 in Austria, 70 in France and Italy, and $1 in West Germany and the UK.[77] By 1975, they had risen to $3.90 in the FRG, $2.80 in Britain, $2.70 in France, $2.40 in Italy, and $1.50 in Spain. Many younger voters, motivated by new political causes from nuclear disarmament and feminism to the green movement and opposition to immigration, were no longer interested in the milieux of their parents and the politics of redistribution. One West German poll in 1978 declared that half of those between the ages of seventeen and twenty-three–5.4 million young people—were dissatisfied with state and society.[78] With more citizens having left school at eighteen and a higher percentage having gone to university, the political agenda was likely to change. '1968' came to symbolize the rupture, as Daniel Cohn-Bendit—one of the students' leaders at the new campus of Nanterre on the edge of Paris—intimated to *Paris-Match*: 'We will begin by

284 EUROPEAN INTEGRATION SINCE THE 1920S

destroying—then little by little action will teach us what we must build.'[79] The discussion of welfare—on a national and European level—became more fraught in this context, despite increases in social spending.

The sudden expansion of higher education in France, which had more than 500,000 students by 1968 (an increase of 67,000 in a single year) and a drop-out rate of more than 50 per cent, had explosive, albeit limited, effects. An opinion poll of students in November revealed that 56 per cent thought that the 'May days' were a reflection of anxiety about future employment and 35 per cent blamed the inadequate state of university facilities, compared to 12 per cent who believed that they were an attempt to transform society in its entirety.[80] Political transformation was more incremental than the events of 1968 suggested. Voters had gradually begun to treat public services as consumers or, more rarely, as independent citizens, alienated by the apparent pettiness, unresponsiveness, and wastefulness of burgeoning, invasive bureaucracies. By the 1990s, the press in Germany was discussing the advent of a society of graduates (after the number of apprentices had dropped by 750,000 in the 1980s to 600,000 per annum), with more disposable income: according to *Die Zeit*, the proportion of income spent on consumer goods had increased to almost 50 per cent by 1985.[81] These citizen-consumers were more dissatisfied with the alleged corruption of single-party dominance (in Italy) or opaque coalitions (in Austria, the Netherlands, Belgium, and Denmark) and they began to 'float' between parties. In the United Kingdom, where the alternation of the two-party system was transparent, successive governments were criticized for their opportunistic 'stop-go' policies, as they sought electorally advantageous short-term gains at the expense of long-term growth. Facing questions about their own legitimacy, governments found it harder and harder to manage—and to justify their management of—more and more complex welfare states. The 'state grew, and as it grew, its very success became its problem', wrote Tony Blair in his memoirs.[82]

The social groupings, alliances, and compromises on which the welfare state had been based no longer seemed to exist by the 1970s. Their disappearance made later arguments about a European Social Model seem more problematic. Social class no longer seemed self-evident, as Bauman's *Memories of Class: The Prehistory and After-life of Class* spelled out in 1982, underlining the 'self-assembly' of class and the 'economization' of class conflict in industrial society, followed by 'the rise and fall of economic growth', the 'limits of social engineering', the 'phenomenon of cumulative deprivation', and the 're-politicization of politics'.[83] With the shrinkage of the manufacturing workforce and the relocation of factories, particularly in high-tech and lighter industries, to the edges of cities, where they employed more non-unionized female and immigrant workers, the bastions of working-class culture, associations, districts, union, and party organization began to crumble. Thatcher's Britain became a by-word for the transformation, as 179,000 jobs were shed in car manufacturing in the first term of the

Conservative government between 1979 and 1983, 173,000 in textiles, 110,000 in iron and steel, 51,000 in coal mining, 42,000 in shipbuilding, and 23,000 in machine tools.[84] The losses in other European economies were similar over the course of the 1970s and 1980s. From 1973–74 to 1985–87, the industrial workforce in the United Kingdom had dropped from 49.2 to 30.2 per cent of the whole, in Belgium from 48.3 to 28.7 per cent and in Sweden from 40.6 to 30.2 per cent.[85] Within a generation (1970–93), manufacturing had shrunk from 32.4 to 18.9 per cent of GDP in the UK, from 32.1 to 17.7 per cent in Belgium, and from 28.3 to 16.8 per cent in Sweden. The jobs which remained, together with those in new industries, were often more precarious, with workers menaced by the prospect of unemployment, which had become 'structural' by the 1980s. In the UK, it had reached 13.2 per cent and in Belgium 14 per cent by 1984. Union membership remained high, but went into decline, at different rates, during the same decade: from 55.4 per cent (13.5 million) in 1979 to 33.7 per cent (9.9 million) by 1990 in the UK and from 55.9 to 51.2 per cent in Belgium.[86] Such reductions, when combined, helped to diminish the importance of the principal political cleavage in European politics. Some indices suggested that class-based votes in Britain and Germany had halved—as a percentage—during the 1950s, 1960s, and 1970s, with Sweden starting from a higher point of around 50 per cent and descending to less than 35.[87] In France, 49 per cent of workers had voted for the Communist Party in 1951, but only 20 per cent by 1986. Twenty-nine per cent of the working-class vote by that date went to the RPR and UDF.[88] Socialist and Social Democratic parties could no longer rely unthinkingly on their electorate, assuming that further increases in social spending would meet with its approval.

European Community member states were becoming service societies, complicating but not nullifying older debates about 'industrial society'. In the UK, whereas industrial employment decreased by 2.2 million between 1971 and 1983, the number of jobs in the service sector—catering, leisure, business services, and the public sector—increased by 1.7 million.[89] Such shifts affected the ways in which the welfare state was viewed. Yet it is easy to be distracted by the mythology of neo-liberalism and ignore the reality of continuing social spending, on which the case for a European Social Model rests. In the United Kingdom under the Conservatives, in particular, a wealth-creating private sector was pitted against an unproductive, interfering, and restrictive public sector (the 'nanny state').[90] Spending cuts were an important component of the programme, as Nigel Lawson spelled out to a meeting of Swiss bankers in 1981: 'The right definition involves a mixture of free markets, financial discipline, firm control over public expenditure, tax cuts, nationalism, "Victorian values" (of the Samuel Smiles self-help variety), privatization and a dash of populism.'[91] The core of Thatcherite Conservatism, as the political scientist Andrew Gamble put it in 1984, consisted of 'accepting the priority given to the control of inflation; renouncing protectionism . . . to shield any sector of the British economy from the need to be competitive; and accepting

286 EUROPEAN INTEGRATION SINCE THE 1920S

a much smaller state sector, with lower taxation, selective rather than universal welfare provision, as well as a permanent weakening of trade union organizations'.[92]

Monetarism came first for Tory 'radicals', or 'sado-monetarists' as the former Labour Chancellor, Denis Healey, labelled them.[93] What they wished to do, in Lawson's opinion in 1980, was to restore the 'two basic propositions' of the 'pre-Keynesian period' before the Second World War: 'The first is that changes in the quantity of money determine, at the end of the day, changes in the general price level; the second is that government is able to determine the quantity of money.'[94] Cuts to public expenditure included a wave of privatizations, reversing post-war nationalization and raising billions for the public purse: £3.9 billion for British Telecom, £5.4 billion for British Gas, £5.1 billion for the water boards, £5 billion for electricity, £2.5 billion for British Steel, £1.4 billion for Rolls Royce, £1.3 billion for British Airports, £900 million for British Airways, and £294 million for Jaguar cars.[95] A second set of cuts were linked to a reform of the welfare state—the civil service, NHS, education, and prisons especially—which was less successful.[96] In such an historical context, doubts about the existence of a European Social Model are understandable but misplaced. Although Thatcher was critical of civil servants, who—she believed—saw themselves entrusted with the 'orderly management of decline', she continued to trust in 'a strong state'.[97] Many Conservative reforms were unpopular (unlike privatization), met with resistance and issued in greater central control, as John Ashworth, the Vice Chancellor of Salford University and former government adviser, lamented: 'They are privatising everyone else and nationalising us.'[98] The citizens of the service society, though not defining themselves as Labourite or working-class, continued to support public services.[99] Government expenditure in the UK did not drop significantly during the Conservative era, averaging 43.5 per cent of GDP in 1974–85, 42.9 per cent in 1986–90, and 42.3 per cent in 1995.[100] 'Whatever the enormous impact of the Thatcher reforms had been on the private sector of the 1980s, we had inherited a public sector largely unreformed,' wrote Blair: 'The state was still as it had been since 1945.'[101] The difference was that the spending of other European states—for example, France (39.4 to 54.5 per cent in 1995), Germany (44.4 to 49.7 per cent) and Italy (34.4 to 53.8 per cent)—had increased markedly.[102] US government spending stood at 32.3 per cent of GDP in 1975–84 and 36.5 per cent in 1995. A specifically European social model had endured and, typically, expanded during an age of neo-liberalism.

The supposed absence of a viable 'European Social Model' has been criticized by proponents and opponents of federalism, or the 'Community method'. For Fritz Scharpf, 'social Europe' is a 'road not taken', beginning with the failure of the Socialist premier of the French Fourth Republic, Guy Mollet, 'to make the harmonization of social regulations and fiscal burdens a precondition for the integration of industrial markets'.[103] If harmonization could have been included in the Treaty of Rome, becoming subject to European Court of Justice rulings at a time when the six founding members had a similar Bismarckian model of work-based social insurance, Scharpf contends, it would have forced governments and the European Commission 'to define the line of demarcation between the spheres of market competition and protected social and cultural concerns at the European level', boosting the European Community's political legitimacy and facilitating further political integration.[104] Instead, the need for unanimity in the Council over 'subsidiary competence' provisions (Article 100), or supplementary social measures relating to 'the establishment or functioning of the common market', together with the granting of extra powers linked to the operation of the market (Article 235), meant that the EEC was caught in a 'joint-decision trap', which prevented further social measures.[105]

At the same time, far-reaching internal-market and monetary-union reforms have 'reduced the capacity of member states to influence the course of their own economies and to realize self-defined socio-political goals', excluding the possibility of altering exchange rates, giving state aid, running deficits beyond the level prescribed by the stability and growth pact, and 'using public-sector industries as an employment buffer'.[106] Since Scharpf rules out increasing taxation to fund higher social spending on the national level (presumably on grounds of competitiveness, even though taxation is the main reason for discrepancies of social expenditure in Europe), he assumes that 'the only national options which remain freely available under European law are supply-side strategies involving lower tax burdens, further deregulation and flexibilization of employment conditions'.[107] His solution is to call for the 'Europeanization' of 'social Europe' through the establishment of 'constitutional parity' between social goals and the rules of economic integration, not least because the 'open method of coordination' (OMC) has not worked.[108] The Common Agricultural Policy (CAP) is one example of both a redistributive social and market-based economic policy, but Scharpf concedes that it is 'much-maligned'.[109] The main challenge which he identifies is the creation of a multi-speed framework, allowing different degrees and types of social integration for Southern, Central, and Eastern European states which have a per-capita GNP (purchasing power) ranging from half (Greece) to between one-third and one-sixth (Central and Eastern Europe) of that of Denmark (in 2002).[110]

For Giandomenico Majone, such disparities are a reason not to attempt the integration of social policy on the European level, meaning that the ESM will remain a 'mirage'.[111] The Treaty of Rome (1957) had listed 'social fields'—employment, labour law, working conditions, vocational training, social security, health and safety, collective bargaining, and right of association—where members could cooperate (Article 118), but it had not required cooperation and it had restricted the role of the European Commission.[112] The Single European Act (1986) gave the Community an enhanced role in the areas of regional development (Title V on economic and social cohesion) and social regulation (Article 100A and 118A, plus Title VII on the environment), allowing measures to be adopted by qualified-majority voting in matters of health and safety and the 'working environment'. The Treaty on European Union (1992) contained further competencies in the fields of consumer and environmental protection, health and safety and the length and regulation of the working day. It was accompanied by an annexe, 'The Protocol on Social Policy', which was largely declaratory and recognized that 'the Community and the Member States shall implement measures which take account of the diverse forms of national practices, in particular in the field of contractual relations, and the need to maintain the competitiveness of the Community economy' (Article 1).[113] Subsequently, this 'Social Chapter' was given 'quasi-constitutional status' by the Treaty of Amsterdam (1997), after the UK opt-out ended under an incoming New Labour government. It outlined twelve types of social rights, including provisions for industrial democracy and collective bargaining on a European level, but it refrained from going beyond social regulation and it stood in contrast to the 'dense web of welfare institutions covering most citizens "from cradle to grave"' on the national level.[114] For Tony Blair, who had done most to entrench the 'Social Chapter', 'We thought it was about basic employment rights like paid holidays and was a necessary feature of a just society', not a hindrance to competitiveness, as Tories claimed.[115] As such, it was believed to supplement existing national legislation, rather than replacing it.

Governments of wealthier member states, particularly Socialist and Social Democratic ones, have feared a 'race to the bottom' or a lowering of standards and 'social dumping', defined by a European Commission report on *The Social Dimension of the Internal Market* in 1988 as 'the fear that national social progress will be blocked or, worse, that there will be downward pressure on social conditions (wages, level of social protection, fringe benefits, etc.) in the most advanced countries, simply because of the competition...from certain countries, where average labour costs are significantly lower'.[116] Average hourly labour costs in 2003 ranged from €20.63 in Denmark to €1.88 in Slovakia.[117] The alternative of a European social policy and welfare provision, however, seems unrealistic and unnecessary, not least because poorer countries have tended to increase their social expenditure, rather than engaging in a race to the bottom. A European standard might reduce aggregate social welfare (wealthier countries are used to greater provision), in Majone's opinion: 'the variety of welfare state models coexisting in Europe' prevents harmonization, and there is little public support for a transfer (with only one-third of respondents, mainly from poorer member states, backing the idea).[118] 'State-like ambitions', which would be necessary for the pursuit and funding of a European welfare state, 'are bound to be counterproductive for a *sui generis* polity like the EU'.[119] The European Social Model, for all its variations, has come into being on the national level, where it is likely to stay. Welfare states, the single market and the European Union are nonetheless linked, as Giddens points out, since leaders and—to a more limited extent—citizens seem to accept that 'market-correcting' social protection and 'market-making' economic integration belong together.[120] In other words, member states continue to maintain the idea and reality of an ESM. Given their role in 'market-making' within the Council of Ministers, they are well placed to do so.

Regional Inequalities and Social Convergence

The convergence of European countries in the post-war era should be understood from the vantage point of those who had experienced the period before 1945. Willy Brandt returned from exile in the neutral haven of Sweden, where he had sat out the war with other Socialists, to Bremen, 'a city on the edge of life'.[121] Even the new mayor called it 'A burned out field of craters', with 'a port that was one no longer'.[122] It seemed to many at the time that reconstruction, both physical and psychological, would take fifty years or more.[123] 'When I look out of the window, the empty holes and destroyed façades of the burned-out houses on the other side of the street stare back,' wrote Wolfgang Langhoff, the director of Düsseldorf's theatre: it was a sight 'which brought the heart of a returnee'—he had gone into exile in Switzerland—to a standstill, but to which he had become accustomed.[124] What would become of them, 'if the destruction becomes normal'? 'Getting used to things is the most terrible force and an obstacle to any forward development,' he wrote.[125] In *Wandlungen der deutschen Familie der Gegenwart* (1953), the sociologist Helmut Schelsky estimated that one-third of the West German population had been affected by 'one of the typical social fates'—as war widows (1.5–2.5 million), the seriously wounded (2.5 million), bombing victims (4.5–6 million), and the displaced and downgraded (1.5–2.5 million).[126] There were no statistics for unemployment until 1949, but it still stood at 11 per cent in 1950; there were 7.3 million more women than men, and 40 per cent of families remained 'incomplete'. For such citizens, the prosperous, outwardly similar lifestyles and working conditions of Europeans, which were being discussed a generation later, were unimaginable.

Historians agree that there has been economic and social convergence in Europe, but they disagree about its extent and causes. Some scholars have paid more attention to longer-term trends and to globalization.[127] Others have underlined the accelerating effect of European integration. Kaelble had asked in 1987 whether a single European society was emerging.[128] By 2017, after the rejection of a European constitution, the eurozone crisis and Brexit, he was asking 'how pronouncedly did European societies really converge after the 1950s and where are the limits?'[129] The most obvious limits involved nations and regions as 'important points of reference for identity', variegated according to 'differences in particular sets of values' relating to religion, national consciousness, family, and sexual morality.[130] Although sharing information, member states continued to control social policy, following 'completely different paths', and national economies (or global companies) remained the focus of industrial disputes, despite the existence of European enterprises.[131] The creation of the ECSC in 1951 and the EEC in 1957 brought together 'very different actors, economically and socially', from an agrarian state such as Italy, the service economy of the Netherlands and the industrial societies of Belgium and West Germany.[132] The 'next challenge for convergence' came from the southern enlargement of 'dictatorship-damaged countries'—Spain, Portugal, and Greece—in the 1980s, followed by the eastern enlargement of 'many new member states, not only with completely different political memories and expectations, but also with different social formations', in 2004–07.[133] In addition to this challenging thirty-year cycle of enlargement, social convergence 'occurred very unevenly on geographical grounds', with Belgium much more integrated from the start than Hungary.[134] North–South and East–West divisions have not been overcome. They were exposed by the eurozone crisis, with southern states such as Italy and Greece facing 'new divergences'—for example, unemployment, which rose from 7 to 13 per cent (compared to 11 per cent in the EU as a whole)—and with richer states emerging 'very differently'.[135] French and Belgian respondents to the Eurobarometer survey in 2012 were more sceptical than previously about the existence of common European values; German, Austrian, Finnish, and British respondents less so, with significant divergences over national debt and immigration (49 per cent seeing it as useful, 43 per cent against).[136] The crisis, in Kaelble's opinion, had left lasting scars:

> The number of opponents of the European Union not only remained higher than before the crisis, it resulted in a new geography of support and rejection. Before the crisis, the South of Europe supported the European Union, whilst, in the North, Scandinavia and Great Britain especially were sceptical. This geography of support changed. The South now supports the European Union far less. The opponents are most numerous in Greece and Cyprus, they are significant in Italy, less strong in Portugal and not at all so in Spain. The northern and eastern part of the EU continues to support the European Union. Support only became greater in Scandinavia. In the special case of Great Britain, the backers of the Union even became a majority in the autumn of 2016, the first time for a long time. In eastern and central Europe, too, support for the European Union remained high, in Poland just as in the Baltic republics, Romania and Bulgaria. Only in Austria, the Czech Republic and Hungary was scepticism in a majority.[137]

Scepticism increased in France, Belgium, the Netherlands, and Germany, but 'supporters were usually a majority'.[138] Overall, the crisis of 2010–12 'did not threaten the social convergence of Europe at its core', with support for the EU returning to its 2009 level by 2015.[139]

Post-war convergence was, in part, the consequence of movement and communication and, in part, economic transformation. 'One could not have imagined in the 1950s how many Europeans would study at other European universities, how many Europeans would migrate within Europe, how many would travel to other countries of Europe on holiday or for business, how easily one can communicate with other European countries and how intensive the exchanges between twinned cities and villages would become,' writes Kaelble (born in 1940): 'Passive, less intensive acquaintance with European countries in one's own land increased markedly, too, via imported consumer goods, new radio and TV broadcasters, and visitors and migrants from other European countries.'[140] Although movement between American states was two to three times greater than in the EU, with over three million US citizens migrating in 2000 compared to 1.3 million Europeans moving from one member state to another in 2014, the difference is 'not fundamental', in the Berlin historian's judgement, not least because migration results from complex combinations of 'push' and 'pull', with improving prospects in one region reducing emigration to another.[141]

The transformation of Western and Southern Europe had been underway since the 1950s, 'not only in respect of gross domestic product', but also 'central social matters', including differences in the organization of work, unemployment, training, the performance of the welfare state, urbanization, consumption, inequality, and even birth rates, marriage, and life expectancy.[142] It was built on the 'lessening of social inequality' during the 'boom' years, as countries across the world—including India, Indonesia, Argentina, and South Africa, according to Thomas Piketty and Anthony Atkinson—witnessed a diminution of income and asset inequality between the 1940s and 1970s.[143] As the Russian-American economist Anthony Smith Kuznets pointed out in the 1950s, the trend was the result of the restructuring and functioning of the capitalist world economy as well as state intervention.[144] High levels of income taxes on the rich, the introduction of taxes on wealth, actions by unions, social insurance, training, and education all mitigated the impact of inequality in Western Europe, but were 'much too disunited' to cause a common trend on their own.[145] Rather, they were added to an improvement in the income of farmers as a result of increased productivity, raising low wages in the economy in its entirety, and to the virtual elimination of illiteracy in southern Europe, likewise pushing up the wages of the lowest paid. They were also connected to the lowering of class distinctions through education, with the reforms of the 1960s having an effect by the 1970s, and through consumption: 'With the advent of mass consumption, many instruments of social exclusion were taken out of the hands of the upper and middle strata, since large parts of their lifestyle became accessible to a significant section of the population.'[146] Throughout, there was an intersection between the 'growing together of European societies', aided by the European Community's creation of an internal market, removal within the Schengen area of border controls, and convergence as a consequence of 'global entanglements' (the end of the Cold War, cheap flights, the privatization of radio and television, the internet, and global trade in goods).[147]

292 EUROPEAN INTEGRATION SINCE THE 1920S

Even though the causes were diverse, the result—the convergence of European societies—seems difficult to deny.

The principal questions for the European Union concern the degree of social— as opposed to economic—integration and the significance of what Hans-Ulrich Wehler has termed an 'accelerating intensification of social inequalities' since the 1980s.[148] This intensification is the result of a growing inequality of labour income, which differs from country to country and is historically specific, according to Piketty and Atkinson. In Europe (the UK, France, Germany, and Sweden), the income share of the top ten per cent was over 45 per cent in 1900, dropping during the First World War, the Great Depression, and Second World War to just over 30 per cent by 1950, dipping under 30 per cent during the 1970s, before rising after 1980 to 35 per cent by 2010 (see Table 6.6).[149] By contrast, the top decile in the United States enjoyed around 40 per cent of income share in 1900, rising to 45 per cent in the 1920s and falling to less than 35 per cent during the Great Depression and Second World War, at which level it remained between 1950 and 1970, before climbing to 48 per cent between 1970 and 2010.[150] The decline of the top ten per cent's share of income is 'entirely due to the fall of top capital incomes'—since 'top wage shares actually did not decline at all'—and is attributable to 'severe shocks to their capital holdings during the 1914–45 period (destruction, inflation, bankruptcies etc.)'.[151]

Since this pattern was common to a variety of European and English-speaking industrialized economies (the United States, Canada, Australia, New Zealand, the UK, Ireland, France, Germany, and the Netherlands) in Atkinson and Piketty's study of top incomes in the twentieth century, the main questions concern

Table 6.6 Share of top ten per cent in total income in Europe and the United States, 1900–2010

	Europe*	US	UK	Germany	France	Sweden
1900	45.9	40.5	47.1	45.0	45.5	45.9
1910	45.8	40.9	47.4	43.7	46.6	45.6
1920	40.2	44.7	41.4	38.7	42.0	35.8
1930	40.8	45.1	39.3	42.0	43.1	37.6
1940	37.8	36.5	33.9	34.4	33.5	33.3
1950	33.2	33.7	30.3	33.2	33.8	29.4
1960	33.2	34.1	29.4	31.0	36.1	30.1
1970	31.0	33.4	28.3	31.4	32.7	26.4
1980	31.2	37.5	32.6	31.6	31.1	22.4
1990	34.8	42.4	38.4	33.8	32.4	25.0
2000	35.7	46.9	40.2	35.7	33.0	27.0
2010	36.9	47.9	41.6	36.1	33.0	28.3

* Europe denotes the UK, Germany, France, and Sweden here.

Source: adapted from Thomas Piketty online data at www.piketty.pse.ens.fr/files/capital21c/supp/TS9.4.

'the non-recovery of top capital incomes during the post-1945 period' and the divergence in income share between continental Europe and the Anglophone countries.[152] Atkinson and Piketty's answer is that 'the introduction of high income and estate tax progressivity (there was virtually no tax progressivity prior to 1914, and top rates increased enormously between 1914 and 1945) made it impossible for top capital holders to fully recover'.[153] It also made it easier to limit the rise in top income shares, which 'have remained fairly stable in France and other continental European countries over the past three decades' but which 'have increased enormously in the US, where they are now back to their interwar levels'.[154] The UK, Canada, Australia, and New Zealand 'tend to be somewhere between the European pattern and the US pattern'.[155] The 'rise of US top income shares is not due to the revival of top capital incomes, but rather to the very large increases in top wages (especially top executive compensation)', Piketty writes: 'As a consequence, top executives (the "working rich") have replaced 'top capital owners (the "rentiers") at the top of the US income hierarchy over the course of the twentieth century', contrasting with 'the European pattern', where high capital incomes are still predominant at the top of the distribution (albeit at lower levels than at the beginning of the twentieth century)'.[156] Over time, 'capital accumulation by the 'working rich' is likely to lead to the revival of top capital incomes', which might require—he suggests in *Capital in the Twenty-First Century* (2013)— a rethinking of income tax and a global tax on capital.[157] Up to the present, it has entailed a degree of social and economic divergence between mainland Europe and English-speaking 'post-industrial' societies. It also lay behind Ronald Reagan's advisors' repeated question to French officials in the early 1980s to explain 'the difference between your economic policy and that of a Communist country'.[158]

The social consequences of economic inequality are better known than those of equality. Within Europe, the United Kingdom provides the main example of an increase in income inequality, which occurred largely during the 1980s, when the real income of the richest twenty per cent grew at 3.6 per cent per annum, the middle group at 2.1 per cent and the poorest at 0.4 per cent.[159] Because of the recession of the early 1990s, there was a small reversal under John Major (1990–97) and, because of targeted redistribution under New Labour (particularly designed to reduce child poverty), there was a stabilization of the real income growth of each quintile under Tony Blair (1997–2008), when the annual income of the poorest twenty per cent grew at 2.2 per cent and that of the richest at 2.0 per cent.[160] The social and cultural by-products of these shifts are contested— Mark Garnett's story of politics, society, and popular culture since 1975 singles out anger, fear, greed, and lust, together with charity, faith, hope, and (mainly under New Labour) apathy—but they have also been fitful and confused, entangled with changing lifestyles, levels of education, and instances of affiliation (class, ethnicity, gender, and region).[161] Although the Blair government halted the increase of income inequality during the 2000s, followed by an uneven period of 'austerity',

294 EUROPEAN INTEGRATION SINCE THE 1920S

Brexit, and low economic growth, which squeezed low and high incomes, the Gini coefficient of income inequality has remained high in the United Kingdom since 1990 at 0.34–0.37, on a scale between 0.24 (Slovakia in 2019) and 0.478 (Costa Rica).[162] The Czech Republic (0.25), Slovenia, Belgium (0.26), Denmark, Finland, Sweden, Austria (0.28), Poland, the Netherlands, Germany, and Hungary (0.29) are all among the most economically egalitarian countries in the world, contrasting with the UK (0.37) and the United States (0.39). Such differences underpin the conception of a European Social Model and the idea that the EU can protect Europeans against the worst effects of globalization.

To the opponents of Thatcherism, the increase in inequality in the UK was intended, tied to an ideology of individualism, enterprise, de-regulation, monetary policy, and financial globalization, and unleashing a series of unintended social and cultural effects. 'Sexy greedy *is* the late eighties,' Caryl Churchill had one of her characters declare in *Serious Money* (1987).[163] Many Tories themselves were more ambivalent, partly because the new money of the City after the 'big bang' on 27 October 1986 seemed vulgar. The dynamics of financial de-regulation appeared to militate against Martin Wiener's influential thesis in *English Culture and the Decline of the Industrial Spirit, 1850–1980* (1981) that middle-class offspring and university graduates continued to think of science and manufacturing as boring, dirty or 'ungentlemanly', preferring to go into the City (or the civil service).[164] Wiener argued that such prejudices had damaging consequences for the quality of management, invention, technical competence, and the availability and stability of industrial finance (since the City provided shorter-term or more expensive capital than was available in continental Europe, Japan, or the United States). De-regulation appeared to have levelled the social distinction between industry and finance without remedying short-termism. Those Tories who had made their fortune in the City of the 'big bang' such as John Redwood and Peter Lilley— also leading Eurosceptics and later supporters of Brexit—were less equivocal about de-regulation's effects.[165]

For its part, New Labour, which came to power in 1997 to the tune of 'Things can only get better' (by D:ream), were anxious, in Blair's words, to ensure that 'power, wealth and opportunity must be in the hands of the many not the few', but also to insist that 'economic dynamism and social justice must go hand in hand', focusing on the creation and maintenance of 'the right environment for enterprise and wealth creation' as a policy priority.[166] Although Peter Mandelson's notorious comment about New Labour being 'intensely relaxed about people getting filthy rich' is usually misrepresented, since he included the qualifier 'as long as they pay their taxes' in the same sentence, Alastair Campbell's recollection in his diaries on 10 October 1999 is revealing of Blair's relative position in Europe: 'Chirac pronounced, "Tony is a modern socialist. That means he is five miles to the right of me"—"And I'm proud of it", said Tony.'[167] Sarkozy, too, marvelled that Blair, whom he lauded as 'talented, brilliant and friendly', 'was to be found to my right on many issues, and sometimes quite markedly'.[168] In historical perspective, the creation of a British exception was recent—the UK's Gini coefficient had been below 0.25 in 1979, making it one of the world's most egalitarian economies—and its significance was limited.[169] For Europe as a whole, enlargement in 1981–86 (Southern Europe) and 2004–07 (Central and Eastern Europe) was more important, challenging basic assumptions about social and economic convergence.

Proportionally, the enlargement of 1973, which had increased the population of the European Community by one-third (64.3 million), was more significant than that of 1981 (Greece) and 1986 (Spain and Portugal), which constituted a 22 per cent increase (58.3 million), and 2004 (Central and Eastern Europe, the Baltic states, Cyprus, and Malta) and 2007 (Bulgaria and Romania), which expanded the EU by 26 per cent (104.8 million). However, the enlargements of 2004–07, given that they almost doubled the number of states (from fifteen to twenty-seven), appeared to necessitate further institutional change, streamlining voting procedures and rebalancing the weighting of votes in the Council and European Parliament, which had been attempted at the Amsterdam Intergovernmental Conference (1997), continued at Nice (2001), and was completed at Lisbon (2007). Both the Mediterranean and the Central and Eastern European enlargements raised social and economic questions, which were not manifest in 1973 and 1995 (Austria, Sweden, Finland), when the new entrants seemed to have compatible economies and systems of social security. Using the EU-15 average GDP per person in 1995 as an index of 100, Austria entered with 110, Sweden with 106, and Finland 97; Denmark had entered in 1973 with a GDP per capita of 121 and the UK 104, compared to the EU-6 index of 108.[170] Whereas Denmark devoted more of its GDP to social spending than the EU-6 (21.8 per cent compared to 19.8), the UK and Ireland spent slightly less (16.6 and 15.3).[171] By contrast, in 1995, all of the new entrants devoted more to social spending than the EU average of 27.1 per cent of GDP: 28.7 per cent in Austria, 30.9 per cent in Finland, and 35.0 per cent in Sweden.[172] The incorporation of such states barely affected the social and economic balance of the European Community and EU.

The situations of Greece, Spain, and Portugal on entry were fundamentally different from those of Western European and Scandinavian states. Greece's official index of GDP per person on entry was 69 ($2,309), compared to the EC-9 average of 106, Spain's was 72 ($2,384), and Portugal's 54 ($1,504), compared to an EC-10 average of 98.[173] Greece was allocating 13.9 per cent of GDP to social expenditure, Spain 18.2, and Portugal 13.0, compared to a European Community average of 24.2 per cent (of a much larger real income).[174] Whereas EU-15 states spent an average of €7,000 per person on social protection in 2003, Poland allocated €1,100.[175] What was more, the respective populations had only recently emerged from dictatorships and were still employed in large numbers in fishing and agriculture (16.6 per cent of GDP in Greece, 11.8 per cent in Portugal, and over 10 per cent in Spain), increasing the Community's agricultural population by 55 per cent in 1981–86 and putting further pressure on a Common Agricultural Policy that was already seen to be wasteful, with its notorious butter mountains and milk lakes.[176] The discrepancies of enlargement in 2004 and 2007 were even greater than in the 1980s, with the populations of most accession states having vivid memories of Communism, Soviet domination, and the disruption of democratic transition and economic liberalization in the 1990s. Compared to the EU-15's index of GDP per person (purchasing power) of 109 in 2004 (or a gross figure of €25,400), the Czech Republic's index was 70 (€8,500), Poland's 47 (€5,100), and Latvia's 43 (€4,800).[177] Bulgaria's index in 2007 was 37 (€3,800) and Romania's 42 (€5,800), compared to an EU-15 index of 110 (€27,900).[178] Denmark's GDP per head by that time was €41,500. From this point of view, as *The Economist* had noted in October 2002, enlargement seemed to be 'Europe's Mexico option':

A far-fetched comparison? Not at all. Look at the numbers, and the parallels are really quite close. According to the OECD, Mexico's GDP per capita measured in purchasing-power terms is $9,100; the figure for Poland, the largest of the current applicants, is $9,600. (Measure the figures in unadjusted dollars and the Mexicans are about 50% richer.) Mexico's population is just shy of 100m; the ten countries lined up to join the EU, plus Romania and Bulgaria which are hoping to join soon after, total just over 100m too. Transparency International's index of global corruption puts Mexico and Poland roughly on a par.[179]

There were differences between Poland and Mexico which explain what occurred in the decade or so after 2004. Like other accession states, Poland had a larger agricultural sector than EU-15 states, including Mediterranean ones (see Table 6.7). Its large industrial sector and comparatively small service sector, however, were not merely the residue of the Communist era or an indication of an ongoing transition; they were also the result of foreign direct investment (FDI)—with German companies the most active investors—and of the successful transformation of companies during the 1990s. The capital stock of FDI in Slovenia, the Czech Republic, Hungary, and Poland increased from $82 billion in 2000 to $222 billion by 2005.[180] Germany bought about one-third of the Czech Republic's, Hungary's, Poland's, and Slovakia's exports in 2004, often from German-owned subsidiaries.[181] 82 per cent of investment in Hungary, 89 per cent of industrial exports, 73 per cent of sales, and 47 per cent of employment were attributable to foreign companies; in Poland, foreign firms accounted for 63 per cent of investment, 59 per cent of exports, 49 per cent of sales, and 29 per cent of employment.[182] European enterprises were attracted by lower wages, but also by Central and Eastern European and Baltic states' urban, educated populations, in which a higher percentage of young people stayed at school until eighteen (typically 80–90 per cent) than in Western Europe (70–80 per cent) or in a state

Table 6.7 Economic and social indicators in the EU-15 and accession states in 2004

	GDP per head (€)	Social protection (% GDP)	Social spending (€ in 2003)	Employment rate:men	Employment rate:women	Secondary education (%)*	Uni (% 18-24)	% labour force in agriculture	% labour force in industry
EU-15	25,400	28.0	7,000	72.7	56.8	73.7	23	3.9	24.2
Denmark	36,000	30.0	—	79.7	71.6	74.8	—	3.6	21.5
UK	28,800	27.6	—	77.8	65.6	76.4	—	0.9	17.9
Germany	26,800	30.5	—	70.8	59.2	72.8	—	2.2	26.4
France	26,500	30.6	—	68.9	57.4	79.8	—	3.6	21.1
Italy	23,300	26.1	—	70.1	45.2	72.9	—	4.4	29.0
Spain	19,600	20.2	—	73.8	48.3	61.1	—	5.7	29.9
Slovenia	13,000	25.4	3,000	70.0	60.5	89.7	—	10.5	36.4
Czech Rep	8,500	19.9	1,600	72.3	56.0	90.9	—	4.0	37.8
Estonia	6,700	14.3 (2001)	800	66.4	60.0	82.3	—	5.8	34.7
Hungary	6,200	20.9	1,600	61.8	47.8	93.7	30	—	—
Poland	5,100	—	1,100	57.2	46.2	89.5	38	19.2	26.8
Latvia	4,800	14.3	600	66.4	58.5	76.9	—	12.5	26.5
Romania	2,700	—	—	63.4	52.1	74.8	—	36.2 (2002)	29.9 (2002)
Turkey	3,400	—	—	67.8	24.3	41.8	—	—	—

*Percentage of 20–24 year olds who have completed secondary education to 18 or 19.

Source: European Commission, *The Social Situation in the European Union, 2005–6* (Brussels, 2006), 130–57; European Commission, *Eurostat Yearbook: A Statistical Eye on Europe, 2005* (Luxembourg, online); I. T. Berend, *From the Soviet Bloc to the European Union: The Economic and Social Transformation of Central and Eastern Europe since 1973* (Cambridge, 2009), 229.

like Turkey (42 per cent), which had a comparable GDP per capita. By 2004, 38 per cent of Poles and 30 per cent of Hungarians aged 18–24 were attending university, compared to 23 per cent in the EU-15.[183] In 1989, 14 per cent of Poles and 10 per cent of Hungarians had been at university.[184] In his memoirs, Sarkozy goes out of his way to explain that a country such as Poland, which had a population the same size as that of Spain and was 'the largest country of Eastern Europe', could not be ignored, in part because its citizens had liberated themselves 'so courageously from the chains of Communism'.[185] Arguably, the struggle against Communism had only come back into the field of view of Western European leaders as a result of post-Communist states' rates of economic growth.

After a period of economic turbulence during the early-to-mid-1990s, the economies of the Central and Eastern European and Baltic states grew rapidly, benefiting from association agreements with the EU (Hungary's agreement coming into force in February 1994, for example) and the promise of accession, once criteria agreed at the June 1993 European Council in Copenhagen, concerning democratic institutions, a functioning market economy and the obligations of membership ('adherence to the aims of political, economic and monetary union'), had been met.[186] In the ten-year period between 1993 and 2003, the EU-15's annual GDP per capita growth was 2.1 per cent, whereas Poland, Latvia, Estonia, and Slovakia registered 4–5 per cent.[187] In 2005, the Czech Republic grew at 4.9 per cent, Hungary at 4.5 per cent, and Poland at 3.7 per cent.[188] Although such differences in growth rates seem small, their cumulative effect was great. Between 1998 and 2007, the ten accession states of 2004 had grown by 67 per cent, compared to 26 per cent for the EU-15.[189] Despite the financial crash of 2007–08 and eurozone crisis of 2010–12, economies in the 'new Europe' have continued to grow more quickly than those in the EU-15, with Slovenia and the Czech Republic overtaking or catching up with Greece and Portugal (see Table 6.8). Much of their growth has been connected to the single market, on which they had come to rely before accession, rather than on EU regional funds and other aid, to which they gained limited access after 2004. In that year, the Czech Republic sent 83.8 per cent of its exports to and sourced 82.5 per cent of its imports from the EU-25.[190]

There is a gap between statistics and citizens' experiences. Have Eastern and Western Europeans become more alike? Their memories of the recent past are different. In the aftermath of the 'Velvet Revolution', amidst the instability of economic collapse and a transition from dictatorship, the dangers were obvious.[191] 'The return of freedom to a place that became morally unhinged has produced something that it clearly had to produce, and therefore something we might have expected,' commented the writer, dissident, and President of Czechoslovakia, Vaclav Havel in an article called 'Paradise Lost' in the New York Review of Books in April 1992:

Table 6.8 GDP per capita (€) and real GDP growth rates (%), 2010–19

	2010		2015		2019	
	GDP/ capita	GDP growth	GDP/ capita	GDP growth	GDP/ capita	GDP growth
EU-28	25,510	1.9	26,670	2.3	28,610	1.5
Denmark	43,840	1.9	45,630	2.3	49,720	2.8
UK	29,830	2.1	31,780	2.4	32,910	1.4
Germany	31,940	4.2	34,130	1.5	35,840	0.6
France	30,690	1.9	31,540	1.1	33,270	1.5
Italy	26,930	1.7	25,640	0.8	26,910	0.3
Spain	23,040	0.2	23,080	3.8	25,200	2.0
Greece	20,150	−5.5	16,870	−0.4	17,750	1.9
Portugal	16,990	1.7	16,620	1.8	18,630	2.5
Slovenia	17,750	1.3	17,990	2.2	20,700	3.2
Czech Rep	15,020	2.4	16,290	5.4	18,330	2.3
Estonia	11,150	2.7	13,330	1.8	15,760	5.0
Hungary	9,960	1.1	11,210	3.8	13,270	4.6
Poland	9,400	3.7	10,890	4.2	13,000	4.5
Latvia	8,520	−4.4	10,790	4.0	12,510	2.0
Romania	6,200	−3.9	7,290	3.0	9,110	4.1

Source: Eurostat, *Economic Indicators* (2021); Eurostat, *Real GDP Growth Rates* (2021).

But it has turned out to be far more serious than anyone could have predicted: an enormous and blindingly visible explosion of every imaginable human vice. A wide range of questionable or at least ambivalent human tendencies, quietly encouraged over the years and, at the same time, quietly pressed to serve the daily operation of the totalitarian system, has suddenly been liberated, as it were, from its straitjacket and given free rein at last. The authoritarian regime imposed a certain order—if that is the right expression for it—on these vices (and in doing so 'legitimized' them, in a sense). This order has now been broken down, but a new order that would limit rather than exploit these vices, an order based on a freely accepted responsibility to and for the whole of society, has not yet been built, nor could it have been, for such an order takes years to develop and cultivate.[192]

Havel's dismay at rapidly growing criminality, the 'collective sewage' of the mass media (and 'especially the gutter press'), and more 'dangerous symptoms' of 'hatred among nationalities, suspicion, racism, even signs of fascism' was characteristic of the times, but was unusual insofar as it emanated from a serving president, writing for an American literary magazine.[193] The fact that Havel professed his lingering optimism—'I am persuaded time and time again that a huge potential of good will is slumbering within our society'—served to underline the seriousness of the malaise, troubled by 'vicious demagogy, intrigue, and deliberate lying, politicking, an unrestrained, unheeding struggle for purely particular

300 EUROPEAN INTEGRATION SINCE THE 1920s

interests, a hunger for power, unadulterated ambition, fanaticism of every imaginable kind; new and unprecedented varieties of robbery, the rise of different mafias; the general lack of tolerance, understanding, taste, moderation, reason'.[194] In politics, where a 'lack of civility is merely a reflection of the more general crisis of civility', the president was worried about 'an extravagant hunger for power and a willingness to gain the favour of a confused electorate by offering them a colourful range of attractive nonsense':

> Demagogy is everywhere, and even matters as serious as the natural longing of a people for autonomy fuel power plays and stimulate deliberate lying to the public. Many members of the so-called *nomenklatura* who, until very recently, were faking their concern for social justice and the working class, have cast aside their masks and, almost overnight, have openly become a class of speculators and thieves. Many a once-feared Communist is now an unscrupulous capitalist shamelessly and unequivocally laughing in the face of the same worker whose interests he once claimed to defend.
>
> Citizens are becoming more and more clearly disgusted with all this, and their disgust is understandably directed against the democratic government that they themselves have elected. Exploiting this situation, many unsavoury characters have been gaining popular favour with ideas such as, for instance, the need to throw the entire government into the Vltava River.[195]

For many voters, 'politics' was new. Polls showed that they were less worried by political 'nonsense' than by economic hardship.

When asked by pollsters in 1993–94 'whether our present political system by comparison with the Communist one is better, the same or worse' in respect of freedom of association, expression, movement, conscience and 'an interest in politics', more than 90 per cent in Bulgaria and Romania and more than two-thirds in Poland and the Czech Republic replied that it was 'better now', but under a quarter considered their 'overall household economic situation' better than it had been five years ago, with 76 per cent in Hungary saying that it was worse (see Table 6.9). Although a majority in Poland thought that parliament might be closed and parties abolished in 1991–95 and about one-third believed that a 'strong man' or dictator should rule in the place of parliament (compared to half of respondents in Russia), these results were outliers in Central and Eastern Europe, becoming marginal by the turn of the century: only 10 per cent in Poland thought parliament might be shut down by 1998.[196] Given anti-Soviet feeling and criticism of corrupt Communist regimes in the Eastern bloc, there was broad support for the democratic successor states, with 74 per cent preferring the present system over the old system in Poland in January–February 1992, compared to 36 per cent in Russia.[197] There was much less support for liberalization and the introduction of market economies, which introduced new levels of risk.

Table 6.9 Perceptions of the economic basket of goods versus the political basket of goods in the Communist and current systems, 1993–94 ('better now' / 'worse now')

	Bulgaria	Czech Rep	Slovakia	Hungary	Poland	Romania
Overall household economic situation*	16/58	23/49	18/62	6/76	17/62	21/65
Per capita GDP (1993) in 1990 international dollars	4,933	7,169***	7,169	5,507	5,010	2,843
Join any organization they want**	95/5	90/1	88/3	81/2	79/2	94/1
Free to say what they want	90/11	84/3	82/4	73/8	83/4	94/2
Travel and live where they want	95/5	96/1	87/2	75/4	75/5	90/2
Live without fear of unlawful arrest	88/11	73/4	62/5	59/4	71/5	81/1
Take an interest in politics or not	97/3	84/0	81/1	—	69/5	92/1
Free to decide whether to practise a religion	98/2	94/0	96/1	83/1	70/6	95/1

* 'When you compare your overall household economic situation with five years ago, would you say that in the past it was better, the same, or worse?'

** 'Please tell me whether our present political system by comparison with the Communist one is better, the same or worse in the following areas.'

*** The Czech Republic and Slovakia are taken together by Maddison.

Source: adapted from J. J. Linz and A. Stepan, *Problems of Democratic Transition and Consolidation: Southern Europe, South America and Post-Communist Europe* (Baltimore, MD, 1996), 182, and A. Maddison, *The World Economy: Historical Statistics* (Paris, 2003), 101.

According to the New Europe Barometer in 1992, 67 per cent of Central and Eastern Europeans replied that they were 'coping'—that is, spending savings and not borrowing money—but only 32 per cent (in a different poll) were coping and satisfied with their lives, with 35 per cent dissatisfied and coping, and 27 per cent dissatisfied and not coping.[198] 47 per cent in Bulgaria were failing to cope. By 1995, 52–4 per cent of Romanians and Bulgarians, 44 per cent of Poles, 30 per cent of Hungarians, and 25 per cent of Czechs were living in poverty, with an income of 35–45 per cent of the average wage.[199] In 1989, only 4 per cent of Czechs, 10 per cent of Hungarians, and 15 per cent of Bulgarians—contrasting with 25 per cent of Poles and 34 per cent of Romanians—had been poor.

The official shrinkage of Central and Eastern European economies was dramatic: the Czech Republic reported a 12 per cent contraction by 1992–93, Hungary more than 20 per cent, Romania more than 30 per cent, and Latvia 49 per cent.[200] Such statistics were unreliable, since growing one's own food and participating in the black market had been features of life under Communism and continued to be so during the transition. Richard Rose claims that citizens were active in nine economies, with 72 per cent of households in a range of Central and Eastern European countries having at least one member with a regular job and 39 per cent with a pension or welfare benefits (the official, monetized economy), 68 per cent growing their own food, 64 per cent exchanging goods and favours with neighbours (the social, non-monetized economy), and 34 per cent using foreign currency, receiving bribes or working in the shadow economy (uncivil, monetized economies).[201] There is every indication that these activities, and the shortages which prompted them, caused anguish and suffering. At the start of the transition, two-thirds of citizens polled by the New Europe Barometer said that they were not earning enough to buy the things they needed: only 11 per cent in Hungary in 1992 stated that they were earning enough and less than 20 per cent in Latvia and Lithuania.[202] Only three countries—Slovenia, the Czech Republic, and Slovakia—did not register decreases in male life expectancy during the early 1990s.[203] Emigration was common: official figures before accession are underestimates (approximately 20,000–40,0000 annually from Poland, for example), based on applications for permanent residency abroad. They rose abruptly from 2008 onwards (to 200,000–300,000 per annum in Poland), when the definition changed to include those migrating for twelve months or longer.[204] In eastern Germany, from which movement after unification was easier and where the statistics are reliable, 1.7 million people—more than one-tenth of the population—moved to West Germany between 1989 and 1999.[205] Westward migration stood at around 100,000 per year—most of them young—during the 2000s. It is likely that these citizens' experiences of hardship and migration affected their outlook over the long term.

EU leaders were anxious about enlargement in 2004, worried by the anti-immigration agenda of tabloid newspapers and the far right, and they took steps to mitigate its effects. In previous enlargements (1973, 1981, 1986, and 1995), the negotiations had taken a similar form, with the *acquis communautaire* split into chapters, on each of which the candidate state presented a position paper outlining its economic and political situation.[206] The member states and the European Commission then arrived at a 'common position' on each chapter, which became the basis of a negotiation about terms of entry and the length of different transition periods. The Copenhagen criteria, which referred to democracy, markets, and adherence and which supplemented the newly inserted clause of the Treaty on European Union about accession (stressing 'liberty, democracy, respect for human rights and fundamental freedoms and the rule of law'), created a process of accession, subject to the scrutiny of EU monitors before and after entry.[207] The provisions, together with pre-accession funding from the European Investment Bank (EIB) via the 'Phare' programme for scientific and technical development, were specifically designed for post-Communist accession states, whose polities and economies needed to be reconstructed. Candidate governments were encouraged to participate in the Lisbon strategy, the negotiation of a Constitutional Treaty and other policy discussions prior to entry. Strict requirements were placed on the implementation of the *acquis* after entry, unlike in previous enlargements, where implementation was left to the new member states.

Agenda 2000: For a Stronger and Wider Union, which was presented by the European Commission in July 1997, accepted that 'A first wave of accessions will affect the budgetary positions of all the member states, reducing the positive balances of net beneficiaries'—Spain, Portugal, Greece, Ireland, and Belgium, which were taking most of the regional funds under Delors II, agreed after Maastricht—'and increasing the negative ones of others'.[208] It proposed that the EU's budget should remain at 1.4 per cent of European GDP, that no country should receive more than 4 per cent of GDP in transfers from the Union, and that new entrants' farmers would not receive direct payments agreed in the CAP reform of 1992. This last goal was modified in the accession agreements, which imposed a ten-year transition period (rising from one-quarter of the normal level) and production quotas to limit competition with producers elsewhere in Europe. The aims of EU leaders were not entirely defensive, however. Structural funds—the European Regional Development Fund, European Social Fund, European Agricultural Guidance and Guarantee Fund and the EIB—were established to reduce 'disparities between the levels of development of the various regions and the backwardness of the least favoured regions or islands, including rural areas' (Art. 130b of the Treaty Establishing the European Community of the Single European Act).[209] In 1999, the aims of the SEA were made into three objectives: the development and structural adjustment of regions lagging behind, with less than 75 per cent of the EU GDP per capita average (Objective 1); the economic and social conversion of areas facing structural difficulties, whether industrial decline or rural depopulation (Objective 2); and the modernization of systems of education, training, and employment (Objective 3). A Cohesion Fund was also established in 1993, after Maastricht, for transport and the environment in states with less than 90 per cent GDP per capita. 60 per cent of funds were initially allocated to Spain and 15 per cent each to Greece and Portugal. Although such funds were important for individual projects, the history of Central and Eastern European states, whose growth began in the mid-1990s before accession and continued on a similar trajectory afterwards, suggests that their overall effect has been secondary.

By 2013, instead of dragging down Europe, the eastern half of the continent was now a major contributor to growth and wealth all over Europe, wrote the *Washington Post* journalist, Anne Applebaum.[210] Four years earlier, a cartoon in

304 EUROPEAN INTEGRATION SINCE THE 1920S

The Economist had imagined the leaders of Germany, France, and the UK, Angela Merkel, Nicolas Sarkozy, and Gordon Brown, sitting in a luxury restaurant, contemplating the bill, on which 'for the rescue of Eastern Europe' was written, with horror: 'The bill that could break up Europe', ran the title of the article beside the cartoon, predicting economic collapse in states which had spent too much and lacked political stability.[211] After the events of the past four years, 'we should really toss out every stereotype, every cliché and every assumption that has ever been made about Europe's political geography,' Applebaum continued: 'East versus West, North versus South, none of it really makes sense of what is going on any more.'[212] British banks owed much more than the combined government debt of Poland and the Czech Republic, whose bonds paid 2 per cent, compared to 5 per cent for Italy, 6 per cent for Portugal, and 10 per cent for Greece. Latvia and Slovakia had experienced crises, but they made cuts and returned to a growth rate of 4–5 per cent per annum. 'Old' Europe's exports to the 'new Europe' had doubled over the previous decade, with the UK's rising from €2.2 billion in 1993 to €10 billion in 2011, France from €2.7 to €16 billion and Germany from €15 to €95 billion. In this sense, enlargement was not a cause of the crisis, but an inhibitor: 'alternative elites', including economists, had planned and then set up new liberal democracies and market economies which worked.

What mattered most, it seemed to Applebaum in 2013, was the desire of leaders and citizens to create 'normal' European states:

> If the existence of an alternative elite was important, however, it was even more important for that alternative elite to have a clear sense of direction. And in the case of the Central Europeans, there was never any doubt about this direction. When working as a journalist in the region in 1989 and 1990, people told me again and again, 'we want to be normal'. And 'normal' in 1989 and 1990 meant Western Europe, Western European democracy and capitalism, a Western European welfare state, Western European political parties, Western European media. There was no desire for experimentation: the question was 'do we move faster towards Europe?' or 'do we move slower towards Europe?' Those who moved faster avoided being stuck halfway.[213]

Applebaum's anecdotes about pro-European attitudes were borne out by polling evidence, showing that Germany and Sweden were the countries that Central and Eastern Europeans most wanted to emulate (31 and 32 per cent in the Czech Republic in 1991, for instance, compared to 14 per cent who thought the United States was a suitable model).[214] The removal of Communist elites by organized dissidents, the lack of a class of oligarchs, forty rather than seventy years of Soviet domination, active opposition movements during the 1970s and 1980s, the presence of an independent church, and a strong sense of historical or cultural particularity all helped the states of the Baltic and Central and Eastern Europe to effect a rapid transition from dictatorship during the 1990s, creating a set of economic and political distinctions between these regions and those of South East Europe and the Soviet successor states.[215]

The fears of Jacques Delors and Jacques Santer, the major sponsors of EU structural funds, that enlargement and the creation of a single market would create a core, especially around the 'golden triangle' of Paris, London, and Frankfurt, and a periphery of agricultural and post-industrial regions have not been realized. Even before the enlargements of 2004 and 2007 created the quickest growing regions in Europe, the Irish economy had grown from a deficit of 40 per cent per capita to an average 20 per cent higher than that of the EU-15. Spain had reduced its deficit from 30 to 15 per cent per capita and Portugal from 45 to 25 per cent over the same period.[216] Regional agglomerations of cities, often transnational, have developed, particularly in and around the Alps, linking Northern Italy, Rhône-Alpes, Southern Germany, Austria, and Switzerland, all of which have GDP per capita incomes well above the EU average (typically 10–30 per cent higher).[217] In 1998, the GDP per capita of Inner London was 243.4, Hamburg 185.5, Luxembourg 175.8, Brussels, 168.8, Vienna 162.8, and Upper Bavaria 161.2.[218] Twenty years later, Inner London (West) was 619.5 and Inner London (East) 165.4, Hamburg was 197.4, Luxembourg 263.0, Brussels 203.3, Vienna 149.8, and Upper Bavaria 178.5 (see Map 6.1).[219] By this time, however, Bucharest (152.2), Bratislava (173.4), and Warsaw (155.9) all had higher average per person incomes than Vienna.

In the East, along the entirety of the EU's border with Belarus, Ukraine, and Moldova are largely agricultural regions with indices of 40–50. Yet these disparities have not created a European core and periphery but, rather, a series of poorer areas within national economies and within the competence of member states' governments. The 'Mezzogiorno' in Italy has long been the anti-model and remains so, with Sicily (58.6), Calabria (56.3), and Campania (61.4) contrasting with Lombardy (127.6) and Trentino (125.5). Other cases of national disparity and division include Greece, where Ipeiros is still one of the poorest regions in the EU (41.8 in 1998 and 48.6 in 2018), and the United Kingdom, where both agricultural regions such as Cornwall (71.1) and the Scottish Lowlands (62.8) exist alongside post-industrial and mixed areas such as West and South Wales (66.6), the North East (69.3) and South Yorkshire (71.2). There has been nothing inevitable or specifically European about such trends. Post-unification governments in the Federal Republic of Germany, for example, which were concerned about eastern Germany becoming a Central European 'Mezzogiorno without the Mafia', have succeeded in increasing standards of living in the new *Bundesländer* (85–90).[220] In Spain, regions such as Extramadura were amongst the poorest areas in the EU twenty years ago (50.2) but have seen marked improvements (66.7). States like Denmark, Finland, Sweden, and the Netherlands have eradicated 'poor' regions altogether. These figures need to be viewed with caution, not least because

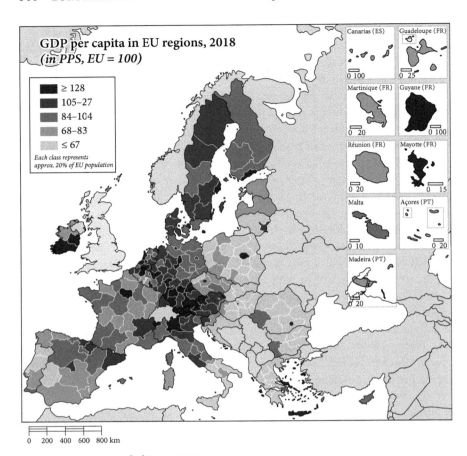

Map 6.1 GDP per inhabitant 2018
Source: Eurostat, at https://en.m.wikipedia.org/wiki/File:Eurostat_GDP_Regions_2018.png

poverty and wealth are often juxtaposed (for instance, in Inner London), yet they do reflect important changes in citizens' opportunities and enjoyment of life. Latvia (69.3), which was the poorest of the accession countries in 2004, now has higher average incomes (GDP per capita) than large parts of Wales, southern Scotland, and the North East of England. The successes of market-led convergence in Europe expose the failures of policy-makers, under pressure from competition in expanding European and global markets, on a national level.

What Is It to Be a European?

'No one in the village had ever seen the sea—except for the Dutch people, the mayor and József Puszka, who had been there during the war,' writes Geert

Mak in the 'Prologue' of *In Europe* (2004).[221] The houses lined a small stream, 'a handful of yellowed, crumbling farms, green gardens, bright apple trees, two little churches, old willows and oaks, wooden fences, chickens, dogs, children, Hungarians, Swabians, Gypsies'.[222] In the village of Vásárosbéc in Southern Hungary, 'time had stopped in 1925'.[223] 'There was not a mechanical sound to be heard: only voices, a dog, a rooster, a gaggle of geese overhead, a wooden wagon creaking down the road, the mayor's scythe,' the Dutch journalist continued: 'Later in the afternoon the ovens were lit; a thin blue veil of smoke floated across the rooftops. Now and then a pig squealed.'[224] Mak was criss-crossing Europe during 'the final months of the millennium', commissioned by the newspaper that he worked for, the *NRC Handelsblad*. What struck him was the variety of lives: not just the difference between East and West, but the different temporalities which citizens inhabited:

> Europe, as I saw in the course of that year, is a continent in which one can easily travel back and forth through time. All the different stages of the twentieth century are being lived, or relived, somewhere. Aboard Istanbul's ferries it is always 1948. In Lisbon it is forever 1956. At the Gare de Lyon in Paris, the year is 2020. In Budapest, the young men wear our fathers' faces.[225]

Vásárosbéc, in 1999, was 'preparing for its country's entry into the European Union'.[226] Over the last three years, 'six more Dutch people have arrived and bought at least a dozen houses', attracted by the low prices of Eastern Europe and by the prospect of a fresh start, 'the sort of people with a past one runs into everywhere at the continent's edge: back taxes, a disastrous divorce, a bankrupt business, trouble with the law'.[227] One of them had had a self-portrait painted on the side of the house, 'on horseback, waving a cowboy hat, ready to tame the Wild East'; another had spent more than €100,000, transforming his home 'into a little mansion, where he spends three weeks each year'.[228] He has overlooked the fact that his neighbour is the village's 'robber headman, who lives with his eight children in what is more or less a pigsty' and who has already tested the 'locked shutters of the Dutchman's El Dorado'.[229] The neighbour's children 'already cavort in the man's pool', Mak goes on.[230] Do Europeans share a 'lived experience'?

Attempts to identify specific sets of European 'values' have had a mixed reception.[231] McCormick draws heavily on the European Values Survey (EVS), which has investigated attitudes to citizenship, family, religion, the workplace, society, and well-being since the early 1980s, together with the World Values Survey (WVS), which—in addition to incorporating EVS findings—has used two axes (individual 'self-expression' and community-based 'secular-rational' values), showing that European societies tend to de-emphasize religion, patriotism, authority, and family values, and that individuals 'value liberty, conformity and

308 EUROPEAN INTEGRATION SINCE THE 1920s

trust in others'.[232] He admits that his findings do not apply to 'the notable exception' of most ex-Communist states, 'which are strong on secular-rational values but weak on self-expression', and to Ireland, Poland, Portugal, and Romania, 'which are weaker on the secular-rational scale'.[233] Overall, many of the responses are associated with 'liberal democracies', combined with an appreciation of welfare and equality:

> Europeanism is associated with preferences for state regulation of markets and social welfare with a view to promoting economic equality and opportunity. But when it comes to questions of how far the state should be allowed to make moral decisions for individuals, or to define personal choices, Europeans are less tolerant of government. The tightening of security in response to international terrorism has resulted in something of a reversal of late, but this has not impinged upon core European preferences in regard to such issues as gender equality, abortion, homosexuality, access to alcohol and drugs, euthanasia, censorship and religion. On these and related matters, Europeanism represents positions that are liberal and progressive, and that often stand in notable contrast to the values of other societies, particularly in the Islamic world.[234]

McCormick's selected values relating to multiculturalism, secularism and capital punishment are unlikely to guarantee cohesion, however. Although 110 countries still had the death penalty in 2010 and none in the EU (with France the last to use it in Western Europe in 1977), the majority of South American states had stopped executions earlier in the twentieth century (Argentina in 1956, Peru in 1979, Columbia in 1909) or even in the nineteenth (Brazil in 1876, Ecuador in 1884), despite a history of extra-judicial killing under dictatorships, during civil wars and in the pursuit of criminal gangs. Many African countries ceased executions in the second half of the twentieth century (Kenya in 1987, South Africa in 1989, Ghana in 1993, Cameroon in 1997). Canada stopped executing people in 1962, New Zealand in 1957, and Australia in 1967.[235] Giscard was shocked to find in the mid-1970s that 'public opinion was persuaded that the President of the Republic "decided" to apply the death penalty and that, ultimately, he alone decided'.[236] Notwithstanding the actions of the Council of Europe, which created the European Convention on Human Rights in 1953, it is hard to detect anything specifically European about the abolition of capital punishment. The same is true of multiculturalism, with definitions, prescriptions, and sanctions varying from country to country. As McCormick himself concedes, the Pew Global Attitudes Survey in 2008 found that negative attitudes to Muslims and Jews were more prevalent in Europe than in the United States and that they were increasing in number, with half of Spanish, German, and Polish, 38 per cent of French, and 23 per cent of British and American respondents having unfavourable opinions about Muslims, and half of Spaniards, 36 per cent of

Poles, 20–5 per cent of French and German, but only 7–9 per cent of Britons and Americans, having negative views of Jews.[237]

There are larger numbers of non-believers or supporters of secularism in many European countries in Western and Eastern Europe than in the rest of the world, with under 20 per cent professing a belief in God in Estonia in 2005 and under 50 per cent in Germany, Hungary, Bulgaria, France, the UK, and Denmark, for instance, yet more than 70 per cent professed such a belief in Ireland, Italy, Poland, and Greece, as they did in the United States.[238] The reasons for what Peter Berger has termed 'Eurosecularity' are diverse, dating back to the need for religious toleration in regions of fragmented principalities and large Protestant populations (the Low Countries and the German lands), those with established Protestant churches (Britain), or dealing with the varied effects of the Enlightenment and urbanization, nineteenth and early twentieth-century struggles between liberals and Catholics (Italy and France), the legacy of Communism, and post-war cultural emancipation. Between 50 and 90 per cent of Europeans, except in Austria, Ireland, Greece, Portugal, Italy, and Poland, thought that religion was not important in a Gallup survey in 2007–08, compared to 33 per cent in the USA, 10–30 per cent in most of Latin America, and 0–20 per cent in most African and Muslim states, but in this and other surveys they were similar to respondents in Australia, Canada, New Zealand, Japan, South Korea, and China (see Table 6.10).[239] 68.7 per cent of Australians, 75.7 per cent of Japanese and 64.1 per cent of South Koreans stated that religion was not very or not at all important in their lives in the World Values Survey of 2017–20, compared to 61.1 per cent of Germans, 18.1 per cent of Greeks, and 21.5 per cent of Romanians.

Swedes who considered themselves 'not a religious person' (56.2) or a 'convinced atheist' (6.5) were certainly secular in international comparison, but so were Japanese respondents (52.2 and 11.2 per cent, respectively). There has been a notable increase in religious indifference and secularism ('not at all religious') in the United States, South Korea, Chile, and Mexico over the last two decades, and a more moderate shift towards indifference (3.7–10.4 per cent) in Turkey. Communist countries such as China and post-Communist states like Estonia are, from a reading of surveys, the least religious countries in the world. Such patterns extend beyond Europe or the 'West' of the Cold War. They are also difficult to decipher, since those who are polled have different points of reference, with many Europeans considering themselves religious, tolerant, and liberal. What seems clear, however, is that neither secular nor religious values could underpin a European identity or way of life. When an early draft of the European constitution referred in its preamble to the 'cultural, religious and humanist inheritance of Europe', pointing to the civilizations of Greece and Rome and the 'philosophical currents of the Enlightenment', but not to Christianity, as its sources, Pope John Paul II called in public for a 'reference to the religious and in particular to the Christian heritage of Europe' and tried to convince Valéry Giscard d'Estaing, the

Table 6.10 'How important is religion in your life?' or 'Independently of whether you go to church or not, would you say you are a religious person, not a religious person or a convinced atheist?'

	2017/2020 Very	Rather	Not very	Not at all	1999/2004 Very	Rather	Not very	Not at all	1981/1984 Religious	Not	Atheist
Germany	13.9	24.6	35.2	25.9	—	—	—	—	—	—	—
Greece	54.8	26.8	11.9	6.2	—	—	—	—	—	—	—
Romania	47.3	30.8	16.6	4.9	—	—	—	—	—	—	—
Spain	—	—	—	—	21.9	27.3	30.9	19.3	—	—	—
Sweden	—	—	—	—	10.6	24.2	42.3	22.2	30.8	56.2	6.5
USA	37.1	23.6	21.9	16.5	56.9	25.4	12.4	4.9	81.4	15.4	1.1
Australia	13.8	15.0	28.0	40.7	—	—	—	—	55.8	37.3	4.4
Japan	4.6	9.9	33.6	42.1	6.4	13.1	31.6	12.4	24.0	52.2	11.2
S. Korea	10.3	25.6	47.7	16.4	23.2	28.9	31.3	16.4	—	—	—
China	3.3	9.7	43.4	42.8	2.5	6.3	25.3	59.9	—	—	—
Indonesia	98.1	1.8	0.1	0.0	98.1	1.8	0.1	0.0	—	—	—
Iran	70.5	22.0	3.3	4.1	78.9	14.9	3.3	1.2	—	—	—
Turkey	60.0	28.4	10.4	1.0	80.3	13.1	3.7	2.7	—	—	—
Brazil	45.1	39.5	10.4	4.7	—	—	—	—	—	—	—
Chile	20.7	34.3	29.6	14.7	46.3	33.4	14.2	5.4	—	—	—
Mexico	50.4	24.1	14.9	10.5	67.7	19.8	8.9	3.1	74.7	16.9	2.3
Zimbabwe	87.7	10.9	1.2	0.3	77.6	14.3	5.6	2.4	—	—	—

Source: World Values Survey, various years.

chair of the European Convention, in private to include such a reference.[240] The Vatican—and the Christian Democrats and other Conservatives in the European People's Party (EPP) who supported it—failed, with the redrafted preamble alluding only to 'the universal values of the inviolable and inalienable rights of the human person, freedom, democracy, equality, and the rule of law', which had developed out of a European cultural, religious, and humanist inheritance.[241] Neither Christianity nor the Enlightenment provided a suitable cultural and ethical foundation for the European Union. French and Dutch voters, only one-third of whom believed in God (with another third professing a belief in a 'spirit or life force'), went on to reject the constitution later in May and June 2005.[242]

There is a series of long-running disputes in sociology about whether it makes sense to talk of collectively held sets of values in 'advanced' economies. For Daniel Bell in *The Coming of Post-Industrial Society* (1973), class and class consciousness, which rested on the notion of private property, were in the process of being replaced by separate but connected realms—economy, polity, and culture—which cut across society, with social structures corresponding to axial principles of economic efficiency and rationality, the regulation of power, and the mediation between different interests in a polity organized through reference to the principle of equality.[243] Bell had argued earlier, at a conference of the Congress for Cultural Freedom in Milan in 1955 (organized by Raymond Aron, who put forward a similar thesis), that economic and social planning was replacing class conflict and was presaging the 'end of ideology'.[244] Cultural meaning was tied to the principle of self-expression. Classes, which were connected to production, wealth, and property, were disintegrating.[245] Knowledge had become more important than property: 'The concept of a post-industrial society is not a picture of a complete social order; it is an attempt to describe and explain an axial change in the social structure (defined as the economy, the technology and the stratification system) of the society.'[246] Underlying the shift was the transformation from goods to services:

In pre-industrial societies—still the condition of most of the world today—the labour force is engaged overwhelmingly in the extractive industries: mining, fishing, forestry, agriculture. Life is primarily a game against nature.... Pre-industrial societies are agrarian societies structured in traditional ways of routine and authority.

Industrial societies—principally those around the North Atlantic littoral plus the Soviet Union and Japan—are goods-producing societies. Life is a game against fabricated nature. The world has become technical and rationalized. The machine predominates, and the rhythms of life are mechanically paced.... The unit is the individual, and the free society is the sum total of individual decisions as aggregated by the demands registered, eventually, in a market.... Traditional elements remain. Work groups intervene to impose their own rhythms and 'bogeys' (or output restrictions) when they can. Waste runs high.

312 EUROPEAN INTEGRATION SINCE THE 1920s

Particularism and politics abound. These soften the unrelenting quality of industrial life. Yet the essential, technical features remain.

A post-industrial society is based on services. Hence, it is a game between persons. What counts is not raw muscle power, or energy, but information. The central person is the professional, for he is equipped, by his education and training, to provide the kinds of skill which are increasingly demanded in the post-industrial society. If an industrial society is defined by the quantity of goods as marking a standard of living, the post-industrial society is defined by the quality of life as measured by the services and amenities—health, education, recreation, and the arts—which are now deemed desirable and possible for everyone.[247]

It was likely that cultural distinctiveness would persist: 'Just as various industrial societies—the United States, Great Britain, Nazi Germany, the Soviet Union, post-World War II Japan—have distinctively different political and cultural features, so it is likely that the various societies that are entering a post-industrial phase will have different political and cultural configurations.'[248] Yet the overarching changes occurring in post-industrial societies were hollowing out particular cultures, as employees carried out similar, interchangeable roles, knowledge, and technical competence assumed greater significance, and individuals placed an emphasis on self-expression. Although post-industrial society is 'communal' rather than individual, because it requires social cooperation, 'increased conflict or deadlocks result' from many different groups wanting many different things and refusing to bargain or to accept trade-offs.[249] Social life becomes more difficult 'because political claims and social rights multiply, the rapidity of social change and shifting cultural fashion bewilders the old, and the orientation to the future erodes the traditional guides and moralities of the past'.[250] Professionalism becomes critical, 'but it clashes, too, with the populism which is generated by the claims for more rights and greater participation in the society'.[251] Classes—and other social groups—were being replaced by managers or elites and the managed or governed: 'The essential division in modern society today is not between those who own the means of production and an undifferentiated "proletariat" but the bureaucratic and authority relations between those who have powers of decision and those who have not, in all kinds of organizations, political, economic and social.'[252] There were competing forces in politics (cooperation and equality), the economy (the need for efficiency and knowledge) and culture (self-expression), which seemed to have issued in fragmentation, the creation of elites (information and decision-making), a continuing assault on tradition, and a transition from 'solid' machines, interests, and classes to 'liquid' relations, movement, a sense of time, and 'instant living', as Bauman later labelled it.[253]

There is nothing specifically European about the transformation which Bell described. Indeed, his study referred primarily to the United States and encompassed the 'West' as a whole, including Japan, Canada, and Australia. At the same time, however, there was no contradiction between internationalism and Europeanism, at least for elites. INSEAD, Sciences Po, Leuven, Brussels, Amsterdam, Göttingen, Freiburg, Uppsala, Aarhus, and Barcelona all taught in English by the early twenty-first century, joining Trinity College Dublin, UCD, Oxford, Cambridge, LSE, Imperial, and many other UK universities to produce tens of thousands of English-speaking, continental European graduates every year. In 2018–19, 143,025 EU students were attending a UK university, in addition to Erasmus students.[254] About 25,000 German, French, and Spanish students were at a US university. Graduates typically worked for a range of multinational companies, with the 'well-dressed young people who flitted through the business-class lounges of international airports brandishing EU passports and corporate American Express cards...probably more international in their culture than any group of Europeans since the aristocratic diplomats of the nineteenth century', in Richard Vinen's words.[255] In multinational companies, the language was usually English ('bad English', in the estimation of the head of ABB, a Swiss-Swedish engineering group), even when no native-speakers were present.[256] Increasingly, in EU circles, too, English had started to replace French, especially after the entry of Sweden and Finland in 1995 and the Central and Eastern European states in 2004–07, for whom English was the language of international business. 42 per cent of European Union documents were in English by 1997 and 40 per cent in French, noted Boutros Boutros-Ghali, *Secrétaire Général de la Francophonie* (and former Secretary-General of the UN).[257]

Such forms of 'lived Europeanism' did not merely concern a small elite.[258] Freedom of movement affected everyone, even if—like the residents of Vásárosbéc—their role was largely passive, observing the arrival of visitors from elsewhere in Europe. By the 2000s, around 135,000 students per year went on Erasmus placements in other member states.[259] Millions were working for small and medium-sized enterprises outside their home country: by 2019, 17.9 million Europeans—or just under 6 per cent of the workforce—were living and working in another member state, with 46 per cent residing in the UK and Germany and 28 per cent in France, Italy, and Spain.[260] About one-third of those changing member state between 2011 and 2019 were highly educated, with a university degree.[261] Business, administration and law have been the most common areas of expertise of highly-skilled migrants.[262] In the UK, almost half of EU workers were highly skilled, in France and Spain one-third, and in Germany one-quarter.[263] There was also an intermediary group of skilled workers, making up another 15 per cent of the cohort in retail and the service sector. In other words, about half of the active population moving around Europe is skilled and about half take up semi-skilled and non-skilled work; 58 per cent of 'movers' come from Romania, Poland, Italy, Portugal, and Bulgaria; 56 per cent are between the ages of twenty and forty-nine; and just over half of those who move stay for ten years or more in their host country.[264]

The majority of those who move acquire the language of their host country. In large enterprises and universities especially, English is widely spoken, drawing on a much larger pool of English-speakers in the EU and reflecting a common expectation that English serves as a lingua franca.[265] Just under half claimed that they were motivated to keep up their language for work and almost 80 per cent for social reasons. More than 70 per cent of those with a second language in Germany, Sweden, Denmark, Finland, France, and Greece spoke English. Unlike in the 1950s, 1960s, and 1970s, large numbers of Europeans have lived, studied and worked—even if only for short business trips—in other member states, where they have been able to communicate with the locals, whom they have frequently befriended and—quite often—married. The impact of mass tourism is less certain, with one-quarter of respondents travelling abroad—mainly within the EU—as early as 1997. It seems likely that travel, too, has had an impact on individual contacts and mutual perceptions.[266] Northern European retirement to the South has played an important part in these contacts, with 5 per cent of the total outflow of citizens in 2020 comprised of those who are sixty or above, moving to countries such as Croatia, Italy, France, Spain, and Portugal.[267]

The movement of people within the European Union has had varied effects. Right-wing parties and the tabloid press have frequently inveighed against 'EU migrants', usually as part of a broader campaign against immigration in general.[268] The actual patterns of migration and responses to them have been complex, however. Many European capitals, which have long traditions as cosmopolitan hubs, and other large cities, such as Barcelona and Hamburg, have become home to significant groups of EU nationals. One-third of Frankfurt's and Brussels's population and more than one-tenth of London's residents—or 1,103,000 people—have come from elsewhere in the EU.[269] Subject to qualification, inhabitants of these metropolitan areas—with large universities, service industries, and public administration—have looked on migration within (and outside) the European Union more favourably than other areas of the country. In the Brexit referendum in June 2016, taking place in the EU's most 'sceptical' member state, 59.9 per cent of voters in London, 60.4 in Manchester, 61.7 in Bristol, 50.7 per cent in Newcastle, 60.0 in Cardiff, and 66.6 in Glasgow voted to remain in the European Union, ignoring scare stories in the press about migration from the EU.[270]

A significant proportion of EU 'movers' in the UK—a total estimated at the time to be 3.7 million (but in fact almost 6 million), including children born in the UK and 320,000 Irish nationals—live outside these metropolitan areas: in 2016, an estimated 21,000 Poles lived in Northamptonshire, 15,000 in Nottinghamshire, and 22,000 in Lincolnshire, for example, predominantly in small towns, doing a range of jobs in agriculture and industry.[271] During the referendum campaign, the press focused on these towns—for example, Grantham, the birthplace of Margaret Thatcher—hinting that there was a link between migration and the Leave vote.

LIVING EUROPE 315

Table 6.11 To be European in the future, 2004

	National only	National and European	European and national	European only	Don't know
EU-15	41	46	6	4	3
Male	38	48	7	5	3
Female	43	44	6	4	3
15-24	34	54	7	4	4
55+	48	42	4	3	2
Self-employed	33	52	9	3	4
Managers	25	56	11	6	2
White-collar	29	54	9	5	3
Manual workers	45	43	4	5	3
House persons	51	38	5	3	3
Unemployed	50	38	7	3	2
Retired	49	41	4	4	2
Left school at 15	53	36	4	4	3
At 16–19	43	44	6	4	3
University 20+	26	58	8	5	3
EU membership a 'good thing'	25	59	9	5	2
A 'bad thing'	69	22	3	2	4
Neither good nor bad	46	42	5	5	3

Source: Eurobarometer 61 (2004), Annexes, 131.

Yet there was little correlation in the Brexit vote between towns with a large proportion of EU migrants and those without. Barnsley and its surrounding area in South Yorkshire (with a population of 239,000) voted by 68.3 per cent to leave yet had a population of around 4,000 Poles and 1,000 Romanians, or a mere 2 per cent of the total.[272]

How citizens feel about EU migration and immigration as a whole is notoriously variable and depends on shifting political and media agendas.[273] Whether citizens feel European or exclusively national has altered less over time, as has been seen (see Table 6.11). Here, there has been a clearer generational, occupational, and educational correlation; 66 per cent of 15–24 year-olds across Europe felt themselves to be European in 2004, compared to 52 per cent of those over 55; 75 per cent of managers, compared to 55 per cent of manual workers; and 74 per cent of university graduates, compared to 47 per cent of those leaving school at 15.[274] 17 per cent of managers felt themselves to be solely or mainly European.[275] In part, such attitudes derived from movement, networks, and contacts, and, in part, from assumptions, perceptions, ideas, and beliefs.

Public Spheres

Many citizens' assumptions about secondary political issues such as 'Europe' are shaped in the public sphere.[276] Arguably, the European issue remains secondary precisely because of the public sphere. In June 2014 (Ipsos MORI), a year-and-a-half after David Cameron's pledge to offer an in/out referendum, the 'EU/Europe/Euro' was considered the eighth 'most important issue facing Britain today', with 12 per cent of respondents mentioning it, after immigration (39 per cent), the economy (33), unemployment (28), the NHS (24), poverty/inequality (16), education (15), and housing (14).[277] The problem with public spheres in the EU, from the point of view of pro-Community politicians and commentators, is that they are, primarily, national and, secondarily, global, not European. Between the 1950s and 1990s, when the internet started to compete with it, television was the principal medium, with the bulk of programmes produced by public—or nationally licensed—broadcasters until de-regulation in the 1990s, when the number of TV stations mushroomed: there were 103 stations across the European Community in 1990, seventy-five of which were general; by 2003, there were 1,132, with 261 general channels and with the rest specializing in news, sport, entertainment, films, shopping, music, and culture.[278] Most viewers continued to get their news from national broadcasters, but there were, by the turn of the century, eighty-eight news channels being offered by different satellite and cable networks (CNN, Sky, Euronews). When news went online in the 2000s, many users continued to go to newspaper or magazine apps (42 per cent), together with news aggregators (14 per cent) and simple searches (21 per cent), which channelled users to the same news sites, yet the suppliers of information had become more varied. Twenty-two per cent in 2018 claimed that they got their news from social media, but this proportion minimizes the shift which has occurred within the production of 'news'.[279]

Most of the media landscape was domestic and American. In a sample week in 2000, 51 per cent of UK drama was domestic and 49 per cent American, with no European productions at all.[280] Similar figures were registered in other member states.[281] More than 70 per cent of imported TV productions in Western Europe between 1997 and 2001 were American. In 2018, US media giants (Disney, Discovery, Warner Media, Comcast) continued to capture more than twice the market share (11 per cent) of their EU rivals (Bertelsmann, Mediaset, BBC, France Televisions), which gained 5 per cent of non-domestic markets.[282] About one-quarter of European TV channels and pay-on-demand services are based in the UK.[283] Other media are similar, with the exception of print media, which are domestic (though often foreign-owned). In 2004, 71 per cent of films shown in the EU were produced or co-produced by American companies; in 2018, 62.3 per cent were American, which was the lowest figure since 2012.[284] Only 2.1 per cent of films were produced in the rest of the world, meaning that 35.6 per cent were

European, yet 70 per cent of these were shown in their 'home', national market, rather than in other member states. 18 out of 20 of the top box office films in the EU in 2018 were American, with the remaining two British. In this media landscape, it has been difficult for the European Union to foster a sense of European identity or for EU leaders to put forward their own version of events.[285]

The media, in Hans-Jörg Trenz's opinion, are 'a kind of natural constraint to transnationalization', dividing news into domestic and international sections, setting agendas and paying attention 'to those foreign events that are most closely tied to domestic politics and interests'.[286] Newspapers and broadcasters frame events and people, who are portrayed 'as friends or enemies of the nation'.[287] These structural biases do not rule out sympathetic coverage of EU policy-making, not least because the European press corps in Brussels has expanded—from 500 to over 900 journalists between 1990 and 2002 alone—and because it is self-reinforcing, dependent, on international news agencies (including *Agence Europe* for the EU) and contacts in EU institutions for stories and original information.[288] With the partial exception of UK broadsheets, journalists working for quality newspapers have tended to act as advocates of integration and 'progressive Europeanism'.[289] One report found that negative references to the EU in editorials of newspapers in the Netherlands, France, Italy, Spain, and Germany comprised less than five per cent of the total.[290] According to another study, the EU figured in about one-third of articles in broadsheets by 2003, more than doubling in salience since 1982, compared to national news stories.[291] 'In those policy fields where Europe matters, European actors and actors from other member states are frequently covered in national media, and national actors, including the media themselves, often refer to European dimensions of issues,' concludes Ruud Koopmans, even if this new focus on heads of state and government, cabinet ministers, and central banks leaves deputies and party actors—'those actors from the core of the political system who are directly accountable to the electorate'— much less well represented.[292]

How do media 'frame' the European Union in their reportage? 19.8 per cent of relevant frames—in the press of France, Germany, Italy, Spain, the Netherlands, UK, and Switzerland in the 1990s and early 2000s—alluded to the functioning of the economy, 12.8 per cent to democracy, rights, and citizenship, 10.9 per cent to sovereignty, 8.8 per cent to security and peace, and 8.2 per cent to equality and cohesion.[293] More than 90 per cent of articles covering 'European' themes referred to the EU, confirming that 'Europe' and the European Union were becoming the same thing in much of the coverage.[294] For Thomas Risse, writing in 2010, it seemed that 'the constitutional debates of the past ten years appear to show an emerging community of communication that discusses the future of European integration as an issue of common concern, irrespective of the various positions toward it', adopting a stance of 'us as Europeans', even though national newspapers express different preferences and strongly disagree among themselves.[295]

318   EUROPEAN INTEGRATION SINCE THE 1920S

However, it is difficult to prove that journalists are debating a subject 'as Europeans', particularly as studies have shown that 'Europe' had become a point of identification ('we') in only 5 per cent of cases by the late 1990s, compared to 40 per cent of cases for the nation-state.[296] By 2014, Risse was asking himself whether the 'extraordinary presence of supranational EU actors as well as executive actors from other countries' during the eurozone crisis was a sign, as 'conventional wisdom has it, that the crisis has led to a re-nationalization of public spheres, pitting, say, "lazy Greeks" against "German Nazis" dictating austerity policies to the rest of Europe', or whether—somewhat improbably—it was an encouraging sign of democratic deliberation and the politicization of the European question.[297]

Although the EU receives more coverage than it did in the 1970s and 1980s, it is misleading to equate it with the reportage of domestic politics. The majority of references to the EU in the quality press are 'instrumental', asking what a given government or member state stands to gain: 85 per cent were framed in this way around the turn of the century.[298] Newspapers had varying emphases in accordance with such national priorities: thus, whereas the *Guardian* (18.8 per cent) and *The Times* (22.4) concentrated in 2000 on the possibility of a British entry into the eurozone, the Austrian *Standard* (41.6) and *Presse* (39.2) focused on the 'Haider affair', and the *Frankfurter Allgemeine Zeitung*, the *Süddeutsche Zeitung*, *El Pais*, *Le Monde*, *La Stampa*, and *Repubblica* all gave priority to the euro, which was to enter into circulation in their respective countries at the start of 2001.[299] Arguably more important than the coverage in broadsheets has been that in the regional and tabloid press, in which the proportion of negative claims about the EU is four times higher than in quality newspapers.[300] These publications have often been tempted to highlight political scandals, intrigue, and hypocrisy in order to sell copy.[301] 'Infotainment' and 'dumbing down' have been standard components of popular reportage, easier to direct at European targets when they came into view during crises and conflicts between different governments.[302] In television news, with its broader audience, stories about the European Union have accounted for less than 5 per cent of broadcasts, except during EU summits, when they constituted about 10 per cent of coverage.[303]

In the debates about a European constitution, the eurozone crisis, migration, and Brexit, much press reportage of the EU was negative, leading to 'renationalization'.[304] Seventy per cent of 'claimants' in relevant newspaper reports in France in 2005 consisted of French national politicians and commentators discussing domestic subjects.[305] EU leaders made up only 13.5 per cent of claimants in France and 18 per cent in Germany during this period. A similar dynamic was visible during the eurozone crisis, with populist backlashes 'likely in the media frenzy to attribute blame to established political actors'.[306] In the UK, the Brexit debacle stimulated 'a first-order EU blame game' and saw pro-European politicians and leaders being punished.[307] As William Pfaff had noted in the *New York Review of Books* during the debate about a European constitution, 'a gap of comprehension between European political elites and the European public' seemed to have opened up, with elites underestimating 'forces of national identity and ambition in each of the twenty-five nations', yet it was not clear how far national presses had stoked up these forces or were merely representing them.[308] What was evident was that there was no European public sphere—or European media—to counteract national presses or the nationalism of voters.

The terms of the debate about a public sphere had been set by Jürgen Habermas and the constitutional lawyer Dieter Grimm in the long run-up to the referendums on a European constitution.[309] To Grimm, a European public sphere did not exist in the 1990s—nor has it since—and, therefore, the European Union could not become a democratic, state-like polity. 'Democracies are characterized by having political rule in them legitimated not transcendentally, traditionally or through elites, but consensually,' he wrote in 'Does Europe Need a Constitution?' (1995): 'The people...are permeated by divergence of opinion and interests, out of which negotiation or majority decision in the political process must first create unity, which can of course change.'[310] Elections, designed to give sectional interests a role in the political system, and free communication, 'without which the elections could not work', are meant to stop the bodies and persons exercising state power from becoming separated from the people, yet in large states further channels and checks are required in the form of additional organizations to assert voters' views and interests and a 'social process of interest mediation and conflict control'.[311] This mediation process is 'not running satisfactorily even at nation-state level' and, on a European level, 'even the pre-requisites are largely lacking': 'There is no Europeanized party system, just European groups in the Strasbourg parliament, and, apart from that, loose cooperation among programmatically related parties.'[312] European associations and citizens' groups have not emerged and 'a search for European media, whether in print or broadcast, would be completely fruitless'.[313] There is pressure to Europeanize the party system and interest groups, especially affecting officials and leaders, but the 'prospects for Europeanization of the communications system are absolutely non-existent':

A Europeanized communications system ought not to be confused with increased reporting on European topics in national media. These are directed at a national public and remain attached to national viewpoints and communication habits. They can accordingly not create any European public nor establish any European discourse. Europeanization in the communications sector would by contrast mean that there would be newspapers and periodicals, radio and television programmes, offered and demanded in a European market and thus creating a nation-transcending communicative context.[314]

320 EUROPEAN INTEGRATION SINCE THE 1920s

Grimm's threshold for a European public sphere—common media and a *lingua franca* for a European public—is higher than Risse's because it is intended to bear the weight of a constitutionally defined, state-like polity. The lack of a common language, with 'even English and French...foreign languages to over 80 percent of the Union population', and the 'absence of a European communications system' mean that public discourse remains 'for the time being bound by national frontiers, while the European sphere will remain dominated by professional and interest discourses conducted remotely from the public'.[315] Under such conditions, the 'full parliamentarization of the European Union' would loosen the Union's ties back to the member states', since 'the European Parliament is by its construction not a federal organ but a central one'.[316] It would not be compensated by closer ties to the people, since there 'is as yet no European people'.[317] To create a federation and to move 'from treaties to a constitution' would remove legitimation by states, instituting a *Kompetenzkompetenz* (the competence to decide about competencies) for European institutions in the stead of a primacy of Community law—as at present—resting on a 'member states' order issued in the treaties', without creating a new source of popular legitimacy on the European level.[318]

Habermas rejects Grimm's argument. The critical point for the Frankfurt philosopher is to create the conditions for democratic deliberation, which allows ethics, politics, history, culture, and identity to be debated and constantly re-established. 'I see the nub of republicanism in the fact that the forms and procedures of the constitutional state together with the democratic mode of legitimation simultaneously forge a new level of social integration,' he writes in his 'Reply to Grimm' (1997): 'Democratic citizenship establishes an abstract, legally mediated solidarity among strangers.'[319] Nation-states themselves had at once fostered and were constituted by this form of social integration, 'realized in the form of a politically socializing communicative context'.[320] Grimm is said to have left open the question of whether there is a pre-existent culture or identity (a *Volksnation* or, even, a Schmittian '*völkischen* homogeneity'): 'What unites a nation of citizens as opposed to a *Volksnation* is not some primordial substrate but rather an intersubjectively shared context of possible understanding.'[321] It is doubtful whether Grimm's reference to democracy requiring 'a collective identity, if it wants to settle its conflicts without violence, accept majority rule and practise solidarity', presupposes a 'primordial', 'pre-political', or 'independent' identity, yet it does point to a difference of emphasis, with the constitutional lawyer underlining a changing but shared content of politics and the philosopher championing procedures which allow debate to take place:

> The ethical-political self-understanding of citizens in a democratic community must not be taken as a historical-cultural *a priori* that makes democratic will-formation possible, but rather as the flowing contents of a circulatory process

that is generated through the legal institutionalization of citizens' communication. This is precisely how national identities were formed in modern Europe.[322]

A European constitution, in Habermas's opinion, would have an 'inducing effect', establishing a 'politically necessary communicative context', redirecting citizens' attention to new European centres of power, addressing the 'democratic deficit' and allowing the EU as a 'regionally comprehensive regime' to tackle global questions which have escaped the control of nation-states.[323] 'The debates on national economic competitiveness and the international division of labour in which we are engaged make us aware of quite another gap—a gap between the nation-state's increasingly limited manoeuvrability, and the imperatives of modes of production interwoven worldwide,' he goes on: 'If there is to be at least some substantive maintaining of the welfare state and some avoiding the further segmentation of an underclass, then institutions capable of acting supranationally must be formed.'[324] He concedes, though, that the 'ambitious functional requirements of democratic will-formation'—the core notion of 'a political public sphere which enables citizens to take positions at the same time on the same topics of the same relevance', 'a freedom-valuing political culture', a 'liberal associational structure of a civil society', and political parties to mediate between 'spheres of informal public communication' and institutionalized deliberation and decision processes'—have not been met: they can 'scarcely be fulfilled in the nation-state framework; this is all the more true for Europe'.[325] In other words, Habermas agrees with Grimm that a European public sphere does not exist. His dispute turns on the ease with which such a sphere could be created in future and the dangers which its creation—and the constitutional and political reforms designed, in part, to bring it about—would entail. The following chapters examine these political reforms and the debates which have accompanied them.

Notes

1. U. Frevert, *Mächtige Gefühle: Von A wie Angst bis Z wie Zuneigung. Deutsche Geschichte seit 1900* (Frankfurt, 2020).
2. J. McCormick, *Europeanism*, 215–16.
3. Ibid., 157–62, 215–21.
4. H. Kaelble, *Auf dem Weg zu einer europäischen Gesellschaft. Eine Sozialgeschichte Westeuropas 1880–1980* (Munich, 1987), 149.
5. Ibid.
6. H. Kaelble, 'Identification with Europe and Politicization of the EU since the 1980s', in J. T. Checkel and P. J. Katzenstein (eds), *European Identity* (Cambridge, 2009), 204.
7. Ibid., 204–5.
8. Ibid., 204; R. Girault (ed.), *Identité et conscience européenne au XXe siècle* (Paris, 1994).
9. Z. Bauman, *Europe: An Unfinished Adventure* (Cambridge, 2004), 4, 125–9: the sociologist does, though, repeat Tzvetan Todorov's list of European 'values', not realities, approvingly: rationality, justice, democracy, an 'autonomous society', and 'citizens endowed with individual liberty and individual responsibility for the ways they use it'.

10. Ibid.
11. Ibid., 98–9.
12. Ibid., 99.
13. Ibid., 101.
14. Ibid., 108, 110.
15. A. Giddens, *Europe in the Global Age* (Cambridge, 2007), 3.
16. Ibid.
17. Ibid., 2. See also Z. Bauman, *Europe: An Unfinished Adventure*, 91–123; and G. Therborn, *European Modernity and Beyond: The Trajectory of European Societies, 1945–2000* (London, 1995), 55–178. Ulrich Beck and Edgar Grande, *Cosmopolitan Europe* (Cambridge, 2007), 94–170, 192–223, examine the same themes, but they re-examine and question the borders of both the nation-state and the EU as repositories of social security and as means of mitigating risk.
18. A. Giddens, *Europe in the Global Age*, 62, 126.
19. Ibid., 9–10; G. Esping-Andersen, *The Three Worlds of Welfare Capitalism* (Cambridge, 1990).
20. A. Giddens, *Europe in the Global Age*, 6.
21. Ibid., 5–6, 16.
22. Ibid., 10.
23. Ibid., 32–40.
24. Ibid., 12.
25. Ibid., 36–8.
26. Ibid., 35.
27. Ibid.
28. Ibid., 11.
29. Ibid. 207.
30. Ibid., 208.
31. J. Chirac, *My Life in Politics*, 173–4.
32. Ibid., 174–5.
33. Ibid., 177.
34. Ibid.
35. *American Enterprise*, quoted in R. Wegs and R. Ladrech, *Europe since 1945: A Concise History*, 4th edn (New York, 1996), 201.
36. Pew Global Attitudes Project, 'Pervasive Gloom about the World Economy' (Washington, DC, 2012), 3. The breakdown of figures is 73 per cent in Italy (67 in 2012), 72 per cent in the UK (61), 68 per cent in Poland (68), 67 per cent in Spain (47), 65 per cent in Germany (69), 59 per cent in the Czech Republic (50), and 56 per cent in France (58).
37. Ibid., 1.
38. Ibid.
39. Ibid. The figures are: 29 per cent in Poland (52 per cent in 2008), 19 per cent in France (19 in 2008), 16 per cent in the Czech Republic, 15 per cent in the UK (30), 6 per cent in Spain and Italy, and 2 per cent in Greece. Only the Federal Republic of Germany diverged from this path, with 53 per cent saying that the national economic situation was good in 2008 and 73 per cent in 2012, which belied much German media coverage of the eurozone crisis and the FRG's ability to act as a creditor of Greece.
40. J. McCormick, *Europeanism*, 126–7. Similarly, a large percentage of Americans—82 per cent—thought that parents should be responsible for providing food, clothing, and housing for their children (up to eighteen), but a smaller number of Europeans (66 per cent of French respondents, 50–9 per cent of British, German, Italian, and Spanish).
41. H. Kaelble, 'Was Prometheus Most Unbound in Europe?', *Journal of European Economic History*, 15 (1986), 72.
42. Ibid., 75–6.
43. C. Crouch, 'Class Politics and the Social Investment Welfare State', in M. Keating and D. McCrone (eds), *The Crisis of Social Democracy in Europe* (Edinburgh, 2015), 156–68.
44. A. Marwick, *Class: Image and Reality in Britain, France and the USA since 1930* (Basingstoke, 1990), 268.
45. M. Weber, *Wirtschaft und Gesellschaft*, 5th edn. (Tübingen, 1976), 1–30; J. Scott, *Stratification and Power: Structures of Class, Status and Command* (Cambridge, 1996), 48–186.
46. H. Schmidt, *Weggefährten*, 181.
47. M. Djilas, *The New Class* (New York, 1957); R. Dahrendorf, *Class and Class Conflict in an Industrial Society* (London, 1957); R. Aron, *La Lutte des classes* (Paris, 1964).
48. J. P. Nettl, *The Soviet Achievement* (New York, 1967), 254.

LIVING EUROPE   323

49. R. Scase, 'English and Swedish Concepts of Class', in F. Parkin (ed.), *The Social Analysis of Class Structure* (London, 1974), 149–77.
50. J. Goldthorpe, *The Affluent Worker* (Cambridge, 1968–69), *The Social Grading of Occupations* (Oxford, 1974), *Social Mobility and Class Structure in Modern Britain* (Oxford, 1980).
51. C. Thélot, *Tel père, tel fils* (Paris, 1982), 46.
52. D. Merllié and J. Prévot, *La Mobilité sociale* (Paris, 1991), 62.
53. R. Scase, 'English and Swedish Concepts of Class', in F. Parkin (ed.), *The Social Analysis of Class Structure* (London, 1974), 149–77.
54. H. Kaelble, *Auf dem Weg zu einer europäischen Gesellschaft*, 59.
55. Ibid., 60–1.
56. See, above all, Gérard Noiriel, *Workers in French Society in the Nineteenth and Twentieth Centuries* (New York, 1990), who does not question the existence of class and who sees the 1950s and 1960s as the high point of militancy, despite other reservations.
57. D. Sassoon, *One Hundred Years of Socialism: The West European Left in the Twentieth Century* (New York, 1996), 198–9.
58. H. Kohl, *Erinnerungen 1930–1982*, vol. 1, 277.
59. D. Sassoon, *One Hundred Years of Socialism*, 141.
60. Ibid., 139.
61. P. Flora, *State, Economy and Society in Western Europe, 1815–1975* (London, 1983), 338; P. Flora and A. J. Heidenheimer (eds), *The Development of Welfare States in Europe and America* (New Brunswick, 1981), 2 vols.
62. D. Sassoon, *One Hundred Years of Socialism*, 140.
63. D. Sassoon, *Contemporary Italy: Economy, Society and Politics since 1945*, 2nd edn (London, 1997), 208–20.
64. P. P. Donati, 'Social Welfare and Social Services in Italy since 1950', in R. Girod, P. de Laubier, and A. Gladstone (eds), *Social Policy in Western Europe and the USA, 1950–1985* (London, 1985), 101–11; G. Vicarelli, 'The Creation of the NHS in Italy, 1961–1978', *Dynamis*, 39 (2019), 21–43.
65. W. Kaiser, *Christian Democracy and the Origins of the European Union* (Cambridge, 2007), 177.
66. Ibid., 164.
67. See G. Galli and A. Prandi, *Patterns of Political Participation in Italy* (New Haven, CT, 1970).
68. P. Ignazi and E. S. Wellhofer, 'Religion, Rurality and Voting: Secularization, Landownership and Italian Electoral Behaviour, 1953–2008', *West European Politics*, 36 (2013), 925.
69. A. De Gasperi, quoted in P. Ginsborg, *A History of Contemporary Italy: Society and Politics, 1943–1988* (London, 1990), 144.
70. Quoted in N. Kogan, *A Political History of Italy: The Postwar Years* (New York, 1983), 61.
71. D. Sassoon, *Contemporary Italy*, 196.
72. C. M. Warner, 'Religious Parties in a Secularizing Political Space: The Case of Italy', *Asian Security*, 4 (2008), 66; C. M. Warner, 'Christian Democracy in Italy: An Alternative Path to Religious Party Moderation', *Party Politics*, 19 (2012), 256–76. The divorce law was defended by a majority of 60 per cent, with a turn-out of 87 per cent.
73. V. B. Lewis, 'Development in Catholic Social Teaching: John XXIII to Paul VI', in G. V. Bradley and E. C. Brugger (eds), *Catholic Social Teaching* (Cambridge, 2019), 142.
74. K. van Kersbergern, *Social Capitalism: A Study of Christian Democracy and the Welfare State* (London, 1995).
75. See D. Dutton, *British Politics since 1945: The Rise, Fall and Rebirth of Consensus*, 2nd edn (Oxford, 1997); B. Harrison, 'The Rise, Fall and Rise of Political Consensus in Britain since 1940', *History*, 84 (1999), 301–24; R. Toye, 'From "Consensus" to "Common Ground": The Rhetoric of the Postwar Settlement and Its Collapse', *Journal of Contemporary History*, 48 (2013), 3–23; N. Rollings, 'Butskellism, the Postwar Consensus and the Managed Economy', in H. Jones and M. Kandiah (eds), *The Myth of Consensus: New Views of British History, 1945–1964* (Basingstoke, 1996), 97–119.
76. N. Barr, 'The Phillips Machine', *LSE Quarterly*, 4 (1988), 321; P. Howlett, 'The "Golden Age", 1955–1973', in P. Johnson (ed.), *Twentieth-Century Britain: Economic, Social and Cultural Change* (London, 1994), 320–39. See A. Hicks, *Social Democracy and Welfare Capitalism: A Century of Income Security Politics* (Ithaca, NY, 1999), 153–221.
77. M. Larkin, *France since the Popular Front: Government and People, 1936–1986* (Oxford, 1988), 205.
78. G. Eley, *Forging Democracy: The History of the Left in Europe, 1850–2000* (Oxford, 2002), 420.
79. Ibid., 321.
80. Ibid., 318.
81. *Die Zeit*, 23 May 1986.

82. T. Blair, *A Journey*, 213.
83. Z. Bauman, *Memories of Class: The Pre-history and After-life of Class* (London, 1982).
84. G. Eley, *Forging Democracy*, 386.
85. Ibid., 385.
86. Ibid., 391.
87. S. M. Lipset, 'Whatever Happened to the Proletariat', *Encounter*, June 1981, 21.
88. 34 per cent went to the Parti Socialiste. J. R. Wegs and R. Ladrech, *Europe since 1945*, 178.
89. G. Eley, *Forging Democracy*, 386.
90. R. Leach, *Political Ideology in Britain*, 3rd edn (Basingstoke, 2015), 57–91.
91. N. Lawson, *The View from No. 11: Memoirs of a Tory Radical* (London, 1993), 64.
92. R. Vinen, *Thatcher's Britain: The Politics and Social Upheaval of the 1980s* (London, 2009), 304–5.
93. Ibid., 109.
94. Nigel Lawson, speech to the Bow Group, 4 August 1980, R. Vinen, *Thatcher's Britain*, 110–11.
95. S. Jenkins, *Thatcher and Sons: A Revolution in Three Acts* (London, 2006), 92.
96. Dennis Kavanagh's report in *Thatcherism and British Politics: The End of Consensus?* (Oxford, 1987), runs: 'The government has made minor cuts on welfare and some changes of a largely symbolic nature. It has protected spending on the NHS and welfare state, and attempts to contain social security expenditure have been thwarted by the massive rise in unemployment.'
97. Her comment about a strong state came in an interview with Simon Jenkins in 1990: ibid., 106. See also M. Thatcher, *Path to Power*, 48.
98. S. Jenkins, *Thatcher and Sons*, 124.
99. K. O. Morgan, *Britain since 1945: The People's Peace*, 3rd edn (Oxford, 2001), 493–4. Likewise, New Labour, which tried to appeal to similar voters, stressed that the debate was not about the value of public services, but the means of delivery. T. Blair, *A Journey*, 212: 'For public services to be equitable, and free at the point of use, they did not all need to be provided on a monopoly basis within the public sector, controlled in a rigid way by national and local bureaucracies often deeply resistant to innovation and genuine local autonomy.' For more on Frank Field's initial design for the welfare state, which was modified, see S. Heywood, *What Does Jeremy Think? Jeremy Heywood and the Making of Modern Britain* (London, 2021), 71–4.
100. European Commission, *European Economy* (1995), 235.
101. T. Blair, *A Journey*, 214.
102. European Commission, *European Economy* (1995), 223–35.
103. F. W. Scharpf, 'The European Social Model: Coping with the Challenges of Diversity', *Journal of Common Market Studies*, 40 (2002), 646.
104. Ibid. There have of course been some consequences of citizens themselves taking employers, retailers, producers, and governments to the ECJ, but these remain marginal, and certainly not akin to the construction of a European social state from below: M. Eigmüller, 'Europeanization from Below: The Influence of Individual Actors on the EU Integration of Social Policies', *Journal of European Social Policy*, 23 (2013), 363–75.
105. F. W. Scharpf, 'The Joint-Decision Trap: Lessons from German Federalism and European Integration', *Public Administration*, 66 (1988), 239–78.
106. F. W. Scharpf, 'The European Social Model: Coping with the Challenges of Diversity', *Journal of Common Market Studies*, 40 (2002), 648.
107. Ibid., 649.
108. Ibid., 666.
109. Ibid., 649. Other authors have been more positive, even though it is difficult to see CAP as a model for the creation of a European welfare state: Ann-Christina Knudsen, *Farmers on Welfare: The Making of Europe's Common Agricultural Policy* (Ithaca, NY, 2009), has argued that CAP was based on the logic of welfare state provisions; Gilbert Noël, 'Les finalités de la politique agricole commune 1958–1972. Marché et cohesion économique et sociale', in A. Varsori (ed.), *Inside the European Community: Actors and Policies in European Integration* (Baden-Baden, 2006), 283–300, shows that policy-makers were aware of the social dimension of CAP from the start, not least because the idea had been pursued on a national level since the late nineteenth century, as Guido Thiemeyer has indicated in *Vom 'Pool Vert' zur Europäischen Wirtschaftsgemeinschaft. Europäische Integration, Kalter Krieg und die Anfänge der Gemeinsame Europäischen Agrarpolitik 1950–1957* (Munich, 1999).
110. F. W. Scharpf, 'The European Social Model: Coping with the Challenges of Diversity', *Journal of Common Market Studies*, 40 (2002), 650. See also F. W. Scharpf, *Governing in Europe* (Oxford, 1999), 187–204, arguing that governments have been constrained by 'negative integration' (removal of restrictions to trade) and by competition—on economic grounds—between national

systems of regulation. His solution is to explore whether a European 'law of unfair regulatory competition' could be developed.

111. G. Majone, *Europe as the Would-be World Power*, 128–50. He is arguing against federalists such as the Belgian Prime Minister Guy Verhofstadt and the German intellectual Jürgen Habermas, who had contended that the Dutch and French 'no' to a European constitution in referenda in 2005 were a rejection of a neo-liberal market and a demand 'for a more welfare-orientated Union'.

112. Ibid., 131–2.

113. Protocol on Social Policy, Treaty on European Union (1992).

114. G. Majone, *Europe as the Would-be World Power*, 134. The name 'Social Chapter' was used synonymously with the Protocol or 'Social Agreement' of 1992. According to Gerda Falkner, 'The EU's Social Dimension', in Michelle Cini (ed.), *European Union Politics* (Oxford, 2003), 267, 'Because of the UK opt-out (or the 'opt-in' of the other member states), the EU after Maastricht (from November 1993) had two different legal bases for the adoption of social policy measures. The EC Treaty's social provisions remained valid for all member states. As introduced in the 1986 Single European Act, they allowed for minimum harmonization as well as for qualified majority voting (QMV) in the area of worker health and safety provisions only. By contrast, the innovative social policy provisions of the Social Agreement, applicable to all but the UK, comprised what had been perceived during the IGC as an amendment to the social provisions of the Treaty. These constituted an extension of Community competence into a wide range of social policy issues, including working conditions; the information and consultation of workers; equality between men and women with regard to labour market opportunities and treatment at work (as opposed to only equal pay before); and the integration of persons excluded from the labour market.' The right of association and the right to strike, social security, termination of workers' contracts, the representation of workers' interests, conditions of employment for other EU nationals, and financial contributions for job creation all remained excluded from the TEU or subject to unanimity in the Council. Most of the fifty-one new directives on social policy since 1974 (together with thirteen changes and seven geographical extensions) concern health and safety, gender equality and working conditions.

115. T. Blair, *A Journey*, 25.

116. Quoted in A. Sapir, 'Trade Liberalization and the Harmonization of Social Policies: Lessons from European Integration', in J. N. Bhagwati and R. E. Hudec (eds), *Fair Trade and Harmonization* (Cambridge, MA, 1996), vol. 1, 559.

117. G. Majone, *Europe as the Would-be World Power*, 139.

118. Ibid., 143–5. On the lack of public support, see H. Obinger, S. Leibfried, and F. G. Castles, 'Bypasses to a Social Europe? Lessons from Federal Experience,' *Journal of European Public Policy*, 12 (2005), 545–71; on the absence of a race to the bottom, see M. Ferrara, A. Hemerijk, and M. Rhodes, 'The Future of the "European Social Model" in the Global Economy', *Journal of Comparative Policy Analysis*, 3 (2001), 163–90.

119. G. Majone, *Europe as the Would-be World Power*, 234.

120. A. Giddens, *Europe in the Global Age*, 207. On market correction, see F. W. Scharpf, 'The European Social Model: Coping with the Challenges of Diversity', *Journal of Common Market Studies*, 40 (2002), 649.

121. W. Brandt, *Erinnerungen*, new edn. (Berlin, 1999), 142.

122. Ibid. There are many such accounts, crossing political lines: see, for instance, the CSU leader Franz Josef Strauß, *Die Erinnerungen*, 64: 'After twelve years, of which six were at war, the "Thousand Year Reich" was over. Germany stood before the greatest pile of rubble in its history.... In this period of 1945 and after, in which it was a question of survival, eating, heating, shelter, the finding of close relatives again, in short naked existence, we asked ourselves the question: how should we go on?' Strauß was born in 1915.

123. H. Glaser, *Die Kulturgeschichte der Bundesrepublik Deutschland. Zwischen Kapitulation und Wärhungsreform 1945–1948* (Frankfurt, 1985), vol. 1, 45.

124. Quoted ibid., 21.

125. Ibid.

126. H. Schelsky, *Wandlungen der deutschen Familie der Gegenwart* (Stuttgart, 1953), 48.

127. See, for instance, Colin Crouch, *Social Change in Western Europe* (Oxford, 1999).

128. H. Kaelble, *Auf dem Weg zu einer europäischen Gesellschaft*, 149.

129. H. Kaelble, 'Die Gesellschaften der EU. Zusammenwachsen und Krise 1957–2017', *Zeitschrift für Staats- und Europawissenschaften*, 15 (2017), 157.

130. Ibid., 163.

131. Ibid., 163–4.

326 EUROPEAN INTEGRATION SINCE THE 1920S

132. Ibid., 158.
133. Ibid.
134. Ibid.
135. Ibid., 169–70.
136. Ibid., 170: overall, those believing in the existence of shared European values dropped from 54 to 49 per cent.
137. Ibid., 171.
138. Ibid.
139. Ibid., 172.
140. Ibid., 159.
141. Ibid., 160: US figures for 2014 and Eurostat figures for 2000 are not available. EU migration was artificially low in 2014 because of the effects of the eurozone crisis.
142. Ibid.
143. H. Kaelble, 'Abmilderung der sozialen Ungleichheit? Das westliche Europa während des Wirtschaftsbooms der 1950er bis 1970er Jahre', *Geschichte und Gesellschaft*, 40 (2014), 595–6; A. B. Atkinson and T. Piketty, *Top Incomes over the Twentieth Century: A Contrast between Continental European and English-speaking Countries* (Oxford, 2006); T. Piketty, *Capital in the Twenty-First Century* (Cambridge, 2014).
144. Kuznets argued that 'income inequality should follow an inverse U-shape along the development process, first rising with industrialization and then declining, as more and more workers join the high productivity sectors of the economy': T. Piketty, 'Top Incomes over the Twentieth Century: A Summary of Main Findings', in A. B. Atkinson and T. Piketty, *Top Incomes over the Twentieth Century*, 9. Kuznets's curve was based on US data from 1913 to 1948.
145. H. Kaelble, 'Abmilderung der sozialen Ungleichheit? Das westliche Europa während des Wirtschaftsbooms der 1950er bis 1970er Jahre', *Geschichte und Gesellschaft*, 40 (2014), 604–5.
146. Ibid., 607.
147. H. Kaelble, 'Die Gesellschaften der EU. Zusammenwachsen und Krise 1957–2017', *Zeitschrift für Staats- und Europawissenschaften*, 15 (2017), 164–5.
148. H.-U. Wehler, 'Wie hoch ist Europas "Preis der Freiheit"?', in H.-U. Wehler, *Essays zur Geschichte* (Munich, 2014), 67. He was commenting on Andreas Wirsching, *Der Preis der Freiheit. Geschichte Europas in unserer Zeit* (Munich, 2012).
149. Thomas Piketty, *Capital in the Twenty-First Century* (Cambridge, MA, 2014), 409, claims that these four European countries 'are quite representative of European diversity' and that 'the curve would not look very different if we included other northern and southern European countries for which data are available, or if we weighted the average by the national income of each country'. It is surprising that no example of a southern European country is given here, since the timing of the movement away from agriculture and development of the welfare state were different, for instance.
150. Ibid.
151. T. Piketty, 'Top Incomes over the Twentieth Century', in T. Piketty, *Top Incomes over the Twentieth Century: A Contrast between Continental European and English-speaking Countries* (Oxford, 2007), 9–10.
152. Ibid., 10. The authors concentrate on industrialized economies. For wider reflections, see A. B. Atkinson and T. Piketty (eds), *Top Incomes: A Global Perspective* (Oxford, 2010).
153. T. Piketty, 'Top Incomes over the Twentieth Century', in T. Piketty, *Top Incomes over the Twentieth Century*, 9–10.
154. Ibid., 11. See also A. B. Atkinson, *Incomes and the Welfare State: Essays on Britain and Europe* (Cambridge, 1995).
155. T. Piketty, 'Top Incomes over the Twentieth Century', in T. Piketty, *Top Incomes over the Twentieth Century*, 9–10.
156. Ibid.
157. Ibid. T. Piketty, *Capital in the Twenty-First Century*, 630–99.
158. Richard Allen and Ed Meese had asked the question at the Ottawa meeting of the G7 in July 1981: P. Short, *Mitterrand*, 335.
159. M. Brewer, A. Goodman, A. Muriel, and L. Sibieta, *Poverty and Inequality in the UK* (London, 2007), 15. This is an Institute for Fiscal Studies briefing paper.
160. Ibid. The figures run until 2005–06. The other quintiles were between 1.9 per cent p.a. and 2.4 per cent p.a., for those between 20 and 39 per cent.
161. M. Garnett, *From Anger to Apathy: The Story of Politics, Society and Popular Culture in Britain since 1975* (London, 2007).

162. P. Bourquin, J. Cribb, T. Waters, and X. Xu, *Living Standards, Poverty and Inequality in the UK: 2019* (London, 2019), 16–17. This is an IfS briefing paper. For global Gini coefficients, see OECD, 'Income Inequality' (2021).
163. L. L. Doan, '"Sexy Greedy Is the Late Eighties": Power Systems in Amis's *Money* and Churchill's *Serious Money*', *Minnesota Review*, 34 (1990), 69–80.
164. See R. Vinen, *Thatcher's Britain*, 178–208; M. J. Wiener, *English Culture and the Decline of the Industrial Spirit, 1850–1980* (Cambridge, 1981).
165. See J. Redwood, *Singing the Blues: 30 Years of Tory Civil War* (London, 2004).
166. Respectively, Tony Blair's speech to the Labour Party Conference in 2001 and his launch of the Labour Party manifesto in 2005, in V. Bogdanor, 'Social Democracy', and R. Taylor, 'New Labour, New Capitalism', in A. Seldon (ed.), *Blair's Britain, 1997–2007* (Cambridge, 2007), 175, 214.
167. A. Campbell, *The Blair Years: Extracts from the Campbell Diaries* (London, 2007), 250. On Mandelson, see M. Keating and D. McCrone (eds), *The Crisis of Social Democracy in Europe* (Edinburgh, 2013), 228–32.
168. N. Sarkozy, *Le Temps des tempêtes*, 77.
169. M. Brewer, A. Goodman, A. Muriel, and L. Sibieta, *Poverty and Inequality in the UK* (London, 2007), 19. Brexit, of course, is linked in various ways to such recent British divergence. The significance of Brexit to Britons contrasts with its importance—which can be read from media coverage—for other Europeans. Arguments for long-term British exceptionalism are commonplace, but remain unconvincing: see, for example, S. Sweeney, *The Europe Illusion: Britain, France, Germany and the Long History of European Integration* (London, 2019), and R. Tombs, *The Sovereign Isle: Britain In and Out of Europe* (London, 2021).
170. The figures are for purchasing power (PPP).
171. Office for Official Publications of the European Communities, *50 Years of Figures on Europe* (Luxembourg, 2003), 45, 59.
172. Ibid.
173. Ibid., 45. See also M. Gilbert, *European Integration*, 158–9.
174. Office for Official Publications of the European Communities, *50 Years of Figures on Europe*, 59.
175. European Commission, *Eurostat Yearbook: A Statistical Eye on Europe, 2005* (Luxembourg, online).
176. See E. da Conceição-Heldt, 'EU Agricultural and Fisheries Policies: An Economic and Environmental Disaster!', in H. Zimmermann and A. Dür (eds), *Key Controversies in European Integration*, 161–8; I. Garzon, *Reforming the Common Agricultural Policy: History of a Paradigm Change* (Basingstoke, 2007).
177. European Commission, *The Social Situation in the European Union, 2005–6* (Luxembourg, 2006), 146.
178. European Commission, *The Social Situation in the European Union, 2008* (Luxembourg, 2009), 170.
179. *Economist*, 5 October 2002.
180. I. T. Berend, *From the Soviet Bloc to the European Union: The Economic and Social Transformation of Central and Eastern Europe since 1973* (Cambridge, 2009), 115.
181. Ibid., 167.
182. Ibid., 115.
183. I. T. Berend, *From the Soviet Bloc to the European Union*, 229.
184. Ibid.
185. N. Sarkozy, *Le Temps des tempêtes*, 106.
186. European Commission, *European Union Enlargement: A Historic Opportunity* (Luxembourg, 2003), 37.
187. I. T. Berend, *From the Soviet Bloc to the European Union*, 259.
188. Ibid., 260.
189. R. Rose, *Understanding Post-Communist Transformation: A Bottom Up Approach* (London, 2009), 193.
190. I. T. Berend, *From the Soviet Bloc to the European Union*, 167.
191. D. Ost, *The Defeat of Solidarity: Anger and Politics in Postcommunist Europe* (Ithaca, NY, 2005), 60–120, examines how 'market populism' was connected to a turn to the right and how dissidents and democrats lost control of politics in the new regime.
192. V. Havel, 'Paradise Lost', *New York Review of Books*, 9 April 1992.
193. Ibid.
194. Ibid.
195. Ibid.

196. Centre for the Study of Public Policy, *New Europe Barometer, 1991–2008*.
197. I. Boeva and V. Shironin, 'Russians between State and Market', *Studies in Public Policy*, 205 (1992), 19–22.
198. R. Rose, *Understanding Post-Communist Transformation*, 79–80.
199. I. T. Berend, *From the Soviet Bloc to the European Union*, 189.
200. Ibid., 75.
201. Ibid., 77.
202. Ibid.
203. Ibid., 85.
204. Eurostat, *Emigration Statistics* (2020). Poland, with 40 million inhabitants, and Romania, with 30 million, with around 200,000 leaving every year, have been the main countries of emigration in Central and Eastern Europe. It is worth noting that the principal countries of emigration in the EU are the United Kingdom, with 300,000 to 400,000 leaving annually, France, with 200,000 to 300,000, and the FRG, with around 250,000, rising to more than 500,000 over recent years.
205. L. Kettenacker, *Germany 1989: In the Aftermath of the Cold War* (London, 2009), 197–8.
206. See Anna Michalski, 'The Enlarging European Union', in D. Dinan (ed.), *Origins and Evolution of the European Union* (Oxford, 2006), 271–92.
207. Ibid., 273. Also, M. Baun, *A Wider Europe: The Process and Politics of European Union Enlargement* (Lanham, MD, 2000).
208. European Commission, *Agenda 2000: For a Stronger and Wider Union* (Luxembourg, 1997), 67.
209. After Amsterdam, this became Article 159.
210. A. Applebaum, 'Does Eastern Europe Still Exist?', *Prospect*, 20 March 2013.
211. *The Economist*, 28 February 2009.
212. A. Applebaum, 'Does Eastern Europe Still Exist?', *Prospect*, 20 March 2013.
213. Ibid. See also Applebaum's account of her trip through Lithuania, Belarus and Ukraine after the fall of the Wall in *Between East and West: Across the Borderlands of Europe* (New York, 1994).
214. Freedom House, *Democracy, Economic Reform and Western Assistance* (1991), 154.
215. For instance, J. Zielonka, *Europe as Empire: The Nature of the Enlarged European Union* (Oxford, 2006), 23–43.
216. A. Rodríguez-Pose, *The European Union: Economy, Society and Polity* (Oxford, 2002), 36.
217. Ibid., 38, referring to the disparity in 1998.
218. Ibid., 37.
219. European Commission, *Eurostat Regional Yearbook* (2020).
220. L. Kettenacker, *Germany 1989*, 186–203.
221. G. Mak, *In Europe: Travels through the Twentieth Century* (London, 2004), xi.
222. Ibid.
223. Ibid., xii.
224. Ibid., xi.
225. Ibid., xii.
226. Ibid., xv.
227. Ibid.
228. Ibid.
229. Ibid.
230. Ibid.
231. For a defence of social-scientific method in this field, see H. Thome, 'Value Change in Europe from the Perspective of Empirical Social Research', in H. Joas and K. Wiegandt (eds), *The Cultural Values of Europe* (Liverpool, 2008), 277–319.
232. J. McCormick, *Europeanism*, 168.
233. Ibid.
234. Ibid.
235. M. Tonry (ed.), *The Handbook of Crime and Punishment* (Oxford, 1998), 739–76.
236. V. Giscard d'Estaing, *Le Pouvoir et la vie*, vol. 1, 260.
237. J. McCormick, *Europeanism*, 174.
238. Eurobarometer, 'Social Values, Science and Technology', June 2005, 9; J. McCormick, *Europeanism*, 177.
239. Gallup World View 2007–08, in J. McCormick, *Europeanism*.
240. B. F. Nelsen and J. L. Guth, *Religion and the Struggle for the European Union: Confessional Culture and the Limits of Integration* (Washington, DC, 2015), 290.
241. Ibid. The Chair of the EPP, Hans-Gert Pöttering, consoled himself that 'many of our values, which we define as Christian, have been included: human dignity, the dignity of older people and

the dignity of children, too'. Many outside the EPP disagreed with him that such values were 'Christian' in all but name: F. Foret, *Religion and Politics in the European Union: The Secular Canopy* (Cambridge, 2015), 58.

242. Eurobarometer, 'Social Values, Science and Technology', June 2005, 9.
243. D. Bell, *The Coming of Post-Industrial Society* (New York, 1973).
244. D. Bell, *The End of Ideology: On the Exhaustion of Political Ideas in the Fifties* (Glencoe, IL, 1960). See M. Conway, *Western Europe's Democratic Age, 1945–1968*, 3–4, on the background to the conference.
245. See also R. Dahrendorf, *Classes and Class Conflict in Industrial Society* and A. Giddens, *The Class Structure of the Advanced Societies* (London, 1973).
246. D. Bell, *The Coming of Post-Industrial Society*, 119.
247. Ibid., 126–7.
248. Ibid., 119.
249. Ibid., 128.
250. Ibid.
251. Ibid.
252. Ibid., 119.
253. Z. Bauman, *Liquid Modernity* (Cambridge, 2000), 53–201.
254. Universities UK, *International Student Recruitment Data* (2016).
255. R. Vinen, *A History in Fragments: Europe in the Twentieth Century* (London, 2000), 581.
256. Ibid., 583.
257. Ibid.
258. See E. Recchi and A. Favell, *Pioneers of European Integration* (Cheltenham, 2009).
259. N. Fligstein, *Euroclash*, 182–5.
260. European Commission, *Annual Report on Intra-EU Labour Mobility 2020* (Luxembourg, 2021), 13. 13 million of a work force of 227.4 million were of working age (20–65).
261. Ibid., 49, 60, 62–3: Many were involved in scientific and technical work (5 per cent of working-age EU migrants in 2019), education (5 per cent), information and communication (3–4 per cent), finance (2 per cent), the arts (2 per cent), or running small businesses (3–4 per cent). Overall, professionals made up 18 per cent of the group, which is roughly the same as the percentage of citizens of host countries (21 per cent), senior managers and administrators comprised 5 per cent, technicians 5 per cent, and clerks and office workers 5–10 per cent, or more than one-third in total.
262. Ibid., 75.
263. Ibid.
264. Ibid., 32, 34.
265. N. Fligstein, *Euroclash*, 148–9. 61.6 per cent—and 82.4 per cent of 15–24 year-olds—said that they spoke a second language in 2000, with 57.5 per cent of them speaking English, 15.6 per cent French, 11.3 per cent German and 1.8 per cent Spanish.
266. Ibid., 153. More than 40 per cent of Dutch and German respondents travelled abroad in 1997.
267. European Commission, *Annual Report on Intra-EU Labour Mobility 2020* (Luxembourg, 2021), 116.
268. See Anna McKeever, *Immigration Policy and Right-wing Populism in Western Europe* (Basingstoke, 2020) for further literature, which is extensive.
269. *Frankfurter Allgemeine Zeitung*, 26 June 2017. By June 2017, 51.2 per cent of Frankfurt's population had a 'background of migration', with more than 60 per cent of migrants—or one-third of the city as a whole—from elsewhere in the European Union. The figures for Paris— 590,504 out of 12,174,880 in the Parisian region, or 5 per cent—and London—1,103,000, excluding Irish and Cypriot nationals, out of 8.9 million (Greater London), or 12.5 per cent— are lower as a proportion but nonetheless are the equivalent of large cities (such as Amsterdam and Genoa): Institut national de la statistique et des études économiques (2015) and the Office for National Statistics, *Population of the UK by Country of Birth and Nationality* (2018).
270. BBC News, EU Referendum Results, June 2016.
271. The Migration Observatory, 'There Were an Estimated 3.7 Million EU Citizens Living in the UK in 2019' (2020); Office for National Statistics, *Population of the UK by Country of Birth and Nationality* (2016). Just under 6 million EU citizens had applied for 'settled status' in the UK by 2021.
272. BBC News, EU Referendum Results, June 2016; Office for National Statistics, *Population of the UK by Country of Birth and Nationality* (2016). See also Telford and Wrekin in the West Midlands, which voted by 63.2 per cent to leave, had a population of 2000 Poles and 1000

330 EUROPEAN INTEGRATION SINCE THE 1920S

Romanians from a population of 169,000, or just under 2 per cent; and Blaenau Gwent in the Welsh valleys, with a population of 69,000, was home to about 1000 Poles, constituting 1.5 per cent of its population, but it voted by 62.0 per cent to leave the EU.

273. For the UK, see E. Kaufmann, 'Levels or Changes? Ethnic Context, Immigration and the UK Independence Party Vote', *Electoral Studies*, 48 (2017), 57–69; E. Kaufmann and G. Harris, '"White Flight" or Positive Contact? Local Diversity and Attitudes to Immigration in Britain', *Comparative Political Studies*, 48 (2015), 1563–90; I. R. Gordon, 'In What Sense Left Behind by Globalisation? Looking for a Less Reductionist Geography of the Populist Surge in Europe', *Cambridge Journal of Regions, Economy and Society*, 11 (2018), 95–113.

274. Eurobarometer 61 (2004), Annexes, 135.

275. There were a similar set of correlations on the question of enlargement: Eurobarometer 61 (2004), Annexes, 135, which asked whether respondents were 'for or against the enlargement of the European Union to include ten new countries this May': managers were 50 per cent for, 35 per cent against; white-collar workers 47 for, 37 against; the self-employed 47 for, 38 against; manual workers 37 for, 42 against; the unemployed 34 for, 47 against and the retired 38 for, 44 against. Those between 15 and 24 were 50 for, 30 against, whereas those over 55 were 38 for, 44 against. Those who had left higher education after the age of 20, were 51 for, 36 against, those who left at 16–19 were 37 for, 43 against. Amongst those who thought EU membership a good thing, 60 were for, 26 against; those considering it a bad thing, were 20 for, 67 against.

276. Ben Page's analysis of the Blair years, 'Culture and Attitudes', in A. Seldon (ed.), *Blair's Britain, 1997–2007*, 436–67, does not consider 'Europe' a major political question. For recent historical research on the media and public sphere, see E. Bunout, M. Ehrmann, and F. Clavert (eds), *Digitised Newspapers—A New Eldorado for Historians: Reflections on Tools, Methods and Epistemology* (Berlin, 2023); E. Bergamini and E. Mourlon-Druol, 'Talking about Europe: Exploring 70 Years of News Archives', *Bruegel Working Paper*, 4 (2021), 1–41; F. Papadia, E. Bergamini, E. Mourlon-Druol, and G. Porcaro, 'Interest in European Matters: A Glass Three-Quarters Full?', *Bruegel Working Paper*, 5 (2021), 2–21; E. Mourlon-Druol, H. Müller, G. Porcaro, and T. Schmidt, 'You'll Never Talk Alone: What Media Narratives on European Reforms Reveal about a Polity in the Making', *Bruegel Working Paper*, 19 (2022), 1–56; M. Herzer, *The Media, European Integration and the Rise of Euro-Journalism, 1950s–1970s* (Basingstoke, 2019).

277. Ipsos MORI, June 2014: 'What do you see as the most/other important issues facing Britain today?' 47 per cent of those over 55 mentioned race/immigration and 55 per cent of those living in the South East of England, excluding London, where 28 per cent mentioned it (the same figure as for those aged 28–34). Only 3 per cent of all respondents thought that Europe was the most important issue. About 20 per cent of over 55s mentioned it as an important issue, compared to 4 per cent of the 25–34 age group. Interestingly, at this stage (before it was taken up by the press), most mentions came from the ABs ('social grade'), 21 per cent of whom mentioned it, not the C1, C2 and DEs, only 7–11 per cent of whom mentioned it all.

278. N. Fligstein, *Euroclash*, 201, referring to the European Audiovisual Laboratory's findings.

279. European Audiovisual Observatory,*Yearbook 2019/20*, 29. On social media, see C. Galpin and H.-J. Trenz, 'Participatory Populism: Online Discussion Forums on Mainstream News Sites during the 2014 European Parliament Election', *Journalism Practice*, 13 (2019), 781–98.

280. N. Fligstein, *Euroclash*, 200.

281. Ibid.: 56 per cent of TV drama in Germany was domestic and 44 per cent American; 43 per cent in Italy was domestic, 51 per cent American, and 6 per cent European; and, in France, 75 per cent was domestic and 25 per cent American.

282. European Audiovisual Observatory, *Yearbook 2019/20*, 33.

283. Ibid., 31.

284. Ibid., 44; N. Fligstein, *Euroclash*, 197.

285. See, for instance, J. Gerhards, 'Westeuropäische Integration und die Schwierigkeiten der Entstehung einer europäischen Öffentlichkeit', *Zeitschrift für Soziologie*, 22 (1993), 96–110.

286. H. J. Trenz, 'Understanding Media Impact on European Integration: Enhancing or Restricting the Scope of Legitimacy of the EU?' *European Integration*, 30 (2008), 297; C. O. Meyer, *Europäische Öffentlichkeit als Kontrollsphäre. Die Europäische Kommission, die Medien und politische Verantwortung* (Berlin, 2002); K. Hafez, *Mythos Globalisierung. Warum die Medien nicht grenzenlos sind* (Wiesbaden, 2005).

287. H. J. Trenz, 'Understanding Media Impact on European Integration: Enhancing or Restricting the Scope of Legitimacy of the EU?', *European Integration*, 30 (2008), 297.

LIVING EUROPE   331

288. P. J. Humphreys, *Mass Media and Media Policy in Western Europe* (Manchester, 1996); R. Hummel, 'Journalistisches Feld und europäische Öffentlichkeit', in W. R. Langenbucher and M. Latzer (eds.), *Europäische Öffentlichkeit und medialer Wandeln* (Wiesbaden, 2006), 296–304. There are still national filters, of course, since the journalists report back to news rooms in their own countries: C. Galpin and H. J. Trenz, 'Converging towards Euroscepticism? Negativity in News Coverage during the 2014 European Parliament Elections in Germany and the UK', *European Politics and Society*, 20 (2019), 260–76. One notorious, unfortunate example was the Brussels *Daily Telegraph* correspondent, Boris Johnson, who wrote stories about bananas and condoms for his UK readers: a 1991 article, 'Italy Fails to Measure Up on Condoms', for example, recorded that 'Brussels bureaucrats have shown their legendary attention to detail by rejecting new specifications for condom dimensions', notwithstanding demands from Italian rubber manufacturers for a narrower minimum width. Willy Hélin, whom Johnson quoted ('this is a very serious business'), denounced the report as a 'load of bullshit' in 2019 from his hospital bed: 'We were not interested in sizes. We had had requests from medical institutions across Europe to check on the safety of condoms. That has nothing to do with the size of dicks.' Johnson was 'the paramount of exaggeration and distortion and lies. He was a clown—a successful clown': 'How Boris Johnson's Brussels-bashing Stories Shaped British Politics', *Guardian*, 14 July 2019.

289. H. J. Trenz, 'Understanding Media Impact on European Integration: Enhancing or Restricting the Scope of Legitimacy of the EU?' *European Integration*, 30 (2008), 302.

290. Ibid.

291. S. Sifft, M. Brüggemann, K. Kleinen von Königslöw, B. Peters, and A. Wimmel, 'Segmented Europeanization: Exploring the Legitimacy of the European Union from a Public Discourse Perspective', *Journal of Common Market Studies*, 45 (2007), 136. The EU was the main story in 14 per cent of articles. Trenz, 'Media Coverage on European Governance: Testing the Performance of National Newspapers', *European Journal of Communication*, 19 (2004), 291–319, produces similar figures: one out of three political articles mention EU affairs and one out of five report directly on a European political issue.

292. R. Koopmans, 'Who Inhabits the European Public Sphere? Winners and Losers, Supporters and Opponents in Europeanized Political Debates', *European Journal of Political Research*, 46 (2007), 205.

293. J. Díez Medrano, 'The Public Sphere and the European Union's Political Identity', in J. T. Checkel and P. J. Katzenstein (eds.), *European Identity* (Cambridge, 2009), 98.

294. H.-J. Trenz, *Europa in den Medien. Die europäische Integration im Spiegel nationaler Öffentlichkeit* (Frankfurt, 2006), 227.

295. T. Risse, *A Community of Europeans? Transnational Identities and Public Spheres* (Ithaca, NY, 2010), 166.

296. H. Wessler, B. Peters, M. Brüggemann, K. Kleinen von Königslöw, and S. Sifft, *Transnationalization of Public Spheres* (Basingstoke, 2008), 50–1. Risse's response to this research is to contend that 'It remains unclear what these results mean': T. Risse, *A Community of Europeans?* 162.

297. T. Risse, 'No Demos? Identities and Public Spheres in the Euro Crisis', *Journal of Common Market Studies*, 52 (2014), 1207–15.

298. H.-J. Trenz, 'Media Coverage on European Governance: Exploring the European Public Sphere in National Quality Newspapers', *European Journal of Communication*, 19 (2004), 309: 38 per cent were framed 'normatively', and 27 per cent in terms of identity.

299. H.-J. Trenz, 'Die mediale Ordnung des politischen Europas. Formen und Dynamiken der Europäisierung politischer Kommunikation in der Qualitätspresse', *Zeitschrift für Soziologie*, 34 (2205), 201.

300. H. J. Trenz, 'Understanding Media Impact on European Integration: Enhancing or Restricting the Scope of Legitimacy of the EU?' *European Integration*, 30 (2008), 302.

301. C. Galpin and H.-J. Trenz, 'Converging towards Euroscepticism? Negativity in News Coverage during the 2014 European Parliament Elections in Germany and the UK', *European Politics and Society*, 20 (2019), 260–76.

302. N. Postman, *Amusing Ourselves to Death: Public Discourse in the Age of Showbusiness* (London, 1985); M. J. Wolf, *The Entertainment Economy: How Mega-Media Forces Are Transforming Our Lives* (London, 1999).

303. J. Peter, C. H. De Vreese, and H. A. Semetko, 'EU Politics on Television News: A Cross-National Comparative Study', *European Union Politics*, 4 (2003), 305–27, examining coverage in 2000; C. H. De Vreese, 'News, Political Knowledge and Participation', *Acta Politica*, 41 (2006), 317–41.

332 EUROPEAN INTEGRATION SINCE THE 1920s

304. R. Vetters, E. Jentges, and H.-J. Trenz, 'Whose Project Is IT? Media Debates on the Ratification of the EU Constitutional Treaty', *Journal of European Public Policy*, 16 (2009), 419–20.
305. Ibid.
306. P. Statham and H.-J. Trenz, 'Understanding the Mechanisms of EU Politicization: Lessons from the Eurozone Crisis', *Comparative European Politics*, 13 (2015), 299; 665.C. Galpin and H.-J. Trenz, 'In the Shadow of Brexit: The 2019 European Parliament Elections as First-Order Polity Elections?' *Political Quarterly*, 90 (2019), 665–6.
307. P. Statham and H.-J. Trenz, 'Understanding the Mechanisms of EU Politicization: Lessons from the Eurozone Crisis', *Comparative European Politics*, 13 (2015), 299.
308. Quoted in J. Díez Medrano, 'The Public Sphere and the European Union's Political Identity', in J. T. Checkel and P. J. Katzenstein (eds.), *European Identity*, 84.
309. For commentary and contextualization, see J.-W. Müller, 'In the Shadows of Statism: Peculiarities of the German Debates on European Integration', in J. Lacroix and K. Nicolaïdis (eds), *European Stories*, 87–104.
310. D. Grimm, 'Does Europe Need a Constitution?', in P. Gowan and P. Anderson (eds), *The Question of Europe* (London, 1997), 250. The article was originally published in 1995 in the *European Law Journal*.
311. Ibid.
312. Ibid., 251–2.
313. Ibid., 252.
314. Ibid.
315. Ibid., 253–4.
316. Ibid., 254.
317. Ibid.
318. Ibid., 256.
319. J. Habermas, 'Reply to Grimm', in P. Gowan and P. Anderson (eds.), *The Question of Europe*, 262.
320. Ibid.
321. Ibid.
322. Ibid., 262–4.
323. Ibid., 261, 264.
324. Ibid., 261.
325. Ibid., 263.

7
Member States

In a recent three-part series of articles in the *London Review of Books*, which begins with a long, biographical critique of the works of Luuk van Middelaar and ends with an exegesis of the commentaries of Ferdinand Mount, Peter Oborne, and Geoffrey Wheatcroft, three Conservative opponents of Brexit, Perry Anderson catalogues the shortcomings of the European Union.[1] The thrust of his argument is that the individual institutions and overall configuration of the EU have failed to provide a democratic apparatus, social benefits, or economic growth for European citizens. 'Democratic systems have effective oppositions that may one day govern,' he writes in 'The European Coup': 'The European Union is organized in such a way that it does not. But since it is good form to regret its "democratic deficit", it would be better if it at least appeared to do so.'[2]

The European Court of Justice (ECJ) was established by former Nazis and fascists, among others, and remains 'hidden from public scrutiny' and closed to 'admission of dissent', contends Anderson.[3] By 1964, in a case about the nationalization of the Italian electricity industry (*Costa v. Enel*), the ECJ had ruled that European law had supremacy over national law: in Dieter Grimm's judgement, as a former member of the *Bundesverfassungsgericht*, the decisions were 'revolutionary because the principles they announced were not agreed on in the treaties' and 'almost certainly would not have been agreed on had the issues been raised'.[4] The Treaty of Rome granted the ECJ the right of judicial review exclusively 'with respect to acts of the Union institutions', not those of national governments or other actors in member states, in Thomas Horsley's words, 'Yet in effect, this is exactly what the court now undertakes on a routine basis.'[5] The Court of Justice is 'the only Union institution whose activities are not routinely scrutinised (by itself or by others) for compliance with the EU treaties,' writes Horsley.[6] In liberal democracies, the rulings of supreme courts 'are subject to alternation or abrogation by elected legislatures', but 'those of the ECJ are not', Anderson goes on: 'They are irreversible. Short of amendment of the treaties themselves, requiring the unanimous agreement of all member states, "which as everyone knows, is all but out of the question", as Grimm writes, there is no recourse against them.'[7]

The European Central Bank (ECB), which was formed to manage the single currency entering circulation in 1999, has proved equally difficult to control and its proceedings—'unlike those of the Fed or the Bank of England, but in keeping with those of the European Court of Justice'—remain secret.[8] 'The Treaty of Maastricht conferred absolute independence on the bank, which operates without

---

European Integration since the 1920s: Security, Identity, and Cooperation. Mark Hewitson, Oxford University Press.
© Mark Hewitson 2024. DOI: 10.1093/oso/9780198915942.003.0008

334 EUROPEAN INTEGRATION SINCE THE 1920S

any of the counterweights—Congress, the White House, the Treasury—that surround the Fed, embedding it in a political setting where it is publicly accountable,' claims Anderson: 'Unlike any other central bank, the independence of the ECB isn't merely statutory, its rules or aims alterable by parliamentary decision—it is subject only to treaty revision.'[9] When currencies and economies, such as those of Greece, were allowed to enter the eurozone, conceived by European leaders as a political 'prestige' project rather than a functioning monetary and economic system, the euro came close to collapse and the ECB resorted to 'getting around European rules', in the words of the former head of research at the bank, Lucrezie Reichlin, in 2012.[10] Like the ECJ, there is no body to police the ECB and make it accountable, it is held.

The political system of the EU depends on the relationship between the European Commission, Parliament, and Council. Unlike many Conservative critics, Anderson accepts that the Commission, since Delors, 'has had to play second fiddle to the European Council', even if it continues to control the rule-book 'as an instrument of power within the Union—the *acquis communautaire*, impenetrable to its citizens, but inescapable for its states, forming the primary means of the *Gleichschaltung* of Eastern Europe to EU norms, over which commissioners presided as proconsuls from Brussels'.[11] The *acquis* was originally 'put together as a codification of EEC regulations to which the UK, Denmark and Ireland would have to adapt on entry into the Community in 1973, when it already came to 2,800 pages', but it now totals 90,000 pages, making it 'the longest and most formidable written monument of bureaucratic expansion in human history'.[12] Nevertheless, in terms of decision-making and, even, agenda-setting, the Commission—together with a European Parliament largely ignored by voters—is subordinate to the European Council: 'the Commission is formally vested with the sole power to propose legislation for the Union, but here the reality differs', for 'more than two-thirds of its proposals are now hatched jointly with the representatives of the member states in the dense undergrowth of Brussels, in which COREPER—which brings together permanent envoys to the EU—holds pride of place, and then rubber stamped by the relevant Council of Ministers when passed up to it'.[13]

It is not immediately apparent why Anderson is opposed to member states wresting back more control over the power to propose legislation (and, later, to discuss, amend, and veto it), but he seems to accept van Middelaar's argument about the transformative atmosphere of the Council, or an 'intermediate sphere composed of its member states as they deliberate in the Council of Ministers and its apex, the European Council', which is distinct from the 'inner sphere' of the Commission, Court of Justice and Parliament, and an 'outer sphere comprising Europe understood as a continent—including states that are not part of the Community—in the world of powers at large, where borders and wars obtain'.[14] The great merit of the Dutch historian's account, Anderson maintains, is that 'he puts the Council where it belongs, as not just the formal apex, but the overmastering instance of the EU, the last but one part of its architecture to come into being, but the most salient of all':

> Van Middelaar leaves little doubt of the much lower regard in which he holds the Commission, a useful but humdrum factory of rules, and the Parliament, a windy cavern of words. The Council, by contrast, is the seat of authoritative decisions. The Commission and the Parliament are given to utopian temptations of European federalism, for which he barely hides his scorn. The Council is the vehicle of the true sense in which Europe has moved, and is continuing to move, towards ever greater union, as a club of states bound together by a common project that does not extinguish their identities as nations, but joins them in a common destiny, a new form of *Schicksalsgemeinschaft*.[15]

Van Middelaar gives 'a graphic, if tactful, description of the psychological and political mechanisms that generate such consensus', and he is broadly supportive of the 'coups' and 'faits accomplis' that the European Council has managed to deliver in the face of events (as it moved from 'the politics of rules' to 'the politics of events').[16] Anderson is less impressed, criticizing decision-making 'behind closed doors, in deliberations of which no minutes are kept, that issue in announcements under the seal of consensus'.[17] The EU's record of dealing with events—migration, the eurozone crisis, war in Ukraine—has been poor.[18]

Anderson's arguments only make sense in respect of an integral, self-contained polity, rather than a confederation of states. Why does he assume, like van Middelaar, that the European Council is a secretive, consensual European institution, instead of a meeting place of member states' governments, acquiring its own administration (COREPER) and supplementing other forums, such as the Council of Ministers, bilateral meetings and intergovernmental conferences? The conflicting interests and points of view of member states have dogged decision-making in respect of the eurozone crisis, migration, and Russia and Ukraine, just as they affected the EU's actions in Yugoslavia in the 1990s. As Anderson admits, 'the more advanced states of Eastern Europe, once their elites were safely inside the Union, became less submissive to it', constituting 'another of the unintended consequences, or counter-finalities, of which there have been so many in the history of integration'.[19] He refers to Christopher Bickerton's claim that nation-states have become member states, which is held to express 'a fundamental change in the political structure of the state, with horizontal ties between national executives taking precedence over vertical ties between governments and their own societies', but what evidence does he—or Bickerton—marshal in support of the claim?[20] The transition from struggling 'class compromise between capital and labour' in European social democracies to neo-liberalism by the early 1980s, with the 'relaunching of the dynamic of integration under Delors' as 'the outcome of a

336 EUROPEAN INTEGRATION SINCE THE 1920S

pattern of domestic political change in which policy priorities had become fiscal retrenchment, wage repression and a return to financial orthodoxies of classical stamp', seems unlikely to have produced deeper integration and national governments' acceptance of 'a set of external constraints' established through the 'constitutionalization' of the European Community by the ECJ.[21]

Neo-liberal governments were especially wary of 'red tape', judicial interference, and the 'corporatism' of neighbouring states, which appeared to have been condoned by the European Community but which was subject to challenge—in the European Court of Justice—under the terms of the Single European Act (1986), with its objective of removing non-tariff barriers. Why, and to what extent, had national governments limited their own powers 'in order to contain the political power of domestic populations', 'binding themselves through an external set of rules, procedures and norms' in order 'to limit popular power' and replacing 'an internal working out of popular sovereignty that serves to *unite* state and society' with 'an externalisation of constraints to national power intended as a way of separating popular will from the policy-making process', as Bickerton contends?[22] The British political scientist's principal aim is to show that 'the active subject, namely the people, is not doing the binding', but such contentions rest on the assumption that national governments, which depend on the support of their peoples, have given up powers definitively to European institutions.[23] This chapter asks whether, and in what circumstances, governments have ceded such powers, investigating how ministers, parties, commentators, and publics have sought to influence or determine the shape and scope of the European Union over time.

The Politics of Integration

Historically, there has not been a creeping, often secret, giving up of powers by member states and a corresponding accumulation of competencies by European institutions. Rather, there has been regular discussion and negotiation by national governments—involving the delegation, defence, and repatriation of powers—about how best to cooperate on a European level in the context of post-war internationalization, the Cold War, globalization, and the emergence of a multipolar international order, which includes regional powers such as the façade democracies of Russia and Turkey and global powers such as the increasingly sectarian democracy of India and the Communist dictatorship of China. The plan for a European Defence Community (1950–54), which also provided for a European constituent assembly and constitution, was more radical than the Treaties of Maastricht (1992) and Lisbon (2007).[24] Mark Pollack's thesis about the 'creeping competence' of the EU up to the early 1990s rested on European regulations and directives, together with distributive and redistributive effects, in the fields of the environment, consumer protection, technology, education, and

MEMBER STATES 337

regional and cultural policy, yet has the EU overridden the preferences of member states in respect of consumer protection and the environment or, even, played a major role in policy areas such as education and culture?[25] By 2000, Pollack was less certain about the redistributive significance of EU policy-making, given the 'economic limits' placed on spending by 'German donor fatigue, the drive to fiscal austerity and Eastern Enlargement' in the 1990s, but he remained confident about 'the continued pace of regulation', which he measured by counting European directives in different fields.[26]

The success of the neo-functional approach—and of later theories of 'Europeanization'—'depended upon national governments not noticing—in effect—the gradual draining away of their lifeblood to Brussels', William Wallace wrote in 1982, but it was characteristic of 'a mixture of description and prescription, which marked the literature on European integration in the 1960s' and 'encouraged observers to focus on the development of the Brussels authorities, rather than to investigate the response of national governments to the process of integration'.[27] The questions which Stanley Hoffmann—and later proponents of intergovernmentalism—asked about the varying significance and different levels of policy-making, with national governments reserving the main areas of 'high politics' for themselves (and objecting when Community regulations impinged on them) are mentioned by Pollack but not answered.[28] For his part, an advocate of 'policy networks' such as John Peterson, who has distinguished between a 'meso level' (policy-shaping by 'non-political' Directorates-General, national civil servants, and private actors), systemic level (policy-setting by institutions such as the Council of Ministers, COREPER, the Commission, and the European Council as a 'court of last resort') and a "super-systemic level" (history-making decisions taken by the governments of member states, often within the Council and sometimes within parameters set by the ECJ), argues that 'eventual outcomes are shaped in crucial ways in the policy-making process' of the EU ('more than in most national systems'), that 'policy networks are particularly rife in EU governance because the EU lacks formal institutions which can facilitate bargaining between interested actors', and that the meso-level has been 'largely overlooked'.[29] Nevertheless, he fails to evaluate the relative importance of decision-making on each level and to explain decision-makers' interactions over time.[30]

European integration has always depended on the relationship—or series of relationships—between the proponents and leaders of European institutions and the governments of European states.[31] Despite the 'collapse of so many nation-states in 1939–40' and the need from 1945 onwards to reconstruct national economies, as Milward has pointed out, the relationship between nation-states and fledgling institutions on the European level was unequal from the start.[32] To talk of 'dialectical federalism' or to understand 'the dynamics of European integration' primarily as the result of the interventions and leadership of EU institutions, which are familiar with 'complex multilateral negotiating situations' and are capable of choosing between 'multiple possible acceptable solutions', is misleading, since it obscures the enduring role of national governments, which have retained decisive powers in the Council of Ministers, the European Council, at intergovernmental conferences, bilateral meetings, and as 'masters of the treaties'.[33] The early hagiography of the 'heroic' founders of the European Communities, working in borrowed headquarters with improvised administrations, makes sense in this context. Europe's nation-states, by contrast, although their economies were on a war footing (producing goods for the German war effort) and their cities damaged, had government buildings intact and officials in place, ready to implement plans which had already been discussed during the war.[34] Monnet himself, a former cognac salesman and Deputy Secretary General of the League of Nations during the interwar period, had worked hard to secure the independence of the Commissariat for the Plan within the French state, answerable directly to President de Gaulle. Initially, a Directorate for the Plan had been designed—under a different head—as one of four directorates within the Ministry for the National Economy. Monnet had manoeuvred himself into position, drawing on the resources and know-how of the French administration and securing the agreement of the Communist Minister for the National Economy, François Billoux, in December 1945 because of the 'temporary nature of the Commissariat': ministers 'only accepted this method because they know that the Commissariat and the Commissions will disappear in six months [and] because they consider them to be temporary', wrote the later head of the ECSC.[35] He would use similar types of improvisation on the European level in the early 1950s, but without the machinery and resources of a state. In such circumstances, it was imperative to gain the backing of national governments.

The pattern of relationships between the officials and leaders of European institutions, national governments, economic interest groups, journalists, parties, and publics was an enduring one, albeit subject to incremental change, as regulation increased and habits of cooperation developed, and it was affected by historical ruptures, such as the oil crisis of 1973 and the end of the Cold War in 1989–90. These relationships continued to hinge on the actions of governments, including informal coalitions and rivalries between the states themselves. The predominance of national governments did not rule out federalism, as the varying stances of Robert Schuman and Joschka Fischer demonstrated, but it tended to ensure that the costs and benefits of supranational arrangements and institutions were weighed up against perceived national interests in the context of the recent history, diplomatic connections, and economic and military power of different European states. Even proponents of supranationalism such as Schuman, who was Prime Minister of France in 1947–48 and Minister of Foreign Affairs in 1948–53, asked of the European Coal and Steel Community, 'Why should we have recourse to this idea, to this new-fangled supranational institution?'[36] His answer ran along national lines and addressed the question of a future German military threat and balance of power:

> I will tell you quite simply that it is to enable Germany to accept restrictions on her own sovereignty.... And if we wish to make Germany accept these restrictions, we must set her an example...we cannot retain for ourselves more power in the sector concerned than Germany will have.... It will mean identical renunciation on both sides and in the most delicate matters, such as the army and the production of coal and steel, products essential to the preparation for war and the formulation of policy.[37]

Everything had to be worked out between the post-war states, as the Schuman Declaration, which put forward the idea of a 'pooling of coal and steel production' to provide 'for the setting up of common foundations for economic development as a first step in the federation of Europe', spelled out on 9 May 1950:

> A united Europe was not achieved and we had war.
> Europe will not be all at once, or according to a single plan. It will be built through concrete achievements which first create a *de facto* solidarity. The coming together of the nations of Europe requires the elimination of the age-old opposition of France and Germany. Any action must in the first place concern these two countries.
> With this aim in view, the French government proposes that action be taken immediately on one limited but decisive point.[38]

For Adenauer, replying to the Schuman Declaration in the Bundestag on 14 June 1950, the French initiative offered the Federal Republic of Germany the chance to put the past behind it and regain status and sovereignty: 'There is no better way of persuading the French people of the peaceable will of the German people', clearing away 'obstacles of a psychological nature between Germany and France forever' and guaranteeing peace in Europe.[39] The Schuman Plan was 'conceived for France and Germany', but 'it was expected from the start that other countries'—Luxembourg, Belgium, and the Netherlands—'could join'.[40] In 1950–51, it was the initiative of the French government for the sake of peace and access to German raw materials and markets, the strong desire of Adenauer's government to regain sovereignty and the willingness of the Benelux countries and Italy to join the ECSC which appeared to be decisive.

In the first phase of European integration, as European institutions were being formed, the British government could have stymied Schuman's and Monnet's plans, especially if it had convinced Washington not to get involved. Bevin had already ensured that the Council of Europe remained an intergovernmental organization 'consisting of a ministerial committee meeting in private and a

340   EUROPEAN INTEGRATION SINCE THE 1920S

consultative body meeting in public', in the words of the joint communiqué of the UK, France, and the Low Countries, which had signed the Treaty of Brussels 'for collaboration in economic, social and cultural matters, and for collective self-defence', in 1948.[41] On this basis, David Bruce, the US ambassador in Paris, thought—in April 1950—that 'there will be no real European integration'.[42] 'The UK tended to exert a retarding influence on Western European plans for closer political and economic integration,' George Kennan told the State Department in September 1949: 'The UK was most wary of entering into any arrangements which might tend to derogate from her sovereignty and she was continuously preoccupied with her Empire commitments. The net result was that UK participation tended to place a ceiling on Western European attainments towards unification.'[43] In his speech at the Quai d'Orsay on 20 June, which opened an intergovernmental conference on the plan for a coal and steel community, Schuman hinted at the fluidity of inter-state relations in Europe, which continued to depend on the consent—or, at least, lack of opposition—of the United Kingdom, as the principal European economic and military power. 'We would have very much preferred that England was also present at our discussions,' he declared: 'We cannot conceive Europe without it.'[44] He pledged to keep the British government informed of the negotiations and hoped that its 'doubts and scruples' would give way before 'more concrete demonstrations' of the effectiveness of the ECSC, preparing 'the way for future cooperation'.[45]

Monnet, as the Foreign Office official Sir Roger Makins testified, did not expect the UK to join the ECSC. 'Now, look, does this mean that if we are not prepared to accept the principle of a Federal Europe, that we're not in, we're not wanted?' asked the British officials at the three-power meeting of Britain, the United States, and France at the Hyde Park Hotel on 11 May 1950: 'Yes, that is the position,' replied Monnet, having already shown the plans to the Americans and gained their support.[46] Precisely because the Schuman Declaration advanced a narrow economic plan, which many thought would fail, London refrained from opposing it, not least because the Labour government had nationalized the coal and steel industries and UK planners continued to look to extra-European markets, with 40 per cent of British exports and re-exports going to Commonwealth countries in 1948.[47] 'It is considered that where German essential goods compete with the United Kingdom, it will be better for Germany to supply Europe, and ourselves to concentrate on extra-European markets,' reported the Interdepartmental Committee on Coordination of the German Economy with the United Kingdom in March 1949, mindful of Britain's capacity as an occupying power: 'German exports to European destinations now would relieve the pressure on the United Kingdom and assist us in increasing our supplies for home re-equipment and for those other markets where for overall balance of payments reasons we urgently require to increase our exports and where we think we stand the best chance of obtaining long-term goodwill.'[48] As Edwin Plowden, the British Chief Planning Officer, expressed it later:

> I don't think that we really believed in the vision [Monnet] had of forming a nucleus around which a new Europe could be built. After all, for I don't know how many hundreds of years, Britain had kept out of Europe. And suddenly to ask it to give up its external, its worldwide, role in order to join with a Europe which was down and out at the time, required a vision which I'm quite sure I hadn't got and I doubt whether very many people in the United Kingdom had. Some may now think they had, but I don't think they did.[49]

In a Cabinet paper of January 1948, Bevin could be found speculating that Britain should be able to develop its own power 'to equal that of the United States of America and the USSR', 'provided we can organise a Western European system such as I have outlined...backed by the power and resources of the Commonwealth and the Americas', but he intended to organize Europe from the outside.[50] Unlike the EDC, which Anthony Eden—'in every sense a NATO man', in the words of Anthony Nutting, minister of state at the Foreign Office—wished to keep Britain out of, the ECSC did not threaten the UK's interests sufficiently for Bevin to try to stall or derail it.[51]

The Franco-German Shaping of Europe

In the second phase of integration from the mid-1950s to the early 1970s, the establishment of a Franco-German axis, in which France was the dominant partner, removed the UK's de facto veto.[52] Harold Macmillan, who was Foreign Secretary in Eden's new government in April 1955, believed that European 'federalism' was on the wane but he also betrayed his assumption that Britain's own power in Europe was declining, as he deliberated in June about whether to join the Spaak committee, which was tasked with creating a common market: 'We had always been inclined to say rather loosely that we did not mind other European Powers federating if they wished, but in fact if they did so and became really strong it might be very embarrassing for us. Europe would be handed over to the Germans, a state of affairs which we had fought two world wars to prevent.'[53] Macmillan, who was one of the most pro-European Conservatives and who had insisted on sending a representative, not merely an observer, to the Spaak committee, continued to resist the assumption, which was widely held in government circles, that Spaak's initiative would fail, if the UK were not involved.[54] From the Treasury, to which he had been moved as Chancellor of the Exchequer in December 1955, he asked what would happen, if the Six were to go ahead:

342 EUROPEAN INTEGRATION SINCE THE 1920S

What then are we to do? Are we to just sit back and hope for the best? If we do that it may be very dangerous for us; for perhaps Messina will come off after all and that will mean Western Europe dominated in fact by Germany and used as an instrument of the revival of power through economic means. It is really giving them on a plate what we fought two wars to prevent.[55]

Macmillan's obsession with Germany and its past, rather than appreciating the new realities of post-war European politics, was typical of other Conservatives, yet his solution, which was 'to reconcile our position as head of the sterling area and as head of the Commonwealth with some degree of European cooperation' at the same time as putting forward the idea of a Free Trade Area ('Plan G'), showed how the UK's position had altered.[56]

London's plan of a Free Trade Area was designed to both surround and include the EEC, resting on the competing, occasionally contradictory, motives of different groups in the Foreign Office, Treasury, and Board of Trade, which ranged from a desire to prevent the failure of the common market to the expectation that some members of the EEC might be tempted by an FTA as a better alternative.[57] Others wanted to torpedo the EEC from outside, by dividing Western Europe into 'Sixes and Sevens' and trying to prove that a European Free Trade Association (EFTA) could work better than a common market (see Map 7.1).[58] As Prime Minister (from January onwards), Macmillan spelled out his strategy to his ally Peter Thorneycroft, President of the Board of Trade, in July 1957:

We must not be bullied by the activities of the Six. We could, if we were driven to it, fight their movement if it were to take the form of anything that was prejudicial to our interests. Economically, with the Commonwealth and other friends, including the Scandinavians, we could stand aside from a narrow Common Market. We also have some politico-military weapons.... We must take the lead in widening their project, or, if they will not cooperate with us, in opposing it.[59]

Macmillan by 1957 had little to offer the Six, however, and little idea of how the Free Trade Area would run: 'In my view, agreement to some kind of managing board and abide by a majority on decisions which come within the general fabric would be a very good offer from us. We could call it supranational and they would like this.'[60] The Prime Minister's insouciance about the difference between supra-nationality, which—by any normal definition—he could not accept, and cooperation was telling, as was his misjudgement of the UK's position: 'If they behaved badly we would resign from the whole affair.'[61] When the Six opted not to join the affair, Macmillan was powerless.

French governments had come to take the lead in European negotiations by the mid-1950s. Because of divisions within, and the fragmentation of, the main parties

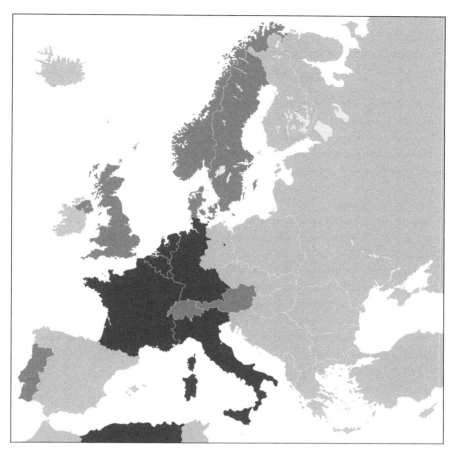

Map 7.1 EFTA and the EEC, 1960–72
Note: Algeria became independent, leaving the EEC, in 1962.
Source: https://en.wikipedia.org/wiki/Inner_Six#/media/File:Inner_Six_and_Outer_Seven.svg

in the Fourth Republic, French ascendancy did not imply continuity, as the shift from Mendès France's failure to ratify the EDC in 1954, via Mollet's 'choice for the community' in 1956–57, to de Gaulle's decision to leave an empty chair at the European Community table in June 1965 demonstrates.[62] Mollet became premier in 1956 after the SFIO had lost twelve seats in the legislative elections of January, leaving the party ninety-five seats out of 595, compared to 150 Communists and 214 on the 'centre-right'. President René Coty asked the Socialist leader to head the government in part because he, like the president, was 'pro-Community', but also in part because he opposed Algerian independence.[63] Most parties were opposed to the establishment of supranational institutions and a common market. Mollet himself was doubtful about such a market, favouring the founding of Euratom much more unequivocally than that of the EEC, yet he had decided that the relaunched project of the Six should succeed. According to the recollection of Robert Marjolin, the former Secretary General of the OEEC, 'the French administration and most important professional groups expressed their fears and their hostility to the project of the Common Market':

> Until then, no one thought that an enterprise of this type could even take shape, much less be completed. Yet suddenly there is a text which has been accepted formally by no one but whose outline prefigures, to a large extent, what could become a European customs union. Above all, we knew that certain members of the government, and not the least considerable, including the President of the Conseil Guy Mollet and the Minister of Foreign Affairs Christian Pineau are favourably inclined towards it. There is a small group of Europeans—Jean Monnet, myself, others—who have resolved to make Europe rise from the failure of the EDC. But the obstacles are immense. They are almost all the expression of a fear which has seized hold of French business circles and, above all, the administration concerning the idea that the mass of protections of all kinds which accumulated during the pre-war, wartime and post-war eras could disappear one day and that French industry would have to face foreign competition without customs dues in the form of contingency payments or state subsidies. In the face of this idea, the interested parties felt naked on a desolate plain, where a glacial wind was blowing.
>
> For my part, I was delighted.[64]

Marjolin was in favour of 'commercial liberty' and was tempted to dramatize his role, exaggerating the obstacles in the path of 'Europeans' like himself, but he nonetheless gave a sense of the strength of opposition to the EEC among businessmen, senior civil servants, and politicians.[65]

There was nothing inevitable about the French government's choice for the Community in 1957. Even for Mollet, 'Europe' co-existed with other priorities, some of which it contradicted. After the Suez crisis in 1956, Socialists—along with other politicians—were loath to relinquish control of Algeria and were anxious to pursue a traditional policy of power, including the development of an independent nuclear deterrent, which was in tension with policies of social justice and economic development in Europe, as Mollet's statement to the National Council of the SFIO hinted in December 1956:

> France is very ambitious; and the Socialist Party is more so for France than France is often aware of being for itself. We have decided that we shall defend France in the international context of NATO. That presupposed an army, NATO, with its costs. We have decided that we would make Europe. We have decided that we would aid, that we would participate in aid to, the under-developed countries. We have decided that we would aid all

the countries of Africa. All this represents tens and hundreds of billions. We have decided that we would save North Africa. We have also decided, in a Socialist-led government, that we would make the necessary effort to equip the country with the investments and equipment it needs to be able to play its part in the international market. Finally we have decided for the same reason, because we are Socialists, that we would sort out the main injustices there are in this country.[66]

As a consequence, Mollet's plans for Europe were limited to Euratom, which seemed to combine a French aspiration to become a nuclear power with European cooperation and control of Germany, and a common market, which promised to stimulate economic growth and allow a phased transition to freer trade. Although a minority of Socialists were critical, like Antoine Mazier, of the thirst for power ('We are living in the illusion of colonial greatness'), most wanted, in the manner of Jean Le Bail, to retain a global role: 'Is France going to become a Sweden, or remain a great power?... One becomes a second-rate power, but one does not choose to be one, and there is not a Socialist who would not seek to defend the national heritage we need.'[67] Given that Mollet and other Socialists did not seek to resurrect the EDC, they pursued such power on a national and international level.

In Germany, 'European integration' existed alongside the security and economic interests of the new West German state. By February 1958, opinion polls revealed that 30 per cent of respondents demanded more 'national self-confidence', with 33 per cent in the same survey preferring to 'ally closely with and in all friendship with America, in order to make the Western world invincible' and 36 per cent wanting to 'free ourselves from all military alliances and remain neutral like Switzerland or Austria'.[68] These divisions in public opinion, even on the question of security, gave politicians considerable scope to pursue Germany's 'national interest' and to adopt different positions on Europe, of which much of the public had little knowledge.[69] In June 1957, before the Treaty of Rome was ratified in the Bundestag, 73 per cent of those polled agreed in general with 'the idea of the common market' and only 9 per cent opposed it, but only 64 per cent had heard of the common market and only 52 per cent were sure that the FRG was a member.[70] Robert Margulies, a supporter of free trade from the *Freie Demokratische Partei* (FDP), felt free to say 'No to Spaakistan'—the exotic world of a common market being designed by the Spaak committee.[71] Ludwig Erhard— along with other 'ordo-liberal' economists such as Alfred Müller-Armack— opposed a European Community which looked likely to allow state support and to impose a high common external tariff.[72] In the mid-1950s, 75 per cent of German exports went to countries outside the bloc of the Six. Adenauer, aided by the shifting position of the SPD, made the decision to back 'a clear, positive

German position on European integration', as he spelled out in a letter to all *Bundesminister* on 19 January 1956:

> The decisive statesmen of the West see the cornerstone of development in this European integration, as my talks, in particular, with Pinay and Spaak and very specific American political opinions have shown. This view is, without doubt, correct. If integration succeeds, we will be able to use the weight of a united Europe, as an important new element, in the negotiation of both security and reunification. On the other hand, we cannot expect serious concessions from the Soviet Union as long as the disunity of Europe gives it hope to draw this or that state onto its side and, in this way, to destroy the solidarity of the West and to introduce the gradual attachment of Europe to its system of satellites. In addition, the lasting order of our relationship with France is only possible on the path to European integration. If integration should fail because of our opposition or hesitation, the consequences are unforeseeable.[73]

For the German Chancellor, European integration was needed in order to secure the vital security interests of the Federal Republic, rather than as a good in its own right.[74]

The uneven course of integration hinged above all on Franco-German cooperation and competition.[75] French efforts to control Germany were central in 'history-making' decisions; most notably, in 1950 as the US sought to hasten German rearmament during the Korean War (1950–54), in 1955–56 as the FRG joined NATO, around 1970 at the time of Willy Brandt's *Ostpolitik*, and in 1990–92 after German unification. It was to be expected, recorded Charles de Gaulle, after discussing 'Europe at length' during his first meeting with Adenauer in September 1958, that the German Chancellor 'agree with me that there could be no question of submerging the identity of our two nations in some stateless construction'.[76] 'Germany had drawn distinct advantages from the mystique of integration', and Adenauer 'was grateful to its French protagonists such as Jean Monnet and Robert Schuman for their gifts'.[77] His goal, as 'Chancellor of a defeated, divided and threatened Germany', was to support a 'West European system which would ensure his country not only equal rights but also commanding influence, would provide powerful support against the East, and by its very existence would encourage the United States to remain in Europe and thus maintain its guarantee to Federal Germany'.[78] 'From a national point of view', France 'had no real need of an organization of Western Europe, since the war had damaged neither its reputation nor its territorial integrity', but it 'was in favour of a practical and, if possible, political *rapprochement* of all European states because her aim was general peace and progress'.[79] It was 'prepared to implement the Treaty of Rome' on 'condition that its national identity remained unaffected'.[80]

For de Gaulle, Adenauer, and many others, there was a close relationship between Europe and the nation-state.

For the German Chancellor, the 'highest commandment' was 'the consolidation of the West' in the mid-1950s.[81] From the vantage point of 1967, he was content to agree with Ernst Friedländer, the President of the Europa-Union, that 'We in Germany must learn to see reunification, not as a national problem, but as a problem for the whole of Europe', since 'reunification nationalism' risked splitting Germany from Western as well as Eastern Europe.[82] On the surface, Adenauer's objectives in the 'decision at Messina' were extensive. 'Integration, initially amongst the Six, is to be pursued with *all* relevant methods, both on the level of general integration (horizontal) and in respect of unified part-integration (vertical)', he recorded in his memoirs: 'Here, from the start, the creation, where possible, of agreed, common institutions is to be sought in order, in the spirit of great political objectives, to bring about a firm binding together of the Six.'[83] However, the Chancellor's priorities remained security and commerce, as they had been in 1956:

> The negotiations concerning the creation of a common European market—i.e. a market which is similar to an internal market—which have progressed very well, must, with great emphasis, be brought to a conclusion. In the process, European organs with powers of decision must be created in order to secure the functioning of the market and, at the same time, to promote political progress.[84]

This form of political integration, which was linked to the functioning of a common market, was likely to be limited. The European 'Community' (*Gemeinschaft*) had to consist of more than existing international organizations—'The OEEC terms are not sufficient'—'for the sake of reunification amongst other things', but it did not extend far, compared to the ambitious plans for the EDC and EPC, and it would probably take time.[85] At the heart of the European project were Franco-German relations, which were 'of decisive importance'.[86] Although Bonn was not able to accede to Paris's offer of bilateral military cooperation because other members of the Western European Union and NATO 'would protest', it was able to find a 'middle way', mindful of French fears of Germany's *Ostpolitik* and its 'dangerousness', as one German Foreign Office report put it.[87] Franco-German bilateral relations and Europeanism were believed by Adenauer to be complementary. Intergovernmentalism and limited supranationalism in economic affairs existed side-by-side.

348 EUROPEAN INTEGRATION SINCE THE 1920S

The Economics of Integration and the Rise of Germany

In the third phase of integration from the early 1970s to the early 1990s, the Franco-German relationship remained central, but the weighting of each partner changed, with Bonn assuming a leadership role in the European Monetary System (EMS), which—according to Marjolin—was 'the most important decision of the 1970s' on the European level.[88] The other significant European achievements of the decade, in the opinion of the Secretary General of the OEEC (1948–55) and former Commissioner (1958–67), were the enlargement of the EEC in 1973, the creation of a European Council, the election of the European Parliament by universal suffrage and the devising of a Community procedure to address the crisis of the steel industry in the late 1970s, yet none of them implied a diminished role for member states. Concerted action over steel was largely a practical matter. The entry of the UK, Ireland, and Denmark 'reinforced the ego-centrism of the governments, their tendency only to attach importance to that which satisfies a national interest, to the detriment of efforts tending to consolidate European unity; it weakened institutions, to a certain degree, because the number of members had increased; and it helped to make the Luxembourg "compromise" into sacred practice, which was applied to all questions, even those which were only of minor significance'.[89] The establishment of a European Council in 1974, which brought together heads of state and government three times per year and was pushed through by Paris and Bonn against resistance from smaller member states, 'facilitated the discussion at the highest level of the great economic and political problems which arose in the Community', but it consisted of 'intergovernmental cooperation in the field of foreign policy' and 'did not create a European executive in any way'.[90] Decisions taken 'at the heart of the European Council are always made unanimously or are not made at all', with the result that member states retained their veto.[91] In theory, the introduction of a directly elected European Parliament in 1979 could have been 'an important step towards the creation of a political Europe', if 'new powers have been conferred on it, giving it, at the level of the Community and in the affairs of the Community, a position comparable to that of a parliament in a nation-state', but 'We know that this was not the case.'[92]

For Giscard D'Estaing, who was president between May 1974 and May 1981, the direct election of the European Parliament constituted a 'cornerstone of the edifice' of Europe, first discussed at the European summit in Paris in December 1974 and recommended by the Tindemans report in January 1976.[93] It was characteristic, he went on, 'of the leaders in office in Germany, France, Italy, the Benelux and Ireland', who were 'in agreement that the union of Europe should be considered a political project, a project which changes as time passes', and who understood it as 'a project of reconciliation between Europeans that was evolving towards the construction of a political power on a global scale'.[94] 'Only the British and Danes remained doubtful,' he maintained:[95]

MEMBER STATES 349

It was exceptionally lucky that Helmut Schmidt, Giulio Andreotti, Pierre Werner and Gaston Thorn in Luxembourg, Léo Tindemans in Belgium and I shared the same European convictions. For us, the European union is a project 'in itself', for which we must—at the same time—determine the best architecture and the surest pathway, and not merely a meeting place where the member states come to debate their national interests.[96]

There was, however, a broad spectrum between the narrow discussion of national interest and supranational coordination or imposition. Giscard professed himself closer to the strand of Europeanness associated with Robert Schuman, 'Catholic and Germanic', defending 'local liberties': 'Without pushing the analogy too far, one can detect the source, to an extent, in the interior of the Holy Roman Empire. Its capital is Aix-la-Chapelle rather than Brussels.'[97] By the same token, the French president distanced himself from Jean Monnet's conception of Europe, which was 'a construction parallel—not necessarily identical—to that of the United States': 'His democratic model is Anglo-Saxon. The label "United States of Europe" describes his project well.'[98] The reform of the European Parliament accorded with the modest aspirations of a president who was 'repelled' by 'the invasion on the part of the governmental sphere—a typically French malady, alas—of all forms of political and social activity'.[99]

The French right opposed the reform, dividing between those who 'refuse the project purely and simply' and those who 'think that it is not necessary to go so fast or so far'.[100] Jacques Chirac resigned as premier in the summer of 1976 over the question of the direct election of the European Parliament among other things, going on to denounce Giscard's party, the *Union pour la Démocratie Française* (UDF), as a 'party of foreigners' in December 1978.[101] The Communists accused the government of 'practising a policy of national resignation'.[102] Yet Giscard's response was to treat such reactions with amusement, laughing out loud despite the fact that his mouth was full—he was having 'a most agreeable, most comfortable breakfast, the one that I prefer, with its smell of hot coffee in the porcelain pots and the flaky aroma of the croissants'—when he heard that Chirac was putting himself forward at the head of the RPR list: 'the great political leaders cannot let a general election pass without putting forward their candidature, even if they do not have the slightest intention of carrying out the functions of the office'.[103] Michel Debré's objection, which he took to the *Conseil constitutionnel*, that the reform was 'unconstitutional because, in reality, it transfers a part of national sovereignty to the European Parliament' was treated as an act of manipulation, designed for effect.[104] The Constitutional Council dismissed Debré's case on 30 December 1976. Direct election had the potential, which was not realized in the event, to reinforce the legitimacy of the European Parliament, making it more visible, but it did not constitute a transfer of powers or sovereignty.

350 EUROPEAN INTEGRATION SINCE THE 1920s

The second 'cornerstone' of the European edifice, in Giscard's estimation, was the European Monetary System, linking member states' currencies—except pound sterling—from 13 March 1979 onwards.[105] With hindsight, the president saw the system, particularly the creation of a European Currency Unit (ECU), as 'a technical and silent revolution, without barricades and the spilling of blood', which comprised a first stage—'without doubt the most difficult'—towards the creation of a single European currency.[106] It not only put 'an end to a period of torments and monetary disorder which cost consumers and citizens dear'; it also introduced 'a new solidarity amongst the states of Europe', Giscard contended.[107] Marjolin was much more dismissive, though agreeing that the EMS represented 'progress towards the formation of a zone of monetary stability'.[108] It was reasonable to suggest that, at least at certain times, participation in the European Monetary System had led 'several countries to adopt difficult measures of economic, financial and monetary policy, which brought them closer to other European countries or, at least, prevented them from moving still further away'.[109] Yet 'it would be absurd to speak of this practical and extremely useful arrangement as a stage on the way to the creation of a European monetary union'.[110] Although the 'notion of an economic and monetary union was, in reality, closer to that of a political union, federation or confederation than to that of a customs union', since it implied 'a European political power, a community budget and an integral system of central banks', 'All that demanded profound transformations for which member states were evidently not ready.'[111] Writing his memoirs in the early 2000s, Giscard hinted that there was a linear movement from 1979 to 1999 (with the use of the ECU as a common European currency), yet what is striking about his account is how little attention he devotes to the ramifications of the EMS and to political integration.[112] Even in the critical third volume of his memoirs, covering the years 1978–81, 'Europe: The Great Voyage' is only one chapter (chapter 7) out of eighteen, which are devoted to domestic politics (chapters 1–4, 9–18) and world affairs (chapters 5–6, 8).[113] In the first two volumes, there is no chapter at all on Europe. The former president describes the European Council meeting in Venice on 12–13 June 1980, which is one of very few European events mentioned, but he concentrates mainly on Afghanistan, the United Nations, the magic of the Grand Canal, and Margaret Thatcher's clothing.[114] He gives so little space to European affairs because he did not anticipate that they would replace a traditional focus on domestic and foreign policy.[115]

Giscard's priorities were shared by the West German Chancellor, Helmut Schmidt, who indicated in a secret note to the Chancellery after a meeting with the French President and Harold Wilson in July 1974 that all were agreed that the European Commission should not transform itself into a European government.[116] For the Chancellor, who had unexpectedly assumed the post on 16 May 1974 after Willy Brandt's resignation following the disclosure that his personal assistant Günter Guillaume was an East German spy, 'Close cooperation with France and the self-integration of Germany is in our own fundamental interest, too.'[117] Despite their different backgrounds, with Giscard the proprietor of a chateau from the *haute bourgeoisie* and Schmidt living in the working-class settlement of Neue Heimat in Hamburg, they came to have 'unconditional trust' in each other and cultivated a 'personal friendship', which contrasted with their relationship with Harold Wilson, whose 'real opinions' were 'difficult to understand correctly' behind his 'tactical skill', and Margaret Thatcher, whose 'penetrating, national egoism' was off-putting: 'she tended, to our discomfort, to announce every compromise with her as a "victory" at home—which in our eyes was a defeat for the European idea'.[118] Schmidt's own Europeanism, though, was largely cooperative, notwithstanding his admiration for Jean Monnet, in whose 'private' committee he had participated—along with Giscard—as a young SPD politician.[119] His support for 'European integration' should be understood in this limited bilateral and multilateral sense:

> As far as the strategic grounds for the bilateral German–French cooperation (*Zusammenarbeit*) and the integration of both our states in the European Community are concerned, Giscard and I probably made the mistake of not speaking out sufficiently clearly in public. There was, indeed, a desire in both countries for reconciliation and agreement about bilateral cooperation, but our goal of the self-integration (*Selbsteinbindung*) of both our nations and states was widely misunderstood in the public sphere as idealism. Giscard and I both failed to explain, in sufficiently clear words, that we were both, in fact, following central, national interests on either side.[120]

As late as the mid-1990s, Schmidt continued, 'there are many influential people, in both France and Germany, who are not sufficiently aware of the strategic, national interest in the advancement of European integration'.[121] Schmidt backed Giscard's proposal for a European Council, where national interests could be discussed and compromises agreed between national heads of state and government, but his interest in the direct election of the European Parliament was slight, going along with the proposal in order to please the FDP and factions of his own party, the SPD.[122]

Schmidt's aims in office were largely social and economic, relating above all to welfare.[123] He comprehended foreign policy, at least in part, in these terms. 'Never since the world economic crisis of the thirties have domestic political, foreign political, and political-economic actions of the rulers (and of the parliament) of Germany had such a strong mutual dependency...as in the last years,' the Chancellor wrote in his confidential 'Marbella paper' in December 1976: 'That would seem to be no less true, indeed perhaps more so, for *the year 1977, which will again stand under the primacy of economic policy*.'[124] European cooperation on currency during the 1970s was essential for the stability of the deutschmark and the price of West German exports. Within the 'snake', the FRG's exports as a percentage of GDP had increased by 4.8 per cent between 1972 and 1976, compared to a fall of 1 per cent between 1969 and 1972, as currencies began to float. For this reason, the Chancellor counselled that 'It would be unwise to break out of the snake', even if 'one would not have to support the others', since 'one would also lose influence over the EC partners, in that they would pursue economic and stabilization policies which would cause their own currencies to fall'.[125] The EMS was negotiated against the backdrop of France, Italy, and the UK's earlier withdrawal from the snake and a depreciation of 12 per cent between October 1977 and February 1978 of the dollar against the deutschmark.[126] West Germany 'would either have to let the mark rise into the stratosphere, with disastrous results for exports,...investment [and] employment, or the Bundesbank would have to buy vast quantities of dollars to keep the exchange rate down, an action that would increase the German money supply and involve serious inflationary dangers', warned the President of the Commission, Roy Jenkins: 'Chancellor Schmidt therefore had strong incentives to look for a system in which changes in the dollar rate would be less disturbing to the stability of exchange rates vis-à-vis Germany's main trading partners.'[127]

As the Chancellor had indicated to the SPD in his 'Guiding Thoughts on Our Foreign Policy' in January 1975, 'We live today...in a universal system of mutually dependent nations, marked by total interdependence of political and economic development.'[128] The fact that West Germany had become, 'in the eyes of the world, *de facto* economically the second world power of the West', in the opinion of the Marbella paper, meant that the German government was pushed towards multilateralism everywhere, not merely in the EEC, but in the newly-formed G7 and at the Helsinki Conference (see Map 7.2). The country's 'unwanted and dangerous rise to the second world power of the West' would arouse suspicions 'in the consciousness of other governments—including especially the Soviet leadership!'[129] Cooperation in Europe, given Germany's past, was the main way of allaying fears about the rise of the West German state, which could provoke 'a revival of memories not only of Auschwitz and Hitler but also of Wilhelm II and Bismarck...perhaps as much in the West as in the East'.[130] As a consequence, it was 'necessary for us, so far as at all possible, to operate not nationally and independently but in the framework of the European Community and of the Alliance'.[131] The Chancellor made no distinction between cooperation within NATO and the EEC: 'This *attempt to cover (abdecken) our actions multilaterally will only partially* succeed, because we will (necessarily and against our own will) become a leadership factor in both systems.'[132] The international system of security and the European economic system were, it seemed, comparable.[133]

Kohl and Mitterrand—and especially the cohabitation governments of Chirac—were different from Schmidt and Giscard, but they were obliged to pay attention to the economic aspects of European integration, as the DM became

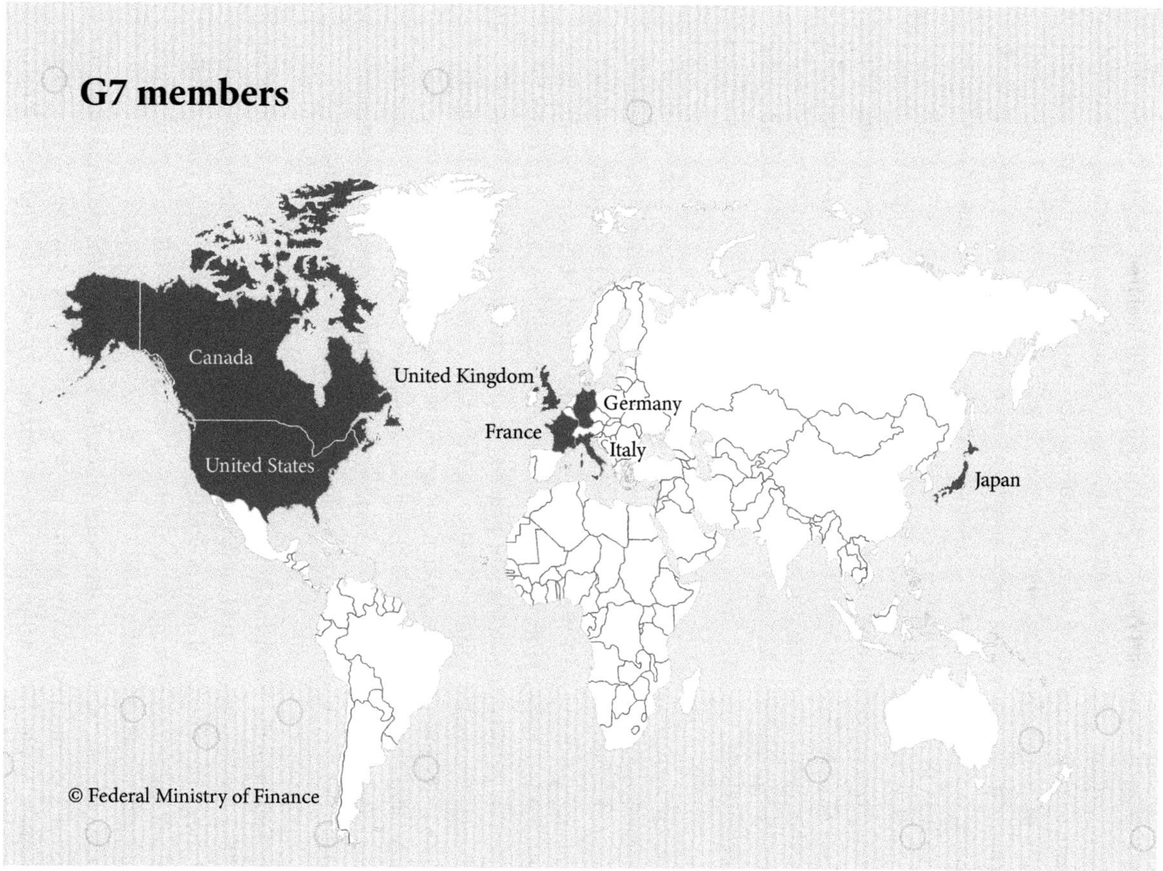

G7 members

© Federal Ministry of Finance

Map 7.2 The Group of Seven (G7)

Source: https://www.bundesfinanzministerium.de/

the dominant currency within the EMS and as the member states backed the project of a single market. The new CDU Chancellor regularly reiterated his support for European integration, linking it—as a former Minister-President of Rheinland-Pfalz—to the Franco-German relationship. There were three *leitmotifs* of the Franco-German Treaty of Friendship, Kohl declared on its twenty-fifth anniversary on 22 January 1988 at the Elysée Palace: 'First, the ties, which had grown over the course of many centuries, between our historical and cultural points of commonality; second, the ever closer co-existence of the French and Germans in the years after 1945; and, third, a common commitment to the work of European unity (*Einigung*).'[134] The cooperation of West Germany and France 'was a first, decisive step on the way to the political union of Europe', claimed the Chancellor, contrasting the warmth of his friendship with Mitterrand ('Good friends', ran a caption of a photograph of the two leaders in his memoirs, arm-in-arm at Chambord in March 1987) with the irritations of his relationship with Thatcher (who 'always caused me headaches', in the words of another caption).[135] The German question required a European solution, albeit one also backed by the United States:

> We Germans always had to remain aware that the German question, the question of the division of our country, could only be answered in an order of peace for the whole of Europe. The way there was via a strong European Community and the Atlantic partnership of Western Europe with the United States and Canada. It was our task to ensure that Europe was strong and capable of action. In order to do this, we needed stamina and patience in order to bear setbacks. Above all, though, we needed a firm will not to be deflection from our goal of a European union. Resignation and stagnation always meant retreat. Small, even the smallest, steps in the right direction could bring about progress, progress in the prospect of the unity of Europe. Our task was and remains that Europe remains a continent in which, for our children and grandchildren, it is worth living and working.[136]

The shadow of the European Union is discernible in such recollections, published in 2005. It is also visible in Hans-Dietrich Genscher's memoirs, which came out in 1995. Yet the details of any political reform were sketchy, with much of the relevant text concentrating on economics and social benefits (a Europe 'worth living and working' in).[137]

The only occasion in his memoirs when Kohl mentions the political mechanisms of the European Community in the 1980s is the passing of the Single European Act in 1986, as he lists new competencies (research and development, the environment, structural policy), the formal incorporation of European Political Cooperation (foreign policy) in the EC and the involvement of the European Parliament in the accession of other states.[138] Yet, even on this occasion, the Chancellor dwelled longer on the creation of an internal market, with the free movement of goods, persons, services, and capital, and on qualified majority voting in the European Council on economic matters.[139] For his Christian Democratic coalition partner, Franz Josef Strauß, who was more interested in NATO and the superpowers, the European Community and European Parliament were expressions of an empty 'multilateralization', alongside the UN, OECD, and Helsinki process, which were favoured by the left as a type of 'multilateral, German congress policy', but which also deprived the FRG of the foreign policy of a normal nation-state.[140]

The Foreign Secretary Hans-Dietrich Genscher, who was the architect of multilateralism in the Bavarian leader's view, was at once more specific and optimistic, contending that his joint initiative in January 1981 with the Italian Foreign Minister Emilio Colombo ignited a 'rocket' and paved the way for a European union.[141] Although the European Council in Stuttgart on 19 June 1983 limited itself 'only' to a 'solemn declaration' (*feierliche Erklärung*), the 'Genscher-Colombo initiative' had 'put the European Union back on the table' and set a course for the future, in the Foreign Secretary's retrospective account: 'Indeed, the Kohl/Genscher government did not let it be, and our engagement was rewarded emphatically with the European Council in Strasbourg seven years later, in December 1989.'[142] In the event, the movement towards a European Union required the stimulus of German unification in 1989/90, Mitterrand's course alteration after the U-turn of the Socialist government of Pierre Mauroy in March 1983, and the existence of a coalition of member states backing a single market in 1985, with the position paper of the UK government in June competing with the 'constitutional draft for the European Union' presented by Kohl and Mitterrand before the June summit of the European Council in Milan.[143] The British and Franco-German plans eventually came to converge in their advocacy of a single market, qualified majority voting on matters relating to the market and the establishment of a secretariat for EPC. Politically, Genscher's and Colombo's conception of a 'European union' had consisted merely of an underlining of 'the role of the European Council', a 'strengthening of European Political Cooperation' and support for 'human rights as the foundation of our common foreign policy'.[144] There was no talk within the West German government of federalism or supranationality in the 1980s. At the Fontainebleau summit in June 1984, 'we agreed to the creation of an *ad hoc* committee for institutional questions, whose task was to disseminate suggestions for the more effective functioning of the Community in questions of political cooperation', under the chairmanship of the Irish Senator James Dooge, but the findings of the Dooge Report were rejected in detail by individual member states.[145] As a consequence, the decision to make 'the European Council into an organ of the Community', with QMV in matters affecting the single market, was the main political innovation of the SEA, serving to reinforce the intergovernmental role of member states.[146]

Politics and economics were connected, but the latter usually took precedence.[147] Genscher introduced the West German presidency of the European Council on 20 January 1988 with the intention of ending the dispute over structural funds—or the 'so-called Delors Package, which was put forward by the Commission in 1987'—asserting that the 'internal market is not only a great labour market, an internal market also means production in the best location, improvement of structural conditions of production, and, above all, a common mastering of deep-seated structural problems'.[148] The Delors I package was adopted in 1988, raising spending on structural policies from 17 to 27 per cent of the EU budget by 1993. Yet Genscher admitted that his priority was the 'realization of the internal market', together with closer cooperation on foreign policy.[149] It was, as Kohl spelled out, in the FRG's interest to consolidate the market of 318 million people—compared to 221 million in the United States and 264 million in the USSR—to which 51 per cent of West German exports went in 1986.[150] From his first European Council summit in Copenhagen (December 1982) onwards, it was evident to the West German Chancellor that 'our primary task [was] to maintain a free internal market'.[151] Copenhagen was 'above all about the economic and social situation of the Community': 'Again and again, there was a temptation to undertake a solitary national path and to introduce national exceptions in the budget and in economic, currency and trade policy.'[152] It would, though, 'have been disastrous to give in to these temptations', for a 'break with economic solidarity would have only heightened the economic crisis' of the early 1980s.[153] By that time, 'I believed that we in Europe had become too comfortable', a state of affairs which stood in contrast to the 1950s, when the European Community had created a 'zone of freedom, political stability and exemplary cooperation' after centuries of division on the continent, noted Kohl in 1983: 'Too many people had come to believe that the Community functioned on its own.'[154] As a result, 'we stood before serious problems', including a 'broad palette' of 'budgetary, finance, agricultural, trade and currency problems', with the EEC in danger of 'stagnating' and 'the solidarity amongst member states' at risk of 'loosening'.[155]

The Chancellor seems to have understood 'European integration' (*europäische Einigung*) principally as a means of addressing such economic difficulties. Both he and Genscher continued throughout the 1980s to believe that French priorities were similar, particularly in respect of monetary policy and the alignment of currencies.[156] Shortly after winning the Bundestag election of 6 March 1983, Kohl had received a note, via his Finance Minister, from Mitterrand, stating his fear that the franc was about to crash out of the European Monetary System and underlining 'the particular importance of the conduct of Germany in the field of European policy and, especially, in respect of the currency question'.[157] Against the advice of Gerhard Stoltenberg, the West German Finance Minister, and Otto Pöhl, the head of the Bundesbank, the Chancellor agreed to raise the value of the deutschmark and lower that of the franc and lira, passing 'the test of German-French partnership' and setting Mitterrand on 'a market-oriented course' and, 'more clearly than before, on course for Europe'.[158] This market orientation appeared to have remained in place, with Genscher confident in 1988 that, 'For France, economic and monetary union had precedence, for economic and political reasons.'[159] Such priorities persisted, as has been seen, during the collapse of the Soviet bloc and the unification of Germany, setting limits on political 'deepening' and ensuring that EMU, which had been set in train by Genscher's establishment of an expert committee in the European Council in Hanover in June 1988, became the main legacy of Maastricht.[160]

Yugoslavia and the Triangulation of Europe

The fourth phase of European integration between 1992 and 2007 was characterized by the uncertain triangular relations between France, Germany, and the UK in the aftermath of Maastricht and the Cold War, as the Yugoslav wars, the economic costs of German unification and the prospect of enlargement complicated long-standing sets of priorities and habits of cooperation on the part of member states.[161] Given the economic and political stresses of the post-unification era, Kohl's government was more inward-looking after 1992 than it had been until that point. 'What is happening in eastern Germany at present is something that has never yet occurred in a time of peace,' reported *Der Spiegel* in April 1991: 'an entire industrial region is being run into the ground'.[162] By the end of 1991, the GDP of the new *Bundesländer* had dropped to 60 per cent of their 1989 level. Wages by 1994 were 70 per cent of West German levels, but productivity was 39 per cent, with the number of those employed dropping by a third (by 1993) from 9.7 to 6.2 million, taking account of 1.7 million who had emigrated to the West and 0.5 million who commuted to the West to work.[163] Only 17 per cent of East Germans characterized the economic situation as good or very good in 1994, falling to 12 per cent by 1998.[164] Unemployment in western Germany increased from 6.3 per cent in 1991 to 9.2 per cent in 1994, with transfer payments from West to East totalling around 620 billion DM in 1991–95 and the FRG's national debt doubling between 1989 and 1995.[165] 80 per cent of East Germans felt that they were second-class citizens in 1997 and 70 per cent of West Germans criticized their eastern counterparts for 'wanting to live like westerners and work like they used to do in the East'.[166] Understandably, members of the government often felt overwhelmed by events at home. 'Many tasks which now presented themselves to us were not foreseeable in 1990,' wrote Kohl in his memoirs: 'Many expectations were not confirmed in the way that we and others had assumed.'[167] The Chancellor's estimate was that 'we had to spend 4 to 5 per cent of GDP yearly' for reconstruction 'over a long period'.[168] Although he paid lip service to the need to use the rest of the 1990s 'for the integration of Europe', his actual narrative focused on

358 EUROPEAN INTEGRATION SINCE THE 1920s

domestic policy and his forecast for 'the next eight years up to 2000' had 'nothing to do with another period of office for Kohl'.[169] Despite staying on until electoral defeat in 1998, he had wanted to stand down after the election of 1994.[170]

Having agreed to economic and monetary union at Maastricht, the Kohl government had no option but to accept the timetable for the introduction of what became the euro, attempting ensure that the European Central Bank was located in Frankfurt and that 'a future European currency must be as stable as the D-Mark'.[171] Yet the fulfilment of 'these constraining requirements of the Maastricht Treaty', which presented 'serious challenges for all of us, and especially for us Germans', seemed to be predominantly an internal matter, with little prospect of altering the FRG's policy towards Europe.[172] France—along with most other member states—was different. The government, political parties, and public all focused on 'Europe' to an unprecedented degree, not least because Mitterrand had opted to ratify the Treaty on European Union by referendum.[173] After asking the public what it thought, the president did not like what he found. 'I am personally wounded when I see how the "yes" voters as much as the "no" voters justify themselves with arguments about a German danger,' he declared on 13 September 1992, one week before the vote: 'First of all it shows a lack of confidence in oneself. Then it implies that there are demons which are specific to Germany, when the fact is that every people must be vigilant about its own. To understand Germany and Germans demands more respect of them.'[174] As is well-known, the voters also showed little respect for the EU, voting only narrowly in favour of the Maastricht Treaty by 51 to 49 per cent. More than half of those polled had thought that France benefited from its membership of the European Community in the 1980s, but only 27 per cent in 1994.

Political parties, too, were divided. In Mitterrand's own Socialist Party, the former Minister of Defence Jean-Pierre Chévènement opposed EMU and the 'yes' campaign, and the Finance Minister Pierre Bérégovoy was against a single currency and a German-dominated European Central Bank, preferring a hard ECU and looser cooperation of central banks. In the RPR, the former Minister of Social Affairs and Employment (1986–88), Philippe Séguin, and the former and future Interior Minister (1986–88, 1993–95), Charles Pasqua, both headed the 'no' campaign. The former Finance Minister and future premier Edouard Balladur (1986–88, 1993–95) likewise opposed a single currency. For his part, Chirac, who became president in 1995 after the right had won the legislative elections of March 1993, was non-committal, hinting at 'une autre politique' of leaving the EMS or abandoning the transition to EMU. Although eventually coming out in favour of 'yes' in 1992, the RPR leader was under pressure from his party base. According to the journalist and former advisor François Bonnemain, 'He is a convinced European whose entourage is rather Eurosceptical.'[175] In the debate between leaders of the RPR, which occurred before the European Parliament elections in 1994, Chirac, backed by Alain Juppé, argued that 'Europe is constructing itself, irremediably, so that we might as well follow such a movement as tilt after windmills.'[176] Pasqua and Séguin continued to oppose him, dividing the electorate and ensuring that the anti-European, far-right-wing list of Philippe de Villiers gained 12.4 per cent in 1994, compared to only 25.6 per cent for the RPR and UDF.

'Euroscepticism' in the 1990s was an admixture of different ingredients. Kohl, who was used to adopting the convenient rhetoric of Europeanism, seemed mystified:

> Perhaps precisely because of these advances [towards economic and monetary union], the word 'Euroscepticism' did the rounds. At the beginning of the 1980s, the talk was still of 'Eurosclerosis'. To this extent, things had got better amongst the pessimists: we had gone from a serious illness to a sensitivity disorder (*Befindlichkeitsstörung*), as the new fashion calls it. Yet, notwithstanding our decisiveness on the path to Europe, we had to comprehend the questions and concerns of our citizens. We had to take them seriously, because they were a reality—those fears, too, which were unfounded. That demanded from all of us who had pledged ourselves to the idea of a united Europe to do what was necessary to win the hearts and minds of our citizens for European integration (*Einigung*).[177]

There were many types of Euroscepticism, with varying national constituencies over time: a utilitarian concern to question the supposed benefits of integration and reassess what had been ruled out (re-nationalization, for instance); political doubts about the possibility of double allegiance to the EU and nation-state, and about a democratic deficit; value-based scepticism about the European Court of Justice and the EU Charter of Fundamental Rights, which seemed to have gained precedence over national legislation; and cultural anxieties about 'identity', including ridicule of the EU's attempts to create meaningful European symbols and affiliations.[178] The rise of 'sceptical' and anti-European parties between 1992 and 2007—23-25 per cent in EP elections in Denmark in the 1990s, 12-13 per cent in France, 14 per cent in Austria, 14.5 per cent in Sweden and 15.6 per cent in the UK in 2004—was difficult to ignore.[179] They were supported by the tabloid press—with the Austrian *Neue Kronen Zeitung*, owned by Mediaprint, having three million readers from a population of eight million, for example—and they could point to opinion polls showing indifference among voters about whether the EU were scrapped altogether, ranging from 30 to almost 60 per cent (in Spain, which had traditionally been Europhile).[180] Unsurprisingly, Chirac's retrospective narrative compares the political project of European integration to a 'path' and a 'journey', which could seem 'slow and laborious', but which had created 'a peaceful, united continent capable of taking on the challenges of a world [in the 1990s and 2000s] that was itself in the throes of upheaval'.[181] Nonetheless, the president was now extraordinarily sensitive to popular and political opposition to 'Europe', which had seen the RPR leader 'booed during the entire first half' of his

360   EUROPEAN INTEGRATION SINCE THE 1920s

speech to party executives prior to the referendum of 1992—something that had 'never happened to me since the creation of the party'.[182] In 2004–05, he was well aware of the dangers of holding another referendum on a European constitution, blaming Tony Blair for his own 'abrupt announcement' in favour of a popular vote 'without first taking the trouble to alert his European partners'.[183] By this time, it was evident to Chirac that the European 'journey' was comparable to 'a mountain path that is never climbed without difficulty and where there is the ever-present risk of falling or stumbling across an obstacle'.[184] The domestic politics of 'Europe' had become problematic.

At the same time, the diplomatic and military entanglements of the EU in the wake of the Cold War altered relations between member states.[185] The outbreak of war in Yugoslavia occurred before the signature of the Treaty of Maastricht and the establishment of a Common Foreign and Security Policy (CFSP), with fighting occurring in Croatia from January 1991 onwards. Splits between member states had already surfaced after Saddam Hussein's invasion of Kuwait in August 1990 and the subsequent Gulf War in January–February 1991, with Paris and Bonn pursuing separate negotiations for the release of hostages in defiance of the European Council decision in October 1990 to act jointly. The UK provided 36,000 and France 16,000 troops for the American-led invasion, with Italy providing aeroplanes and three warships, the Netherlands a small naval force and Germany, prevented by the Basic Law from deploying troops out of the NATO area, supplying token air support and a third of the funding for the entire operation. 'As I look at our allies in the Gulf,' wrote George Bush in his diary on 17 October 1990: 'the Brits are strong, and the French are French.... The rest of the Europeans do not want to use force.'[186] The European Community lacked the means to coordinate its members, even though CFSP was being discussed at the same time as the war was being waged. The American political scientist George Ross attended the Commission's lunchtime Cabinet meetings in January 1991, as Delors's staff—headed by the Chef de Cabinet Pascal Lamy—discussed 'whether there would be a Common Foreign and Security Policy': 'The moment made it inevitable that the first subject of informal conversation would be the Gulf War. "Insider" information from corridor gossip and diplomatic cyphers machine-gunned around the table until Lamy changed the subject.'[187] The Gulf War at once constituted the backdrop to discussion of a Common Foreign and Security Policy and exposed its future defects. Looking back in March 1991, Delors conceded that, 'once it became obvious that the situation would have to be resolved by armed combat, the Community had neither the institutional machinery nor the military force to allow it to act as a community'.[188] In Yugoslavia, as the conflicting parties descended into the continent's worst series of wars since the Second World War, the European Community sought to intervene as a bloc, sending a 'troika' of foreign ministers from Italy, Luxembourg, and the Netherlands (past, present, and future EC presidencies) in April 1991 to offer aid in return for the

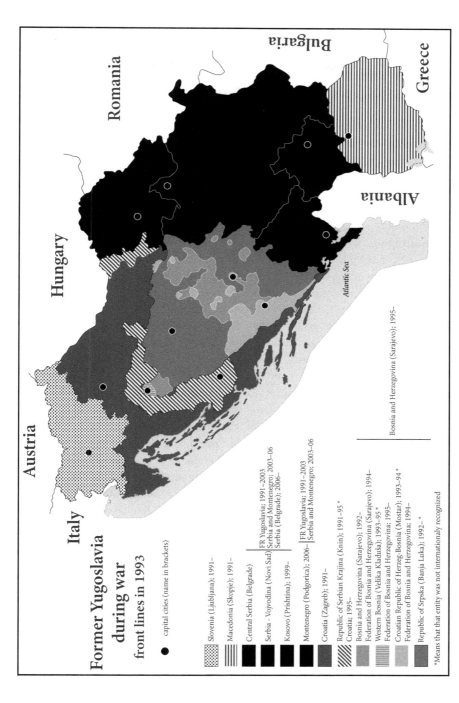

Map 7.3 The Former Yugoslavia at war, 1993
Source: https://en.m.wikipedia.org/wiki/File:Map_of_war_in_Yugoslavia_1993.png

362   EUROPEAN INTEGRATION SINCE THE 1920s

maintenance of the integrity of the Yugoslav state (see Map 7.3). When, on 30 May 1991, Slobodan Milošević told Delors—on a trip to Belgrade—that the condition for Croatian independence was the surrender of 'Serb territories' in Croatia, it became clear that the European Community was powerless to prevent conflict. The EC peace plan devised at the conference at The Hague in September–October 1991, which was chaired by Peter Carrington and backed by Russia and the United States, was ignored by the warring parties. It was in these circumstances that the larger member states started to act on their own.

The paragraphs on a Common Foreign and Security Policy in the Treaty on European Union, which had been drafted before the meeting of the heads of government at Maastricht on 9 December 1991, enjoined member states, not only to define and implement a common policy, but also to refrain from actions contrary to the interests of the EU or likely 'to impair its effectiveness as a cohesive force in international relations'.[189] In order to achieve concerted and convergent action, governments were asked to inform and consult with one another in the Council.[190] Before the Maastricht Treaty had been signed, however, the German government had recognized Slovenia and Croatia as independent states on 23 December 1991, without consulting with other member states and in contravention of the European Community agreement that the independence of Yugoslav republics by 15 January 1992 would depend on their respect for human rights and rights of minorities, democracy, and the peaceful resolution of disputes over borders, subject to the findings of the French judge, Robert Badinter. Bonn feared—correctly, as Badinter's report spelled out—that Croatia would fail to meet these thresholds. In his memoirs, Kohl plays down his disagreement with the UK and France, which had long been wary of intervening in the internal affairs of Yugoslavia, commenting merely that 'Slovenia had already announced that it accepted the specified catalogue [of rights and duties], and Croatia had agreed to follow with a corresponding announcement'.[191] Three days after the meeting of the Council of Foreign Ministers in Brussels on 16 December, the German cabinet decided, in its last meeting of the year, formally to recognize 'the Yugoslav republics'.[192] 'At the time, it was claimed by some countries that the situation in Yugoslavia was exacerbated by the recognition,' Kohl goes on, refusing to name his French and British critics: 'That was proved false, however.'[193] His claim was that fear of further acts of recognition pushed the conflicting parties to accept the United Nations' peace plan, demonstrating that 'the Yugoslav policy within the European Community had an effect'.[194] Mitterrand 'was not correctly informed insofar as he criticized the Germans for distancing themselves, with the early recognition of Slovenia and Croatia, from the decisions of Maastricht,' the Chancellor wrote:

> It was true, though, that recognition certainly did not mark the start of a common European foreign policy. It was too early for this. Now as then, the EC was, for the most part, an economic community, and we were only beginning to build a

political union in Europe. Thus, no one could expect of the EC that such difficult foreign-policy questions could be resolved without friction.[195]

Kohl's stated reasons for acting as he did—'a particular duty in matters of national self-determination', the fact that 'no country in Europe' had so many Croats living in it as Germany, the belief that talking with each other in Yugoslavia might help overcome 'the hatred between the warring parties'—were quite different from those of decision-makers elsewhere.[196]

Initially, Kohl could argue that Bonn and Paris were still in agreement over Yugoslavia, which dominated the agenda of the EU and Franco-German summits during 1992–94, since 'Mitterrand was reinforced in his belief in a limited intervention' by the fear that a 'military operation would be highly precarious and could issue in a second Vietnam'.[197] The president was well aware of what was occurring in Yugoslavia, having been informed early in 1991 by the Yugoslav President and ally of Milošević, Borisav Jović, that 'It is not easy to delimit the territory between the different peoples because we are all mixed together. There is a risk of Civil War, a tragedy for the Balkans and for Europe.'[198] As the Serb population of Krajina proclaimed its intention to secede from Croatia in April 1991, the French president confided to Attali, 'This is the beginning of the end.'[199] During the summer of 1991, French policy-makers and the military created contingency plans for a European peacekeeping force, including the deployment of 10,000 French troops, but Mitterrand was unenthusiastic about going ahead, backed up by John Major, who told him that 'I am not sending my army anywhere.'[200] Early agreement with Germany about the difficulties of a military intervention barely concealed fundamental disagreement about foreign policy, with Paris, London, and Madrid, mindful of separatism in Corsica, Northern Ireland, and the Basque Country, supporting the maintenance of a federal Yugoslav state and rejecting Bonn's rush to recognize Slovenia and Croatia immediately after their declarations of independence in June 1991. After the failure of Carrington's EC peace talks in October, Mitterrand refrained from bringing about a public breach with Kohl for the sake of the Treaty on European Union, as Roland Dumas, the Minister of Foreign Affairs, noted him saying in late 1991: 'The break-up of Yugoslavia is a drama. That of the Community would be a disaster.'[201]

Increasingly, however, France and the United Kingdom were drawn into the war in Bosnia, providing the largest contingents of the UN Protection Force (UNPROFOR) and, by the summer of 1995, setting up a Franco-British-Dutch rapid reaction force, backed by NATO air strikes (3,515 sorties against 338 Bosnian Serb targets). 'For well-known constitutional reasons, we could not take part in military actions,' wrote Kohl, limited to humanitarian aid as the 'shocking news about the situation of human rights in Bosnia-Herzegovina' reached European capitals and were shown on television, leaving citizens critical—'in Germany, too'—of their governments' 'inadequate...efforts to end the conflict'.[202]

364 EUROPEAN INTEGRATION SINCE THE 1920s

In these circumstances, French and British 'realism' gained the upper hand, as the French president spelled out to the German Chancellor on 3 December 1992:

Mitterrand: Do you intend to send German troops [to Bosnia]?

Kohl: No.

Mitterrand: Then let us be realists and speak frankly. Izetbegovic is pushing for the internationalization of the war. It is our interest that all of it stops as soon as possible....The Serbs are in the wrong from A to Z, but we don't have the material means to use force to stop them.... The solution is a consensus of the three ethnic groups.[203]

As France, the UK, and US increasingly resorted to limited force—air power and rapid response on the ground—to stop Serb incursions, Germany—along with other member states—was left to follow events.[204] The Dayton Agreement, signed on 14 December 1995, was an American-brokered accord which was brought about by the military collaboration of the United States, France, and Britain. 'Mr Chirac insisted on having the signing ceremony at the Elysée Palace...in part to stake a French claim to credit for the agreement', having lost 56 soldiers in Bosnia, and in part because 'French diplomats [had] complained that Mr Holbrooke had run roughshod over his European colleagues in Dayton', reported the *New York Times*.[205] Kohl and Carl Bildt, representing the EU, were at the signing ceremony, but played little role in the negotiation of the agreement.

The replacement of Mitterrand by Chirac as president on 17 May 1995 transformed the relationship between France, Germany, and the UK under the pressure of events in Yugoslavia. The RPR leader was critical of American and European caution earlier in the conflict.[206] 'In what was a failure to assume the full weight of their responsibilities, the great powers had from the beginning made the mistake of refusing to threaten a military intervention that probably would have been enough to dissuade the aggressors from all sides while there was still time,' he wrote in his memoirs, referring in a veiled fashion to the stance of Germany, along with other member states: 'Instead, they limited themselves to exclusively humanitarian actions that, although doubtless vital, became the substitute for a real political strategy.'[207] The new president's description of the situation in Bosnia in the summer of 1995 revealed how relationships in Europe and NATO were changing, as France endeavoured to end the 'deadly encircling of Sarajevo' (dating back to 1994) and to force 'western governments out of their wait-and-see attitude'.[208] After one hundred peacekeeping soldiers had been taken hostage by the forces of Ratko Mladić in late May 1995, 'I immediately decided to take charge of the affair', writes Chirac, 'furious at seeing our soldiers humiliated in this way'.[209] 'I was determined to put an end to an anomaly that meant that these same missions did not operate according to their own rules but, as was the case in

Yugoslavia, conformed to the objectives conceived by diplomats or inspired by intellectuals,' the president continues: 'Also, there could be no more question of depending on nothing more than the goodwill of a UN-based authority whose procrastinations had led to the dramatic consequences that had once again been seen in Sarajevo.'[210] Convinced by the end of May that 'firmness was paying off', Chirac 'no longer had any doubt that a rapid reaction force should be set up immediately in Bosnia with the role of guaranteeing the security of the peace-keeping forces and allowing UNPROFOR to ensure that the security zones and free passage of humanitarian aid were respected'.[211]

Chirac's allies were the UK—'The British Prime Minister, John Major, gave me his agreement in principle'—and the United States, where Republicans in Congress eventually agreed '"not to get in the way of your plan when many of your soldiers are there"—on condition, however, that the United States was not involved in any way, financial or military, in the creation of this force, for which France and Great Britain alone would assume the cost'.[212] After Mladić's 'appalling operation of ethnic cleansing against the Muslim population' at Srebrenica on 6–11 July 1995, Chirac—faced with US assessments that military intervention was 'too risky'—telephoned John Major 'to warn him in his turn of the extreme gravity of the situation and to encourage him not to give in':

> 'We claim to be the upholders of democracy and the defenders of human rights,' I said to the British Prime Minister. 'We have sent soldiers and formed the rapid reaction force together, and now we are powerlessly watching our television screens and seeing ethnic cleansing in which thousands of women are going to be raped and thousands of men will have their throats slit and then be thrown to their graves! If I were Serbian, I would be laughing as Hitler must have laughed in Munich when he met Chamberlain and Daladier. We are in the same situation.'[213]

Confronted by 'a situation in which genocide is taking place with impunity before our eyes', which he could not accept, Chirac saw Major, 'whom I knew was himself furious at what was happening in Bosnia', as 'a sure and determined interlocutor' and as his principal military ally.[214] Arguably, these momentous events helped the UK to create a triangular relationship with France and Germany at the core of the European Union during Chirac's presidency between 1995 and 2007.

Relations between the UK, France, and Germany were not always straightforward in the period after 1992. Even during the war in Kosovo in 1998–99, which centred on a NATO aerial bombing campaign (March–June 1999) against the attempts of the Yugoslav army to quash the Kosovo Liberation Army (KLA) and remove Albanians—a large majority of the population—from the province, Paris and London disagreed about the deployment of ground forces, which the British Prime Minister thought necessary 'to have an immediately deterrent effect on

Milošević' and which he 'continually put pressure on the other allied leaders' to accept.[215] 'I tried to explain to him, in vain, that a land offensive would only worsen the conflict by giving the Serbs, who were seasoned soldiers, the opportunity of fierce resistance and would lead the two sides into an endless war that would be enormously costly in terms of human lives,' wrote Chirac, but Tony Blair 'categorically rejected my arguments'.[216] The young Prime Minister admitted subsequently that he 'knew little' about 'contemporary foreign affairs' and had had his 'own attitude to foreign policy' 'completely changed' by the Kosovo conflict.[217] From the outset, he wrote a decade later, 'I was extraordinarily forward in advocating a military solution', provoking 'the irritation of many of our allies and the consternation of a large part of our system' as he sought a resolution of the conflict, not merely 'pacification'.[218] The 'strengths and weaknesses of Europe in this type of situation were laid painfully bare', he continued: 'brilliant at ringing statements of intent, which then evaporated into thin air when the consequences of seeing them through became apparent.'[219]

Over the war in Iraq in March–April 2003, the division between the UK (and Spain and Italy), on the one hand, and France and Germany, on the other, was more pronounced, with Europe 'now split down the middle', in Blair's view, as 'thirteen out of the twenty-five members were in favour' and the 'ten new accession countries came out strongly for the US position—and were roundly abused by Jacques Chirac for it!'[220] There 'were nations for whom the American alliance was a fundamental part of their foreign policy', who tended to back the United States, and 'there were those for whom the alliance was important, but not fundamental', who 'backed off', believing that the 'conflict would harm relations between the West and Islam', the Prime Minister contended.[221] The British Foreign Secretary, Jack Straw, openly opposed his French counterpart Dominique de Villepin at the United Nations on 7 March 2003, as the UK and the US sought a second Security Council resolution providing 'a clear timeline to an ultimatum' and authorizing the use of force:

'Dominique...said that the choice before us was disarmament by peace or disarmament by war. Dominique that is a false choice.' In his speech he had referred to a lot of diplomatic pressure on Iraq from the Non-Aligned Movement, the Arab League and the EU, adding, disingenuously, that the US and UK forces had 'lent support' to that pressure. I picked this apart. We had to back our diplomacy with a credible threat of force. 'I wished we lived in a different world where this was not necessary, but sadly we live in this world and the choice, Dominique, is not ours as to how this disarmament takes place, the choice is Saddam's.'[222]

Chirac's question about the same event was, 'what use would such a resolution serve for Great Britain and the United States, determined as they were to go to war with or without the mandate of the United Nations, other than exposing them to probable rejection by the majority of the members of the Council?'[223] On 10 March, the French president released what Straw labelled 'his wrecking ball', declaring in a live television interview that 'Ma position, c'est que quelles que soient les circonstances, la France votera "non"', effectively deterring those states with additional votes in the Security Council—'the Africans, and Chile and Mexico'—from supporting the second resolution.[224] What was evident, but barely mentioned at the time, were the equal and opposing roles played by Britain and France in Europe in respect of foreign policy.[225] As the French President had met Blair at a summit in Brussels in October 2002, 'Chirac had called him in, totally patronised him, tried to say the whole thing'—a Franco-German deal about enlargement and CAP, with a threat to re-examine the British rebate—'was sorted because France and Germany had decided and that was that,' noted Alastair Campbell in his diary.[226] As Schröder's interpreter had asked him 'Wow, what was all that about?' as Chirac stormed off, and 'TB said he didn't care about him losing it', the Prime Minister spelled out why: 'The French have to accept that they should treat the UK as an equal in Europe. "He can present me as an American poodle if he wants, but we're not putting up with his shit any more. We do it on our terms now."'[227]

For Blair, it was natural that the UK should play a central part in the discussions about the nature and future of Europe in the early twenty-first century. The 'challenge Europe faced' had been transformed, with the EU—'partly due to strong British insistence'—enlarged to twenty-five member states and still recovering 'from an immensely divisive period over Iraq', which had been 'particularly painful' since 'France and Germany had been in the "no" camp'.[228] 'After years of internal wrangling, a consultation exercise had resulted in a Constitution for Europe which now had been rejected,' he recalled: 'So, *quo vadis*?'[229] Although constrained at home by the 'truly hysterical behaviour of the Eurosceptic media', resting on newspapers 'with a combined daily circulation of around eight million—a situation unique in Europe in terms of pervasion'—which was 'wildly and irredeemably hostile to Europe' and which 'misrepresented what Europe was doing', the Prime Minister deliberately sought to put the UK at the centre of EU politics:

> In general terms, for me, Europe was a simple issue. It was to do with the modern world. I supported the European ideal, but even if I hadn't, it was utterly straightforward: in a world of new emerging powers, Britain needed Europe in order to exert influence and advance its interests. It wasn't complicated. It wasn't a psychiatric issue. It was a practical question of realpolitik.
>
> I regarded anti-European feeling as hopelessly, absurdly out of date and unrealistic. It was also the product of a dangerous insularity, a myopia about

368   EUROPEAN INTEGRATION SINCE THE 1920s

the world that I thought affected adversely the whole psychology of the country. It was a kind of post-empire delusion.[230]

As the leader of Singapore, Lee Kuan Yew, had 'told Margaret' and repeated to Blair, 'Britain can't afford to be out of Europe in the world as it is. It's just not realistic.'[231] The Indian Prime Minister, Manmohan Singh, 'told me the same thing'.[232] Blair's theory about 'our problem with Europe is that we didn't invent it' and, then, 'when Macmillan sensibly decided we should join, de Gaulle said, "Non",' leaving 'us a national narrative about the EU that was deeply unhelpful'.[233] The difference forty years later was that the UK stood close to the centre of 'Europe', which even a 'pragmatic European' such as Straw, who 'was on the No side' in 'the great arguments in the sixties and seventies about whether Britain should be in the Common Market', could accept without further comment.[234]

The centrality of Britain in the European Union helped to place limits on supranationality. Although much less explicit than Joschka Fischer, conceding that 'for me, the question of a European constitution was far less important than the question of a European social model', Gerhard Schröder was broadly in favour of creating, 'not only a prospering trade region', but also 'a political space' in Europe, which alone would allow the legitimization of the constitutional process.[235] 'The six core countries, which had come together on 25 March 1957 as the European Economic Community,...had half a century to overcome nationalistic tendencies, which are still the strongest force of resistance against a deepening and widening of integration', the Chancellor contended in 2006, before going on to point out—apparently in appreciation—that the EU 'had agreed on a binding canon of values', that the European Court of Justice ensured 'that EU guidelines are converted into national law', and that the European Commission 'naturally' regulates 'more and more what was originally reserved for national governments', with 'over fifty percent of all laws in national parliaments...adaptations to European law'—'an increasing tendency'.[236]

Straw and Blair were more obstructive, with the Foreign Secretary coming to believe—after an early article in *The Economist* in its support, about which, now, 'I cringe'—that 'the Convention on the Future of Europe turned out to be a *folie de grandeur*':

> My expectation was that the Convention on the Future of Europe would do what it said on the tin—bring the EU 'closer to its citizens...[with] European institutions...less unwieldy and rigid...more efficient and open'. I was particularly pleased that the Declaration had recognized that it should not be 'intervening, in every detail, in matters by their nature, better left to Member States' and regions' elected representatives.' It started out well enough.
>
> I thought it might be possible to reduce the fundamentals of the EU's operation from hundreds of pages to something as concise as the US constitution, and to

MEMBER STATES 369

deal with the need to change the way the EU now operated, with a membership up from six when it started to the twenty-seven members it would have by 2007.[237]

In the event, the 'euro-enthusiasts' in the Convention 'had had a field day, with one unnecessary, and inflammatory, section after another' in the draft 'constitution', giving the impression 'that it would lead to a new relationship between member states and the Union, 'a country called Europe'.[238] When the French and Dutch populations voted against the constitution, 'I could not contain my delight, I'm afraid.'[239] Blair was different—'He was a true believer, in a way I had never been'—and he continued, like Chirac, to defend the constitution, as a means—as the president put it—of making 'the necessary institutional changes' required by enlargement.[240] Yet the British Prime Minister remained critical of Europe's 'own delusion'—or that of insiders—'that the way to make Europe stronger was simply to integrate its decision-making processes' or, in other words, 'more qualified majority voting, more powers to the European Parliament, more areas for European legislation etc.'[241] When the French and German governments put forward the 'pro-European' Belgian Prime Minister Guy Verhofstadt as the next President of the Commission in June 2004, Blair objected, successfully installing the Portuguese Prime Minister José Manuel Barroso instead, who was 'plainly the better choice if you wanted Europe to reform in a non-federalist direction'.[242] For Straw, Verhofstadt, who was Flemish in a Belgian state which 'barely exists' and is 'linguistically and culturally split', 'had little direct emotional comprehension of what it meant to come from a nation with a strong and enduring sense of itself'.[243] His blocked appointment constituted 'the first time that the twin-engine motor of Europe had been stalled in respect of such a big issue', Blair recalled: 'My relationship with Gerhard Schröder never recovered.'[244] The incident demonstrated, though, what could happen when the UK stood 'at the centre of things'.[245]

The fifth phase of European integration since 2007 has been characterized by multipolarity, with new blocs and divisions created by enlargement (East versus West), the eurozone crisis and increasing migration to the EU (South versus North). For the Red–Green coalition government in Germany, the 'widening in the East' (*Osterweiterung*) in 2004 (Poland, the Czech Republic, Slovakia, Hungary, Estonia, Latvia, and Lithuania) and 2007 (Romania and Bulgaria), was at once 'an historic task of the European Union' and a challenge, since movements in Central and Eastern Europe which had been 'united in opposition against Communist political elites' and had been on the 'way to regaining national independence' now 'had to be ready to give up important parts of their new sovereignty to this Europe that was still foreign to them'.[246] The New Labour government in the United Kingdom saw enlargement consolidating a shift towards a more durable form of confederal cooperation. 'An abiding tension inside the EU is between those who want a deeper union and those who want a wider one,' recalled Straw: 'In the UK we've long come down on the wider side of the equation. A larger union suits us.'[247] The benefits of widening were both economic and political, internal and external, helping to explain why the UK government has supported the accession of Turkey.[248] 'One of the reasons we were in the vanguard for the east European states was that their free market and pro-NATO stances provided potential for us to strengthen a natural alliance within the Union, against that led by France and Germany,' wrote Straw in 2012: 'There was a bigger strategic argument too—the more that all of geographical Europe could be bound into the Union, the less the risk of violent conflict between states; the greater the prospect for the democratic idea across the Continent.'[249] For the former Foreign Secretary, 'This is why the EU is a noble project; why it is worth—most of the time—working round its irritations, frustrations, pomposities, and the ever-present efforts of a self-serving administration in Brussels to extend its powers at the expense of those of the nation-state', for 'there was no guarantee that the newly "liberated" states [of the collapsing Soviet bloc] would move to Western-style democracies; nor, later in the decade, that the new Balkan states would stop resorting to extreme violence to resolve their ethnic and territorial arguments'.[250] When Blair addressed the European Parliament on 23 June 2005, as the head of the incoming presidency after the rejection of the European constitution, many MEPs 'were ready to jeer', given his record on Iraq, the British rebate, and the constitutional question, but they ended up applauding him.[251] 'I praised Europe,' he noted: 'I also mocked the pretensions of the endless constitutional focus, pointing out that each time we said that the purpose of such an obsession was to bring us "closer to the people" we lost even more of their support.'[252] In the British Prime Minister's opinion, Europe was 'pinned between those who talked of social Europe, which basically meant more regulation, and those who wanted Europe to be only a market and nothing else'—in other words, 'sceptics versus federalists'.[253] It is doubtful that many of his listeners were convinced by his triangulation—as part of 'a debate over classic third-way politics'—of a social Europe and a free market, or federalism and scepticism, and a middle way.[254] Arguably, though, the 'big impact' of the speech rested on the continuing open-endedness of the debate about Europe.[255]

Few European governments since 2007, including the new grand coalition of Angela Merkel in Germany (November 2005 onwards) and new presidency of Nicolas Sarkozy in France (May 2007–May 2012), have had fixed or easily identifiable views on Europe.[256] As the last decade or so has demonstrated, there is nothing inevitable about European integration. At certain historical junctures, the conditions in which decision-makers acted appear to have made cooperation or a delegation of powers easier or more likely. In the late 1940s and early 1950s, leaders' experiences of and lessons drawn from the Second World War, the collapse of states and notion of a 'zero hour' (or loss of memory), the replacement of pre-war political elites and founding (or re-establishment) of liberal democracies, the need to reconstruct economies and establish a new trading system, the imposition of a *pax americana* and fear of Soviet intervention all permitted and, in some respects, encouraged post-war governments to cooperate and to establish new European institutions. Likewise, in the 1980s and 1990s, the perceived disintegration of the nation-state, the end of the Cold War, a widely held belief that economic 'liberalization' was required, the apparent convergence of welfare systems and disquiet about the inability of national governments to deal on their own with the environment, international crime, immigration, and information technology seemed to make contemporaries more amenable to integration. To an extent, the institutions established and treaties signed in these periods, together with a welter of regulations and networks of 'insiders', developed their own momentum, yet they were also checked and limited by member states, with their varying governments, parties, and political cultures.

Although the ways in which such governments have combined have always been complicated, with the formation of loose groupings and a distinction between large and small states, they have become more varied and complex over time, as the European Community and EU have grown from six members to twenty-eight and as their competencies have increased. Despite repeatedly expressed fears of German ascendancy or, even, hegemony, the FRG has only 18.5 per cent of the EU's population (2020), 22 per cent of its nominal GDP, and, until 2014 (when QMV was tied to population and a majority of member states), 8.5 per cent of the vote in the European Council. Notwithstanding the spread of qualified majority voting and co-decision (involving a veto for the European Parliament) to a wider range of policy areas, there is less chance of proponents of supranationality in a single state or group of states imposing their will on others. The governments of large and medium-sized member states have, in any event, usually been eager to retain critical powers and competencies in the main fields of policy-making. The next chapter examines their delegation and defence of these powers.

Notes

1. P. Anderson, 'The European Coup', *London Review of Books*, vol. 42, 17 December 2020, 9–23; 'Ever Closer Union?', *London Review of Books*, vol. 43, 7 Jan. 2021, 25–34; 'The Breakaway', *London Review of Books*, vol. 43, 21 Jan. 2021, 3–10.
2. P. Anderson, 'The European Coup', *London Review of Books*, vol. 42, 17 December 2020, 23.
3. P. Anderson, 'Ever Closer Union?', *London Review of Books*, vol. 43, 7 January 2021, 25, relying on Vera Fritz, *Juges et avocats généraux de la Cour de Justice de l'Union européenne 1952–1972* (Frankfurt, 2018).
4. Quoted in *London Review of Books*, vol. 43, 7 January 2001, 26; D. Grimm, *The Constitution of European Democracy* (Oxford, 2017).
5. P. Anderson, 'Ever Closer Union?', *London Review of Books*, vol. 43, 7 January 2021, 26; T. Horsley, *The Court of Justice of the European Union as an Institutional Actor*, 125.
6. T. Horsley, *The Court of Justice of the European Union as an Institutional Actor*, 5. Joseph Weiler has written extensively on this topic, pointing out reasons for national governments and courts

372 EUROPEAN INTEGRATION SINCE THE 1920S

accepting ECJ rulings and their later, successful objections to them: see, for instance, J. H. H. Weiler, 'A Quiet Revolution: The European Court of Justice and Its Interlocutors', *Comparative Political Studies*, 26 (1994), 510–34; J. H. H. Weiler, 'A Constitution for Europe? Some Hard Choices', *Journal of Common Market Studies*, 40 (2002), 563–80.

7. P. Anderson, 'Ever Closer Union?', *London Review of Books*, vol. 43, 7 January 2021, 27. It is not clear why the scope of ECJ activity could not be included in treaty revisions such as those of Maastricht, Amsterdam, Nice, and Lisbon or a decision of the European Council to make a 'light amendment'.

8. Ibid., 30.

9. Ibid.

10. Ibid., 30–1. The comment about the euro as a 'prestige' project comes from G. Majone, *Europe as the Would-be World Power: The EU at Fifty* (Cambridge, 2009), 108. See also G. Majone, *Rethinking the Union of Europe Post-Crisis: Has Integration Gone Too Far?* (Cambridge, 2014), 20–57.

11. P. Anderson, 'Ever Closer Union?', *London Review of Books*, vol. 43, 7 January 2021, 29.

12. Ibid.

13. Ibid., 28.

14. P. Anderson, 'The European Coup', *London Review of Books*, vol. 42, 17 December 2020, 12.

15. Ibid., 16.

16. Ibid., 20.

17. Ibid., 16.

18. Ibid., 20–3, referring to L. van Middelaar, *Alarums and Excursions: Improvising Politics on the European Stage* (Newcastle, 2019).

19. P. Anderson, 'Ever Closer Union?', *London Review of Books*, vol. 43, 7 January 2021, 29. Nicolas Sarkozy, *Le Temps des tempêtes*, 106–7, claimed afterwards that Angela Merkel's plan to convene a meeting of twenty-six member states, without Poland (which was refusing to sign), would have been unacceptable.

20. C. Bickerton, *European Integration: From Nation-States to Member States* (Oxford, 2012), vii.

21. P. Anderson, 'Ever Closer Union?', *London Review of Books*, vol. 43, 7 January 2021, 31.

22. Ibid.; C. Bickerton, *European Integration*, 67.

23. C. Bickerton, *European Integration*, 67.

24. M. A. Pollack, 'Creeping Competence: The Expanding Agenda of the European Community', *Journal of Public Policy*, 88 (1994), 95–144; M. A. Pollack, 'The End of Creeping Competence? EU Policy-Making since Maastricht', *Journal of Common Market Studies*, 38 (2000), 519–38; S. Princen and M. Rhinard, 'Crashing and Creeping: Agenda-setting Dynamics in the European Union', *Journal of European Public Policy*, 13 (2006), 1113–32.

25. M. A. Pollack 'Creeping Competence: The Expanding Agenda of the European Community', *Journal of Public Policy*, 88 (1994), 97: 'I shall argue that the institutional decision rules of the Community institutions have a decisive effect on task expansion for all three policy types' (regulation, distribution, and redistribution).

26. M. A. Pollack, 'The End of Creeping Competence? EU Policy-Making since Maastricht', *Journal of Common Market Studies*, 38 (2000), 527, 530.

27. W. Wallace, 'Europe as a Confederation: The Community and the Nation-State', *Journal of Common Market Studies*, 21 (1982), 64–5.

28. M. A. Pollack 'Creeping Competence: The Expanding Agenda of the European Community', *Journal of Public Policy*, 88 (1994), 100–2; S. Hoffmann, 'Obstinate or Obsolete? The Fate of the Nation-State and the Case of Western Europe', *Daedalus*, 95 (1966), 862–915.

29. J. Peterson, 'Decision-making in the European Union: Towards a Framework for Analysis', *Journal of European Public Policy*, 2 (1995), 86.

30. More recently, Peterson, 'Junker's Political European Commission', *Journal of Common Market Studies*, 55 (2017), 349–67, has sought to examine European institutions in light of the 'new intergovernmentalism', or 'integration without traditional forms of delegation', as Bickerton, Hodson and Puetter (eds), *The New Intergovernmentalism: States and Supranational Actors in the Post-Maastricht Era* (Oxford, 2015), 4–5, have put it.

31. Jacques Attali gives a good account of how bilateral relations worked, intersecting with governments' relationship with European institutions. France's main relations were with Germany, given the regular meetings between Mitterrand and Kohl which took place in accordance with the terms of the Franco-German Friendship Treaty: for instance, on 24 April (Trèves), 27 June (La Haye), 26 August (Heidelberg), 27 October (Frankfurt), 28 October 1986 (Bonn), where the leaders discussed CAP, more 'dynamic' European questions—which France and Germany initiated—such as Airbus and TGV connections to the East, and the Cold War. There were also regular meetings

between the French and British governments: for example, 16 October 1986 (London), 20 November 1986 (the annual Franco-British summit in Paris), 29 July 1987 (Paris), at which the Middle East and the Cold War were the main topics of conversation; and Franco-Italian meetings, often prior to the meetings of the G5 and G7: for instance, 28 November 1986 (Paris) and 25 February 1987 (Paris). J. Attali, *Verbatim 1986–1988* (Paris, 1995), vol. 2, 57–9, 103–5, 141–2, 179–83, 189–92, 205–6, 209–10, 263–4, 266–8, 346–7, 368–71, 473–4.

32. A. Milward, *The European Rescue of the Nation-State*, 2nd edn (London, 2000), 25.

33. E. F. Delaney, 'The European Constitution and Europe's Dialectical Federalism', in N. W. Barber, M. Cahill, and R. Ekins (eds.), *The Rise and Fall of the European Constitution* (Oxford, 2019), 73–87; D. Beach, *The Dynamics of European Integration: Why and When EU Institutions Matter* (Basingstoke, 2005), 2–4, 16–34, 245–58: although Beach concedes that 'EU institutions are not the motors of integration that supranationalists have contended', he continues to focus largely on their actions and interventions.

34. See A. Shennan, *Rethinking France: Plans for Renewal, 1940–1946* (Oxford, 1989); P. Addison, *The Road to 1945: British Politics and the Second World War* (London, 1977); G. J. Ikenberry, 'Creating Yesterday's New World Order: Keynesian "New Thinking" and the Anglo-American Postwar Settlement', in J. Goldstein and R. O. Keohane (eds), *Ideas and Foreign Policy: Beliefs, Institutions and Political Change* (Ithaca, NY, 1993), 57–86.

35. F. Billoux and J. Monnet, quoted in L. A. Brunet, 'The Creation of the Monnet Plan, 1945–1946: A Critical Re-Evaluation', *Contemporary European History*, 27 (2018), 33–4.

36. R. Schuman, *French Policy towards Germany since the War* (Oxford, 1954), quoted in G. F. Treverton, *America, Germany and the Future of Europe* (Princeton, NJ), 103.

37. Ibid.

38. Schuman Declaration, 9 May 1950, at https://europa.eu/european-union/about-eu/symbols/europe-day/schuman-declaration_en.

39. K. Adenauer, 14 June 1950, in B. Lefort (ed.), *Une Europe inédite. Documents des archives Jean Monnet* (Lille, 2001), 666–7.

40. Ibid., 660.

41. Quoted in D. W. Urwin, *The Community of Europe: A History of European Integration since 1945*, 2nd edn (London, 1995), 32, 34. See also John W. Young, *Britain and European Unity, 1945–1992* (Basingstoke, 1993), who holds that the British government in the late 1940s and early 1950s had little room for manoeuvre, and Christopher Lord, *Absent at the Creation: Britain and the Formation of the European Community, 1950–2* (Aldershot, 1996), and Edmund Dell, *The Schuman Plan and the British Abdication of Leadership in Europe* (Oxford, 1995), who contend that it did, but failed to act.

42. D. Bruce, 25 April 1950, quoted in C. A. Wurm, 'Britain and West European Integration, 1948–9 to 1955: Politics and Economics', in J. Noakes, P. Wende, and J. Wright (eds), *Britain and Germany in Europe, 1949–1990* (Oxford, 2002), 42.

43. G. F. Kennan, quoted in A. Bullock, *Ernest Bevin, Foreign Secretary, 1945–1951* (London, 1983), 703.

44. Robert Schuman's speech to the Six at the Quai d'Orsay, 20 June 1950, at https://www.cvce.eu/obj/discours_de_robert_schuman.

45. Ibid.

46. M. Charlton, *The Price of Victory* (London, 1983), 99.

47. K. O. Morgan, *Labour in Power, 1945–1951* (Oxford, 1984), 391–2.

48. Quoted in A. S. Milward, *The European Rescue of the Nation-State*, 2nd edn, 364.

49. Quoted in M. Charlton, *The Price of Victory*, 87.

50. E. Bevin, 'The First Aim of British Foreign Policy', 4 January 1948, in S. Wall, *Reluctant European*, 36.

51. Anthony Nutting, in M. J. Dedman, *The Origins and Development of the European Union, 1945–95* (London, 1996), 78. Eden was aware of the changing dynamics of 'nuclearization', pushing him further towards NATO and further away from the EDC: see G. Schmidt, 'European Security: Anglo-German Relationships, 1949–1956', in J. Noakes, P. Wende, and J. Wright (eds), *Britain and Germany in Europe*, 115–40. As Eden told the House of Commons, 'The whole essence of the EDC lay in its supranational character, leading to a federal structure for Europe. That might be a good thing or it might not: I am not prepared to argue that. Some people were all for it and some were against it, but, so far, no party in this country has been willing to subscribe to that conception for ourselves. Therefore, it was not possible for Britain to make the kind of contribution towards a federal structure which we can make to this present arrangement [the Western European Union]'. Quoted in K. Ruane, *The Rise and Fall of the European Defence Community: Anglo-American*

374 EUROPEAN INTEGRATION SINCE THE 1920S

Relations and the Crisis of European Defence, 1950–55 (Basingstoke, 2000), 182. Harold Macmillan, *Tides of Fortune, 1945–55* (London, 1969), 480, remarked that the failure of the EDC and the European Political Community was 'a good result for us'.

52. L. Warlouzet, 'The EEC/EU as an Evolving Compromise between French Dirigism and German Ordoliberalism, 1957–1995', *Journal of Common Market Studies*, 57 (2019), 77–93.

53. H. Macmillan to officials at the Foreign Office, 29 June 1955, in A. S. Milward, 'Childe Harold's Pilgrimage', in J. Noakes, P. Wende, and J. Wright (eds), *Britain and Germany in Europe*, 56.

54. Ibid., 50: Sir Harold Caccia, one of three Under-Secretaries in the Foreign Office, believed that the Six were so unlikely to go ahead without the UK that it was a waste of time to report on their activities. Rab Butler noted, even after the event, that there was 'not the slightest possibility of the Messina "common market" coming into existence.... The only troublesome point was whether we should strive to kill it or let it collapse of its own weight', in M. Charlton, *The Price of Victory*, 198. Macmillan, too, recalled that 'We thought they wouldn't succeed', in A. Moravcsik, *The Choice for Europe: Social Purpose and State Power from Messina to Maastricht* (Ithaca, NY, 1998), 128.

55. H. Macmillan to Sir Edward Bridges, Permanent Under-Secretary at the Treasury, 1 February 1956, in A. S. Milward, 'Childe Harold's Pilgrimage', in J. Noakes, P. Wende, and J. Wright (eds), *Britain and Germany in Europe*, 57–8.

56. A. S. Milward, 'Childe Harold's Pilgrimage', in J. Noakes, P. Wende, and J. Wright (eds), *Britain and Germany in Europe*, 57–8.

57. See J. Ellison, *Threatening Europe: Britain and the Creation of the European Community, 1955–58* (Basingstoke, 2000), 12–92, 153–76.

58. Ibid., 13–36, 95–128.

59. H. Macmillan to P. Thorneycroft, 15 July 1957, in A. S. Milward, 'Childe Harold's Pilgrimage', in J. Noakes, P. Wende, and J. Wright (eds), *Britain and Germany in Europe*, 58.

60. H. Macmillan to F. A. Bishop, 16 July 1957, ibid.

61. Ibid. See also N. P. Ludlow, 'A Waning Force: The Treasury and British European Policy, 1955–63', *Contemporary British History*, 17 (2003), 87–104; S. Wall, *Reluctant European*, 47–8: Rab Butler, who was chair of the OEEC, told Michael Charlton, 'At that time, Britain was regarded as the normal chairman of Europe.... I remember giving almost my final dinner in Paris to the OEEC...and making a remark saying that excavations were proceeding at Messina at which we were not taking part...I always remember that because it was, in my view, a definite lack of foresight on the part of myself, and a much bigger lack of foresight on the part of Treasury, and a very big lack of foresight on the part of the Foreign Office.... That is where we started to go wrong in regard to the EEC of today.'

62. The term 'choice for the Community' comes from Craig Parsons, *A Certain Idea of Europe*, 90–116, deriving from Andrew Moravcsik's *The Choice for Europe*.

63. C. Parsons, *A Certain Idea of Europe*, 107–8.

64. R. Marjolin, *Le travail d'une vie. Mémoires 1911–1986* (Paris, 1986), 282.

65. Ibid.

66. S. Berstein, 'The Perception of French Power by the Political Forces', in E. Di Nolfo (ed.), *Power in Europe? Great Britain, France, Germany and Italy and the Origins of the EEC, 1952–1957* (Berlin, 1992), vol. 2, 347.

67. Ibid., 348.

68. W. Loth, 'From the "Third Force" to the Common Market: Discussions about Europe and the Future of the Nation-State in West Germany, 1945–57', in D. Geppert (ed.), *The Postwar Challenge, 1945–1958* (Oxford, 2003), 204.

69. It is worth noting that this would also have been true of Kurt Schumacher, if the SPD had been voted into office in 1949, as had been expected. Peter Merseburger, *Der Schwierig Deutsche. Kurt Schumacher*, 469, points out that the SPD leader had given a 'strict no' to the Council of Europe.

70. DIVO Institute poll, in W. Loth, 'From the "Third Force" to the Common Market', in D. Geppert (ed.), *The Postwar Challenge, 1945–1958*, 209.

71. Ibid., 205.

72. See A. C. Mierzejewski, *Ludwig Erhard: A Biography* (Chapel Hill, NC, 2004). In general, 'ordo-liberals' looked to the freeing of global markets under US leadership: V. R. Berghahn, 'Ordoliberalism, Ludwig Erhard and West Germany's "Economic Basic Law"', *European Review of International Studies*, 2 (2015), 37–47.

73. K. Adenauer to all federal ministers, 19 January 1956, in K. Adenauer, *Erinnerungen 1955–1959* (Stuttgart, 1967), vol. 2, 253–4. On the SPD, see R. Hrbek, *Die SPD, Deutschland und Europa*

MEMBER STATES   375

1945–1957 (Bonn, 1972), 255–62, and J. Bellers, *Reformpolitik und EWG-Strategie der SPD* (Munich, 1979), 79–91.

74. H.-P. Schwarz, 'Adenauer und Europa', *Vierteljahreshefte für Zeitgeschichte*, 27 (1979), 471–521, argues that Adenauer had left traditional ways of thinking about the nation-state behind, seeking to combine the internal interests of Germany with its external situation in Europe. See also H.-P. Schwarz, *Konrad Adenauer: A German Politician and Statesman in a Period of War, Revolution and Reconstruction* (Providence, RI, 1995–7), 2 vols.

75. See U. Lappenküper, *Die deutsch-französischen Beziehungen 1949–1963. Von der 'Erbfeindschaft' zur 'Entente élémentaire'* (Munich, 2001); M. Koopmann, Das schwierige Bündnis. *Die deutsch-französischen Beziehungen und die Außenpolitik der Bundesrepublik Deutschland 1948–1965* (Baden-Baden, 2000).

76. C. de Gaulle, *Memoirs*, vol. 2, 177.

77. Ibid. See U. Lappenküper, *Die deutsch-französischen Beziehungen 1949–1963*, 1201–32; H. Köhler, *Adenauer. Eine politische Biographie*, vol. 2, 444–54.

78. C. de Gaulle, *Memoirs*, vol. 2, 177. Also G. J. Martin, *General de Gaulle's Cold War* (New York, 2013).

79. C. de Gaulle, *Memoirs*, vol. 2, 177.

80. Ibid.

81. K. Adenauer, *Erinnerungen*, vol. 2, 243. This relationship with the 'West', especially the United States, had been slow to develop and was valued accordingly, as something precious but fragile: T. W. Maulucci, 'Konrad Adenauer's April 1953 Visit to the United States and the Limits of the German–American Relationship in the Early 1950s', *German Studies Review*, 26 (2003), 577–96; H. Köhler, *Adenauer. Eine politische Biographie* (Frankfurt, 1997), vol. 2, 93–133.

82. K. Adenauer, *Erinnerungen*, vol. 2, 252–3.

83. Ibid., 254. See W. Weidenfeld, *Konrad Adenauer und Europa. Die geistigen Grundlagen der westeuropäischen Integrationspolitik des ersten Bonner Bundeskanzlers* (Bonn, 1976).

84. K. Adenauer to federal ministers, 19 January 1956, K. Adenauer, *Erinnerungen*, vol. 2, 254.

85. Ibid.

86. Ibid. Adenauer was comparing them to the relations between Italy and the FRG, which were significant, but less important than Franco-German relations. H.-P. Schwarz (ed.), *Adenauer und Frankreich. Die deutsch-französischen Beziehungen 1958–1969* (Bonn, 1990).

87. K. Adenauer, *Erinnerungen*, vol. 2, 262. The Foreign Office report was from autumn 1954. Also R. J. Granieri, *The Ambivalent Alliance: Konrad Adenauer, the CDU/CSU and the West, 1949–1966* (New York, 2003), 70–109.

88. R. Marjolin, *Le travail d'une vie*, 355. On the EMS, see E. Moulon-Druol, *A Europe Made of Money: The Emergence of the European Monetary System* (Ithaca, NY, 2012); L. Warlouzet, 'The EEC/EU as an Evolving Compromise between French Dirigism and German Ordoliberalism, 1957–1995', *Journal of Common Market Studies*, 57 (2019), 77–93; L. Warlouzet, *Governing Europe in a Globalizing World: Neoliberalism and Its Alternatives Following the 1973 Oil Crisis* (London, 2018). Michèle Weinachter, *Valéry Giscard d'Estaing et l'Allemagne. Le double rêve inachevé* (Paris, 2004), 69–70, shows that Giscard was closer to de Gaulle than Pompidou, who wanted to pay more attention to the United Kingdom. 'He has always been convinced—for as long as I have known him'—of the centrality of the Franco-German relationship, recalled Raymond Barre: 'From this point of view, he was in the absolute line of General de Gaulle more than that of Pompidou. Pompidou looked in the English direction. Giscard never looked in the English direction.' In 1975, even Monnet pleaded with Giscard to develop better relations with the UK, but to no avail.

89. R. Marjolin, *Le travail d'une vie*, 354.

90. Ibid., 355. On the resistance of smaller states, see U. Krotz and J. Schild, *Shaping Europe*, 118.

91. R. Marjolin, *Le travail d'une vie*, 354.

92. Ibid.

93. V. Giscard d'Estaing, *Le pouvoir et la vie. Choisir* (Paris, 2006), vol. 3, 273.

94. Ibid.

95. Ibid.

96. Ibid., 274. See S. Berstein and J.-F. Sirinelli (eds), *Les années Giscard. Valéry Giscard d'Estaing et l'Europe 1974–1981* (Paris, 2006).

97. V. Giscard d'Estaing, *Le pouvoir et la vie*, vol. 3, 274.

376   EUROPEAN INTEGRATION SINCE THE 1920S

98. Ibid. M. Weinachter, 'Le tandem *Valéry Giscard d'Estaing*—Helmut Schmidt et la gouvernance européenne', in W. Loth (ed.), *La gouvernance supranationale dans la construction européenne* (Brussels, 2005), 205–38.

99. V. Giscard d'Estaing, *Le pouvoir et la vie*, vol. 3, 275. See W. Wessels, *Der Europäische Rat. Stabilisierung statt Integration? Geschichte, Entwicklung und Zukunft der EG-Gipfelkonferenzen* (Bonn, 1980), 122.

100. V. Giscard d'Estaing, *Le pouvoir et la vie*, 276. On the hesitancy of Paris because of domestic opposition, despite Giscard's support for direct election, see M. Weinachter, *Valéry Giscard d'Estaing et l'Allemagne. Le double rêve inachevé* (Paris, 2004), 439.

101. C. Parsons, *A Certain Idea of Europe*, 160; A. Moravscik, *The Choice for Europe*, 260.

102. V. Giscard d'Estaing, *Le pouvoir et la vie*, 276.

103. Ibid., 281. Mitterrand chose to do the same.

104. Ibid., 277.

105. S. Berstein, J.-C. Casanova, and J.-F. Sirinelli (eds), *Les années Giscard. La politique économique 1974–1981* (Paris, 2009).

106. V. Giscard d'Estaing, *Le pouvoir et la vie*, 296. See M. Waechter, *Helmut Schmidt und Valéry Giscard d'Estaing. Auf der Suche nach Stabilität in der Krise der 1970er Jahren* (Bremen, 2011).

107. V. Giscard d'Estaing, *Le pouvoir et la vie*, 296. A. E. Gfeller, *Building a European Identity: France, the United States and the Oil Shock, 1973–1974* (New York, 2012).

108. R. Marjolin, *Le travail d'une vie*, 355.

109. Ibid.

110. Ibid. Bernard Clappier, the head of the Banque de France and Giscard's representative at the talks with German counterparts about monetary cooperation, leading to the EMS, stated that the 'kernel' of any agreement would be exchange-rate stabilization and everything else—a European unit of account, mandatory interventions, other financing provisions—would be 'symbolic': A. Moravscik, *The Choice for Europe*, 252; J. Story, 'The Launching of the EMS: An Analysis of Change in Foreign Economic Policy', *Political Studies*, 36 (1988), 404–5.

111. R. Marjolin, *Le travail d'une vie*, 358.

112. This is not to argue that EMU had no effect on policy over the longer term, but rather to suggest that it did not produce institutional reform in other areas: for the long-term effects, see D. Jossilin, 'Between Europe and a Hard Place: French Financial Diplomacy from 1995–2002', *French Politics, Culture and Society*, 22 (2004), 57–75.

113. V. Giscard d'Estaing, *Le pouvoir et la vie. Choisir* (Paris, 2006), vol. 3, 273–311.

114. Ibid., vols 1–2, 733–7.

115. Détente and relations with the superpowers remained central: M. Meimeth, *Frankreichs Entspannungspolitik der 70er Jahre zwischen Status quo und friedlichem Wandel. Die Ära Georges Pompidou und Valéry Giscard d'Estaing* (Baden-Baden, 1990).

116. H. Miard-Delacroix, 'Helmut Schmidt et les institutions européennes', in M.-T. Bitsch (ed.), *Le couple France-Allemagne et les institutions européennes* (Brussels, 2001), 424.

117. H. Schmidt, *Weggefährten und Reflexionen* (Berlin, 1996), 258.

118. Ibid., 264. D. Petter, *Auf dem Weg zur Normalität. Konflikt und Verständigung in den deutsch-französischen Beziehungen der 1970er Jahre* (Munich, 2014); M. Weinachter, *Valéry Giscard d'Estaing et l'Allemagne. Le double rêve inachevé* (Paris, 2004); G.-H. Soutou, 'Staatspräsident Valéry Giscard d'Estaing und die deutsche Frage', in K. Hildebrand, U. Wengst, and A. Wirsching (eds), *Geschichtswissenschaft und Zeiterkenntnis von der Aufklärung bus zur Gegenwart* (Munich, 2008), 373–82.

119. H. Schmidt, *Weggefährten und Reflexionen*, 253. He noted, with little obvious regret, that Monnet's aim of overcoming 'the principle of unanimity and of achieving a 'thoroughgoing' European currency system and foreign and defence policy had not been realized, even by the 1990s.

120. Ibid., 262.

121. Ibid.

122. U. Krotz and J. Schild, *Shaping Europe*, 118; T. Birkner, *Comrades for Europe? Die 'Europarede' Helmut Schmidts 1974* (Bremen, 2005).

123. This is Andrew Moravcsik's argument about Schmidt's European policy in *The Choice for Europe*, 250–9. H. Schmidt, 'Der Politiker als Ökonom', in H. Schmidt, *Kontinuität und Konzentration*, 2nd edn (Bonn, 1976), 36–52. On Schmidt's domestic priorities, see M Rupps, *Helmut Schmidt. Eine politische Biographie* (Stuttgart, 2002).

124. Quoted in Timothy Garton Ash, *In Europe's Name: Germany and the Divided Continent* (London, 1993), 85.

125. In A. Moravscik, *The Choice for Europe*, 251.
126. E. Mourlon-Druol, *A Europe Made of Money*, 30–64.
127. Ibid., 251–2.
128. H. Schmidt, 'Guiding Thoughts on Our Foreign Policy', 17 January 1975, in K. Spohr, *The Global Chancellor: Helmut Schmidt and the Reshaping of the International Order* (Oxford, 2016), 17–18.
129. H. Schmidt, the 'Marbella paper', December 1976, in T. Garton Ash, *In Europe's Name*, 87.
130. Ibid.
131. Ibid.
132. Ibid.
133. There were also close ties between the emerging G7 and the EEC, of course: E. Mourlon-Druol and F. Romero (eds), *International Summitry and Global Governance: The Rise of the G7 and the European Council, 1974–1991* (London, 2014); J. v. Karczewski, 'Weltwirtschaft ist unser Schicksal'. *Helmut Schmidt und die Schaffung der Weltwirtschaft* (Bonn, 2008); E. Böhm, *Die Sicherheit des Westens. Enstehung und Funktion der G7-Gipfel 1975–1981* (Munich, 2014).
134. H. Kohl, *Erinnerungen 1982–1990* (Munich, 2005), vol. 2, 600. E. Gaddum, *Die deutsche Europapolitik in den 80er Jahren. Interessen, Konflikte und Entscheidungen der Regierung Kohl* (Paderborn, 1994); M. Haeussler, 'The Conviction of a Realist: Concepts of "Solidarity" in Helmut Schmidt's European Thought, 1945–82', *European Review of History*, 24 (2017), 955–72.
135. H. Kohl, *Erinnerungen*, vol. 2, 601, 448–9, 61.
136. Ibid., 158.
137. Ibid.
138. Ibid., 589. For Kohl's political priorities, see K. Dreher, *Helmut Kohl. Leben mit Macht* (Stuttgart, 1998); K.-R. Korte, *Deutschlandpolitik in Helmut Kohls Kanzlerschaft. Regierungsstil und Entscheidungen 1982–1989* (Stuttgart, 1998); H.-P. Schwarz, *Helmut Kohl. Eine politische Biographie* (Munich, 2012).
139. H. Kohl, *Erinnerungen 1982–1990*, vol. 2, 589.
140. F. J. Strauß, *Die Erinnerungen* (Berlin, 1989), 564.
141. H.-D. Genscher, *Erinnerungen* (Berlin, 1995), 362.
142. Ibid., 366.
143. H. Haftendoorn, *Coming of Age: German Foreign Policy since 1945* (Lanham, MD, 2006), 312–13.
144. H.-D. Genscher, *Erinnerungen*, 364.
145. Ibid., 370.
146. Ibid., 374.
147. J. Leaman, *The Political Economy of Germany under Chancellors Kohl and Schröder* (New York, 2009), 43–98; R. Zohlnhöfer, *Die Wirtschaftspolitik der Ära Kohl 1982–1989* (Opladen, 2001).
148. H.-D. Genscher, *Erinnerungen*, 382.
149. Ibid.
150. H. Kohl, *Erinnerungen*, vol. 2, 157–8, 680.
151. Ibid., 99.
152. Ibid., 98.
153. Ibid.
154. Ibid., 155.
155. Ibid.
156. K. Dyson and K. Featherston, *The Road to Maastricht: Negotiating Economic and Monetary Union* (Oxford, 1999), 256–85, 306–69.
157. H. Kohl, *Erinnerungen*, vol. 2, 108.
158. Ibid., 111.
159. H.-D. Genscher, *Erinnerungen*, 387.
160. U. Krotz and J. Schild, *Shaping Europe*, 190–9; K. Dyson and K. Featherstone, *The Road to Maastricht: Negotiating Economic and Monetary Union* (Oxford, 1999), 757–8; W. Loth, 'Helmut Kohl und die Währungsunion', *Vierteljahreshefte für Zeitgeschichte*, 61 (2013), 455–80.
161. A case could be made for the inclusion of Italy, given Giulio Andreotti's role in setting an early date for stage 2 of EMU—January 1994—at the European Council in Rome in October 1990, against the wishes of an isolated Margaret Thatcher, but Italian governments played little role in later events, with the exception of Gianni de Michaelis's attempt to entice the Montenegrin government away from Belgrade with the promise of European aid in October 1991: P. Ginsborg, *Italy and Its Discontents, 1980–2001* (London, 2001), 246–8; on de Michaelis, see L. Silber and A. Little, *The Death of Yugoslavia*, 195.
162. 'Eine Industrieregion zerbricht', 15 April 1991, in U. Herbert, *A History of Twentieth-century Germany* (Oxford, 2019), 932.

378 EUROPEAN INTEGRATION SINCE THE 1920s

163. Ibid., 932–3.
164. Ibid., 939.
165. Ibid., 936.
166. Ibid., 940.
167. H. Kohl, *Erinnerungen 1990–1994* (Munich, 2007), vol. 3, 472.
168. Ibid., 473.
169. Ibid., 480.
170. Ibid.
171. Ibid., 616. M. Schmidt (ed.), *The Chancellor of the Unification: Germany and Europe* (Budapest, 2016); F. van Esch, 'Why Germany Wanted EMU: The Role of Helmut Kohl's Belief System and the Fall of the Wall', *German Politics*, 21 (2012), 34–52.
172. H. Kohl, *Erinnerungen 1990–1994*, vol. 3, 616–17.
173. F. Schotters, 'Mitterrand's Europe: Functions and Limits of "European Solidarity" in French Policy during the 1980s', *European Review of History*, 24 (2017), 973–90.
174. Quoted in R. Tiersky, *François Mitterrand*, 196.
175. P. Madelin, *Jacques Chirac. Une biographie* (Paris, 2002), 488.
176. Ibid., 523. H. Drake, 'Jacques Chirac's Balancing Acts: The French Right and Europe', *South European Society and Politics*, 10 (2005), 297–313.
177. H. Kohl, *Erinnerungen*, vol. 3, 617.
178. C. Leconte, *Understanding Euroscepticism* (Basingstoke, 2010), 43–67. Also P. Taggart and A. Szczerbiak, *Opposing Europe: The Comparative Party Politics of Euroscepticism* (Oxford, 2005–08), 2 vols; B. Wessels, 'Discontent and European Identity: Three Types of Euroscepticism', *Acta Politica*, 42 (2007), 287–306; C. De Vreese, 'A Spiral of Euroscepticism: The Media's Fault?', *Acta Politica*, 42 (2007), 271–86; M. Lubbers and P. Scheepers, 'Political versus Instrumental Euroscepticism: Mapping Euroscepticism in European Countries and Regions', *European Union Politics*, 6 (2006), 223–42; N. Sitter, 'The Politics of Opposition and European Integration in Scandinavia: Is Euro-Scepticism a Government-Opposition Dynamic?', *West European Politics*, 24 (2001), 22–39.
179. The figures come from C. Leconte, *Understanding Euroscepticism*, 119, and include parties which were 'Eurocritical', Eurosceptic and anti-European. Most were in the last category.
180. Ibid., 187.
181. J. Chirac, *My Life in Politics* (Basingstoke, 2012), 307.
182. Ibid., 121.
183. Ibid., 309.
184. Ibid., 307.
185. J. Glaurdić, *The Hour of Europe: Western Powers and the Breakup of Yugoslavia* (New Haven, CT, 2011).
186. G. Bush and B. Scowcroft, *A World Transformed* (New York, 1998), 383.
187. G. Ross, 'Inside the Delors Cabinet', *Journal of Common Market Studies*, 32 (1994), 503.
188. G. Ross, *Jacques Delors and European Integration*, 97–8.
189. D. Buchan, *Europe: The Strange Superpower* (Aldershot, 1993), 46.
190. Ibid. See also M. Gilbert, *European Integration*, 196.
191. H. Kohl, *Erinnerungen*, vol. 3, 405.
192. Ibid.
193. Ibid., 406. See also Daniele Conversi, *German-bashing and the Breakup of Yugoslavia* (Seattle, WA, 1998), who elaborates on these arguments.
194. H. Kohl, *Erinnerungen*, vol. 3, 406.
195. Ibid.
196. Ibid., 407–8. M. Libal, *Limits of Persuasion: Germany and the Yugoslav Crisis, 1991–1992* (Westport, CT, 1997).
197. H. Kohl, *Erinnerungen*, vol. 3, 462. Yugoslavia was uppermost at the meeting of Kohl, Mitterrand, and Edouard Balladur, the new neo-Gaullist prime minister, at Beaune in early 1993 and at Bonn in December of the same year: ibid., 584, 639.
198. B. Jović, quoted in P. Short, *Mitterrand*, 519. Also C. Jones, 'François Mitterrand's Visit to Sarajevo, 28 June 1992', *Diplomacy and Statecraft*, 28 (2017), 296–319.
199. F. Mitterrand to J. Attali, April 1991, in P. Short, *Mitterrand*, 519.
200. Ibid., 520.
201. Ibid.
202. H. Kohl, *Erinnerungen*, vol. 3, 462, 507, 647. A. Dalgaard-Nielsen, *Germany, Pacifism and Peace Enforcement* (Manchester, 2006), 70–80.

MEMBER STATES 379

203. F. Mitterrand to H. Kohl, 3 December 1992, in R. Tiersky, *François Mitterrand*, 205.
204. Hanns Maull and Bernhard Stahl, 'Durch den Balkan nach Europa? Deutschland und Frankreich in den Jugoslawienkreigen', *Politische Vierteljahresschrift*, 43 (2002), 82–111, admit that there was a rift between France and Germany over Yugoslavia in the early 1990s but argue that it was resolved by the time of the war in Kosovo in 1999.
205. *New York Times*, 15 December 1995. R. F. Kuisel, *The French Way: How France Embraced and Rejected American Values and Power* (Princeton, NJ, 2012), 212–42; C. Cogan, 'Mitterrand, France and NATO: The European Transition', *Journal of Transatlantic Studies*, 9 (2011), 257–67; A. Macleod, 'French Policy toward War in the Former Yugoslavia: A Bid for International Leadership', *International Journal*, 52 (1997), 243–64.
206. R. F. Kuisel, *The French Way*, 230–70.
207. J. Chirac, *My Life in Politics*, 156.
208. Ibid.
209. Ibid.
210. Ibid., 157.
211. Ibid.
212. Ibid., 159.
213. Ibid., 160, 162.
214. Ibid., 162–3.
215. Ibid., 222. C. Wagnsson, *Security in a Greater Europe: The Possibility of a Pan-European Approach* (Manchester, 2008), 25–47.
216. J. Chirac, *My Life in Politics*, 222.
217. T. Blair, *A Journey* (London, 2010), 224, 227.
218. Ibid., 227. O. Daddow, ' "Tony's War"? Kosovo and the Interventionist Impulse in British Foreign Policy', *International Affairs*, 85 (2009), 547–60; C. Hill, 'Putting the World to Rights: Tony Blair's Foreign Policy Mission', in A. Seldon and D. Kavanagh (eds), *The Blair Effect, 2001–5* (Cambridge, 2005), 384–409.
219. T. Blair, *A Journey*, 227.
220. Ibid., 423. S. B. Dyson, *The Blair Identity: Leadership and Foreign Policy* (Manchester, 2009), 70–131.
221. T. Blair, *A Journey*, 423.
222. J. Straw, *Last Man Standing: Memoirs of a Political Survivor* (London, 2012), 387–8.
223. J. Chirac, *My Life in Politics*, 278; P. Rieker, *French Foreign Policy in a Changing World: Practising Grandeur* (Basingstoke, 2017), 87–106.
224. J. Straw, *Last Man Standing*, 388–9; S. Recchia, 'Did Chirac say "Non"? Revisiting UN Diplomacy on Iraq, 2002–2003', *Political Science Quarterly*, 130 (2015), 625–54.
225. Spain was treated more dismissively by the French president, who 'deplored the unconditional support that the Spanish leader José María Aznar gave the Anglo-American arguments and the extremely critical judgements that he continually made of France', leading to 'a particularly stormy debate about this when he passed through Paris on February 26': J. Chirac, *My Life in Politics*, 279. C. Wagnsson, *Security in a Greater Europe*, 73–127; L. Warlouzet, 'Britain at the Centre of European Cooperation, 1948–2016', *Journal of Common Market Studies*, 56 (2014), 955–70.
226. A. Campbell, *Alastair Campbell Diaries: The Burden of Power* (London, 2012), vol. 4, 340, 25 October 2002.
227. Ibid.
228. T. Blair, *A Journey*, 532. S. Serfaty, *Architects of Delusion: Europe, America and the Iraq War* (Philadelphia, PA, 2011).
229. T. Blair, *A Journey*, 532. S. B. Dyson, *The Blair Identity*, 47–69.
230. T. Blair, *A Journey*, 533.
231. Ibid., 534.
232. Ibid. P. Riddell, 'Europe', in A. Seldon and D. Kavanagh (eds), *The Blair Effect*, 362–83; O. Daddow, *New Labour and the European Union: Blair and Brown's Logic of History* (Manchester, 2011).
233. T. Blair, *A Journey*, 534. Much of the debate about Euroscepticism in the UK relates to the right-wing press and to the Conservative Party, with disagreement about how real the dangers and risks were: Jeremy Heywood, the Cabinet Secretary and head of the civil service under David Cameron, apparently believed that the pressure for a referendum on Europe was rising, even though 'he still felt that people were too negative about Britain's position in Europe', but he also had to accept Cameron's 'political decision', without challenging its necessity: S. Heywood,

380   EUROPEAN INTEGRATION SINCE THE 1920S

What Does Jeremy Think? Jeremy Heywood and the Making of Modern Britain (London, 2021), 390–1.
234. J. Straw, *Last Man Standing*, 416.
235. G. Schröder, *Entscheidungen. Mein Leben in der Politik* (Hamburg, 2006), 328, 333.
236. Ibid., 335.
237. J. Straw, *Last Man Standing*, 416–17.
238. Ibid., 418–19.
239. Ibid., 421.
240. J. Chirac, *My Life in Politics*, 307.
241. T. Blair, *A Journey*, 534–5.
242. Ibid., 537. For criticism of Blair's stance, see M. Redgrave, 'Europeanising the National Interest: Tony Blair's and New Labour's Lost Objective', *Journal of Contemporary European Studies*, 16 (2008), 421–32. Alastair Campbell, *Alastair Campbell Diaries: Outside, Inside, 2003–2005* (London, 2016), vol. 5, 306, 1 September 2004, noted how this hinged on deals with Italy and other states: 'TB had clearly just about had it with Schroeder. He said he was very friendly to his face but at it the whole time with Chirac. He had been to Silvio and had suggested France-Germany-Italy trilateralism. Berlusconi had said no. TB said he would much prefer to deal with left-minded people but these guys are weak.'
243. J. Straw, *Last Man Standing*, 415.
244. T. Blair, *A Journey*, 537. The Prime Minister, ibid., 539, recalled that 'my friendship with Gerhard dimmed', from early joint enthusiasm for a 'third way' and 'social Europe' to divisions over foreign policy and EU institutions: 'He got over Iraq, but he was furious over Guy and the presidency of the Commission. At the dinner where Guy's appointment was blocked, he rounded on me in a very personal way. I tried to explain that Guy was not someone whose direction for Europe I could agree with. It wasn't personal on my part. Gehard made it clear: it was on his, and that was that.'
245. Ibid.
246. G. Schröder, *Entscheidungen*, 334.
247. J. Straw, *Last Man Standing*, 423.
248. Ibid., 431–2; T. Blair, *A Journey*, 540: 'I was and am in favour of Turkey's accession.'
249. J. Straw, *Last Man Standing*, 423.
250. Ibid., 424.
251. T. Blair, *A Journey*, 538.
252. Ibid.
253. Ibid.
254. Ibid.
255. Ibid.
256. This was also true of New Labour under Gordon Brown, who failed to show up for the signing of the Lisbon Treaty on 13 December 2007 and got 'hammered' for it, in Campbell's opinion: A. Campbell, *Alastair Campbell Diaries: From Crash to Defeat, 2007–2010* (London, 2018), vol. 7, 88, 14 December 2007.

8
Europolity

The European Union, in Habermas's opinion, 'owes its existence to the efforts of political elites who could count on the passive consent of their more or less indifferent populations, as long as the peoples could regard the Union as also being in their economic interest'.[1] The legitimacy of the EU rested on outcomes, not the citizens' 'political will'.[2] 'This state of affairs is explained not only by the history of its origins but also by the legal constitution of this unique formation', with the European Central Bank, the Commission and the European Court of Justice intervening most profoundly in the lives of European citizens 'even though these institutions are the least subject to democratic controls'.[3] The European Council, which had taken the initiative during the eurozone crisis, is 'made up of heads of government whose role in the eyes of their citizens is to represent their respective national interests in distant Brussels', the German philosopher continues.[4] Although the European Parliament was meant to be a 'bridge between the conflict of opinions in the national arenas and the momentous decisions taken in Brussels', the bridge is 'almost devoid of traffic'.[5] The European Union is neither a 'state-like' entity nor a 'normal' liberal, democratic polity. The old questions remain in place, therefore. What role should the European Union have and how can it function most effectively?

The financial crash and eurozone crisis had proved to Habermas that the existing institutions of the EU lacked legitimacy and were ill-suited to solving Europe's economic and political problems.[6] Up to 'the present day there remains a gulf at the European level between the citizens' opinion and will formation, on the one hand, and the policies actually adopted to solve the pressing problems, on the other,' he declared in April 2013: 'What unite the European citizens today are the Eurosceptical mindsets that have become more pronounced in all of the member countries during the crisis, albeit in each country for different and rather polarizing reasons.'[7] The 'blueprint' of the European Commission, Presidency of the Council and ECB in December 2012, which contemplated the possibility of 'eurobonds', a debt repayment fund, the right to levy taxes on the EU level and 'integrated guidelines' for member states' fiscal and economic policies, seemed to have created the need for the Monetary Union 'to be expanded into a real Political Union' in order to legitimate 'cross-border transfer payments with corresponding transnational redistribution effects'.[8] 'There are only two coherent strategies for dealing with the current crisis,' Habermas wrote in the *Frankfurter Allgemeine Zeitung* on 3 August 2012, along with the economists Peter Bofinger and Julian

---

European Integration since the 1920s: Security, Identity, and Cooperation. Mark Hewitson, Oxford University Press.
© Mark Hewitson 2024. DOI: 10.1093/oso/9780198915942.003.0009

382 EUROPEAN INTEGRATION SINCE THE 1920s

Nida-Rümelin: 'a return to national currencies across the EU, which would expose each individual country to the unpredictable fluctuations of highly speculative foreign exchange markets, or the institutional underpinning of a collective fiscal, economic, and social policy within the eurozone, with the further aim of restoring policy-makers their lost capacity for action in the face of market imperatives at a transnational level.'[9] The authors' preference of a political union alone appeared capable of preserving European welfare states: 'Only a politically united core Europe offers any hope of reversing the process—already far advanced—of transforming a citizens' democracy built on the idea of the social state into a sham democracy governed by market principles.'[10] For the first time 'in the history of capitalism', it seemed, 'a crisis triggered by the most advanced sector, the banks, could only be resolved by governments getting their citizens, in their capacity as taxpayers, to stump up for the losses incurred', leaving the latter 'rightly outraged'.[11] For Habermas, Bofinger, and Nida-Rümelin, there should not be 'communitarization through the back door', without thorough-going political reform after a 'broad public debate', since 'a free-floating European technocracy' lacks 'the impulse and the strength to contain and redirect the profit-oriented imperatives of investment capital into socially compatible channels'.[12] Only 'feedback from the pressing dynamics of a mobilized political public sphere' could direct and legitimize a European executive or administration.[13]

'Solidarity', which was linked historically to a belief in 'a universal community of faithful believers' in world religions but which developed in a political sense during and after the French Revolution, is required in order to convince citizens to consent to economic transfers and to push governments, not to compete against their neighbours, but to pursue economic growth in all member states.[14] For Habermas, such solidarity derives from political associations or shared political interest and presupposes '*political* contexts of life, hence contexts that are legally organized and in this sense artificial ones'.[15] It was not likely to develop from the de facto 'executive federalism' of the EU, especially if 'the establishment of a common economic government' crossed '*the red line of the classical understanding of sovereignty*', which entailed the abandonment of the 'idea that the nation-states are "the sovereign subjects of the treaties"', without translating the democratic mechanisms and legitimacy of these states to the European level.[16] Procedurally, 'the dethronement of the European Council' within a political union 'would mean *switching over from intergovernmentalism to the community method*', with the European Parliament and Council acting on an equal basis as the ordinary legislative procedure was extended to cover aspects of economic and other areas of governance currently falling under the competence of member states.[17]

Although Habermas maintains that the 'European federal state is the wrong model, demanding more solidarity than the historically autonomous European nations are willing to contemplate', he concedes that the fundamental threshold between intergovernmentalism and supranationalism would have been traversed.[18] His contention that 'the step to supranational democracy need not be conceived as a transition to a "United States of Europe"' rests on the weak and unconvincing claim that member states will retain their statehood, despite ceding most decision-making powers: '"Confederation" versus "federal state" is a false alternative (and a specific legacy of the constitutional discussion in nineteenth-century Germany). The nation-states can well preserve their integrity as states within a supranational democracy by retaining both their roles of the implementing administration and the final custodian of civil liberties.'[19] Governments and polities reduced to the implementation of decisions made elsewhere and the defence of citizens' civil liberties would not be 'state-like'. The German philosopher himself admits that national governments have 'no interest in disempowering themselves' and would be reluctant to call in the European Council for a constituent assembly to revise the treaties, removing references to member states as their 'sovereign subjects'.[20] Even the creation of a core political union out of the monetary union of eurozone members 'would depend essentially on the consent of countries preferring to stay out'.[21] 'In the worst case', he warns, 'principled resistance' on the part of those countries could be overcome 'by a re-foundation of the Union (based on existing institutions)'.[22] His hope in 2012–13 was that the Federal Republic of Germany, as the main paymaster of the EU, 'holds the key to the fate of the European Union in its hand', since it had the means to underwrite 'solidarity' through economic transfers (in the 'blueprint') and a corresponding political reform to establish the community method.[23] The refusal of Merkel's coalition government to play such a role, subsequently declining to take up Emmanuel Macron's plan for political reform, has left 'the European integration process...on a downward curve', close to the point of no return.[24]

Critics of Habermas, such as the British philosopher Simon Glendinning, object that the 'new European configuration', which is 'in the making', consists of institutions founded on treaties between nation-states.[25] Thus, the European Council—and the governments of member states—had taken the initiative in the eurozone crisis, arriving at decisions 'collectively, by achieving consensus among these heads of government and their varied senses of both the EU's and their own interests and priorities'.[26] For Glendinning, this type of decision-making constituted a 'pooling' of sovereignty; for Habermas, it is the EU's principal fault: 'Through what can only be seen as an unprecedented act of radical self-sacrifice of sovereignty, Habermas calls on today's member states to take steps, as soon as possible, toward what he calls "a supranational democracy"', or 'an international state which is formed by a fundamental "transfer of competences from the national to a European level"'.[27] Such a 'dethronement' would overcome 'national particularisms' and establish a 'common government for Europe', which would 'involve something more than we have seen before': 'Not a further pooling of sovereignty over some policy field, not the further extension of Union competences permitted by treaties between nation-states, but a "decision", a sovereign

384 EUROPEAN INTEGRATION SINCE THE 1920s

decision on the part of each member state, to give up the power to make sovereign decisions'.[28] The German philosopher anticipates opposition from Eurosceptics but, in Glendinning's opinion, he ignores a middle way, which recalls Immanuel Kant's idea of a 'voluntary association of states willing to co-exist peacefully while nevertheless retaining their sovereignty'.[29] Habermas had discounted this solution as a 'weak', 'sterile', and 'conceptually flawed' transitional stage, yet he had misunderstood Kant and seized on an alternative solution which would, 'if it were ever realized, likely lead to disaster for Europe'.[30] Solidarity, which 'belongs historically to a politics of friendship or "fraternity"', is comprehended by Habermas in a 'radically discontinuous' sense, not designed to come to the assistance of a state such as Greece during the eurozone crisis, but 'to submerge it in a tsunami of political overcoming'.[31] The 'quasi-hegemony' of a single power is 'not in the least ruled out in the formation of an international state'.[32] The aim of the EU should not be 'to build a new singularity but an enduring multiplicity'.[33] 'A European Union that could both "preserve and secure" this diversity and simultaneously institute conditions of increasing international tolerance "likely to prevent war" is not a weak idea'; it is a great idea, resting on existing forms of intergovernmental cooperation and limited pooling of sovereignty, concludes Glendinning.[34]

The dispute between advocates of federalism and varying forms of 'community method', on the hand, and intergovernmentalism or confederalism, on the other hand, is a long-standing one. Historically, political theorists and social scientists have been tempted either to imagine another, better world or to predict how institutions will develop. Because the European Union is a unique type of polity, it has been particularly susceptible to enquiries about its trajectory or 'finality'. The 'task of selecting and justifying variables and explaining their hypothesized interdependence cannot be accomplished without an agreement as to possible conditions to which the process is expected to lead,' wrote Ernst Haas in an essay on the 'joy and anguish of pre-theorizing' in 1971: 'In short, we need a dependent variable.'[35] Politicians, too, have asked the same questions, especially those running European institutions, who have every incentive to expand their jurisdictions and to turn them into something else. This chapter, by contrast, investigates the historical parameters and practices which affected the decision-making of European governments and officials. To what extent has a pooling of sovereignty occurred and was it the result of deliberate negotiation or a barely noticed accumulation of competencies?

The Failure of Federalism

There were many theorists of federalism in the 1940s and 1950s, particularly in Italy and the United Kingdom, proffering a range of wares.[36] Although they agreed on the foundation of constitutional autonomy, they had varying opinions about a division of powers and the desirability of specific outcomes.[37] Formally, as Reginald Harrison has indicated, federalists were sceptical about 'human nature and about the potential for good will and cooperation among states', specifying the competencies and powers of carefully defined agencies in a founding constitution.[38] More generally, they were suspicious of nationalism and nation-states, after the era of dictatorships and war in Europe during the 1930s and early 1940s, with a federation designed to keep the constituent parts—national groups and former states—in check and to prevent the domination of one over others, at the same time as harnessing the powers of the parts against an external threat, such as the USSR.[39] Their suspicions often persisted in the post-war era of superpowers, freer trade, and European integration.[40]

Federalists were a 'small nucleus of non-conformists seeking to point out that the national states have lost their proper rights since they cannot guarantee the political and economic safety of their citizens', wrote Altiero Spinelli, one of the authors of the Ventotene 'Manifesto for a Free and United Europe' (1941) and a leader of the European federalist movement, as late as 1972: 'They also insist that European union should be brought about by the European populations, and not by diplomats, by directly electing a European constituent assembly, and by approval, through a referendum, of the constitution that this assembly would prepare.'[41] During and immediately after the war, the group of federalists had seemed larger and more mainstream, with European resistance movements expressing their hope of European unity and the *Union Européenne des Fédéralistes* (UEF), the umbrella organization of national associations of federalists, counting 150,000 members. The UEF's aim of working 'for the creation of a European federation which shall be a constitutive element of a world federation' seemed utopian, but its narrower objective of fostering European integration met with considerable support among European politicians, many of whom were members of the European Parliamentary Union and the United Europe Movement (UEM), founded by Winston Churchill in May 1947.[42] The 'Congress of Europe' at The Hague, which was convened by the various organizations, was attended by 200 deputies from national assemblies and 700 dignitaries—including former and serving prime ministers such as Churchill, Konrad Adenauer, Alcide De Gasperi, Georges Bidault, Paul Reynaud, Léon Blum, Paul-Henri Spaak, and Paul van Zeeland—in May 1948.[43] Nothing came of the call of the Congress's Political Committee, chaired by the former French premier Paul Ramadier, for a constituent 'European Assembly' to create a federal state and 'an economic and political union', which would provide the only 'solution to both the economic and political aspects of the German problem' and 'assure security and social progress'.[44] Both the ambition and the failure of the call were noteworthy.

There were good reasons for wanting to integrate European economies, military planning and political decision-making after the Second World War, yet these were not dissimilar to those of the 1920s.[45] The need to reverse relative economic decline, rebuild legitimate political structures, avoid radicalization at home and abroad, improve relations between continental states, and escape cultural decadence and complacency was widely recognized. 'A number of fervent Europeans', wrote Robert Marjolin, former colleague of Monnet and the Secretary General of the OEEC from 1948 to 1955, 'were quite a strong force during the fifties and early sixties':

> For them, federal Europe was within reach, if the political will were there. Practically speaking, once the first step had been taken in this direction, events would necessarily follow on from one another and inevitably lead to the desired result. This is the gist of the so-called theory of *engrenage* (chain reaction) or the 'spill-over effect'. It is set out in the fullest detail in what may be regarded as the political testament of Walter Hallstein, who, as a close collaborator of Konrad Adenauer, then as President of the EEC Commission from 1958 to 1967, played a large part in the construction of the Common Market.
>
> The forces which the Europeans had let loose in deciding to create a common market, so Hallstein's thinking went, must inevitably take Europe to economic union, then to political union.... Trade policy was an essential part of foreign policy, itself closely bound up with defence policy.... Thus, a process that began modestly with the establishment of a customs union and a common agricultural or commercial policy would reach its logical outcome: a European federation, or as others would name it, the United States of Europe.[46]

Such fervent Europeans shared many of the motives of their contemporaries in the late 1940s and 1950s, but they often drew different inferences. Marjolin himself 'did not believe that the concept of nationality could be displaced [by the concept of "Europe"] within a single generation, or even several generations, merely by creating new institutions', observed the American official George Ball: 'Patriotism had been the coalescing force animating Germany's neighbours to resist her ravaging armies in two world wars, and Britain, in Marjolin's view, was not ready for Europe. He did not think—as Monnet did—that deeply entrenched habits of thought could be quickly modified in the pressure chambers of new institutions.'[47] Marjolin, according to Ball, addressed the same problems as Monnet with similar intentions, but 'from different angles of attack'.[48] Given the crisis-ridden conditions of the continent since the First World War, European cooperation was likely to be modest and reversible.

The terms of the debate about Europe after 1945 remained confused. Most of the main protagonists except the British were willing to contemplate giving up sovereignty in specific spheres, but they disagreed about how much and which types of power and in which fields of policy-making and administrative activity. Out of office, Churchill, who had earlier been seen as a federalist, was willing to hand over to European authorities—or 'integrate'—areas of administration, but not instances of decision-making: 'We are ready to play an active part in all plans for integration on an intergovernmental basis,' he explained to René Pleven in 1950 on the subject of the European Defence Community, before warning that 'defence considerations, our Commonwealth connections and the Sterling Area inhibit us from subordinating ourselves...to any European supranational authority'.[49] As for the Labour government between 1945 and 1951, a future Conservative ministry would have to stop 'short of actual membership' of a supranational organisation with the power to make decisions.[50] The Italian government of De Gasperi, which had put forward the notion of a European Political Community (EPC)—with a continental constituent assembly to draw up a common constitution—alongside the European Defence Community, was equally conscious in 1951, from an opposing point of view, that 'a renunciation of sovereignty, like that foreseen,...could not be put into effect by governments or accepted by parliaments without the creation, in response, on the federal level, of an organism in which the powers that the National Assemblies were giving up could be entrusted and which would have the authority to exercise them in the same right as national parliaments.... The organism enjoying such powers should be, according to the Italian delegation, the European Assembly.'[51]

The terms 'federal' and 'federation', however, were ambiguous, regularly used in a very vague, positive sense or in reaction to a specific proposal. Thus, when Churchill averred, on returning to office in 1951, that 'I never thought that Britain or the British Commonwealth should, either individually or collectively, become an integral part of a European federation, and have never given the slightest support to the idea,' he was referring to the supranational federation of the ECSC, EDC, and EPC.[52] By contrast, when de Gaulle instructed his *commissaires* to undertake 'a detailed study of a project for a federation of western Europe' in October 1943, he had a much more limited form of economic cooperation in mind, which he later—in March 1944—described as a 'form of western grouping that rests principally on an economic foundation and is as broad as possible'.[53] By August 1949, at the time of the campaign of federalists to turn the Advisory Assembly of the newly founded Council of Europe into a constituent assembly of a future European federation, de Gaulle could be found outlining his plan not for a federation but a confederation—'unity will initially take the form of a confederation'—in order to highlight the fact that 'each state retains its sovereignty', except for 'those areas which nations will hand over to the community so as to create unity there.'[54] In a similar spirit, de Gaulle's close collaborator, the RPF politician Michel Debré, proposed a 'pact for a union of European states' in early 1950, which—like the general's plan—envisaged the 'giving up of sovereignty of participating states' in specified areas of defence and the economy, but not in other spheres of government.[55] The purpose of terms such as 'confederation' and 'union' was to distinguish between different degrees and levels of decision-making,

388   EUROPEAN INTEGRATION SINCE THE 1920S

but it was frequently obscured by the participation of Debré, Jacques Chaban-Delmas, and other national-minded politicians within organizations such as the *Union Européenne des Fédéralistes*, which continued to call for a European 'federation'. Even within the European networks of Socialists and Christian Democrats, which are rightly seen as one of the principal forums for the propagation and implementation of transnational ideas, there were fundamental disagreements about the nature and desirable extent of 'federation'. 'European planning, much less than national planning,' declared Alexandre Verret, of the *Mouvement pour les Etats-Unis socialistes d'Europe* (MEUSE), in July 1949, 'cannot count on the spontaneous adhesion of the "masses", for Europe is too weak an organic reality, which has not yet blossomed, to make them believe in the same manner as the national idea, with profound echoes in the collective and individual subconscious'.[56] Whether to integrate decision-making in the field of defence and what form of political community to create, if any, remained matters of contention.

To federalists such as De Gasperi, a European Political Community was needed in the early 1950s to safeguard the principle of supranationality: 'Either Europe will be established now or it won't be established at all, and that would be a sad day for all countries.'[57] In the event, 'Europe' was not established in the form anticipated by De Gasperi, after the failure to ratify the EDC and EPC. Reform occurred in limited economic spheres, where the need for cooperation had been widely recognized by political elites in the 1920s. French diplomats such as Massigli and ministers like Bidault opposed the proposal for a European Political Community, even after executive power had been vested in the unanimity of a Council of Ministers. The EPC was a 'sprawling monster', which would lead to the loss of France's autonomy in the international order, asserted Bidault, leader of the Christian Democratic MRP, in 1953.[58] The Gaullist Debré was just as emphatic in his rejection of the EDC, at least in retrospect: 'As regards the organisation of Europe as described by the treaty, and as expanded by the complementary project for a Political Community, it implies at this point the disappearance of France.... The federalists are the enemies of the nation-state and want to replace it with Community Europe. That is what is unacceptable.'[59] Instead, integration proceeded through the pooling of coal, iron, and steel, with the formation of the ECSC by the Treaty of Paris (1951). The terms and goals of the treaty were limited—in earlier discussions the pro-European Conservative Harold Macmillan had dismissed Monnet's project as 'a plan to have a plan'—and any subsequent 'spill-over' into other areas was resisted by individual governments, including those in France.[60] Paul van Zeeland, the Belgian Foreign Minister, was critical of the EDC project precisely because Monnet and other federalists seemed to be 'forcing the pace, apparently in the hope of achieving European unity by the back door, and loading down the European army proposal with a top-heavy superstructure borrowed from the Schuman plan'.[61] When the ratification of the

EDC failed, Spaak—van Zeeland's successor—eventually accepted that such failure was 'predictable', resolving with Monnet to return to the more promising task of economic integration: 'Spaak turned up and his first words were, "Obviously, it's a disaster.... Can we do anything in the economic field?" And they were off.... Monnet said, "Yes, we must try",' reported André Staercke, the later Belgian permanent representative to NATO.[62] The product of Spaak's and Monnet's deliberations and those of the Dutch Foreign Minister Johan Willem Beyen—the European Economic Community—was carefully circumscribed, like the ECSC, not least because the French government was wary of the free-trading ramifications of a common market. Tariffs, it was agreed, would be reduced gradually in three four-year stages. Initially, the French government only agreed formally to the first stage.[63] 'Europe' for many ministers was a limited and fragile entity until the late 1960s and beyond.

The proponents of federalism or, less specifically, the 'community method' did not disappear after the failure—from the point of view of advocates of a European federation—of The Hague Congress, the Council of Europe and the European Political Community. Rather, many invested their hopes in the more modest supranational characteristics of the ECSC and EEC, and associated expectations of spill-over from one economic sector to another, with cumulative political effects. As a result, the history of the European Community has been punctuated with struggles between 'fervent Europeans' and defenders of the member states. The 'empty chair' crisis in 1965–66, which is often portrayed as an example of de Gaulle's intransigence, involved a fundamental disagreement about the competencies of the European Commission and 'endangered' the EEC itself, in the French leader's opinion.[64] The dispute was entangled with the Common Agricultural Policy, which had been funded by national contributions until June 1965 but which Walter Hallstein, the president of the Commission, proposed would be paid from the EEC's 'own resources', namely the common external tariff levied on industrial and agricultural products.[65] The principal issue, however, concerned the powers and independence of a supranational European Commission, as Hallstein had spelled out in a speech at Chatham House in December 1964, when he pointed out that the Treaty of Rome provided for a transition to qualified majority voting in the Council of Ministers and required unanimity to amend a Commission proposal (Article 149) from January 1966 onwards.[66] He went on to label state sovereignty a myth and to call for the unity of European states on the world stage, if they were to count at all: to this end, further political integration would be needed, spearheaded by the Commission. In such a context, Hallstein's proposal to alter the procedure for setting the budget, which had been decided in the Council of Ministers after consultation with the Assembly, was seen as an attempt to make the EEC financially independent of the member states, establishing—in de Gaulle's phrase—'a great independent financial power': according to the proposed procedure, the Commission would

390 EUROPEAN INTEGRATION SINCE THE 1920s

submit a draft budget to the Council of Ministers, which would hand an amended version to the Assembly, which in turn could make amendments by a simple majority before sending the budget back to the Commission for approval or rejection.[67] The Council could only reject the budget at this stage by a vote of five member states out of six and amend individual points by four votes out of six. The reform created a 'kind of government of the Community', in Marjolin's words, with the absurd prospect of the Commission, together with Luxembourg and Belgium, imposing a budget against the wishes of Germany, France, and Italy.[68]

Supranationality and Intergovernmentalism

De Gaulle had long sought to check the powers of the Commission, inducing the French ambassador in Denmark and member of the Free French Forces in London, Christian Fouchet, to draw up a plan for a 'Union of the European Peoples', 'without supranational institutions', and with a powerful Council of member states which would set its own budget (Title IV) and take questions and consider recommendations from a European Parliament (Title II).[69] The plan was presented to member states in October–November 1961. A revised version was submitted in January 1962 and was stymied by the Belgian and Dutch governments, partly because 'Our partners fear that in this domain, the fact of *Franco-German domination is establishing itself,*' as de Gaulle had remarked to Adenauer in May 1961: 'This is not entirely false, but what can we do about that? For the first time in their history, France and Germany can collaborate closely. They should not allow themselves to be stopped by their partners' objections.'[70] The German, Italian, and Luxembourg governments had responded favourably, albeit ambivalently, to the Fouchet plan. Their role at the Council of Ministers meeting on 28 June 1965, encouraged by Hallstein, was less ambiguous, as they threatened to renege on a promise to fund CAP if France were to fail to compromise with the Commission on control of the budget. Yet, when the French withdrew their permanent representative from Brussels on 6 July, leaving an empty chair and making unanimity impossible, the other governments refused to push matters to a head (despite Ludwig Erhard's plea to the Italian government on 7 July to 'face the General as a Community'), prompting the Commission to give up its attempt to seize control of the budget.[71] At a press conference on 9 September, the French President pressed home his advantage:

we know—and heaven knows how well we know it—that there is a different conception of European federation in which, according to the dreams of those who have conceived it, the member countries would lose their national identities, and which ... would be ruled by some sort of technocratic body of elders, stateless and irresponsible.[72]

Paris had already blocked the Commission's attempt to gain control of the budget and circumvent the Council of Ministers by granting greater powers to the European Assembly.

The dispute turned, in the autumn of 1965, on the question of qualified majority voting and the possibility of a member state having a veto on matters of self-defined national interest, which the governments of the 'five' initially opposed at the meeting of the Council and Commission on 17–18 January in Luxembourg. They had, however, agreed to the French Minister of Foreign Affairs Couve de Murville's demand for a rotating presidency for the Commission and for member states to have a preventive veto over the Commission's proposals to the Council, allowing them to quash initiatives at the outset.[73] At the reconvened meeting on 28–29 January, the member states supposedly agreed to disagree in the 'Luxembourg Compromise', with the third point noting that 'there is a divergence of views on what should be done in the event of a failure to reach complete agreement', yet the fourth point concluded 'that this divergence does not prevent the Community's work being resumed in accordance with the normal procedure' and, critically, the second point noted that 'the French delegation considers that, where very important issues are at stake, discussion must be continued until unanimous agreement is reached', which amounted to the concession of a national veto.[74] The Dutch Minister of Foreign Affairs, Joseph Luns, claimed that the outcome was a 'tie', belying his earlier insistence that a veto would bring about the 'paralysis' of the European Community.[75] Brussels insiders were tempted to downplay the significance of the compromise. One former president of the European Court contended that there was no crisis 'because the law took its course'; another claimed that compromise was 'a spurious element of Community law, bound to fade out gradually'.[76] Emile Noël, the general-secretary of the Commission, declared in 1967 that 'There is nothing in the Accords of Luxembourg.'[77]

The veto was a political reality, however, with far-reaching consequences, even if member states also accepted the need for qualified majority voting in specified areas. De Gaulle had entrenched the principle of national contributions to the Community budget, making it beholden to its national paymasters, and he had set limits on the Commission's initiation of proposals, which were to be discussed— and could be blocked—in the Council of Ministers. The French President's own summary to his ministers in Paris was that 'supranationality has gone. France will remain sovereign.'[78] As such, it seemed to be in accordance with his earlier statement to the press on 15 May 1962 that 'at present no other Europe is possible than that of the states, aside of course from that of myths, fictions and parades', which he reiterated in 1965: 'However big the glass which is proffered from outside, we prefer to drink from our own glass, while at the same time clinking glasses with those around us.'[79] The agreement to qualified majority voting in the Council of Ministers was more than a clinking of glasses, ensuring the continuing cooperation of member states and supranational institutions. 'Why had we broken things off?' de Gaulle had asked in the midst of the crisis in January 1966: 'Because the Commission claimed an exorbitant role', which the other member states 'seemed ready to concede'.[80] Marjolin maintained that those states, too, 'did not want the majority vote any more than the French government did and they sacrificed it to the French with no great pain, and some even with secret relief'.[81] Even if his recollections were coloured by his preferences at the time and his subsequent reading of history, the European Commissioner for Economic and Financial Affairs demonstrated the importance of the compromise for the functioning of the EEC.

Once de Gaulle had resigned on 28 April 1969, after losing a referendum on the reform of local government, proponents of greater integration tried again to reform the European Community. At The Hague summit on 1–2 December 1969, which had originally been proposed by Georges Pompidou, the heads of the member states' governments agreed to look once more at the possibility of financing the EEC from its own resources, pushing ahead with economic and monetary union, creating the grounds for a common foreign policy ('political unification'), strengthening the Community's institutions (especially the Assembly) and enlarging the bloc (by negotiating with the UK, Ireland, Denmark, and Norway). Although the French government refused to allow the Assembly greater control over the budget, the Six agreed in April 1970 that the EEC could be financed through tariffs on imports and up to 1 per cent of revenue from VAT. The Werner Report—named after the committee chair Pierre Werner, who was the prime minister of Luxembourg—was presented in October, concluding that 'economic and monetary union is an objective realizable in the course of the present decade'.[82] It advised that the Council of Economics and Finance Ministers become the 'centre of decision' by 1974, setting parameters for member states' fiscal policies and central banks, which would be asked to reduce the 'margins of fluctuation' between currencies by intervening in markets.[83] 'The centre of decision for economic policy will exercise independently, in accordance with the Community interest, a decisive influence over the general economic policy of the Community, ran the report.[84] Notwithstanding the fact that the turbulence of the currency and financial markets in the early 1970s, as the value of the dollar—no longer convertible into gold—began to fall, and the oil crisis of 1973 meant that the timetable of the Werner Report was abandoned officially at a meeting in December 1974, it had been adopted in principle by member states at a Council of Ministers in the spring of 1971. The plan to strengthen the Assembly, drafted by the French political scientist Georges Vedel, was more successful, though falling far short of the original proposal to give it powers of co-decision (or veto), which it eventually acquired in 1992: at the Paris summit of December 1974, leaders of member states agreed to the direct election of what became—by the time of the first election in 1979—a European Parliament, with a vaguer pledge that 'the competence of the European Assembly will be extended, in particular by granting it certain powers in the Community's legislative process'.[85]

Together with enlargement in 1973, experimentation with the currency 'snake' from 1972 to 1974 and the European Monetary System from 1979 onwards, and the inauguration of European Political Cooperation in October 1970, providing for 'regular exchanges and consultations' to facilitate 'a better mutual understanding on the great international problems', the member states sought to improve and consolidate the powers of European institutions (see Map 8.1).[86] The negotiation was not a straightforward struggle between 'federalists' and defenders of the nation-state or, more cooperatively, 'intergovernmentalists'. Alliances and proposals for reform were unpredictable, as the shift from de Gaulle to Pompidou— and, then, to Giscard d'Estaing, who introduced the European Council in 1974— demonstrated.[87] Even British governments, despite paying attention to awkward elements in both the Labour and Conservative Parties, seemed willing to reform and reinforce European institutions. The Conservative Prime Minister Edward Heath 'wants to replace the old, comfortable class-ridden Britain by a tougher, more competitive society with better rewards for the able', wrote Andrew Roth, the American-born political correspondent of the *Manchester Evening News*, in

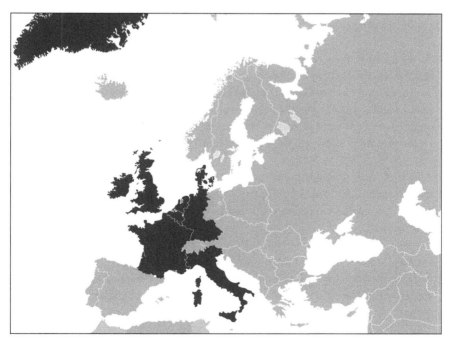

Map 8.1 The EEC enlargement of 1973
Source: https://en.wikipedia.org/wiki/1973_enlargement_of_the_European_Communities#/media/File:EC09-1973_European_Community_map_enlargement.svg

394   EUROPEAN INTEGRATION SINCE THE 1920S

1972: 'Part of his enthusiasm for entry into the Common Market derives from his belief that intensified competition will stimulate those worthy of survival and purge the incompetents.'[88] In private, Heath thought that the Commission, in particular, was guilty of 'constantly barging ahead with regulations drawn up to suit themselves and then coming along, more or less with a take-it-or-leave-it attitude'.[89] Geoffrey Rippon, the Conservative MP for Hexham and Heath's chief negotiator for entry into the EEC, reassured him that contacts with Brussels 'would give a rapidly increasing number of officials from home departments first-hand experience of dealing with the Community and so make a very effective contribution to the spread of European-mindedness throughout Whitehall'.[90] Through cooperation and compromise, the British would have the chance themselves to shape European politics.

By January 1977, Roy Jenkins—who had been one of sixty-nine pro-EEC Labour MPs to revolt against the party whip to back Heath's negotiated terms of entry in October 1971—had become the first British President of the European Commission. In the first Jean Monnet lecture at the European University Institute in Florence on 27 October 1977, he reiterated his support for economic and monetary union at the same time as spelling out its political implications, including a central government within a 'multi-tiered', confederal polity to deal with external relations, regional aid, and industrial policy, which would be funded—he was willing to conjecture—by 5–7 per cent of the gross Community product:

> Do we intend to create a European union or do we not?...There would be little point in asking the peoples and governments of Europe to contemplate union, were it not for the fact that real and efficient sovereignty over monetary issues already eludes them to a high and increasing degree. The prospect of monetary union should be seen as part of the process of recovering the substance of sovereign power. At present we tend to cling to its shadow.[91]

For Jenkins, such changes constituted a step as bold as that taken by the 'last generation' who had signed the Treaty of Rome in 1957.[92] They were, however, 'confederal' in nature, underlining the limits as well as the dynamics of reform on the European level.

Jacques Delors became the eighth President of the European Commission on 7 January 1985, replacing the little-known Gaston Thorn (1981–85). By the time he had completed his second term in January 1995, Europe was transformed, with a single market (SEA, 1986), a common travel area (Schengen, 1985) and a European Union—inaugurated at Maastricht (1992)—consisting of 'European citizens' and cooperating more fully in the fields of justice and home affairs (asylum, borders, drugs, judicial cooperation, police intelligence), foreign policy and defence (as long as it was 'compatible with the common security and defence policy' of NATO), and monetary union, for which criteria and a timetable were agreed.[93] Critically, the European Parliament was given a veto—in the co-decision procedure—over legislation concerning the free movement of workers, education, and culture programmes, European-wide infrastructure and research and development, the provision of services and the harmonization of national laws to conform with the single market. Yet there were restrictions placed on supranational institutions. The German delegation at Maastricht had wanted to emphasize the powers of the European Parliament to demonstrate to the German public that Europe was becoming more democratic (corresponding to the model of the Federal Republic), in the opinion of the French negotiator, Pierre de Boissieu, but they failed to achieve their objective.[94] The same was true of Ruud Lubbers, the Dutch Prime Minister, for whom 'The less defence and intergovernmental agreement there is, the more there will be of the European Parliament and of the Americans, and Lubbers will be happy.'[95]

For his part, Delors had long put forward the idea of a European federation, with a political executive answerable to the European Parliament and national assemblies—for example, on 23 January 1990—but he had been slapped down by Mitterrand, his principal sponsor: 'That idiot! Why is he interfering? No one in Europe would ever want that! By being an extremist, he is going to make what is realisable fail.'[96] The French President, in Attali's words, 'liked to recall that he was one of the rare French politicians who had participated in the Congress of The Hague in 1948, which was the birth act'.[97] Delors accepted this verdict, adding that Mitterrand had 'unblocked' Europe in the 1980s, altering the *Parti socialiste*'s suspicion of the EEC and favouring the accession of Spain and Portugal against the majority of French socialists: 'For my part, I knew he was a life-long European.'[98] Arguably, the president's interest had always been primarily economic, as a means of resisting American domination through money and of resolving the problems of the French economy, even if such priorities had political ramifications. 'For François Mitterrand, Europe could not simply be reduced to such a great market,' recalled Attali: 'the Single Act was not, for him, an end in itself, but was a necessary stage on the way to a single currency, a common social charter and political integration; its realization, and its enactment, became his obsession, to the point that it was one of the pretexts by which he convinced himself to put himself forward again in 1988.'[99] The choice for Mitterrand was between following the Bundesbank and bowing to US pressure or delegating powers to European institutions, which the French government could influence in the making of economic policy.[100] The main consequence was that political reforms were limited and realistic, with the European Parliament gaining a restricted right of co-decision and the Commission receiving no extra powers in 1992, with its ability to make proposals subjected to parliamentary scrutiny.[101]

It was critical for Mitterrand to achieve a fixed commitment from the other member states on the introduction of a single European currency. When John Major objected over lunch at Downing Street on 2 December 1991 that any member state, not just the United Kingdom, should have an opt-out clause, the French President refused, since 'That would amount to saying that we haven't made a final choice in favour of the single currency'.[102] Although praising the British Prime Minister for being 'courageous', having been 'more prepared to commit to Europe'—in Major's own words—than 'ever before', Mitterrand was not willing to abandon 'what we are meeting for in Maastricht'.[103] The introduction of the European Currency Unit (ECU) was set for 1 January 1999. The French President was less interested in the political aspects of the Treaty on European Union, which remained open-ended.

Symbolically, the Maastricht Treaty (1992) seemed to embody a more defined political entity—a European Union, as adumbrated in the aspiration of the Treaty of Rome (1957) for 'an ever closer union among the peoples of Europe'—and to create a direct connection between the EU and its citizens, as Article 8 spelled out: 'Citizenship of the Union is hereby established. Every person holding the nationality of a Member State shall be a citizen of the Union'.[104] Yet the meaning of Article 8 remained unclear, with Danes voting against ratification of Maastricht in the first referendum in June 1992 in part because EU citizenship was not held to be equivalent to Danish citizenship. With the backing of other European governments, Article 17 of the Treaty of Amsterdam (1997) specified that 'Citizenship of the Union shall complement and not replace national citizenship'.[105] In effect, priority was given to national citizenship, and associated rights and duties, over European citizenship, as the long and painful negotiation of citizens' rights during the Brexit process has made plain.[106]

Even the phrase 'ever closer union of the peoples of Europe', which was included in the opening declaration of the TEU (angering Eurosceptics in the British Conservative Party), was a watered-down version of the 'Solemn Declaration on European Union' signed by heads of state and government on 19 June 1983 in Stuttgart, which underlined governments' commitment, 'on the basis of an awareness of a common destiny and the wish to affirm the European identity [sic]...to progress towards an ever closer union among the peoples and Member States of the European Community'.[107] Their endeavour aimed 'to continue the work begun on the basis of the Treaties of Paris and Rome and to create a united Europe, which is more than ever necessary in order to meet the dangers of the world situation, capable of assuming the responsibilities incumbent on it by virtue of its political role, its economic potential and its manifold links with other peoples'.[108] The declaration was solemn but without effect. Its pledge to involve member states rather than merely 'peoples', which had more rhetorical force than legal or political substance, was not included in a binding treaty.

Luuk van Middelaar's case about the 'politicization of the club' after 1992, with the European Council defining 'basic policy guidelines' and taking 'strategic decisions', is best understood as an extension and formalizing of member states' powers, not as a change or rupture.[109] The Union itself did not, as van Middelaar admits, have a 'legal personality', with some lawyers arguing that momentous actions such as the deployment of troops were carried out by 'the member states jointly' and with others pointing out that the Council had signed an accord with the former Yugoslavia 'on behalf of the European Union' in April 2001.[110] For the Dutch historian, the EU was left 'in a twilight zone', but its position was consistent with that of an organization bound by the treaties of member states.[111]

Reforming the European Union

Few governments envisaged a European federation on Delors's model.[112] They did struggle to reform the political institutions of the EU in the 1990s and 2000s, however, partly to meet the challenges of EMU and to cope with the increased demands and numbers of representatives resulting from enlargement in 1995, 2004, and 2007, as the Union grew from a Western and Southern European club of twelve member states with a population of 350,909,000 to twenty-seven states with 494,297,000. One exception to this pragmatic proclivity was the new German SPD-Green coalition government of Gerhard Schröder and Joschka Fischer (1998–2005). 'The introduction of the euro was not only the crowning-point of economic integration, it was also a profoundly political act, because a currency is not just another economic factor but also symbolizes the power of the sovereign who guarantees it,' declared the German Minister of Foreign Affairs on 12 May 2000 at the Humboldt University in Berlin, in a speech marking the fiftieth anniversary of the Schuman Plan: 'A tension has emerged between the communitarization of economy and currency on the one hand and the lack of political and democratic structures on the other, a tension which might lead to crises within the EU if we do not take productive steps to make good the shortfall in political integration and democracy, thus completing the process of integration.'[113]

Fischer was a special case, as a pro-European Green, a '68er' with no memory of National Socialism (he was born in 1948) and a member of the German student movement (even though he left school early and never attended university), but he, too, was aware above all of the challenges posed by enlargement (see Map 8.2):

Thus we in Europe are currently facing the enormously difficult task of organizing two major projects in parallel:

1. Enlargement as quickly as possible. This poses difficult problems of adaptation both for the acceding states and for the EU itself. It also triggers fear and anxiety in our citizens: are their jobs at risk? Will enlargement make Europe even less transparent and comprehensible for its citizens? As seriously as we must tackle these questions, we must never lose sight of the historic dimension of eastern

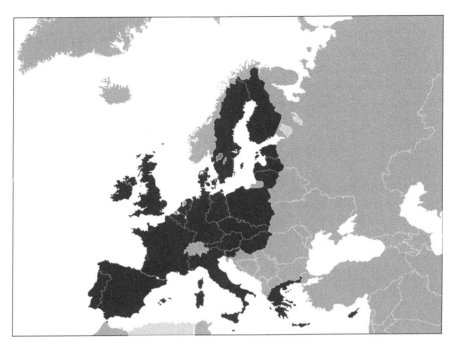

Map 8.2 The enlargement of the EU in 2004
Source: https://en.wikipedia.org/wiki/2004_enlargement_of_the_European_Union#/media/File: EU25-2004_European_Union_map_enlargement.svg

enlargement. For this is a unique opportunity to unite our continent, wracked by war for centuries, in peace, security, democracy, and prosperity.

Enlargement is a supreme national interest, especially for Germany. It will be possible to lastingly overcome the risks and temptations objectively inherent in Germany's dimensions and central situation through enlargement and simultaneous deepening of the EU. Moreover, enlargement—consider the EU's enlargement to the south—is a pan-European programme for growth....

2. Europe's capacity to act. The institutions of the EU were created for six member states. They just about still function with fifteen. While the first step towards reform, to be taken at the upcoming intergovernmental conference and introducing increased majority voting, is important, it will not in the long term be sufficient for integration as a whole. The danger will then be that enlargement to include 27 or 30 members will hopelessly overload the EU's ability to absorb, with its old institutions and mechanisms, even with increased use of majority decisions, and that it could lead to severe crises.[114]

Fischer's federalism—which ended with him joining the Spinelli Group in 2010—only manifested itself once he had—in the same speech—removed 'my Foreign

Minister's hat altogether in order to suggest a few ideas both on the nature of this so-called finality of Europe and on how we can approach and eventually achieve this goal'.[115] He was anxious to warn 'all the Eurosceptics on this and the other side of the Channel...not to immediately produce the big headlines again, because firstly this is a personal vision of a solution to the European problems. And, secondly, we are talking here about the long term, far beyond the current intergovernmental conference. So no one need be afraid of these ideas.'[116]

Fischer's idea comprised a 'transition from a union of states to full parliamentarization as a European federation, something Robert Schuman demanded 50 years ago'.[117] Like Habermas, the Minister of Foreign Affairs thought that nation-states could retain an important role in a federation. 'Only if European integration takes the nation-states along with it into such a Federation, only if their institutions are not devalued or even made to disappear, will such a project be workable despite all the huge difficulties,' he continued: 'In other words, the existing concept of a federal European state replacing the old nation-states and their democracies as the new sovereign power shows itself to be an artificial construct which ignores the established realities in Europe.'[118] To this end, Fischer proposed a 'division of sovereignty between Europe and the nation-state', outlining how a European Parliament could represent a 'Europe of the nation-states and a Europe of the citizens'.[119] His solution was—not uncannily—like that of the Federal Republic of Germany:

> In my opinion, this can be done if the European Parliament has two chambers. One will be for elected members who are also members of their national parliaments. Thus there will be no clash between national parliaments and the European parliament, between the nation-state and Europe. For the second chamber a decision will have to be made between the Senate model, with directly-elected senators from the member states, and a chamber of states along the lines of Germany's Bundesrat. In the United States, every state elects two senators; in our Bundesrat, in contrast, there are different numbers of votes.[120]

For the 'executive', 'one can decide in favour of developing the European Council into a European government, i.e. the European government is formed from the national governments, or—taking the Commission structure as a starting-point— one can opt for the direct election of a president with far-reaching executive powers', with 'various other possibilities between these poles'.[121] In order to create greater transparency, a 'constituent treaty' could 'lay down what is to be regulated at European level and what has still to be regulated at national level', resting on 'a clear definition of the competences of the Union and the nation-states respectively', with 'core sovereignties and matters which absolutely have to be regulated at European level being the domain of the Federation, whereas everything else would remain the responsibility of the nation-states'.[122] He was confident—'with an eye to our friends in the United Kingdom, because I know that the term "federation" irritates many Britons'—that the 'nation-states will continue to exist and at European level they will retain a much larger role than the *Länder* in Germany'.[123] Fischer—unlike Habermas—did not mention ownership of the treaty and *Kompetenzkompetenz*, but he implied that they would rest with the European Union 'when European finality is attained'.[124] In the meantime, enhanced cooperation on the part of a core of member states might be necessary, even if it 'means nothing more than increased intergovernmentalization under pressure from the acts and the shortcomings of the "Monnet Method"'.[125] By contrast, 'steps towards a constituent treaty—and exactly that will be the precondition for full integration—require a deliberate political act to re-establish Europe'.[126] Few other European ministers agreed with Fischer, as the debate about a European constitution was to demonstrate.

The 'European Convention', established by the European Council at Laeken (Belgium) in December 2001 and chaired by Valéry Giscard d'Estaing, Giuliano Amato (a former Italian prime minister), and Jean-Luc Dehaene (a former Belgian premier), was initially tasked with solving some of the institutional problems of the EU discussed, and partly tackled, in the Treaty of Amsterdam (1997), which had extended the use of the 'co-decision procedure', reinforced the role of the European Parliament and allowed 'enhanced cooperation', and in the Treaty of Nice (2001), which altered voting weights and introduced a double (member states and weighted votes) or, even, treble majority voting system in the Council (including 62 per cent of the EU's population, when a member state requested it). The Convention's assignment seemed compatible with previous attempts at practical institutional reform, but Giscard and other members—thirty deputies from national parliaments, sixteen MEPs, fourteen nominees of national governments, and two representatives of the Commission—soon began to talk of drafting a 'constitution'.[127] As Amato recalled, the Convention had received only a 'cautious mandate' from the member states in the European Council:

Incredibly enough (under the light of the later difficulties in the governance of the Eurozone and of the last-minute rush in inventing new instruments to face them) nothing was planned, nor even discussed for the euro. Our governments and the European institutions seemed satisfied with the unsatisfactory arrangement they had agreed upon in Maastricht, namely the coordination of national economic and fiscal policies, as a sufficient source of convergence and stability.

In relation to the enlargement there was, at least, a debate around the issue of 'deepening': was it, or was it not, an essential prerequisite of a successful 'widening'? It is a fact that our governments could not initially agree on any form of deepening, and the Intergovernmental Conference of Nice in December 2000 limited its efforts to the few innovations that were simply inescapable to make the enlargement possible: basically, the redistribution of seats in the Parliament, and of the voting rights in the Council.

However, the demand for wider reforms was not utterly ignored.[128]

A preparatory report for the European Council in December 2001 provided a list of issues still to be dealt with—'more precise delimitation of powers between the Union and the States, reflecting subsidiarity; the status of the Charter of Fundamental Rights; simplification of the Treaties; and the role of national parliaments in the European architecture (I added this final item by hand and it proved essential to gain the consent of the UK)'—'but it is hard to find evidence in it that deepening was the real aim', wrote Amato.[129] The Laeken Declaration of December 2001 addressed 'a much wider list of questions, including the "democratic deficit" of the Union and its possible remedies.[130] The prospect of a European Constitution was raised only in the final words and only for the long-run future: "The question ultimately arises as to whether this simplification and re-organization might not lead in the long run to the adoption of a constitutional text."'[131] The Convention had not been given 'an explicit mandate to write a text (constitutional or not), but just "to consider the key issues arising for the Union's future development and try to identify the various possible responses",' Amato admitted.[132] José Manuel Aznar, the Spanish prime minister who was acting as President of the European Council when the Convention convened in late February 2002, talked of 'furthering integration' and of the 'constitutionalization of the European Union' in his inaugural speech, but his objectives were incremental, seeking to attain 'a sustainable and effective Europe' based on citizens' equal enjoyment of an 'internal market, the single currency and the European social model'.[133] He was aware that 'the consolidation of the European project' was 'not, as might appear, an easy task', requiring 'pluralistic constitutionalization' because of the 'many legal systems of...Member States' and carrying the risk that those states 'go back to each of us doing on our own what until now we have done together'.[134]

The draft 'Treaty Establishing a Constitution for Europe' which was presented by Giscard to the European Council meeting in Thessalonica on 20 June 2003 seemed to be a radical alteration of existing treaty arrangements. It began by quoting Thucydides: 'Our Constitution...is called a democracy because power is in the hands not of a minority but of the greatest number.'[135] Amongst other things, the draft treaty simplified the rules of qualified-majority voting in the Council (a 'dual majority', comprising a majority of member states and 60 per cent of the EU's population); it reduced the size of the Commission (fifteen instead of up to twenty-seven Commissioners); it required that all measures passed by the Council of Ministers have parliamentary assent; and it spelled out in an expansive fashion the areas in which the EU had exclusive competence (competition policy, common commercial policy, customs, fisheries, monetary policy for the Eurozone), shared responsibility (internal market, environment, transport,

402 EUROPEAN INTEGRATION SINCE THE 1920S

energy, health and safety, aspects of social policy) and little say (subsidiarity), which could be stalled but not blocked at the proposal stage—preventing discussion in the Council of Ministers—by a 'reasoned opinion' presented by a national parliament and backed by parliaments in a third or more of member states.[136] The final version of the constitution retained much of the federalizing spirit of the draft.[137] Article I-15 enjoined member states to 'coordinate their economic policies within the Union', although leaving it to the Council of Ministers to adopt actual measures (by QMV), and allowed the EU to 'take initiatives to ensure coordination of Member States' social policies'.[138] Article I-16 stated that 'The Union's competence in matters of common foreign and security policy shall cover all areas of foreign policy and all questions relating to the Union's security, including the progressive framing of a common defence policy that might lead to a common defence.'[139] 'Member States shall actively and unreservedly support the Union's common foreign and security policy in a spirit of loyalty and mutual solidarity and shall comply with the Union's action in this area,' it went on: 'They shall refrain from action contrary to the Union's interests or likely to impair its effectiveness.'[140] In Amato's view, there were also other notable 'ingredients of a constitutional architecture': 'not only the flag, the anthem and the motto, as has been frequently pointed out, but also more substantial innovations, such as the reduction of the Commission's members to 15, the separation of legislative and non-legislative acts, the adoption of co-decision as the ordinary legislative procedure and the legal force given to the Charter of Fundamental Rights'.[141] On 'other crucial issues', however, 'traditional patterns prevailed', recorded the former Vice-Chair of the European Convention.[142]

What were such 'traditional patterns'? For Amato, they were both theoretical and practical. Article I-11 of the Treaty Establishing a Constitution for Europe pointed out that 'The limits of Union competences are governed by the principle of conferral' by member states, serving to restrict the attainment of 'the objectives set out in the Constitution': 'Competences not conferred upon the Union in the Constitution remain with the Member States.'[143] It was critical in the Vice-Chair's opinion, that 'competences were conferred on the Union not by it, but by the states', on 'the basis of the principle of conferral', as 'the first in the list of the fundamental principles on the allocation of powers and of the consequent acts'.[144] This provision limited and, in certain circumstances, could override Article I-10, stating that 'The Constitution and law adopted by the Union's institutions in exercising competences conferred on it shall have primacy over the law of the Member States.'[145] By contrast, 'the supremacy clause of a federal constitution', such as that of the United States, invested ultimate authority, power and competence in the 'Constitution and the Laws of the United States' as 'the Supreme Law of the Land', 'any Thing in the Constitution of Laws of any State to the Contrary notwithstanding'.[146] 'Compare this final part of the US supremacy clause to Article I-5 of the Convention's text,' went on Amato: 'By such an article (now Article 4 of the TEU), the Union is obliged to respect a detailed list of features of the national identity of its Member States, and currently this is considered the main European legal basis of those "counter-limits" that national Constitutional Courts are entitled to erect against Regulations and Directives, despite their supposed primacy.'[147] Practically, the position of the member states was strengthened in the treaty by the creation of a President of the European Council (with a thirty-month renewable term) and a Foreign Minister. Revisions to the draft treaty by Council ensured that the constitutional establishment of a 'legal personality' for the EU (Article 6), whereby the EU Minister of Foreign Affairs could sign international agreements on behalf of the member states, was subject to unanimity in the European Council, meaning that each government exercised a veto. The Council also reduced the number of policy areas subject to a European Parliament veto (formerly 'co-decision', renamed 'ordinary legislative procedure'), increased the thresholds for QMV (to 55 per cent of member states and 65 per cent of the EU's population), and reserved the right to switch—by a unanimous vote—to majority voting or to co-legislation with the European Parliament (from special to ordinary legislative procedure).[148] Crucially, as Amato pointed out, national governments kept control of the purse: 'any decision on new financial resources to be assigned to the Union needed (as it still needs) approval by the Member States'.[149] For these reasons, the Convention put forward a constitutional 'treaty', which was compatible with intergovernmentalism or confederalism, in the Vice-Chair's judgement, not a 'constitution': 'A union of states is what we have now [in 2019], but it is also what we would have had, had our Constitutional Treaty been approved as it was—and not under the disguising structure of the Lisbon Treaty.'[150] Amato's verdict is shared by legal scholars such as Joseph Weiler.[151]

The critical questions concerned the attitudes of the member states, rules about future revision of the constitution and the likelihood that the constitution would be ratified. According to Amato's retrospective account, the 'federalists' fought a 'lost battle' over a European constitution.[152] Giscard himself 'had proposed the writing of a "Constitutional Treaty", in other words an international act containing a Constitution, the force of which, therefore, was not expected to come from the citizens of Europe, but from the states'.[153] The dynamic soon changed when the members of the Convention met, 'particularly when most of them represent parliaments, not governments, and when they meet in a hemicycle—as happens in the European Parliament'—pushing them beyond the limits of their mandate (Laeken Declaration): 'The arguments against a truly federal Constitution were more than robust, but it is beyond doubt that the momentum for the federal move arrived *with* the Convention, and neither before nor after.'[154] The governments of the member states stood their ground, however:

> The fact of the matter is that in the Convention two opposite points of view were confronting each other: on the one side, the position of the representatives of

most of the governments, expecting from the Convention not more integration, but more clarity and more simplification. On the other side, the position of the representatives of the European Parliament and of the Commission, firmly in favour of more integration. The only surprise came from the representatives of national parliaments, who more frequently stood on the side of their colleagues from the European Parliament than on the side of their governments; quite likely on the assumption that, by doing so, they were better interpreting the will of their citizens rather than the interests of their governmental machineries.[155]

The 'eagerness of the Convention did not necessarily change the expectation of (several) Member States and their governments', noted Amato: 'Did a Constitution necessarily mean more integration? Couldn't it be just a better definition of the relationship between the states and the Union, to the advantage of the former?'[156] The German government of Schröder and Fischer was keen to increase the weight of the European Parliament and was seen—after Fischer's speech at the Humboldt University—as a champion of federalism. Jacques Chirac was less enthusiastic, signing up to the so-called 'ABC proposal' (Aznar-Blair-Chirac) for a permanent president of the European Council as a means of giving the organ of the member states greater visibility and continuity. 'To tell you the truth, there was a real problem, the German and the French vision were not exactly the same,' the French President told a press conference at the Elysée Palace on 14 January 2003:

To be clear, Germany was preoccupied with the necessity of a better integration and, accordingly, wished to markedly reinforce the power of the Commission... and, for that purpose, make the European Parliament elect the President of the Commission. To be honest, France was very reserved on that orientation. By contrast, France was very attached to a President of the European Council and, in order to do so, wanted the President of the European Council to be elected for a long period, five years or two-and-a-half years with the possibility of one re-election.[157]

The government of Tony Blair in the UK, preoccupied with the outbreak and course of the war in Iraq in 2003 and more concerned about the imminent enlargement of the EU in 2004 than about the European Convention, went further, aiming to block or nullify the initiative: 'Despite the British government's best hopes and intentions, the Convention had turned into a damage-limitation exercise as far as the UK was concerned, its integrationist thrust being more than the government could readily swallow,' wrote Stephen Wall, the UK's Permanent Representative to the EU until 2000 and Blair's senior official advisor on EU issues until 2004.[158]

According to Wall, the Irish Presidency in 2004—after that of Silvio Berlusconi, who 'was simply told' by Chirac and Schröder 'that no agreement would be reached under his chairmanship'—had 'moved the IGC to an agreement on a European Constitutional Treaty better suited to British taste', 'with consummate professionalism'.[159] On the principal question of the future revision of the constitutional treaty, 'the Convention did not get far with self-renewal', in van Middelaar's preliminary verdict.[160] The final version of the treaty, signed by the heads of state and government in Rome on 29 October 2004, provided a veto for any member state: 'If, two years after the signature of the treaty amending this Treaty, four fifths of the Member States have ratified it and one or more Member States have encountered difficulties in proceeding with ratification, the matter shall be referred to the European Council.'[161] (Article IV-443) Various groups of MEPs had proposed that four-fifths or five-sixths of member states would suffice for future revision, with the Vice-Chair of the Convention Amato avowing that 'the professor of constitutional law in him would commit suicide if unanimity was retained'.[162] When it was, in effect, retained, partly because of opposition to revision by majority on the part of the British, Irish, and Swedish governments, the politician in Amato—as his fellow Vice-Chair Dehaene put it—managed to live with it.[163] In van Middelaar's opinion, 'one unforeseen and one unseen' circumstance served to alter this position on unanimity, with the final iteration of the treaty—and the subsequent Lisbon Treaty (2007)—containing the possibility of 'light amendment' by a unanimous vote in the European Council (without the need for treaty change, an intergovernmental conference and ratification) for matters of internal policy which do not increase the competencies of the EU (Article IV-445, which was not in the draft treaty and was 'unforeseen').[164] The 'unseen' circumstance concerned so-called 'passerelles' (footbridges), or the possibility of the European Council, again by a unanimous vote, moving to qualified majority voting or to the ordinary legislative procedure (in cases governed by special legislative procedures), in which the European Parliament became a co-legislator (Article IV-444). Yet member states retained a veto in all such cases: van Middelaar's thesis rests on the supposition that they would act differently in the 'club' atmosphere, subject to collective pressures, of the European Council.[165] The negotiation of the constitutional treaty itself, which took place bilaterally and at the Council summits of Laeken (14–15 December 2001), Athens (16–17 April 2003), Thessalonica (20 June 2003) and Brussels (16–17 October 2003, 25–6 March 2004) as well as at the intergovernmental conference in Rome between 4 October 2003 and 18 June 2004, suggested that heads of state and government, and their advisors, were capable of compromise and adaptation in different settings but they were also willing to defend their own positions and 'national interests'.

The combination of the reiteration of the 'fundamental principle' of conferral, the consolidated powers of the European Council and the unanimity procedure for future amendment reassured some ministers that the constitutional treaty was worthy of their support. Eighteen out of twenty-five member states had ratified it by 29 May 2005, when 55 per cent of French voters rejected it in a referendum, followed on 1 June by 61 per cent of Dutch voters.[166] Blair himself had vowed to fight a referendum—'Let the issue be put and let the battle be joined!'—in favour of ratification, but he was forced into it, reneging on a promise to Chirac that he would not allow a popular vote.[167] The French President subsequently bowed to pressure to do the same.[168] Yet neither was convinced that he could win. Blair had come to power in 1997 after travelling to Australia to persuade Rupert Murdoch to back Labour. The price of such support, coinciding with the need to convince voters sceptical of 'Europe', was a defensive orientation towards the EU, as the leader of the Labour Party spelled out in *The Sun* on 22 April 1997: 'Let me make my position on Europe absolutely clear. I will have no truck with a European super-state. If there are moves to create that dragon, I will slay it.'[169] By 23 November 2001, at a speech on Europe at Birmingham University, just before Laeken, the Prime Minister had moderated his tone—'Blair used a series of negative arguments, mostly about the risks of non-engagement' and about the need for reform, since the EU was a 'success, but a flawed success', in Wall's summary—but he was aware of the constant 'anti-EU propaganda of the Murdoch press', which 'both reflected and augmented public scepticism'.[170] Against this background, he rejected the argument of the Foreign Secretary, Jack Straw, in favour of a referendum on the grounds that the House of Lords would require a referendum, forcing the government to use the Parliament Act to override it and delay a vote until after the general election of 2005, and allowing the Conservatives to use anti-European sentiment and the thwarting of the popular will during the election campaign. Blair replied to Straw that, 'once a referendum was promised, it would dominate politics to the exclusion of all else' and that 'Persuading Labour voters to turn out to vote on the minutiae of a treaty which was, in substance, less important than the Single European Act or the Maastricht Treaty would be a lost cause.'[171] By the spring of 2004, the Prime Minister had changed his mind:

> The Constitution for the EU had been agreed. With deep misgivings, I accepted we had to promise a referendum on it. We wouldn't get the Constitution through the House of Lords without it, and even the Commons vote would have been in doubt. My statement met with predictably and justifiably raucous cheering from Tories, who knew my heart wasn't in it.
>
> Jacques Chirac was also aggrieved as he felt it presented him with a real problem. In this, he was right. If Britain promised a referendum, it put enormous pressure on France to do the same. But truthfully, I couldn't avoid it, and as Jack Straw insistently advocated, better to do it apparently willingly than be forced to do it by a vote. However, it reminded me how far I had to go to persuade British

opinion of the merits of being in the mainstream of Europe. As ever, the difficulty was that the Eurosceptics were organised and had savage media backing; those in favour of a constructive attitude were disorganised and had the usual progressive media 'backing', i.e. spending more time criticising their own side than rebutting the propaganda of the other.[172]

Blair thought—at least with hindsight—that he might have succeeded in a referendum campaign, but he conceded that 'Our polls were resolutely against success and not many people believed we could shift them', including his own advisors.[173] Even if French and Dutch voters supported the constitutional treaty, which remained in the balance—in Blair's opinion—with the polls 'unclear', most observers assumed that the UK electorate would say 'no'.[174] The likelihood of this outcome gave the decisions of 2004 the air of a rehearsal.

To Blair, the failure to ratify the constitutional treaty in 2005 was the expression of broader, more profound popular discontentment with European affairs. 'I have sat through Council conclusions after Council conclusions describing how we are "reconnecting to the people of Europe". Are we?' Blair asked the European Parliament on 23 June 2005, at the start of the British Presidency: 'It is time to give ourselves a reality check.'[175] Most European leaders were more circumspect, resolving to put many of the provisions of the constitutional treaty—the President of the European Council and High Representative for Foreign Affairs, the 'double majority' voting system, ordinary legislative procedure (for 95 per cent of EU legislation) and a withdrawal clause (now Article 50)—into a more routine revision of the Treaties of Rome in the form of the Lisbon Treaty (2007), akin to Maastricht, Amsterdam, and Nice. References to an EU flag and anthem were removed, as was the Charter of Fundamental Rights, although all continued to exist (with British, Polish, and Czech opt-outs from the Charter). Vaclav Klaus, the Czech leader and a supporter of an 'organization of European states', condemned the Lisbon Treaty as a threat to the Czech Republic as 'a sovereign state'.[176] The Irish electorate rejected the treaty in a referendum—the only one held—by 53 to 47 per cent on 12 June 2008, voting again to approve it in October 2009. Yet the treaty itself was more moderate than the constitutional treaty of 2004, with no pretence of being a self-standing document or act of foundation. In 2009, the *Bundesverfassungsgericht* ruled that the German government's ratification of the Lisbon Treaty was constitutional, as long as the Bundestag and Bundesrat increased their scrutiny of European policy and member states continued to be allowed to determine their economic, social, and cultural form. The member states had to be able to preserve national democratic life and to remain 'masters of the treaties', recorded the German constitutional court in Karlsruhe, which had arrived at similar rulings in 1974 and in 1993, after Maastricht.[177] Although the court's interference in European affairs (in order to protect rights guaranteed in the *Grundgesetz*, or Basic Law) has received greater attention, it also confirmed

408 EUROPEAN INTEGRATION SINCE THE 1920s

that member states had kept control of European treaties—and their revision—
and that the fundaments of nationally determined economic, social, and cultural
life remained in place.

A European Confederation

The history of member states' interactions with European institutions often
diverges from the main theories of European integration. Some theorists have
treated the European Community and EU as if they are transitional, paying more
attention to the end point (or *'finalité'*) of the process. Advocates of a federal
system of government usually make this assumption, even if they distinguish
between federalism as an ideology, which can be 'centralist', 'de-centralist', or
'balanced' (Preston King), and a federation, which in most iterations is a state-like
entity with the ultimate say over competencies and a constitutional delineation of
jurisdictions and functions.[178] Both European commentators such as Hendrik
Brugmans and Americans such as Carl Friedrich stressed that the movement
towards federal institutions could be gradual, with the latter concentrating on
federalizing tendencies rather than constitutional principles.[179] If Friedrich's question was 'What function does a federal relationship have?—rather than what
structure', he nonetheless continued to relate process to a more or less defined
form of federal government—'a static, and therefore permanent, type of governmental relationship'—albeit in order to challenge such a definition.[180]

For Amatai Etzioni, in his work on *Political Unification* (1965), the end point
remained critical:

> A political community is a community that possesses three kinds of integration:
> (a) it has an effective control over the means of violence (though it may 'delegate'
> some of this control to member units); (b) it has a centre of decision-making that
> is able to affect significantly the allocation of resources and rewards throughout
> the community; and (c) it is the dominant focus of political identification for the
> large majority of politically aware citizens.[181]

Given that this type of polity failed to materialize on the European level, theorists
have sought to understand the 'process' or 'transition' in varying ways, beginning
with neo-functionalists' attempts to examine 'international integration by indir-
ection, by trial and error, by miscalculation on the part of the actors desiring
integration, by manipulation on the part of the actors desiring integration, by
manipulation of elite social forces on the part of small groups of pragmatic
administrators and politicians in the setting of a vague but permissive public
opinion'.[182] This investigation of 'incrementalism' was primarily economic, deliberately eschewing the political focus of federalism.[183] More recently, theories of

'Europeanization'—or the 'incremental process reorienting the direction and shape of politics to the degree that EC political and economic dynamics become part of the organizational logic of national politics and policy-making'—have extended the notion of gradually changing norms and patterns of interaction to 'policy-networks specialising in the creation of authoritative European rules'.[184] Law, economics, and politics are combined in such accounts. Scholars of the 'constitutionalization' of political relations have examined the gradual accretion of more formal laws, distinguishing the process which has brought it about from more overtly political federalizing tendencies.[185] Although these processes are historical, theorists have tended to focus on the present and to try to predict what will happen in the future.

Much of the scholarly interest in the European Union has been generated by its apparent uniqueness. Proponents of comparative politics such as Simon Hix have asked why there should be 'a general theory of the EU' when we 'do not have a general theory of American or German politics' and they have sought to use concepts of representation, political cleavages, party formation, coalition-building, the articulation of interests and questions of distribution to understand EU politics, which are kept separate from 'integration', the pooling of sovereignty and creation of supranational institutions by member states within theories of international relations.[186] Hix nevertheless recognizes that 'the political system of the European Community' is only 'part formed' and 'largely *sui generis*'.[187]

In many respects, the interest of political scientists in the 'new institutionalism' of James March and Johan Olsen, who aim to 'explore some ways in which the institutions of politics, particularly administrative institutions, provide order and influence change in politics', has served to underline the unique characteristics of the European Union by focusing attention on supranational institutions in the making, rather than on the relationships between new European institutions and existing member states within a wider social context and international order.[188] Whereas March and Olsen look at institutions configured historically and legally within states as the predominant locus of political organization, positing that the 'state is not only affected by society but also affects it', scholars of EU institutions often bracket out such states (much as Hix excludes broader forms of economic and social integration from his 'middle-range' theory), concentrating on the internal sets of rules established by institutions as formal, legal entities (rational-choice institutionalism), as 'cognitive scripts, categories and models that are indispensable for action (sociological institutionalism) or as historically evolving "normative vessels" (historical institutionalism)'.[189] If institutions are defined as 'formal rules, compliance procedures and standard operating practices that struc-ture relationships between individual units of the polity and the economy', in Peter Hall's words, how are we to understand 'the polity' and 'the economy'?[190] Usually, scholars investigate the single market and EU institutions. In the former case, there are, at least, established rules within a sphere of EU competency and

410 EUROPEAN INTEGRATION SINCE THE 1920s

jurisdiction, even if the intersection of local, national, and global markets, and the institutions which govern them (from municipal authorities to the WTO) is also relevant.[191] In the latter case, the rules governing the relationship between EU institutions and member states are in the process of being established, with states remaining the 'masters of the treaties'.[192]

Criticism of 'new institutionalism' has tended to focus on the distinction between the creation and operation of European institutions or on the intrusion of wider sets of discourses, norms, and beliefs, or 'polity ideas'.[193] A 'sociological turn in EU institutionalism' could 'move institutionalists beyond their fascination with the formal rules and arrangements of "the most densely institutionalized international organization in the world"', in the opinion of Jane Jenson and Frédéric Mérand, yet it promises to 'uncover the parts that actors—from taxi drivers producing subterranean forms of political legitimacy to military officers pragmatically involved in the Europeanization of military practices—play in the theatre of European integration', to locate 'the real spaces in which "European" practice occurs', and to examine the social relations of power within EU institutions, and between them and European citizens.[194] Attention is rarely paid in these studies to the formal and informal relations of power between European institutions and member states.[195]

In theory, the other main approach to European integration within comparative politics, which has examined multilevel governance and policy networks, can encompass the dynamic relationship between member states and EU institutions. In an intriguingly titled article—'Of Blind Men, Elephants and International Integration' (1972)—which is often cited by exponents of the 'governance turn', Donald Puchala compares the analysis of integration to blind people feeling different parts of an elephant and describing what they feel.[196] His thesis that 'contemporary international integration can be thought of as a set of processes that produce and sustain a Concordance System at the international level' incorporates nation-states as 'major component units of the system', with national governments remaining 'central actors in it': although 'contemporary international integration does in fact go "beyond the nation-state" both organizationally and operationally, it nonetheless does not go very far beyond'.[197] However, the fact that 'the most complex Concordance Systems'—such as the European Community—'may include actors in four organizational arenas—the subnational, the national, the transnational and the supranational'—makes them different from an 'exclusively government-to-government or "billiard ball" system of traditional world politics' and has prompted commentators to focus on 'any number of within- and between-arena interactions', which tend to become 'highly institutionalized', with 'organizational networks' characterized by 'routinized procedures', producing a concordance system which 'is much more bureaucratic than it is diplomatic'.[198]

Bargaining among actors over 'the achievement of convergent or collective ends is the predominant style of interaction' within the system, writes Puchala, reducing

political conflict to 'divergent views about "ways to cooperate" rather than...
fundamental incompatibilities in the interests of various actors', as exponents
of 'Realism' in international relations expect.[199] Pragmatism, resulting from the
collapse of traditional ideologies, and perceptions of international interdependence
or, at least, 'perceptions of national inadequacy' are prevalent.[200] At the same time,
the atmosphere in the European Community is different:

> the 'atmosphere' within the Concordance System, especially in councils where
> common programs are formulated and decided upon, is one of high mutual
> sensitivity and responsiveness. To begin with, actors within the system tend to
> possess a good deal more information about one another and about one
> another's goals, objectives, preferences and needs than is common in more
> traditional diplomacy where emphasis is upon one's own needs and upon ways
> to fulfil these regardless of what the other fellow may want. But even more
> important, actors within the Concordance System feel some compulsion to see
> to it that their partners' needs as well as their own are fulfilled in decisions made
> and programs executed. All of this may sound rather strange to the student of
> traditional international relations. Nevertheless, it is precisely this atmosphere
> of shared compulsion to find mutually rewarding outcomes, this felt and
> shared legitimacy in concession-making, and this reciprocal sensitivity to needs
> that markedly distinguishes between the new international politics of the
> Concordance System and the traditional politics of the Machiavellian world.[201]

The principal questions, though, concern the framework for an analysis of
disagreements, competing national interests and the evolution of competencies,
especially in circumstances where 'the mass populations of the nation-states
within the system' do not 'accord legitimacy to the structures and processes of
the system' and do not 'defer to the outcomes of the bargaining outcomes of the
multi-arena system', contrary to Puchala's expectations.[202]

Few, if any, theorists of multilevel governance have devised convincing answers
to such questions. The premise that supranational institutions exist and that
much EU activity is technical is unobjectionable. 'Low politics this may be, in
the Hoffmann terminology, but it is probably the nine-tenths of the EU "policy
iceberg" that is below the water line,' Jeremy Richardson has written: 'There is an
increasing amount of political activity at this level within the EU and some means
has to be found of analysing and conceptualising it.'[203] Theories of multilevel
governance attempt to account for such political activity, with 'governance' suggesting a less decisive set of legal competencies and political powers than
'government'.[204] Proponents of the theory are aware of 'state-centric' approaches
in international relations, including liberal intergovernmentalism, against which
they frame their own arguments. 'The multilevel governance model does not reject
the view that state executives and state arenas are important, or that these remain

the *most* important pieces of the European puzzle,' write Gary Marks and Liesbet Hooghe. 'However, when one asserts that the state no longer monopolizes European level policy-making or the aggregation of domestic interests, a very different polity comes into focus.'[205] Decision-making competencies were 'shared by actors at different levels rather than monopolized by state executives', with 'supranational institutions—above all, the European Commission, the European Court and the European Parliament'—having 'independent influence in policy-making that cannot be derived from their role as agents of state executives', Marks and Hooghe continue.[206] Collective decision-making entails 'a significant loss of control for individual state executives', with political arenas becoming 'interconnected rather than nested' and sub-national actors operating 'in both national and supranational arenas, creating transnational associations in the process' and encouraging the growth of 'policy networks'.[207] The principal endeavour of theorists of multilevel governance has been to explain why 'states allow competencies to be shifted out of their hands to supranational or subnational institutions', allowing their own sovereignty to be weakened.[208]

A liberal intergovernmentalist such as Moravcsik has replied that 'states receive something important in return'.[209] Historians of the nation-state such as Milward and Vibeke Sørensen claim that member states' 'principal national interest will be not only to define and limit the transfer of sovereignty very carefully but also meticulously to structure the central institutions so as to preserve a balance of power within the integrationist framework in favour of the nation-states themselves'.[210] Advocates of theories of multilevel governance, by contrast, argue that national governments may accept 'the benefits of more efficient delivery of collective policies' or wish 'to avoid responsibility for certain policies', insulating decision-making from political pressures.[211] Member states are subject to qualified majority voting in the European Council in specified areas 'from the internal market to trade, agriculture and the environment', distinguishing the EU from international organizations such as the UN or WTO.[212] The notion of a veto (the Luxembourg compromise) 'is available to national governments only under restricted conditions' and is subject to 'the willingness of other state executives to tolerate its use in a particular case'.[213] Although states retain 'ultimate sovereignty by virtue of their continuing monopoly of the means of legitimate coercion within their respective territories' and as a result of their ability to withdraw, since 'the EU itself has no armed forces with which to contest that decision', they are 'constrained by the economic and political sanctions—and consequent political-economic dislocation—that it would almost certainly face if it revoked its treaty commitments and pulled out of the European Union'.[214] Given the difficulty of withdrawing or deploying a veto, national governments have been constrained in their attempts 'to control supranational agents', which have benefited from 'unintended consequences of institutional change, 'informational asymmetries' (the Commission is a 'small and thinly staffed organization' but has 'a unique informational base', given 'its position as interlocutor with national governments, subnational authorities and numerous interest groups') and the willingness of member states to accept 'detailed regulation as a response to mistrust' of other member states and companies.[215] These constraints on member states matter, with governments no longer controlling competition and state aid within their borders and no longer having the right to conduct trade negotiations. Yet the focus on areas where EU institutions are active—particularly trade—tends to obscure other policy-making areas where member states have preserved their powers, jurisdictions, and competencies. How and why did they remain 'sovereign' in the midst of 'integration' and 'internationalization'?

Few would deny that policy-making on the European level depends on an unprecedented relationship between supranational institutions, whose powers and competencies are the result of a gradual accretion and long-term delegation by member states, and national governments, which are answerable to an increasingly unpredictable coalition of political parties, media and voters, against a backdrop of international organizations, global commerce, multinational companies, and transnational interest groups. Many scholars have sought to go beyond what Thomas Risse labels 'the sterile controversy of neofunctionalism versus intergovernmentalism', availing themselves of insights from both international relations theory and comparative political analysis.[216] Risse's own additive effort to combine work on transnational politics, policy networks and multilevel governance, historical institutionalism, and social constructivism, incorporating theories of communicative action, also fails to explain why the EU has developed as it has, partly because it leaves questions about the nature of a European political order unanswered, and partly because it puts 'history-making' decisions and 'issue areas that are only loosely integrated' to one side, stating merely that they depend on 'the domestic structure of those member states involved in the major bargains' and on 'the degree of previous Europeanization—institutional path dependence— of the policy area to be regulated'.[217]

Richard Bellamy and Dario Castiglione address the first question about the nature and legitimacy of a European polity (the structure in which 'collective decisions can be made about particular issues') and regime (the particular 'form of governance', determining the style and scope of politics).[218] The internal legitimacy of a polity requires that the '*subjects* who make and have to obey collective decisions must recognize each other as equal citizens and acknowledge the designated decision-making body as rightfully holding sway over a given sphere of their lives, be that sphere territorially or functionally defined', with recognition 'both contingently conditioned by such factors as language, culture, historical accident and geography, and more deliberately agreed to by various forms of tacit, express or hypothetical consent, from referenda and oaths of allegiance to military service or mere residence'.[219] The external legitimacy of a polity rests on its ability to meet 'formal and substantive criteria, such as are found in

414   EUROPEAN INTEGRATION SINCE THE 1920s

international law', facilitating its recognition by other states and non-citizens.[220] Like advocates of multilevel governance, Bellamy and Castiglione 'assume sovereignty to be partially dispersed between different policy spheres involving different subjects, for which different sorts of "regime" might be appropriate', making the EU 'very different, therefore, from a standard, albeit somewhat idealized, conception of a federal nation-state', in which 'there is a strong political allegiance to the boundaries of the "polity" and the competences of the subunits are relatively clear'.[221] There are 'multiple channels of political representation for different sorts of political subjects' in the 'proto-European polity': 'member states in the Intergovernmental Conferences and Councils of Ministers, national political parties in the EP, selected functional interests in the Economic and Social Committee (ESC) and subnational territorial units in the Committee of the Regions'.[222] The European Union, they conclude, is a 'polycentric "polity"' possessing a multi-level "regime"', whose internal legitimacy rests on 'a series of dialogues among the multiple European constituencies' within a 'mixed constitution'.[223] Although they admit that the EU rests on different, sometimes incompatible, types of representation and democracy—with the European Parliament seeking to represent the common good of a 'European people', which does not exist, national governments pursuing their own interests in the Council, and national parliaments and elections seeking to hold national governments to account—they can be balanced by linking European decision-making to national politics through the creation of European Committees and the discussion of EU legislation in national parliaments.[224] Faced with the diversity of Europe's political cultures and the shallowness of European affiliations, there is little alternative, in Bellamy and Castiglione's view, to the existing 'balance and separation of powers produced by the European Union's unique mix of intergovernmental, supranational and transnational decision-making mechanisms'.[225] This interpretation of European governance rests, in part, on an acknowledgement of historical conditions and contradictions.

Like many other commentators, Bellamy and Castiglione assume that intergovernmental forms of cooperation, including within the Council, consist largely of the pursuit of national self-interest: 'National governments and their ministers operate largely as authorized substitutes [for their citizens] and very occasionally as mandated delegates of domestic interests, though with limited electoral accountability for what they do at the EU level given the low salience of Europe in domestic elections.'[226] Moravcsik, in their reading, proposes 'a tripartite argument whereby national governments first define an ordering of preferences in response to the domestic pressures of societal groups, second, bargain amongst themselves to realize these interests and, third, choose appropriate institutions to realize them' in a context where 'all interests are assumed to be pursued economically'.[227] Moravcsik himself agrees that the European Community can be analysed as 'a successful intergovernmental regime designed to manage economic interdependence through a negotiated policy of coordination'.[228] Whereas most of his predecessors had treated the EC as a sui generis phenomenon, in part because of the 'expectation that Europe would develop in a federal direction, which led neo-functionalists to stress the uniqueness of its institutional structure, rather than analogies to other forms of interstate cooperation'.[229] For his part, the American proponent of liberal intergovernmentalism aims to incorporate general theories of international political economy over the past two decades, such as the studies of Robert Keohane and Joseph Nye, in order to explain integration 'in terms of theories of interdependence, regimes or other generalizable phenomena'.[230] Implicitly, there had been a change in the four dimensions of policy-making, which defined European integration: '(1) the *geographical scope* of the regime; (2) the *range* of issues in which policies are coordinated; (3) the *institutions* of joint decision-making, implementation and enforcement; (4) the *direction and magnitude of substantive domestic policy adjustment*', all of which were related to policy coordination.[231] Moravcsik's approach rests on both comparison with other forms of international interdependence, which have been intergovernmental, and a 'liberal' assumption that 'private individuals and voluntary associations with autonomous interests, interacting in civil society, are the most fundamental actors in politics', obliging governments to represent their preferences in external negotiations.[232] Liberals are state-centric in a different sense from 'realists'. 'The approach taken here departs decisively… from those theories in international relations, most notably realist and neo-realist approaches, which treat states as "billiard balls" or "black boxes" with fixed preferences for wealth, security or power,' he writes: 'Instead, governments are assumed to act purposively in the international arena, but on the basis of goals that are defined domestically. Following liberal theories of international relations, which focus on state-society relations, the foreign policy goals of national governments are viewed as varying in response to shifting pressures from domestic social groups, whose preferences are aggregated through political institutions.'[233] Diplomatic actions are 'constrained simultaneously by what other states will accept and what domestic constituencies will ratify', making the success of a negotiation dependent on a government bargaining 'on these two tables' and giving diplomats and other negotiators some freedom of manoeuvre in this 'two-level game'.[234]

Liberal theories of economic interdependence posit that 'increasing transborder flows of goods, services, factors or pollutants create "international policy externalities" among nations, which in turn create incentives for policy coordination'.[235] Governments seeking to negotiate and coordinate policy on a European level are assumed to be highly rational.[236] Intergovernmental bargaining theory assumes, first, that 'treaty-amending negotiations take place within a non-coercive system of unanimous voting in which governments can and will reject agreements that would leave them worse off than unilateral policies'; second, that 'the transaction costs of generating information and ideas are low relative to the benefits of interstate cooperation'; and, third, that 'the distribution of benefits reflects relative bargaining power, which is shaped in turn by the pattern of policy interdependence'.[237] Outcomes are seen to depend on '(1) the value of unilateral policy alternatives relative to the status quo, which underlies credible threats to veto; (2) the value of alternative coalitions, which underlies credible threats to exclude; and (3) the opportunities for issue linkage or side-payments, which underlie "package deals"'.[238] The formation of preferences and weighing up of interests in this fashion seems most suited to market transactions, with the internal market deemed to be 'at the core of the EC' and the creation of the single market occupying much of Moravcsik's attention: 'The most basic EC policies—including internal market policy, agricultural policy, competition policy, industrial policy, and research and development policy—are designed to liberalize or eliminate distortions in markets for private goods and services.'[239] By contrast, 'the costs and benefits created by political cooperation for private groups are diffuse and uncertain', with private producers taking little interest in them and 'partisan elites' taking over, deploying symbolic and ideological arguments, rather than calculated and concrete ones, and intermittently being constrained by mass publics.[240]

Economic decision-making is assumed by Moravcsik to be insulated—with national positions 'instrumental' in this sphere—from decisions about EU institutions and their powers in a broader sense.[241] Critics have pointed to the imperfection of knowledge, which has affected decision-making and worked to the advantage of European institutions 'at the centre of a network of knowledge', and the inadequacy of Robert Putnam's notion of a 'two-level game', when agenda-setting and decision-making was occurring on multiple levels in the European Union.[242] Historically, there is little indication that decision-makers have managed or, even, sought to keep economic cooperation separate from other spheres of policy-making, including foreign and security policy, as federalists' and neo-functionalists' hopes of political spill-over demonstrated in the 1950s and 1960s.[243] Although it is true that states have found it easier to agree on an internal market than on other areas of policy and the institutional form of the European Community, there is every sign that their decisions, which were not purely rational, but emotional, contingent, and socially conditioned, were affected by historical 'lessons' concerning the maintenance of peace, the place of Europe in the world, the threat of Communism, the balance of power during the Cold War, the dangers of protectionism in the 1920s and 1930s, and the need to follow the lead of the United States in economic affairs as well as military and diplomatic ones.[244] How far they were likely to go in order to achieve economic cooperation and to set up common European institutions was affected, in certain circumstances, by such considerations. What 'Europe' was—its configuration of institutions and perceived record at any given time—at once depended on and conditioned the assumptions and actions of national governments. Governance affected integration, with citizens—as Bellamy and Castiglione rightly suggest—having demands and beliefs (about the political order, among other things), not merely preferences.[245]

Moravcsik's response to such criticism, at least in retrospect, has been to refer to '"regime theory", which treats international institutions as instruments to help states implement, elaborate, enforce and extend incomplete contracts under conditions of uncertainty'.[246] Such institutions can constrain state sovereignty in two ways: first, by means of pooling, 'when governments agree to decide future matters by voting procedures other than unanimity'; and, second, through delegation, 'when supranational actors are permitted to take certain autonomous decisions, without an intervening interstate vote or unilateral veto'.[247] These constraints on state sovereignty have come to encompass a wider range of fields unconnected to the internal market—with intergovernmental institutions in areas such as drug approval, anti-terrorist activity, the security of borders, sharing information, coordinating policies, and initiating investigations—and they have involved more thorough-going forms of delegation or pooling, including qualified majority voting (QMV) in the Council, agenda-setting by the European Council and the Commission, the European Parliament's co-decision powers, the structure of the CAP, some of the functions of the European Central Bank (ECB), and the European Court of Justice's powers of adjudication.[248] From the point of view of governments, pooling and delegation created a degree of entanglement: 'While states ultimately reserve the sovereign right to withdraw from the EU and its policies, such withdrawal is in practice extremely difficult, because regime-based cooperation is so advantageous to states in realizing the material and ideal goals of their domestic constituents.'[249] These entanglements were also frequently made bearable, in ways which Moravcsik tends to neglect, by the belief of policy-makers that long-term cooperation within European institutions was desirable for deeply held, 'historical' reasons. At the same time, the cautious fashion in which national governments, anxious to retain their own powers, formed European institutions had long-term consequences, with the 'European constitutional settlement' imposing 'tight constraints on EU policy' which exceed those constraining national systems of 'consociational or consensus democracy' in the Netherlands or Austria in the 1950s and 1960s, federalism in Switzerland or Canada, or a separation of powers and reduced fiscal competencies in the United States.[250] 'The result is as much confederal as federal, and almost eliminates any threat of a European superstate,' writes the political scientist, placing a 'set of substantive, fiscal, administrative, legal and procedural constraints on EU policy-making...embedded in treaty and legislative provisions that have the force of constitutional law'.[251]

Modern states have acquired a panoply of competencies—taxation, the provision of welfare, defence and police powers, education, cultural policy, non-economic civil litigation, the funding of civilian infrastructure, and regulation unconnected to cross-border economic activity—that remain within their purview, with the 'core of EU activity and its strongest constitutional prerogatives' lying 'almost exclusively in the area of trade in goods and services, the movement of factors of production, the production of and trade in agricultural commodities, exchange rates and monetary policy, foreign-aid and trade-related environmental, consumer and competition policy', in Moravcsik's judgement.[252] These tasks have remained the core of EU activity even after the Treaty of Lisbon (2007). The EU 'employs fewer people than a modest European city' and its ability to tax is capped at 1.3 per cent of GDP. It has 'no police, military force of significant investigatory capacity' and implements very few of its own regulations.[253] Until Lisbon, even everyday EU directives had to be promulgated under rules that require the support of between 74 and 100 per cent of the weighted votes of territorial representatives in the Council of Ministers—'a level of support higher than required for legislation in any existing national polity or, indeed, to amend nearly any national constitution in the world today'.[254] Although EU rules are enforced in the core area of trade, in other areas member states can join international organizations (for example, the UN Security Council or bodies dealing with human rights, defence, border controls, or environmental policy) or they can act as a 'core' within EU institutions (enhanced cooperation or 'coalitions of the willing' in social, monetary, defence, and immigration policies).[255] Governments have also been able to opt out. The increasing number of opt-outs distinguishes the European Union from national federations.[256]

For Moravcsik, talk of a democratic deficit is misleading, not least because the late twentieth and early twenty-first centuries have been a period of 'the "decline of parliaments" and the rise of courts, public administrations and the "core executive"', with accountability deriving 'not through direct participation in majoritarian decision-making, but instead through complex systems of indirect representation, selection of representatives, professional socialization, *ex post* review, and balances between branches of government'.[257] Within 'the multilevel governance system prevailing in Europe', the European Union has most autonomy in those spheres 'in which many advanced industrial democracies, including most member states of the EU, insulate themselves from direct political contestation'; namely, central banking, constitutional adjudication, criminal and civil prosecution, technical administration, and economic diplomacy.[258] More importantly, the EU is not a federation, but functions as a confederation, relying on a separation of powers rather than parliamentary sovereignty.[259] Democratically elected governments of member states dominate 'the still largely territorial and intergovernmental structure of the EU', wielding power through the European Council, 'the EU's dominant institution'.[260] 'In the Council of Ministers, which imposes the most important constraint on everyday EU legislation, permanent representatives, ministerial officials and the ministers themselves from each country act under constant instruction from national executives, just as they would at home,' the American political scientist notes, referring—in *The Choice for Europe*—to a range of historical case studies from the 1950s to the 1990s.[261] The combination of the direct accountability of the European Parliament, which citizens elect but are largely ignorant of, and indirect accountability of national governments, which voters care about and trust to act on their behalf in 'Europe', underpins the legitimacy of the European Union. Viewed historically, ministers have not always acted rationally in carefully circumscribed economic spheres. Moravcsik's political economy model is plausible because it coincides with such ministers' other, largely national, imperatives over time.

The advocates of a 'new intergovernmentalism' are unconvinced by Moravcsik's argument about legitimacy, which they label as 'Panglossian in its optimism', and his case about a cautious delegation of powers and limited integration in specific areas, largely concerning markets, against which they have pitted their own hypotheses about an increase in the scope of EU activity after Maastricht, rendered possible because of the undoing of 'very different political bargains struck between competing social forces' within the national structures of post-war capitalism.[262] After 1992, the European Union not only completed the transition from single market to monetary union and expanded from fifteen to twenty-eight members, it also 'increased its involvement in socio-economic governance and justice and home affairs', acquiring its own foreign and security policy, its own foreign policy representative and a European diplomatic service, write Christopher Bickerton, Dermot Hodson, and Uwe Puetter.[263] Since 'the basic constitutional features of the Union have remained remarkably stable', with member states refusing at Maastricht, Amsterdam, Nice and Lisbon to concede 'substantial powers to the European Commission or the Court of Justice of the EU', most of the integration is attributable to the deliberation and consensus-building of national governments in the Council and to '*de novo* bodies' such as the European External Action Service (EEAS), which member states have established and continue to control.[264] Bickerton explains this 'paradox' of less supra-nationalism and more integration by referring to a shift from nation-states in the 1950s and 1960s to 'member states' from the 1980s onwards, in which power and authority derive from 'the participation by national governments in transnational networks of rule', yet it is difficult to believe that 'cooperation with officials from other member states', even if a 'core activity of national bureaucracies', has transformed statehood and separated politics, which is still national, from bureaucracy, given the continuing concentration of resources and competencies on the national level.[265]

Critics such as Frank Schimmelfennig and Simon Bulmer have questioned whether there is not still a mixture of activities carried out by existing supra-national bodies (the European Commission, Court of Justice, the European Parliament) and new ones (the European Central Bank), together with intergovernmental bodies (the Council), and whether intergovernmental cooperation

420   EUROPEAN INTEGRATION SINCE THE 1920s

has increased after Maastricht.[266] 'New policies have often been introduced through intergovernmental policy coordination and cooperation,' declares Schimmelfennig: prime examples are European Political Cooperation (1970), various forms of monetary policy, from the Monetary Committee (1958), and the 'snake' of 1972 to the European Monetary System (1979), the TREVI anti-terrorist intergovernmental network (1975), the beginnings of regional policy (1975), and the Schengen agreement (1985).[267] Bickerton, Hodson, and Puetter show that these types of intergovernmental initiatives continued and, at times, intensified in the 1990s, 2000s, and 2010s. What was more, the spheres of intergovernmental coordination expanded and the part played by political parties and the public increased. 'The ambition to specify exactly how domestic politics matter for the European integration process has long been at the heart of intergovernmental concerns', with liberal intergovernmentalists focusing on domestic interest groups and systematizing the role played by socio-economic interests, individual leaders, and political ideology, claim the new intergovernmentalists: 'Our understanding of domestic politics is broader and...it includes problems of legitimacy and authority and treats the preference formation process itself as an input into institutional change at the EU level'.[268] National governments, political parties and publics all had their own conceptions of what 'Europe' was and what it was for. Their interactions with European institutions and other member states had become increasingly complicated. How should historians make sense of these interactions?

In important respects, the European Community functions as a confederation, or 'a union of states in a body politic'.[269] A 'treaty of union founds a body that possesses personality, but it is more than merely the technical, "legal" personality of the typical interstate organization,' writes Murray Forsyth: 'The "personality" formed by union is an original capacity to act akin to that possessed by the states themselves', with states 'locked together' as 'regards the exercise of fundamental powers'.[270] Internally, a confederation makes laws for its members, but 'it is not the constituted unity of one *people* or *nation*, but a unity constituted by *states*', as a fragile, treaty-constituted political body' and a '"half-way house" between interstate and intrastate relations'.[271] In the European Community, 'the confederal elements are again conspicuous', in Forsyth's view: 'The Community is based on a treaty which is more than a conventional interstate treaty', resembling instead a 'constitutive treaty' and establishing 'common institutions which are capable of passing laws that are directly binding throughout the territory of the community'.[272] In an economic confederation such as the EEC, the 'economy of each state has not ceased to exist, but it has been placed within a new economy— that of the Community as a whole'.[273] The idea of 'supranationality', implying 'complete independence' of nation-states, was introduced in contradistinction to traditional 'intergovernmental' institutions, but supranational institutions have remained subordinate to the Council, 'in which are gathered the representatives of the member states' and which has 'the final power of legislative decision'.[274] Since the Luxembourg compromise in 1966, the position of the Council of Ministers and COREPER 'has strengthened in relation to that of the Commission': 'The pivotal role of the Committee of Permanent Representatives deserves particularly to be noted', for, as a consequence of 'its permanency, its close links with the member states, and the "instructions" which pass to it from them, it is in some ways more analogous to the governing body of the customary confederation than any other body in the European Community'.[275] The requirement of unanimity in the Council on vital matters of state interest 'also conforms closely to confederal practice', as does the Court of Justice's 'supremacy' or 'law-making power', 'acting within the area set out by the founding treaty' and existing alongside the supremacy or law-making power of member states.[276] Since a 'fully democratic form of government presupposes a deep-rooted underlying sense of oneness or nationality', creating a 'trust binding together government and governed whatever the outcome of the ballot box', in Forsyth's opinion, the European Parliament could not function like the assembly of a nation-state.[277] Rather, it should be a 'critical body' alongside a confederal government.[278]

Contemporaries have generally avoided the terminology of a confederation in respect of the European Union, with critics and opponents preferring to see it merely as a market or as a 'super-state', and strong supporters striving for a federation or for more extensive supranational institutions. For political analysts of the EEC, in Forsyth's judgement, 'There has been a strong tendency... to stress over and over again that it is *sui generis*, a completely new and peculiar form of political life'.[279] Moreover, they have succumbed to 'an unfortunate tendency... to apply paradigms and models to the Community in which reference to the state is either completely avoided, or kept to an absolute minimum,' he goes on: 'Even the word "supranational", which has so often been used to differentiate the European Economic Community from other, merely "international" organizations, is scarcely conducive to clear thinking because it deflects the eye from the main constituent elements of the Community.'[280] Arguably, the main constituents are still the member states, whose governments have been wary of ceding powers, competencies. and jurisdictions to the European Commission, Court of Justice, and European Parliament other than in clearly defined areas of mutual advantage, starting with the internal market. Since they remain 'masters of the treaties', they have usually managed to block attempts by European institutions—even if backed by a coalition of member states—to share or take control of the most important spheres of policy-making (welfare, taxation, education, foreign policy, defence, and culture). The end of the Cold War and enlargement have, on the one hand, created a greater need, externally, to

422 EUROPEAN INTEGRATION SINCE THE 1920s

coordinate foreign and security policy and, internally to reform and streamline forms of governance, and, on the other, they have created a more unstable environment abroad and greater diversity, together with more independent member states, within the EU.[281] In a period of globalization, cooperation between European states, including through the mediation of supranational institutions and through direct contact with each other in the Council, seems more necessary than ever. Both forms of cooperation are compatible with the unarticulated practices of a confederation.

Notes

1. J. Habermas, 'Democracy, Solidarity and the European Crisis', lecture on 26 April 2013 at Leuven University.
2. Ibid.
3. Ibid.
4. Ibid.
5. Ibid.
6. Before the Eurozone crisis, although still critical of the democratic deficit of the EU, Habermas had been more confident that 'a latent, rather Europe-friendly, mood predominates among the citizens of the member states, with the exception of Great Britain and the Scandinavian countries': J. Habermas, 'European Politics at an Impasse: A Plea for a Policy of Graduated Integration', in J. Habermas, *Europe: The Faltering Project* (Cambridge, 2009), 102, which was first published in 2008 in German. See also U. Beck, *German Europe* (Cambridge, 2013), for a similar approach from a sociological starting point.
7. J. Habermas, 'Democracy, Solidarity and the European Crisis'.
8. Ibid.
9. *Frankfurter Allgemeine Zeitung*, 3 August 2012.
10. Ibid.
11. Ibid.
12. Ibid.; J. Habermas, 'Democracy, Solidarity and the European Crisis', lecture on 26 April 2013 at Leuven University.
13. Ibid.
14. Ibid.
15. Ibid.
16. Ibid.
17. Ibid.
18. *Frankfurter Allgemeine Zeitung*, 3 August 2012.
19. J. Habermas, 'Democracy, Solidarity and the European Crisis', 26 April 2013.
20. Ibid.
21. Ibid.
22. Ibid.
23. Ibid. For Beck, *German Europe*, 80, 'Germany has undoubtedly profited political, morally and economically from Europe, from the euros and also from the crisis. Pressing for European political union is therefore very much in its interest.'
24. J. Habermas, 'New Perspectives for Europe', lecture at the Goethe University (Frankfurt), 21 September 2018. Beck, *German Europe*, 45–65, refers to Merkel as 'Merkiavelli', using 'hesitation as a means of coercion'.
25. S. Glendinning, 'Europe Should Reject Jürgen Habermas' Vision of a Federal European State', *EUROPP*, 3 September 2013.
26. Ibid.
27. Ibid.
28. Ibid. The references to 'dethronement' and 'particularisms' come from J. Habermas, 'Democracy, Solidarity and the European Crisis', lecture on 26 April 2013 at Leuven University. Habermas had pressed for an immediate solution to the European problem in the wake of the rejection of a European constitution and at the start of the financial crisis. See J. Habermas, 'An Avantgardistic

Instinct for Relevances: The Role of the Intellectual and the European Cause', in J. Habermas, *Europe: The Faltering Project*, 56: 'Others find my main current preoccupation, the future of Europe, abstract and boring. Why should we get worked up about such a tame issue? My answer is simple: if we don't succeed in making the key question of the *finalité*—the ultimate goal—of European unification into the topic of a European-wide referendum by the time the next European election comes around in 2009, then the neoliberal orthodoxy will have decided the future of the European Union.'

29. S. Glendinning, 'Europe Should Reject Jürgen Habermas' Vision of a Federal European State', EUROPP, 3 September 2013.
30. Ibid.
31. Ibid.
32. Ibid.
33. Ibid., citing John Stuart Mill.
34. Ibid.
35. E. B. Haas, 'The Study of Regional Integration: Reflections on the Joy and Anguish of Pretheorizing', in L. N. Lindberg and S. A. Scheingold (eds), *European Integration: Theory and Research* (Cambridge, MA, 1971), 18.
36. S. Fabbrini, *Federalism and Democracy in the European Union and the United States* (London, 2005); M. Burgess, *Comparative Federalism: Theory and Practice* (New York, 2006); P. King, *Federalism and Federation* (London, 1982); J. Pinder and R. Mayne, *Federal Union: The Pioneers* (Basingstoke, 1990); M. Forsyth, 'The Political Theory of Federalism: The Relevance of Classical Approaches', in J. J. Hesse and V. Wright (eds), *Federalizing Europe?* (Oxford, 1996); J. Bednar, *The Robust Federation* (Cambridge, 2008); J. H. Weiler, 'Federalism without Constitutionalism: Europe's Sonderweg', in K. Nicolaidis and R. Howse (eds), *The Federal Vision* (Oxford, 2001), 54–70.
37. M. Burgess, 'Federalism and Federation in Western Europe', in M. Burgess (ed.), *Federalism and Federation in Western Europe* (London, 1986), 18.
38. R. Harrison, *Europe in Question: Theories of Regional International Integration* (London, 1974), 44.
39. For David McKay, *Rush to Union: Understanding the European Federal Bargain* (Oxford, 1996), 40, the advent of the Cold War was the main reason that 'the conditions for a federal bargain were absent in the 1945–50 period'. He, too, though pays tribute to Milward's insight that twenty out of the twenty-six European nation-states had been annexed, occupied, or turned into satellite states between 1938 and 1940, creating a rupture in a European and global order of nation-states.
40. On the intersection of the two periods, see T. Milani, 'From Laissez-Faire to Supranational Planning: The Economic Debate within Federal Union, 1938–1945', *European Review of History*, 23 (2016), 664–85; T. Milani, 'Retreat from the Global? European Unity and British Progressive Intellectuals, 1930–45', *International History Review*, 42 (2019), 99–116.
41. A. Spinelli, 'The Growth of the European Movement since the Second World War', in M. Hodges (ed.), *European Integration* (London, 1972), 68.
42. W. Lipgens, *A History of European Integration, 1945–1947* (Oxford, 1987), 376. The UEM had 3000 members, largely drawn from political elites (including right-wingers).
43. J. Pinder, 'Federalism and the Beginnings of European Union', in K. Larres (ed.), *A Companion to Europe since 1945* (Oxford, 2009), 29.
44. W. Lipgens, *A History of European Integration*, 657–84.
45. On continuities in France, see R. Boyer, 'Les bureaux d'eetudes du ministere des Affaires étrangères et l'Europe pendant la Seconde Guerre mondiale', in R. Girault and G. Bossuat (eds), *Europe brisée, Europe retrouvée* (Paris, 1994), 133–52; on Belgium, see G. Duchenne, *Esquisses d'une Europe nouvelle. L'européisme dans la Belgique de l'entre-deux-guerres 1919–1939* (Brussels, 2008), 531–638.
46. R. Marjolin, 'What Type of Europe', in D. Brinkley and C. Hackett (eds), *Jean Monnet: The Path to European Unity* (Basingstoke, 1991), 172–3, extracted from Marjolin's memoirs, published in English in 1989.
47. Ibid., 172.
48. Ibid., 171.
49. Quoted in A. Adamthwaite, 'Sir Anthony Eden: Pro- or Anti-European? The Making of Britain's European Policies', in G. Bossuat (ed.), *Inventer l'Europe. Histoire nouvelle des groupes d'influence et des acteurs de l'unitee européenne* (Berne, 2003), 249.
50. Ibid.
51. Memorandum of the Italian delegation at the EDC talks, 9 October 1951, cited in D. Preda, 'De Gasperi, Spinelli et le project de communauté politique et européenne', in Bossuat (ed.), *Inventer l'Europe*, 343. R. T. Griffiths, 'Europe's First Constitution: The European Political Community', 1952–1954', in S. Martin (ed.), *The Construction of Europe* (Dordrecht, 1994), 19–39.
52. Adamthwaite, 'Eden', in Bossuat (ed.), *Inventer l'Europe*, 249.

424 EUROPEAN INTEGRATION SINCE THE 1920s

53. Cited in Loth, 'De Gaulle und Europa', *Historische Zeitschrift*, 253 (1991), 631.
54. Ibid., 640.
55. Ibid., 641.
56. Quoted in G. Bossuat, 'Les euro-socialistes de la SFIO: Réseaux et influences', in G. Bossuat (ed.), *Inventer l'Europe*, 422.
57. Preda, 'De Gasperi', in Bossuat (ed.), *Inventer l'Europe*, 344.
58. Quoted in Réau, 'Integration or Cooperation?', in Geppert (ed.), *Postwar Challenge*, 256. Also, G. H. Sootou, 'Georges Bidault et la construction européenne 1944-1954', *Revue d'histoire diplomatique*, 105 (1991), 269-72.
59. Ibid., 257, citing Debré's memoirs, published in 1984. More generally, E. Fursdon, *The European Defence Community* (London, 1980).
60. Eden in F. Duchêne, *Monnet*, 209; on resistance to federalism, see Bossuat, 'Les hauts fonctionnaires', *Journal of European Integration History*, 1 (1995), 100-1.
61. F. Duchêne, *Monnet*, 232.
62. Ibid., 262-3.
63. Bossuat, 'Les hauts fonctionnaires', *Journal of European Integration History*, 1 (1995), 102-4.
64. C. de Gaulle, quoted in J. Vanke, 'Charles de Gaulle's Uncertain Ideas of Europe', in D. Dinan (ed.), *Origins and Evolution of the European Union* (Oxford, 2006), 157. The account of the crisis in W. van Meurs, R. de Bruin, L. van de Grift, C. Hoetink, K. van Leeuwen, and C. Reijnen, *The Unfinished History of European Integration* (Amsterdam, 2013), 82-4, although quite balanced, is characteristic, presenting Hallstein's proposal as 'ambitious'. It met resistance because Hallstein did not 'proceed very tactically', putting the proposal to the European Parliament before the Council of Ministers, in contravention of previous practice. Arguably, the proposal was rejected by the French government because it brought up a fundamental question of governance.
65. J. Lambert, 'The Constitutional Crisis, 1965-1966', *Journal of Common Market Studies*, 4 (1966), 202; N. P. Ludlow, *The European Community and the Crises of the 1960s: Negotiating the Gaullist Challenge* (London, 2006), 65. In May 1966, de Gaulle told his government that the agricultural question 'was the whole question', 'in the background of all the debates and all the difficulties', but this was partly for a home audience, after the constitutional question had been resolved: A. Peyrefitte, *C'était de Gaulle* (Paris, 2000), vol. 3, 185.
66. M. Gilbert, *European Integration*, 98. J. P. J. White, 'Theory Guiding Practice: The Neofunctionalists and the Hallstein EEC Commission', *Journal of European Integration History*, 9 (2003), 111-31.
67. Quoted in J. Lambert, 'The Constitutional Crisis, 1965-1966', *Journal of Common Market Studies*, 4 (1966), 216.
68. R. Marjolin, *Architect of European Unity: Memoirs, 1911-1986* (London, 1989), 350.
69. For Marjolin's description of the failure of the Fouchet Plan, see R. Marjolin, *Le travail d'une vie*, 324-7.
70. C. de Gaulle to K. Adenauer, 20 May 1961, quoted in J. Vanke, 'Charles de Gaulle's Uncertain Ideas of Europe', in D. Dinan (ed.), *Origins and Evolution of the European Union*, 154.
71. L. Erhard, 7 July 1965, in L. van Middelaar, *The Passage to Europe: How a Continent Became a Union*, new edn (New Haven, CT, 2020), 59.
72. C. de Gaulle, 9 September 1965, quoted in D. W. Urwin, *The Community of Europe: A History of European Integration since 1945*, 2nd edn (London, 1995), 111.
73. M. Gilbert, *European Integration*, 102.
74. Extraordinary session of the Council, *Bulletin of the European Communities*, 3 (1966).
75. J. M. A. H. Luns, quoted in L. van Middelaar, *The Passage to Europe*, 61-2.
76. Andreas Donner and Pierre Pescatore, ibid., 63.
77. Ibid.
78. C. de Gaulle, 2 February 1966, in A. Peyrefitte, *C'était de Gaulle* (Paris, 1997), vol. 2, 620.
79. C. de Gaulle, *Mémoires d'espoir* (Paris, 1994), 792-3; D. W. Irvin, *The Community of Europe*, 112.
80. A. Peyrefitte, *C'était de Gaulle* (Paris, 2000), vol. 3, 183-5.
81. R. Marjolin, *Architect of European Unity*, 356.
82. Quoted in Mark Gilbert, *European Integration*, 111, whose excellent account forms the basis of this paragraph. See also the *Journal of European Integration History*, 9 (2003).
83. M. Gilbert, *European Integration*, 111.
84. Ibid.
85. Ibid., 146.
86. Ibid., 112.
87. E. Mourlon-Druol, 'Filling the EEC Leadership Vacuum? The Creation of the European Council in 1974', *Cold War History*, 10 (2010), 315-39.

88. A. Roth, *Heath and the Heathmen* (London, 1972), 5.
89. E. Heath, quoted in S. Wall, *Reluctant European: Britain and the European Union from 1945 to Brexit* (Oxford, 2020), 116.
90. Ibid.
91. R. Jenkins, 27 October 1977, in M. Gilbert, *European Integration*, 142.
92. Ibid. See also N. P. Ludlow, *Roy Jenkins and the European Commission Presidency, 1976–1980: At the Heart of Europe* (Basingstoke, 2016).
93. G. Ross, *Jacques Delors and European Integration*, 169.
94. P. de Boissieu, two weeks before the Maastricht summit, quoted in R. Tiersky, *François Mitterrand: A Very French President* (New York, 2000), 192.
95. Ibid.
96. J. Attali, *Verbatim* (Paris, 1993), vol. 1, 331. Luuk van Middelaar, *The Passage to Europe*, 186, points out, Delors had declared on French TV at this time that 'My objective is that before the end of the millennium Europe should have a true federation.'
97. J. Attali, *Verbatim*, vol. 1, 289.
98. J. Delors, *La France par l'Europe* (Paris, 1988), 178–9.
99. J. Attali, Verbatim, vol. 1, 299.
100. R. Tiersky, *François Mitterrand*, 193–4.
101. L. van Middelaar, *The Passage to Europe*, 191. Mitterrand was dismissive of both the Commission and European Parliament, asking Lubbers in the summer of 1991, during a visit to the Elysée, 'But what are you saying now? The Commission is zero, the Parliament is zero, and zero plus zero is zero.'
102. Quoted in P. Short, *Mitterrand: A Study in Ambiguity* (London, 2013), 516.
103. Ibid.
104. Article 8, Treaty on European Union (1992).
105. Article 17.1, Treaty of Amsterdam (1997).
106. In theory, the EU could have guaranteed the rights of British citizens of the European Union, but it was never likely to do so, given the complicated and fractious negotiations taking place and the real costs—healthcare, in particular—which this would have entailed for member states.
107. European Council, 'Solemn Declaration on European Union', *Bulletin of the European Communities*, 6 (1983), 25–9.
108. Ibid. Attempts to link European institutions to a European culture and identity were present from the start: see, above all, J. Krumrey, *The Symbolic Politics of European Integration: Staging Europe* (Basingstoke, 2018), which concentrates on the 1950s and examines European leaders' discussion of the diplomatic statute of the European Community, the nature of a European Parliament and the decision about where to locate institutions, presaging the idea of a 'capital of Europe'.
109. L. van Middelaar, *The Passage to Europe*, 193–4.
110. Ibid., 194–5.
111. Ibid., 195.
112. The argument counters that of Mark Gilbert, *European Integration*, 226, among others, who contends that 'The yearning for federalism died hard among the Union's leaders', with the European Council setting up a 'European Convention' at Laeken in December 2001 for this reason.
113. J. Fischer, 'From Confederacy to Federation—Thoughts on the Finality of European Integration', speech by Joschka Fischer at the Humboldt University in Berlin, 12 May 2000, 6, available at https://ec.europa.eu/.
114. Ibid., 7–8. Fischer's family had fled from Hungary just after the Second World War. According to A. Hyde-Price and C. Jeffery, 'Germany in the European Union: Constructing Normality', *Journal of Common Market Studies*, 39 (2001), 697–8, the Foreign Minister's stance was different from that of Schröder and Edmund Stoiber, the Minister-President of Bavaria and leader of the CSU, both of whom 'have expressly qualified the Eurovision held by Kohl'. See also A. Hyde-Price, *Germany and European Order: Enlarging NATO and the European Union* (Manchester, 2000); V. Handl and C. Jeffery, 'Germany and Europe after Kohl: Between Social Democracy and Normalization?', *German Studies Review*, 24 (2001), 55–82; S. Bulmer, C. Jeffery, and S. Padgett (eds), *Rethinking Germany and Europe: Democracy and Diplomacy in a Semi-Sovereign State* (Basingstoke, 2010); S. Bulmer and W. E. Paterson, 'Germany and the European Union: From "Tamed Power" to Normalized Power?', *International Affairs*, 86 (2010), 1051–73.
115. J. Fischer, 'From Confederacy to Federation', 12 May 2000, 8.
116. Ibid.
117. Ibid., 9.

118. Ibid., 10.
119. Ibid.
120. Ibid.
121. Ibid., 10–11.
122. Ibid., 11.
123. Ibid.
124. Ibid.
125. Ibid., 15.
126. Ibid.
127. Giscard already mentioned a 'Constitution for European citizens' in his 'Introductory Speech to the Convention on the Future of Europe', 19, Brussels, 26 February 2002, at http://european-convention.europa.eu/.
128. G. Amato, 'The Cautious Mandate to the 2002 Convention', in N. W. Barber, M. Cahill and R. Ekins (eds), *The Rise and Fall of the European Constitution* (London, 2019), 11.
129. Ibid., 11–12.
130. Ibid., 12.
131. Ibid.
132. Ibid.
133. J. M. Aznar, 'Address by the President of the European Council at the Inaugural Meeting of the Convention on the Future of Europe', 5, Brussels, 28 February 2002.
134. Ibid., 3–4.
135. Preamble of a 'Draft Treaty Establishing a Constitution for Europe', 3, at http://european-convention.europa.eu/.
136. The 'Protocol on the Role of National Parliaments in the European Union' and the 'Protocol on the Application of the Principles of Subsidiarity and Proportionality', ibid., 231, still gave the Commission the right to maintain its proposal, once a review had taken place. In other words, national parliaments had no veto.
137. Thomas Christiansen and Christine Reh, *Constitutionalizing the European Union* (Basingstoke, 2009), 62–4, argue that the Convention itself, for a variety of reasons, developed its own dynamic.
138. European Communities, *Treaty Establishing a Constitution for Europe* (Luxembourg, 2005), 23.
139. Ibid.
140. Ibid.
141. G. Amato, 'The Cautious Mandate to the 2002 Convention', in N. W. Barber, M. Cahill, and R. Ekins (eds), *The Rise and Fall of the European Constitution*, 13.
142. Ibid.
143. European Communities, *Treaty Establishing a Constitution for Europe*, 20.
144. G. Amato, 'The Cautious Mandate to the 2002 Convention', in N. W. Barber, M. Cahill, and R. Ekins (eds), *The Rise and Fall of the European Constitution*, 13–14.
145. Ibid., 13.
146. Ibid., 14.
147. Ibid. This argument counters those of Thomas Horsley, *The Court of Justice of the European Union as an Institutional Actor: Judicial Lawmaking and Its Limits* (Cambridge, 2018), which is one of the principal props of Perry Anderson's recent case in 'Ever Closer Union?' *London Review of Books*, 7 January 2021, vol. 43, 25–34. See also P. Lindseth, *Power and Legitimacy: Reconciling Europe and the Nation-State* (Oxford, 2010).
148. These are the so-called 'passerelles' or footbridges which would have allowed the European Council to change the treaty without an intergovernmental conference and ratification in member states, as was usual when treaties were amended: L. van Middelaar, *Passage to Europe*, 123–4.
149. G. Amato, 'The Cautious Mandate to the 2002 Convention', in N. W. Barber, M. Cahill, and R. Ekins (eds), *The Rise and Fall of the European Constitution*, 14.
150. Ibid., 15.
151. Even before the 'constitution' was put forward, Weiler had warned: 'This "constitutional" document could still be signed by its "high contracting parties" and sent for ratification in each of the 25 Member States in accordance with their constitutional requirements, just like any other treaty of significance. In such a case, Europe would not have a constitution but a constitutional Treaty.' See J. H. H. Weiler, 'A Constitution for Europe? Some Hard Choices', *Journal of Common Market Studies*, 40 (2002), 565. There were many factors working against the adoption of a constitution by a federal state in the making: enlargement, with which the constitution was commonly associated, seemed to have happened historically, whereas a constitution required

legal justification and legitimation; a European or federal *demos* did not exist; the notion of social solidarity and agreement about the nature of a welfare state, which could be subjected to European legislation, was decreasing, as basic principles were being questioned; and national constitutional and supreme courts did not recognize the ultimate primacy of the ECJ, as the actions of the *Bundesverfassungsgericht* had made plain.

152. G. Amato, 'The Cautious Mandate to the 2002 Convention', in N. W. Barber, M. Cahill, and R. Ekins (eds), *The Rise and Fall of the European Constitution*, 12.
153. Ibid.
154. Ibid., 12–13.
155. Ibid., 13.
156. Ibid., 12.
157. J. Chirac, 14 January 2003, in U. Krotz and J. Schild, *Shaping Europe: France, Germany and Embedded Bilateralism from the Elysée Treaty to Twenty-First Century Politics* (Oxford, 2013), 123.
158. S. Wall, *Reluctant European: Britain and the European Union from 1945 to Brexit* (Oxford, 2020), 249.
159. Ibid.
160. L. van Middelaar, *Passage to Europe*, 122.
161. Ibid., 197.
162. Quoted ibid., 121.
163. Ibid. Peter Hain, representing the UK government had told the Convention in late April 2003 that he would not sign the draft treaty if it left open the possibility of future revision of the constitutional treaty without unanimity.
164. Ibid., 122–3.
165. Ibid., 125.
166. Ibid.
167. A. Rawnsley, *The End of the Party* (London, 2010), 257–9.
168. S. Tierney, *Constitutional Referendums: The Theory and Practice of Republican Deliberation* (Oxford, 2012), 11.
169. Quoted in S. Wall, *Reluctant European*, 229.
170. Ibid., 242.
171. Ibid., 253.
172. T. Blair, *A Journey* (London, 2010), 501.
173. Ibid., 530.
174. Ibid.
175. Quoted in S. Wall, *Reluctant European*, 255.
176. V. Klaus, quoted in M. Gilbert, *European Integration*, 242.
177. L. van Middelaar, *Passage to Europe*, 116.
178. P. King, *Federalism and Federation* (London, 1982); M. Burgess (ed.), *Federalism and Federation in Western Europe* (London, 1986).
179. H. Brugmans, *Fundamentals of European Federalism* (London, 1948); C. J. Friedrich, *Trends in Federalism in Theory and Practice* (New York, 1968).
180. C. J. Friedrich, *Trends in Federalism*, 21; C. J. Friedrich, 'Federalism, Regionalism and Association', *European Journal of Political Research*, 2 (1974), 389.
181. A. Etzioni, *Political Unification: A Comparative Study of Leaders and Forces* (New York, 1965), 4. For a good summary, see B. Rosamond, *Theories of European Integration*, 23–31.
182. E. Haas, *The Uniting of Europe*, 3rd edn, xii. He went on to link federalism to a lack of confidence: 'The national ideologies of the ruling elites in 1950 were therefore far from ebullient, self-confident, assertive or hostile. On the contrary, national consciousness and the objective national situation combined to make desirable a search for policy alternatives that would guarantee security and welfare, peace and plenty without repeating the nationalist mistakes of an earlier generation of statesmen. The result was the drive for a united Europe—maximally by way of federal institutions, minimally through a tight network of intergovernmental organizations, and, after 1952, most consistently by way of supranational "communities" devoted to specific functional tasks with great indirect political importance' (xvii).
183. Ibid.
184. Respectively, R. Ladrech, 'Europeanization of Domestic Politics and Institutions: The Case of France,' *Journal of Common Market Studies*, 32 (1994), 70; and S. Bartolini, T. Risse, and B. Strnth, 'Between Europe and the Nation-State: The Reshaping of Interests, Identities and Political Representation' (Florence, 1999), 2, at http://www.iue.it/. There are many definitions.

428 EUROPEAN INTEGRATION SINCE THE 1920S

See, for instance, P. Graziano and M. P. Vink (eds), *Europeanization: New Research Agendas* (Basingstoke, 2007), 7: 'we thus understand Europeanization very broadly as the *domestic adaptation to European regional integration*'.

185. See, for instance, T. Christiansen and C. Reh, *Constitutionalizing the European Union*, 52–4: the purpose of such works on 'constitutionalization' is to distance such processes, as a normative good, from a federal finality. For an analysis of the primacy of the political in federalism, see C. Pentland, *International Theory and European Integration* (London, 1973).

186. S. Hix, 'CP, IR and the EU! A Rejoinder to Hurrell and Menon', *West European Politics*, 19 (1996), 804; S. Hix, 'The Study of the European Community: The Challenge to Comparative Politics', *West European Politics*, 17 (1994), 1–30. For a more recent use of such concepts, see S. Hix, *What's Wrong with the European Union and How to Fix It* (Cambridge, 2008).

187. S. Hix, 'The Study of the European Community: The Challenge to Comparative Politics', *West European Politics*, 17 (1994), 1. J. Caporaso and A. Stone Sweet, 'Conclusion: Institutional Logics of European Integration', in A. Stone Sweet, W. Sandholtz, and N. Fligstein (eds), *The Institutionalization of Europe* (Oxford, 2001), 222–3, contend that 'we strongly reject the view that Europe or regional integration are somehow *sui generis* objects of inquiry', but they go on to admit that 'the Europe of the past half-century is treated as providing social scientists with rich opportunities for evaluating propositions about how new political systems emerge and evolve'. The main points of comparison for political scientists, however, are existing liberal democracies.

188. J. G. March and J. P. Olsen, *Rediscovering Institutions: The Organizational Basis of Politics* (New York, 1989), 16.

189. Ibid., 17; J. G. March and J. P. Olsen, 'The New Institutionalism: Organizational Factors in Political Life', *American Political Science Review*, 78 (1984), 734–49; P. Hall and R. C. R. Taylor, 'Political Science and the Three New Institutionalisms', *Political Studies*, 44 (1996), 948.

190. P. Hall, *Governing the Economy: The Politics of State Intervention in Britain and France* (Cambridge, 1986), 19.

191. See, especially, K. A. Armstrong and S. Bulmer, *The Governance of the Single European Market* (Manchester 1998); K. A. Armstrong, 'Regulating the Free Movement of Goods: Institutions and Institutional Change', in J. Shaw and G. More (eds), *New Legal Dynamics of European Union* (Oxford, 1995), 164–91; S. Bulmer, 'The Governance of the European Union: A New Institutionalist Approach', *Journal of Public Policy*, 13 (1993), 351–80.

192. For an example of an essay going beyond internal consideration of institutions to the legal and inter-institutional context, see N. Fligstein and J. McNichol, 'The Institutional Terrain of the European Union', in W. Sandholtz and A. Stone Sweet (eds), *European Integration and Supranational Governance* (Oxford, 1998), 59–91.

193. J. Lindner and B. Rittberger, 'The Creation, Interpretation and Contestation of Institutions: Revisiting Historical Institutionalism', *Journal of Common Market Studies*, 41 (2003), 445–73; M. Jachtenfuchs, *Die Konstruktion Europas. Verfassungsideen und institutionelle Entwicklung* (Baden-Baden, 2002); M. Jachtenfuchs, T. Diez, and S. Jung, 'Which Europe? Conflicting Models of a Legitimate European Political Order', *European Journal of International Relations*, 4 (1998), 409–45. Alec Stone Sweet, Wayne Sandholtz, and Neil Fligstein (eds), *The Institutionalization of Europe*, 2–3, try to explain 'why law-making competences tended to migrate, from the national towards the EC level, faster and further in some policy domains than others' in accordance with two logics: first, 'rising levels of cross-national exchange', pressuring 'public authorities to develop modes of supranational governance' and undermining national modes of governance, with actors engaged in transnational exchange working 'to eliminate national barriers to their activities'; and, second, 'these and other actors, such as individuals and interest groups interested in policy reform more generally, would lobby in national political arenas, putting pressure on governments to design or support the expansion of European policies in EU policy domains'. In addition, EU institutions have developed their own momentum, with the EU becoming a 'powerful regulatory state' (16–17). See also W. Sandholtz and A. Stone Sweet (eds), *European Integration and Supranational Governance* (Oxford, 1998).

194. J. Jenson and F. Mérand, 'Sociology, Institutionalism and the European Union', *Comparative European Politics*, 8 (2010), 85–6.

195. Political scientists are aware of the wider field of relations in which EU institutions operate, of course. Thus, Thomas Christiansen, 'Tensions of European Governance: Politicized Bureaucracy and Multiple Accountability in the European Commission', *Journal of European Public Policy*, 4 (1997), 73–90, investigates the conflicting accountability of the Commission to member states and to European citizens, but he examines national influence, for example via commissioners,

within the Commission rather than relations between member states, COREPER, the European Council and the Commission.

196. D. J. Puchala, 'Of Blind Men, Elephants and International Integration', *Journal of Common Market Studies*, 10 (1971), 267–84.
197. Ibid., 277.
198. Ibid., 278–9.
199. Ibid., 280.
200. Ibid., 281.
201. Ibid., 282.
202. Ibid., 282–3.
203. J. Richardson, 'Policy-making in the EU: Interests, Ideas and Garbage Cans of Primeval Soup', in J. Richardson (ed.), *European Union: Power and Policy-making* (London, 1996), 5.
204. J. Richardson, 'Policy-Making in the EU: Familiar Ambitions in Unfamiliar Settings?', in A. Menon and V. Wright (eds), *From the Nation-State to Europe* (Oxford, 2001), 97: 'The most distinctive feature (and probably the most ignored) of the European Union is the absence of a recognizable government. Thus, European *governance*, rather than government, is clearly the most appropriate label for a system of policy-making which displays a considerable diffusion of power'.
205. G. Marks, L. Hooghe, and K. Blank, 'European Integration from the 1980s: State-centric vs. Multi-level Governance', *Journal of Common Market Studies*, 34 (1996), 346.
206. Ibid.
207. Ibid. On policy networks, see J. Peterson, 'Decision-making in the European Union: Towards a Framework for Analysis', *Journal of European Public Policy*, 2 (1995), 69–93; J. Peterson, 'Policy Networks and European Union Policy-making: A Reply to Kassim', *West European Politics*, 18 (1995), 389–407; H. Kassim, 'Policy Networks and European Union Policy-making: A Sceptical View', *West European Politics*, 17 (1994), 15–27.
208. G. Marks, L. Hooghe, and K. Blank, 'European Integration from the 1980s: State-centric vs. Multi-level Governance', *Journal of Common Market Studies*, 34 (1996), 347.
209. Ibid., citing A. Moravcsik, 'Why the European Community Strengthens the State: Domestic Politics and International Cooperation', a talk given to the American Political Science Association on 1–4 September 2004 in New York.
210. A. Milward and V. Sørensen, 'Interdependence or Integration? A National Choice', in A. Milward, R. Ranieri, F. Romero, and V. Sørensen (eds), *The Frontier of National Sovereignty: History and Theory, 1945–1992* (London, 1993), 19.
211. G. Marks, L. Hooghe, and K. Blank, 'European Integration from the 1980s: State-centric vs. Multi-level Governance', *Journal of Common Market Studies*, 34 (1996), 349.
212. Ibid., 350: here 'majoritarian principles of decision-making are confined to symbolic issues'.
213. Ibid., 351.
214. Ibid., 352.
215. Ibid., 355.
216. T. Risse-Kappen, 'Exploring the Nature of the Beast: International Relations Theory and Comparative Policy Analysis Meet the European Union', *Journal of Common Market Studies*, 34 (1996), 59.
217. Ibid., 66, 68.
218. R. Bellamy and D. Castiglione, 'Legitimizing the Euro-"Polity" and Its "Regime"', *European Journal of Political Theory*, 2 (2003), 8–11.
219. Ibid., 10–11.
220. Ibid., 11.
221. Ibid., 21.
222. Ibid., 27.
223. Ibid., 28.
224. R. Bellamy and D. Castiglione, 'Three Models of Democracy, Political Community and Representation in the EU', *Journal of European Public Policy*, 20 (2013), 220. On the absence of a 'European public', see R. Bellamy and D. Castiglione, 'Democracy by Delegation? Who Represents Whom and How in European Governance', *Government and Opposition*, 46 (2011), 101–25.
225. R. Bellamy and D. Castiglione, 'Lacroix's European Constitutional Patriotism: A Response', *Political Studies*, 52 (2004), 190.
226. R. Bellamy and D. Castiglione, 'Three Models of Democracy, Political Community and Representation in the EU', *Journal of European Public Policy*, 20 (2013), 215.

430 EUROPEAN INTEGRATION SINCE THE 1920s

227. R. Bellamy and D. Castiglione, 'Legitimizing the Euro-"Polity" and Its "Regime"', *European Journal of Political Theory*, 2 (2003), 16.
228. A. Moravcsik, 'Preferences and Power in the European Community: A Liberal Intergovernmentalist Approach', *Journal of Common Market Studies*, 31 (1993), 474.
229. Ibid., 477.
230. Ibid.
231. Ibid., 479.
232. Ibid., 483.
233. Ibid., 481.
234. A. Moravcsik, 'Integrating International and Domestic Theories of International Bargaining', in P. B. Evans, H. K. Jacobsen, and R. D. Putnam (eds), *International Bargaining and Domestic Politics: Double-Edged Diplomacy* (London, 1993), 15; R. D. Putnam, 'Diplomacy and Domestic Politics: The Logic of Two-level Games', in P. B. Evans, H. K. Jacobsen, and R. D. Putnam (eds), *International Bargaining and Domestic Politics: Double-Edged Diplomacy* (London, 1993), 431–68.
235. A. Moravcsik, 'Preferences and Power in the European Community: A Liberal Intergovernmentalist Approach', *Journal of Common Market Studies*, 31 (1993), 485.
236. Ibid., 480–2.
237. A. Moravcsik, *The Choice for Europe*, 60–2.
238. Ibid., 63.
239. A. Moravcsik, 'Preferences and Power in the European Community: A Liberal Intergovernmentalist Approach', *Journal of Common Market Studies*, 31 (1993), 488. In addition to *The Choice for Europe*, which focuses above all on the Single European Act and negotiation of the Maastricht Treaty, see A. Moravcsik, 'Negotiating the Single European Act: National Interests and Conventional Statecraft in the European Community', *International Organization*, 45 (1991), 19–56.
240. A. Moravcsik, 'Preferences and Power in the European Community: A Liberal Intergovernmentalist Approach', *Journal of Common Market Studies*, 31 (1993), 494.
241. Ibid., 494–5.
242. See, Daniel Wincott, 'Institutional Interaction and European Integration: Towards an Everyday Critique of Liberal Intergovernmentalism', *Journal of Common Market Studies*, 33 (1995), 607, to which Moravcsik replied in 'Liberal Intergovernmentalism and Integration: A Rejoinder', *Journal of Common Market Studies*, 33 (1995), 611–28. See also A. Moravcsik, 'A New Statecraft? Supranational Entrepreneurs and International Cooperation', *International Organization*, 53 (1999), 267–306; O. R. Young, 'Comment on "A New Statecraft?"', *Journal of Common Market Studies*, 805–9; A. Moravcsik, 'Theory and Method in the Study of International Negotiation: A Rejoinder to Oran Young', *Journal of Common Market Studies*, 811–14. On multilevel government in this context, see D. L. Smith and J. L. Ray, 'The 1992 Project', in D. L. Smith and J. L. Ray (eds), *The 1992 Project and the Future of Integration in Europe* (New York, 1993), 8–9.
243. This is not to claim that Moravcsik ignores other spheres of policy-making—as his critique of Sebastian Rosato, *Europe United: Power Politics and the Making of the European Community* (Ithaca, NY, 2011) makes plain—rather that the relationship between decisions in different spheres is left open. A. Moravcsik, 'Did Power Politics Cause European Integration? Realist Theory Meets Qualitative Methods', *Security Studies*, 22 (2013), 775–6: 'Few deny that geopolitics has had some impact on integration, especially in the 1950s. The leading undergraduate textbook on European integration correctly reflects the broad scholarly agreement that in establishing the European Coal and Steel Community (ESCS), France had to find a solution against the USSR (mediated in part by the United States) and fear of German power. I know of no major account of the EDC—after all, a military alliance—that denies that it was proposed to accommodate German rearmament within the imperatives of Western alliance policies against the USSR. Even the European Economic Community (EEC), an economic arrangement, has customarily been explained in part as an instrument in German Chancellor Konrad Adenauer's strategy of embedding Germany within the West and preventing war between France and Germany, thereby strengthening the Western alliance.... In the *Choice for Europe*, I tested economic and geopolitical factors against each other, concluding that in nearly half (seven of fifteen) of national negotiating involvements, geopolitical and related ideological factors had an important impact, and in three cases—including German policy in the EEC negotiations, the only case where my work overlaps with Rosato's—they fundamentally altered the outcome.'

244. J. T. Checkel and A. Moravcsik, 'A Constructivist Research Program in European Studies?', *European Union Politics*, 2 (2001), 219–49: Moravcsik's concern to put forward 'testable' hypotheses makes it difficult to account for wider sets of motivations and to examine the relationship between ideas and actions. See also A. Moravcsik, 'Is Something Rotten in the State of Denmark? Constructivism and European Integration', *Journal of European Public Policy*, 6 (1999), 669–81.

245. R. Bellamy and D. Castiglione, 'Legitimizing the Euro-"Polity" and Its "Regime"', *European Journal of Political Theory*, 2 (2003), 8; R. Bellamy and D. Castiglione, 'Three Models of Democracy, Political Community and Representation in the EU', *Journal of European Public Policy*, 20 (2013), 212.

246. A. Moravcsik, 'Preferences, Power and Institutions in 21st-century Europe', *Journal of Common Market Studies*, 56 (2018), 1654. His reference to this topic in *Choice for Europe*, 67–8, does not mention 'regime theory' as such, but does discuss the pooling and delegation of sovereignty.

247. A. Moravcsik, *Choice for Europe*, 67.

248. A. Moravcsik, 'Preferences, Power and Institutions in 21st-century Europe', *Journal of Common Market Studies*, 56 (2018), 1655.

249. Ibid., 1654.

250. A. Moravcsik, 'In Defence of the "Democratic Deficit": Reassessing Legitimacy in the European Union', *Journal of Common Market Studies*, 40 (2002), 606–7.

251. Ibid., 607.

252. Ibid., 607, 615: none of the most important political issues according to opinion polls—health, education, law and order, welfare and taxation—are 'primarily an EU competence'.

253. Ibid., 608–9.

254. Ibid., 609.

255. Ibid., 610.

256. Ibid.

257. Ibid., 613. See also G. Majone (ed.), *Regulating Europe* (London, 1996) and G. Majone, 'Europe's Democratic Deficit', *European Law Journal*, 4 (1998), 5–28.

258. A. Moravcsik, 'In Defence of the "Democratic Deficit": Reassessing Legitimacy in the European Union', *Journal of Common Market Studies*, 40 (2002), 613.

259. Ibid., 610.

260. Ibid., 612.

261. Ibid. A. Moravcsik, *The Choice for Europe*, 13: the volume seeks to take 'a first step' in the direction of providing 'a reliable "social history" of European integration'.

262. C. J. Bickerton, D. Hodson, and U. Puetter, 'The New Intergovernmentalism: European Integration in the Post-Maastricht Era', *Journal of Common Market Studies*, 53 (2015), 716, 708.

263. Ibid., 703.

264. Ibid., 703–5.

265. C. J. Bickerton, 'A Union of Member States', in C. J. Bickerton, D. Hodson, and U. Puetter (eds), *The New Intergovernmentalism: States and Supranational Actors in the Post-Maastricht Era* (Oxford, 2015), 54–9. See also C. J. Bickerton, *European Integration: From Nation States to Member States* (Oxford, 2012).

266. F. Schimmelfennig, 'What's the News in "New Intergovernmentalism"? A Critique of Bickerton, Hodson and Puetter', *Journal of Common Market Studies*, 53 (2015), 723–30; S. Bulmer, 'Understanding the New Intergovernmentalism: Pre- and Post-Maastricht in EU Studies', in C. J. Bickerton, D. Hodson, and U. Puetter (eds), *The New Intergovernmentalism*, 289–304.

267. F. Schimmelfennig, 'What's the News in "New Intergovernmentalism"? A Critique of Bickerton, Hodson and Puetter', *Journal of Common Market Studies*, 53 (2015), 725–6.

268. C. J. Bickerton, D. Hodson, and U. Puetter, 'The New Intergovernmentalism: European Integration in the Post-Maastricht Era', *Journal of Common Market Studies*, 53 (2015), 707.

269. M. Forsyth, *A Union of States*, 7.

270. Ibid., 15.

271. Ibid., 15–16.

272. Ibid., 184.

273. Ibid., 184.

274. Ibid., 184–5.

275. Ibid., 185.

276. Ibid., 185–6.

432 EUROPEAN INTEGRATION SINCE THE 1920s

277. Ibid., 186.
278. Ibid.
279. Ibid., 5.
280. Ibid.
281. Integration has, therefore, become more 'differentiated': for further literature on this topic, see F. Schimmelfennig and T. Winzen, *Ever Looser Union? Differentiated European Integration* (Oxford, 2020).

Conclusion

What difference does a history of European integration make to our understanding of contemporary events? This study seeks to make the case, along with other historical works, for an analysis of overlapping processes of integration over a broader terrain and longer period than those usually considered by political scientists and specialists of international relations. It argues that the conditions pushing policy-makers towards cooperation in Europe during the 1920s, issuing in the 'Locarno system' and informing Briand's attempt to create an intergovernmental 'United States of Europe', persisted during the post-war era. The need to cooperate economically, to compete with extra-European powers and to prevent national antagonisms on the continent spilling over into war had been widely recognized in the aftermath of both the First and Second World Wars. Faced with the prospect of economic dislocation and decline, ideological conflict and dictatorship, international crises and industrialized warfare, ministers, officials, politicians, intellectuals, and publicists considered European solutions to intimidating, new problems at the same time as conducting domestic experiments (democratization, state intervention, welfare, economic planning, and redistributive taxation), reaching bilateral or multilateral agreements (the Locarno Treaty, the Franco-German trade treaty of 1927, the International Steel Cartel, the Marshall Plan, GATT, and Bretton Woods) and participating in international organizations (the League of Nations, UN, NATO, and OEEC). The Cold War at once underlined the significance of such long-standing challenges and altered governments' priorities, as military defence against a single ideological foe became uppermost and forced states to accept the tutelage of a superpower.[1] European cooperation after 1945 was interwoven with—and often subordinate to—these wider sets of events.

Notwithstanding the scale of the domestic challenges facing post-war governments and their need to adapt to a bi-polar global order, a common mythology of 'Europe', popularized during the interwar and post-war eras, remains central to an understanding of integration.[2] In limited spheres, governments were able to justify a transfer of powers, competencies or sovereignty to European—rather than multilateral or international—institutions.[3] Although leaders and intellectuals failed to agree on the necessity and form of a European polity, on appropriate spheres of activity for European institutions and on the territorial extent of Europe, they nonetheless found it easier to imagine and to set up supranational European organizations than other regional or global ones. Such 'integration'—a

---

European Integration since the 1920s: Security, Identity, and Cooperation. Mark Hewitson, Oxford University Press.
© Mark Hewitson 2024. DOI: 10.1093/oso/9780198915942.003.0010

434   EUROPEAN INTEGRATION SINCE THE 1920s

term coined by American Marshall planners in the late 1940s as a vaguer analogue of 'union'—might have been possible in the 1920s, as an outgrowth of Franco-German reconciliation; it found echoes in Churchill's eve-of-defeat offer of a Franco-British Union, partly based on a draft by Monnet and Pleven, to the ministry of Paul Reynaud on 16 June 1940; and it came into being with the signing of the Treaty of Paris, founding the European Coal and Steel Community in 1951.[4] It rested less on convergence between European states, whose economic, social, cultural, and political differences had been exacerbated by the national and ideological conflicts of the interwar and war years, than on a shared sense of a common European plight and set of needs.[5] Convergence has become more important over time, as the competencies of European institutions have increased and citizens have become more active participants in European politics.[6]

Leaders' and citizens' feelings about and perceptions of 'Europe' proved to be durable, but they were also defensive and unstable, linked to a series of crises which threatened to reawaken national rivalries and conflicts, as seemed to be the case in respect of the German question (the Saarland, partition, eastern borders, rearmament, and industrial 'hegemony'), or which risked subsuming Europe altogether, as in the struggle against Communism during the onset of the Cold War.[7] 'Without Stalin and his aggressive policies, without the threat with which he confronted the free world, the Atlantic Alliance would never have been born and the movement for European unity, embracing Germany as an integral part, would never have had the astonishing success which it has in fact enjoyed,' wrote Paul-Henri Spaak in his memoirs, at once tying 'Europeanism' to 'Atlanticism' and revealing their precariousness, at least in the immediate post-war era.[8] 'Europeanism', or an affiliation with Europe resting on a putatively common set of values or interests, was often subordinate, in the minds of opinion- and decision-makers, to national interests and, in the realm of foreign policy and defence, to other international commitments. In the discussion and negotiation of a European Defence Community, contemporaries were able to witness the rapid re-surfacing of anti-German sentiment, disagreements about the emerging global order—with Anthony Eden only agreeing to station British troops in Germany under the aegis of NATO—and a demonstration of the primacy of allegiance to the United States, as the fears and enmities of the Cold War worsened.[9]

While it is true that national interests and international commitments some-times coincided with European integration, they were not bound to do so, as could be seen during acts of national self-assertion—for instance, the UK's opposition to 'federalism' in 1949–51 and 1955–58 or France's precipitation of the 'empty chair crisis' between June 1965 and January 1966—and during periods of international crisis, whether the unpredictable corollary of de-colonization (the partition of India, the Suez crisis in 1956, the Algerian War) or the Cold War (the Berlin blockade in 1948–49, the Korean War, Soviet intervention in the GDR in 1953 and

CONCLUSION 435

Hungary in 1956, or the second Berlin crisis of 1958).[10] At such moments, it was not clear whether national and international crises would also become crises of European integration, in Ludger Kühnhardt's sense.[11] Certainly, a limited, hard-fought *acquis communautaire* in the areas of coal and steel production, nuclear power and the regulation and running of a common market seemed insecure and reversible until the 1960s, at the earliest, in the face of the global and domestic conflicts which had helped to foster integration in the first place. Most of the conditions which had complicated attempts at European cooperation in the 1920s—the changing policies of the United States and the menace of US isolationism, Soviet expansionism, and the strength of home-grown Communism, the Janus-faced nature of the Franco-German relationship, the uncertain role of European states in the world, and the unpredictable consequences of nationalism, imperialism, and world war—remained in place in the late 1940s and 1950s.

Historians of European integration usually begin in 1945, or 1939, with defeat or a supposed 'zero hour', signalling the reconstruction of European states and economies.[12] Yet it could be contended that they overstate the significance of the rupture and pay undue attention to economic reconstruction, overlooking the fact that a government like that of Belgium accepted minimal direct assistance from the European Recovery Program (Marshall Aid) and that even German industry had retained much of its plant, its large companies and their detailed plans for the post-war era.[13] Similarly, state bureaucracies, although purged of high-level 'collaborators', remained more or less intact, as the transition from the Third Republic via the Vichy regime to the Fourth Republic demonstrated.[14] Many agencies and cadres of the state did not collapse, and returning or re-emerging political elites and parties were quick to dispel fears of a potential power vacuum. Consequently, officials', politicians', and ministers' priorities were not merely dictated by frequent emergencies; they were also characterized by a historical understanding of the crises of the interwar era, which they had been able to reflect upon in internal or external exile.[15] Policy-makers were not simply motivated by the need to restore the nation-state and rebuild economies, as the foundation of future welfare states; they were guided by longer-standing concerns, such as a desire to strengthen Europe against extra-European powers, to compensate for or halt the loss of empire, to reverse 'decline', to escape the worst effects of nationalism, to stop the spread of Communism, and to prevent a lapse or relapse into dictatorship, as had occurred in Greece, Spain, and Portugal.[16] As Gerhard Schröder noted in 2006, 'European integration is reliable.'[17] 'All members of the union have profited from it. Neither Spain nor Portugal, Ireland nor Greece would be in a similarly positive economic and social position today without the European Union.' He went on: 'The European way is a history of success—partly because it is proof that a common economic area, in which national prejudices are overcome and national sovereign rights are subordinated, is a path towards peace.'[18] Economics and foreign policy seemed to have had mutually beneficial effects within a European polity.

436   EUROPEAN INTEGRATION SINCE THE 1920s

All such problems were connected to persuasive narratives about Europe. They ought to be addressed, it appeared to many leaders in the 1920s and in the 1940s and 1950s, on a European or international level. In this respect, the decision-makers and commentators of the interwar and post-war eras were not as different as they might seem, in spite of the existence of influential advocates of supra-national institutions within continental administrations after 1945, but not beforehand.[19] The most important decisions in both periods were taken, as Milward rightly suggests, by governments pursuing national interests, but how were such interests defined and how far could they be achieved through the cooperation of European states? External security was fundamental for leaders and voters alike, but it was difficult to overcome historical antagonisms and coordinate activities in this area without the intercession of the United States. As a consequence, governments tended to favour various forms of economic inte-gration, which were relatively uncontroversial at home and abroad, and to rule out political integration, or the delegation of sovereignty to new institutions, not only in the spheres of diplomacy and defence, but also in other areas of government, including social policy, education, and law and order, which were barely discussed.[20] Although economic integration proved more straightforward than political integration, it continued to depend on foreign policy and domestic politics.[21] European leaders wanted to cooperate economically in the interwar and post-war periods, but they failed in the 1920s and early 1930s and succeeded in the 1950s, in part, because the *pax americana* which came into being after 1945 was more stable and more consistently enforced than the Versailles Peace Treaty and, in part, because the Weimar Republic—one of the parties in the pivotal Franco-German relationship—succumbed to dictatorship, whereas the Federal Republic of Germany and the Fourth Republic did not.[22] As a result of such changing conditions, it seemed, at various junctures, that the choice for Europe was highly uncertain.

Cold War Europe

As Tony Judt has indicated, the European Community was created in a 'special context' after 1945.[23] Notwithstanding the continuity of European leaders' eco-nomic goals, the international environment in which they worked had been transformed. The unexpected onset of the Cold War and the emergence of two global superpowers allowed the integration of West Germany into Western Europe, against a backdrop of memory loss—or a willingness on the part of citizens to 'put recent history behind them'—in Italy, France, Belgium, and the Netherlands, as well as Germany.[24] It also encouraged them to ally with each other and with the United States in order to deter the Soviet Union. State intervention and economic planning during the Second World War helped to convince contemporaries that they could pool economic control, at least in part, in a 'multinational authority'; the disastrous economic history of the 1930s and 1940s combined with pent-up, post-war demand to make special measures, including European cooperation, appear necessary or acceptable to different political constituencies; and the defeat of a majority of states in Europe made most populations wary of military spending or adventure.[25] 'These were unrepeatable, one-time transformations,' writes Judt: 'That is to say, Western Europe will probably never again have to catch up on thirty years of economic stagnation or half a century of agrarian depression or rebuild after a disastrous war', aided by the United States in the unprecedented context of the Cold War.[26]

Adenauer was quicker—in January 1948—than many of his compatriots to realize that the 'saving of Europe' was only achievable 'via the USA'.[27] For about one hundred years, 'great changes have occurred in Europe and on the earth in its entirety,' wrote the West German Chancellor in his memoirs, published in 1966: 'Europe, which still gave the whole world its direction before the First World War, was torn apart. This continent was economically and politically so powerless that it would have been extraordinarily endangered after the end of the war without the help of the United States.'[28] By the 1950s, Adenauer's position had become orthodox. Likewise, in Italy, the Christian Democrats turned themselves into a pro-American party, on the right side against the Communists in the Cold War.[29] Other countries followed suit. In the Netherlands, as elsewhere, the population was largely preoccupied with the 'Herculean task' of 'the reconstruction of a devastated and plundered land' and 'a fundamental change in the political and economic relations with the Dutch East Indies', in the words of Jan van den Brink, the Minister of Economic Affairs in the Drees-van Schaik government (1948–51).[30] Confronted by the prospect of a plan for 'little Europe' in the form of the Schuman Plan for the ECSC, the cabinet was divided between proponents of the 'Germany memorandum', presented in 1949 by Max Kohnstamm of the Ministry of Foreign Affairs, which argued that the recovery of the Netherlands depended on German reconstruction in Western Europe, and 'Atlanticists' who feared that the plan ran counter to the interests of the United States and the UK.[31] In the event, Washington itself was changing position from that outlined by Chip Bohlen of the US State Department in October 1949—'The French ... feel that while we are still giving lip-service to ... the general unification of Europe, in reality, we are as a matter of basic policy envisaging future developments more along the lines of Anglo-American partnership, with the continent ... as a sort of junior partner'—to that settled on by Dean Acheson, the Secretary of State, at around the same time: 'Recent trends suggest that the most likely tight grouping of the character we have in mind would be a continental union including France, Italy, Belgium, Western Germany and possibly the Netherlands.'[32] During the Korean War (1950–54), this American policy of German and Western European reconstruction within a 'continental union', as one of the cornerstones of a 'Western' economic bloc, was believed to complement a US-led alliance structure, which had the North Atlantic Treaty Organization at its core. It was vital for European states, given their reliance on the United States, that economics and European cooperation, on the one hand, and security during the early Cold War, on the other, were believed to be complementary by successive American administrations.

European institutions were set up in such circumstances. Federalism failed under these conditions. Spaak, who had been inspired by Bevin's speech in the House of Commons on 22 January 1948 ('never before had Britain been so outspoken in proclaiming its readiness to help promote the unity of Western Europe, nor has it ever shown such courage since'), was surprised by the subsequent caution of the British and French proposals, prior to the signature of the Treaty of Brussels on 4 March 1948.[33] The first argument of the proposals warned that 'Nothing must be done to irritate or worry the USSR', with a call to emphasize the 'German threat' instead.[34] The second argument 'was even more unexpected', prohibiting 'a premature conclusion of a multilateral defence agreement, for, we were told, the Americans might use this as a pretext for assuming that the security of Europe was assured and, consequently, for withdrawing their troops'.[35] Security and economics were connected, not least because the United States was only 'ready to play an active part in the defence of Europe on condition that Germany's resources, including its manpower, were used', yet its insistence 'troubled a great many consciences', especially in France, where 'memories of the war, the invasion, the defeat and the occupation were still fresh'.[36] The rapid drafting of the Pleven Plan, which 'called for the creation of a European army geared to the political institutions of a united Europe', 'was but an emotional reaction to the idea that a German army might emerge' under American auspices, in Spaak's opinion.[37] Its failure, with Pierre Mendès France's disappointing and anger-inducing decision not to ratify the treaty to establish a European Defence Community, demonstrated the inability of Europeans to coordinate their own defence policy and to defend themselves.[38]

The United States, which had supported the EDC, and the UK and France, which—in the end—had not, proved reluctant to relinquish control of diplomatic and military matters.[39] For a similar reason, they thwarted federalists' 'offensive' in the second session of the Council of Europe to create 'supranational authorities' and to build what one opposing British Labour MP termed a 'united Europe'.[40] 'The British were not only outspoken, they were united', continued Spaak, who 'had hoped too fervently for Britain's participation to give up easily so long as there seemed the slightest chance of its realization': 'there was no difference in this respect between Conservative and Labour', with Macmillan—who came into office in the second Churchill government on 26 October 1951—spelling out his rejection of 'the very notion of supra-nationality'.[41] What London preferred, instead of the 'legislative approach' of federalists, was 'what they called the

CONCLUSION   439

"functional approach".'.[42] 'Their idea was that a united Europe should be created by solving one by one the practical problems of the moment', advising 'those who wish to take the federal path [to] do so by all means', the former Belgian Prime Minister went on: '"We [the British], for our part, have no intention of following their example, though we do see their point of view." Thus, the idea of a "Little Europe" took shape, comprising France, Germany, Italy, and the Benelux countries.'[43] To Spaak's 'cruel...disillusionment', Churchill—whose Zurich speech had kept alive the hope that he was a federalist—adopted the same position once back in office: Europe would not only be 'little', but also economic and incremental.[44]

Historical mistrust between governments and populations after the Second World War militated against the establishment of a European federation. Monnet explained to Sir Roger Makins at the British Foreign Office in May 1950 that the UK was 'not wanted', if it was 'not prepared to accept the principle of a Federal Europe', but he was in no position to impose a federal blueprint on European governments.[45] Instead, the French head of planning agreed with Spaak that the failure of the EDC and European Political Community in 1954 had been a 'disaster', which had overloaded the European army proposal with a 'top-heavy' political 'superstructure' (in Paul van Zeeland's words), and he agreed to do something more limited 'in the economic field'.[46] Monnet intended—in the opinion of one British official—to create a 'nucleus around which a new Europe could be built'.[47] The idea was shared by other federalists such as Hallstein, who aimed 'to take Europe to economic union, then to political union', with the connections between trade policy, foreign policy, and defence eventually leading to unification in these spheres, too, and issuing—in Marjolin's summary of Hallstein's objectives—in 'a European federation, or as others would name it, the United States of Europe'.[48]

Such flights of fancy have distracted many scholars. Marjolin's point was that 'nationality', habits of thought, and historical enmities could not simply be 'displaced' in the 'pressure chambers of new institutions'.[49] Both his testimony and that of 'insiders' confirmed that federalists had had to concentrate on specific industrial sectors—coal and steel—for which they had designed 'supra-national' institutions in the narrow sense, separate from those of member states. Few contemporaries understood what 'supranational' meant: as late as 1957, Macmillan could be found speculating that 'some kind of managing board' for his planned Free Trade Area (which became EFTA) could be labelled 'supra-national' in order to make it popular with the other members.[50] Neither the terms nor the substance of the debate about European institutions, which was over-shadowed by the more pressing questions of domestic politics and foreign policy, were familiar to contemporaries, even those—like Macmillan—who considered themselves pro-European and backed cooperation on the European level. 'Pro-Community' advocates hoped that the habits, methods, and advantages of

440　EUROPEAN INTEGRATION SINCE THE 1920s

such cooperation would 'spill over'—in a phrase which was used at the time—into contiguous sectors of the economy and other spheres of governance. Could such a model be extended to wider fields of policy-making, however?

Intergovernmental Cooperation

Histories of European integration and the European Community, together with political studies of the EU, tend to overstate the role of the founders of European institutions and understate the longer-term significance of national governments.[51] An insider's view of the institutions as they evolved—such as that provided by Haas in *The Uniting of Europe*—is necessary.[52] In the 1950s and 1960s, the Community project seemed to be proceeding according to plan, with the effective development of the European Coal and Steel Community (the subject of Haas's study) and the creation of the European Economic Community, which transferred many of the practices and institutions—albeit in modified form (the High Authority, Assembly and Court of Justice)—from the ECSC to the EEC. Even critics such as John Gillingham accept that the '"liberal framework document" for a customs union regulated by a "competition principle"', included at the insistence of the 'ordo-liberal' Ludwig Erhard and banning the 'abuse of dominant positions by trusts and, through state aid, public corporations as well', enjoyed a certain amount of success, reinforcing the institutional structure of the EEC.[53] The same institutions, though, were also established, reformed, and limited through deliberate acts of governments, in whose territories they operated and from whose coffers they have been funded. Thus, because of the different expectations and competing interests of national governments, many of which feared the impact of a freeing of trade and a loss of control over vital sources of income and areas of policy-making, the EEC's institutions were weaker and less supranational than those of the ECSC: the High Authority was nominated jointly, making it more independent than the European Commission, which was headed by Commissioners appointed by national governments; the ECSC had its own source of revenue, deriving from tariffs on coal and steel, whereas the European Community relied on the contributions of member states; and, notwithstanding the transfer of the Assembly of the ECSC's power of censure, by means of which it could dismiss the High Authority by a two-thirds vote, to the European Parliament (Art. 144 of the Treaty of Rome), it was not used at all until 1972 and not threatened successfully until 1999.[54] Although the 'history-making decisions' of member states are referred to regularly and turning-points at intergovernmental conferences and European Council meetings have been studied in detail, the more routine decision-making of governments, which found expression in Councils of Ministers but which was prepared and discussed in internal and bi-lateral meetings, has received less attention.[55]

CONCLUSION   441

Governments' decisions, resistance, agreements, and compromises did most to create the parameters within which the EU functions. Such parameters were often established through struggles between advocates of supranationality and proponents of intergovernmental cooperation. American observers in the late 1940s such as David Bruce, the US ambassador in Paris, were unambiguous that the United Kingdom, with its imperial commitments, did not want to enter agreements which might 'derogate from its sovereignty', preventing the type of 'real European integration' desired by Monnet and Schuman.[56] The fact that Britain was 'not ready for Europe', as Marjolin had put it (in the recollection of the American official George Ball), did not stop 'fervent Europeans' from setting up supranational institutions, but it did restrict their scope.[57] Likewise, Hallstein's attempt to create a self-contained EEC, funded from its own tariffs on industrial and agricultural goods and operating in the Council of Ministers on the basis of qualified majority voting, was blocked by de Gaulle in 1965–66, acting as the head of the EEC's most powerful state. Those who had conceived of a 'European federation', which would cause member states to 'lose their national identity', declared the French president in September 1965, were eventually defeated.[58] Hallstein's most notable successor in the 1970s, Roy Jenkins, failed to achieve his own, more confederal version of a self-contained European Community, to be paid for—in theory—by a levy of 5–7 per cent of the gross Community product.[59] Jacques Delors, who became President of the Commission with Mitterrand's backing in January 1985, was more successful, overseeing the Single European Act (1986) and Treaty on European Union (1992), with its timetable for economic and monetary union. However, when he advanced his long-cherished dream of a European federation in 1990, declaring on television that 'My objective is that before the end of the millennium Europe should have a true federation', he was promptly called an 'idiot' by the French President, who accused him of risking EMU and a series of more moderate political gains—which were later incorporated in the Maastricht Treaty—for a project that few member states could accept.[60] National governments were unlikely to give up their most important powers and competencies, in the French President's view, even in the disconcerting circumstances of 1989–90. Correspondingly, when the European Convention presented its 'Treaty Establishing a Constitution for Europe' in June 2003, the governments of the member states ensured that they 'conferred' competencies and remained the subjects of the treaty, meaning that Europe would still have been a 'union of states'—in the opinion of the Vice-Chair of the Convention and former Italian Prime Minister, Giuliano Amato—if the constitutional treaty had been passed. In the event, it was rejected by the voters of France and the Netherlands in 2005, necessitating the incorporation of a more restricted set of provisions in what Amato called the 'disguising structure' of the Lisbon Treaty.[61]

Ministers have approached the EU as representatives of their own governments and constituents. Their role as representatives has often co-existed with a belief in

442 EUROPEAN INTEGRATION SINCE THE 1920S

Europe, as Chirac—who presided over the French 'no' in 2005—made plain in his memoirs, dispelling rumours, which his own statements in the early 1990s had done much to fuel, that he was a reluctant European and was wary of economic and monetary union. 'Ultimately, the very future of the construction of Europe was at stake; it could not have been realized or pursued without the shared vision and objectives of the Franco-German partnership,' he wrote of his assumption of the presidency in 1995, as he sought to allay the German Chancellor's fears about the future of EMU.[62] 'This singular alliance' between France and Germany was not based principally on our common interests but in fact was based on the many contradictions that it was vitally important to each of us to overcome, knowing all too well from experience how destructive conflict between us could be.'[63] For his part, Kohl was moved by 'the emotion and anxious sensitivity of a generation for whom the reconciliation and alliance of our two nations remained the essential guarantee of lasting peace on the continent', in Chirac's opinion.[64]

The French President's approach to the European Union was largely practical and openly self-interested, however, accepting that both France and Germany had overcome their 'similar weakness' after the Second World War, with the latter emerging from the conflict 'physically and morally destroyed' and the former, 'even if in the winning camp,...no less marked by the terrible trials of defeat and occupation', before regaining 'their self-esteem' and asserting 'their place among the great nations' through cooperation in Europe.[65] 'The truth is that from the beginning I was a European, not from passion but from reason, desirous of defending French interests within the Union at the same time as striving to get it to adopt a more responsible and coherent means of operating—two aims that were often difficult to reconcile,' wrote Chirac with hindsight.[66] His understanding of the workings of the European Community, which in its early years—with the exception of the Common Agricultural Policy—'was nothing but a long series of disappointments', betrayed his intergovernmental bias, which looked back to de Gaulle, without whose will 'this treaty would doubtless have gone unheeded, like so many others': 'The principal authority envisaged for its [the EEC's] functioning was the...Council [of Ministers], formed by representatives from the various governments but aided by an assembly of appointed members and a commission to deal with executive functions, as well as a court of justice.'[67] His position was redolent of that of his Prime Minister Jean-Pierre Raffarin, whom he blamed for the failure of the referendum vote in 2005 and whose programme for government, as 'a loyal European', had declared the premier 'favourable to enlargement' and to 'a federation of nation-states'.[68] It also revealed the assumption, made explicit by Chirac's successor Nicolas Sarkozy, that 'To lead Europe is not a right of the French, it is a duty, because if we don't do it, no one will do it in our stead!'[69]

Member states collaborate with European institutions, but they have retained overall control of the trajectory of European politics. Occasionally, when ministers such as Joschka Fischer have indicated a desire to strengthen the European

CONCLUSION 443

Parliament or, even, the Commission, they have been overruled by other governments. Though a renegade capable of opposing Donald Rumsfeld over the invasion of Iraq in a public forum at the Bayerischer Hof Hotel in Munich in 2003, the Minister of Foreign Affairs was careful to take off his 'Foreign Minister's hat' when he put forward his conception of a 'European federation' on the fiftieth anniversary of the Schuman Plan in 2000.[70] Over time, the European Commission, which had been touted as an executive-in-the-making in the 1960s, 1970s, and 1980s, has become less influential, continuing to oversee the single market and to run programmes connected, albeit tangentially, to market transactions, from research and development to the environment.[71] Through the Council of Ministers, the European Council established in 1974, the President of the Council and High Representative of Foreign Affairs (in the 2007 Lisbon Treaty), and COREPER, which has provided the Council with a permanent administrative apparatus made up of diplomats and other officials from member states, national governments have been able to assert control over European affairs.

The ministers of the Benelux countries had 'pressed for a role for governments in the European mechanism' in 1950, because 'They alone bore democratic responsibility towards their populations' and had 'national aims in view', writes van Middelaar, before going on to reiterate the aspiration of the Treaty of Rome that 'The Council shall consist of a representative of each Member State at ministerial level, who may commit the government of the Member State in question.'[72] For the Dutch historian, the atmosphere of the 'club', together with the extension of qualified majority voting, ensures that joint EU decisions override national biases and interests—this is the second, broader meaning of 'supra-nationalism', in addition to the creation of independent European authorities—yet there is also an opportunity to 'duck this responsibility' of representing a joint European decision, succumbing to the 'great temptation to claim only the successes and to blame "Brussels" for any failures'.[73] Equally, ministers are likely to approach Councils of Ministers meetings with national points of view, steering discussions in their own direction and avoiding contentious questions for other members. Most policy areas—including health, education, law and order, welfare, taxation, foreign policy, and defence—are still the primary responsibility of member states, meaning that a failure to reach a decision is not critical.[74] Where decisions were needed, for example for the reform of the EU itself after enlargement (to make mechanisms and institutions designed for six members work for twenty-seven), there is every indication that national governments have fought for their own positions and have safeguarded the powers of member states as a whole. Although it is true that national vetoes have rarely been used, it is difficult to gauge the effectiveness of the threat, however unlikely, of a veto.[75]

The new public interest in European affairs since the 1990s, with the end of the so-called 'permissive consensus', made governments warier of compromising perceived national interests. 'Europe' remained a second-order political question, with only 12 per cent of respondents in the UK considering it 'an important issue facing Britain today' in 2014, shortly before the Cameron government—partly for internal party reasons, partly to stem marginal electoral losses on the right (UKIP)—included the pledge of a referendum in the Conservative Party manifesto of 2015.[76] About one-fifth of those over fifty-five thought it an important issue, compared to less than one-twentieth of those aged 25–34. Only 3 per cent believed that 'Europe' was the most important issue facing the UK at that time. The subsequent Brexit campaign, after the Tories won the 2015 election, showed how the press, together with social media, could work to the disadvantage of the European Union, with newspapers having a 'natural' bias towards 'home', rather than 'foreign', news, which is covered separately.[77] In European broadsheets, coverage of European affairs had increased from about one-sixth to one-third of articles between 1982 and 2003, compared to national news stories, yet the framing of the coverage generally conformed to a national scheme of 'them' and 'us'.[78] According to one study, 'Europe' had only become a point of identification—'we'—in five per cent of relevant articles.[79] The EU itself was the main focus of around one-eighth of domestic and European articles.[80] In the popular tabloid press, the situation for the European Union is far worse, with the number of negative articles on the EU four times higher than in quality newspapers.[81] The United Kingdom in the early twenty-first century was an outlier in this respect, with 'Eurosceptic media' drawing on tabloid newspapers which had a combined readership of 16–24 million (out of an electorate of 45 million), in Tony Blair's frustrated and critical estimation, yet Austria, with its Eurosceptic *Kronen-Zeitung*, the Federal Republic of Germany, with its national-minded *Bild-Zeitung*, and many other member states were not fundamentally different.[82] Much social media coverage rested on newspaper and magazine articles (42 per cent) and news aggregators (14 per cent).[83] Other media—TV, film, music—were largely domestic or American. National broadcasters regularly tried to be balanced in their reportage, but their selection of stories was typical of the print media, with the EU figuring in less than five per cent of news broadcasts.[84] It has proved difficult in these circumstances to have impartial debates about the European Union and it has been tempting for politicians to blame 'Europe'.

A Confederation of Nation-States

Given such public pressures, national biases, and government self-interest, it is not surprising that the EU has functioned as a confederation of nation-states.[85] To Habermas, the opposition between '"confederation" versus "federal state"' is 'false', yet it distinguishes between states which decide to cooperate over the long term in certain policy areas, providing themselves with the institutional framework to do so, and component parts of a larger, state-like system of government.[86] Enlargement has at once made the creation of a federal state less likely and increased the number of calls to bring one into being, since a confederation of twenty-seven states appears unwieldy. The inability of the European Union to deal with the problems confronting it—climate change, migration, and economic and monetary union—have overlaid and exacerbated, in Habermas's opinion, long-standing 'legitimation crises' of modern states, which had proved unable to control the effects of global capitalism and to safeguard the welfare state on a national level.[87] For the German philosopher, the answer is to switch from 'intergovernmentalism to the community method', giving the EU greater, more decisive executive power and solving its 'democratic deficit', with the foundation of a 'a supranational democracy' and with the European Parliament and Council acting—via the existing 'ordinary legislative procedure'—in the spheres currently under the control of member states.[88]

Critics have doubted whether Europe's fragmented public spheres, diverse cultures, and historical antagonisms would foster solidarity and loyalty to a European government, predicting a deterioration of political trust and the aggravation of Euroscepticism instead.[89] Nevertheless, it is hard to deny that there has been an 'economization' of politics over the last century or so, rendering the political consequences of economic integration unavoidable, and that there has been a transfer of competencies and powers from the national to the European level.[90] The Court of Justice, in particular, has ignored 'the application *to the Court* of the EU Treaty framework as a tool to determine the internal constitutionality of its institutional activities', which have been 'dynamic' in 'the exercise of its interpretative functions', in Thomas Horsley's view.[91] The Court, he contends, 'routinely invokes its own institutional responses', 'developed without regard to the Treaty framework as constitutional touchstones' governing 'the conditions under which EU law applies within national legal systems', but he also concedes that '*neither* the Treaty framework *nor* Member States and their national courts recognise the Court's powerful claim to act as the "Trustee" of what *it* sees as the guiding principles of European integration'.[92] National courts—most notably, the *Bundesverfassungsgericht*—have been willing to challenge and reject the Court of Justice's rulings on the basis of their own interpretations of the European treaty framework.[93] The ECJ itself has operated 'a bifurcated jurisprudence..., which, on the hand, extensively interpreted the reach of the jurisdiction/competences/powers granted to the Community and, on the other hand, had taken a self-limiting approach towards the expansion of Community jurisdiction/competence/powers when exercised by the political organs'.[94] More importantly, member states have reserved the right, as 'masters of the treaties', to legislate and to reform EU institutions, including the Court. 'Unlike the governments of most federal states, the governments of the Member States, jointly and severally, could control the legislative expansion of Community jurisdiction/competences/powers', wrote Joseph Weiler in 2002, meaning that 'nothing that was done could be done

446 EUROPEAN INTEGRATION SINCE THE 1920s

without the assent of all states'.[95] Root-and-branch reform requires the unanimity of member states, but it can be incremental, involving changes in the monitoring of institutions' compliance with the treaties, and it is usually subject to political pressure, which can alter the interpretation of rules and laws without the need for treaty revision.[96]

The Court of Justice was allowed more scope of interpretation when there was greater agreement amongst member states about the nature and desirability of European integration.[97] Few, if any, commentators question the fact—confirmed by the *Bundesverfassungsgericht* in 1974, 1993, and 2009—that member states remain 'masters of the treaties'.[98] Given that the European Union has found it harder and harder to justify itself over time, with the decline of religious-inspired 'political messianism', and normative and social, or output-based, legitimacy, it is unlikely, in Weiler's view, that European institutions will replace national ones in the legal or political order.[99] Through the development of the European Council and COREPER, member states have ensured that national governments constitute the fulcrum of the European political order, or system of governance, which has been constructed through trial, error, and contestation in order to permit enduring forms of cooperation between states. Decision-making is often slow and executive actions are modest in scale, as was demonstrated in the eurozone and migration crises, precisely because the EU is not state-like, requiring negotiation between governments which disagree. For the same reasons, the resulting European agencies, such as the European Border and Coast Guard Agency (Frontex, founded in 2005 and headquartered in Warsaw) and the European Stability Mechanism (ESM, created in 2012 and providing €500 billion of loans to states in financial difficulty), can seem tentative, but they are designed to supplement national agencies and constitute an improvement on existing states of affairs, compared to the unilateral actions or ad hoc multilateral agreements of individual states.[100]

Fritz Scharpf's 'joint-decision trap'—'frustration without disintegration and resilience without progress'—appears to correspond to these confederal compromises: 'In the absence of a European government with a popular base of its own, all possibilities of institutional transformation are entirely determined by the self-interests of national governments', with 'even those among them which most vigorously support activist and expansionary European policies... likely to hedge their bets when it comes to relinquishing their veto powers'.[101] At the same time, 'the "reluctant Europeans" among member governments have been much more willing to accept disagreeable compromises on substantive policy than to weaken their own institutional control over the substance of future decisions'.[102] Whether this situation constitutes a 'trap' is doubtful. Rather, it describes the willingness of member states to compromise on matters of policy, while retaining control of decision-making. For Scharpf, the European Community—in 1988—was 'an institutional arrangement whose policy outcomes have an inherent (non-accidental)

CONCLUSION 447

tendency to be sub-optimal—certainly when compared to the policy potential of unitary governments of similar size and resources', but one which represented 'a "local optimum" in the cost-benefit calculations of all participants that might have the power to change it', with any institutional change likely to be 'large-scale' in order to be effective, 'implying the acceptance of short-term losses for many, or all, participants'.[103] By 2006, Scharpf had come to prefer the term 'joint-decision mode' and had conceded, 'after the accession of the United Kingdom in the early 1970s and after eastern enlargement', 'the hopes for a common "European social model" had already become unrealistic', along with 'harmonized taxes on capital incomes,...harmonized industrial rules, or...a Keynesian concertation between European monetary policy and national fiscal and wage policies'.[104] His priority now was 'the need to accommodate diversity' by means of 'enhanced cooperation' and 'opt-outs', loosening 'the stranglehold of existing European law', instead of by 'majority decisions that violate politically salient preferences in the Member States [which] would destroy the legitimacy of EU institutions'.[105] Such 'variable geometry' or 'differentiation' corresponds to continuing differences between member states.[106]

Given the persistence of national—and other—differences, disputes about and struggles over the form and trajectory of the European Union are to be expected. Cooperation and political integration have always depended on wider processes of economic, social, and cultural convergence, as well as on instances of identification and historical understanding. Increasingly, during the post-war era, the relationship between 'identity' and 'ways of life' has become a fraught one. 'The nation-state is a political configuration of modernity', yet 'modernity is a curious condition, for in some respects it is characterized by flux and impermanence, what Baudelaire in his classic formulation identified as "the transitory, the fugitive, the contingent"', writes Philip Schlesinger: 'It is this aspect of modernity that has been emphasized in the recent vogue for "postmodernity", whose proponents have been apt to think that the old collectivities may no longer confer identities that command special attention.'[107] Whereas some commentators have contended that 'post-Fordist "flexible accumulation"' has led to 'neo-tribalism', others 'have quite explicitly argued for the obsolescence of the nation-state and heralded this as opening up potential new spaces of tolerance for the "stranger"'.[108] Given that 'Europe is simultaneously undergoing processes of centralization and fragmentation' and the 'political and economic developments in the integration process... are out of phase with the cultural', in Schlesinger's opinion, 'what European identity *might be* still remains an open question'.[109] It is evident, however, that 'the principle of the nation-state as a locus of identity and political control', not least because it had been reaffirmed by 'ethno-nationalist awakenings in the former Communist bloc' and 'neo-nationalist separatisms or racist nationalisms' in Western Europe during the 1990s, would remain in place.[110] The 'deixis of little words' and 'flaggings of nationhood', in Michael Billig's terminology, had not

448   EUROPEAN INTEGRATION SINCE THE 1920s

disappeared, helping to create the 'depths and mechanisms of our identity, embedded in routines of social life', and reminding us 'that we are "us", different from "them"'.[111] Virtually all citizens to some extent, and a sizeable constituency to a large extent, appear to have been moved by such mechanisms. In 2004, for instance, almost two-thirds of respondents to a Eurobarometer poll in the UK professed that they felt solely British and two-fifths of their counterparts in the Kingdom of Belgium felt themselves to be Belgian alone.[112] Such citizens' rejection or ignorance of the EU has been a serious obstacle to the creation of a European set of allegiances.

There is little to suggest that the population—or significant part—of any member state is 'post-national'. Although 'national pride' ratings in Europe are low in global comparison, with Nigerian and Brazilian respondents more than two times and Americans more than three times more likely to profess themselves 'very proud' of their nationality (in 2003) than Czech or Dutch respondents, identification with the nation-state remains more common than affiliation with 'Europe'.[113] In regular Eurobarometer surveys, a much higher proportion of respondents believe themselves to be national in the first instance: in 2004, 87.3 per cent across the continent considered themselves mostly national, for example.[114] In 2010, more than 90 per cent replied that they felt very or fairly attached to their nation-state.[115] Yet, for many citizens, such sentiments were not exclusive: in the same survey, 53 per cent said that they were very or fairly attached to the EU. A majority—52 per cent—had a positive view of the EU in 2007, before the financial crisis, and a large minority—45 per cent—after it (in 2019).[116] In 2011, just under two-thirds felt that they were 'definitely' or 'to some extent' citizens of the European Union.[117] A relatively small number of citizens—around 15 per cent in Belgium, France, and Germany in 2004—felt that they were primarily European and a much larger group—between 41 and 48 per cent—considered themselves to be primarily national and secondarily European.[118] Those who felt partly or largely European were more likely to speak a second language and to have travelled for work or as students. There is also a correlation between age, level of education, and 'Europeanism', albeit a comparatively weak one, differing from one country to another.[119] The United Kingdom before 2016 was usually an outlier in such surveys, with only 40 per cent believing themselves to be citizens of the European Union in 2011.[120] Wariness about national affiliations and allegiances were just as pronounced in Britain as elsewhere, but citizens' feelings of attachment to Europe were—according to surveys—not as strong as in other member states, on the whole. At some points, especially during the eurozone crisis, the popularity of the EU has waned, and there has often been a disparity between popular perceptions of 'benefit' and 'attachment', particularly in net donor countries such as the Federal Republic of Germany. Nonetheless, a significant number of European citizens seem to have been positive about the European Union for much of the time, in keeping with the expectations of scholars

CONCLUSION 449

such as Anthony Smith, who—despite stressing the 'antiquity' and 'cultural foundations' of nations—has pointed out that 'human beings have multiple identities' and
'that such identities may be concentric rather than conflictual'.[121] In modernity,
there has been 'a successive differentiation' and 'enlargement' of processes of identification, in Smith's view.[122] Affiliations with Europe comprise one aspect—
prompted by politics but perpetuated by travel, trade, and communication—of
such differentiation.[123]

Despite many attempts, it has not proved possible to define a specifically
European culture or set of values. John McCormick's claim that secularism,
multiculturalism, and abolition of the death penalty mark out European particularity is unconvincing, with many states beyond Europe favouring abolition and
many populations and governments in the European Union having an uneven
record of religious and cultural toleration and integration. Australia, Canada, New
Zealand, Japan, South Korea, and China are more secular than many EU member
states, with 86.2 per cent of Chinese and 68.7 per cent of Australian respondents
in 2017–20 saying that they were not religious, compared to 18.1 per cent of
Greeks.[124] Arguably, however, similarity mattered more than particularity, helping
to convince Europeans to cooperate with each other in different fields.[125] Here,
contiguous models of liberal democracy, free trade within mixed economies,
industrial and post-industrial society, higher education, and the welfare state
have all been influential, not only in giving Europeans the sense that they are
similar, but in defining common sets of aspirations for the future. The principal
enlargement of the European Union in 2004, together with the challenges of
meeting convergence criteria before then, were rendered less problematic by the
rapid economic growth of the accession states and the fact that Germany and
Sweden were considered the countries most worthy of emulation, mentioned by
one-third of Czechs in the early 1990s, compared to the United States, which was
selected by one-seventh of respondents as a model.[126] Central and Eastern
European countries were not merely enmeshed in economic supply chains, with
three-quarters or more of investment, industrial exports, and sales in Hungary,
and just under half of those employed, attributable to foreign companies by
2005, for example; they had also caught up economically, with Hungary's GDP
per capita rising from about one-quarter to almost one-half of the EU average
between 2004 and 2019.[127] Furthermore, they boasted a higher proportion of
university graduates than the EU-15.[128] Many differences—and stereotypes
about difference—remain intact, reinforced by historical enmities and current
political divisions, which can be seen in widespread (and warranted) criticism of
the Law and Justice Party in Poland and Fidesz in Hungary, but there is still much
more of a sense that other Europeans are 'like us' than there was before 1945 or,
even, 1989.

Europeans are bound together less by history than by historical 'lessons', born
of antagonism and conflict.[129] The perceived 'self-destruction' of Europe created

conditions in which economic and diplomatic cooperation seemed desirable. The gradual attainment of a safe area in Europe—a 'security community'—was part of this defensive project, designed to protect European states against each other and against the economic power of the United States and the military threat of the Soviet Union. The European Community was correspondingly limited: it was established as a common market within an American-dominated military and diplomatic order, in which there was scope for economic competition but little opportunity to extend its role as an international organization. Although the habits of cooperation and the reality of interdependence in the European Union served to defuse tensions between member states, they failed to secure compliance or to promote agreement externally, as the EU sought to act in and beyond its borderlands, with less committed, more conditional backing from the United States, after the end of the Cold War. Its record in Yugoslavia, Libya, Syria, and Ukraine (before 2022), where it has worked with France and the United Kingdom above all, has been poor. A daunting array of problems remain unresolved, making the trajectory of the EU uncertain. Yet individual states have also proved incapable of coordinating their actions and even NATO has performed unevenly in recent conflicts from Croatia and Bosnia to Crimea.[130] The ability of the EU to foster habits of cooperation between members and to act as a magnet for neighbouring states remains significant.

This study has sought to explain why the European Union, member states, and European citizens have followed the course that they have, attempting to work out, in the process, who or what they are, and how they came to be what they are, rather than speculating about what they might become.[131] Historical constraints have frequently prevented Europeans from advancing as far as the founders and sponsors of the EU have desired, ensuring that the European Council and the governments of member states have remained the principal agents—and differentiated historical forms of intergovernmentalism and confederalism are arguably the most plausible explanations—of change and resistance within the European Union, even if such agents have also faced reversals and had to overcome challenges.[132] The existence of continuities and 'turning points', periods of acceleration and stasis, relative stability and destabilization have all been characteristic of 'integration', as have persisting political cultures, institutions, and diplomatic and economic conditions in an era of rupture and extremes.[133] What Mark Gilbert has called the 'orthodox', or 'Whig', history of European integration is unlikely to be convincing in these circumstances.[134] All the same, it is possible to argue that integration has occurred, in however discontinuous and fragmented a form.[135] Although national governments, which are accountable to voters, domestic media, and public opinion, have had to adjust to changing historical conditions (economic globalization, the end of the Cold War, the politics of identity at home and abroad) and an evolving set of European institutions, together with a rotating series of leaders, they have managed, to date, to retain control of politics on the

CONCLUSION   451

European level. This limited but mutable history of European integration differs, in important respects, from the faster-moving, progressive or disruptive, future-oriented accounts of political scientists, philosophers, federalists, and Eurosceptics, including those who brought about Brexit on a prospectus of fear, hope, and loathing. A European state such as the United Kingdom can exist beyond the orbit of the European Union (and the European Economic Area), but why would it choose to do so?[136] What 'Leavers' were breaking away from was not evident in 2016, in spite of all the anger and the arguments, with scare stories about the accession of Turkey, the creation of a European army and the existence of a European superstate finding a ready audience. What the EU is and does, and why, as an apparatus of long-term cooperation of nation-states and changing populations, is an historical question with a contemporary relevance. It should not be lost from view in a miasma of dreams, expectations, anxieties, and disappointments.

Notes

1. U. Kotz, K. K. Patel, and F. Romero (eds), *Europe's Cold War Relations: The EC towards a Global Role* (London, 2019); W. Loth (ed.), *Europe, Cold War and Coexistence, 1953–1965* (London, 2004); P. Ludlow (ed.), *European Integration and the Cold War: Ostpolitik-Westpolitik, 1965–1973* (London, 2007); L. Crump and S. Erlandsson (eds), *Margins for Manoeuvre in Cold War Europe: The Influence of Smaller Powers* (London, 2019).
2. See, especially, the essays in M. Spiering and M. J. Wintle (eds), *Ideas of Europe since 1914* (Basingstoke, 2002). I have written about this at greater length in M. Hewitson and M. D'Auria (eds), *Europe in Crisis: Intellectuals and the Idea of Europe, 1917–1957* (New York, 2012), 1–9, 323–31.
3. On American-led internationalism and internationalization, see J. M. Cooper, Jr. (ed.), *Reconsidering Woodrow Wilson: Progressivism, Internationalism, War and Peace* (Baltimore, 2008); D. F. Schmitz, *The Triumph of Internationalism: Franklin D. Roosevelt and a World in Crisis, 1933–1941* (Washington, D.C., 2007); E. E. Spalding, *The First Cold Warrior: Harry Truman, Containment and the Remaking of Liberal Internationalism* (Kentucky, 2006).
4. On the Franco-British Union, see A. Shlaim, 'Prelude to Downfall: The British Offer of Union to France, June 1940', *Journal of Contemporary History* 9 (1974), 27–63, who stresses that the offer was born of desperation, although having 'a respectable intellectual parentage'; D. W. J. Johnson, 'Britain and France in 1940', *Transactions of the Royal Historical Society* 22 (1972), 141–57; R. Mayne et al. (eds), *Cross Channel Currents: 100 Years of Entente Cordiale* (London, 2004), 87–108; D. Reynolds, *In Command of History: Churchill Fighting and Writing the Second World War* (New York, 2005), 168–9; R. Jenkins, *Churchill* (London, 2002), 619–20.
5. On convergence, see especially H. Kaelble, *Sozialgeschichte Europas 1945 bis zur Gegenwart* (Munich, 2007); H. Kaelble, *A Social History of Western Europe, 1880–1980* (Oxford, 1990); H. Kaelble, *Nachbarn am Rhein: Entfremdung und Annäherung der französischen und deutschen Gesellschaft seit 1880* (Munich, 1991); H. Kaelble, *Social Mobility in the Nineteenth and Twentieth Centuries: Europe and America in Comparative Perspective* (New York, 1986); H. Kaelble (ed.), *The European Way* (New York, 2004). Most historians of twentieth-century Europe have emphasized divergences and conflicts, from E. Hobsbawm, *An Age of Extremes: The Short Twentieth Century, 1914–1991* (London, 1994), 21–224, to Bernard Wasserstein, *Barbarism and Civilization: A History of Europe in Our Time* (Oxford, 2007), 80–519.
6. E. Balibar's *We, the People of Europe? Reflections on Transnational Citizenship* (Princeton, NJ, 2004), was part of this shift. It first appeared in French in 2001.
7. N. Lewkowicz, *The German Question and the International Order, 1943–1948* (Basingstoke, 2010); P. Alter, *The German Question and Europe: A History* (London, 2000); J. McAllister, *No Exit: America and the German Problem, 1943–1954* (Ithaca, 2002). On a global Cold War, see, in particular, J. Gaddis, *We Now Know: Rethinking Cold War History* (Oxford, 1998); and J. Gaddis, *The Cold War: A New History* (London, 2006).

452   EUROPEAN INTEGRATION SINCE THE 1920s

8. P.-H. Spaak, *The Continuing Battle: Memoirs of a European* (London, 1971), 141.
9. D. C. Large, 'Grand Illusions: The United States, the Federal Republic of Germany and the European Defence Community, 1950–1954', in J. M. Diefendorf et al. (eds), *American Policy and the Reconstruction of West Germany*, 375–94; L. Köllner et al., *Die EVG-Phase* (Munich, 1990); H. E. Volkmann and W. Schwengler (eds), *Die Europäische Verteidigungsgemeinschaft* (Boppard, 1985); T. P. Ireland, *Creating the Entangling Alliance* (Westport, Conn., 1981); F. H. Heller and J. R. Gillingham (eds), *NATO: The Founding of the Atlantic Alliance and the Integration of Europe* (New York, 1992); A. Grosser, *The Western Alliance* (London, 1980); S. Dockrill, *Britain's Policy for West German Rearmament* (Cambridge, 1991); and P. Winand, *Eisenhower, Kennedy and the United States of Europe* (New York, 1993). W. Loth, 'Die EWG und das Projekt der Europäischen Politischen Gesellschaft', in R. Hudemann (ed.), *Europa im Blick der Historiker* (Munich, 1995), 191–201, argues—unconvincingly—against this line, positing that the EDC failed because it was not supranational enough.
10. In addition to the literature on the UK, see J. Palayret et al. (eds), *Visions, Votes and Vetoes: The Empty Chair Crisis and the Luxembourg Compromise Forty Years On* (Berne, 2006); N. P. Ludlow, *The European Community and the Crises of the 1960s: Negotiating the Gaullist Challenge* (London, 2007); N. P. Ludlow, *Dealing with Britain: The Six and the First UK Application to the EEC* (Cambridge, 1997). On international crises, see A. Shlaim, *The United States and the Berlin Blockade, 1948–1949* (Berkeley, 1983); D. F. Harrington, 'The Berlin Blockade Revisited', *The International History Review* 6 (1984), 88–112; P. Lowe, *The Korean War* (New York, 2000); W. Stueck, *The Korean War: An International History* (Princeton, 1995); L. S. Kaplan, 'The Korean War and US Foreign Relations: The Case of NATO', in F. H. Heller (ed.), *The Korean War* (Lawrence, Kans., 1977); R. G. Hughes, *Britain, Germany and the Cold War: The Search for Détente, 1949–1967* (London, 2007), 6–89; G. Schmidt (ed.), *Zwischen Bündnissicherung und priviligierter Partnerschaft. Die deutsch-britische Beziehungen und die Vereinigten Staaten von Amerika 1955–1963* (Bochum, 1995); R. Steininger et al. (eds), *Die doppelte Eindämmung. Europäische Sicherheit und deutsche Frage in den Fünfzigern* (Munich, 1993); J. M. Schick, *The Berlin Crisis, 1958–1962* (Philadelphia, 1971); J. Arenth, *Der Westen tut nichts! Transatlantische Kooperation während der zweiten Berlin-Krise (1958–1962)* (Frankfurt, 1993); C. Bremen, *Die Eisenhower-Administration und die zweite Berlin-Krise 1958–1961* (Berlin, 1998). On decolonization, see F. Heinlein, *British Government Policy and Decolonisation, 1945–1963* (London, 2002); R. Hyam, *Britain's Declining Empire: The Road to Decolonisation, 1918–1968* (Cambridge, 2007); N. White, *Decolonisation: The British Experience since 1945* (London, 1999); J. Darwin, *Britain and Decolonisation* (New York, 1988); R. F. Betts, *France and Decolonisation, 1900–1960* (London, 1991); M. Connelly, *A Diplomatic Revolution: Algeria's Fight for Independence and the Origins of the Post-Cold War Era* (Oxford, 2002); I. M. Wall, *France, the United States and the Algerian War* (Berkeley, 2001); T. Shaw, *Eden, Suez and the Mass Media: Propaganda and Persuasion during the Suez Crisis* (London, 2009); J. Pearson, *Sir Anthony Eden and the Suez Crisis: Reluctant Gamble* (Basingstoke, 2002); W.S. Lucas, *Divided We Stand: Britain, the United States and the Suez Crisis* (London, 1991); D. Carlton, *Britain and the Suez Crisis* (Oxford, 1989); S. C. Smith (ed.), *Reassessing Suez 1956* (Aldershot, 2008).
11. L. Kühnhardt (ed.), *Crises in European Integration: Challenge and Response, 1945–2005* (Oxford, 2009), 1–18.
12. See, especially, A. S. Milward, *The European Rescue of the Nation-State*; A. S. Milward, *The Reconstruction of Western Europe, 1945–51* (London, 1984). Many studies of national governments have been influenced by Milward: see, for instance, much of the literature on the UK; J. W. Young, *Britain and European Unity, 1945–1992* (London, 1993), 1–52; W. Kaiser, *Using Europe, Abusing the Europeans: Britain and European Integration, 1945–1963* (Basingstoke, 1997); D. Gowland and A. Turner, *Reluctant Europeans: Britain and European Integration, 1945–1998* (London, 1999); and D. Gowland, A. Turner, and A. Wright, *Britain and European Integration since 1945* (London, 2009); S. George, *Britain and European Integration since 1945* (Oxford, 1992); N. J. Crowson, *The Conservative Party and European Integration since 1945: At the Heart of Europe?* (London, 2009), 14–44, 71–104.
13. On Belgium, see D. C. Reymen, 'The Economic Effects of the Marshall Plan Revisited', in J. Agnew and J. N. Entrikin (eds), *The Marshall Plan Today: Model and Metaphor* (London, 2004), 82–126. On Germany, W. Abelshauser, 'Kriegswirtschaft und Wirtschaftswunder: Deutschlands wirtschaftliche Mobilisierung für den Zweiten Weltkrieg und die Folgen für die Nachkriegszeit', *Vierteljahreshefte für Zeitgeschichte* 47 (1999), 503–38; N. Finszch and J. Martschukat (eds), *Different Restorations: Reconstruction and 'Wiederaufbau' in the United States and Germany, 1865–1945–1989* (Oxford, 1996); S. Reich, *The Fruits of Fascism: Postwar Prosperity in Historical*

CONCLUSION   453

Perspective (Ithaca, 1990); J. Gimbel, *Science, Technology and Reparations: Exploitation and Plunder in Postwar Germany* (Stanford, 1990); V. R. Berghahn, *The Americanization of West German Industry, 1945–1973* (Oxford, 1986); R. G. Stokes, *Divide and Prosper: The Heirs of I.G. Farben under Allied Authority, 1945–1951* (Berkeley, 1988); P. Hayes, *Industry and Ideology: IG Farben in the Nazi Era* (Cambridge, 1987), 213–384; W. Abelshauser et al., *German Industry and Global Enterprise: BASF* (Cambridge, 2009), 332–61; N. Gregor, *Daimler-Benz in the Third Reich* (New Haven, 1998), 76–108, 218–46; S. Tolliday, 'Enterprise and State in the West German *Wirtschaftswunder: Volkswagen* and the Automobile Industry, 1939–1962', *Business History Review* 69 (1995), 273–350.

14. R. O. Paxton, *Vichy France: Old Guard and New Order, 1940–1944* (New York, 1972); S. Fishman et al. (eds), *France at War: Vichy and the Historians* (Oxford, 2000); R. Gildea, *Marianne in Chains: In Search of the German Occupation, 1940–1945* (New York, 2002); J. Jackson, *France: The Dark Years, 1940–1944* (Oxford, 2003); S. Kitson, 'From Enthusiasm to Disenchantment: The French Police and the Vichy Regime, 1940–1944', *Contemporary European History* 11 (2002), 371–90; A. Shennan, *Rethinking France: Plans for Renewal, 1940–1946* (Oxford, 1989); M. Margairaz, *L'Etat, les finances et l'économie. Histoire d'une conversion 1932–1952* (Paris, 1991); R. Kuisel, *Capitalism and the State in Modern France: Renovation and Economic Management in the Twentieth Century* (Cambridge, 1981), and R. Kuisel, 'Vichy et les origines de la planification économique 1940–1946', *Le Mouvement sociale* 98 (1977), 77–101.

15. A. Glees, *Exile Politics during the Second World War: The German Social Democrats in Britain* (Oxford, 1982); D. Orlow, 'Delayed Reaction: Democracy, Nationalism and the SPD, 1945–1966', *German Studies Review* 16 (1993), 77–102; A. Rödder, *Die deutschen sozialistischen Exilgruppen in Grossbritannien* (Hanover, 1968); J. Herf, *Divided Memory* (Harvard, 1997), 13–68; E. Lacina, *Emigration 1933–1945* (Stuttgart, 1982); S. M. Di Scala, *Renewing Italian Socialism* (Oxford, 1988), 3–32; W. Kaiser, *Christian Democracy and the Origins of European Union* (Cambridge, 2007), 119–90; and W. Kaiser, 'Cooperation of European Catholic Politicians in Exile in Britain and the USA during the Second World War', *Journal of Contemporary History* 35 (2000), 439–65; I. Tombs, 'Une identité européenne assiégée? Les exiles socialistes à Londres, 1939–1945', *Revue d'histoire moderne et contemporaine* 46 (1999), 263–79; W. Loth, *Sozialismus und Internationalismus. Die französischen Sozialisten und Nachkriegsordnung Europas, 1940–1950* (Stuttgart, 1977); C. W. Nettelbeck, *Forever French: Exile in the United States, 1939–1945* (Oxford, 1991); N. Atkin, *The Forgotten French: Exiles in the British Isles, 1940–1944* (Manchester, 2003); J. P. and M. Cointet, *La France à Londres, 1940–1943* (Brussels, 1990); G. Adams, *Political Ecumenism: Catholics, Jews and Protestants in de Gaulle's Free France, 1940–1945* (Montreal, 2006); M. Conway and J. Gotovitch (eds), *Europe in Exile: European Exile Communities in Britain, 1940–1945* (New York, 2001).

16. G. Sapelli, *Southern Europe since 1945: Tradition and Modernity in Portugal, Spain, Italy, Greece and Turkey* (London, 1995); J. Kurth and J. Petras, *Mediterranean Paradoxes: The Politics and Social Structure of Southern Europe* (Oxford, 1994); K. Featherstone, *Political Change in Greece: Before and after the Colonels* (Basingstoke, 1987); S. Payne, *The Franco Regime, 1936–1975* (Madison, 1987); J. J. Linz and A. Stepan, *Democratic Transition and Consolidation* (Baltimore, 1996), 3–86; J. J. Linz and A. Stepan (eds), *The Breakdown of Democratic Regimes* (Baltimore, 1978), vols 1–2.

17. G. Schröder, *Entscheidungen*, 366.

18. Ibid. Not for the last time, his comments were quickly overtaken by events, with the onset of the eurozone crisis.

19. See M. Hewitson, 'Europe and the Fate of the World: Crisis and Integration in the Late 1940s and 1950s' and 'Inventing Europe and Reinventing the Nation-State in a New World Order', in M. Hewitson and M. D'Auria (eds), *Europe in Crisis*, 35–81.

20. See L. Warlouzet, *Le choix de la CEE par la France: l'Europe économique en débat de Mendès-France à de Gaulle 1955–1969* (Paris, 2011); K. K. Patel and J. Schot, 'Twisted Paths to European Integration: Comparing Agriculture and Transport Policies in a Transnational Perspective', *Contemporary European History*, 20 (2011), 383–403; N. P. Ludlow, 'The Emergence of a Commercial Heavy-Weight: The Kennedy Round Negotiations and the European Community of the 1960s', *Diplomacy and Statecraft*, 18 (2007), 351–68; L. Coppolaro, 'In Search of Power: The European Commission in the Kennedy Round Negotiations, 1963–1967', *Contemporary European History*, 23 (2014), 23–41. For the period after the EEC was established, see L. Warlouzet, *Governing Europe in a Globalizing World: Neoliberalism and Its Alternatives Following the 1973 Oil Crisis* (London, 2018); E. Mourlon-Druol, 'Integrating an International Political Economy Dimension into European Integration History: The Challenges of the 1970s', *Journal of European Integration History*, 17 (2011), 335–41.

454   EUROPEAN INTEGRATION SINCE THE 1920S

21. E. Mourlon-Druol, *A Europe Made of Money*, 7, points out that this was even true of monetary policy, where 'technicalities mattered economically *and* politically'.
22. P. Krüger, 'Das doppelte Dilemma: Die Aussenpolitik der Republik von Weimar zwischen Staatensystem und Innenpolitik', *German Studies Review* 22 (1999), 247–67, and P. Krüger, *Die Aussenpolitik der Republik von Weimar* (Darmstadt, 1985).
23. T. Judt, *A Grand Illusion? An Essay on Europe* (1996), 4.
24. Ibid., 28–30.
25. Ibid., 25–7, 30.
26. Ibid., 33.
27. K. Adenauer to S. J. Vogel, 26 January 1948, in H.-P. Schwarz, 'Adenauer und Europa', *Vierteljahreshefte für Zeitgeschichte*, 27 (1979), 482.
28. K. Adenauer, *Erinnerungen 1953–1955* (Stuttgart, 1966), vol. 2, 301.
29. See P. P. D'Attore, 'Americanism and Anti-Americanism in Italy', in Stirk and Willis (eds), *Shaping Postwar Europe*, 43–52.
30. Quoted in M. Segers, *The Netherlands and European Integration, 1950 to the Present* (Amsterdam, 2020), 57.
31. Ibid., 63–7.
32. Ibid., 46, 75–6. Acheson quoted in K. Schwabe (ed.), *Die Anfänge des Schuman-Plans 1950/51* (Baden-Baden, 1988), 218.
33. P.-H. Spaak, *The Continuing Battle*, 143.
34. Ibid., 147.
35. Ibid.
36. Ibid., 154–5.
37. Ibid., 155.
38. Ibid., 171.
39. See Kevin Ruane, *The Rise and Fall of the European Defence Community: Anglo-American Relations and the Crisis of European Defence, 1950–55* (Basingstoke, 2000), on the variety and mutability of British attitudes to the EDC. French opinions, too, were divided.
40. Ibid., 211.
41. Ibid., 213, 215.
42. Ibid., 212.
43. Ibid.
44. Ibid., 219–21.
45. M. Charlton, *The Price of Victory*, 99. The words are those of Makins, which Monnet confirmed.
46. F. Duchêne, *Monnet*, 232, 262–3.
47. E. Plowden, speaking retrospectively, in M. Charlton, *The Price of Victory*, 87.
48. R. Marjolin, 'What Type of Europe', in D. Brinkley and C. Hackett (eds), *Jean Monnet: The Path to European Unity* (Basingstoke, 1991), 172–3, taken from Marjolin's memoirs, published in English in 1989.
49. Ibid., 172.
50. H. Macmillan to officials at the Foreign Office, 29 June 1955, in A. S. Milward, 'Childe Harold's Pilgrimage', in J. Noakes, P. Wende, and J. Wright (eds), *Britain and Germany in Europe*, 58.
51. Recent works such as Mark Gilbert's *European Integration: A Political History*, 1, have sought deliberately to avoid such a focus: 'this book is a narrative general history that inserts the story of European integration into the wider history of this period', incorporating 'imperial decline and decolonization; the threat and then fall of communism; the impact of American foreign, fiscal, and monetary policy; and the democratization of the Mediterranean countries and the nations of central Europe'. Earlier works such as D. Urwin's *A History of European Integration since 1945*, 2nd edn. (1995), paid attention to the Cold War and the United States (chapter 2) and de Gaulle (chapter 8), but largely concentrated on the development of European institutions and policy-making.
52. E. B. Haas, *The Uniting of Europe: Political, Social and Economic Forces, 1950–1957* (Notre Dame, IN, 1958).
53. J. R. Gillingham, *The EU: An Obituary* (London, 2016), 28–9.
54. V. Herman and J. Lodge, *The European Parliament and the European Community* (Basingstoke, 1978), 49: 'Article 144 was not formally invoked—nor the threat of it even seriously hinted at—in the first fourteen years of the of the Community's existence.' Successful use of the threat of invocation, as it is understood here (as the ultimate consequence of the threat), led to the early resignation of the Santer Commission in 1999. More generally, see M. Gilbert, 'Narrating the Process: Questioning the Progressive Story of European Integration', *Journal of Common Market Studies*, 46 (2008), 641–62.

CONCLUSION   455

55. The classic account of history-making decisions is J. Peterson, 'Decision-making in the European Union: Towards a Framework for Analysis', *Journal of European Public Policy*, 2 (1995), 86. Emmanuel Mourlon-Druol, *A Europe Made of Money*, 267, is an exception in this respect, underlining, in the field of monetary policy, that a major trend in the second half of the 1970s 'was the ability of the newly created European Council to provide the political impetus needed to create a new European scheme'. He arrives at this conclusion through a study of the policies of selected member states vis-à-vis the European Monetary System.

56. D. Bruce, 25 April 1950, quoted in C. A. Wurm, 'Britain and West European Integration, 1948—9 to 1955: Politics and Economics', in J. Noakes, P. Wende, and J. Wright (eds), *Britain and Germany in Europe, 1949-1990*, 42.

57. R. Marjolin, 'What Type of Europe', in D. Brinkley and C. Hackett (eds), *Jean Monnet: The Path to European Unity* (Basingstoke, 1991), 172.

58. C. de Gaulle, 9 September 1965, quoted in D. W. Irvin, *The Community of Europe*, 111.

59. N. P. Ludlow, *Roy Jenkins and the European Commission Presidency, 1976–1980: At the Heart of Europe* (Basingstoke, 2016), 120–7, on the MacDougall Report. The figure seemed unrealistic and the plan was not adopted, but they were discussed.

60. L. van Middelaar, *The Passage to Europe*, 186; J. Attali, *Verbatim*, vol. 1, 331.

61. G. Amato, 'The Cautious Mandate to the 2002 Convention', in N. W. Barber, M. Cahill, and R. Ekins (eds), *The Rise and Fall of the European Constitution*, 15.

62. J. Chirac, *My Life in Politics*, 153.

63. Ibid., 154.

64. Ibid.

65. Ibid.

66. Ibid., 45.

67. Ibid., 43–4. Chirac actually refers to a 'European Council', which only came into being in the mid-1970s (introduced by Giscard), but which he appears—perhaps tellingly—to date back to the origins of the EEC.

68. Ibid., 310; J.-P. Raffarin, *Je marcherai toujours à l'affectif. Souvenirs* (Paris, 2012), 273.

69. N. Sarkozy, *Le Temps des tempêtes* (Paris, 2020), vol. 1, 109.

70. *Spiegel International*, 17 February 2011, giving an exposition of Fischer's memoirs; J. Fischer, 'From Confederacy to Federation—Thoughts on the Finality of European Integration', speech by Joschka Fischer at the Humboldt University in Berlin, 12 May 2000, 6, available at https://ec.europa.eu/.

71. This idea has been an enduring one: see A. Wille, *The Normalization of the European Commission: Politics and Bureaucracy in the EU Executive* (Oxford, 2013). Laurent Warlouzet, 'The Centralization of EU Competition Policy: Historical Institutionalist Dynamics from Cartel Monitoring to Merger Control, 1956–91', *Journal of Common Market Studies*, 54 (2016), 725–41, argues that the European Commission took advantage of the unintended consequences of Council decisions to gain control of key aspects of the functioning of the market. Arguably, though, governments were reasonably content, over time, to leave control of cartels and mergers, together with other market functions, to the European Commission.

72. L. van Middelaar, *The Passage to Europe*, 294.

73. Ibid.

74. A. Moravcsik, 'In Defence of the "Democratic Deficit": Reassessing Legitimacy in the European Union', *Journal of Common Market Studies*, 40 (2002), 607, 615.

75. The European constitution paid considerable attention to the veto: L. van Middelaar, *The Passage to Europe*, 122–4.

76. Ipsos MORI, June 2014. The losses were significant in European Parliament elections, with proportional representation and the chance to register a protest vote, but were likely to be marginal in general elections.

77. H. J. Trenz, 'Understanding Media Impact on European Integration: Enhancing or Restricting the Scope of Legitimacy of the EU?' *European Integration*, 30 (2008), 297.

78. S. Sifft, M. Brüggemann, K. Kleinen von Königslöw, B. Peters, and A. Wimmel, 'Segmented Europeanization: Exploring the Legitimacy of the European Union from a Public Discourse Perspective', *Journal of Common Market Studies*, 45 (2007), 136.

79. H. Wessler, B. Peters, M. Brüggemann, K. Kleinen von Königslöw, and S. Sifft, *Transnationalization of Public Spheres* (Basingstoke, 2008), 50–1.

80. S. Sifft, M. Brüggemann, K. Kleinen von Königslöw, B. Peters, and A. Wimmel, 'Segmented Europeanization: Exploring the Legitimacy of the European Union from a Public Discourse Perspective', *Journal of Common Market Studies*, 45 (2007), 136. See also H. J. Trenz, 'Media Coverage on European Governance: Testing the Performance of National Newspapers', *European Journal of Communication*, 19 (2004), 291–319.

456 EUROPEAN INTEGRATION SINCE THE 1920s

81. H. J. Trenz, 'Understanding Media Impact on European Integration: Enhancing or Restricting the Scope of Legitimacy of the EU?' *European Integration*, 30 (2008), 302.
82. T. Blair, *A Journey*, 533. The estimated readership here is based on two to three times the circulation figure. See Chapter 6.
83. C. Galpin and H.-J. Trenz, 'Participatory Populism: Online Discussion Forums on Mainstream News Sites during the 2014 European Parliament Election', *Journalism Practice*, 13 (2019), 781–98.
84. J. Peter, C. H. De Vreese, and H. A. Semetko, 'EU Politics on Television News: A Cross-National Comparative Study', *European Union Politics*, 4 (2003), 305–27, examining coverage in 2000; C. H. De Vreese, 'News, Political Knowledge and Participation', *Acta Politica*, 41 (2006), 317–41.
85. The literature on a European confederation is small, with few historical works. See, for instance, G. Majone's treatment of 'The Confederal Option' in *Dilemmas of European Integration*, 209–18. D. Calleo, *Rethinking Europe's Future* (Princeton, NJ, 2001), 373, calls the EU a 'hybrid confederacy'.
86. J. Habermas, 'Democracy, Solidarity and the European Crisis', 26 April 2013.
87. J. Habermas, *Legitimitätsprobleme im Spätkapitalismus* (Frankfurt, 1973); J. Habermas, *Europe: The Faltering Project* (Cambridge, 2009).
88. J. Habermas, 'Democracy, Solidarity and the European Crisis', 26 April 2013. See also J. Habermas, P. Bofinger, and J. Nida-Rümelin, *Frankfurter Allgemeine Zeitung*, 3 August 2012.
89. S. Glendinning, 'Europe Should Reject Jürgen Habermas' Vision of a Federal European State', *EUROPP*, 3 September 2013.
90. M. A. Pollack, 'Creeping Competence: The Expanding Agenda of the European Community', *Journal of Public Policy*, 88 (1994), 95–144; M. A. Pollack, 'The End of Creeping Competence? EU Policy-Making since Maastricht', *Journal of Common Market Studies*, 38 (2000), 519–38.
91. T. Horsley, *The Court of Justice of the European Union as an Institutional Actor: Judicial Lawmaking and Its Limits* (Cambridge, 2018), 260.
92. Ibid., 263–4. See also P. Lindseth, *Power and Legitimacy: Reconciling Europe and the Nation-State* (Oxford, 2010).
93. Joseph Weiler, 'A Constitution for Europe? Some Hard Choices', *Journal of Common Market Studies*, 40 (2002), 572, has argued that, if a true constitution were to come into being, 'Sooner or later, "supreme" courts in the Member States would realize that the "socio-legal contract" announced by the ECJ in its major constitutionalizing decisions—namely, that the Community constitutes a new legal order...for the benefit of which the states have limited their sovereign rights, *albeit within limited fields*—had been shattered. Although these "supreme" courts had accepted the principles of the new legal order, supremacy and direct effect, the fields seemed no longer limited. In the absence of Community legal checks, they would realize, it would fall upon them to draw the jurisdictional lines between the Community and its Member States.'
94. Ibid.
95. Ibid. See also J. H. H. Weiler, 'Does Europe Need a Constitution? Demos, Telos and the German Maastricht Decision', *European Law Journal*, 1 (1995), 219–58.
96. T. Horsley, *The Court of Justice of the European Union as an Institutional Actor*, 280–3, on the monitoring of compliance. Ibid., 42: revision of the treaties also requires ratification by individual member states, in addition to unanimity in Council. The so-called 'passerelle' clauses allow a shift to QMV in specific, secondary spheres of activity, but only after a unanimous vote in Council.
97. See J. H. H. Weiler, 'A Quiet Revolution: The European Court of Justice and Its Interlocutors', *Comparative Political Studies*, 26 (1994), 510–36.
98. Article 48 of the Treaty on European Union.
99. J. H. H. Weiler, 'In the Face of the Crisis: Input Legitimacy, Output Legitimacy and the Political Messianism of European Integration', *Journal of European Integration*, 34 (2012), 825–41; J. H. H. Weiler, 'The Political and Legal Culture of European Integration: An Exploratory Essay', *International Journal of Constitutional Law*, 9 (2011), 678–94. His notion of 'political messianism' derives from his work on Christian Democracy: J. H. H. Weiler, *L'Europe chrétienne. Une excursion* (Paris, 2007).
100. L. van Middelaar, *Alarums and Excursions*, 21–64, 91–114.
101. F. W. Scharpf, 'The Joint-Decision Trap: Lessons from German Federalism and European Integration', *Public Administration*, 66 (1988), 267–8.
102. Ibid., 268.
103. Ibid., 271.
104. F. W. Scharpf, 'The Joint-Decision Trap Revisited', *Journal of Common Market Studies*, 44 (2006), 856.
105. Ibid., 856–7.

CONCLUSION 457

106. On variable geometry and differentiated integration, see K. Holzinger and F. Schimmelfennig, 'Differentiated Integration in the European Union: Many Concepts, Sparse Theory, Few Data', *European Journal of Political Research*, 19 (2012), 292–305; F. Schimmelfennig, 'Good Governance and Differentiated Integration: Graded Membership in the European Union', *European Journal of Political Research*, 55 (2016), 789–810; F. Schimmelfennig, D. Leuffen, and B. Rittberger, 'The European Union as a System of Differentiated Integration: Interdependence, Politicization and Differentiation', *Journal of European Public Policy*, 22 (2015), 764–82.

107. P. Schlesinger, 'Europeanness: A New Cultural Battlefield?' *Innovation*, 5 (1992), 12.

108. Ibid., 13, citing Michel Maffesoli and Zygmunt Bauman, respectively.

109. Ibid., 22.

110. Ibid.

111. M. Billig, *Banal Nationalism*, 174–5.

112. Eurobarometer 91, 2004, in N. Fligstein, *Euroclash*, 143.

113. World Values Survey, 2003/4, at http://www.wordvaluessurvey.org.

114. Eurobarometer 91, 2004, in N. Fligstein, *Euroclash*, 141.

115. H. Zimmermann and A. Dür, 'Can There Be a Common European Identity?', in H. Zimmermann and A. Dür (eds), *Key Controversies in European Integration*, 95.

116. J. McCormick, *Europeanism*, 101; Eurobarometer 92 (2019), First Results, 8.

117. H. Zimmermann and A. Dür, 'Can There Be a Common European Identity?', in H. Zimmermann and A. Dür (eds), *Key Controversies in European Integration*, 95.

118. Eurobarometer 91, 2004, in N. Fligstein, *Euroclash*, 143; J. McCormick, *Europeanism*, 100–1.

119. Eurobarometer 61 (2004), Bericht, 21; Annexes: Tables, 40–4.

120. Eurobarometer 75, 2011, 52.

121. A. D. Smith, *The Antiquity of Nations* (Cambridge, 2004); A. D. Smith, *The Cultural Foundations of Nations: Hierarchy, Covenant and Republic* (Oxford, 2008); A. D. Smith, 'National Identity and the Idea of European Unity', *International Affairs*, 68 (1992), 67.

122. A. D. Smith, 'National Identity and the Idea of European Unity', *International Affairs*, 68 (1992), 58–9.

123. On the attempts of the founders and early sponsors of the European Community to force this issue, claiming a type of symbolic sovereignty, see J. Krumrey, *The Symbolic Politics of European Integration: Staging Europe* (Basingstoke, 2018).

124. World Values Survey, 2017–20.

125. When asked in the 2019 Eurobarometer whether 'People in the European Union have a lot of things in common', 51 per cent agreed that they did and 43 per cent disagreed, with 9 per cent totally disagreeing. Interestingly, 54 per cent in the UK agreed and 37 per cent disagreed, and 77 per cent in Sweden agreed and only 22 per cent disagreed. Some countries with higher numbers of citizens who felt 'European' had larger numbers of sceptics, including Belgium (46 per cent agree, 53 per cent disagree) and France (41 per cent agree, 53 per cent disagree): 'Europeans in 2019', Special Eurobarometer 486, Annex, T54.

126. Freedom House, *Democracy, Economic Reform and Western Assistance* (1991), 154.

127. I. T. Berend, *From the Soviet Bloc to the European Union: The Economic and Social Transformation of Central and Eastern Europe since 1973* (Cambridge, 2009), 115. European Commission, *The Social Situation in the European Union, 2005–6* (Brussels, 2006), 130–57; European Commission, *Eurostat Yearbook: A Statistical Eye on Europe, 2005* (Luxembourg, online); Eurostat, *Economic Indicators* (2021); Eurostat, *Real GDP Growth Rates* (2021).

128. 30 per cent compared to 23 per cent.

129. O. Calligaro, *Negotiating Europe*, 104–14.

130. This has been in contrast to NATO's role in the war between Russia and Ukraine.

131. The study's historical approach differs from those of intergovernmentalists by explaining why governments—beyond answerability to the domestic preferences of voters—have agreed to delegate powers and competencies in some areas, but not in others, at different times: for an interesting discussion of the challenges posed by historical crises for theories of intergovernmentalism, see F. Schimmelfennig, 'Liberal Intergovernmentalism and the Crises of European Union', *Journal of Common Market Studies*, 56 (2018), 1578–94.

132. Piers Ludlow's analysis of de Gaulle's role in the 1960s is a good example of this type of historical understanding: N. P. Ludlow, *The European Community and the Crises of the 1960s* (London, 2006), 118–19. See also historians' criticism of Andrew Moravcsik's treatment of de Gaulle: A. Moravcsik, 'De Gaulle between Grain and Grandeur: The Political Economy of French EC Policy, 1958–1970', *Journal of Cold War Studies*, 2 (2000), Nos 2 and 3, 3–43, 4–68; R. Lieshout,

M. L. L. Seegers, and A. M. van der Vleuten, 'De Gaulle, Moravcsik and *The Choice for Europe*: Soft Sources, Weak Evidence', *Journal of Cold War Studies*, 6 (2004), 89–139; C. Parsons, *A Certain Idea of Europe*, 29; and C. Parsons, 'Showing Ideas as Causes: The Origins of the European Union', *International Organization*, 56 (2002), 47–84. On differentiated integration, see F. Schimmelfennig and T. Winzen, *Ever Looser Union? Differentiated European Integration* (Oxford, 2020).

133. It is notable that Eric Hobsbawm, *Age of Extremes: The Short Twentieth Century, 1914–1991* (London, 1994), 239–40, 276–7, 559–60, barely discusses the European Community in his history of ruptures and advances. Mark Mazower, *Dark Continent: Europe's Twentieth Century* (London, 1998), 290–366, likewise concentrates on global and domestic politics, including that of welfare states, and on the 'Americanization of Europe'. The same is true of Richard Vinen, *A History in Fragments: Europe in the Twentieth Century* (London, 2000), 316–17, 359–61, 580–3, 628–9, and Bernard Wassertein, *Barbarism and Civilization: A History of Europe in Our Time* (Oxford, 2007), 455–7, 521–4, 631–4, 709–13. In part, such reluctance seems to derive from the apparent disjunction between the seismic shifts of international and domestic politics, on the one hand, and the apparently pedestrian 'progress' and marginality of EC/EU politics, on the other. Tony Judt, *Postwar*, 153–60, 526–34, 713–91, is an exception in this respect. See also S. Berger and C. Tekin (eds), *History and Belonging: Representations of the Past in Contemporary European Politics* (New York, 2018).

134. See M. Gilbert, 'Narrating the Process: Questioning the Progressive Story of European Integration', *Journal of Common Market Studies*, 46 (2008), 641–8, for a summary of this progressive historical literature.

135. I have attempted to show how such integration related to the military and diplomatic conditions of the Cold War (and post-Cold War), domestic debates about history and identity, the dynamics of global trade, variable types of social convergence, and the European policies of member states, all of which militate against Gilbert's emphasis, ibid., 658, on the political contingency of 'narrative': 'not only is politics a highly contingent affair, but what we currently think of as the "true story" of the EU is to a great degree contingent, too'. On explanation and contingency, with which most historians of integration would agree, see the discussion of François Furet *In the Workshop of History* (Chicago, 1982) in the Introduction.

136. Nicolas Sarkozy, *Le Temps des tempêtes*, 356–7, claimed that Brexit was a 'catastrophe for them and for us'. His two mistakes were, first, to think that London was the United Kingdom or, even, England and, second, to believe that David Cameron had 'the force, courage and charisma vis-à-vis his troops that Tony Blair had on his'. 'I was always convinced that Europe had a great need of the United Kingdom and that the obverse was also true—that the latter ran the risk of becoming a caricature and turning in on itself without the former, which would be against its nature.'

Bibliography

Primary Sources

Polls, Surveys and Reports

Centre for the Study of Public Policy, *New Europe Barometer, 1991–2008*
Eurobarometer 48, 1997
Eurobarometer 60, 2003, First Results
Eurobarometer 61, April 2004
Eurobarometer, 'Social Values, Science and Technology', June 2005
Eurobarometer 75, Spring
Eurobarometer 77, 2012, First Results
Eurobarometer 92, 2019, First Results
European Audovisual Observatory, *Yearbook 2019/20*
European Commission, 'Speech by the Right Hon. Roy Jenkins, President of the European Communities, on the Occasion of the Opening of the Spanish Negotiations, Brussels, 3 February 1979, *Archive of European Integration*, at http://aei.pitt.edu, *The Social Situation in the European Union*, 2008 (Luxembourg, 2009), 312
European Commission, *European Economy*, 46 (December 1990)
European Commission, *European Economy*, 6 (1995)
European Commission, *Economics of Transition*, 4 (1996)
European Commission, *Agenda 2000: For a Stronger and Wider Union* (Luxembourg, 1997)
European Commission, *50 Years of Figures on Europe* (Luxembourg, 2003)
European Commission, *European Union Enlargement: A Historic Opportunity* (Luxembourg, 2003)
European Commission, *The Social Situation in the European Union, 2005–6* (Luxembourg, 2006)
European Commission, *The Social Situation in the European Union*, 2008 (Luxembourg, 2009)
European Commission, 'The Historical Development of European Integration' (2018), at www.europarl.europa.eu
European Commission, 'EU Customs Union: Facts and Figures' (2019)
European Commission, *Annual Report on Intra-EU Labour Mobility 2020* (Luxembourg, 2021)
European Communities, *Bulletin of the European Communities*, 3 (1966)
European Communities, 'Declaration on European Identity', *Bulletin of the European Communities*, 12 (1973), 118–22
European Communities, 'Portugal's Application for Accession to the Communities', *Bulletin of the European Communities*, 3 (1977)
European Communities, *External and Intra-European Union Trade: Statistical Yearbook*, (Luxembourg, 2003)
European Communities, *Treaty Establishing a Constitution for Europe* (Luxembourg, 2005)
European Convention, 'Draft Treaty Establishing a Constitution for Europe' (2004), at http://european-convention.europa.eu/
European Convention, 'Protocol on the Role of National Parliaments in the European Union' and the 'Protocol on the Application of the Principles of Subsidiarity and Proportionality' (2004), at http://european-convention.europa.eu/
European Council, 'Solemn Declaration on European Union', *Bulletin of the European Communities*, 6 (1983)
Eurostat, *Eurostat Yearbook: A Statistical Eye on Europe, 2005* (Luxembourg, 2005, online)
Eurostat, 'World Trade in Goods and Services: An Overview' (2019)

460 BIBLIOGRAPHY

Eurostat, *Emigration Statistics* (2020)
Eurostat, *Regional Yearbook* (2020)
Freedom House, *Democracy, Economic Reform and Western Assistance* (1991)
Institut national de la statistique et des études économiques (2015)
Ipsos MORI, June 2014
Migration Observatory, 'There Were an Estimated 3.7 Million EU Citizens Living in the UK in 2019' (2020)
OECD Outlook 64 (1998)
Office for National Statistics, *Population of the UK by Country of Birth and Nationality* (2016)
Office for National Statistics, *Population of the UK by Country of Birth and Nationality* (2018)
Pew Global Attitudes Project, 'Pervasive Gloom about the World Economy' (Washington, DC, 2012)
United Nations, *Annual Trade Statistics* (New York, 1980–2000)
United Nations Conference on Trade and Development, *World Investment Report: The Shift towards Services* (New York, 2004)
Universities UK, International Student Recruitment Data (2016)
World Trade Organization, *World Trade Statistical Review 2019* (Geneva, 2019)
World Values Survey, 2003–04, at http://www.wordvaluessurvey.org
YouGov, 'How Britain Voted at the EU Referendum', 27 June 2016

Documents and Speeches

R. Bullen and M. E. Pelly (eds), *Documents on British Policy Overseas*, series ii, vol. I, *The Schuman Plan, the Council of Europe and Western European Integration 1950–1952* (London, 1986)
Bundesministerium des Inneren unter Mitwirkung des Bundesarchivs (ed.), Deutsche Einheit: Sonderedition aus den Akten des Bundeskanzleramtes 1989/90 (Munich, 1998)
W. Churchill, 'Sinews of Peace' speech, 5 March 1946, National Archives, FO 371/51624
J. Fischer, 'From Confederacy to Federation—Thoughts on the Finality of European Integration', speech by Joschka Fischer at the Humboldt University in Berlin, 12 May 2000, 6, available at https://ec.europa.eu/
G. Ford, H. Kissinger, and B. Scowcroft, memorandum of a conversation, 23 August 1974, National Security Adviser Collection 036600070, National Archives and Records Administration, Washington D.
V. Giscard d'Estaing, 'Constitution for European citizens', in his 'Introductory Speech to the Convention on the Future of Europe', 19, Brussels, 26 February 2002, at http://european-convention.europa.eu/
M. Gorbachev, 'Europe as a Common Home', 6 July 1989, at https://digitalarchive.wilsoncenter.org/document/speech-mikhail-gorbachev-council-europe-strasbourg-europe-common-home
G. F. Kennan, 'Long Telegram', 22 February 1946, in US Department of State (ed.), *Foreign Relations of the United States, 1946* (Washington, DC, 1969), vol. 6, 696–709
G. F. Kennan, 'The Sources of Soviet Conduct', *Foreign Affairs*, July 1947
G. F. Kennan memo, 28 February 1948, in US Department of State (ed.), *Foreign Relations of the United States, 1948* (Washington DC, 1976), vol. 1, 509–29
H. Kissinger, G. Ford, and B. Scowcroft, memorandum of a conversation, 15 August 1974, Collection 036600162, National Archives and Records Administration
R. Schuman's speech to the Six at the Quai d'Orsay, 20 June 1950, at https://www.cvce.eu/obj/discours_de_robert_schuman
Schuman Declaration, 9 May 1950, at https://europa.eu/european-union/about-eu/symbols/europe-day/schuman-declaration_en
M. Thatcher, 'Bruges Speech', 20 September 1988, at https://www.cvce.eu/en/education/unit-content/

Newspapers, Periodicals, and Broadcasters

'Nobel for EU Praised in European, Not British, Press', Agence France Presse, 13 October 2012
'Labour Votes to Leave the EEC', BBC News, 26 April 1975
'EU Referendum Results', BBC News, June 2016

'"That Was Chilling": Ten Years since the Financial Crash', BBC News, 9 August 2017
'Brexit: How Will the New Tariff System Work', BBC News, 13 March 2019
'Brexit News: Britons FURIOUS after EU Superstate Plot Exposed', *Daily Express*, 5 August 2021
T. Shipman, 'Ridicule as Nobel Peace Prize is Given to the EU', *Daily Mail*, 13 October 2012
'The EU Diplomat Row Shows Bexiteers Right—Brussels Does Aim to Become a Superstate', *Daily Telegraph*, 21 January 2021
E. O'Doherty, 'Does European Culture Exist?', *Dublin Review of Books*, 1 July 2013
Economist, *Europe's Economies: The Structure and Management of Europe's Ten Largest Economies* (London, 1978)
'Bull? Or Albatross', *Forbes*, 30 March 1992
'Synthesis Europa', *Frankfurter Allgemeine Zeitung*, 13 May 1950
L. Harding and I. Traynor, 'Peace Prize: Ray of Light Pierces EU's Gloom as Nobel Committee Takes Long View', *Guardian*, 13 October 2012
'How Boris Johnson's Brussels-bashing Stories Shaped British Politics', *Guardian*, 14 July 2019
'First Test for New Europe', *Independent*, 28 June 1991
EU Risks Being Split Apart, Says Sarkozy', *Irish Times*, 9 December 2011
'A Europe at Peace', *Irish Times*, 11 December 2012
'Mr. Bevin's Statement on the Pact: "No Ganging Up" against Any Country', *Manchester Guardian*, 19 March 1949
'Today's Signature of Atlantic Treaty: Arms for the West; Mr Acheson's Explanations to Eager Statesmen', *Manchester Guardian*, 2 April 1949
'Lessons of the Brussels Treaty: Framework for Atlantic Defence Organization', *Manchester Guardian*, 5 April 1949
'If the Missiles Go, Peace May Stay', *New York Times*, 29 April 1987
'Some Western Nations Split off on Yugoslavia', *New York Times*, 3 July 1991
'European Community Freezes Arms Sales and Aid', *New York Times*, 6 July 1991
'Fraying at the Edges', *New York Times*, 4 February 2010
'A Talk with Helmut Schmidt', *New York Times Magazine*, 16 September 1984
T. Adams, 'We're Out of the European Union. Just How Did We Get Here?', *Observer*, 27 December 2020
F. O'Toole, 'So Long, We'll Miss You', *Observer*, 27 December 2020
'Orbán, Le Pen, Salvini Join Forces to Blast EU Integration', *Politico* 2 July 2021
A. Applebaum, 'Does Eastern Europe Still Exist?', *Prospect*, 20 March 2013
Interview with Helmut Schmidt, *Der Spiegel*, 6 January 1975
W. Isaacson, 'Is One Germany Better than Two?', *Time*, 20 November 1989
'Britain and America in Peace', *Times*, 6 March 1946
'Headway in the West', *Times*, 6 March 1948
'Russia and Her Allies', *Times*, 9 March 1946
'The Three Powers', *Times*, 14 March 1946
'European Unity', *Times*, 11 March 1948
'Unity to Retain Freedom', *Times*, 22 April 1948
'Mr. Churchill's Call to Europe', *Times*, 8 May 1948
'The Six Powers', *Times*, 22 July 1952
'Urgent Problems of the Six and the Seven', *Times*, 17 March 1960
'Problems for Britain in Links with the Six', *Times*, 30 June 1960
'Britain Drawn by Grip of Europe', *Times*, 3 May 1962
'Britain Puts New Proposals to E.E.C.', *Times*, 12 April 1962
'No Opposition to Britain on E.E.C.', *Times*, 15 May 1962
'Mr. Wilson Ready for Europe—On Terms', *Times*, 19 March 1966
'Mr. Heath Stakes All on Europe Link', *Times*, 29 March 1966
'Viewpoint', *Times*, 7 May 1974
C. Bremner, 'EU Leaders Squabble over Their Peace Prize', *Times*, 20 October 2012
'Bull's Story Is a Tear-Jerker', *Wall Street Journal*, 29 June 2000

462 BIBLIOGRAPHY

'IBM, Groupe Bull of France Form Alliance: Paris Moves to Help State-Owned Firm Meet Japanese Competition', *Washington Post*, 29 January 1992
'Ein Gesamtkonzept, aber wie', *Die Zeit*, 3 March 1989
H. Schmidt, 'Einer unserer Brüder', *Die Zeit*, 24 July 1987

Political Diaries, Correspondence, and Memoirs

K. Adenauer, *Erinnerungen 1953–1955* (Stuttgart, 1966–7), 3 vols
K. Adenauer, *Memoirs, 1945–53* (London, 1966)
J. Attali, *Verbatim* (Paris, 1993), vol. 1
J. Baker, *The Politics of Diplomacy* (New York, 1995)
T. Blair, *A Journey* (London, 2010)
W. Brandt, *Erinnerungen* (Frankfurt, 1989)
W. Brandt, *My Life in Politics* (London, 1992)
G. Brown, *My Life, Our Times* (London, 2017)
G. Bush and B. Scowcroft, *A World Transformed* (New York, 1998)
A. Campbell, *The Blair Years: Extracts from the Campbell Diaries* (London, 2007)
A. Campbell, *The Alistair Campbell Diaries* (London, 2011–18), vols 3–5
J. Chirac, *My Life in Politics* (Basingstoke, 2009)
J. Delors, *La France par l'Europe* (Paris, 1988)
C. de Gaulle, *Mémoires d'espoir* (Paris, 1970–1), 2 vols
H.-D. Genscher, *Erinnerungen* (Berlin, 1995)
V. Giscard d'Estaing, *Le Pouvoir et la vie* (Paris, 2004–7), vols 1–3
V. Havel, 'Paradise Lost', *New York Review of Books*, 9 April 1992
S. Heywood, *What Does Jeremy Think? Jeremy Heywood and the Making of Modern Britain* (London, 2021)
H. Kissinger, *The White House Years* (Boston, 1979)
H. Kohl, *Erinnerungen* (Munich, 2004–05), 3 vols
N. Lawson, *The View from No. 11: Memoirs of a Tory Radical* (London, 1993)
H. Macmillan, *Tides of Fortune, 1945–55* (London, 1969)
J. Major, *The Autobiography* (London, 1999)
R. Marjolin, *Le travail d'une vie. Mémoires 1911–1986* (Paris, 1986)
J. Moch, *Une si longue vie* (Paris, 1976)
J. Monnet, *Mémoires*
M. Nicholson, *Natasha's Story* (London, 1994)
A. Peyrefitte, *C'était de Gaulle* (Paris, 1997–2000), vols 2–3
J.-P. Raffarin, *Je marcherai toujours à l'affectif* (Paris, 2012)
A. Rawnsley, *The End of the Party* (London, 2010)
J. Redwood, *Singing the Blues: 30 Years of Tory Civil War* (London, 2004)
G. Ross, *Jacques Delors and European Integration* (Cambridge, 1995)
G. Ross, 'Inside the Delors Cabinet', *Journal of Common Market Studies*, 32 (1994), 499–523
N. Sarkozy, *Le Temps de tempêtes* (Paris, 2020), vols 1
H. Schmidt, 'Der Politiker als Ökonom', in H. Schmidt, *Kontinuität und Konzentration*, 2nd edn (Bonn, 1976), 36–52
H. Schmidt, *Weggefährten und Reflexionen* (Berlin, 1996)
G. Schröder, *Entscheidungen. Mein Leben in der Politik* (Hamburg, 2006)
P.-H. Spaak, *The Continuing Battle: Memoirs of a European* (Boston, MA, 1971)
F. J. Strauß, *The Grand Design: A European Solution to German Reunification* (New York, 1966)
F. J. Strauß, *Die Erinnerungen* (Berlin, 1989)
J. Straw, *Last Man Standing: Memoirs of a Political Survivor* (London, 2012)
H. Teltschik, *329 Tage. Innenansichten der Einigung* (Berlin, 1993)
M. Thatcher, *The Downing Street Years* (London, 1993)
M. Thatcher, *Path to Power* (London, 1995)
S. Wall, *The Official History of Britain and the European Community: From Rejection to Referendum, 1963–1975* (London, 2012), vol. 2

BIBLIOGRAPHY   463

S. Wall, *Reluctant European: Britain and the European Union from 1945 to Brexit* (Oxford, 2020)
W. Zimmermann, *Origins of a Catastrophe: Yugoslavia and Its Destroyers* (New York, 1996)

Pamphlets, Treatises, and Contemporary Commentary

T. W. Adorno, 'The Culture Industry Reconsidered' (1963), *New German Critique*, 6 (1975), 12–19
P. Anderson, 'Depicting Europe', *London Review of Books*, 20 September 2007
P. Anderson, 'The European Coup', *London Review of Books*, vol. 42, 17 December 2020, 9–23
P. Anderson, 'Ever Closer Union?', *London Review of Books*, vol. 43, 7 January 2021, 25–34
P. Anderson, 'The Breakaway', *London Review of Books*, vol. 43, 21 January 2021, 3–10
A. Applebaum, *Between East and West: Across the Borderlands of Europe* (New York, 1994)
H. Arendt, *The Origins of Totalitarianism* (New York, 1951)
R. Aron, 'Historical Sketch of the Great Debate', in R. Aron and D. Lerner (eds), *France Defeats EDC* (New York, 1957)
R. Aron, *La Lutte des classes* (Paris, 1964)
R. Aron, *Plaidoyer pour l'Europe décadente* (Paris, 1977)
A. B. Atkinson and T. Piketty, *Top Incomes over the Twentieth Century: A Contrast between Continental European and English-speaking Countries* (Oxford, 2006)
E. Balibar, *We, the People of Europe? Reflections on Transnational Citizenship* (Princeton, NJ, 2004)
E. Balibar, *Europe, constitution, frontière* (Bordeaux, 2005)
Z. Bauman, *Memories of Class: The Pre-history and After-life of Class* (London, 1982)
Z. Bauman, 'Soil, Blood and Identity', *Sociological Review*, 40 (1992), 675–701
Z. Bauman, *Liquid Modernity* (Cambridge, 2000)
Z. Bauman, *Europe: An Unfinished Adventure* (Cambridge, 2004)
S. de Beauvoir, *La force des choses* (Paris, 1963)
U. Beck, *German Europe* (Cambridge, 2013)
U. Beck and E. Grande, *Cosmopolitan Europe* (Cambridge, 2007)
D. Bell, *The End of Ideology: On the Exhaustion of Political Ideas in the Fifties* (Glencoe, IL, 1960)
D. Bell, *The Coming of Post-Industrial Society* (New York, 1973)
N. Bobbio, *Ideological Profile of the Twentieth Century in Italy* (Princeton, 1995)
P. Bourdieu, *Practical Reason: On the Theory of Action* (Palo Alto, CA, 1998)
H. Brugmans, *Fundamentals of European Federalism* (London, 1948)
R. von Coudenhove-Kalergi, *L'Europe unie* (Paris, 1938)
R. Dahrendorf, *Class and Class Conflict in an Industrial Society* (London, 1957)
R. Dahrendorf, *Plädoyer für die Europäische Union* (Munich, 1973)
G. Delanty, *Inventing Europe: Idea, Identity, Reality* (Basingstoke, 1995)
G. Delanty, *Formations of European Modernity: A Historical and Political Sociology of Europe*, 2nd edn (Basingstoke, 2018)
G. Delanty and C. Rumford, *Rethinking Europe: Social Theory and the Implications of Europeanization* (London, 2005)
A. Demangeon, *Le déclin de l'Europe* (Paris, 1920)
M. Djilas, *The New Class* (New York, 1957)
H. M. Enzensberger, *Ach Europa* (Frankfurt, 1987)
G. Esping-Andersen, *The Three Worlds of Welfare Capitalism* (Cambridge, 1990)
C. J. Friedrich, 'The Unique Character of Totalitarian Society', in C. J. Friedrich (ed.), *Totalitarianism* (New York, 1953)
C. J. Friedrich, *Trends in Federalism in Theory and Practice* (New York, 1968)
F. Fukuyama, *The End of History and the Last Man* (London, 1992)
M. Gauchet, *La démocratie contre elle-même* (Paris, 2002)
M. Gauchet, 'Comment l'Europe divise la France', *Le débat*, 136 (2005), 4–19
M. Gauchet, *La condition politique* (Paris, 2005)
A. Giddens, *The Class Structure of the Advanced Societies* (London, 1973)
A. Giddens, *The Consequences of Modernity* (Cambridge, 1990)

464 BIBLIOGRAPHY

A. Giddens, *Europe in the Global Age* (Cambridge, 2007)
A. Giddens, *The Crisis of the European Union* (Cambridge, 2012)
S. Glendinning, 'Europe Should Reject Jürgen Habermas's Vision of a Federal European State and Instead Create an Enduring Association between Sovereign Nations', EUROPP blog (LSE), 3 September 2013
M. Glenny, *The Rebirth of History: Eastern Europe in the Age of Democracy* (London, 1990)
M. Glenny, *The Fall of Yugoslavia: The Third Balkan War*, 3rd edn (London, 1996)
J. Goldthorpe, *The Affluent Worker* (Cambridge, 1968–69)
J. Goldthorpe, *The Social Grading of Occupations* (Oxford, 1974)
J. Goldthorpe, *Social Mobility and Class Structure in Modern Britain* (Oxford, 1980)
G. Grass, 'Short Speech of a Rootless Cosmopolitan' (1990), in *Two States—One Nation?* (New York, 1990)
D. Grimm, 'Does Europe Need a Constitution?', in P. Gowan and P. Anderson (eds), *The Question of Europe* (London, 1997), 250–6
D. Grimm, *The Constitution of European Democracy* (Oxford, 2017)
J. Habermas, *Staatsbürgerschaft und nationale Identität: Überlegungen zur europäischen Zukunft* (St Gallen, 1990)
J. Habermas, 'Reply to Grimm', in P. Gowan and P. Anderson (eds), *The Question of Europe* (London 1997), 262–4
J. Habermas, *Die postnationale Konstellation: Politische Essays* (Frankfurt, 1998)
J. Habermas, *Europe: The Faltering Project* (Cambridge, 2009)
J. Habermas, *The Crisis of the European Union* (Cambridge, 2012)
J. Habermas, 'Democracy, Solidarity and the European Crisis', in A.-M. Grozelier, B. Hacker, W. Kowalsky, J. Machnig, H. Meyer, and B. Unger (eds), *Roadmap to a Social Europe* (Falkensee, 2013), 4–13
M. Horkheimer and T. W. Adorno, *Dialektik der Aufklärung* (Amsterdam, 1947)
K. Jaspers, *The Question of German Guilt* (New York, 1947)
S. Jenkins, *Thatcher and Sons: A Revolution in Three Acts* (London, 2006)
B. de Jouvenel, *Vers les Etats d'Europe* (Paris, 1930)
T. Judah, *The Serbs: History, Myth and the Destruction of Yugoslavia* (New Haven, CT, 1997)
H. Kelsen, 'Is a Peace Treaty with Germany Legally Possible and Politically Desirable?', *American Political Science Review*, 41 (1947), 1188–93
J. M. Keynes, *The Economic Consequences of the Peace* (London, 1919)
H. von Keyserling, *Das Spektrum Europas* (Heidelberg, 1928)
M. Kundera, 'The Tragedy of Central Europe', *New York Review of Books*, 7 April 1984
H. D. Lasswell, *Politics: Who Gets What, When, How* (New York, 1950)
S. M. Lipset, 'Whatever Happened to the Proletariat?', *Encounter*, 56 (1981), 18–34
G. Mak, *In Europe: Travels through the Twentieth Century* (London, 2004)
P. Manent, *Democracy without Nations? The Fate of Self-Governance in Europe* (Wilmington, DE, 2007)
H. Marcuse, *Reason and Revolution* (Oxford, 1941)
H. Marcuse, *Eros and Civilization* (London, 1956)
D. Marsh, *The Germans* (London, 1989)
V. Meier, *Yugoslavia: A History of Its Demise* (London, 1999)
F. Meinecke, *Die deutsche Katastrophe* (Wiesbaden, 1946)
J. P. Nettl, *The Soviet Achievement* (New York, 1967)
F. Neumann, *Behemoth* (London, 1942)
F. Neumann, *The Democratic and the Authoritarian State* (New York, 1957)
P. Nora, 'Between Memory and History: *Les Lieux de Mémoire*', *Representations*, 26 (1989), 7–25
J. Nye, *Bound to Lead: The Changing Nature of American Power* (New York, 1990)
J. Nye, *Soft Power: The Means to Success* (New York, 2004)
J. Nye, 'Soft Power: The Evolution of a Concept', *Journal of Political Power*, 14 (2021), 196–208
J. Ortega y Gasset, *Revolt of the Masses* (London, 1932)

BIBLIOGRAPHY 465

J. Ortega y Gasset, 'The Unity and Diversity of Europe', in J. Ortega y Gasset, *Toward a Philosophy of History* (New York, 1941), 43–83
T. Piketty, *Capital in the Twenty-First Century* (Cambridge, 2014)
J. G. A. Pocock, 'Deconstructing Europe', *London Review of Books*, 19 December 1991
F. Pollock, *Automation: Materialien zur Beurteilung der ökonomischen und sozialen Folgen* (Frankfurt, 1956)
K. Popper, *The Open Society and Its Enemies* (London, 1945), 2 vols
K. Popper, *The Poverty of Historicism* (London, 1957)
R. D. Putnam, 'Diplomacy and Domestic Politics', *International Organization*, 42 (1988), 427–61
R. D. Putnam, 'Diplomacy and Domestic Politics: The Logic of Two-level Games', in R. D. Putnam, P. B. Evans, H. K. Jacobsen, and R. D. Putnam (eds), *International Bargaining and Domestic Politics: Double-Edged Diplomacy* (London, 1993), 431–68
G. Ritter, *Europa und die deutsche Frage* (Munich, 1948)
J. Rupnik, *L'Autre Europe: Crise et fin du communisme* (Paris, 1993)
J.-P. Sartre, 'Le fantôme de Staline', *Les Temps modernes*, 129–31 (1956–57), 577–697
H. Schelsky, *Wandlungen der deutschen Familie der Gegenwart* (Stuttgart, 1953)
C. Schmitt, *Der Begriff des Politischen*, new edn (Berlin, 1963)
L. Silber and A. Little, *The Death of Yugoslavia*, revised edn (London, 1996)
O. Spengler, *Der Untergang des Abendlandes*, revised edn (Munich, 1923)
A. Spinelli, 'The Growth of the European Movement since the Second World War', in M. Hodges (ed.), *European Integration* (London, 1972), 43–68
D. Sternberger, 'Verfassungspatriotismus' (1979), in *Schriften* (Frankfurt, 1992), vol. 10, 3–16
T. Todorov, *The New World Disorder: Reflections of a European* (Cambridge, 2005)
M. Weber, *Wirtschaft und Gesellschaft* (Tübingen, 1921)
S. Zweig, *The World of Yesterday* (London, 1953)

Secondary Literature

T. Abe, 'The "Japan Problem": The Trade Policy between the European Countries and Japan in the Last Quarter of the 20th Century', *Entreprises et histoire*, 80 (2015), 13–35
W. Abelshauser, 'Kriegswirtschaft und Wirtschaftswunder: Deutschlands wirtschaftliche Mobilisierung für den Zweiten Weltkrieg und die Folgen für die Nachkriegszeit', *Vierteljahreshefte für Zeitgeschichte* 47 (1999), 503–38
W. Abelshauser et al., *German Industry and Global Enterprise: BASF* (Cambridge, 2009)
M. Abramovitz, 'Catching Up, Forging Ahead and Falling Behind', *Journal of Economic History*, 46 (1986), 385–406
M. Abramovitz, 'The Catch Up Factor in Postwar Economic Growth', *Economic Inquiry*, 38 (1990), 1–18
G. Adams, *Political Ecumenism: Catholics, Jews and Protestants in de Gaulle's Free France, 1940–1945* (Montreal, 2006)
A. Adamthwaite, 'Britain and the World, 1945–1949': The View from the Foreign Office', in J. Becker and F. Knipping (eds), *Power in Europe? Great Britain, France, Italy and Germany in a Postwar World, 1945–1950* (Berlin, 1986), vol. 1, 9–26
A. Adamthwaite, 'Overstretched and Overstrung: Eden, the Foreign Office and the Making of Policy', in E. Di Nolfo (ed.), *Power in Europe? Great Britain, France, Germany and Italy and the Origins of the EEC, 1952–1957* (Berlin, 1992), vol. 2, 19–42
A. Adamthwaite, *Grandeur and Misery: France's Bid for Power in Europe, 1914–1940* (1995)
A. Adamthwaite, 'Sir Anthony Eden: Pro- or Anti-European? The Making of Britain's European Policies', in G. Bossuat (ed.), *Inventer l'Europe. Histoire nouvelle des groupes d'influence et des acteurs de l'unitee européenne* (Berne, 2003), 245–56
P. Addison, *The Road to 1945: British Politics and the Second World War* (London, 1977)
R. Adler-Nissen and K. Kropp (eds), *A Sociology of Knowledge of European Integration: The Social Sciences in the Making of Europe* (London, 2016)
H. Adomeit, *Imperial Overstretch: Germany in Soviet Policy from Stalin to Gorbachev* (Baden-Baden, 1998)

BIBLIOGRAPHY

D. H. Aldcroft and S. Morewood, *The European Economy since 1914*, 5th edn (London 2013)

B. W. E. Aldford, *British Economic Performance, 1945–1975* (1988)

M. S. Alexander and J. F. V. Keiger, *France and the Algerian War, 1954–1962: Strategy, Operations and Diplomacy* (London, 2002)

M. S. Alexander and J. F. V. Keiger (eds), *The Algerian War and the French Army, 1954–1962: Experience, Image, Testimony* (Basingstoke, 2002)

P. Alter, *The German Question and Europe: A History* (London, 2000)

G. Amato, 'The Cautious Mandate to the 2002 Convention', in N. W. Barber, M. Cahill, and R. Ekins (eds), *The Rise and Fall of the European Constitution* (London, 2019)

D. M. Anderson and D. Branch, *Allies at the End of Empire: Loyalists, Nationalists and the Cold War, 1945–76* (London, 2017)

A. Andry, E. Mourlon-Druol, H. A. Ikonomou, and Q. Jouan, 'Rethinking European Integration History in Light of Capitalism: The Case of the Long 1970s', *European Review of History*, 26 (2019), 553–72

B. Anzulovic, *Heavenly Serbia: From Myth to Genocide* (London, 1999)

O. Appelqvist, 'Rediscovering Uncertainty: Early Attempts at a Pan-European Post-War Recovery', *Cold War History*, 8 (2008), 327–52

J. Arenth, *Der Westen tut nichts! Transatlantische Kooperation während der zweiten Berlin-Krise (1958–1962)* (Frankfurt, 1993)

B. von Ark, 'Convergence and Divergence on the European Periphery: Productivity in Eastern and Southern Europe in Retrospect', in B. van Ark and N. Crafts (eds), *Quantitative Aspects of Post-War European Growth* (Cambridge, 1996), 271–326

K. Armstrong and S. J. Bulmer, 'Regulating the Free Movement of Goods: Institutions and Institutional Change', in J. Shaw and G. More (eds), *New Legal Dynamics of European Union* (Oxford, 1995), 164–91

K. Armstrong and S. J. Bulmer, *The Governance of the Single European Market* (Manchester, 1998)

D. Art, *The Politics of the Nazi Past in Germany and Austria* (Cambridge, 2006)

D. Art, 'Why 2013 Is Not 1933: The Radical Right in Europe', *Current History*, 112 (2013), 88–93

D. Artaud, 'A propos de l'occupation de la Ruhr', *Revue d'histoire moderne et contemporaine*, 17 (1970), 1–21

D. Artaud, *La question des dettes interalliees et la reconstruction de l'Europe, 1917–1929* (Lille, 1978)

D. Artaud, 'Die Hintergründe der Ruhrbesetzung 1923: Das problem der Interallierten Schulden', *Vierteljahreshefte für Zeitgeschichte*, 1979, 241–59

D. Artaud, 'La question des dettes interalliées et la reconstruction de l'Europe', *Revue historique*, 530 (1979), 363–82

N. Atkin, *The Forgotten French: Exiles in the British Isles, 1940–1944* (Manchester, 2003)

P. P. D'Attore, 'Americanism and Anti-Americanism in Italy', in P. M. R. Stirk and D. Willis (eds), *Shaping Postwar Europe*, 43–52

M. D'Auria, 'The Ventotene Manifesto: The Crisis of the Nation-State and the Political Identity of Europe', in M. Spiering and M. Wintle (eds), *European Identity and the Second World War* (Basingstoke, 2011), 141–58

M. D'Auria, 'Junius and the "President Professor": Luigi Einaudi's European Federalism', in M. Hewitson and M. D'Auria (eds), *Europe in Crisis: Intellectuals and the European Idea, 1917–1957* (New York, 2012), 289–304

A. Bachoud, J. Cuesta, and M. Trebitsch (eds), *Les intellectuals et l'Europe de 1945 à nos jours* (Paris, 2000)

J. H. Backer, *The Decision to Divide Germany* (Durham, NC, 1978)

H. Badinger and N. Maydell, 'Legal and Economic Issues in Completing the EU Internal Market for Services: An Interdisciplinary Perspective', *Journal of Common Market Studies*, 47 (2009), 693–717

T. Bahcheli and S. Noel, 'Ties That No Longer Bind: Greece, Turkey and the Fading Allure of Ethnic Kinship in Cyprus', in T. J. Mabry and J. McGarry (eds), *Divided Nations and European Integration* (University Park, PA, 2013), 313–40

C. Bailey, *Between Yesterday and Tomorrow: German Visions of Europe, 1926–1950* (New York, 2013)

R. Bailey, *The European Connection: Implications of EEC Membership* (Oxford, 1983)

P. Bajon, 'The European Commissioners and the Empty Chair Crisis of 1965–66', *Journal of European Integration History*, 15 (2009), 105–25

B. Balassa (ed.), *European Economic Integration* (Amsterdam, 1975)

A. Balcells, *Catalan Nationalism* (London, 1996)

M. Balfour, *Germany: The Tides of Power* (London, 1992)

G. Ballor, 'Agents of Integration: Multinational Firms and the European Union', *Enterprise and Society*, 2 (2020), 886–92

D. Balsom, 'Wales', in M. Watson (ed.), *Contemporary Minority Nationalism* (London, 1990), 8–23

T. Banchoff, *The German Problem Transformed: Institutions, Politics and Foreign Policy, 1945–1995* (Ann Arbor, MI, 1999)

O. Bange and G. Niedhart (eds), *Helsinki 1975 and the Transformation of Europe* (New York, 2008)

O. Bange and P. Villaume (eds), *The Long Détente: Changing Concepts of Security and Cooperation in Europe, 1950s–1980s* (Budapest, 2017)

S. H. Barnes and R. Pierce, 'Public Opinion and Political Preferences in France and Italy', *Midwest Journal for Political Sciences*, 15 (1971), 643–60

G. Barraclough, *European Unity in Thought and Action* (Oxford, 1963)

S. Bartolini, T. Risse, and B. Strnth, 'Between Europe and the Nation-State: The Reshaping of Interests, Identities and Political Representation' (Florence, 1999), 2, at http://www.iue.it/

M. Baun, *A Wider Europe: The Process and Politics of European Union Enlargement* (Lanham, MD, 2000)

R. Bavaj, 'Germany and "Western Democracies": The Spatialization of Ernst Fraenkel's Political Thought', in R. Bavaj and M. Steber (eds), *Germany and 'the West': The History of a Modern Concept* (New York, 2015), 183–99

J. Baylis, *The Diplomacy of Pragmatism: Britain and the Formation of NATO, 1942–1949* (Basingstoke, 1993)

D. Beach, *The Dynamics of European Integration: Why and When EU Institutions Matter* (Basingstoke, 2005)

J. M. Beck, *Territory and Terror: Conflicting Nationalisms in the Basque Country* (London, 2004)

S. O. Becker, T. Fetzer, and D. Novy, 'Who Voted for Brexit? A Comprehensive District-Level Analysis', *Economic Policy*, 32 (2017), 601–50

C. Becker-Schaum, P. Gassert, M. Klimke, W. Mausbach, and M. Zepp (eds), *The Nuclear Crisis: The Arms Race, Cold War Anxiety and the German Peace Movement of the 1980s* (New York, 2016)

W. Becker, 'Views of the Foreign Policy Situation among the CDU Leadership, 1945–1957, in E. Di Nolfo (ed.), *Power in Europe? Great Britain, France, Germany and Italy and the Origins of the EEC, 1952–1957* (Berlin, 1992), vol. 2, 351–71

J. Bednar, *The Robust Federation* (Cambridge, 2008)

D. Beetham, *Max Weber and the Theory of Modern Politics*, 2nd edition (Cambridge, 1985)

R. L. Beisner, *Dean Acheson: A Life in the Cold War* (Oxford, 2009)

R. Bellamy 'Liberalism and Nationalism in the Thought of Max Weber', *History of European Ideas*, 14 (1992), 499–507

R. Bellamy and D. Castiglione, 'Legitimizing the Euro-"Polity" and Its "Regime"', *European Journal of Political Theory*, 2 (2003), 7–34

R. Bellamy and D. Castiglione, 'Lacroix's European Constitutional Patriotism: A Response', *Political Studies*, 52 (2004), 187–93

468   BIBLIOGRAPHY

R. Bellamy and D. Castiglione, 'Democracy by Delegation? Who Represents Whom and How in European Governance', *Government and Opposition*, 46 (2011), 101–25

R. Bellamy and D. Castiglione, 'Three Models of Democracy, Political Community and Representation in the EU', *Journal of European Public Policy*, 20 (2013), 206–23

J. Bellers, *Reformpolitik und EWG-Strategie der SPD* (Munich, 1979)

I. T. Berend, *From the Soviet Bloc to the European Union: The Economic and Social Transformation of Central and Eastern Europe since 1973* (Cambridge, 2009)

I. T. Berend, *The History of European Integration: A New Perspective* (London, 2016)

M. Berezin, *Illiberal Politics in Neoliberal Times: Culture, Security and Populism in the New Europe* (Cambridge, 2009)

E. Bergamini and E. Mourlon-Druol, 'Talking about Europe: Exploring 70 Years of News Archives', *Bruegel Working Paper*, 4 (2021), 1–41

S. Berger, *The Search for Normality. National Identity and Historical Consciousness in Germany since 1800* (Oxford, 1997)

S. Berger, *Inventing the Nation: Germany* (London, 2004)

S. Berger and C. Tekin (eds), *History and Belonging: Representations of the Past in Contemporary European Politics* (New York, 2018)

V. R. Berghahn, *The Americanization of West German Industry, 1945–1973* (Cambridge, 1986)

V. R. Berghahn, 'The Debate on "Americanization" among Economic and Cultural Historians', *Cold War History*, 10 (2010), 107–30

V. R. Berghahn, 'Ordoliberalism, Ludwig Erhard and West Germany's "Economic Basic Law"', *European Review of International Studies*, 2 (2015), 37–47

H. Berghoff and U. A. Balbier (eds), *The East German Economy, 1945–2010: Falling Behind or Catching Up?* (Cambridge, 2013)

S. Berstein, 'French Power', in J. Becker and F. Knipping (eds), *Power in Europe? Great Britain, France, Italy and Germany in a Postwar World, 1945–1950* (Berlin, 1986), vol. 1, 163–84

S. Berstein, 'The Perception of French Power by the Political Forces', in E. Di Nolfo, *Power in Europe? Great Britain, France, Germany and Italy and the Origins of the EEC, 1952–1957* (Berlin, 1992), vol. 2, 333–50

S. Berstein and J.-F. Sirinelli (eds), *Les années Giscard. Valéry Giscard d'Estaing et l'Europe 1974–1981* (Paris, 2006)

P. Betts, *Ruin and Renewal: Civilising Europe after the Second World War* (London, 2020)

R. F. Betts, *France and Decolonisation, 1900–1960* (London, 1991)

C. J. Bickerton, *European Integration: From Nation-States to Member States* (Oxford, 2012)

C. J. Bickerton, D. Hodson, and U. Puetter, 'The New Intergovernmentalism: European Integration in the Post-Maastricht Era', *Journal of Common Market Studies*, 53 (2015), 703–22

C. J. Bickerton, D. Hodson, and U. Puetter (eds), *The New Intergovernmentalism: States and Supranational Actors in the Post-Maastricht Era* (Oxford, 2015)

R. Bideleux and I. Jeffries, *A History of Eastern Europe* (London, 1998)

R. Biermann, *Zwischen Kreml und Kanzleramt: Wie Moskau mit der deutschen Einheit rang* (Paderborn, 1997)

F. Biess, *German Angst: Fear and Democracy in the Federal Republic of Germany* (Oxford, 2020)

M. Billig, *Talking of the Royal Family* (London, 1992)

M. Billig, *Banal Nationalism* (London, 1995)

T. Birkner, *Comrades for Europe? Die 'Europarede' Helmut Schmidts 1974* (Bremen, 2005)

A. Blair, *The European Union since 1945* (London, 2014)

M. Bleaney, *The Rise and Fall of Keynesian Economics: An Investigation of Its Contribution to Capitalist Development* (Basingstoke, 1985)

E. Böhm, *Die Sicherheit des Westens. Enstehung und Funktion der G7-Gipfel 1975–1981* (Munich, 2014)

T. Börzel and T. Risse, 'Conceptualizing the Domestic Impact of Europe', in K. Featherstone and C. Radaelli (eds), *The Politics of Europeanization* (Oxford, 2003), 57–80

I. Boeva and V. Shironin, 'Russians between State and Market', *Studies in Public Policy*, 205 (Glasgow, 1992)

BIBLIOGRAPHY   469

V. Bogdanor, 'Social Democracy', in A. Seldon (ed.), *Blair's Britain, 1997–2007* (Cambridge, 2007), 164–82

V. Bojičić, 'The Disintegration of Yugoslavia: Causes and Consequences of Dynamic Inefficiency in Semi-command Economies', in D. A. Dyker and I. Vejvoda (eds), *Yugoslavia and After* (London, 1996), 65–83

A. Boltho (ed.), *The European Economy: Growth and Crisis* (Oxford, 1982)

A. Boltho, 'Export-led Growth or Growth-led Exports? Western Europe in the "Golden Age"', *European Journal of Comparative Economics*, 17 (2020), 185–203

E. Bonino, A. King, C. Larass, A. Matutes, N. Notat, and A. Pelinka, *How Much Popular Support Is There for the EU?* (Brussels, 1997)

M. J. Bordo, R. Macdonald, and M. J. Oliver, 'Sterling in Crisis, 1964–1967', *European Review of Economic History*, 13 (2009), 437–59

G. Bossuat, *La France, l'aide américaine et la construction européenne 1944–1954* (Paris, 1992)

G. Bossuat, 'Les euro-socialistes de la SFIO. Réseaux et influence', in Bossuat, G. and G. Saunier (eds), *Inventer l'Europe. Histoire nouvelle des groupes d'influence et des acteurs de l'unite europeenne* (Brussels, 2003), 409–30

G. Bossuat (ed.), *L'Europe et la mondialisation* (Paris, 2006)

G. Bossuat and G. Saunier (eds), *Inventer l'Europe. Histoire nouvelle des groupes d'influence et des acteurs de l'unité européenne* (Brussels, 2003)

C. Bottici and B. Challand, *Imagining Europe: Myth, Memory and Identity* (Cambridge, 2013)

P. Bourquin, J. Cribb, T. Waters, and X. Xu, *Living Standards, Poverty and Inequality in the UK: 2019* (London, 2019)

R. Boyce, *The Great Interwar Crisis and the Collapse of Globalization* (Basingstoke, 2009)

R. Boyer, 'Les bureaux d'eetudes du ministere des Affaires eetrangeres et l'Europe pendant la Seconde Guerre mondiale', in R. Girault and G. Bossuat (eds), *Europe brisée, Europe retrouvée* (Paris, 1994), 133–52

F. Bozo, 'Mitterrand's France, the End of the Cold War and German Unification: A Reappraisal', *Cold War History*, 7 (2007), 455–78

F. Bozo, 'La France face à l'unification allemande', in J.-P. Cahn and U. Pfeil (eds), *Allemagne, 1974–1990: De l'Ostpolitik à l'unification* (Villeneuve d'Ascq, 2009), 285–301

F. Bozo, *Visions of the End of the Cold War in Europe, 1945–1990* (New York, 2012)

G. V. Bradley and E. C. Brugger (eds), *Catholic Social Teaching* (Cambridge, 2019)

J. Brand, *The National Movement in Scotland* (Londo, 1978)

B. F. Braumoeller, 'The Myth of American Isolationism', *Foreign Policy Analysis*, 6 (2010), 349–71

Z. Bray and M. Keating, 'European Integration and the Basque Country in France and Spain', in T. J. Mabry and J. McGarry, *Divided Nations and European Integration* (Philadelphia, PA, 2013), 127–56

C. Bremen, *Die Eisenhower-Administration und die zweite Berlin-Krise 1958–1961* (Berlin, 1998)

I. Bremmer and R. Taras (eds), *Nations and Politics in the Communist Successor States* (Cambridge, 1993)

F. Brettschneider, *Wahlumfragen: Empirische Befunde zur Darstellung in den Medien und zum Einfluss auf das Wahlverhalten in der Bundesrepublik Deutschland und den USA* (Munich, 1991)

J. J. Breuilly, *Nationalism and the State* (Manchester, 1985)

J. J. Breuilly, 'Imagined Communities and Modern Historians', *Nations and Nationalism*, 22 (2016), 625–59

J. J. Breuilly, 'Nation, Nation-state and Nationalism', in E. Hanke, L. Scaff, and S. Whimster (eds), *The Oxford Handbook of Max Weber* (Oxford, 2020), 185–205

M. Brewer, A. Goodman, A. Muriel, and L. Sibieta, *Poverty and Inequality in the UK* (London, 2007)

A. Brill, *Abrgrenzung und Hoffnung: 'Europa' in der deutschen, britischen und amerikanischen Presse 1945–1980* (Göttingen, 2014)

D. Brinkley, *Jean Monnet: The Path to European Unity* (Basingstoke, 1991)

D. Brinkley and C. Hackett (eds), *Jean Monnet: The Path to European Unity* (Basingstoke, 1991)

470 BIBLIOGRAPHY

S. N. Broadberry, C. Giordano, and F. Zollino, 'Productivity', in G. Toniolo (ed.), *The Oxford Handbook of the Italian Economy since Unification* (Oxford, 2013), 187–226

S. Brockmann, *Literature and German Unification* (Cambridge, 2006)

R. Brubaker, *Nationalism Reframed: Nationhood and the National Question in the New Europe* (Cambridge, 1996)

R. Brubaker, *Citizenship and Nationhood in France and Germany* (Cambridge, MA, 1998)

H. Brugmans, *Fundamentals of European Federalism* (London, 1948)

H. Brugmans, *L'Idée européenne* (1970)

B. Bruneteau, 'The Construction of Europe and the Concept of the Nation-State', *Contemporary European History* 9 (2000), 245–60

L. A. Brunet, 'The Creation of the Monnet Plan, 1945–1946: A Critical Re-Evaluation', *Contemporary European History*, 27 (2018), 23–41

W. Brus, 'Evolution of the Communist Economic System: Scope and Limits', in D. Stark and V. Nee, *Remaking the Economic Institutions of Socialism: China and Eastern Europe* (Palo Alto, 1989), 255–77

D. Buchan, *Europe: The Strange Superpower* (Aldershot, 1993)

I. Budge and K. Newton, *The Politics of the New Europe: Atlantic to Urals* (London, 1997)

C. Buffet, *Mourir pour Berlin: La France et l'Allemagne* (Paris, 1991)

J. Bugakski, *Nations in Turmoil* (Boulder, CO, 1995)

A. Bullock, *Ernest Bevin, Foreign Secretary, 1945–1951* (London, 1983)

S. J. Bulmer, 'The Governance of the European Union: A New Institutionalist Approach', *Journal of Public Policy*, 13 (1994), 351–80

S. J. Bulmer and W. E. Paterson, 'Germany and the European Union: From "Tamed Power" to Normalized Power?', *International Affairs*, 86 (2010), 1051–73

S. J. Bulmer, S. Bulmer, C. Jeffery, and S. Padgett (eds), *Rethinking Germany and Europe: Democracy and Diplomacy in a Semi-Sovereign State* (Basingstoke, 2010)

S. J. Bulmer, S. Bulmer, C. Jeffery, and S. Padgett (eds), 'Understanding the New Intergovernmentalism: Pre- and Post-Maastricht in EU Studies', in C. J. Bickerton, D. Hodson, and U. Puetter (eds), *The New Intergovernmentalism: States and Supranational Actors in the Post-Maastricht Era* (Oxford, 2015), 289–304

J. Bulpitt, *Territory and Power in the United Kingdom* (Colchester, 2008)

R. F. Bunn, *German Politics and the Spiegel Affair: A Case Study of the Bonn System* (Baton Rouge LA, 1968)

E. Bunout, M. Ehrmann, and F. Clavert (eds), *Digitised Newspapers—A New Eldorado for Historians: Reflections on Tools, Methods and Epistemology* (Berlin, 2023)

L. Buonanno and N. Nugent, *Policies and Policy Processes of the European Union* (Basingstoke, 2013)

M. Burgess, 'Federalism and Federation in Western Europe', in M. Burgess (ed.), *Federalism and Federation in Western Europe* (London, 1986), 15–33

M. Burgess, *Federalism and the European Union: The Building of Europe, 1950–2000* (London, 2000)

M. Burgess, *Comparative Federalism: Theory and Practice* (New York, 2006)

E. Bussière, *La France, la Belgique et l'organisation économique de l'Europe* (Paris, 1991)

E. Bussière (ed.), *Europa. L'idée et l'identité européennes de l'antiquité grecque au XXe siècle* (Anvers, 2001)

E. Bussière, 'Premiers schemas européens et économie internationale durant l'entre-deux-guerres', *Relations internationales*, 123 (2005), 51–70

E. Calandri, 'The Western European Union Armaments Pool: France's Quest for Security and European Cooperation in Transition, 1951–55', *Journal of European Integration History*, 1 (1995), 37–63

D. Calleo, *Europe's Future: The Grand Alternatives* (New York, 1965)

D. Calleo, *The German Problem Reconsidered: Germany and the World Order, 1870 to the Present* (Cambridge, 1978)

D. Calleo, *Rethinking Europe's Future* (Princeton, NJ, 2001)

BIBLIOGRAPHY 471

O. Calligaro, *Negotiating Europe: EU Promotion of Europeanness since the 1950s* (Basingstoke, 2013)

O. Calligaro, 'From "European Cultural Heritage" to "Cultural Diversity"? The Changing Core Values of European Cultural Policy', *Politique européenne*, 45 (2014), 60–85

O. Calligaro, 'Legitimation through Remembrance? The Changing Regimes of Historicity of European Integration', *Journal of Contemporary European Studies*, 23 (2015), 330–43

O. Calligaro and K. K. Patel, 'The True "EURESCO"? The Council of Europe, Transnational Networking and the Emergence of European Community Cultural Policies, 1970–90', *European Review of History*, 24 (2017), 399–422

J.-Y. Camus and N. Lebourg, *Far-Right Politics in Europe* (Cambridge, MA, 2017)

R. Caplan, *Europe and the Recognition of New States in Yugoslavia* (Cambridge, 2009)

M. J. Carley, 'Behind Stalin's Moustache: Pragmatism in Early Soviet Foreign Policy, 1917–1941', *Diplomacy and Statecraft*, 12 (2001), 159–74

D. Carlton, *Britain and the Suez Crisis* (Oxford, 1989)

G. de Carmoy, *The Foreign Policies of France, 1944–1968* (Chicago, 1970)

F. Caron, *An Economic History of Modern France* (London, 1979)

M. Carreras, '"What Do We Have to Lose?" Local Economic Decline, Prospect Theory, and Support for Brexit', *Electoral Studies*, 62 (2019), online

E. Carter, *How German Is She? Postwar West German Reconstruction and the Consuming Woman* (Ann Arbor, MI, 1997)

N. D. Cary, 'Reassessing Germany's Ostpolitik: From Détente to Refreeze', *Central European History*, 33 (2000), 235–62

N. D. Cary, 'Reassessing Germany's Ostpolitik: From Refreeze to Reunification', *Central European History*, 33 (2000), 369–90

N. Caspersen, *Contested Nationalism: Serb Elite Rivalry in Croatia and Bosnia in the 1990s* (New York, 2010)

J. L. Chabot, *Aux origines intellectuelles de l'Union européenne* (Grenoble, 2005)

J. Chace, 'Sharing the Atom Bomb', *Foreign Affairs*, 75 (1996), 129–44

G. R. Chafetz, *Gorbachev, Reform and the Brezhnev Doctrine: Soviet Policy toward Eastern Europe, 1985–1990* (Westport, CT, 1993)

M. Charlton, *The Price of Victory* (London, 1983)

J. T. Checkel and P. J. Katzenstein (eds), *European Identity* (Cambridge, 2009)

J. T. Checkel and P. J. Katzenstein, 'The Politicization of European Identities', in J. T. Checkel and P. J. Katzenstein (eds), *European Identity* (Cambridge, 2009), 1–26

J. T. Checkel and A. Moravcsik, 'A Constructivist Research Programme in EU Studies?', *European Union Politics*, 2 (2001), 219–49

R. Chin, *The Guest Worker Question in Postwar Germany* (Cambridge, 2009)

C. S. Christensen (ed.), *Analyzing Political Tensions between Ukraine, Russia and the EU* (Hershey, PA, 2020)

T. Christiansen, 'Tensions of European Governance: Politicized Bureaucracy and Multiple Accountability in the European Commission', *Journal of European Public Policy*, 4 (1997), 73–90

T. Christiansen and C. Reh, *Constitutionalizing the European Union* (Basingstoke, 2009)

T. Christiansen, K. E. Jørgensen, and A. Wiener (eds), *The Social Construction of Europe* (London, 2001)

P. Claeys and N. Loeb-Mayer, 'Trans-European Party Groupings: Emergence of New and Alignment of Old Parties in the Light of the Direct Elections to the European Parliament', *Government and Opposition*, 14 (1979), 455–78

A. Clayton, *The French Wars of Decolonization* (London, 2014)

D. Clayton and D. M. Higgins, '"Buy British": An Analysis of UK Attempts to Turn a Slogan into Government Policy in the 1970s and 1980s', *Business History*, 64 (2020), 1260–80

D. Coen and J. Richardson (eds), *Lobbying the European Union: Institutions, Actors and Issues* (Oxford, 2009)

472 BIBLIOGRAPHY

C. Cogan, 'Mitterrand, France and NATO: The European Transition', *Journal of Transatlantic Studies*, 9 (2011), 257–67

J. P. Cointet and M. Cointet, *La France à Londres, 1940–1943* (Brussels, 1990)

A. Cole, *François Mitterrand: A Study in Political Leadership* (London, 1994)

S. Collini, *Absent Minds: Intellectuals in Britain* (Oxford, 2006)

R. Colquhoun, *Raymond Aron* (London, 1986), 2 vols

E. da Conceição-Heldt, 'EU Agricultural and Fisheries Policies: An Economic and Environmental Disaster!', in H. Zimmermann and A. Dür (eds), *Key Controversies in European Integration* (Basingstoke, 2012), 161–8

M. Connelly, *A Diplomatic Revolution: Algeria's Fight for Independence and the Origins of the Post-Cold War Era* (Oxford, 2002)

I. Connor, *Refugees and Expellees in Post-war Germany* (Manchester, 2007)

W. Connor, *Ethnonationalism: The Quest for Understanding* (Princeton, NJ, 1994)

D. Conversi, *German-bashing and the Breakup of Yugoslavia* (Seattle, WA, 1998)

M. Conway, 'The Rise and Fall of Western Europe's Democratic Age, 1945–1973', *Contemporary European History*, 13 (2004), 67–88

M. Conway, *Western Europe's Democratic Age, 1945–1968* (Princeton, NJ, 2020)

M. Conway and V. Depkat, 'Towards a European History of the Discourse of Democracy: Discussing Democracy in Western Europe, 1945–1960', in M. Conway and K. K. Patel (eds), *Europeanization in the Twentieth Century* (Basingstoke, 2010), 132–56

M. Conway and J. Gotovitch (eds), *Europe in Exile: European Exile Communities in Britain, 1940–1945* (New York, 2001)

E. Conze, M. Klimke, and J. Varon (eds), *Nuclear Threats, Nuclear Fear, and the Cold War of the 1980s* (New York, 2017)

V. Conze, *Das Europa der Deutschen: Ideen von Europa in Deutschland zwischen Reichstradition und Westorientierung 1920–1970* (Munich, 2005)

D. Cook, *The Culture Industry Revisited: Theodor W. Adorno on Mass Culture* (New York, 1996)

J. M. Cooper, Jr. (ed.), *Reconsidering Woodrow Wilson: Progressivism, Internationalism, War and Peace* (Baltimore, 2008)

M. Copelovitch, J. Frieden, and S. Walter, 'The Political Economy of the Euro Crisis', *Comparative Political Studies*, 49 (2016), 811–40

G. Cophornic, 'SFIO et UEO: La recherche d'une unité', in R. Girault and G. Bossuat (eds), *Europe brisée, Europe retrouvée* (Paris, 1994), 257–82

L. Coppolaro, *The Making of a World Trading Power: The European Economic Community (EEC) in the GATT Kennedy Round Negotiations, 1963–67* (Farnham, 2013)

L. Coppolaro, 'In Search of Power: The European Commission in the Kennedy Round Negotiations, 1963–1967', *Contemporary European History*, 23 (2014), 23–41

L. Coppolaro, 'In the Shadow of Globalization: The European Community and the United States in the GATT Negotiations of the Tokyo Round, 1973–1979', *International History Review*, 40 (2018), 752–73

F. Costiglia, *Awkward Dominion: American Political, Economic and Cultural Relations with Europe, 1919–1933* (Ithaca, NY, 1987)

V. Cotesta, 'Rosenzweig, Schmitt and the Concept of Europe', in M. Hewitson and M. D'Auria (eds), *Europe in Crisis: Intellectuals and the European Idea, 1917–1957* (New York, 2012), 169–82

N. Crafts and M. Magnani, 'The Golden Age and the Second Globalization in Italy', in G. Toniolo (ed.), *The Oxford Handbook of the Italian Economy since Unification* (Oxford, 2013), 69–107

N. Crafts and T. C. Mills, 'Europe's Golden Age: An Econometric Investigation of Changing Trend Rates of Growth', in B. van Ark and N. Crafts (eds), *Quantitative Aspects of Post-War European Growth* (Cambridge, 1996), 415–31

N. Crafts and G. Toniolo, 'Postwar Growth: An Overview' and B. Eichengreen, 'Institutions and Economic Growth: Europe after World War II', in N. Crafts and G. Toniolo (eds), *Economic Growth in Europe since 1945* (Cambridge, 1996), 1–72

BIBLIOGRAPHY   473

L. Cram, 'Identity and European Integration: Diversity as a Source of Integration', *Nations and Nationalism*, 15 (2009), 109–28

L. Cram, 'Does the EU Need a Navel? Implicit and Explicit Identification with the European Union', *Journal of Common Market Studies*, 50 (2012), 71–86

M. Creswell and M. Trachtenberg, 'France and the German Question, 1945–1955', *Journal of Cold War Studies*, 5 (2003), 5–28

O. Croci, 'Not a Zero-Sum Game: Atlanticism and Europeanism in Italian Foreign Policy', *International Spectator*, 43 (2008), 137–55

W. C. Cromwell, 'The Marshall Plan, Britain and the Cold War', *Review of International Studies*, 8 (1982), 233–49

C. Crouch, *Social Change in Western Europe* (Oxford, 1999)

C. Crouch, 'Class Politics and the Social Investment Welfare State', in M. Keating and D. McCrone (eds), *The Crisis of Social Democracy in Europe* (Edinburgh, 2015), 156–68

N. J. Crowson, *The Conservative Party and European Integration since 1945: At the Heart of Europe?* (London, 2009)

L. Crump and S. Erlandsson (eds), *Margins for Manoeuvre in Cold War Europe: The Influence of Smaller Powers* (London, 2019)

Z. Csergö and J. M. Goldgeier, 'Kin-State Activism in Hungary, Romania and Russia: The Politics of Ethnic Demography', in T. J. Mabry and J. McGarry, *Divided Nations and European Integration* (Philadelphia, PA, 2013), 89–126

D. Cuccia, *There Are Two German States and Two Must Remain? Italy and the Long Path from the German Question to Reunification* (Hildesheim, 2019)

B. Cumings, '"Revising Postrevisionism," or, The Poverty of Theory in Diplomatic History', *Diplomatic History*, 17 (1993), 539–69

O. Daddow, *New Labour and the European Union: Blair and Brown's Logic of History* (Manchester, 2011)

O. Daddow, '"Tony's War"? Kosovo and the Interventionist Impulse in British Foreign Policy', *International Affairs*, 85 (2009), 547–60

A. Dalgaard-Nielsen, *Germany, Pacifism and Peace Enforcement* (Manchester, 2006), 70–80

O. Dann, *Nation und Nationalismus in Deutschland*, 3rd edn (Munich, 1993)

J. v. Dannenberg, *The Foundations of Ostpolitik* (Oxford, 2008)

W. Danspeckgruber, 'Self-Determination and Regionalization in Contemporary Europe', in W. Danspeckgruber (ed.), *The Self-Determination of Peoples: Community, Nation and State in an Interdependent World* (Boulder, CO, 2002), 165–200

W. Danspeckgruber, 'Self-Determination in Our Time: Reflections on Perception, Globalization and Change', in J. Fisch (ed.), *Die Verteilung der Welt: Selbstbestimmung und das Selbstbestimmungsrecht der Völker* (Munich, 2011), 307–31

J. Darwin, *Britain and Decolonisation* (New York, 1988)

A. Daum, *Kennedy in Berlin* (Cambridge, 2008)

N. Davies, *Rising '44: The Battle for Warsaw* (New York, 2004)

N. Davies, *God's Playground* (Oxford, 2005)

P. Davies, *The National Front in France* (London, 2012)

M. Dedman, *The Origins and Development of the European Union, 1945–1995: A History of European Integration* (London, 1996)

C. Defrance, *La Politique culturelle de la France sur la rive gauche du Rhin, 1945–1955* (Strasbourg, 1994)

A. Deighton (ed.), *Britain and the First Cold War* (Basingstoke, 1990)

A. Deighton, *The Impossible Peace: Britain, the Division of Germany and the Origins of the Cold War* (Oxford, 1990)

A. Deighton (ed.), *Building Postwar Europe: National Decision-Makers and European Institutions, 1948–63* (Basingstoke, 1995)

E. F. Delaney, 'The European Constitution and Europe's Dialectical Federalism', in N. W. Barber, M. Cahill, and R. Ekins (eds), *The Rise and Fall of the European Constitution* (Oxford, 2019), 73–87

474 BIBLIOGRAPHY

E. Dell, *The Schuman Plan and the British Abdication of Leadership in Europe* (Oxford, 1995)

J.-F. Deniau, *La découverte de l'Europe* (Paris, 1994)

B. Denitch, *Ethnic Nationalism: The Tragic Death of Yugoslavia*, revised edn (Minnesota, 1996)

A. DePorte, *Europe between the Superpowers: The Enduring Balance* (New Haven, CT, 1979)

K. W. Deutsch, *Political Community and the North Atlantic Area* (Princeton, NJ, 1957)

R. Dietl, 'In Defence of the West: General Lauris Norstad, NATO Nuclear Forces and Transatlantic Relations, 1956–1963', *Diplomacy and Statecraft*, 17 (2006), 347–92

J. Diez Medrano, *Divided Nations: Class, Politics and Nationalism in the Basque Country and Catalonia* (Ithaca, NY, 1995)

J. Diez Medrano, 'The Public Sphere and the European Union's Political Identity', in J. T. Checkel and P. J. Katzenstein (eds), *European Identity* (Cambridge, 2009, 81–107

D. Dinan, *Europe Recast: A History of European Union* (Basingstoke, 2004)

D. Dinan, 'The Historiography of European Integration', in D. Dinan (ed.), *Origins and Evolution of the European Union* (Oxford, 2006), 297–324

P. Dine, *Images of the Algerian War: French Fiction and Film, 1954–1992* (Oxford, 1994)

L. L. Doan, '"Sexy Greedy Is the Late Eighties': Power Systems in Amis's Money and Churchill's Serious Money', *Minnesota Review*, 34 (1990), 69–80

A. Dobson, *An Introduction to the Politics and Philosophy of José Ortega y Gasset* (Cambridge, 1989)

S. Dockrill, *Britain's Policy for West German Rearmament* (Cambridge, 1991)

A. Doering-Manteuffel, *Wie westlich sind die Deutschen? Amerikanisierung und Westernisierung im 20. Jahrhundert* (Göttingen, 1999)

A. Doering-Manteuffel, 'Perceptions of the West in Twentieth-Century Germany', in R. Bavaj and M. Steber (eds), *Germany and 'the West': The History of a Modern Concept* (New York, 2015), 81–96

M. Dogan, 'The Decline of Nationalisms within Western Europe', *Comparative Politics*, 26 (1994), 281–305

P. P. Donati, 'Social Welfare and Social Services in Italy since 1950', in R. Girod, P. de Laubier, and A. Gladstone (eds), *Social Policy in Western Europe and the USA, 1950–1985* (London, 1985), 101–11

N. Doumanis, *Inventing the Nation: Italy* (London, 2001)

S. Dowrick and D.-T. Nguyen, 'OECD Comparative Economic Growth 1950–1985: Catch-Up and Convergence', *American Economic Review*, 79 (1989), 1010–30

J. Dragović-Soso, *'Saviours of the Nation': Serbia's Intellectual Opposition and the Revival of Nationalism* (London, 2002)

D. Drake, *Intellectuals and Politics in Postwar France* (Basingstoke, 2002)

H. Drake, 'Jacques Chirac's Balancing Acts: The French Right and Europe', *South European Society and Politics*, 10 (2005), 297–313

K. Dreher, *Helmut Kohl. Leben mit Macht* (Stuttgart, 1998)

F. Duchêne, *Jean Monnet: The First Statesman of Interdependence* (New York, 1994)

G. Duchenne (ed.), *Réseaux économiques et construction européenne* (Brussels, 2004)

G. Duchenne, *Esquisses d'une Europe nouvelle. L'européisme dans la Belgique de l'entre-deux-guerres 1919–1939* (Brussels, 2008)

J. Dülffer, '"No More Potsdam!" Konrad Adenauer's Nightmare and the Basis of His International Orientation', *German Politics and Society*, 25 (2007), 19–42

J. Dumbrell, 'Varieties of Post-Cold War American Isolationism', *Government and Opposition*, 24 (1999), 24–43

R. H. Dumke, 'Reassessing the Wirtschaftswunder: Reconstruction and Postwar Growth in West Germany in an International Context', *Oxford Bulletin of Economics and Statistics*, 52 (1990), 451–91

M. Dumoulin (ed.), *The European Commission, 1958–72: History and Memories* (Luxembourg, 2007)

D. H. Dunn, 'Isolationism Revisited: Seven Persistent Myths in the Contemporary American Foreign Policy Debate', *Review of International Studies*, 31 (2005), 237–61

BIBLIOGRAPHY   475

J.-B. Duroselle, *La Décadence, 1932–1939* (Paris, 1979)
J.-B. Duroselle, *L'idée d'Europe au XXe siècle: Des mythes aux réalités* (Brussels, 1996)
J.-B. Duroselle, *France and the Nazi Threat: The Collapse of French Diplomacy, 1932–1939* (New York, 2004)
D. Dutton, *British Politics since 1945: The Rise, Fall and Rebirth of Consensus*, 2nd edn (Oxford, 1997)
K. Dyson, 'The Ambiguous Politics of Western Germany: Politicization in a "State" Democracy', *European Journal of Political Research*, 7 (1979), 375–96
K. Dyson, *The State Tradition in Western Europe* (Oxford, 1980)
K. Dyson (ed.), *European States and the Euro: Europeanization, Variation, and Convergence* (Oxford, 2002)
K. Dyson, 'Norman's Lament: The Greek and Euro Area Crisis in Historical Perspective', *New Political Economy*, 15 (2010), 597–608
K. Dyson, *States, Debt, and Power: 'Saints' and 'Sinners' in European History and Integration* (Oxford, 2014)
K. Dyson, 'Playing for High Stakes: The Eurozone Crisis', in D. Dinan, N. Nugent, and W. E. Paterson (eds), *The European Union in Crisis* (London, 2017), 54–76
K. Dyson and K. Featherston, *The Road to Maastricht: Negotiating Economic and Monetary Union* (Oxford, 1999)
S. B. Dyson, *The Blair Identity: Leadership and Foreign Policy* (Manchester, 2009), 70–131
J. Eatwell and M. Milgate, *The Fall and Rise of Keynesian Economics* (Oxford, 2011)
L. J. Edinger, *Kurt Schumacher: A Study in Personality and Political Behaviour* (Palo Alto, CA, 1965)
E. Edwards Spalding, *The First Cold Warrior: Harry Truman, Containment and the Remaking of Liberal Internationalism* (Lexington, KY, 2006)
M. A. Eger, 'Even in Sweden: The Effect of Immigration on Support for Welfare State Spending', *European Sociological Review*, 26 (2010), 203–17
M. Eigmüller, 'Europeanization from Below: The Influence of Individual Actors on the EU Integration of Social Policies', *Journal of European Social Policy*, 23 (2013), 363–75
M. Eilstrup-Sangiovanni (ed.), *Debates on European Integration: A Reader* (Basingstoke, 2006)
C. Eisenberg, 'The Cold War in Europe', in J.-C. Agnew and R. Rosenzweig (eds), *A Companion to Post-1945 America* (Oxford, 2002), 406–25
G. Eley, *Forging Democracy: The History of the Left in Europe, 1850–2000* (Oxford, 2002)
J. Ellison, *Threatening Europe: Britain and the Creation of the European Community, 1955–58* (Basingstoke, 2000)
D. W. Ellwood, *Rebuilding Europe: Western Europe, America and Postwar Reconstruction* (London, 1992)
J. Elvert, 'The "New European Order" of National Socialism: Some Remarks on Its Sources, Genesis and Nature', in D. Gosewinkel (ed.), *Anti-Liberal Europe: A Neglected Story of Europeanization* (New York, 2015), 105–27
F. van Esch, 'Why Germany Wanted EMU: The Role of Helmut Kohl's Belief System and the Fall of the Wall', *German Politics*, 21 (2012), 34–52
A. Etzioni, *Political Unification: A Comparative Study of Leaders and Forces* (New York, 1965)
S. Fabbrini, *Federalism and Democracy in the European Union and the United States* (London, 2005)
G. Falkner, 'The EU's Social Dimension', in M. Cini (ed.), *European Union Politics* (Oxford, 2003), 310–22
A. Favell, *Eurostars and Eurocities: Free Moving Urban Professionals in an Integrating Europe* (Oxford, 2007)
K. Featherstone, *Political Change in Greece: Before and after the Colonels* (Basingstoke, 1987)
C. H. Feinstein (ed.), *The Managed Economy: Essays in British Economic Policy and Performance since 1929* (Oxford, 1982)
M. Ferrara, A. Hemerijk, and M. Rhodes, 'The Future of the "European Social Model" in the Global Economy', *Journal of Comparative Policy Analysis*, 3 (2001), 163–90

476 BIBLIOGRAPHY

D. K. Fieldhouse, *Unilever Overseas: The Anatomy of a Multinational, 1895–1965* (London, 1978)

D. K. Fieldhouse, *Western Imperialism in the Middle East, 1914–1958* (Oxford, 2008)

A. P. Fimister, *Robert Schuman: Neo-Scholastic Humanism and the Reunification of Europe* (Saarbrücken, 2008)

G. Fink (ed.), *Stress of War, Conflict and Disaster* (Oxford, 2010)

P. Finney, 'Still "Marking Time"? Text, Discourse and Truth in International History', *Review of International Studies*, 27 (2001), 291–308

N. Finszch and J. Martschukat (eds), *Different Restorations: Reconstruction and 'Wiederaufbau' in the United States and Germany, 1865–1945–1989* (Oxford, 1996)

O. Fioreto, *Reconstructions: Multilateralism and European Varieties of Capitalism after 1950* (Oxford, 2010)

C. Fischer, *A Vision of Europe. Franco-German Relations during the Great Depression, 1929–1932* (Oxford, 2017)

G. Fischer and R. Strauss (eds), *Europe's Income, Wealth, Consumption and Inequality* (Oxford, 2020)

S. Fishman, 'Shaping, Not Making, Democracy: The European Union and the Post-Authoritarian Political Transformations of Spain and Portugal', *South European Society and Politics*, 8 (2003), 31–46

S. Fishman et al. (eds), *France at War: Vichy and the Historians* (Oxford, 2000)

A. Fitzgibbons, *Keynes's Vision* (Oxford, 1988)

F. J. Fleron, E. P. Hoffmann, and R. F. Laird, *Classic Issues in Soviet Foreign Policy: From Lenin to Brezhnev* (New York, 1991)

N. Fligstein, *Euroclash: The EU, European Identity and the Future of Europe* (Oxford, 2008)

N. Fligstein and J. McNichol, 'The Institutional Terrain of the European Union', in W. Sandholtz and A. Stone Sweet (eds), *European Integration and Supranational Governance* (Oxford, 1998), 59–91

N. Fligstein, A. Polykova, and W. Sandholtz, 'European Integration, Nationalism and European Identity', *Journal of Common Market Studies*, 50 (2012), 106–22

P. Flora, *State, Economy and Society in Western Europe, 1815–1975* (London, 1983)

P. Flora and A. J. Heidenheimer (eds), *Development of Welfare States in Europe and America* (London, 1981)

B. J. Foley, 'France: A Case of Eurosclerosis?', in B. J. Foley (ed.), *European Economies since the Second World War* (Basingstoke, 1998), 48–74

A. M. Fonseca, 'From the Iberian Peninsula to Latin America: The Socialist International's Initiatives in the First Years of Brandt's Presidency', in B. Rother and K. Larres (eds), *Willy Brandt and International Relations: Europe, the USA and Latin America, 1974–1992* (London, 2019), 179–94

F. Foret, *Religion and Politics in the European Union: The Secular Canopy* (Cambridge, 2015)

F. Foret and O. Calligaro, 'Governing by Prizes: How the European Union Uses Symbolic Distinctions in Its Search for Legitimacy', *Journal of European Public Policy*, 26 (2019), 1335–53

A. Forster, *Britain and the Maastricht Negotiations* (Basingstoke, 1999)

M. Forsyth, 'The Political Theory of Federalism: The Relevance of Classical Approaches', in J. J. Hesse and V. Wright (eds), *Federalizing Europe?* (Oxford, 1996), 25–45

R. Frank, 'The French Dilemma: Modernistion with Dependence or Independence and Decline', in J. Becker and F. Knipping (eds), *Power in Europe? Great Britain, France, Italy and Germany in a Postwar World, 1945–1950* (Berlin, 1986), vol. 1, 263–82

R. Frazier, 'Did Britain Start the Cold War? Bevin and the Truman Doctrine', *Historical Journal*, 27 (1984), 715–27

N. Frei, *Adenauer's Germany and the Nazi Past: The Politics of Amnesty and Integration* (New York, 2002)

N. Frei, *Vergangheitspolitik: Die Anfänge der Bundesrepublik und die NS-Vergangenheit* (Munich, 2012)

BIBLIOGRAPHY   477

V. Fritz, *Juges et avocats généraux de la Cour de Justice de l'Union européenne 1952–1972* (Frankfurt, 2018)

M. Fulbrook, 'Aspects of Society and Identity in the New Germany', in M. Mertes, S. Muller and H. A. Winkler (eds), *In Search of Germany* (New Brunswick, NJ, 1996), 229–52

M. Fulbrook, *German National Identity after the Holocaust* (Cambridge, 1999)

F. Furet, 'From Narrative History to Problem-oriented History' (1975), in F. Furet, *In the Workshop of History* (Chicago, 1982), 54–67

E. Fursdon, *The European Defence Community: A History* (Basingstoke, 1980)

J. L. Gaddis, 'The Emerging Post-Revisionist Synthesis on the Origins of the Cold War', *Diplomatic History*, 7 (1983), 171–90

J. L. Gaddis, *The Long Peace: Inquiries into the History of the Cold War* (Oxford, 1987)

J. L. Gaddis, *We Now Know: Rethinking Cold War History* (Oxford, 1997)

J. L. Gaddis, *The Landscape of History: How Historians Map the Past* (Oxford, 2002)

J. L. Gaddis, *The Cold War: A New History* (London, 2006)

E. Gaddum, *Die deutsche Europapolitik in den 80er Jahren: Interessen, Konflikte und Entscheidungen der Regierung Kohl* (Paderborn, 1994)

T. Gallagher, 'Nationalism and Romanian Political Culture in the 1990s', in D. Light and D. Phinnemore (eds), *Post-Communist Romania: Coming to Terms with Transition* (Basingstoke, 2001), 104–26

G. Galli and A. Prandi, *Patterns of Political Participation in Italy* (New Haven, CT, 1970)

C. Galpin and H.-J. Trenz, 'Converging towards Euroscepticism? Negativity in News Coverage during the 2014 European Parliament Elections in Germany and the UK', *European Politics and Society*, 20 (2019), 26–76

C. Galpin and H.-J. Trenz, 'In the Shadow of Brexit: The 2019 European Parliament Elections as First-Order Polity Elections?' *Political Quarterly*, 90 (2019), 664–71

C. Galpin and H.-J. Trenz, 'Participatory Populism: Online Discussion Forums on Mainstream News Sites during the 2014 European Parliament Election', *Journalism Practice*, 13 (2019), 781–98

A. Gamble, *Hayek* (Cambridge, 1996)

G. Garavini, *After Empires: European Integration, Decolonization and the Challenge from the Global South, 1957–1986* (Oxford, 2012)

M. Garnett, *From Anger to Apathy: The Story of Politics, Society and Popular Culture in Britain since 1975* (London, 2007)

T. Garton Ash, *The Uses of Adversity* (London, 1989)

T. Garton Ash, *In Europe's Name: Germany and the Divided Continent* (London, 1993)

T. Garton Ash, 'Trials, Purges and History Lessons: Treating a Difficult Past in Post-Communist Europe', in J.-W. Müller (ed.), *Memory and Power in Post-War Europe: Studies in the Presence of the Past* (Cambridge, 2002), 265–82

I. Garzon, *Reforming the Common Agricultural Policy: History of a Paradigm Change* (Basingstoke, 2007)

A. Gat, *Nations: The Long History and Deep Roots of Political Ethnicity and Nationalism* (Cambrdige, 2012)

M. Gehler, *Zeitgeschichte im dynamischen Mehrebenensystem. Zwischen Regionalisierung, Nationalstaat, Europäisierung, internationaler Arena und Globalisierung* (Bochum, 2001)

M. Gehler, W. Kaiser, and B. Leucht (eds), *Netzwerke im europäischen Mehrebenensystem. Von 1945 bis zur Gegenwart* (Vienna, 2009)

T. Geiger and J. Hansen, 'Did Protest Matter? The Influence of the Peace Movement on the West German Government and the Social Democratic Party, 1977–1983', in E. Conze, M. Klimke, and J. Varon (eds), *Nuclear Threats, Nuclear Fear, and the Cold War of the 1980s* (New York 2017), 290–315

E. Gellner, *Nations and Nationalism* (Oxford, 1983)

P. Genschel and M. Jachtenfuchs, *Beyond the Regulatory Polity? The European Integration of Core State Powers* (Oxford, 2013)

478 BIBLIOGRAPHY

S. George, *Britain and European Integration since 1945* (Oxford, 1992)

D. Geppert, 'Bridge over Troubled Water: German Left-Wing Intellectuals between "East" and "West", 1945–1949', in R. Bavaj and M. Steber (eds), *Germany and 'the West': The History of a Modern Concept* (New York, 2015), 262–76

K. J. Gergen, *The Saturated Self* (New York, 1991)

J. Gerhards, 'Westeuropäische Integration und die Schwierigkeiten der Entstehung einer europäischen Öffentlichkeit', *Zeitschrift für Soziologie*, 22 (1993), 96–110

M. H. Geyer, 'Der Kampf um nationale Repräsentation: Deutsch-deutsche Sportbeziehungen und die "Hallstein-Doktrin"', *Vierteljahreshefte für Zeitgeschichte*, 44 (1996), 55–86

M. H. Geyer (ed.), *The Power of Intellectuals in Contemporary Germany* (Chicago, 2001)

A. E. Gfeller, *Building a European Identity: France, the United States and the Oil Shock, 1973–1974* (New York, 2012)

J. G. Giauque, *Grand Designs and Visions of Unity: The Atlantic Powers and the Reorganization of Western Europe, 1955–1963* (Chapel Hill, NC, 2002)

M. Gilbert, 'Narrating the Process: Questioning the Progressive Story of European Integration', *Journal of Common Market Studies*, 46 (2008), 641–62

M. Gilbert, *European Integration: A Political History*, 2nd edn (Lanham, MD, 2021)

R. Gildea, *Marianne in Chains: In Search of the German Occupation, 1940–1945* (New York, 2002)

J. R. Gillingham, *European Integration, 1950–2003: Superstate or New Market Economy* (Cambridge, 2003)

J. R. Gillingham, 'A Theoretical Vacuum: European Integration and Historical Research Today', *Journal of European Integration History* 14 (2008)

J. R. Gillingham, 'The End of the European Dream', in H. Zimmermann and A. Dür (eds), *Key Controversies in European Integration* (Basingstoke, 2012), 19–31

J. Gimbel, *Science, Technology and Reparations: Exploitation and Plunder in Postwar Germany* (Stanford, 1990)

P. Ginsborg, *A History of Contemporary Italy: Society and Politics, 1943–1988* (London, 1990)

P. Ginsborg, *Italy and Its Discontents, 1980–2001* (London, 2001)

R. Girault, 'Decision-Makers, Decisions and French Power', in E. Di Nolfo (ed.), *Power in Europe? Great Britain, France, Germany and Italy and the Origins of the EEC, 1952–1957* (Berlin, 1992), vol. 2, 66–83

R. Girault (ed.), *Identité et conscience européenne au XXᵉ siècle* (Paris, 1994); R. Frank (ed.), *Les identités européennes au XXᵉ siècle* (Paris, 2004)

R. Girault and G. Bossuat (eds), *Europe brisée, Europe retrouvée. Nouvelles réflexions sur l'unité européenne au XXᵉ siècle* (Paris, 1994)

H. Glaser, *Die Kulturgeschichte der Bundesrepublik Deutschland. Zwischen Kapitulation und Wärhungsreform 1945–1948* (Frankfurt, 1985), vol. 1

J. Glaurdić, *The Hour of Europe: Western Powers and the Breakup of Yugoslavia* (New Haven, CT, 2011)

A. Glees, *Exile Politics during the Second World War: The German Social Democrats in Britain* (Oxford, 1982)

F. Gloriant, 'To Adapt to the Cold War Bipolar Order? Or to Challenge It? Macmillian and de Gaulle's Rift in the Face of the Second Berlin Crisis', *Cold War History*, 18 (2018), 465–83

P. Gold, *Gibraltar: British or Spanish?* (London, 2005)

J. B. Goodman, *Monetary Sovereignty: The Politics of Central Banking in Western Europe* (Ithaca, NY, 1992)

I. R. Gordon, 'In What Sense Left Behind by Globalisation? Looking for a Less Reductionist Geography of the Populist Surge in Europe', *Cambridge Journal of Regions, Economy and Society*, 11 (2018), 95–113

E. D. Gordy, *The Culture of Power in Serbia: Nationalism and the Destruction of Alternatives* (University Park, PA, 1999)

D. P. Gorenburg, *Minority Ethnic Mobilization in the Russian Federation* (Cambridge, 2003)

BIBLIOGRAPHY 479

N. Gould-Davies, 'Rethinking the Role of Ideology in International Politics during the Cold War', *Journal of Cold War Studies*, 1 (1999), 90–109

D. Gowland and A. Turner, *Reluctant Europeans: Britain and European Integration, 1945–1998* (London, 1999)

D. Gowland and A. Wright, *Britain and European Integration since 1945* (London, 2009)

R. J. Granieri, *The Ambivalent Alliance: Konrad Adenauer, the CDU/CSU and the West, 1949–1966* (New York, 2003)

V. Gransow and K. Jarausch (eds), *Die Deutsche Vereinigung: Dokumente zu Bürgerbewegung, Annäherung und Beitritt* (Cologne, 1991)

J. Gray, *Isaiah Berlin* (London, 1995)

R. Gray, *The Imperative of Modernity: An Intellectual Biography of Ortega y Gasset* (Berkeley, 1989)

W. G. Gray, *Germany's Cold War: The Global Campaign to Isolate East Germany, 1949–1969* (Chapel Hill, NC, 2003)

P. Graziano and M. Vink (eds), *Europeanization: New Research Agendas* (Basingstoke, 2007)

N. Gregor, *Daimler-Benz in the Third Reich* (New Haven, 1998)

F. Greiner, *Wege nach Europa. Deutungen eines imaginierten Kontinents in deutschen, britischen und amerikanischen Printmedien, 1914–1945* (Göttingen, 2014)

R. T. Griffiths (ed.), *The Netherlands and the Integration of Europe* (Amsterdam, 1990)

R. T. Griffiths, 'Europe's First Constitution: The European Political Community', 1952–1954', in S. Martin (ed.), *The Construction of Europe* (Dordrecht, 1994), 19–39

R. T. Griffiths and A. Asbeek Brusse, 'The Dutch Cabinet and the Rome Treaties', in E. Serra (ed.), *Il Rilancio dell'Europa e i trattati di Roma* (Milan 1989) 461–93

A. Grosser, *The Western Alliance* (London, 1980)

S. Grüner, *Geplantes 'Wirtschaftswunder'? Industrie- und Strukturpolitik in Bayern 1945 bis 1973* (Berlin, 2009)

M. Guibernau, *Catalan Nationalism: Francoism, Transition and Democracy* (London, 2004)

M. Guibernau, 'Nationalism without States', in J. Breuilly (ed.), *The Oxford Handbook of the History of Nationalism* (Oxford, 2013), 592–614

P. Guillen, 'Pierre Mendès France et l'Allemagne', in R. Girault (ed.), *Pierre Mendès France et le rôle de la France dans le monde* (Grenoble, 1991), 39–54

P. Guillen, 'Europe as a Cure for French Impotence? The Guy Mollet Government and the Negotiation of the Treaties of Rome', in E. Di Nolfo (ed.), *Power in Europe? Great Britain, France, Germany and Italy and the Origins of the EEC, 1952–1957* (Berlin, 1992), vol. 2, 505–16

P. Guillen, 'France and the Defence of Western Europe: From the Brussels Pact (March 1948) to the Pleven Plan (October 1950)', in N. Wiggershaus and R. G. Foerster (eds), *The Western Security Community* (Oxford, 1993), 125–48

E. B. Haas, *The Uniting of Europe: Political, Social and Economic Forces, 1950–1957* (Notre Dame, IN, 1958)

E. B. Haas, *Beyond the Nation-State: Functionalism and International Organization* (Palo Alto, CA, 1964)

E. B. Haas, 'The Study of Regional Organization: Reflections on the Joy and Anguish of Pretheorizing', *International Organization*, 24 (1970), 607–46

E. B. Haas, 'The Obsolescence of Regional Integration Theory', *Working Paper: Institute of International Studies* (Princeton, NJ, 1975)

E. B. Haas, 'Turbulent Fields and the Theory of Regional Integration', *International Organization*, 30 (1976), 173–212

E. B. Haas and P. Schmitter, 'Economics and Differential Patterns of Political Integration', *International Organization*, 18 (1964), 705–37

M. Haeussler, 'A "Cold War European"? Helmut Schmidt and European Integration, c. 1945–1982', *Cold War History*, 15 (2016), 427–47

M. Haeussler, 'The Conviction of a Realist: Concepts of "Solidarity" in Helmut Schmidt's European Thought, 1945–82', *European Review of History*, 24 (2017), 955–72

480 BIBLIOGRAPHY

K. Hafez, *Mythos Globalisierung: Warum die Medien nicht grenzenlos sind* (Wiesbaden, 2005)

H. Haftendoorn, *Coming of Age: German Foreign Policy since 1945* (Lanham, MD, 2006)

R. H. Haigh, D. S. Morris, and A. R. Peters, *Soviet Foreign Policy, the League of Nations and Europe, 1917–1939* (Aldershot, 1986)

D. Halikiopoulou and S. Vasilopoulou, 'Support for the Far Right in the 2014 European Parliament Elections: A Comparative Perspective', *Political Quarterly*, 85 (2014), 285–8

I. Hall, *Dilemmas of Decline: British Intellectuals and World Politics, 1945–1975* (Cambridge, 2012)

P. Hall *Governing the Economy: The Politics of State Intervention in Britain and France* (Cambridge, 1986)

F. Halliday, *The Making of the Second Cold War*, 2nd edn (London, 1986)

V. Handl and C. Jeffery, 'Germany and Europe after Kohl: Between Social Democracy and Normalization?', *German Studies Review*, 24 (2001), 55–82

J. Hanhimäki, 'Détente in Europe, 1969–1975', in M. Leffler and O. A. Westad (eds), *The Cambridge History of the Cold War* (Cambridge, 2010), vol. 2, 198–218

J. Hanhimäki, *The Rise and Fall of Détente: American Foreign Policy and the Transformation of the Cold War* (Washington, DC 2013)

R. E. Hannigan, *The Great War and American Foreign Policy, 1914–1924* (University Park, PA, 2017)

W. F. Hanrieder, *West German Foreign Policy, 1949–1963: International Pressure and Domestic Response* (Palo Alto, 1967)

W. F. Hanrieder, *Germany, America, Europe: Forty Years of German Foreign Policy* (New Haven, CT, 1989)

J. K. M. Hanson, *The Civilian Population and the Warsaw Uprising of 1944* (Cambridge, 1982)

R. Harmsen and M. Spiering (eds), *Euroscepticism: Party Politics, National Identity and European Integration* (Amsterdam, 2004)

D. F. Harrington, 'The Berlin Blockade Revisited', *The International History Review* 6 (1984), 88–112

J. Harris, 'Political Thought and the State', in S. J. D. Green and R. C. Whiting (eds), *The Boundaries of the State in Modern Britain* (Cambridge, 2002), 15–28

B. Harrison, 'The Rise, Fall and Rise of Political Consensus in Britain since 1940', *History*, 84 (1999), 301–24

B. Harrison, *Finding a Role? The United Kingdom, 1970–1990* (Oxford, 2010)

M. Harrison, *The Reluctant Ally: France and Atlantic Security* (Baltimore, 1981)

M. Harrison, 'Coercion, Compliance and the Collapse of the Soviet Command Economy', *Economic History Review*, 55 (2002), 397–433

R. J. Harrison, *Europe in Question: Theories of Regional Integration* (London, 1974)

J. van der Harst, *The Atlantic Priority: Dutch Defence Policy at the Time of the European Defence Community* (Brussels, 2003)

C. Harvie, *Scotland and Nationalism: Scottish Society and Politics, 1707 to the Present*, 3rd edn (London, 1998)

D. Haselbach, '"Soziale Marktwirtschaft" als Gründungsmythos: Zur Identitätsbildung im Nachkriegsdeutschland', in D. Mayer-Iswandy (ed.), *Zwischen Traum und Trauma—Die Nation* (Tübingen, 1994), 255–66

D. Hay, *Europe: The Emergence of an Idea* (Edinburgh, 1957)

P. Hayes, *Industry and Ideology: IG Farben in the Nazi Era* (Cambridge, 1987)

J. Hearn, *Rethinking Nationalism: A Critical Introduction* (Basingstoke, 2006)

M. Heimann, 'The Scheming Apparatchik of the Prague Spring', *Europe-Asia Studies*, 60 (2008), 1717–34

F. Heinlein, *British Government Policy and Decolonisation, 1945–1963* (London, 2002)

D. Held, A. McGrew, D. Goldblatt, and J. Perraton, *Global Transformations: Politics, Economics and Culture* (Oxford, 1999)

F. H. Heller and J. R. Gillingham (eds), *NATO: The Founding of the Atlantic Alliance and the Integration of Europe* (New York, 1992)

BIBLIOGRAPHY 481

J. Hellmann, *Emmanuel Mounier and the New Catholic Left, 1930–1950* (Toronto, 1981)

U. Herbert, *A History of Twentieth-century Germany* (Oxford, 2019)

J. Herf, *War by Other Means: Soviet Power, West German Resistance and the Battle of the Euromissiles* (New York, 1991)

J. Herf, *Divided Memory: The Nazi Past in the Two Germanys* (Cambridge, Mass., 1997)

V. Herman and J. Lodge, *The European Parliament and the European Community* (Basingstoke, 1978)

J. G. Hershberg, '"Explosion in the Offing": German Rearmament and American Diplomacy, 1953–1955', *Diplomatic History*, 16 (1992), 511–49

M. Herzer, *The Media, European Integration and the Rise of Euro-Journalism*, 1950s–1970s (Basingstoke, 2019)

J. Hess, 'Europagedanke und nationaler Revisionismus: Überlegungen zu ihrer Verknüpfung in der Weimarer Republik am Beispiel Wilhelm Heiles', *Historische Zeitschrift*, 225 (1977), 572–622

J. Hess, 'Westdeutsche Suche nach nationaler Identität', in W. Michalka (ed.), *Die Deutsche Frage in der Weltpolitik* (Stuttgart, 1986), 9–50

B. Heuser and K. Stoddart, 'Difficult Europeans: NATO and Tactical/Non-strategic Nuclear Weapons in the Cold War', *Diplomacy and Statecraft*, 28 (2017), 454–76

M. Hewitson, 'Conclusion: Nationalism and the Nineteenth Century?', in T. Baycroft and M. Hewitson (eds), *What is a Nation? Europe, 1789–1914* (Oxford, 2006), 312–55

M. Hewitson, *History and Causality* (Basingstoke, 2014)

M. Hewitson and M. D'Auria (eds), *Europe in Crisis: Intellectuals and the European Idea, 1917–1957* (New York, 2012)

A. Hicks, *Social Democracy and Welfare Capitalism: A Century of Income Security Politics* (Ithaca, NY, 1999), 153–221

R. Higgs, 'Wartime Prosperity? A Reassessment of the US Economy in the 1940s', *Journal of Economic History*, 52 (1992), 41–60

C. Hill, 'Putting the World to Rights: Tony Blair's Foreign Policy Mission', in A. Seldon and D. Kavanagh (eds), *The Blair Effect, 2001–5* (Cambridge, 2005), 384–409

L. Hillaker, 'Representing a "Better Germany": Competing Images of State and Society in the Early Cultural Diplomacy of the FRG and GDR', *Central European History*, 53 (2020), 372–92

M. Hilmes, *The Television History Book*, 3rd edn (London, 2004)

P. Hirst and G. Thompson, *Globalization in Question: The International Economy and the Possibilities of Governance* (Cambridge, 1996)

W. I. Hitchcock, *France Restored: Cold War Diplomacy and the Quest for Leadership in Europe, 1944–1954* (Chapel Hill, NC, 1998)

S. Hix, 'The Study of the European Community: The Challenge to Comparative Politics', *West European Politics*, 17 (1994), 1–30

S. Hix, 'CP, IR and the EU! A Rejoinder to Hurrell and Menon', *West European Politics*, 19 (1996), 802–4

S. Hix, *The Political System of the European Union* (Basingstoke, 1999)

S. Hix, *What's Wrong with the European Union and How to Fix It* (Cambridge, 2008)

S. Hix and C. Lord, *Political Parties in the European Union* (Basingstoke, 1997)

F. Hjorth, 'Who Benefits? Welfare Chauvinism and National Stereotypes', *European Union Politics*, 17 (2016), 3–24

S. B. Hobolt, 'The Brexit Vote: A Divided Nation, A Divided Continent', *Journal of European Public Policy*, 23 (2016), 1259–77

E. J. Hobsbawm, *Nations and Nationalism since 1780* (Cambridge, 1990)

E. J. Hobsbawm, *An Age of Extremes: The Short Twentieth Century, 1914–1991* (London, 1994)

C. v. Hodenberg, *Television's Moment: Sitcom Audiences and the Sixties Cultural Revolution* (New York, 2015)

J. Hoff Wilson, *Ideology and Economics: U.S. Relations with the Soviet Union, 1918–1933* (Columbia, MO, 1974)

S. Hoffmann, 'International Systems and International Law', in K. Knorr and S. Verba (eds), *The International System* (Princeton, NJ, 1961), 205–39

482 BIBLIOGRAPHY

S. Hoffmann, 'De Gaulle, Europe and the Atlantic Alliance', *International Organization*, 18 (1964)

S. Hoffmann, 'Obstinate or Obsolete? The Fate of the Nation-State and the Case of Western Europe', *Daedalus*, 95 (1966), 862–915

S. Hoffmann, *The European Sisyphus: Essays on Europe, 1964–1994* (Boulder, CO, 1995)

A. Hofmann, *The Emergence of Détente in Europe: Brandt, Kennedy and the Formation of Ostpolitik* (London, 2007)

M. J. Hogan, *The Marshall Plan: America, Britain and the Reconstruction of Western Europe, 1947–1952* (Cambridge, 1987)

M. J. Hogan, *The Marshall Plan, Britain and the Reconstruction of Western Europe, 1947–1952* (Cambridge, 1987)

M. J. Hogan (ed.), *The End of the Cold War: Its Meaning and Implications* (Cambridge, 1992)

K. Holl, 'Europapolitik um Vorfeld der deutschen Regierungspolitik: Zur Tätigkeit proeuropäischer Organisationen in der Weimarer Republik', *Historische Zeitschrift*, 219 (1974), 33–94

M. Holm, *The Marshall Plan: A New Deal for Europe* (London, 2016)

L. Holmes, *Post-Communism: An Introduction* (Oxford, 1997)

K. Holzinger and F. Schimmelfennig, 'Differentiated Integration in the European Union: Many Concepts, Sparse Theory, Few Data', *European Journal of Political Research*, 19 (2012), 292–305

L. Hooghe and G. Marks, 'A Postfunctionalist Theory of European Integration: From Permissive Consensus to Constraining Dissensus', *British Journal of Political Science*, 39 (2009), 1–23

L. Hooghe and G. Marks, 'Grand Theories of European Integration in the 21st Century', *Journal of European Public Policy*, 26 (2019), 1113–33

A. M. Hornblum, *The Invisible Harry Gold: The Man Who Gave the Soviets the Atom Bomb* (New Haven, CT 2010)

T. Horsley, *The Court of Justice of the European Union as an Institutional Actor: Judicial Lawmaking and Its Limits* (Cambridge, 2018)

M. Hoskin, *Understanding Immigration: Challenges in an Era of Mass Population Movement* (Albany, NY, 2017)

D. Howarth and J. Torfing (eds), *Discourse Theory in European Politics: Identity, Policy and Governance* (Basingstoke, 2005)

R. Hrbek, *Die SPD, Deutschland und Europa 1945–1957* (Bonn, 1972)

R. Hudemann, H. Kaelble, and K. Schwabe (eds), *Europa im Blick der Historiker* (Munich, 1995)

R. G. Hughes, *Britain, Germany and the Cold War: The Search for Détente, 1949–1967* (London, 2007)

R. G. Hughes, *Britain, Germany and the Cold War: The Search for a European Détente, 1949–1967* (London, 2007)

R. Hummel, 'Journalistisches Feld und europäische Öffentlichkeit', in W. R. Langenbucher and M. Latzer (eds), *Europäische Öffentlichkeit und medialer Wandeln* (Wiesbaden, 2006), 296–304

P. J. Humphreys, *Mass Media and Media Policy in Western Europe* (Manchester, 1996)

A. Hurrell, 'Explaining the Resurgence of Regionalism in World Politics', *Review of International Studies*, 21 (1995)

D. Hüser, *Frankreichs 'doppelte Deutschlandpolitik'* (Berlin, 1996)

R. Hyam, *Britain's Declining Empire: The Road to Decolonisation, 1918–1968* (Cambridge, 2007)

A. Hyde-Price, *Germany and European Order: Enlarging NATO and the European Union* (Manchester, 2000)

A. Hyde-Price, and C. Jeffery, 'Germany in the European Union: Constructing Normality', *Journal of Common Market Studies*, 39 (2001), 689–717

P. Ignazi and E. S. Wellhofer, 'Religion, Rurality and Voting: Secularization, Landownership and Italian Electoral Behaviour, 1953–2008', *West European Politics*, 36 (2013), 919–45

G. J. Ikenberry, 'Creating Yesterday's New World Order: Keynesian "New Thinking" and the Anglo-American Postwar Settlement', in J. Goldstein and R. O. Keohane (eds), *Ideas and Foreign Policy: Beliefs, Institutions and Political Change* (Ithaca, NY, 1993), 57–86

T. P. Ireland, *Creating the Entangling Alliance* (Westport, Conn., 1981)

R. Irving, *Adenauer* (London, 2002)

M. Jachtenfuchs, *Die Konstruktion Europas: Verfassungsideen und institutionelle Entwicklung* (Baden-Baden, 2002)

M. Jachtenfuchs, T. Diez, and S. Jung, 'Which Europe? Conflicting Models of a Legitimate European Political Order', *European Journal of International Relations*, 4 (1998), 409–45

J. Jackson, *France: The Dark Years, 1940–1944* (Oxford, 2003)

P. Jackson, 'France and the Problems of Security and International Disarmament after the First World War', *Journal of Strategic Studies*, 29 (2006), 247–80

J. Jacobson, *Locarno Diplomacy: Germany and the West* (Princeton, 1972)

J. Jacobson, 'Strategies of French Foreign Policy after World War I', *Journal of Modern History*, 55 (1983), 78–95

H. James, *The German Slump* (Oxford, 1986)

H. James, 'The Fall and Rise of the European Economy in the Twentieth Century', in T. C. W. Blanning (ed.) *The Oxford History of Modern Europe* (Oxford, 2000), 182–209

P. James and M. B. Steger, 'A Genealogy of "Globalization": The Career of a Concept', *Globalizations*, 11 (2014), 417–34

F. Jameson, *Postmodernism, or the Cultural Logic of Late Capitalism* (London, 1991)

K. H. Jarausch, 'Postnationale Nation: Zum Identitätswandel der Deutschen 1945–1995', *Historicum*, 30 (1995), 30–35

K. H. Jarausch, *After Hitler: Recivilizing Germans, 1945–1995* (Oxford, 2006)

K. H. Jarausch and H. Siegrist (eds), *Amerikanisierung und Sowjetisierung in Deutschland, 1945–1970* (Frankfurt, 1997)

R. Jenkins, *Churchill* (London, 2002)

J. Jenson and F. Mérand, 'Sociology, Institutionalism and the European Union', *Comparative European Politics*, 8 (2010), 74–92

R. Jervis, 'Identity and the Cold War', in M. Leffler and O. A. Westad (eds), *The Cambridge History of the Cold War: Crises and Détente* (Cambridge, 2010), vol. 2, 22–43

J.-F. Jiménez-Diaz and S. Delgado-Fernández (eds), *Political Leadership in the Spanish Transition to Democracy, 1975–1982* (New York, 2016)

D. W. J. Johnson, 'Britain and France in 1940', *Transactions of the Royal Historical Society* 22 (1972), 141–57

P. Johnson (ed.), *Twentieth-Century Britain: Economic, Social and Cultural Change* (London, 1994), 320–39

C. Jones, 'François Mitterrand's Visit to Sarajevo, 28 June 1992', *Diplomacy and Statecraft*, 28 (2017), 296–319

G. Jones, *Renewing Unilever: Transformation and Tradition* (Oxford, 2005)

G. Jones and P. Miskell, 'European Integration and Corporate Restructuring: The Strategy of Unilever, c. 1957–c.1990', *Economic History Review*, 58 (2005), 113–39

M. Jones, 'Great Britain, the United States, and Consultation over the Use of the Atomic Bomb', *Historical Journal*, 54 (2011), 797–828

N. Jordan, 'The Reorientation of French Diplomacy', *English Historical Review*, 117 (2002), 867–88

K. E. Jørgensen (ed.), *Reflective Approaches to European Governance* (Basingstoke, 1997)

D. Jossilin, 'Between Europe and a Hard Place: French Financial Diplomacy from 1995–2002', *French Politics, Culture and Society*, 22 (2004), 57–75

T. Judt, *Past Imperfect: French Intellectuals, 1944–1956* (Berkeley, 1992)

T. Judt, *A Grand Illusion? An Essay on Europe* (London, 1996)

T. Judt, 'The Past Is Another Country: Myth and Memory in Post-War Europe', in J.-W. Müller (ed.), *Memory and Power in Post-War Europe* (Cambridge, 2004), 157–83

T. Judt, *Postwar: A History of Europe since 1945* (London, 2005)

C. Kaddous (ed.), *The European Union in International Organizations and Global Governance* (Oxford, 2015)

H. Kaelble, 'Was Prometheus Most Unbound in Europe?', *Journal of European Economic History*, 15 (1986), 65–104

484 BIBLIOGRAPHY

H. Kaelble, *Auf dem Weg zu einer europäischen Gesellschaft: Eine Sozialgeschichte Westeuropas 1880–1980* (Munich, 1987)

H. Kaelble, *A Social History of Western Europe, 1880–1980* (Oxford, 1990)

H. Kaelble, *Nachbarn am Rhein: Entfremdung und Annäherung der französischen und deutschen Gesellschaft seit 1880* (Munich, 1991)

H. Kaelble, *Europäer über Europa: Die Entstehung des europäischen Selbstverständnisses im 19. und 20. Jahrhundert* (Frankfurt, 2001)

H. Kaelble (ed.), *The European Way* (New York, 2004)

H. Kaelble, *Sozialgeschichte Europas 1945 bis zur Gegenwart* (Munich, 2007)

H. Kaelble, 'Identification with Europe and Politicization of the EU since the 1980s', in J. T. Checkel and P. J. Katzenstein (eds), *European Identity* (Cambridge, 2009), 193–212

H. Kaelble, 'Abmilderung der sozialen Ungleichheit? Das westliche Europa während des Wirtschaftsbooms der 1950er bis 1970er Jahre', *Geschichte und Gesellschaft*, 40 (2014), 591–609

H. Kaelble, 'Die Gesellschaften der EU: Zusammenwachsen und Krise 1957–2017', *Zeitschrift für Staats- und Europawissenschaften*, 15 (2017), 156–72

W. Kaiser, *Using Europe, Abusing the Europeans: Britain and European Integration, 1945–1963* (Basingstoke, 1997)

W. Kaiser, 'Cooperation of European Catholic Politicians in Exile in Britain and the USA during the Second World War', *Journal of Contemporary History* 35 (2000), 439–65

W. Kaiser, 'No Second Versailles: Transnational Contacts in the People and Freedom Group and the International Christian Democratic Union, 1936–1945', in M. Gehler, W. Kaiser and H. Wohnout (eds), *Christdemokratie in Europa im 20 Jahrhundert* (Vienna, 2001), 616–41

W. Kaiser, 'From State to Society? The Historiography of European Integration', in M. Cini and A. Bourne (eds), *Palgrave Advances in European Union Studies* (Basingstoke, 2006), 190–208

W. Kaiser, *Christian Democracy and the Origins of European Union* (Cambridge, 2007)

W. Kaiser and M. Gehler, 'Transnationalism and Early European Integration: The NEI and the Geneva Circle, 1947–1957', *Historical Journal*, 44 (2001), 773–98

W. Kaiser and B. Leucht, 'Informal Politics of Integration: Christian Democratic and Transatlantic Networks in the Creation of the ECSC Core Europe', *Journal of European Integration History*, 14 (2008), 35–50

W. Kaiser and J. Schot, *Writing the Rules for Europe: Experts, Cartels and International Organizations* (Basingstoke, 2014)

W. Kaiser and A. Varsori (eds), *European Union History: Themes and Debates* (Basingstoke, 2010)

L. S. Kaplan, 'The Korean War and US Foreign Relations: The Case of NATO', in F. H. Heller (ed.), *The Korean War* (Lawrence, Kans., 1977), 44–53

Z. Karabell, *Architects of Intervention: The United States, the Third World and the Cold War, 1946–1962* (Baton Rouge, 1999)

E. Karamouzi, *Greece, the EEC and the Cold War, 1974–1979: The Second Enlargement* (Basingstoke, 2014)

J. v. Karczewski, *'Weltwirtschaft ist unser Schicksal'. Helmut Schmidt und die Schaffung der Weltwirtschaft* (Bonn, 2008)

H. Karge, 'Practices and Politics of Second World War Remembrance: (Trans-) National Perspectives from Eastern and South-Eastern Europe', in M. Pakier and B. Stråth (eds), *Contested Histories and Politics of Remembrance* (New York, 2010), 119–46

H. Kassim, 'Policy Networks and European Union Policy-Making: A Sceptical View', *West European Politics*, 17 (1994), 15–27

E. Kaufmann, 'Levels or Changes? Ethnic Context, Immigration and the UK Independence Party Vote', *Electoral Studies*, 48 (2017), 57–69

E. Kaufmann and G. Harris, '"White Flight" or Positive Contact? Local Diversity and Attitudes to Immigration in Britain', *Comparative Political Studies*, 48 (2015), 1563–90

D. Kavanagh, *Thatcherism and British Politics: The End of Consensus?* (Oxford, 1987)

M. Keating, 'Minority Nationalism and the State: the European Case', in M. Watson (ed.), *Contemporary Minority Nationalism* (London, 1990), 174–94

M. Keating, *Nations against the State: The New Politics of Nationalism in Quebec, Catalonia and Scotland*, 2nd edn (London, 2001)

M. Keating and D. McCrone (eds), *The Crisis of Social Democracy in Europe* (Edinburgh, 2013)

J. Ker-Lindsay, *EU Accession and UN Peacemaking in Cyprus* (Basingstoke, 2005)

J. Ker-Lindsay, *The Cyprus Problem: What Everyone Needs to Know* (Oxford, 2011)

K. van Kersbergern, *Social Capitalism: A Study of Christian Democracy and the Welfare State* (London, 1995)

I. Kershaw, 'The "Hitler Myth": Image and Reality in the Third Reich', in D. Crew, *Nazism and German Society, 1933–1945* (London, 1994), 197–215

L. Kettenacker, *Germany 1989: In the Aftermath of the Cold War* (London, 2009)

S. Kieninger, 'Transformation or Status Quo: The Conflict of Stratagems in Washington over the Meaning and Purpose of the CSCE and MBFR, 1969–1973', in O. Bange and G. Niedhart (eds), *Helsinki 1975 and the Transformation of Europe* (New York, 2008), 67–82

S. Kieninger, *Dynamic Détente: The United States and Europe, 1964–1975* (Cambridge, CT, 2016)

S. Kieninger, 'A Preponderance of Stability: Henry Kissinger's Concern over the Dynamics of Ostpolitik', *Journal of Transatlantic Studies*, 17 (2019), 42–60

S. Kim, '"Because the Homeland Cannot Be in Opposition: Analysing the Discourses of Fidesz and Law and Justice (PiS) from Opposition to Power', *East European Politics*, 37 (2021), 332–51

P. King, *Federalism and Federation* (London, 1982)

S. Kitson, 'From Enthusiasm to Disenchantment: The French Police and the Vichy Regime, 1940–1944', *Contemporary European History* 11 (2002), 371–90

A.-C. L. Knudsen, *Farmers on Welfare: The Making of Europe's Common Agricultural Policy* (Ithaca, NY, 2009)

N. Kogan, *A Political History of Italy: The Postwar Years* (New York, 1983)

W. L. Kohl, *French Nuclear Diplomacy* (Princeton, NJ, 1971)

H. Köhler, *Adenauer. Eine politische Biographie* (Frankfurt, 1997), vol. 2

B. Kohler-Koch and B. Rittberger, 'The Governance Turn in EU Studies', *Journal of Common Market Studies*, 44 (2006), 27–49

G. Kolko, *Confronting the Third World: United States Foreign Policy, 1945–1980* (New York, 1988)

L. Köllner et al., *Die EVG-Phase* (Munich, 1990)

J. Kooiman (ed.), *Modern Governance: New Government-Society Interactions* (London, 1993)

M. Koopmann, *Das schwierige Bündnis: Die deutsch-französischen Beziehungen und die Außenpolitik der Bundesrepublik Deutschland 1948–1965* (Baden-Baden, 2000)

R. Koopmans, 'Who Inhabits the European Public Sphere? Winners and Losers, Supporters and Opponents in Europeanized Political Debates', *European Journal of Political Research*, 46 (2007), 183–210

J. Kopstein, *The Politics of Economic Decline in East Germany, 1945–1989* (Chapell Hill, NC, 2000)

K.-R. Korte, *Deutschlandpolitik in Helmut Kohls Kanzlerschaft. Regierungsstil und Entscheidungen 1982–1989* (Stuttgart, 1998)

U. Kotz, K. K. Patel, and F. Romero (eds), *Europe's Cold War Relations: The EC Towards a Global Role* (London, 2019)

M. Kramer, 'Ideology and the Cold War', *Review of International Studies,* 25 (1999), 539–76

M. Kramer, 'The Kremlin, the Prague Spring and the Brezhnev Doctrine', in V. Tismaneanu (ed.), *Promises of 1968: Crisis, Illusion and Utopia* (Budapest, 2011), 285–370

W. Krieger, 'Was General Clay a Revisionist? Strategic Aspects of the United States' Occupation of Germany', *Journal of Contemporary History*, 18 (1983), 165–84

M. Kros and M. Coenders, 'Explaining Differences in Welfare Chauvinism between and within Individuals over Time: The Role of Subjective and Objective Economic Risk, Economic Egalitarianism and Ethnic Threat', *European Sociological Review*, 35 (2019), 860–73

486 BIBLIOGRAPHY

U. Krotz and J. Schild, *Shaping Europe: France, Germany and Embedded Bilateralism from the Elysée Treaty to Twenty-First Century Politics* (Oxford, 2013)

K. Krüger, *Wirtschaftswunder und Mangelwirtschaft. Zur Produktion einer Erfolgsgeschichte in der deutschen Geschichtskultur* (Bielefeld, 2020)

P. Krüger, *Die Aussenpolitik der Republik von Weimar* (Darmstadt, 1985)

P. Krüger, 'European Unity and German Foreign Policy in the 1920s', in P. M. R. Stirk (ed.), *European Unity in Context: The Interwar Period* (London, 1989), 84–98

P. Krüger, 'Hitlers Europapolitik', in W. Benz. H. Buchheim, and H. Mommsen (eds), *Der Nationalsozialismus. Studien zur Ideologie und Herrschaft* (Frankfurt, 1993), 104–32

P. Krüger, 'Das doppelte Dilemma: Die Aussenpolitik der Republik von Weimar zwischen Staatensystem und Innenpolitik', *German Studies Review*, 22 (1999), 247–67

J. Krumrey, *The Symbolic Politics of European Integration: Staging Europe* (Basingstoke, 2018)

L. Kühnhardt, *European Union—The Second Founding: The Changing Rationale of European Integration* (Baden-Baden, 2008)

L. Kühnhardt (ed.), *Crises in European Integration: Challenge and Response, 1945–2005* (Oxford, 2009)

R. F. Kuisel, 'Vichy et les origines de la planification économique 1940–1946', *Le Mouvement sociale* 98 (1977), 77–101

R. F. Kuisel, *Capitalism and the State in Modern France: Renovation and Economic Management in the Twentieth Century* (Cambridge, 1981)

R. F. Kuisel, 'Coca-Cola and the Cold War: The French Face Americanization, 1948–1953', *French Historical Studies*, 17 (1991), 96–116

R. F. Kuisel, *The French Way: How France Embraced and Rejected American Values and Power* (Princeton, NJ, 2012)

C. Kupchan (ed.), *Nationalism and Nationalities in the New Europe* (Ithaca, NY, 1995)

J. Kurth and J. Petras, *Mediterranean Paradoxes: The Politics and Social Structure of Southern Europe* (Oxford, 1994)

H. Kurthen, W. Bergmann, and R. Erb (eds), *Antisemitism and Xenophobia in Germany after Unification* (Oxford, 1997)

Y. Lacaze, *L'Opinion française et la crise de Munich* (Berne, 1991)

E. Lacina, *Emigration 1933–1945* (Stuttgart, 1982)

J. Lacroix, 'Borderline Europe : French Visions of the European Union', in J. Lacroix and K. Nicolaïdis (eds), *European Stories: Intellectual Debates on Europe in National Contexts* (Oxford, 2010), 105–21

J. Lacroix and K. Nicolaïdis (eds), *European Stories: Intellectual Debates on Europe in National Contexts* (Oxford, 2010)

R. Ladrech, 'Europeanization of Domestic Politics and Institutions: The Case of France,' *Journal of Common Market Studies*, 32 (1994), 69–88

W. LaFeber, 'An End to *Which* Cold War?' in M. J. Hogan (ed.), *The End of the Cold War: Its Meaning and Implications* (Cambridge, 1992), 13–20

J. Lambert, 'The Constitutional Crisis, 1965–1966', *Journal of Common Market Studies*, 4 (1966), 195–228

J. R. Lampe, *Yugoslavia as History: Twice There Was a Country*, 2nd edn (Cambridge, 2000)

D. S. Landes, *The Unbound Prometheus: Change and Industrial Development in Western Europe from 1750 to the Present* (Cambridge, 1969)

U. Lappenküper, *Die deutsch-französischen Beziehungen 1949–1963. Von der 'Erbfeindschaft' zur 'Entente élémentaire'* (Munich, 2001)

D. C. Large, 'Grand Illusions: the United States, the Federal Republic of Germany and the European Defence Community, 1950–1954', in J. M. Diefendorf et al. (eds), *American Policy and the Reconstruction of West Germany* (Cambridge, 1993), 375–94

D. C. Large, *Germans to the Front: West German Rearmament in the Adenauer Era* (Chapel Hill, NC, 1996)

M. Larkin, *France since the Popular Front: Government and People, 1936–1986* (Oxford, 1988)

BIBLIOGRAPHY 487

K. Larres, 'Churchill's "Iron Curtain" Speech in Context: The Attempt to Achieve a "Good Understanding on All Points" with Stalin's Soviet Union', *International History Review*, 40 (2018), 86–107

K. Larres and P. Panayi, *The Federal Republic of Germany since 1949: Politics, Society and Economy before and after Unification* (London, 1996)

J. Laughland, *Tainted Source: Undemocratic Origins of the European Idea* (New York, 1997)

P. J. Lavrakas and M. W. Traugott (eds), *Election Polls, the News Media and Democracy* (New York, 2000)

P. Lawrence, *Nationalism: History and Theory* (London, 2005)

M. Lazreg, *Torture and the Twilight of Empire: From Algiers to Baghdad* (Princeton, NJ, 2008)

R. Leach, *Political Ideology in Britain*, 3rd edn (Basingstoke, 2015)

J. Leaman, *The Political Economy of Germany under Chancellors Kohl and Schröder* (New York, 2009)

C. Leconte, *Understanding Euroscepticism* (Basingstoke, 2010)

S. Lee, 'German Decision-Making Elites and European Integration: German "Europolitik" during the Years of the EEC and Free Trade Area Negotiations', in A. Deighton (ed.), *Building Postwar Europe: National Decision-Makers and European Institutions, 1948–63* (Basingstoke, 1995), 38–54

S. Lefèvre, *Les relations économiques franco-allemandes de 1945 à 1955* (Paris, 1998)

M. Leffler, *The Elusive Quest: America's Pursuit of European Stability and French Security, 1919–1933* (Chapel Hill, NC, 1979)

B. Lefort (ed.), *Une Europe inédite: Documents des archives Jean Monnet* (Lille, 2001)

N. Leites and C. de la Malène, 'Paris from EDC to WEU', *World Politics*, 8 (1955), 193–219

A. Lejour, 'Economic Aspects of the Internal Market for Services', in J. Pelkmans, D. Hanf, and M. Chang (eds), *The EU Internal Market in Comparative Perspective: Economic, Political and Legal Analyses* (Brussels, 2008), 115–37

W. Lepenies, *Folgen einer unerhörten Begebenheit: Die Deutschen nach der Vereinigung* (Berlin, 1992)

B. Leucht, K. Seidel, and L. Warlouzet (eds), *Reinventing Europe: The History of the European Union, 1945 to the Present* (London, 2023)

R. B. Levering, V. O. Pechatnov, V. Botzenhart-Viehe, and C. E. Edmondson (eds), *Debating the Origins of the Cold War: American and Russian Perspectives* (Lanham, MD, 2001), 85–178

T. Levitt, 'The Globalization of Markets', *Harvard Business Review*, 61 (1983), 92–102

S. Levsen, 'Authority and Democracy in Postwar France and West Germany, 1945–1968,' *Journal of Modern History*, 89 (2017), 812–50

N. Lewkowicz, *The German Question and the International Order, 1943–1948* (Basingstoke, 2010)

M. Libal, *Limits of Persuasion: Germany and the Yugoslav Crisis, 1991–1992* (Westport, CT, 1997)

U. Liebert, 'Contentious European Democracy: National Intellectuals in Transnational Debates', in J. Lacroix and K. Nicolaïdis (eds), *European Stories: Intellectual Debates on Europe in National Contexts* (Oxford, 2010), 51–77

U. Liebert, 'The Emergence of a European Identity', in H. Zimmermann and A. Dür (eds), *Key Controversies in European Integration* (Basingstoke, 2012)

R. S. Lieshout, M. L. L. Segers, and J. M. van der Vleuten, 'De Gaulle, Moravcsik and *The Choice for Europe*: Soft Sources, Weak Evidence', *Journal of Cold War Studies*, 6 (2004), 89–139

M. Lilla, *New French Thought* (Princeton, NJ, 1994)

L. N. Lindberg, *The Political Dynamics of European Economic Integration* (Palo Alto, CA, 1963)

L. N. Lindberg and S. A. Scheingold (eds), *Regional Integration: Theory and Research* (Cambridge, MA, 1963)

L. N. Lindberg and S. A. Scheingold, *Europe's Would-be Polity: Patterns of Change in the European Community* (Englewood Cliffs, NJ, 1970)

L. Lindlar and C.-L. Holtfrerich, 'Geography, Exchange Rates and Trade Structures: Germany's Export Performance since the 1950s', *European Review of Economic History*, 1 (1997), 217–46

488 BIBLIOGRAPHY

J. Lindner and B. Rittberger, 'The Creation, Interpretation and Contestation of Institutions: Revisiting Historical Institutionalism', *Journal of Common Market Studies*, 41 (2003), 445–73

P. Lindseth, *Power and Legitimacy: Reconciling Europe and the Nation-State* (Oxford, 2010)

J. J. Linz and A. Stepan (eds), *The Breakdown of Democratic Regimes* (Baltimore, 1978), vols 1–2

J. J. Linz and A. Stepan, *Democratic Transition and Consolidation* (Baltimore, 1996)

W. Lipgens, 'European Federation in the Political Thought of Resistance Movements during World War II', *Central European History*, 1 (1968), 5–19

W. Lipgens, *Europa-Föderationspläne der Widerstandsbewegungen 1940–1945* (Munich, 1968)

W. Lipgens, *Die Anfänge der europäischen Einigungspolitik 1945–1950* (Stuttgart, 1977)

W. Lipgens, *A History of European Integration, 1945–1947* (Oxford, 1982)

W. Lipgens and W. Loth (eds), *Documents on the History of European Integration* (Berlin, 1985–88), 3 vols

W. Lippmann, *The Cold War: A Study in U.S. Foreign Policy* (New York, 1947)

T. O. Lloyd, *Empire to Welfare State: English History, 1906–1967* (Oxford, 1970)

J. Lodge, 'Loyalty and the EEC: The Limitations of the Functionalist Approach', *Political Studies*, 26 (1978), 232–48

C. Lord, *Absent at the Creation: Britain and the Formation of the European Community, 1950–2* (Aldershot, 1996)

M. Loriaux, *France after Hegemony: International Change and Financial Reform* (Ithaca, NY, 1991)

R. Lorimer, *Mass Communications: A Comparative Introduction* (Manchester, 1994)

W. Loth, *Sozialismus und Internationalismus. Die französischen Sozialisten und Nachkriegsordnung Europas, 1940–1950* (Stuttgart, 1977)

W. Loth, 'Der "Kalte Krieg" in der historischen Forschung', in G. Niedhart (ed.), *Der Westen und die Sowjetunion* (Paderborn, 1983), 155–75

W. Loth, 'German Conceptions of Europe during the Escalation of the East-West Conflict, 1945–1949', in J. Becker and F. Knipping (eds), *Power in Europe? Great Britain, France, Italy and Germany in a Postwar World, 1945–1950* (Berlin, 1986), vol. 1, 517–36

W. Loth, *The Division of the World, 1941–1955* (London, 1988)

W. Loth, 'De Gaulle und Europa', *Historische Zeitschrift*, 253 (1991), 629–60

W. Loth, 'Die EWG und das Projekt der Europäischen Politischen Gesellschaft', in R. Hudemann (ed.), *Europa im Blick der Historiker* (Munich, 1995), 191–201

W. Loth, *Der Weg nach Europa. Geschichte der europäischen Integration 1939–1957* (Göttingen, 1996)

W. Loth, 'Der Prozess der europäischen Integration', *Jahrbuch fur europaische Geschichte* 1 (2000), 17–30

W. Loth, 'Identity and Statehood in the Process of European Integration', *Journal of European Integration History* 6 (2000), 19–31

W. Loth (ed.), *Crises and Compromises: The European Project, 1963–1969* (Baden-Baden, 2001)

W. Loth, *Overcoming the Cold War: A History of Détente* (Basingstoke, 2002)

W. Loth, 'From the "Third Force" to the Common Market: Discussions about Europe and the Future of the Nation-State in West Germany, 1945–57', in D. Geppert (ed.), *The Postwar Challenge, 1945–1958* (Oxford, 2003), 191–209

W. Loth (ed.), *Europe, Cold War and Co-existence* (London, 2004)

W. Loth, 'Explaining European Integration', *Journal of European Integration History* 14 (2008), 9–26

W. Loth, 'Helmut Kohl und die Währungsunion', *Vierteljahreshefte für Zeitgeschichte*, 61 (2013), 455–80

W. Loth, *Building Europe. A History of European Unification* (Berlin, 2015)

W. Loth and G. Soutou (eds), *The Making of Détente: Eastern Europe and Western Europe in the Cold War, 1965–75* (London, 2010)

P. Lowe, *The Korean War* (New York, 2000)

M. Lubbers and P. Scheepers, 'Political versus Instrumental Euroscepticism: Mapping Euroscepticism in European Countries and Regions', *European Union Politics*, 6 (2006), 223–42

W. S. Lucas, *Divided We Stand: Britain, the United States and the Suez Crisis* (London, 1991)

G. Lucassen and M. Lubbers, 'Who Fears What? Explaining Far-right-wing Preference in Europe', *Comparative Political Studies*, 45 (2012), 547–74

N. P. Ludlow, *Dealing with Britain: The Six and the First UK Application to the EEC* (Cambridge, 1997)

N. P. Ludlow, 'Paying the Price of Victory? Postwar Britain and the Ideas of National Independence', in D. Geppert (ed.), *The Postwar Challenge, 1945–1958* (Oxford, 2003), 259–72

N. P. Ludlow, 'A Waning Force: The Treasury and British European Policy, 1955–63', *Contemporary British History*, 17 (2003), 87–104

N. P. Ludlow, 'The Making of the CAP: Towards a Historical Analysis of the EU's First Major Policy', *Contemporary European History*, 14 (2005), 347–71

N. P. Ludlow, *The European Community and the Crises of the 1960s: Negotiating the Gaullist Challenge* (London, 2006)

N. P. Ludlow, 'The Emergence of a Commercial Heavy-Weight: The Kennedy Round Negotiations and the European Community of the 1960s', *Diplomacy and Statecraft*, 18 (2007), 351–68

N. P. Ludlow (ed.), *European Integration and the Cold War: Ostpolitik—Westpolitik, 1965–1973* (London, 2007)

N. P. Ludlow, 'Widening, Deepening and Opening Out: Towards a Fourth Decade of European Integration History', in W. Loth (ed.), *Experiencing Europe: 50 Years of European Construction 1957–2007* (Baden-Baden, 2009), 33–44

N. P. Ludlow, *Roy Jenkins and the European Commission Presidency, 1976–1980: At the Heart of Europe* (Basingstoke, 2016)

L. Lundberg, 'European Economic Integration and the Nordic Countries' Trade', *Journal of Common Market Studies*, 30 (1992), 157–73

G. Lundestad, *'Empire' by Invitation: The United States and European Integration, 1945–1997* (Oxford, 1998)

P. M. Lützeler, *Die Schriftsteller und Europa* (Munich, 1992)

F. M. B. Lynch, *France and the International Economy, from Vichy to the Treaty of Rome* (London, 1997)

F. M. B. Lynch, 'France and European Integration: From the Schuman Plan to Economic and Monetary Union', *Contemporary European History*, 13 (2004), 117–20

A. J. McAdams, *Germany Divided: From the Wall to Reunification* (Princeton, NJ, 1993)

J. McAllister, *No Exit: America and the German Problem, 1943–1954* (Ithaca, 2002)

P. McCarthy, *The French Socialists in Power, 1981–1986* (New York, 1987)

J. McCormick, *The European Superpower* (Basingstoke, 2007)

J. McCormick, 'Why Europe Works', in H. Zimmermann and A. Dür (eds), *Key Controversies in European Integration* (Basingstoke, 2012), 11–19

J. McCormick, *Why Europe Matters: The Case for the European Union* (Basingstoke, 2013)

J. McCormick, *Europeanism* (Oxford, 2010)

D. B. MacDonald, *Balkan Holocausts? Serbian and Croatian Victim-centred Propaganda and the War in Yugoslavia* (Manchester, 2002)

J. McDougall, *A History of Algeria* (Cambridge, 2017)

J. McDougall, 'The Impossible Republic: The Reconquest of Algeria and the Decolonization of France, 1945–1962', *Journal of Modern History*, 89 (2017), 772–811

J. McGarry and B. O'Leary, 'The Exaggerated Impact of European Integration on the Politics of Divided Nations', in T. J. Mabry, J. McGarry, M. Moore, and B. O'Leary (eds), *Divided Nations and European Integration* (Philadelphia, PA, 2013), 341–91

M. McGwire, 'National Security and Soviet Foreign Policy', in M. P. Leffler and D. S. Painter (eds), *Origins of the Cold War*, 2nd edn (London, 2005), 53–76

D. McKay, *Rush to Union: Understanding the European Federal Bargain* (Oxford, 1996)

A. McKeever, *Immigration Policy and Right-wing Populism in Western Europe* (Basingstoke, 2020)

J. M. MacKenzie, *Propaganda and Empire: The Manipulation of British Public Opinion, 1880–1960* (Manchester, 1986)

A. Macleod, 'French Policy toward War in the Former Yugoslavia: A Bid for International Leadership', *International Journal*, 52 (1997), 243–64

A. Maddison, *Economic Growth in the West* (London, 1964)

A. Maddison, *The World Economy: Historical Statistics* (Paris, 2003)

P. Madelin, *Jacques Chirac: Une biographie* (Paris, 2002)

E. J. Mahan, *Kennedy, de Gaulle and Western Europe* (Basingstoke, 2002)

M. Mandelbaum, 'Causal Analysis in History', *Journal of the History of Ideas*, 3 (1942), 30–50

M. Mandelbaum, *Purpose and Necessity in Social Theory* (Baltimore, 1987)

C. S. Maier (ed.), *The Cold War in Europe* (New York, 1991)

C. S. Maier, *Dissolution: The Crisis of Communism and the End of East Germany* (Princeton, NJ, 1997)

G. Majone, 'The New Institutionalism: Organizational Factors in Political Life', *American Political Science Review*, 78 (1984), 734–49

G. Majone, 'The Rise of the Regulatory State in Europe', *West European Politics*, 17 (1994), 77–101

G. Majone (ed.), *Regulating Europe* (London, 1996)

G. Majone, 'Europe's Democratic Deficit', *European Law Journal*, 4 (1998), 5–28

G. Majone, *Europe as the Would-be World Power: The EU at Fifty* (Cambridge, 2009)

G. Majone, *Rethinking the Union of Europe Post-Crisis: Has Integration Gone Too Far?* (Cambridge, 2014)

P. Major, *The Death of the KPD: Communism and Anti-Communism in West Germany, 1945–1956* (Oxford, 1998)

N. Malcolm, *Kosovo: A Short History* (Basingstoke, 1998)

J. G. March and J. P. Olsen, *Rediscovering Institutions: The Organizational Basis of Politics* (New York, 1989)

M. Margairaz, *L'Etat, les finances et l'économie. Histoire d'une conversion 1932–1952* (Paris, 1991)

E. Mark, 'October or Thermidor? Interpretations of Stalinism and the Perception of Soviet Foreign Policy in the United States, 1927–1947', *American Historical Review*, 94 (1989), 937–62

G. Marks, L. Hooghe, and K. Blank, 'European Integration from the 1980s: State-centric vs. Multi-level Governance', *Journal of Common Market Studies*, 34 (1996), 341–78

G. Marks, F. W. Sharpf, P. C. Schmitter, and W. Streeck (eds), *Governance in the European Union* (London, 1996)

A. J. Marques Mendes, 'The Contribution of the European Community to Economic Growth: An Assessment of the First 25 Years', *Journal of Common Market Studies*, 24 (1986), 261–77

P. Marsh, *The New Industrial Revolution: Consumers, Globalization and the End of Mass Production* (New Haven, CT, 2012)

G. J. Martin, '"Grandeur et dépendances": The Dilemmas of Gaullist Foreign Policy, September 1967 to April 1968', in N. P. Ludlow (ed.), *European Integration and the Cold War: Ostpolitik—Westpolitik, 1965–1973* (London, 2007), 36–52

G. J. Martin, *General de Gaulle's Cold War: Challenging American Hegemony, 1963–68* (New York, 2013)

V. Martin de la Torre, *Europe, a Leap into the Unknown: A Journey Back in Time to Meet the Founders of the European Union* (Bern, 2014)

A. Marwick, *Class: Image and Reality in Britain, France and the USA since 1930* (Basingstoke, 1990)

V. Mastny, *The Cold War and Soviet Insecurity: The Stalin Years* (Oxford, 1996)

R. C. O. Matthews, C. H. Feinstein, and J. C. Odling-Smee, *British Economic Growth, 1856–1973* (Oxford, 1982)

W. Matthews, *The New Left, National Identity and the Break-Up of Britain* (Leiden, 2013)

BIBLIOGRAPHY   491

H. Maull and B. Stahl, 'Durch den Balkan nach Europa? Deutschland und Frankreich in den Jugoslawienkreigen', *Politische Vierteljahresschrift*, 43 (2002), 82–111

T. W. Maulucci, 'Konrad Adenauer's April 1953 Visit to the United States and the Limits of the German–American Relationship in the Early 1950s', *German Studies Review*, 26 (2003), 577–96

T. W. Maulucci, *Adenauer's Foreign Office: West German Diplomacy in the Shadow of the Third Reich* (Ithaca, NY, 2012)

R. Mayne, D. Johnson, and R. Tombs (eds), *Cross Channel Currents: 100 Years of Entente Cordiale* (London, 2004)

K. Maxwell, 'Portugal: "The Revolution of the Carnations", 1974–75', in A. Roberts and T. Garton Ash (eds), *Civil Resistance and Power Politics: The Experience of Non-Violent Action from Gandhi to the Present* (Oxford, 2009), 144–61

M. Mazower, *Dark Continent: Europe's Twentieth Century* (London, 1998)

M. Mazower, *No Enchanted Palace: The End of Empire and the Ideological Origins of the United Nations* (Princeton, NJ, 2009)

L. Mees, *Nationalism, Violence and Democracy: The Basque Clash of Identities* (Basingstoke, 2003)

A. Megill, 'Recounting the Past: "Description", Explanation and Narrative in Historiography', *American Historical Review*, 94 (1989), 627–53

M. Meimeth, *Frankreichs Entspannungspolitik der 70er Jahre zwischen Status quo und friedlichem Wandel: Die Ära Georges Pompidou und Valéry Giscard d'Estaing* (Baden-Baden, 1990)

F. Mérand, *European Defence Policy: Beyond the Nation-State* (Oxford, 2008), 48–9

P. H. Merkl, *German Unification in the European Context* (Palo Alto, CA, 1993)

P. Merseburger, *Der schwierige Deutsche. Kurt Schumacher* (Stuttgart, 1995)

W. van Meurs, R. de Bruin, L. van de Grift, C. Hoetink, K. van Leewen, and C. Reijnen, *The Unfinished History of European Integration* (Amsterdam, 2018)

C. O. Meyer, *Europäische Öffentlichkeit als Kontrollsphäre: Die Europäische Kommission, die Medien und politische Verantwortung* (Berlin, 2002)

W. Meyer, *Mythos Deutsche Mark. Zur Geschichte einer abgeschafften Währung* (Berlin, 2001)

H. Miard-Delacroix, 'Helmut Schmidt et les institutions européennes', in M.-T. Bitsch (ed.), *Le couple France-Allemagne et les institutions européennes* (Brussels, 2001)

A. Michalski, 'The Enlarging European Union', in D. Dinan (ed.), *Origins and Evolution of the European Union* (Oxford, 2006), 271–92

E. Michels, *Guillaume, der Spion. Eine deutsch-deutsche Karriere* (Berlin, 2013)

L. van Middelaar, *The Passage to Europe: How a Continent Became a Union*, new edn (New Haven, CT, 2020)

L. van Middelaar, *Alarums and Excursions: Improvising Politics on the European Stage* (Newcastle, 2019)

K. Middlemas, *Orchestrating Europe* (London, 1995)

A. C. Mierzejewski, *Ludwig Erhard: A Biography* (Chapel Hill, NC, 2004)

T. Milani, 'From Laissez-Faire to Supranational Planning: The Economic Debate within Federal Union, 1938–1945', *European Review of History*, 23 (2016), 664–85

T. Milani, 'Retreat from the Global? European Unity and British Progressive Intellectuals, 1930–45', *International History Review*, 42 (2019), 99–116

J. E. Miller, *The United States and Italy, 1940–1950* (Chapel Hill, 1986)

M. Miller, 'The Approaches to European Institution-Building of Carlo Sforza, Italian Foreign Minister, 1947–51', in A. Deighton (ed.), *Building Postwar Europe: National Decision-Makers and European Institutions, 1948–1963* (Basingstoke, 1995), 55–69

A. S. Milward, 'Allegiance: The Past and the Future', *Journal of European Integration History*, 1 (1995), 7–19

A. S. Milward, 'The Social Basis of Monetary Union', in P. Gowan and P. Anderson (eds), *The Question of Europe* (London 1997), 149–61

A. S. Milward, *The European Rescue of the Nation-State*, 2nd edn (London, 2000)

492   BIBLIOGRAPHY

A. S. Milward, 'Childe Harold's Pilgrimage', in J. Noakes, P. Wende, and J. Wright (eds), *Britain and Germany in Europe* (Oxford, 2002), 49–66

A. S. Milward, *The Rise and Fall of a National Strategy: The UK and the European Community* (London, 2002), vol. 1

A. S. Milward and V. Sorensen (eds), *The Frontier of National Sovereignty: History and Theory, 1945–1992* (Routledge, 1993)

P. Milza, 'Public Opinion and Perception of Power in France at the End of the Fourth Republic', in E. Di Nolfo, *Power in Europe? Great Britain, France, Germany and Italy and the Origins of the EEC, 1952–1957* (Berlin, 1992), vol. 2, 462–76

G. I. Mirsky, *On Ruins of Empire: Ethnicity and Nationalism in the Former Soviet Union* (Westport, CT, 1997)

A. Moravcsik, 'Negotiating the Single European Act: National Interests and Conventional Statecraft in the European Community', *International Organization*, 45 (1991), 19–56

A. Moravcsik, 'Integrating International and Domestic Theories of International Bargaining', in P. B. Evans, H. K. Jacobsen, and R. D. Putnam (eds), *International Bargaining and Domestic Politics: Double-Edged Diplomacy* (London, 1993), 3–42

A. Moravcsik, 'Preferences and Power in the European Community: A Liberal Intergovernmentalist Approach', *Journal of Common Market Studies*, 31 (1993), 473–524

A. Moravcsik, 'Is Something Rotten in the State of Denmark? Constructivism and European Integration', Journal of European Public Policy, 6 (1999), 669–81 A. Moravcsik, 'Liberal Intergovernmentalism and Integration: A Rejoinder', *Journal of Common Market Studies*, 33 (1995), 611–28

A. Moravcsik, *The Choice for Europe: Social Purpose and State Power from Messina to Maastricht* (Ithaca, NY, 1998)

A. Moravcsik, 'A New Statecraft? Supranational Entrepreneurs and International Cooperation', *International Organization*, 53 (1999), 267–306

A. Moravcsik, 'Theory and Method in the Study of International Negotiation: A Rejoinder to Oran Young', *International Organization*, 53 (1999), 811–14

A. Moravcsik, 'Beyond Grain and *Grandeur*: An Answer to Critics and an Agenda for Future Research', *Journal of Cold War Studies*, 2.3 (2000), 117–42

A. Moravcsik, 'De Gaulle between Grain and *Grandeur*: The Political Economy of French EC Policy, 1958–1970, *Journal of Cold War Studies*, 2.2 (2000), 3–43, and 2.3 (2000), 4–68

A. Moravcsik, 'In Defence of the "Democratic Deficit": Reassessing Legitimacy in the European Union', *Journal of Common Market Studies*, 40 (2002), 603–24

A. Moravcsik, 'Did Power Politics Cause European Integration? Realist Theory Meets Qualitative Methods', *Security Studies*, 22 (2013), 773–90

A. Moravcsik, 'Preferences, Power and Institutions in 21st-century Europe', *Journal of Common Market Studies*, 56 (2018), 1648–74

K. O. Morgan, *Labour in Power, 1945–1951* (Oxford, 1984)

K. O. Morgan, *Britain since 1945: The People's Peace*, 3rd edn (Oxford, 2001)

E. Morse, *Foreign Policy and Interdependence in Gaullist France* (Princeton, NJ, 1973)

D. A. Moses, *German Intellectuals and the Nazi Past* (Cambridge, 2007)

K. O. Morgan, 'The Non-German German and the German German: Dilemmas of Identity after the Holocaust', *New German Critique*, 101 (2007), 45–94

E. Mourlon-Druol, 'Filling the EEC Leadership Vacuum? The Creation of the European Council in 1974', *Cold War History*, 10 (2010), 315–39

E. Mourlon-Druol, 'Integrating an International Political Economy Dimension into European Integration History: The Challenges of the 1970s', *Journal of European Integration History*, 17 (2011), 335–41

E. Mourlon-Druol, *A Europe Made of Money: The Emergence of the European Monetary System* (Ithaca, NY, 2012)

E. Mourlon-Druol, and F. Romero (eds), *International Summitry and Global Governance: The Rise of the G7 and the European Council, 1974–1991* (London, 2014)

E. Mourlon-Druol, 'Rich, Vivid and Ignored: History in European Studies', *Politique européenne*, 50 (2015), 56–69

E. Mourlon-Druol, H. Müller, G. Porcaro, and T. Schmidt, 'You'll Never Talk Alone: What Media Narratives on European Reforms Reveal about a Polity in the Making', *Bruegel Working Paper*, 19 (2022), 1–56

S. Moyn, 'Personalism, Community, and the Origins of Human Rights', in S.-L. Hoffmann (ed.), *Human Rights in the Twentieth Century* (Cambridge, 2010), 86–106

C. Mudde, *Populist Radical Right Parties in Europe* (Cambridge, 2007)

C. Mudde, 'The Populist Radical Right: A Pathological Normalcy', *West European Politics*, 33 (2010), 1175–7

C. Mudde, 'The Far Right and the European Elections', *Current History*, 113 (2014), 98–103

C. Mudde, *The Far Right Today* (Cambridge, 2019)

J.-W. Müller, *Another Country: German Intellectuals, Unification and National Identity* (New Haven, CT, 2000)

J.-W. Müller, 'Introduction: The Power of Memory, the Memory of Power and the Power over Memory', in J.-W. Müller (ed.), *Memory and Power in Post-War Europe: Studies in the Present of the Past* (Cambridge, 2002), 1–35

J.-W. Müller, *Constitutional Patriotism* (Princeton, NJ, 2009)

J.-W. Müller, 'On "European Memory": Some Conceptual and Normative Remarks' and S. Berger, 'Remembering the Second World War in Western Europe, 1945–2005', in M. Pakier and B. Stråth (eds), *Contested Histories and Politics of Remembrance* (New York, 2010), 25–37

J.-W. Müller, *Contesting Democracy: Political Ideas in Twentieth-Century Europe* (New Haven, CT, 2011)

J.-W. Müller, *What is Populism?* (London, 2017)

W. Mulligan, *The Great War for Peace* (New Haven, CT, 2014)

R. Münch, 'German Nation and German Identity: Continuity and Change from the 1770s to the 1990s', in B. Heurlin (ed.), *Germany in the Nineties* (Basingstoke, 1996), 13–43

J. M. Mushaben, *From Post-War to Post-Wall Generations: Changing Attitudes towards the National Question and NATO in the Federal Republic of Germany* (Boulder, CO, 1998)

M. Myant, 'Poland—the Permanent Crisis', in R. A. Clarke (ed.), *Poland: The Economy in the 1980s* (London, 1989), 1–28

A. Nafpliotis, *Britain and the Greek Colonels: Accommodating the Junta in the Cold War* (London, 2012)

N. Naimark, *The Russians in Germany: A History of the Soviet Zone of Occupation, 1945–1949* (Cambridge, MA, 1995)

T. Nairn, *The Break-up of Britain: Crisis and Neo-Nationalism*, 2nd edn (London, 1981)

P. Nash, 'Eisenhower, Nuclear Weapons and Arms Control', in C. J. Pach (ed.), *A Companion to Dwight Eisenhower* (New York, 2017), 327–49

H. Nehring, '"Westernization": A New Paradigm for Interpreting West European History in a Cold War Context', *Cold War History*, 4 (2004), 175–91

H. Nehring, 'What Was the Cold War?', *English Historical Review*, 127 (2012), 920–49

M. S. Neiberg, *When France Fell: The Vichy Crisis and the Fate of the Anglo-American Alliance* (Cambridge, MA, 2021)

B. F. Nelsen and J. L. Guth, *Religion and the Struggle for the European Union: Confessional Culture and the Limits of Integration* (Washington, DC., 2015)

B. F. Nelsen and A. Stubb (eds), *The European Union: Readings on the Theory and Practice of European Integration* (Oxford, 2003)

C. W. Nettelbeck, *Forever French: Exile in the United States, 1939–1945* (Oxford, 1991)

M. Neuburger, *The Orient Within: Muslim Minorities and the Negotiation of Nationhood in Modern Bulgaria* (Ithaca, NY, 2004)

M. Newman, 'Léon Blum, French Socialism and European Unity, 1940–1950', *Historical Journal*, 4 (1981), 189–200

494 BIBLIOGRAPHY

A. J. Nicholls, *Freedom with Responsibility: The Social Market Economy in Germany, 1918–1963* (Oxford, 1994)

R. Nichols, *Treason, Tradition and the Intellectual: Julien Benda and Political Discourse* (Lawrence, 1978)

L. A. Nichter, *Richard Nixon and Europe: The Reshaping of the Postwar Atlantic World* (Cambridge, 2015)

K. Nicolaïdis and S. K. Schmidt, 'Mutual Recognition "On Trial": The Long Road to Services Liberalization', *Journal of European Public Policy*, 14 (2007), 717–34

G. Niedhart, 'U.S. Détente and West German *Ostpolitik*: Parallels and Frictions', in M. Schulz and T. A. Schwartz (eds), *The Strained Alliance: U.S.–European Relations from Nixon to Carter* (Cambridge, 2010), 23–44

G. Niedhart, '*Ostpolitik*: Transformation through Communication and the Quest for Peaceful Change', *Journal of Cold War Studies*, 18 (2016), 14–59

G. Niedhart, 'East–West Conflict: Short Cold War and Long Détente', in O. Bange and P. Villaume (eds), *The Long Détente: Changing Concepts of Security and Cooperation in Europe, 1950s–1980s* (Budapest, 2017), 19–30

G. Noël, 'Les finalités de la politique agricole commune 1958–1972: Marché et cohesion économique et sociale', in A. Varsori (ed.), *Inside the European Community: Actors and Policies in European Integration* (Baden-Baden, 2006), 283–300

G. Noiriel, *Workers in French Society in the Nineteenth and Twentieth Centuries* (New York, 1990)

E. Di Nolfo, 'Das Problem der europäischen Einigung als ein Aspekt der italienischen Aussenpolitik 1945–1954', *Vierteljahreshefte für Zeitgeschichte*, 28 (1980), 145–67

P. Nord, *France's New Deal: From the Thirties to the Postwar Era* (Princeton, NJ, 2010)

E. A. Nordlinger, *Isolationism Reconfigured* (Princeton, NJ, 1995)

Z. Norkus, 'Max Weber on Nations and Nationalism: Political Economy before Political Sociology', *Canadian Journal of Sociology*, 29 (2004), 389–418

L. Nuti, *The Crisis of Détente in Europe: From Helsinki to Gorbachev, 1975–1985* (London, 2008)

L. Nuti, F. Bozo, M.-P. Rey, and B. Rother (eds), *The Euromissiles Crisis and the End of the Cold War* (Washington, DC, 2015)

T. Oatley, *Monetary Politics: Exchange Rate Cooperation in the European Union* (Ann Arbor, 1997)

H. Obinger, S. Leibfried, and F. G. Castles, 'Bypasses to a Social Europe? Lessons from Federal Experience,' *Journal of European Public Policy*, 12 (2005), 545–71

P. O'Brien, *Beyond the Swastika* (London, 1996)

D. Oesch, 'Explaining Workers' Support for Right-wing Populist Parties in Western Europe: Evidence from Austria, Belgium, France Norway and Switzerland', *International Political Science Review*, 29 (2008), 349–73

K. Ohmae, *The Borderless World: Power and Strategy in the Interlinked Economy* (New York, 1990)

K. Ohmae, *The Evolving Global Economy: Making Sense of the New World Order* (Cambridge, MA, 1995)

R. Okey, *Eastern Europe, 1740–1985: Feudalism to Communism*, 2nd edn (London, 1992)

P. Oleskog Tryggvason and J. Strömbäck, 'Fact or Fiction? Investigating the Quality of Opinion Poll Coverage and Its Antecedents', *Journalism Studies*, 19 (2018), 2148–67

M. O'Mahoney, 'Measures of Fixed Capital Stocks in the Post-war Period: A Five-country Study', in B. van Ark and N. Crafts (eds), *Quantitative Aspects of Post-War European Growth* (Cambridge, 1996), 165–214

D. Orlow, 'Delayed Reaction: Democracy, Nationalism and the SPD, 1945–1966', *German Studies Review* 16 (1993), 77–102

D. Ost, *The Defeat of Solidarity: Anger and Politics in Postcommunist Europe* (Ithaca, NY, 2005)

N. O'Sullivan, *European Political Thought since 1945* (Basingstoke, 2004)

M. J. Ouimet, *The Rise and Fall of the Brezhnev Doctrine in Soviet Foreign Policy* (Chapel Hill, NC, 2003)

R. Ovendale, *The English-speaking Alliance: Britain, the United States, the Dominions and the Cold War, 1947–1951* (London, 1985)

U. Özkirimli, *Theories of Nationalism: A Critical Introduction*, 3rd edn (New York, 2017)

A. Paczkowski, *Revolution and Counterrevolution in Poland, 1980–1989: Solidarity, Martial Law and the End of Communism in Europe* (Rochester, NY, 2015)

A. Pagden (ed.), *The Idea of Europe* (Cambridge, 2002)

B. Page, 'Culture and Attitudes', in A. Seldon (ed.), *Blair's Britain, 1997–2007* (Cambridge, 2007), 436–67

M. Pakier and B. Stråth, 'Introduction: A European Memory?', in M. Pakier and B. Stråth (eds), *Contested Histories and Politics of Remembrance* (New York, 2010), 1–20

J. Palayret et al. (eds), *Visions, Votes and Vetoes: The Empty Chair Crisis and the Luxembourg Compromise Forty Years On* (Berne, 2006)

F. Papadia, E. Bergamini, E. Mourlon-Druol, and G. Porcaro, 'Interest in European Matters: A Glass Three-Quarters Full?', *Bruegel Working Paper*, 5 (2021), 2–21

R. Papini, *The Christian Democratic International* (Lanham, MD, 1997)

C. Parsons, 'Showing Ideas as Causes: The Origins of the European Union', *International Organization*, 56 (2002), 47–84

C. Parsons, *A Certain Idea of Europe* (Ithaca, New York, 2003)

R. Pastor-Castro, 'The Quai d'Orsay and the European Defence Community Crisis of 1954', *History*, 91 (2006), 386–400

K. K. Patel, *Europäisierung wider Willen: Die Bundesrepublik Deutschland in der Agrarintegration der EWG, 1955–1973* (Munich, 2009)

K. K. Patel, 'Multiple Connections in European Cooperation: International Organizations, Policy Ideas, Practices and Transfers, 1967–1992', *European Review of History*, 24 (2017), 337–57

K. K. Patel, *Project Europe: A History* (Cambridge, 2020)

K. K. Patel and W. Kaiser, 'Continuity and Change in European Cooperation during the Twentieth Century', *Contemporary European History*, 27 (2018), 165–82

K. K. Patel and J. Schot, 'Twisted Paths to European Integration: Comparing Agriculture and Transport in a Transnational Perspective', *Contemporary European History*, 20 (2011), 383–403

A. Paul, 'The EU in the South Caucasus and the Impact of the Russia-Ukraine War', *The International Spectator*, 50 (2015), 30–42

A. Pavković, *The Fragmentation of Yugoslavia: Nationalism and War in the Balkans*, 2nd edn (Basingstoke, 2000)

A. Pavković, H. Koscharsky, and A. Czarnota (eds), *Nationalism and Post-Communism* (Aldershot, 1995)

R. Pawin, 'Retour sur les "Trentes Glorieuses" et la périodisation du second XXe siècle', *Revue d'histoire modern et contemporaine*, 60 (2013), 155–75

M. M. Payk and R. Pergher (eds), *Beyond Versailles: Sovereignty, Legitimacy and the Formation of New Polities after the Great War* (Bloomington, Indiana, 2018)

S. Payne, *The Franco Regime, 1936–1975* (Madison, 1987)

S. Payne, *A History of Fascism, 1914–1945* (London, 1996)

R. O. Paxton, *Vichy France: Old Guard and New Order, 1940–1944* (New York, 1972)

J. Pearson, *Sir Anthony Eden and the Suez Crisis: Reluctant Gamble* (Basingstoke, 2002)

S. Pedersen, *The Guardians: The League of Nations and the Crisis of Empire* (Oxford, 2015)

J. Pelkmans, 'Mutual Recognition in Goods and Services: An Economic Perspective', in F. Kostoris and P. Schioppa (eds), *The Principles of Mutual Recognition in the European Integration Process* (Basingstoke, 2005), 83–128

A. Perez-Agote, *The Social Roots of Basque Nationalism* (Reno, NV, 2006)

J. Peter, C. H. De Vreese, and H. A. Semetko, 'EU Politics on Television News: A Cross-National Comparative Study', *European Union Politics*, 4 (2003), 305–27

J. Peterson, 'Decision-making in the European Union: Towards a Framework for Analysis', *Journal of European Public Policy*, 2 (1995), 69–93

J. Peterson, 'Policy Networks and European Union Policy-making: A Reply to Kassim', *West European Politics*, 18 (1995), 389–407

J. Peterson, 'Junker's Political European Commission', *Journal of Common Market Studies*, 55 (2017), 349–67

J. Peterson and E. Bomberg, *Decision-Making in the European Union* (Basingstoke, 1999)

D. Petter, *Auf dem Weg zur Normalität. Konflikt und Verständigung in den deutsch-französischen Beziehungen der 1970er Jahre* (Munich, 2014)

P. Pierson, 'The Path to European Integration: An Historical Institutionalist Account', *Comparative Political Studies*, 29 (1996), 123–64

P. Pierson, *Politics in Time: History, Institutions and Social Analysis* (Princeton, NJ, 2004)

J. Pinder, 'Federalism and the Beginnings of European Union', in K. Larres (ed.), *A Companion to Europe since 1945* (Oxford, 2009), 25–44

J. Plamenatz, 'Two Types of Nationalism', in E. Kamenka (ed.), *Nationalism: The Nature and Evolution of an Idea* (London, 1970), 22–36

A. v. Plato, 'An Unfamiliar Germany: Remarks on the Past and Present Relationship between East and West Germans', *Oral History*, 21 (1993), 35–42

G. Poggi, 'The Constitutional State of the Nineteenth Century: An Elementary Conceptual Portrait', *Sociology*, 11 (1977), 311–32

G. Poggi, *The Development of the Modern State: A Sociological Interpretation* (Palo Alto, CA, 1978)

G. Poggi, *The State: Its Nature, Development and Prospects* (Cambridge, 1990)

U. G. Poiger, *Jazz, Rock and Rebels: Cold War Politics and American Culture in a Divided Germany* (Berkeley, CA, 2000)

M. A. Pollack, 'Creeping Competence: The Expanding Agenda of the European Community', *Journal of Public Policy*, 88 (1994), 95–144

M. A. Pollack, 'The End of Creeping Competence? EU Policy-Making since Maastricht', *Journal of Common Market Studies*, 38 (2000), 519–38

S. Pollard, *Peaceful Conquest: The Industrialization of Europe, 1760–1970* (Oxford, 1981)

K. Polynczuk-Alenius, 'At the Intersection of Racism and Nationalism: Theorising and Contextualising the "Anti-immigration" Discourse in Poland', *Nations and Nationalism*, 27 (2021) 766–81

M. M. Postan, *An Economic History of Western Europe, 1945–1964* (London, 1967)

M. Poster, *Existential Marxism in Postwar France: From Sartre to Althusser* (Princeton, 1975)

N. Postman, *Amusing Ourselves to Death: Public Discourse in the Age of Showbusiness* (London, 1985)

M. S. Power, *Jacques Maritain, Christian Democrat, and the Quest for a New Commonwealth* (Lampeter, 1992)

P. Preston, *The Triumph of Democracy in Spain* (London, 2001)

G. Pridham, *Christian Democracy in Western Germany: The CDU/CSU in Government and Opposition, 1945–1976* (London, 1977)

S. Princen and M. Rhinard, 'Crashing and Creeping: Agenda-setting Dynamics in the European Union', *Journal of European Public Policy*, 13 (2006), 1113–32

L. Probst, 'Founding Myths in Europe and the Role of the Holocaust', and D. Diner, 'Restitution and Memory: The Holocaust in European Political Cultures, *New German Critique*, 90 (2003), 36–58

S. Pryke, 'National and European Identity', *National Identities*, 22 (2020), 91–105

D. J. Puchala, 'Of Blind Men, Elephants and International Integration', *Journal of Common Market Studies*, 10 (1971), 267–84

A. Rabil, Jr, *Merleau-Ponty: Existentialist of the Social World* (New York, 1967)

S. Radošević, 'The Collapse of Yugoslavia: Between Chance and Necessity', in D. A. Dyker and I. Vejvoda (eds), *Yugoslavia and After* (London, 1996), 28–47

T. Raithel, 'The German Nation and the 2006 FIFA World Cup', in S. Rinke and K. Schiller (eds), *The FIFA World Cup, 1930–2010: Politics, Commerce, Spectacle and Identities* (Göttingen, 2014), 353–71

H. C. Raley, *José Ortega y Gasset: Philosopher of European Unity* (Alabama, 1971)

S. P. Ramet, *Balkan Babel: The Disintegration of Yugoslavia from the Death of Tito to the War for Kosovo* (Boulder, CO, 1999)

S. P. Ramet, *Thinking about Yugoslavia: Scholarly Debates about the Yugoslav Breakup and the Wars in Bosnia and Kosovo* (Cambridge, 2005)

R. J. Ranieri, 'Italy: After the Rewards of Growth, the Penalty of Debt', in B. J. Foley (ed.), *European Economies since the Second World War* (Basingstoke, 1998), 75–101

R. J. Ranieri, *The Ambivalent Alliance: Konrad Adenauer, the CDU/CSU and the West, 1949–1966* (New York, 2003)

R. W. Rauch, Jr, *Politics and Belief in Contemporary France: Emmanuel Mounier and Christian Democracy, 1932–1950* (The Hague, 1972)

W. J. Reader, *Fifty Years of Unilever, 1930–1980* (London, 1980)

E. du Réau, *Edouard Daladier, 1884–1970* (Paris, 1993)

E. du Réau, 'La France et l'Europe d'Aristide Briand à Robert Schuman. Naissance, déclin et redéploiement d'une politique étrangere (1929–1950)', *Revue d'histoire moderne et contemporaine*, 42 (1995)

E. du Réau, *L'idée d'Europe au XXe siècle. Des mythes aux réalités* (Brussels, 1996)

E. du Réau (ed.), *Europe des elites? Europe des peuples? La construction de l'espace européenne 1945–1960* (Paris, 1998)

E. du Réau, 'Integration or Cooperation? Europe and the Future of the Nation-State in France, 1945–1955', in D. Geppert (ed.), *Postwar Challenge: Cultural, Social and Political Change in Western Europe, 1945–1958* (Oxford, 2003), 241–58

E. du Réau, *La construction européenne au XXe siècle. Fondements, enjeux, defies* (Nantes, 2007)

E. du Réau, *L'Europe en construction. Le second vingtième siècle*, 2nd edn (Paris, 2007)

S. Recchia, 'Did Chirac say "Non"? Revisiting UN Diplomacy on Iraq, 2002–2003', *Political Science Quarterly*, 130 (2015), 625–54

E. Recchi and A. Favell, *Pioneers of European Integration* (Cheltenham, 2009)

M. Redgrave, 'Europeanising the National Interest: Tony Blair's and New Labour's Lost Objective', *Journal of Contemporary European Studies*, 16 (2008), 421–32

W. Rees, 'Preserving the Security of Europe', in A. Dorman, S. Croft, W. Rees, and M. Uttley *Britain and Defence, 1945–2000* (London, 2001), 49–68

S. Reich, *The Fruits of Fascism: Postwar Prosperity in Historical Perspective* (Ithaca, 1990)

D. C. Reymen, 'The Economic Effects of the Marshall Plan Revisited', in J. Agnew and J. N. Entrikin (eds), *The Marshall Plan Today: Model and Metaphor* (London, 2004), 82–126

D. Reynolds, 'The "Big Three" and the Division of Europe, 1945–48: An Overview', *Diplomacy and Statecraft*, 1 (1990), 118–23

D. Reynolds, 'Beyond Bipolarity in Space and Time', in M. J. Hogan (ed.), *The End of the Cold War: Its Meaning and Implications* (Cambridge, 1992), 245–56

D. Reynolds (ed.), *The Origins of the Cold War in Europe: International Perspectives* (New Haven, CT, 1994)

D. Reynolds, *One World Indivisible: A Global History since 1945* (London, 2000)

D. Reynolds, *In Command of History: Churchill Fighting and Writing the Second World War* (New York, 2005)

D. Reynolds, *From World War to Cold War: Churchill, Roosevelt and the International History of the 1940s* (Oxford, 2006)

J. Richardson, 'Policy-Making in the EU: Interests, Ideas and Garbage Cans of Primeval Soup', in J. Richardson (ed.), *European Union: Power and Policy-Making* (London, 1996)

J. Richardson, 'Policy-Making in the EU: Familiar Ambitions in Unfamiliar Settings?', in A. Menon and V. Wright (eds), *From the Nation-State to Europe* (Oxford, 2001)

J. L. Richardson, *Germany and the Atlantic Alliance: The Interaction of Strategy and Politics* (Cambridge, CT., 1966)

P. Riddell, 'Europe', in A. Seldon and D. Kavanagh (eds), *The Blair Effect, 2001–5* (Cambridge, 2005), 362–83

D. Rieff, *Slaughterhouse: Bosnia and the Failure of the West* (New York, 1995)

498 BIBLIOGRAPHY

B. Rieger, *The People's Car: A Global History of the Volkswagen Beetle* (Cambridge, MA, 2013)

P. Rieker, *French Foreign Policy in a Changing World: Practising Grandeur* (Basingstoke, 2017)

T. Risse, *A Community of Europeans? Transnational Identities and Public Spheres* (Ithaca, NY, 2010)

T. Risse, 'No Demos? Identities and Public Spheres in the Euro Crisis', *Journal of Common Market Studies*, 52 (2014), 1207–1215

T. Risse-Kappen, 'Exploring the Nature of the Beast: International Relations Theory and Comparative Policy Analysis Meet the European Union', *Journal of Common Market Studies*, 34 (1996)

F. F. Rizi, *Benedetto Croce and the Birth of the Italian Republic, 1943–1952* (Toronto, 2019)

D. R. Roberts, *Croce and the Uses of Historicism* (Berkeley, 1987)

R. Robertson, *Globalization: Social Theory and Global Culture* (London, 1992)

G. Robin, *La diplomatie de Mitterrand, ou le triomphe des apparences 1981–1985* (Paris, 1985)

A. Rödder, *Die deutschen sozialistischen Exilgruppen in Grossbritannien* (Hanover, 1968)

A. Rödder, 'Der Mythos von der frühen Westbindung. Konrad Adenauer und Stresemanns Aussenpolitik', *Vierteljahreshefte für Zeitgeschichte*, 41 (1993), 543–73

A. Rödder, *Stresemanns Erbe: Julius Curtius und die deutsche Aussenpolitik 1929–1931* (Paderborn, 1996)

A. Rodriguez-Pose, *The European Union: Economy, Society and Polity* (Oxford, 2002)

N. Rollings, 'Butskellism, the Postwar Consensus and the Managed Economy', in H. Jones and M. Kandiah (eds), *The Myth of Consensus: New Views of British History, 1945–1964* (Basingstoke, 1996), 97–119

A. Romano, 'Détente, Entente or Linkage? The Helsinki Conference on Security and Cooperation in Europe in US Relations with the Soviet Union', *Diplomatic History*, 33 (2009), 703–22

A. Romano, *From Détente in Europe to European Détente: How the West Shaped the Helsinki CSCE* (Brussels, 2009)

A. Romano, 'The EC Nine's Vision and Attempts at Ending the Cold War', in F. Bozo, M.-P. Rey, B. Rother, and N. P. Ludlow (eds), *Visions of the End of the Cold War, 1945–1990* (New York, 2012), 134–46

A. Romano, 'Pan-Europe: A Continental Space for Cooperation(s)', in A. Romano and F. Romero (eds), *European Socialist Regimes' Fateful Engagement with the West: National Strategies in the Long 1970s* (London, 2021), 31–49

S. de Roode, 'Changing Images of the Nation in England, Germany and the Netherlands: A Comparison', *History Compass*, 7 (2009), 894–916

S. de Roode, *Seeing Europe through the Nation: The Role of National Self-images in the Perception of European Integration in the English, German and Dutch Press in the 1950s and 1990s* (Stuttgart, 2012)

S. Rosato, *Europe United: Power Politics and the Making of the European Community* (Ithaca, NY, 2011)

B. Rosamond, *Theories of European Integration* (Basingstoke, 2000)

R. Rose, *Understanding Post-Communist Transformation: A Bottom Up Approach* (London, 2009)

J. Rosenau, *Along the Domestic-Foreign Frontier: Exploring Governance in a Turbulent World* (Cambridge, 1997)

A. Roth, *Heath and the Heathmen* (London, 1972)

J. Rothschild, *East Central Europe between the Two World Wars* (Seattle, 1974)

V. R. Rothwell, *Britain and the Cold War, 1941–1947* (London, 1982)

H. Rousso, 'Das Dilemma eines europäischen Gedächtnisses', *Zeithistorische Forschungen*, 1 (2004), 363–78

K. Ruane, *The Rise and Fall of the European Defence Community: Anglo-American Relations and the Crisis of European Defence, 1950–55* (Basingstoke, 2000)

M. Rupps, *Helmut Schmidt. Eine politische Biographie* (Stuttgart, 2002)

S. Rutar, 'Nationalism in Southeastern Europe, 1970–2000', in J. Breuilly (ed.), *The Oxford Handbook of the History of Nationalism* (Oxford, 2013), 515–34

H. B. Ryan, 'A New Look at Churchill's "Iron Curtain" Speech', *Historical Journal*, 22 (1979), 895–920

K. Sainsbury, *Churchill and Roosevelt at War: The War They Fought and the Peace They Hoped to Make* (Basingstoke, 1994)

M. Salewski, 'Europa: Idée und Wirklichkeit in der nationalsozialistischen Weltanschauung und politischen Praxis', in O. Franz (ed.), *Europas Mitte* (Göttingen, *1987*), 85–106

W. Sandholtz and A. Stone Sweet (eds), *European Integration and Supranational Governance* (Oxford, 1998)

G. Sapelli, *Southern Europe since 1945: Tradition and Modernity in Portugal, Spain, Italy, Greece and Turkey* (London, 1995)

A. Sapir, 'Trade Liberalization and the Harmonization of Social Policies: Lessons from European Integration', in J. N. Bhagwati and R. E. Hudec (eds), *Fair Trade and Harmonization* (Cambridge, MA, 1996), vol. 1, 543–70

A. Sapir, 'European Integration at the Crossroads: A Review Essay on the 50th Anniversary of Bela Balassa's *Theory of Economic Integration*', *Journal of Economic Literature*, 49 (2011), 1200–29

D. Sassoon, *One Hundred Years of Socialism: The West European Left in the Twentieth Century* (New York, 1996)

D. Sassoon, *Contemporary Italy: Economy, Society and Politics since 1945*, 2nd edn (London, 1997)

R. Saunders, *Yes to Europe! The 1975 Referendum and Seventies Britain* (Cambridge, 2018)

S. M. Di Scala, *Renewing Italian Socialism* (Oxford, 1988), 3–32

S. M. Di Scala and S. Mastellano, *European Political Thought, 1815–1989* (Boulder, Colorado, 1998)

F. W. Scharpf, 'The Joint-Decision Trap: Lessons from German Federalism and European Integration', *Public Administration*, 66 (1988), 239–78

F. W. Scharpf, *Governing in Europe* (Oxford, 1999)

F. W. Scharpf, 'The European Social Model: Coping with the Challenges of Diversity', *Journal of Common Market Studies*, 40 (2002)

F. W. Scharpf, 'The Joint-Decision Trap Revisited', *Journal of Common Market Studies*, 44 (2006), 845–64

P. Scheepers, M. Inserts, and M. Coenders, 'Ethnic Exclusionism in European Countries: Public Opposition to Civil Rights for Legal Migrants as a Response to Perceived Ethnic Threat', *European Sociological Review*, 18 (2002), 17–34

F. Scheid Raine, 'The Iranian Crisis of 1946 and the Origins of the Cold War', in M. P. Leffler and D. S. Painter (eds), *The Origins of the Cold War*, 2nd edn (London, 2005), 93–111

A. Shennan, *Rethinking France: Plans for Renewal, 1940–1946* (Oxford, 1989)

E. Scheuch, *Wie deutsch sind die Deutschen?* (Bergisch-Gladbach, 1991)

J. M. Schick, *The Berlin Crisis, 1958–1962* (Philadelphia, PA, 1971)

K. Schiller and C. Young, *The 1972 Munich Olympics and the Making of Modern Germany* (Berkeley, CA, 2010)

F. Schimmelfennig, 'What's the News in "New Intergovernmentalism"? A Critique of Bickerton, Hodson and Puetter', *Journal of Common Market Studies*, 53 (2015), 723–30

F. Schimmelfennig, 'Good Governance and Differentiated Integration: Graded Membership in the European Union', *European Journal of Political Research*, 55 (2016), 789–810

F. Schimmelfennig, 'Liberal Intergovernmentalism and the Crises of European Union', *Journal of Common Market Studies*, 56 (2018), 1578–94

F. Schimmelfennig and T. Winzen, *Ever Looser Union? Differentiated European Integration* (Oxford, 2020)

F. Schimmelfennig, D. Leuffen, and B. Rittberger, 'The European Union as a System of Differentiated Integration: Interdependence, Politicization and Differentiation', *Journal of European Public Policy*, 22 (2015), 764–82

S. Schirmann (ed.), *Robert Schuman et les pères de l'Europe* (Bern, 2008)

H. Schissler, *The Miracle Years: A Cultural History of West Germany, 1949–1968* (Princeton, NJ, 2001)

H. Schissler, 'Postnationality—Luxury of the Privileged?', *German Politics and Society*, 15 (1997), 8–27

P. Schlesinger, 'Europeanness: A New Cultural Battlefield?' *Innovation*, 5 (1992), 11–23

G. Schmidt, 'Divided Europe—Divided Germany, 1950-63', *Contemporary European History*, 3 (1994), 155–92

G. Schmidt (ed.), *Zwischen Bündnissicherung und priviligierter Partnerschaft. Die deutsch-britische Beziehungen und die Vereinigten Staaten von Amerika 1955–1963* (Bochum, 1995)

G. Schmidt, 'European Security: Anglo-German Relationships, 1949-1956', in J. Noakes, P. Wende, and J. Wright (eds), *Britain and Germany in Europe* (Oxford, 2002), 115–40

M. Schmidt (ed.), *The Chancellor of the Unification: Germany and Europe* (Budapest, 2016)

W. Schmidt, 'Die Wurzeln der Entspannung. Der konzeptionelle Ursprung der Ost- und Deutschlandpolitik Willy Brandts in den fünfziger Jahren', *Vierteljahreshefte für Zeitgeschichte*, 51 (2003), 521–63

W. Schmidt, 'A Prophet Unheard: Willy Brandt's North-South Policy and Its Reception in the United States', in B. Rother and K. Larres (eds), *Willy Brandt and International Relations: Europe, the USA and Latin America, 1974–1992* (London, 2019), 67–84

P. C. Schmitter, 'On the Way to a Post-Functionalist Theory of European Integration', *British Journal of Political Science*, 39 (2009), 211–15

D. F. Schmitz, *The Triumph of Internationalism: Franklin D. Roosevelt and a World in Crisis, 1933–1941* (Washington, D.C., 2007)

G. Schneider and M. Aspinwall (eds), *The Rules of Integration: Institutionalist Approaches to the Study of Europe* (Manchester, 2001)

D. Schoenbaum, *The Spiegel Affair* (Garden City, NY, 1968)

D. Schoenbaum and E. Pond, *The German Question and Other German Questions* (Basingstoke, 1996)

G. Schöpflin, 'Nationalism and Ethnicity in Europe, East and West', in C. A. Kupchan (ed.), *Nationalism and Nationalities in the New Europe*, 37–65

F. Schotters, 'Mitterrand's Europe: Functions and Limits of "European Solidarity" in French Policy during the 1980s', *European Review of History*, 24 (2017), 973–90

H.-P. Schwarz, 'Adenauer und Europa', *Vierteljahreshefte für Zeitgeschichte*, 27 (1979), 471–521

H.-P. Schwarz (ed.), *Adenauer und Frankreich. Die deutsch-französischen Beziehungen 1958–1969* (Bonn, 1990)

H.-P. Schwarz, *Konrad Adenauer: A German Politician and Statesman in a Period of War, Revolution and Reconstruction* (Providence, RI, 1995-7), 2 vols

H.-P. Schwarz, *Helmut Kohl. Eine politische Biographie* (Munich, 2012)

T. A. Schwartz, *America's Germany: John J. McCloy and the Federal Republic of Germany* (Cambridge, MA, 1991)

V. Sebestyen, *Revolution 1989: The Fall of the Soviet Empire* (New York, 2009)

M. Segers, *The Netherlands and European Integration, 1950 to the Present* (Amsterdam, 2020)

K. Seidel, *The Process of Politics in Europe: The Rise of European Elites and Supranational Institutions* (London, 2010)

S. Seidendorf, *Europäisierung nationaler Identitätsdiskurse? Ein Vergleich französischer und deutscher Printmedien* (Baden-Baden, 2007)

S. Serfaty, *Architects of Delusion: Europe, America and the Iraq War* (Philadelphia, PA, 2011)

W. H. Sewell, Jr., *Logics of History: Social Theory and Social Transformation* (Chicago, 2005)

M. A. Shain, 'The Extreme-Right and Immigration Policy-Making: Measuring Direct and Indirect Effects', *West European Politics*, 29 (2006), 270–89

T. Shaw, *Eden, Suez and the Mass Media: Propaganda and Persuasion during the Suez Crisis* (London, 2009)

A. Shearmur, *The Political Thought of Karl Popper* (London, 1996)

A. Shennan, *Rethinking France: Plans for Renewal, 1940–1946* (Oxford, 1989)

M. J. Sherwin, 'The Atomic Bomb and the Origins of the Cold War', in M. P. Leffler and D. S. Painter (eds), *The Origins of the Cold War*, 2nd edn (London, 2005), 58–71

BIBLIOGRAPHY   501

J. Shields, 'The Far Right Vote in France: From Consolidation to Collapse?' *French Politics, Culture and Society*, 28 (2010), 25–45

A. Shlaim, 'Prelude to Downfall: The British Offer of Union to France, June 1940', *Journal of Contemporary History* 9 (1974), 27–63

A. Shlaim, *The United States and the Berlin Blockade, 1948–1949* (Berkeley, 1983)

P. Short, *Mitterrand: A Study in Ambiguity* (London, 2013)

S. Sifft, M. Brüggemann, K. Kleinen von Königslöw, B. Peters, and A. Wimmel, 'Segmented Europeanization: Exploring the Legitimacy of the European Union from a Public Discourse Perspective', *Journal of Common Market Studies*, 45 (2007), 127–55

H.-W. Sinn, *The Euro Trap: On Bursting Bubbles, Budgets and Beliefs* (Oxford, 2014)

N. Sitter, 'The Politics of Opposition and European Integration in Scandinavia: Is Euro-Scepticism a Government-Opposition Dynamic?', *West European Politics*, 24 (2001), 22–39

M. Skey and M. Antonich (eds), *Everyday Nationhood: Theorising Culture, Identity and Belonging after Banal Nationalism* (Basingstoke, 2017)

R. Skidelsky, *John Maynard Keynes* (London, 2000), 3 vols

G. Sluga, *Internationalism in the Age of Nationalism* (Philadelphia, PA, 2013)

G. Sluga and P. Clavin (eds), *Internationalisms: A Twentieth-Century History* (Cambridge, 2016)

A. D. Smith, 'National Identity and the Idea of European Unity', *International Affairs*, 68 (1992), 55–76

A. D. Smith, *The Antiquity of Nations* (Cambridge, 2004)

A. D. Smith, *The Cultural Foundations of Nations: Hierarchy, Covenant and Republic* (Oxford, 2008)

D. L. Smith and J. L. Ray, 'The 1992 Project', in D. L. Smith and J. L. Ray (eds), *The 1992 Project and the Future of Integration in Europe* (New York, 1993), 3–15

J. E. Smith, 'The View from USFET: General Clay's and Washington's Intepretation of Soviet Intentions in Germany, 1945–1948', in H. A. Schmitt (ed.), *US Occupation in Europe after World War II* (Lawrence, KS, 1978), 64–85

J. E. Smith, 'General Clay and the Russians: A Continuation of the Wartime Alliance in Germany, 1945-1948', *Virginia Quarterly Review*, 64 (1988), 20–36

M. B. Smith, 'Peaceful Coexistence at All Costs: Cold War Exchanges between Britain and the Soviet Union in 1956', *Cold War History*, 12 (2012), 537–58

S. C. Smith (ed.), *Reassessing Suez 1956* (Aldershot, 2008)

T. Smith, 'The French Colonial Consensus and People's War, 1946–58', *Journal of Contemporary History*, 9 (1974), 217–47

J. Snyder, *From Voting to Violence: Democratization and Nationalist Conflict* (New York, 2000)

S. A. Sofos, 'Culture, Politics and Identity in Former Yugoslavia', in B. Jenkins and S. A. Sofos (eds), *Nation and Identity in Contemporary Europe* (London, 2003), 252–63

R. Soucy, *Fascist Intellectual: Drieu La Rochelle* (Berkeley, 1979)

G.-H. Soutou, 'Problèmes concernant le rétablissement des relations économiques franco-allemandes après la premiere guerre mondiale', *Francia*, 2 (1974), 580–96

G.-H. Soutou, 'Georges Bidault et la construction européenne 1944–1954', *Revue d'histoire diplomatique*, 105 (1991), 269–72

G.-H. Soutou, *L'alliance incertaine. Les rapports politico-stratégiques franco-allemands, 1954–1996* (Paris, 1996)

G.-H. Soutou, 'The Linkage between European Integration and Détente: The Contrasting Approaches of de Gaulle and Pompidou, 1965-1974', in N. P. Ludlow (ed.), *European Integration and the Cold War: Ostpolitik—Westpolitik, 1965–1973* (London, 2007) 11–35

G.-H. Soutou, 'Staatspräsident Valéry Giscard d'Estaing und die deutsche Frage', in K. Hildebrand, U. Wengst, and A. Wirsching (eds), *Geschichtswissenschaft und Zeiterkenntnis von der Aufklärung bus zur Gegenwart* (Munich, 2008), 373–82

C. Spagnolo, 'Reinterpreting the Marshall Plan: The Impact of the European Recovery Programme in Britain, France, Western Germany and Italy, 1947–1955', in D. Geppert (ed.), *The Postwar Challenge, 1945–1958* (Oxford, 2003), 275–98

502 BIBLIOGRAPHY

E. E. Spalding, *The First Cold Warrior: Harry Truman, Containment and the Remaking of Liberal Internationalism* (Kentucky, 2006)

V. A. Spencer, 'Rethinking Cultural and Political Nationalism', *Politics, Groups and Identities*, 2 (2014), 666–73

M. Spiering and M. J. Wintle (eds), *Ideas of Europe since 1914* (Basingstoke, 2002)

K. Spohr, 'German Unification: Between Official History, Academic Scholarship and Political Memoirs', *Historical Journal*, 43 (2000), 860–88

K. Spohr, 'Precluded or Precedent-Setting? The "NATO Enlargement Question" in the Triangular Bonn-Washington-Moscow Diplomacy of 1990–1991', *Journal of Cold War Studies*, 14 (2012), 4–54

K. Spohr, 'Germany, America and the Shaping of Post-Cold War Europe: A Story of German International Emancipation through Political Unification, 1989–90', *Cold War History*, 15 (2015), 221–43

K. Spohr, *The Global Chancellor: Helmut Schmidt and the Reshaping of the International Order* (Cambridge, 2016)

K. Spohr and D. Reynolds (eds), *Transcending the Cold War: Summits, Statecraft and the Dissolution of Bipolarity in Europe, 1970–1990* (Oxford, 2016)

D. Staritz and A. Sywottek, 'The International Political Situation as Seen by the German *Linksparteien* (SPD, SED and KPD) between 1945 and 1949', in J. Becker and F. Knipping (eds), *Power in Europe? Great Britain, France, Italy and Germany in a Postwar World, 1945–1950* (Berlin, 1986), vol. 1, 213–24

P. Statham and H.-J. Trenz, 'Understanding the Mechanisms of EU Politicization: Lessons from the Eurozone Crisis', *Comparative European Politics*, 13 (2015), 287–306

M. Steber, '"The West", Tocqueville and West German Conservatism from the 1950s and 1970s', in R. Bavaj and M. Steber (eds), *Germany and 'the West': The History of a Modern Concept* (New York, 2015), 230–47

J. Stein, 'National Minorities and Political Development in Post-Communist Europe', in J. Stein (ed.), *The Politics of National Minority Participation in Post-Communist Europe* (New York, 2000), 1–30

Z. Steiner, *The Lights that Failed: European International History, 1919–1933* (Oxford, 2005)

Z. Steiner, *The Triumph of the Dark: European International History, 1933–1939* (Oxford, 2010)

R. Steininger et al. (eds), *Die doppelte Eindämmung. Europäische Sicherheit und deutsche Frage in den Fünfzigern* (Munich, 1993)

C. Sterling, *The Masaryk Case* (New York, 1969)

B. Stiel, *The Marshall Plan: Dawn of the Cold War* (Oxford, 2018)

P. M. R. Stirk, 'Authoritarian and National Socialist Conceptions of Nation, State, and Europe', in P. M. R. Stirk (ed.), *European Unity in Context: The Interwar Period* (London, 1989), 125–48

P. M. R. Stirk, *European Unity in Context: The Interwar Period* (London, 1989)

P. M. R. Stirk, *Twentieth-Century German Political Thought* (Edinburgh, 2006)

J. Stoetzel, 'Defeatism in Western Europe: Reluctance to Fight for the Country', in M. Dogan (ed.), *Comparing Pluralist Democracies: Strains on Legitimacy* (Boulder, CO, 1988), 169–80

R. G. Stokes, *Divide and Prosper: The Heirs of I.G. Farben under Allied Authority, 1945–1951* (Berkeley, 1988)

A. Stone Sweet and W. Sandholtz, 'European Integration and Supranational Governance', *Journal of European Public Policy*, 4 (1997), 297–317

A. Stone Sweet, W. Sandholtz, and N. Fligstein (eds), *The Institutionalization of Europe* (Oxford, 2001)

J. Story, 'The Launching of the EMS: An Analysis of Change in Foreign Economic Policy', *Political Studies*, 36 (1988), 397–412

J. Story and B. Pollack, 'Spain's Transition: Domestic and External Linkages', in G. Pridham (ed.), *Encouraging Democracy: The International Context of Regime Transition in Southern Europe* (New York, 1991), 45–61

B. Stråth, 'Methodological and Substantive Remarks on Myth, Memory and History in the Construction of a European Community', *German Law Journal*, 6 (2003), 255–71

BIBLIOGRAPHY   503

W. Stueck, *The Korean War: An International History* (Princeton, 1995)

J. L. Sullivan, *ETA and Basque Nationalism: The Fight for Euskadi, 1890–1986* (London, 2015)

R. G. Suny, *The Revenge of the Past: Nationalism, Revolution and the Collapse of the Soviet Union* (Palo Alto, CA, 1993)

B. Supple, 'Fear of Failing: Economic History and the Decline of Britain', *Economic History Review*, 47 (1994), 441–58

S. Sweeney, *The Europe Illusion: Britain, France, Germany and the Long History of European Integration* (London, 2019)

P. Taggart and A. Szczerbiak, *Opposing Europe: The Comparative Party Politics of Euroscepticism* (Oxford, 2005–08), 2 vols

E. Tannam, 'The European Union and the Politics in Northern Ireland', *Ethnic and Racial Studies*, 18 (1995), 797–817

E. Tannam, 'The Divided Irish', in T. J. Mabry, J. McGarry, M. Moore, and B. O'Leary (eds), *Divided Nations and European Integration* (Philadelphia, PA, 2013), 251–75

M. Tanner, *Croatia: A Nation Forged in War* (New Haven, CT, 1997)

R. Taras, 'Gomulka's "Rightist-Nationalist Deviation", the Postwar Jewish Communists and the Stalinist Reaction in Poland, 1945–1950', *Nationalities Papers*, 22 (1994), 111–27

P. Taylor, *The End of European Integration: Anti-Europeanism Examined* (London, 2008)

R. Taylor, 'New Labour, New Capitalism', in A. Seldon (ed.), *Blair's Britain, 1997–2007* (Cambridge, 2007), 214–40

G. Thiemeyer, *Vom 'Pool Vert' zur Europäischen Wirtschaftsgemeinschaft: Europäische Integration, Kalter Krieg und die Anfänge der Gemeinsame Europäischen Agrarpolitik 1950–1957* (Munich, 1999)

M. Thomas, *Fight or Flight: Britain, France and Their Roads from Empire* (Oxford, 2014)

R. Thomas, *Serbia under Milošević: Politics in the 1990s* (London, 1999)

R. T. Thomas, *Britain and Vichy: The Dilemma of Anglo-French Relations, 1940–42* (London, 1979)

H. Thome, 'Value Change in Europe from the Perspective of Empirical Social Research', in H. Joas and K. Wiegandt (eds), *The Cultural Values of Europe* (Liverpool, 2008), 277–319

M. Thompson, *Forging War: The Media in Serbia, Croatia, Bosnia and Hercegovina* (Luton, 1999)

S. Tierney, *Constitutional Referendums: The Theory and Practice of Republican Deliberation* (Oxford, 2012)

R. Tiersky, *François Mitterrand: A Very French President* (New York, 2000)

N. Tocci, *EU Accession Dynamics and Conflict Resolution: Catalysing Peace or Consolidating Partition in Cyprus?* (Aldershot, 2004)

S. Tolliday, 'Enterprise and State in the West German Wirtschaftswunder: Volkswagen and the Automobile Industry, 1939–1962', *Business History Review*, 69 (1995), 273–350

I. Tombs, 'Une identité européenne assiégée? Les exiles socialistes à Londres, 1939–1945', *Revue d'histoire moderne et contemporaine* 46 (1999), 263–79

R. Tombs, *The Sovereign Isle: Britain in and out of Europe* (London, 2021)

J. Tomlinson, 'Inventing "Decline": The Falling Behind of the British Economy in the Postwar Years', *Economic History Review*, 49 (1996), 731–57

J. Tomlinson, 'Managing the Economy, Managing the People', in F. Carnevali and J.-M. Strange (eds), *Twentieth-Century Britain: Economic, Cultural and Social Change*, 2nd edn (London, 2007), 233–46

A. S. Tompkins, *Better Active than Radioactive! Anti-Nuclear Protest in 1970s France and West Germany* (Oxford, 2016)

M. Tonry (ed.), *The Handbook of Crime and Punishment* (Oxford, 1998)

A. J. Tooze, 'Who Is Afraid of Inflation? The Long Shadow of the 1970s', *Journal of Modern European History*, 12 (2014), 53–60

R. Toye, 'From "Consensus" to "Common Ground": The Rhetoric of the Postwar Settlement and Its Collapse', *Journal of Contemporary History*, 48 (2013), 3–23

R. Toye, '"This Famous Island Is the Home of Freedom": Winston Churchill and the Battle for "European Civilization"', *History of European Ideas*, 46 (2020), 666–80

504 BIBLIOGRAPHY

M. Trachtenberg, *History and Strategy* (Princeton, NJ, 1991)

M. Trachtenberg, 'France and NATO, 1949–1991', *Journal of Transatlantic Studies*, 9 (2011), 184–94

G. Trausch, 'Der Schuman-Plan zwischen Mythos und Realität', in R. Hudemann, H. Kaelble, and K. Schwabe (eds), *Europa im Blick der Historiker. Europäische Integration im 20: Jahrhundert* (Munich, 1995), 105–28

H.-J. Trenz, 'Media Coverage on European Governance: Testing the Performance of National Newspapers', *European Journal of Communication*, 19 (2004), 291–319

H.-J. Trenz, 'Die mediale Ordnung des politischen Europas. Formen und Dynamiken der Europäisierung politischer Kommunikation in der Qualitätspresse', *Zeitschrift für Soziologie*, 34 (2005), 188–206

H.-J. Trenz, 'The European Public Sphere: Contradictory Findings in a Diverse Research Field', *European Political Science*, 4 (2005), 407–20

H.-J. Trenz, *Europa in den Medien. Die europäische Integration im Spiegel nationaler Öffentlichkeit* (Frankfurt, 2006)

H.-J. Trenz, 'Understanding Media Impact on European Integration: Enhancing or Restricting the Scope of Legitimacy of the EU?' *European Integration*, 30 (2008), 291–309

G. F. Treverton, *America, Germany and the Future of Europe* (Princeton, NJ)

A. Trunk, *Europa, ein Ausweg. Politische Eliten und europäische Integration in den 1950er Jahren* (Munich, 2007)

B. Turner, *Suez 1956: The Forgotten War* (London, 2006)

E. A. Tiryakian, 'Coping with Collective Stigma: The Case of Germany', in D. Rothbart and K. V. Korostelina (eds), *Identity, Morality and Threat* (Lanham, MD, 2006), 329–66

D. Urwin, *The Community of Europe: A History of European Integration since 1945* (London, 1991)

J. C. Van Hook, *Rebuilding Germany: The Creation of the Social Market Economy, 1945–1957* (Cambridge, 2004)

J. Vanke, 'Charles de Gaulle's Uncertain Ideas of Europe', in D. Dinan (ed.), *Origins and Evolution of the European Union* (Oxford, 2006), 141–65

R. Vetters, E. Jentges, and H.-J. Trenz, 'Whose Project Is IT? Media Debates on the Ratification of the EU Constitutional Treaty', *Journal of European Public Policy*, 16 (2009)

G. Vicarelli, 'The Creation of the NHS in Italy, 1961–1978', *Dynamis*, 39 (2019), 21–43

R. Vinen, *A History in Fragments: Europe in the Twentieth Century* (London, 2000)

R. Vinen, *Thatcher's Britain: The Politics and Social Upheaval of the Thatcher Era* (London, 2013)

C. Vögele and M. Bachl (eds), 'The Quality of Public Opinion Poll Coverage in German National Newspapers during Federal Election Campaigns', *International Journal of Public Opinion Research*, 32 (2019), 332–45

H. E. Volkmann and W. Schwengler (eds), *Die Europäische Verteidigungsgemeinschaft* (Boppard, 1985)

C. H. De Vreese, 'News, Political Knowledge and Participation', *Acta Politica*, 41 (2006), 317–41

C. H. De Vreese, 'A Spiral of Euroscepticism: The Media's Fault?', *Acta Politica*, 42 (2007), 271–86

J. van der Waal et al., '"Some Are More Equal than Others": Economic Egalitarianism and Welfare Chauvinism in the Netherlands', *Journal of European Social Policy*, 20 (2010), 350–63

M. Waechter, *Helmut Schmidt und Valéry Giscard d'Estaing. Auf der Suche nach Stabilität in der Krise der 1970er Jahre* (Bremen, 2011)

O. Waever, 'Europe since 1945: Crisis to Renewal', in K. Wilson and J. van der Dussen (eds), *History of the Idea of Europe* (London, 1993), 151–214

O. Waever, 'Insecurity, Security and Asecurity in the West European Non-War Community', in E. Adler and M. Barnett (eds), *Security Communities* (Cambridge, 1998), 69–118

C. Wagnsson, *Security in a Greater Europe: The Possibility of a Pan-European Approach* (Manchester, 2008)

I. M. Wall, *The United States and the Making of Postwar France* (Cambridge, 1991)

I. M. Wall, *France, the United States and the Algerian War* (Berkeley, CA, 2001)

W. Wallace, 'Europe as a Confederation: The Community and the Nation-State', *Journal of Common Market Studies*, 21 (1982), 57–68

W. Wallace (ed.), *The Dynamics of Integration* (London, 1991)

W. Wallace, 'The Nation-State - Rescue or Retreat?', in P. Anderson and P. Gowan (eds), *The Question of Europe* (London, 1997), 21–50

I. Wallerstein, *The Modern World-System* (New York, 1974–2011), 4 vols

J. I. Walsh, *European Monetary Integration and Domestic Politics: Britain, France and Italy* (Boulder, CO, 2000)

W. Ward, *British Culture and the End of Empire* (Manchester, 2001)

L. Warlouzet, 'Relancer la CEE avant la chaise vide: Néo-functionalists vs. fédéralistes au sein de la Commission européenne 1964–1965', *Journal of European Integration History*, 14 (2008), 69–86

L. Warlouzet, *Le choix de la CEE par la France: l'Europe économique en débat de Mendès-France à de Gaulle 1955–1969* (Paris, 2011)

L. Warlouzet, 'European Integration History: Beyond the Crisis', *Politique européenne*, 44 (2014), 98–122

L. Warlouzet, 'The Interdisciplinary Challenge in European Integration History', *Journal of Contemporary History*, 49 (2014), 837–45

L. Warlouzet, 'The Centralization of EU Competition Policy: Historical Institutionalist Dynamics from Cartel Monitoring to Merger Control, 1956-91', *Journal of Common Market Studies*, 54 (2016), 725–41

L. Warlouzet, 'Britain at the Centre of European Co-operation, 1948–2016', *Journal of Common Market Studies*, 56 (2018), 955–70

L. Warlouzet, *Governing Europe in a Globalizing World: Neoliberalism and Its Alternatives Following the 1973 Oil Crisis* (London, 2018)

L. Warlouzet, 'The EEC/EU as an Evolving Compromise between French Dirigism and German Ordoliberalism, 1957–1995', *Journal of Common Market Studies*, 57 (2019), 77–93

L. Warlouzet, *Europe contre Europe: Entre liberté, solidarité et puissance* (Paris, 2022)

C. M. Warner, 'Religious Parties in a Secularizing Political Space: The Case of Italy', *Asian Security*, 4 (2008), 61–78

C. M. Warner, 'Christian Democracy in Italy: An Alternative Path to Religious Party Moderation', *Party Politics*, 19 (2012), 256–76

G. Warner, 'Aspects of the Suez Crisis', in E. Di Nolfo (ed.), *Power in Europe? Great Britain, France, Germany and Italy and the Origins of the EEC, 1952–1957* (Berlin, 1992), vol. 2, 43–65

B. Wasserstein, *Barbarism and Civilization: A History of Europe in Our Time* (Oxford, 2007)

J. R. Wegs and R. Ladrech, *Europe since 1945*, 4th edn (New York, 1996)

H.-U. Wehler, 'Radikalnationalismus und Nationalsozialismus', in J. Echternkamp and S. O. Müller (eds), *Die Politik der Nation. Deutscher Nationalismus in Krieg und Krisen 1760 bis 1960* (Munich, 2002), 203–17

H.-U. Wehler, 'Wie hoch ist Europas "Preis der Freiheit"?', in H.-U. Wehler, *Essays zur Geschichte* (Munich, 2014)

W. Weidenfeld, *Außenpolitik für die Deusche Einheit. Die Entscheidungsjahre 1989/90* (Stuttgart, 1998)

J. H. Weiler, 'A Quiet Revolution: The European Court of Justice and Its Interlocutors', *Comparative Political Studies*, 26 (1994), 510–34

J. H. Weiler, 'Does Europe Need a Constitution? Demos, Telos and the German Maastricht Decision', *European Law Journal*, 1 (1995), 219–58

J. H. Weiler, 'Federalism without Constitutionalism: Europe's Sonderweg', in K. Nicolaidis and R. Howse (eds), *The Federal Vision* (Oxford, 2001), 54–70

J. H. Weiler, 'A Constitution for Europe? Some Hard Choices', *Journal of Common Market Studies*, 40 (2002), 563–80

J. H. Weiler, *The Federal Vision: Legitimacy and Levels of Governance in the United States and the European Union* (Oxford, 2003)

J. H. Weiler, *L'Europe chrétienne. Une excursion* (Paris, 2007)

J. H. Weiler, 'The Political and Legal Culture of European Integration: An Exploratory Essay', *International Journal of Constitutional Law*, 9 (2011), 678–94

J. H. Weiler, 'In the Face of the Crisis: Input Legitimacy, Output Legitimacy and the Political Messianism of European Integration', *Journal of European Integration*, 34 (2012), 825–41

M. Weinachter, *Valéry Giscard d'Estaing et l'Allegemagne. Le double rêve inachevé* (Paris, 2004)

M. Weinachter, 'Le tandem *Valéry Giscard d'Estaing*—Helmut Schmidt et la gouvernance européenne', in W. Loth (ed.), *La gouvernance supranationale dans la construction européenne* (Brussels, 2005), 205–38

B. Wellings and M. Kenny, 'Nairn's England and the Progressive Dilemma: Reappraising Tom Nairn on English Nationalism', *Nations and Nationalism*, 25 (2019), 847–65

A. Werblan, 'Wladyslaw Gomulka and the Dilemmas of Polish Nationalism', *International Political Science Review*, 9 (1988), 143–58

B. Wessels, 'Discontent and European Identity: Three Types of Euroscepticism', *Acta Politica*, 42 (2007), 287–306

W. Wessels, 'An Ever Closer Fusion? A Dynamic Macropolitical View on Integration Processes', *Journal of Common Market Studies*, 35 (1997), 267–99

H. Wessler, B. Peters, M. Brüggemann, K. Kleinen von Königslöw, and S. Sifft, *Transnationalization of Public Spheres* (Basingstoke, 2008)

O. A. Westad, *The Global Cold War: Third World Interventions and the Making of Our Times* (Cambridge, 2005)

J. White, *Political Allegiance after European Integration* (Basingstoke, 2011)

J. White, 'The Spectres Haunting Europe: Reading Contemporary Catalan Nationalism Through the Break-Up of Britain', *European Review*, 26 (2018), 600–15

J. P. J. White, 'Theory Guiding Practice: the Neofunctionalists and the Hallstein EEC Commission', *Journal of European Integration History*, 9 (2003), 111–31

N. White, *Decolonisation: The British Experience since 1945* (London, 1999)

S. Wiederkehr, *Die eurasische Bewegung. Wissenschaft und Politik in russischen Emigration der Zwischenkriegszeit und im postsowjetischen Russland* (Cologne, 2007)

A. Wiener, T. Börzel, and T. Risse (eds), *European Integration Theory*, 3rd edn (Oxford, 2018)

M. J. Wiener, *English Culture and the Decline of the Industrial Spirit, 1850–1980* (Cambridge, 1981)

T. Wieser and E. Kitzmantel, 'Austria and the European Community', *Journal of Common Market Studies*, 28 (1990), 431–49

M. Wilke, *The Path to the Berlin Wall: Critical Stages in the History of Divided Germany* (New York, 2014)

A. Wille, *The Normalization of the European Commission: Politics and Bureaucracy in the EU Executive* (Oxford, 2013)

C. Williams, *Adenauer: The Father of a New Germany* (New York, 2000)

K. Williams, *The Prague Spring and Its Aftermath: Czechoslovak Politics, 1968–1970* (Cambridge, 1997)

P. Winand, *Eisenhower, Kennedy and the United States of Europe* (New York, 1993)

D. Wincott, 'Institutional Interaction and European Integration: Towards an Everyday Critique of Liberal Intergovernmentalism', *Journal of Common Market Studies*, 33 (1995), 597–609

H. A. Winkler, 'Rebuilding of a Nation: The Germans before and after Unification', *Daedalus*, 123 (1994), 107–27

H. A. Winkler, *Der lange Weg nach Westen: Deutsche Geschichte vom 'Dritten Reich' bis zur Wiedervereinigung* (Munich, 2000), 2 vols

M. Winock, 'U.S. Go Home. L'antiaméricanisme français', *L'Histoire*, 50 (1982), 7–20

M. Winock, *Le siècle des intellectuelles* (Paris, 1997)

A. Wirsching, *Der Preis der Freiheit. Geschichte Europas in unserer Zeit* (Munich, 2012)

M. J. Wolf, *The Entertainment Economy: How Mega-Media Forces Are Transforming Our Lives* (London, 1999)

S. Wood, 'Das Deutschlandbild: National Image, Reputation and Interests in Post-War Germany', *Central European History*, 27 (2018), 651–73

BIBLIOGRAPHY 507

C. M. Woodhouse, *The Rise and Fall of the Greek Colonels* (London, 1985)
R. M. Worcester, *British Public Opinion: A Guide to the History and Methodology of Political Opinion* (Cambridge, 1991)
J. Wright, 'Stresemann and Locarno', *Contemporary European History*, 4 (1995), 109–31
J. Wright, *Gustav Stresemann: Weimar's Greatest Statesman* (Oxford, 2002)
C. A. Wurm, 'Britain and West European Integration, 1948–9 to 1955: Politics and Economics', in J. Noakes, P. Wende, and J. Wright (eds), *Britain and Germany in Europe, 1949–1990* (Oxford, 2002), 27–48
J. W. Young, *France, the Cold War and the Western Alliance, 1945–1949: French Foreign Policy and Post-War Europe* (Leicester, 1990)
J. W. Young, *Britain and European Unity, 1945–1992* (Basingstoke, 1993)
J. W. Young, 'British Officials and European Integration, 1944–60', in A. Deighton (ed.), *Building Postwar Europe: National Decision-Makers and European Institutions, 1948–63* (London, 1995)
O. R. Young, 'Comment on "A New Statecraft?"', *International Organization*, 53 (1999), 805–9
P. Zelikow and C. Rice, *Germany Unified and Europe Transformed: A Study in Statecraft* (Cambridge, MA, 1997)
J. Zielonka, *Europe as Empire: The Nature of the Enlarged European Union* (Oxford, 2006)
O. Zimmer, *Nationalism in Europe, 1890–1940* (Basingstoke, 2003)
H. Zimmermann, *Money and Security: Troops, Monetary Policy and West Germany's Relations with the United States and Britain, 1950–1971* (Cambridge, 2013)
H. Zimmermann and A. Dür, 'Can There Be a Common European Identity?', in H. Zimmermann and A. Dür (eds), *Key Controversies in European Integration* (Basingstoke, 2012), 95–6
R. Zohlnhöfer, *Die Wirtschaftspolitik der Ära Kohl 1982–1989* (Opladen, 2001)
V. Zubok and C. Pleshakov, *Inside the Kremlin's Cold War* (Cambridge, MA, 1996)

Index

For the benefit of digital users, indexed terms that span two pages (e.g., 52–53) may, on occasion, appear on only one of those pages.

Abendland 124–5, 128–31
ABN AMRO banking group 214–15
Abyssinia (1936), Italian invasion of 93–5
Acheson Dean 57–8, 62, 101, 437–8
acquis communautaire 111–12, 229, 302–3, 334, 434–5
Adams, Tim 19–20
Adorno, Theodor 125–6, 139–40
Afghanistan 34–5, 56–7, 62–3, 350
Africa 30–1, 39–40, 43–4
Aftenposten 30–1
Agence Europe 317
Agenda 2000 303
Ahlen Programme (1947) 280–2
Albania, 174–7, 365–6
Algerian War 49, 57, 131–2, 344, 434–5
Allied High Commission 50, 66, 103, 252
Allied zones, in Germany 31–2, 37–42, 47–50, 52, 54–5, 95–6, 103, 115, 217
Alphand, Hervé 59, 103
Alsace 233–4
Amato, Giuliano 400–5, 441
Amazon 218–19
Amsterdam (1997), Treaty of 287–8, 295, 396, 400, 407–8, 419
Anderson, Benedict 170, 181–3, 189–90
Anderson, Perry 153, 333–6
Andreotti, Giulio 74, 114, 349
Anglo-Irish Agreement (1985) 112–13
Anglo Irish Bank 214–15
Annales school 13–14
Antall, József 146–7
anti-Semitism 308–9
appeasement 44–6
Apple 218–19
Applebaum, Anne 303–4
Arendt, Hannah 124–5, 139–40
Argentina 110–11, 291–2, 308–9
Armistice Day 201–2
arms race 17–18, 98
Aron, Raymond 107–8, 134, 136–7, 139–41, 144–6, 277–8, 311
Art, David 180

Ashworth, John 286
Asia 4–5, 34, 95–6, 170–1, 201–2, 243–4, 268–9
Athens 30
Atkinson, Anthony 291–3
Atlantic Monthly 171
Atlanticism 64–5, 95–6, 106, 241, 434
Attali, Jacques 73–4, 106, 363, 395
Attlee, Clement 29, 39–40, 221, 280
Augstein, Rudolf 98
austerity 19, 215–16, 293–4, 317–18, 336–7
Austin, John L. 9–10
Australia 274–7, 292–3, 308–9, 312–13, 405–6, 449
Austria 1, 67–8, 70, 96–7, 139, 179–80, 184–7, 195, 203, 251–2, 274–5, 278–80, 282–4, 290, 293–5, 305, 309, 345–6, 359–60, 417, 443–4
Austrian People's Party (*Österreichische Volkspartei*) 114
authoritarianism 124–5, 133–4, 139, 142, 145, 147, 170–1, 183, 188, 299
Aznar, José Manuel 401, 404

Badinter, Robert 362
Baghdad 188–9
Bailey, Christian 32–3
Baker, James 71
Balibar, Etienne 143
Balkans 30–1, 173, 363
Ball, George 98–9, 386
Baltic states 34, 42–3, 176, 184, 295–8
Bank of England 333–4
Barcelona 314
Bardoux, Jacques 108–9
Barnsley 314–15
Barre, Raymond 245
Barroso, Jose Manuel 30, 369
Barthes, Roland 16
Basque nationalism 112–13, 178–9, 363
Basic Law (*Grundgesetz*) 69, 138, 360–2, 407–8
Basic Treaty (1972) 58–9, 69
Bastille Day 201–2
Baudrillard, Jean 143

510 INDEX

Bauman, Zygmunt 143, 269, 312
Beauvoir, Simone de 141–2
Beck, Ulrich 143
Belarus 42–3, 305–6
Belgium 67, 92–3, 100, 108, 139, 179–80,
196, 198–9, 221–2, 235, 248–51,
274–7, 280, 282, 284–5, 289–90, 293–4,
303, 339, 349, 389–90, 400, 435–8,
447–9
Belgrade 52, 172, 360–2
Bell, Daniel 311–13
Bellamy, Richard 413–17
Benda, Julien 124–5, 127–8, 135
Bérégovoy, Pierre 358–9
Berger, Peter 309
Berlin 42–3, 47, 52–6, 58–9, 68–70, 100–1,
134, 397
Berlin Agreement 59
Berlin blockade (1948–9) 35, 37–9, 65, 95–6,
434–5
Second Berlin Crisis (1958) 62–3, 434–5
Berlin Wall 18–19, 30, 47, 54, 63, 171
Fall of the Wall 70, 190–2
Berlin, Isaiah 134, 136–7
Berlusconi, Silvio 405
Bernanos, Georges 124–5, 140–1
Bevin, Ernest 36, 39–42, 50–1, 54–5, 339–41
Beyen, Johan Willem 12, 108–9, 235,
241–2, 388–9
Bickerton, Christopher 335–6, 419–20
Bidault, Georges 385
Bild-Zeitung 215–16, 443–4
Bildt, Carl 364
Billig, Michael 188–90
Billoux, François 338–9
Bismarck, Otto von 352
Black Sea 46
Blum, Léon 385
Bofinger, Peter 381–2
Bohlen, Chip 437–8
Bolkestein, Frits 254–5
Bolsheviks 44–6
Bonnet, Henri 48
Bosnia-Hercegovina 114–15, 171–7, 363–5,
449–50
Bosnian War (1992-5) 114–15, 173–6, 363–5
Bossi, Umberto 184–7
Bourdieu, Pierre 11
Boutros-Ghali, Boutros 312–13
Bracher Karl Dietrich 137, 193–4
Brandt, Willy 49–50, 52, 55–9, 63, 65–6, 106–7,
138, 192, 243, 289, 346–7, 350–1
Bratislava 305
Brazil 151, 195, 308–9

Bretton Woods agreement (1944) 68–9, 91–2,
217, 236, 238, 241–2, 251, 433
Breuilly, John 182–3
Brexit 1, 18–20, 195–6, 199–200, 214, 289–90, 293–4,
314–15, 318–19, 333, 396, 443–4, 450–1
Brezhnev, Leonid 60–1
Brezhnev doctrine 60
Briand, Aristide 12, 92–5, 100–1, 231–3, 433
Brink, Jan van den 437–8
Bristol 314
British Airports 286
British Airways 286
British Gas 286
British Steel 286
British Telecom (BT) 253, 286
Brown, Gordon 181, 195–6, 303–4
Bruce, David 339–40, 441
Brüning, Heinrich 93–5, 98, 100
Brubaker, Rogers 176
Brussels 305
Brussels (1948), Treaty of 130–1, 339–40, 438
Burns, Arthur 252
Busek, Erhard 114
Brzezinski, Zbygniew 65–6
Bucharest 52, 154–5, 305
Budapest 52, 307
Soviet occupation of (1956) 47, 73, 151
Bülow, Bernhard Wilhelm von 93–5
Bulgaria 46, 177, 290, 295–6, 300–1, 309, 313,
369–70
Bulmer, Simon 11
Bundesbank 55–6, 68–9, 351–2, 356–7, 395
Bundesrat 399, 407–8
Bundestag 37–9, 64–6, 104–5, 339, 345–6, 356–7,
407–8
Bundesverfassungsgericht 333, 407–8, 445–6
Bundeswehr 62–3, 65–6
Bush, George 70–4, 106, 360–2
Butler, Rab 283–4

Caetano, Marcello 112
Calabria 305–6
Callaghan, James 63–4
Callanan, Martin 30
Calleo, David 50–1
Camdessus, Michel 238–40
Cameron, David 19–20, 30, 443–4
Cameroon 308–9
Campania 305–6
Campbell, Alastair 294–5, 366–7
Camus, Albert 140–1
Canada 67–8, 110, 274–80, 292–3, 308–9,
312–13, 354, 417, 449
capital punishment 308–9

Capitant, René 134
Cardiff 314
Carnation Revolution (1974) 112
Carrington, Peter (Lord) 360–2
Carter, Jimmy 63–6, 68–9
Cash, Bill 30
Cassis de Dijon case (1979) 247–8
Castiglione, Dario 413–14
Catalonia 112–13, 178–9, 363
Cetniks 175–6
Chaban-Delmas, Jacques 387–8
Chabot, Jean-Luc 92–3
Chamberlain, Austen 92–3
Chamberlain, Neville 44–6, 365
Chambre de commerce internationale 232
Charlemagne 125–6, 214
Charter of Fundamental Rights of the European
   Union (2000) 359–60
Chauvel, Jean 103
Checkel, Jeffrey 154–5
Chévènement, Jean-Pierre 358–9
Chile 309
China 34–6, 49, 57–8, 60, 98, 110, 131–2,
   309–11, 336–7, 449
Chirac, Jacques 183, 245, 271–2, 294–5, 349,
   352–4, 358–60, 364–7, 369, 404–7, 441–2
Christian Democracy 32–3, 114, 142, 144–5,
   194–5, 282–3
Christian Democratic Party (CDUCSU/) 32–3,
   37–9, 50, 54–5, 59, 64–8, 95–6, 242, 280,
   352–4
Christianity 37–9, 55, 65, 124–6, 142, 309–11
Christiansen, Thomas 9–10
Churchill, Caryl 294
Churchill, Winston 35–6, 39–42, 52, 55, 63, 105,
   130–2, 151, 280, 294, 385–8, 433–4, 438–9
Fulton, Missouri speech (1946) 52, 130–1
   Zurich speech (1946) 151, 438–9
citizenship 114, 122, 134, 136–7, 181, 192–4, 199,
   268, 307–8, 317–18, 320, 396
City of London 230–1
class 36, 55, 135, 275–80, 284–6, 291–4, 300,
   304–5, 311, 335–6, 350–1, 393–4
Clinton, Bill 171, 188–9
Coca-Cola 57
Cockfield, Arthur 248
Cohesion Fund 303
Cohn-Bendit, Daniel 283–4
Cold War 6–7, 13, 16–18, 29, 31–2, 34–52, 54–7,
   59–75, 90–1, 96, 98–101, 106, 109, 122,
   130–2, 138–44, 146–7, 149–52, 154–5,
   167–8, 171–2, 176–7, 201–2, 291–2,
   309–11, 336–9, 357–8, 360–2, 370–1,
   416–17, 421–2, 433–40, 449–51

Coldiretti 282
Cole, George 253–4
Colombo, Emilio 355
Columbia 308–9
COMECON 44, 60–1, 70–1, 182–3, 223–6
Comité français de cooperation européenne 93–5
Commisariat Général au Plan 14–15, 51, 98–9,
   337–8
Committee of Permanent Representatives
   (COREPER) 13, 334–7, 420–1,
   442–3, 446
Committee of the Regions 413–14
Common Agricultural Policy (CAP) 113–14,
   153, 217, 225, 233–4, 287, 389–90, 442
Common Assembly (ECSC) 220–1
common external tariff (CET) 64–5, 219–21,
   255–6, 345–6, 389–90
common market 12, 91–2, 105–6, 172, 219–25,
   230, 235–44, 252–6, 286–7, 341–7, 368,
   386, 388–9, 393–4, 434–5, 449–50
   negative market integration 6–7, 153, 218
Common Foreign and Security Policy
   (Maastricht) 8, 29, 115, 217, 360–2,
   401–2
Commonwealth 39–42, 47–8, 148–9, 340–2,
   386–8
Communism 17–18, 31–2, 35–6, 39–40, 42,
   44–7, 50, 52, 54–5, 57–61, 90, 95–6,
   98–100, 130–1, 133–4, 141–7, 168, 170–2,
   174–5, 177–8, 184, 187–8, 214, 223–5,
   237–8, 277–8, 280–2, 284–5, 292–3,
   295–8, 300–5, 307–11, 336–8, 342–4, 349,
   369–70, 416–17, 434–5, 437–8, 447–8
Communist Party of the Soviet Union
   (CPSU) 44, 60
Communist Party of France (PCF) 37–9, 48,
   54–5, 95–6, 268–9
comparative politics 7–12, 409–12
Completing the Internal Market White Paper
   (1985) 248
confederation 66, 103, 106, 125–6, 143, 169,
   335–6, 350, 382–3, 387–8, 408–22,
   444–51
Conference on Security and Cooperation in
   Europe (CSCE) 59, 109
Connor, Walker 170
Conservative Party (UK) 30, 39–40, 166,
   188–9, 203, 238–40, 243–4, 274–5,
   283–6, 333–4, 386–9, 393–4, 396, 420–1,
   438–9, 443–4
Conservative People's Party (Switzerland) 32–3
Consultative Committee (ECSC) 221
constitutional patriotism 138, 192–4
Copenhagen Criteria (1993) 298, 302–3

512 INDEX

Cornwall 305–6
Corsica 363
Costa Rica 293–4
Costa vs Enel case 333
Coty, René 342–4
Coudenhove-Kalergi, Richard von 5, 128–30, 145, 235
Council of Europe (1949) 103, 108–10, 219–20, 308–9, 339–40, 387–90, 438–9
Court of Justice (ECSC) 220–1
Council of Ministers 108–9, 114–15, 220–2, 228, 288–9, 334–41, 349, 365–6, 388–90, 441–3
Courtade, Pierre 143–4
Coutard, Jean 99–100
Couve de Murville, Maurice 42–3, 103, 391
Cripps, Sir Stafford 40–2
Croatia 60–1, 114–15, 132, 172–7, 314, 360–3, 449–50
Croatian Democratic Union (HDZ) 114–15, 175–6
Croatian War (1991) 114–15, 360–3, 449–50
Croce, Benedetto 133–4, 145
Croizat, Ambroise 280–2
Curtius, Robert 93–5, 100
Czech Republic 242–3, 272–5, 290, 293–8, 300–5, 369–70, 407–8, 448–9
Czechoslovakia 46, 58–60, 70, 97, 100–1, 146–7, 151–2, 177–8, 187–8, 190, 195
    Foreign Office (Czech) 187–8
Cyprus 111–12, 114, 215–16, 290, 295

Dahrendorf, Ralf 143, 277–8
Daladier, Edouard 46, 365
Damascus 35–6
Daily Mail 30, 188–9
Daily Telegraph 19–20, 70
Darling, Alistair 214–15
Dawes Plan (1924) 36–7
Dayton Agreement (1995) 364
de Boissieu, Pierre 394–5
De Gasperi, Alcide 39, 282–3, 385–9
de Gaulle, Charles 35–6, 42–3, 49, 57–8, 64–5, 99–100, 103–6, 108–9, 196, 227, 234–6, 245–6, 337–8, 346–7, 368, 387–8, 390–4, 441–2
De Michelis, Gianni 114
De Ruggiero, Guido 133–4
de Villepin, Dominique 366
de Villiers, Philippe 358–9
Debré, Michel 349
Declaration on European Identity (1973) 109–10
decolonization 17–18, 35–6, 47–9, 57, 131–2, 141–2, 146–7, 342–4, 434–5

Dehaene, Jean-Luc 400, 405
Dehio, Ludwig 138–9
Delanty, Gerard 130
Delegation for Regional Development and Planning (France) 178–9
Delors, Jacques 74, 115, 217, 238–40, 303, 305, 334–6, 356, 360–2, 394–5, 441
Delors package (Delors I and II) 303, 356
Democratic Unionist Party (DUP) 112–13
democratization 30–1, 112, 170–3, 184, 433
demography 1, 39–40, 54–5, 145, 169–70, 175–9, 194–5, 215–16, 223–5, 227–8, 249–50, 270–1, 289, 295–8, 302–3, 313–15, 320, 363, 365–6, 371, 397, 400
Demangeon, Albert 123–4
Democrazia Cristiana (DC) 39, 280–3, 309–11, 437–8
de-Nazification 37–9, 56–7
Denmark 139, 166, 198–9, 271, 274–7, 280–2, 284, 287–9, 293–6, 305–6, 309, 314, 334, 348, 359–60, 390, 392–3
départements et territoires d'outre-mer (DOMs-TOMs) 235
DePorte, Anton 36–7
Derrida, Jacques 9–10
desecuritization 90–1
Deutsch, Karl 7–8, 89–90
dictatorship 12, 17–18, 37–9, 65–6, 91–5, 111–12, 124–5, 128–30, 133–7, 139–40, 145, 151, 177, 283–4, 289–90, 295–6, 298, 304–5, 308–9, 336–7, 384–5, 433, 435–6
Diez, Thomas 9–10
Djilas, Milovan 277–8
Dooge, James 355
Drees, Willem 437–8
Dresden 55–6, 73
Drieu La Rochelle, Pierre 135, 145
Dromer, Jean 57
Dubcek, Alexander 59–60
Duhamel, Georges 93–5
Dulles, John Foster 36–7, 66, 108
Dumas, Roland 114–15
Duverger, Maurice 134

East, the 34, 39–40, 43–4, 52, 55, 60, 65–6, 73–4, 98, 100, 151–2, 181, 184, 187–8, 227, 231, 280, 305–6, 346–7, 352, 357–8, 369–70
East Asia 170–1, 243–4, 268–9
East German workers' uprising (1953) 47, 52, 62–3, 95–6, 434–5
Eastern Bloc 57–60, 152, 172, 184, 187–8, 223–6, 277–8, 300–1

Economic and Monetary Union (EMU) 69, 74, 216–17, 249, 256, 298, 300, 356–9, 392–4, 397, 441–2, 444–5, 449

Economic and Social Committee (ESC) 413–14

Economist 29, 179–80, 216, 223, 240, 245, 295–6, 303–4, 368

Ecuador 308–9

Eden, Anthony 341, 434

Eisenhower, Dwight 33–4, 55, 57–8, 62, 66, 252

Eliade, Mircea 143–4

Eliot, T. S. 124–5

Enlightenment 123–6, 154–5, 309–11

Enzensberger, Hans-Magnus 147

Erasmus students 312–13

Erhard, Ludwig 64–5, 91–2, 106–7, 115, 194–5, 227, 240–2, 280–2, 345–6, 440

Esping-Andersen, Gøsta 270–1

Estonia 100–1, 197–8, 254, 298, 309–11, 369–70

ethnicity 168–74, 176–7, 181, 188, 196, 293–4

Etzioni, Amatai 364–5, 369–70, 408–9

Eurasia 36–9, 167–8

Eurogroup 214–16

Europe, ideas of 127–8

    Central Europe 47–8, 59, 151–2, 168, 232–3, 274–7, 290, 304–6

    Eastern Europe 17–18, 30–2, 35–7, 42–4, 46–7, 54–5, 58–61, 74, 100, 106, 109, 114, 124–5, 143–4, 149, 151–2, 167–9, 177–8, 181, 223–5, 230–1, 242–3, 270, 274–5, 287, 294–8, 300–5, 307, 309, 312–13, 334–6, 347, 369–70, 449

    Southern Europe 56–7, 112, 124–5, 170–1, 178–9, 215–16, 250–1, 253–4, 291–2, 294–5

    Western Europe 2–3, 6–7, 12, 17–18, 31–6, 39–44, 47, 49–51, 54–5, 57–62, 64–5, 89–92, 95–6, 98, 105, 108–9, 115, 123–4, 136–7, 142–3, 147–9, 151–2, 168, 172–4, 181, 187–8, 219–20, 222–7, 237–8, 240–2, 251–4, 291–2, 296–8, 304, 308–9, 316–17, 342, 346–7, 354, 387–8, 436–8, 447–8

Europe 1990 plan 247–8

European Agricultural Guidance and Guarantee Fund 303

European army 1, 388–9, 438–9

European Atomic Energy Community (Euratom) 32–3, 67, 219–20, 240–1, 342–5

European Central Bank (ECB) 215–16, 333–4, 358–9, 381, 417, 419–20

European Coal and Steel Community (ECSC) 2–4, 10–12, 32–3, 51–2, 66–7, 92–3, 98, 103, 107–9, 130–1, 136, 142–3, 147–8, 216, 218–25, 233–40, 250–1, 290, 337–41, 387–90, 433–4, 437–8, 440

European Commission 10–11, 13, 112, 149, 214, 216–17, 237–8, 248, 286–9, 302–3, 334, 350–1, 368, 381–2, 389–92, 394–5, 411–12, 419–22, 440, 442–3

European constitution 8, 193–4, 289–90, 307–8, 319, 321, 359–60, 368–70, 399–401, 403, 405, 417

European Convention on Human Rights (ECHR) 113–14, 308–9

European Council 13, 30, 73–4, 106–7, 110–11, 115, 203, 214, 298, 334–8, 348, 350–1, 354–7, 360–2, 371, 381–4, 393–4, 396–7, 399–408, 412–13, 417–19, 440, 442–3, 446, 450–1

    Fontainebleau (1984) 74–5

    Laeken (2001) 400

European Court of Justice (ECJ) 247–8, 286–7, 333–6, 359–60, 368, 381, 419–22, 440, 442, 445–6

European Defence Community (EDC) 12, 34–7, 64–5, 67, 96, 103, 105, 107–9, 130–1, 136, 153, 219–20, 240–2, 336–7, 341–5, 347, 386–9, 434, 438–9

European Economic Community (EEC) 4, 32–4, 57–8, 60–1, 64–5, 67–8, 92–3, 103–5, 108–12, 130–1, 142–3, 147–50, 167–8, 182–3, 190, 218–26, 229, 235, 237–40, 243–4, 250–4, 286–7, 289–90, 334, 342–4, 348, 352, 356, 368, 386, 388–95, 420–2, 440–1

European Free Trade Association (EFTA) 238–40, 342, 439–40

European integration, histories of 2–7, 16

European Investment Bank (EIB) 302–3

European Monetary System (EMS) 67–8, 106–7, 238–40, 348, 350, 356–7, 393–4, 419–20

European Parliament 1, 6–9, 30, 98, 106–9, 113–15, 179–80, 199, 228–9, 235, 295, 309–11, 334, 348–9, 351, 354–5, 358–9, 369–71, 381–2, 385, 390, 392–5, 399–400, 402–5, 407–8, 411–14, 417–22, 440, 444–5

European Payments Union (EPU) 91–2, 238

European People's Party (EPP) 309–11

European Political Community (EPC) 347, 386–90, 439

European Political Cooperation (EPC) 108–11, 354–5, 393–4, 419–20

European Recovery Program, *see* Marshall Aid

European Regional Development Fund 303

European Social Model 153, 217, 270–89, 293–4, 368, 401, 446–7

European Stability Mechanism (ESM) 215–16, 270–1, 287–9, 446

514 INDEX

European Values Survey 307-8
Europeanism 64-5, 92-3, 100-1, 106, 135-7, 172, 178-9, 189-203, 221-2, 268, 308, 312-13, 317, 347, 350-1, 359, 434, 448-9
Europeanization 8-9, 123-4, 150-1, 167, 287, 319, 337, 408-10, 413
Euroscepticism 1, 19, 30, 180, 203, 294, 358-9, 367, 381-4, 396, 398-9, 406-7, 417, 443-6, 450-1
Eurosclerosis 243-4
Eurozone 30, 217, 318, 333-4, 381-3, 400-2
Eurozone crisis 30-1, 179-80, 190, 193-4, 199-200, 214-16
Exchange Rate Mechanism (ERM) 68-9
executive 8-9, 133-4, 139-40, 216, 219-20, 241-2, 318, 335-6, 348, 359-60, 381-2, 388-9, 395, 399-400, 411-13, 418-19, 442-6

Fabius, Laurent 238-40
Falklands War (1982) 110-11
Fannie Mae 214-15
Farage, Nigel 19
fascism 35, 39, 133-5, 139-40, 184-7, 299-300
Faure, Edgar 240-1
Federal Reserve 214-15, 252
federalism 1, 12, 19, 32-3, 143, 172, 286-7, 335, 337-9, 341, 355, 369-70, 382, 384-90, 398-9, 404, 408-9, 434-5, 438
federation 1-3, 66, 71, 98-100, 135-6, 153-4, 172, 192, 201-2, 216, 232, 309-11, 339, 350, 384-90, 395, 397, 399-400, 408, 418-19, 421-2, 439, 441-3
feminism 283-4
Fest, Joachim 55-6
Fidesz (Hungary) 114, 179-80, 449-50
Figaro 30-1, 136
Finland 42-3, 46, 228, 251-2, 271, 293-5, 305-6, 312-14
Fischer, Joschka 218, 338-9, 368, 397, 399-400, 404, 442-3
Fleiderer, Karl-Georg 98
Foreign Direct Investment (FDI) 218, 252-3, 296-8
Forsthoff, Ernst 139-40
Forsyth, Murray 420-2
Fortis banking group 214-15
Fortune magazine 218-19
Foucault, Michel 9-10
Fouchet, Christian 390
Fouchet Plan 104-5, 390
Fraenkel, Ernst 138
France 1, 5, 29-31, 35-6, 42-6, 48-52, 54-8, 60-1, 64-7, 69, 71, 73-4, 89-109, 111-12, 114-15, 123-4, 130-1, 134, 136-7, 139-42, 144-5, 166, 178-81, 184, 187-8, 196, 199-200, 218, 221-8, 230-8, 240-1, 243-6, 251-4, 270-86, 290, 292-3, 303-4, 308-9, 313-14, 316-19, 338-47, 350-4, 357-67, 369-71, 388-92, 404, 406-7, 434-9, 441-2, 448-50
  Treasury 240
  Ministry of Foreign Affairs (Quai d'Orsay) 48, 59, 93-5, 103, 107-8, 131-2, 230-1, 240-1, 339-40
France Telecom 254
Franco, General Francisco 112, 136-7, 141-2, 178-9
Franco-British Union (1940) 433-4
Franco-German Friendship Treaty (1963) 64-5, 104-5, 352-4
Franco-German Trade Treaty (1927) 232-3
Frankfurt 314
Frankfurter Allgemeine Zeitung 30-1, 55-6, 130-1, 149, 318, 381-2
Freddie Mac 214-15
Freie Demokratische Partei (FDP) 54-5, 345-6, 351
Free French Forces 390
Free Trade Area (FTA) 217, 241, 255-6, 342, 439-40
Freedom Party (Austria) 1, 179-80
French Revolution (1789) 192-3, 382
Freud, Sigmund 141-2, 170, 189-90
Friedrich, Carl J. 139-40, 408
Friedländer, Ernst 96, 347
Front National (France) 1, 179-80
Frontex 446
functionalism 123-4, 228-9
Furet, François 13-16

Gaddis, John Lewis 1-2, 34, 42
Gaitskell, Hugh 283-4
Gamble, Andrew 285-6
Garnett, Mark 293-4
Garton Ash, Timothy 66, 146-7, 177-8
Gastarbeiter (guest workers) 194-5
Gat, Azar 154-5, 169-70
Gauck authority 146-7
Gaullism 42-3, 58-9, 99-100, 144-5, 271-2, 388-9
Gehlen, Arnold 138
Gehler, Michael 6-7
Gellner, Ernest 182-3
gender 275-7, 293-4, 308
General Agreement on Tariffs and Trade (GATT) 238, 255-6, 433
Genscher, Hans-Dietrich 73-4, 106, 355-7

INDEX 515

Gergen, Kenneth 188
German People's Party (DVP) 232–3
German question 2–3, 33–4, 50–6, 62, 68–70, 75,
  89–90, 93–5, 101, 106, 131–2, 233–5,
  352–4, 434
German reunification 50, 55–6, 59, 63, 70, 95–6,
  98–100, 194, 346–7
Germany 2–3, 5, 29–33, 36–44, 46–56, 61–75,
  89–90, 96, 123–4, 128–32, 136–7, 184,
  232–7
  Auswärtiges Amt 65–6, 93–5, 100, 347
  Federal Republic of Germany (FRG) 17, 50–9,
    61–75, 91–106, 108, 110–11, 130–41, 147,
    154–5, 184–8, 190–4, 196, 199–200, 218,
    221–3, 225–7, 229–32, 234–40, 242–4,
    247–50, 252–3, 270–2, 274–86, 289–90,
    292–4, 296–8, 302–6, 309, 312–14,
    317–19, 339–42,
    345–58, 360–7, 369–71, 383–4,
    389–90, 398–400, 404, 434, 436–9,
    441–4, 448–9
  German Democratic Republic (GDR) 39,
    54–5, 58–9, 65–6, 69–71, 73–4, 95–7, 106,
    109, 114, 194, 223–5, 434–5
  Imperial Germany 96–7
  Weimar Republic 12, 92–6, 231–3
  Nazi Germany 30–1, 37–9, 46, 50–1, 55, 92–5,
    125–6, 134–5, 137–9, 171–2, 184–7, 194,
    196, 215–16, 236–7, 312,
    318, 333
Ghana 308–9
Gibraltar 112
Giddens, Anthony 143, 188–9, 270–2, 288–9
Gierek, Edward 223–5
Giesen, Bernhard 193–4
Gilbert, Mark 4–5, 450–1
Giscard d'Estaing, Valéry 63–4, 106–7, 111–12,
  223–5, 245–6, 308–11, 348–52, 393–4,
  400–3
Glasgow 314
Glendinning, Simon 127–8, 383–4
Global South, see Third World
globalization 4–7, 47, 146–7, 187–8, 193–6,
  202–3, 244–56, 269–71, 289–90, 293–4,
  336–7, 421–2, 450–1
Goldblatt, David 244–5
Goldthorpe, John 441
Gomulka, Wladyslaw 184
Good Friday Agreement (1998) 112–13
Google 218–19
Gorbachev, Mikhail 60–1, 70–4, 106
Grantham 314–15
Grass, Günter 192
Great Depression 44, 292

Greece 30, 36, 42–4, 47–8, 111–12, 114, 124–5,
  215–16, 218, 269–75, 287, 289–90, 295–6,
  298, 303–6, 309–11, 314, 333–4,
  383–4, 435
  Ancient Greece 124–5, 309–11
Green movement 283–4
Grewe, Wilhelm 138–9
Grimm, Dieter 319–21
Group of Seven (G7) 67–8, 252, 352
Guardian 30, 131, 147–8, 188–9, 318
Guillaume, Günter 350–1
Gulf War (1991) 115, 171, 360–2

Haas, Ernst 3–4, 7–8, 32–3, 149–50, 219–23,
  384, 440
Habermas, Jürgen 65–6, 143, 192–4, 319–21,
  381–4, 399–400
Habsburg monarchy 230–1
Hague, The 385
Hájek, Jirí 59–60
Hall, Peter 409–10
Hallstein, Walter 386, 389–90, 439, 441
Hallstein doctrine 54, 58–9, 194
Hamburg 305, 314
Harden, Maximilian 123–4
Hargreaves, Peter 30
Harrison, Reginald 384–5
Hauptmann, Gerhart 123–4
Havel, Václav 146–8, 298
Hayek, Friedrich 132, 134, 136–7
HBOS (Halifax Bank of Scotland) 214–15
Healey, Denis 286
Heath, Edward 393–4
Heile, Wilhelm 128–30
Held, David 244–5
Heller, Agnes, 127
Helsinki Accords (1975) 59, 109, 352,
  354–5
Heuss, Theodor 98
High Authority (ECSC) 12, 216, 219–21, 440
Hillenbrand, Martin 59
Hirschfeld, Max 240
Hitler, Adolf 44–6, 50–1, 125–6, 144–5
Hix, Simon 409
Hobbes, Thomas 146
Hobsbawm, Eric 184–7
Hodson, Dermot 419
Hoesch, Leopold von 100
Hoffman, Paul 2–3
Hoffmann, Stanley 7–8, 149–50, 337, 411–12
Holbrooke, Richard 364
Holocaust 17–18, 30–1, 131–2, 147, 192–4
Holy Roman Empire 125–6, 349
Honecker, Erich 69–70

516 INDEX

Hooghe, Liesbet 411–12
Hoover, Herbert 44
Hopkins, Harry 29
Horkheimer, Max 125–6, 139–40
Horsley, Thomas 333
Hull, Cordell 44
Hungary 1, 46, 60, 70–1, 95–7, 143–4, 146–7,
    151, 177–80, 199, 242–3, 289–90, 293–4,
    296–8, 300–2, 306–7, 309, 369–70,
    434–5, 449
Hurd, Douglas 114–15
Hurrell, Andrew 90–1
Hussein, Saddam 188–9, 360–2

IBM 225
immigration, see migration
India 291–2, 336–7, 362
    independence 35–6, 47–8, 434–5
Indo-China 35–6, 49, 125–6
Indonesia 291–2
inequality 169, 177, 268–71, 277–8, 291–4, 316
intercontinental ballistic missiles
    (ICBMs) 42–3, 62
intergovernmentalism 6–10, 13, 16, 34–5,
    104–6, 109, 115, 149–50, 193–4, 203,
    222–3, 230, 241, 295, 335–40, 347–8,
    355, 382–4, 386–7, 390–403, 405,
    411–21
    liberal intergovernmentalism 9–10, 149–50,
        411–15, 419–20
    new intergovernmentalism 419–20
International Monetary Fund (IMF) 91–2,
    215–16, 238, 241
international relations, theories of 4–5, 7–12,
    42–3, 65–6, 143, 149–50, 409–20, 433
International Steel Cartel (1926) 231–4, 433
International Values Survey 184–7
Iraq 188–9
Iraq War (2003) 366–7, 369–70, 404, 442–3
Ireland 18–19, 30–1, 110–13, 195, 215–16, 229,
    249–50, 292–3, 295, 303, 307–9, 334–48,
    392–3, 435
Irish Times 30–1
Iron Curtain 43–4, 52, 142–5, 168, 235–6
Islamophobia 308–9
Ismay, Hastings 131–2
Istanbul 307
Italy 1, 37–9, 43–6, 56–7, 89–90, 92–3, 96–7,
    110–11, 132–4, 139, 143, 167, 178–80,
    184–8, 197–8, 220–2, 226–7, 232–3,
    236–8, 243, 246–8, 270–5, 278–84, 286,
    289–90, 303–6, 309, 313–14, 317, 339,
    348, 351–2, 360–2, 366, 384–5, 389–90,
    436–9

Jaguar cars 286
Jameson, Fredric 188
Japan 294, 309, 311–13, 449
Jaruzelski, General Wojciech 110–11
Jasenovac camp 175–6
Jaspers, Karl 124–5
Jenkins, Roy 112, 243–4, 351–2, 394, 441
John XXIII 282–3
John Paul II 309–11
Johnson, Boris 19–20
Johnson, Lyndon Baines 62–3
Joliot-Curie, Frédéric 145
Jouvenel, Bertrand de 134, 145
Jovic, Borisav 175–6, 363
Judt, Tony 12, 31–4, 50–1, 55, 436–7
Juncker, Jean-Claude 214
Juppé, Alain 271–2, 358–9

Kaelble, Hartmut 4–5, 268–9, 289–91
Kaiser, Jakob 37–9
Kaiser, Wolfram 4–7
Kant, Immanuel 384
Karadžic, Radovan 176
Karamanlis, Konstantinos 111–12
Katholieke Volkspartij (KVP) 282
Katzenstein, Peter 154–5
Kelsen, Hans 137
Kennan, George F. 2–3, 43–4, 46
Kenya 308–9
Keohane, Robert 414–15
Keynes, John Maynard 125–6, 242, 339–40
Khrushchev, Nikita 44, 60
King, Preston 408
Kirchheimer, Otto 138
Klaus, Vaclav 407–8
Kobbert, Erich 149
Kohl, Helmut 55–6, 64–8, 70–4, 89–107, 192,
    217, 249–50, 280, 335–59, 362–4, 441–2
Kohnstamm, Max 240, 437–8
Korean War (1950–4) 98–9, 101, 346–7, 434–5,
    437–8
Kosovo 30–1, 171–2, 174–6, 365–6
Kosovo Liberation Army (KLA) 365–6
Kosygin, Alexander 60
Krajina 175–6
Krüger, Peter 100
Kundera, Milan 151
Kurile Islands 34

Labour Party (Netherlands) 241
Labour Party (UK) 36, 39–40, 54–5, 190, 238–40,
    274–5, 280, 286, 340–1, 385–94, 405–6,
    438–9
    New Labour 288–9, 293–5, 369–70

INDEX 517

Lamont, Norman 30
Lamy, Pascal 360–2
Langhoff, Wolfgang 289
Larock, Victor 241
Lasswell, Harold 8–9
Lasterie du Saillant, Charles de 230–1
Latin America 30–1, 36–7, 65–6, 110, 170–1, 201–2, 309, 341
Latvia 100–1, 179–80, 295–6, 298, 302–6, 369–70
Law and Justice Party (Poland) 1, 179–80, 449
Lawson, Nigel 285–6
League of Communists of Yugoslavia (LCY) 172, 174–5
League of Nations 36–7, 93–5, 100, 123–4, 145, 183, 216–32, 236, 337–8, 433
Leahy, Admiral William 42
Le Bail, Jean 345
Lee, Sir Frank 225–6
Lee, Kuan Yew 368
Lega (Italy) 1, 184–7
legislature 8–9, 333
Lehman Brothers 214–15
Leibholz, Gerhard 138
Leipzig 55–6, 70
Leningrad 34, 151
Lepenies, Wolf 193–4
Levitt, Theodore 245
liberalization 247–51, 295–6, 300–1, 370–1
Lilley, Peter 294
Lincolnshire 314–15
Lindberg, Leon 7–8, 10–11, 223
Lipgens, Walter 12, 30–1, 153–4
Lisbon 307
Lisbon Agenda (2000) 271
Lisbon Treaty (2007) 8, 402–3, 405, 407–8, 441–3
Lithuania 100–1, 302, 369–70
Lloyds TSB 214–15
lobby groups 13–14, 232, 253
Locarno (1925), Treaty of 92–5, 100–1, 232–3, 433
Locke, John 146
Lodge, Juliet 123–4, 228–9
Lombardy 305–6
London 19, 113–15, 179–80, 189–90, 214–15, 230–1, 253–4, 305–6, 314, 390
London Report (1981) 110–11
London Review of Books 333–6
L'Oreal 238–40
Lorraine 101, 233–4
Loth, Wilfried 12, 33–4
Loucheur, Louis 231–2

Lubbers, Ruud 394–5
Lukacs, Georg 124–5
Luns, Joseph 391
Luxembourg 115, 221–2, 231–2, 248, 305, 339, 348–9, 360–2, 389–93
Luxembourg compromise (1966) 106–7, 391, 412–13, 420–1
Libya 449–50

Maastricht Treaty, *see* Treaty on European Union
Macedonia 172, 177
Macmillan, Harold 147–8, 196, 225–6, 235, 238–40, 341–2, 368, 388–9, 438–40
Macron, Emmanuel 382–3
Macura, Lazar 175–6
Madagascar 35–6, 131–2
Maier, Reinhold 98
Majone, Giandomenico 216, 287–8
Major, John 188–9, 203, 251, 293–4, 335–65, 395–6
Mak, Geert 306–7
Makins, Sir Roger 340–1
Malta 71, 295
Malraux, André 144–5
Manchester 314
Manchester Evening News 393–4
Mandelson, Peter 294–5
Mann, Klaus 124–5
Mann, Thomas 137
March, James 11, 409–10
Marcuse, Herbert 139–40
Maritain, Jacques 134, 142
Marjolin, Robert 225–7, 230, 236–8, 342–4, 348, 350, 385–6, 389–92, 439–41
Marks, Gary 9, 411–12
Marsh, David 55–6
Marshall, George C. 43–4, 51
Marshall, T. H. 134
Marshall Aid 2–3, 44–6, 65, 91–2, 187–8, 236–8, 240, 435
Marx, Karl 142, 277–8
Marxism 46–7, 123–42
Masaryk, Jan 187–8
Massigli, René 99–100, 388–9
Mauriac, François 55, 144–5
Mauroy, Pierre 106–7, 187–8, 238–40, 355
Mayrisch, Emile 231–2
Mazier, Antoine 345
McCloy, John 252
McCormick, John 197–8, 218–19, 268, 307–9, 449
McGarry, John 113–14
McGrew, Anthony 244–5

518 INDEX

media 13–14, 19–20, 73, 152–5, 170–1, 173, 199–202, 244–5, 268–9, 299–300, 304, 315–21, 367, 406–7, 413, 443–4, 449–50
Mediaprint 359–60
Mediterranean 35–6, 40–4, 57–8, 125–6, 274–5, 295–8
Meinecke, Friedrich 134–5
Memorandum on the Organisation of a Regime of European Federal Union (1930) 229
Mendès France, Pierre 105, 342–4
Mérand, Frédéric 410
Merkel, Angela 30, 214–16, 303–4, 370–1
Merleau-Ponty, Maurice 134, 141–4
Messina meeting (1955) 103, 219–20, 237, 240–1, 342, 347
Mexico 274–5, 295–8, 309–11, 366–7
Mezzogiorno 305–6
Middelaar, Luuk van 333, 335–6, 396–7
Middle Ages 136–7
Middle East 35–6, 40–4, 65–6, 109, 114
migration 1, 152, 177–8, 180, 190, 194–5, 227, 248, 268–71, 283–4, 289–91, 302, 314–16, 318–19, 335–6, 369–71, 407–8, 444–6
Milosevic, Slobodan 174–6, 360–3, 365–6
Milward, Alan 4–6, 9–10, 12, 122–3, 153–4, 184–8, 190, 337–8, 412–13, 436
Mischlich, Robert 103
missile gap crisis 62
Mitteleuropa 50–1, 97, 128–30
Mladic, Ratko 364–5
Moch, Jules 107–8
Moldova 34, 305–6
Mollet, Guy 66, 99–101, 105–8, 241, 286–7, 342–5
Molotov, Vyacheslav 35
monetarism 286
Monnet, Jean 12, 51, 90, 92–3, 98–9, 101, 103, 108–9, 216–17, 219–21, 233–6, 335–41, 344, 346–7, 350–1, 385–6, 388–9, 394, 399–400, 433–4, 439, 441
Montenegro 172, 177
Moravcsik, Andrew 7–8, 10–11, 149–50, 412–17
Morgenthau Plan 67, 103
Morin, Edgar 143–4
Moses, Dirk. A. 137
Mounier, Emmanuel 134, 142
Mount, Ferdinand 333
Mouvement pour les Etats-Unis socialistes d'Europe (MEUSE) 387–8
Mouvement Républicain Populaire (MRP) 99–100, 388–9
Mudde, Cas 180
Müller-Armack, Alfred 345–6
multiculturalism 268–70, 308–9, 449
Multilateral Nuclear Force 62–3

multilevel governance 4–5, 8–9, 11, 150–1, 410–14, 418–19
multinational corporations 13–14, 187–8, 245, 249–51, 253–5, 312–13, 413

Nagy, Imre 47, 95–6
Nairn, Tom 170, 184–7
Nanterre 283–4
narrative history 13–17, 90–1, 152–3, 181, 196, 245–6, 368, 436
National Health Service (NHS) 271–2, 286, 316
nationalism 12, 32–3, 46–7, 91–3, 101, 122, 124–5, 127–8, 134–9, 141, 146, 152, 154–5, 167–80, 182–8, 190–203, 219, 221–2, 229, 235–6, 268, 285–6, 318–19, 347, 384–5, 434–5
Nazi New Order in Europe 33
neo-functionalism 3–4, 8–11, 123–4, 127–8, 149–50, 219–29, 408–9, 414–17
neo-liberalism 92–3, 166, 285–6, 336
Netherlands 56–7, 100, 108, 139, 195, 198–200, 221–2, 229, 235, 242–3, 249–51, 254, 270–1, 280–4, 289–90, 292–4, 305–6, 317–18, 339, 360–2, 417, 436–8, 441
  Foreign Office (Dutch) 240–1, 437–8
Nettl, J. P. 277–8
Neue Kronen Zeitung 359–60
Neumann, Franz 139–40
New Europe Barometer 300–1
new institutionalism 8–9, 11, 409–10, 413
New York Review of Books 151, 298, 318–19
New York Times 29, 62–3, 67–8, 364
New Zealand 292–3, 308–9, 449
Newcastle 314
newspapers, *see* media
Nice (2001), Treaty of 295
Nicholson, Jim 113–14
Nicholson, Michael 115
Nida-Rümelin, Julian 381–2
Nielsen, François 9
Niethammer, Lutz 193–4
Nietzsche, Friedrich 142
Nigeria 195
Nixon, Richard 54, 59, 62, 68–9, 109, 238, 252
Nobel Peace Prize 29
Nora, Pierre 152–3
North America 4–5, 36–7, 43–4, 90–1, 96–7, 251–2, 341
North Atlantic Treaty Organization (NATO) 7–8, 19, 33–5, 40–3, 47, 50, 56–8, 62–9, 71–4, 89–90, 96, 100, 103, 105–6, 108, 111–12, 115, 130–2, 341, 344–7, 352, 354–5, 360–6, 369–70, 388–9, 394–5, 433–4, 437–8, 449–50

North East of England 305–6
Northamptonshire 314–15
Northern Ireland 18–19, 113–14, 178–9, 363
Northern Italy 305
Northern League, *see* Lega
Northern Rock 214–15
Norway 115, 139, 280, 392–3
Nottinghamshire 314–15
NRC Handelsblad 306–7
nuclear disarmament 283–4
Nuclear Planning Group 62–3
nuclear weapons 17–18, 33–4, 42–3, 47, 56–8,
    61–6, 69, 73, 92–3, 95–6, 98–9, 110,
    219–20, 227, 283–4, 344–5, 434–5
Nuffield Social Mobility Study 277–8
Nuremberg trials 37–9
Nutting, Anthony 341
Nye, Joseph 414–15

Obama, Barack 30
Oborne, Peter 333
Observer 18–20
Occupation Statute 65–6
O'Doherty, Enda 126–7
O'Hare, Anne 29
oil crisis (1973) 243, 246–7, 338–9, 392–3
O'Leary, Brendan 113–14
Olsen, Johan 11, 409–10
open method of coordination (OMC) 287
Orbán, Viktor 1, 114
Organisation for European Economic
    Cooperation (OEEC) 2–3, 222, 225–6,
    230, 237–8, 241–2, 251, 335–48,
    385–6, 433
Ortega y Gasset, José 125–6, 128–30, 133, 136–7,
    145–6
Orwell, George 43–4
O'Toole, Fintan 18–19
Ottoman Empire 172, 230–1
Ouchy (1932), Treaty of 235

Pacific (region) 36–7, 43–4, 169
Pais, El 318
Paneuropa movement 128–30
Paris 35, 93–5, 104, 125–6, 178–9, 283–4, 305,
    307, 314
Paris (1951), Treaty of 233–4, 388–9
Parsons, Craig 105–7
Pasqua, Charles 358–9
Patel, Kiran Klaus 16
patriotism 138, 170, 184–7, 192–4, 307–8, 386
Pearl Harbor 42–3
Perraton, Jonathan 244–5
Peru 308–9

Peterson, John 337
Pew Global Attitudes Survey 308–9
Phare programme 302–3
Phillips, A. W. H. 283–4
Pierson, Paul 11
Piketty, Thomas 291–3
Pilzudski, Jósef 46
Pinay, Antoine 240–1, 346
Pius XII 282–3
Plamenatz, John 181
Plato, Alexander von 147
Pleven, René 386–7
Plowden, Edwin 340–1
Pocock, J. G. A. 167–9
Pöhl, Karl Otto 55–6
Poland 1, 39, 46–7, 54–60, 70–1, 110–11, 146–7,
    177–80, 184, 223–5, 242–3, 272–5, 290,
    293–8, 300–4, 307–9, 313, 369–70, 449
policy networks 3–5, 8–9, 150–1, 337, 408–13
political science 1–2, 4–5, 9–11, 13–14, 143, 153,
    169–70, 414–20
politics 7–8, 150–1, 256, 368, 411–12
    high politics 7–8, 150–1, 256, 337
    low politics 7–8, 150–1, 411–12
polity 8–9, 11, 13, 16–17, 149, 288–9, 311,
    319–20, 335–6, 381–422, 433–5
Pollack, Mark 336–7
Pollock, Friedrich 139–40
Pompidou, Georges 57–8, 106–7, 109, 245–6,
    392–4
Poos, Jacques 115
Popper, Karl 131–2, 134, 136–7
Port Arthur 34
Portugal 30, 112, 195, 215–16, 250–1, 270,
    274–7, 289–90, 295–6, 298, 303–4, 307–9,
    313–14, 395, 435
post-functionalism 229
post-modernism 168, 188–9
Potsdam conference (1945) 47, 96
Prague 52, 187–8
Prague Spring 56–7, 60
press, *see* media
Presse 318
Proctor and Gamble 253–4
public opinion 6–7, 12, 14–18, 42, 55, 57–8, 61,
    63, 65–6, 70–1, 93–5, 106–7, 114, 123,
    130, 138–40, 146–7, 151, 154–5, 170–1,
    173–4, 180, 184–7, 193–4, 196, 216, 223,
    229, 242–4, 268, 277–8, 288–9, 300,
    308–9, 316–21
public sphere 316–21
Puchala, Donald 410
Puetter, Uwe 419
Putnam, Robert 416–17

520 INDEX

qualified majority voting (QMV) 287–8, 354–5, 369, 371, 389–92, 401–2, 405, 412–13, 417, 441, 443

Ramadier, Paul 39–40, 385
Rassemblement National, see *Front National*
Rassemblement pour la République (RPR) 245, 284–5, 349, 358–60, 364–5
Ray, Leonard 9
Reagan, Ronald 56–7, 65–6, 69, 293–4
Realism (IR theory) 410–11, 414–15
rearmament 31–2, 62–3, 66, 101, 226–7, 235, 346–7, 434
Redwood, John 294
Regional Economic Planning Boards (UK) 178–9
Reichlin, Lucrezie 333–4
Repubblica 318
Reuter, Edzard 55–6
Reynaud, Paul 385
Reynolds, David 33–5
Rhineland 230–1, 233–4
Rhineland (1936), militarization of 93–5
Rhône-Alpes 305
Richardson, Jeremy 411–12
Rippon, Geoffrey 393–4
Risse, Thomas 317–18
Robin, Gabriel 106–7
Rocard, Michel 106
Rolls Royce 286
Roman Empire 97, 151–2, 309–11
Romania 46, 100–1, 114, 177, 179–80, 290, 295–6, 300–2, 307–8, 313, 369–70
Rome (1957), Treaty of 67, 108–9, 254–5, 286–8, 333, 345–7, 389–90, 394, 396, 440, 443
Rompuy, Herman Van 30
Roosevelt, Franklin D. 29, 35–6
Rosselli, Carlo 133–4
Roth, Andrew 393–4
Rougement, Denis de 124–5
Rotterdam 253–4
Royal Bank of Scotland (RBS) 214–15
Ruhr industry 233–4
Ruhr (1923), occupation of 92–3, 100–3
Rumsfeld, Donald 442–3
Rupnik, Jacques 172
Russia 2–3, 6, 19, 54–5, 65 96–7, 106, 144–5, 167–8, 240, 275–7, 300–1, 335–7, 360–2
Russian Civil War 44–6
Russian Revolution (1917) 47, 128–30
Rutten, Charles 241

Saarland 103, 233–4, 434
Sagladin, Vadim 73–4

Sakhalin 34
Salazar, António de Oliveira 112
Salk, Jane 9
Sandholtz, Wayne 9, 11
Santer, Jacques 305
Sarajevo 115, 364–5
Sarkozy, Nicolas 104, 294–8, 303–4, 370–1, 442
Sargent, Sir Orme 39–40
Sartre, Jean-Paul 124–5, 136, 141–4
Sassoon, Donald 278–80, 282–3
Scandinavia 100–1, 203, 269–71, 290
Schaik, Josef van 437–8
Scharpf, Fritz 286–7, 446–7
Scheingold, Stuart A. 223
Schelsky, Helmut 138
Schengen area 112–13, 291–2, 394–5, 419–20
Scheuner, Ulrich 138–9
Schimmelfennig, Frank 419–20
Schissler, Hanna 193–4
Schlesinger, Philip 447–8
Schlumberger 238–40
Schlüter, Poul 166
Schmid, Carlo 37–9, 147–8
Schmidt, Helmut 52, 55–6, 62–3, 65–70, 106–7, 194–5, 242–3, 246–7, 277–8, 349–54
Schmitt, Carl 133–4, 138–9
Schmitter, Philippe 229
Schröder, Gerhard 154–5, 196, 366–9, 397, 404–5, 435
Schuman, Robert 51–2, 101–3, 108–9, 233–4, 338–41, 346–7, 349, 388–9, 397, 399, 437–8, 441–3
Schuman Declaration (1950) 339–41
Scotland 112–13, 178–9
Scottish Lowlands 305–6
secularism 134, 136, 141, 197–8, 268, 282–3, 307–11, 449
security community 17, 89–90, 92–3, 104, 107–16, 450–1
Séguin, Philippe 358–9
Seidel, Katja 4–5
Serbian Democratic Party (SDS) 176
Sethe, Paul 98
Sforza, Carlo 39
Shipman, Tim 30
Singh, Manmohan 368
Single European Act (1986) 166, 223–5, 247–8, 251–2, 255–6, 287–8, 303, 336, 354–5, 405–6, 441
single market 9–10, 18–19, 217–19, 223–5, 243–4, 248, 250–5, 288–9, 298, 305, 352–5, 394–5, 409–10, 415–16, 419, 442–3
Skourletis, Panos 30

'Slavs' 95–6
Slovakia 19–20, 46, 114, 177–80, 242–3, 252–3, 288–9, 293–4, 298, 302–4, 369–70
Slovenia 60–1, 114–15, 171–3, 175–6, 195, 242–3, 269–98, 302, 362–3
small and medium-sized enterprise (SMEs) 253, 313
Smiles, Samuel 285–6
Smith, Anthony 170, 201–3, 448–9
Smith Kuznets, Anthony 291–2
snake monetary system 68–9, 351–2, 393–4, 419–20
Snyder, Jack 170–3, 177–8
Soares, Mario 112
Social and Democratic Labour Party (SDLP) 113–14
Social Chapter 287–8
social constructivism 9–10, 150–1, 413
Social Dimension of the Internal Market report (1988) 288–9
social market economy 139–40, 236, 242, 282
social mobility 277–80
Socialist Party (Belgium) 47, 241
Socialist Party (France) 99–100, 105–8, 238–40, 286–7, 342–4, 355, 358–9
   Section Française de l'Internationale Ouvrière (SFIO) 99–101, 105, 107–8, 231–2, 335–45
Socialist Party (Italy) 114
Socialist Party of Serbia (SPS) 174–5
Socialist Unity Party (SED) 37–9, 54–5, 70–1, 280
Sofia 52
Soir, Le 30–1
Solidarity (*Solidarnosc*) 56–7, 59–60, 110–11
Sollmann, Wilhelm 49–50, 95–6
Sørensen, Vibeke 412–13
South America, *see* Latin America
South Korea 274–5, 309–11, 449
South Tyrol 112–13
South Yorkshire 308
Southern Germany 305
Soviet Military Authority in Germany (SMAD) 37–9
Soviet Union (USSR) 2–3, 5, 12, 29, 31–2, 34–48, 50–1, 54–66, 69–71, 73–4, 91–2, 95–6, 98–100, 106, 109–11, 122–4, 130–2, 141–7, 168, 171, 176–8, 223–5, 230–1, 277–80, 311–12, 341, 346, 356, 384–5, 436–8, 449–50
Sozialdemokratische Partei Deutschlands (SPD) 32–3, 37–9, 49–50, 52, 54–5, 64–5, 67–8, 95–6, 99–100, 147–8, 232–3, 345–6, 350–2, 397

South Africa 291–2
Spaak, Paul-Henri 12, 47, 100, 103, 105–6, 108, 219–20, 233–4, 237, 241–2, 335–46, 385, 388–9, 434, 438–9
Spain 30, 112, 136–7, 166, 178–9, 199–200, 215–43, 270–7, 283–4, 289–90, 295–8, 303, 305–6, 313–14, 317–18, 359–60, 366, 395, 435
Spanier, David 149
Spanish Civil War 93–5, 136–7, 178–9
Speer, Albert 33
Spender, Stephen 124–5
Spengler, Oswald 123–6, 145
Spiegel 30–1, 98, 110–11, 357–8
Spiegel Affair (1962–3) 52
spill-over 4, 221, 223, 386, 388–90, 416–17
Spinelli, Altiero 385
Spinelli Group 398–9
Srebrenica 365
Staercke, André 388–9
stagflation 243
Stalin, Joseph 14–15, 34–6, 63, 73, 98, 131, 141–5, 434
Stalin's Note (1952) 63
Stalinism 184
   Terror 35, 46
Stampa, La 30–1
Standaard, De 30–1
Standard 318
Star, The 188–9
Stoltenberg, Gerhard 356–7
Stone Sweet, Alec 9, 11
Strategic Arms Limitation Treaty (SALT) 63
Strauß, Franz Josef 52, 62, 90–1, 354–5
Straw, Jack 366–70, 405–7
Stresemann, Gustav 12, 92–6, 231–3
Structural Funds 113–14, 305, 356
Süddeutsche Zeitung 130–1, 318
Sun, The 188–9, 405–6
superpower 2–5, 8, 42, 48, 56–7, 59–60, 65–6, 70, 72–4, 90–101, 115, 138–9, 141–4, 146–7, 151, 187–8, 202–3, 218–19, 354–5, 385, 433, 436–7
superstate 1, 104–5, 417, 450–1
supranationalism 4–13, 32–5, 44, 48, 122–4, 127, 177, 219–29, 233–5, 241–2, 321, 338–9, 342–4, 347, 349, 355, 368, 371, 382–4, 386–97, 409–14, 417, 419–22, 433–4, 436, 438–41, 443–5
Süskind, Patrick 191–2
Sweden 67–8, 198–9, 229, 251–2, 271, 274–8, 280–2, 284–5, 289, 292–5, 304–6, 312–14, 345, 359–60, 449

522 INDEX

Switzerland 67–8, 289, 305, 317–18, 345–6, 417
Syria 19, 131–2, 449–50
Syriza (Greece) 30

Taylor, Charles 193
Taylor, Paul 3–4
Teltschik, Horst 73–4
Temps modernes, Les 141–2
Ten Point Programme (1989) 70–1
Test Ban Treaty (1963) 34–5, 62–3
Thatcher, Margaret 70, 73–4, 96, 166, 244,
    246–8, 255–6, 284–6, 294, 314–15, 350–4
Third Republic (France) 435
Third World 6–7, 17–18, 39–40, 44, 47–8, 60,
    65–6
Thorn, Gaston 349
Thorneycroft, Peter 342
Time magazine 65–6
Times 30, 130–1, 142, 147–9, 188–9, 253–4, 318
Tindemans, Léo 349
Tindemans report (1976) 348
Today newspaper 188–9
Tolstaya, Tatyana 167–8
Toynbee, Arnold 140–1
transactionalism 7–8
Trans-European Networks (TENs) 218–19
Treaty on European Union (1992) 8, 29, 126–7,
    199, 203, 217, 238–40, 333–4, 336–7,
    356–8, 360–2, 385–96, 400, 405–8,
    419–20, 441
Trentino 305–6
Trenz, Hans-Jörg 317
TREVI anti-terrorist network (1975) 419–20
tribalism 136–7, 188, 447–8
Truman, Harry 29
Truman Doctrine 29, 35–6, 54–5
Tsarism 46–7, 230–1
Tudzman, Franjo 114–15
Tüngel, Richard 98
Turkey 36, 42, 47–8, 111–12, 115, 296–8,
    309–11, 336–7, 369–70, 450–1
Tusk, Donald 214

United Kingdom Independence Party
    (UKIP) 179–80, 443–4
Ukraine 114, 177, 305–6, 335–6, 449–50
Ulbricht, Walter 61
Ulster Unionist Party (UUP) 113–14
Unilever 253–4
*Union Démocratique et Socialiste de la
    Résistance* 107–8
Union Européenne des Fédéralistes (UEF) 385
Union pour la Démocratie Française
    (UDF) 284–5, 349, 358–9

United Europe Movement (UEM) 385
United Kingdom 1, 18–20, 35–7, 39–52, 54–5,
    57–8, 60–1, 69, 71, 89–90, 92–3, 100,
    105–6, 111–15, 128–31, 134, 136–9, 143,
    147–9, 166–81, 188–90, 195–6, 198–9,
    222, 226–7, 236, 238, 240–1, 251–6,
    274–8, 280, 283–6, 290, 293–4, 305–6,
    309, 312, 316, 339–41, 363–70, 384–8,
    393–6, 406–7, 438–9, 441, 443–4,
    446–51
    Foreign Office 39–42, 47–8, 131–2,
        340–1, 439
    House of Commons 221, 438
    House of Lords, 406
    Treasury 40–2, 214–15, 341–2
United Nations 110, 350, 362, 366–7,
    Security Council 417–18
United Nations Protection Force
    (UNPROFOR) 363–4
United States 2–3, 6–8, 12, 17, 34–51, 54,
    56–69, 89–93, 96–103, 108, 110–12,
    115, 123–4, 131–2, 134–5, 138–45,
    216, 225–36, 238, 240–3, 251–2,
    268–80, 292–5, 304–5, 308–13, 340–1,
    346–7, 349, 352–4, 356, 360–2, 364–7,
    382–3, 386, 399, 402–3, 416–17, 433–9,
    449–50
    State Department 2–3, 14–15, 91–2, 339–40,
        437–8
    Treasury 333–4
United States of Europe 2–3, 56–7, 64–5,
    91–2, 134–5, 232, 235, 349, 382–3, 386,
    433, 439
Upper Bavaria 305
Uri, Pierre 219–20
Ustaše regime (Croatia) 175–6

Valéry, Paul 123–4
Varsori, Antonio 6–7
Vedel, Georges 392–3
Velvet Revolution 298
Veneto 282
Ventotene Manifesto 385
Verband für europäische Verständigung 128–30
Vergangenheitspolitik 193–4, 196
Verhofstadt, Guy 369
Verret, Alexandre 387–8
Versailles (1919), Treaty of 31–2, 44–6,
    93–6, 100–1, 140–1, 177, 183–4,
    230–3, 437–8
Vicenza 282
Vichy regime 57, 142, 435
Vienna 52, 171, 305
Vietnam War 54, 56–7, 65–6, 363

Vinen, Richard 312–13
Vojvodina 172, 176

Waever, Ole 90
Wales 178–9, 305–6
Walesa, Lech 59–60
Wall, Stephen 404
Wall Street 67–8, 216, 230–1
Wall Street Journal 67–8
Wallace, William 13, 337
Wallerstein, Immanuel 188
Warsaw 52, 73, 151, 184, 305, 446
Warsaw Pact 18–19, 29–61, 70
Washington Post 303–4
Wat, Alexander 269
Weber, Max 181–2
Weber, Werner 133–4
Weiler, Joseph 402–3, 445–6
welfare state 6–7, 12, 17–18, 184, 190,
    193–4, 217, 225–6, 237, 242,
    268–89, 291–2, 304, 321, 381–2,
    435, 444–5, 449
Welt, Die 30–1
Werner, Pierre 349
West, the 17–18, 30–2, 34, 55, 58–75, 90, 95–6,
    98–9, 130–1, 141–7, 151–2, 167–8,
    177–8, 181, 184, 187–8, 223–6, 235–6,
    269, 289–90, 303–4, 306–7, 309–13,
    345–7, 352, 366, 369–70
Western European Union (WEU) 105–6, 108–9,
    115, 147–8, 347
Wheatcroft, Geoffrey 333
Whig history 450–1
White, Jonathan 199–200
Wiener, Martin, 294
Wiener Zeitung 30–1

Wilhelm II, Kaiser 31–2
Wilson, Harold 114, 238–40, 350–1
Winkler, Heinrich August 193–4
Winterbottom, Michael 115
World Bank 91–2, 238
World Trade Organization (WTO) 255–6, 410,
    412–13
World War
  First World War 12–13, 19–20, 33, 44,
    47, 50–1, 96, 101, 122–6, 128–33,
    145–7, 172, 183, 225–6, 230–1, 292,
    386, 437–8
  Second World War 14–15, 17–18, 31–6, 42–3,
    46, 50–1, 57, 61, 91–3, 95–6, 99–101, 103,
    124–32, 134–7, 139, 141–2, 145–7,
    153–4, 174–8, 183–4, 190, 194, 219, 222,
    226–7, 236–8, 242, 253–4, 280, 283–4,
    286, 292, 360–2, 370–1, 385–6, 433,
    436–7, 439, 442
Wormsier, Olivier 240–1
Worsthorne, Peregrine 70

Yalta meeting (1945) 47
Young Plan (1929) 36–7
Yugoslav National Army (JNA) 114, 172–3,
    175–6
Yugoslavia 17–18, 60–1, 89–115, 166–77, 335–6,
    357–71, 396–7, 449–50

Zaire 44
Zeeland, Paul van 385, 388–9
Zeit, Die 62–3, 98, 284
Žižek, Slavoj 143
Zollverein 232–3
Zukunft, Die 123–4
Zweig, Stefan 151